973.917 Car
Caroli, Betty Boyd.
The Roosevelt women

W9-BTI-665
I JOH 00 0 036303 7

THE ROOSEVELT WOMEN

ALSO BY BETTY BOYD CAROLI

Today's Immigrants: Their Stories (with Thomas Kessner)

First Ladies

Immigrants Who Returned Home

Inside the White House

America's First Ladies

973.917
Car

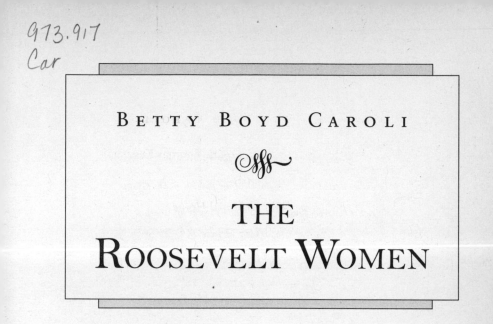

BETTY BOYD CAROLI

THE
ROOSEVELT WOMEN

BASIC BOOKS
A Member of the Perseus Books Group

JOHNSTON PUBLIC LIBRARY
JOHNSTON, IOWA 50131

Copyright © 1998 by Betty Boyd Caroli.

Published by Basic Books, a Member of the Perseus Books Group

All rights reserved. Printed in the United States of America.
No part of this book may be used or reproduced in any manner whatsoever
without written permission except in the case of brief quotations
embodied in critical articles and reviews.
For information address
Basic Books, 10 East 53rd Street, New York, NY 10022.

Designed by Jenny Dossin

Genealogical chart copyright © 1998 by Jeffrey L. Ward

ISBN 0-465-07133-3

TO LIVIO

CONTENTS

"Theodores" — Oyster Bay Roosevelts

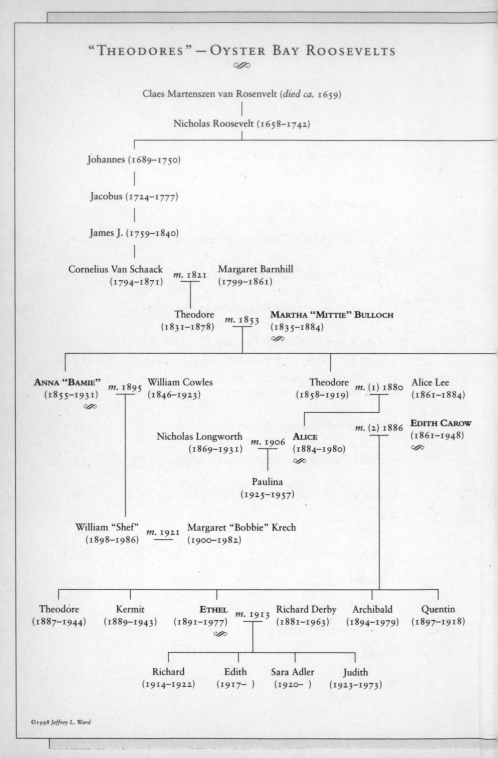

Claes Martenszen van Rosenvelt (*died ca.* 1659)

Nicholas Roosevelt (1658–1742)

Johannes (1689–1750)

Jacobus (1724–1777)

James J. (1759–1840)

Cornelius Van Schaack (1794–1871) — *m.* 1821 — Margaret Barnhill (1799–1861)

Theodore (1831–1878) — *m.* 1853 — **Martha "Mittie" Bulloch** (1835–1884)

Anna "Bamie" (1855–1931) — *m.* 1895 — William Cowles (1846–1923)

Theodore (1858–1919) — *m.* (1) 1880 — Alice Lee (1861–1884)

m. (2) 1886 — **Edith Carow** (1861–1948)

Nicholas Longworth (1869–1931) — *m.* 1906 — **Alice** (1884–1980)

Paulina (1925–1957)

William "Shef" (1898–1986) — *m.* 1921 — Margaret "Bobbie" Krech (1900–1982)

Theodore (1887–1944)

Kermit (1889–1943)

Ethel (1891–1977) — *m.* 1913 — Richard Derby (1881–1963)

Archibald (1894–1979)

Quentin (1897–1918)

Richard (1914–1922)

Edith (1917–)

Sara Adler (1920–)

Judith (1923–1973)

©1998 Jeffrey L. Ward

"Franklins" — Hyde Park Roosevelts

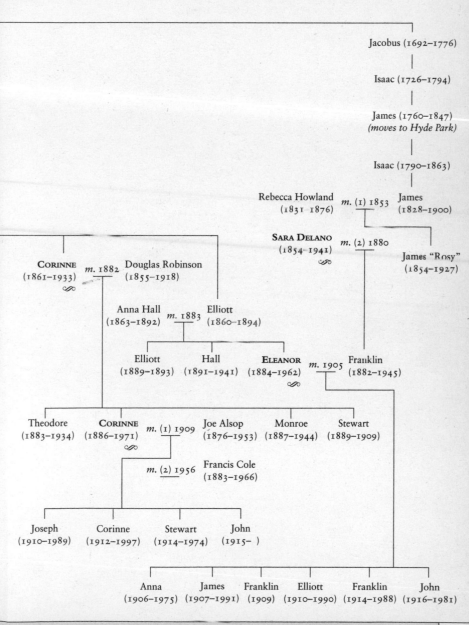

Jacobus (1692–1776)

Isaac (1726–1794)

James (1760–1847)
(moves to Hyde Park)

Isaac (1790–1863)

Rebecca Howland (1831–1876) — *m.* (1) 1853 — James (1828–1900)

Sara Delano (1854–1941) — *m.* (2) 1880 — James "Rosy" (1854–1927)

Corinne (1861–1933) — *m.* 1882 — Douglas Robinson (1855–1918)

Anna Hall (1863–1892) — *m.* 1883 — Elliott (1860–1894)

Elliott (1889–1893)   Hall (1891–1941)   **Eleanor** (1884–1962) — *m.* 1905 — Franklin (1882–1945)

Theodore (1883–1934)   **Corinne** (1886–1971) — *m.* (1) 1909 — Joe Alsop (1876–1953)   Monroe (1887–1944)   Stewart (1889–1909)

m. (2) 1956 — Francis Cole (1883–1966)

Joseph (1910–1989)   Corinne (1912–1997)   Stewart (1914–1974)   John (1915–)

Anna (1906–1975)   James (1907–1991)   Franklin (1909)   Elliott (1910–1990)   Franklin (1914–1988)   John (1916–1981)

PREFACE

MORE THAN FIFTEEN years ago, when I was first encouraged to look into the subject of presidents' wives, I objected that I did not want to study a group of women whose names we knew because of the men they married. Prodded to look more closely, I realized I was wrong—the women deserved scrutiny in their own right, and their famous husbands figured in my study mostly because their prominence helped guarantee that the women's records were preserved. Too often, letters and diaries have been discarded—as inconsequential and unimportant –because they were written by women. Proximity to presidents increased chances for survival.

As I delved into the history of America's First Ladies, I had to face the fact that unraveling women's records raised questions peculiar to them—not a new idea since I had often encountered it during the twenty years that I taught women's history at the City University of New York. The choice of spouse, the number of children, and the health of aging parents all shaped women's lives without much touching men's. Presidential wives, often outspoken and independent at the time of marriage, had to learn to move in their husbands' shadows, and I wondered how they felt about that. The answer was complicated, varying from woman to woman, and I sympathized with their plight.

After I completed *First Ladies* (Oxford, 1987 and 1995), several of them called out for full-length studies of their own, but the Roosevelt women called loudest. Since Eleanor almost always topped the lists of outstanding First Ladies, not only those compiled by presidential scholars but also by *Good Housekeeping* readers, I was curious about her models. Much attention had been given to Marie Souvestre, her teacher at Allenswood, and to various political associates and friends, but I wondered about early role models within the Roosevelt family. One of only a handful of women to have a close relative precede them to the White House, Eleanor might have gained something from her aunt Edith, I reasoned. Did she? The quest for that answer led me to Theodore's sisters, and for a while I contemplated writing a book called *Eleanor and Her Aunts*. The realization that other Roosevelt women deserved inclusion persuaded me to widen my scope.

Because most of the women treated here died too long ago for any living person to have a clear memory of them, I turned to their letters. Thousands have been catalogued, ready for reading, and I was impressed once again by the fact that future generations will have more trouble studying ours—because e-mail and the telephone have largely replaced pen on paper. I tried to use the letters judiciously. Some were dictated to employees, resulting in errors on names, and the calligraphy on some was nearly indecipherable. I had to remember that correspondence is limited to people who are separated, so reading the letters between a mother and one daughter, for example, can skew the picture, revealing a lot about their relationship but very little about an equally important connection between the same mother and another daughter who lived close by.

Once again I was impressed by the fact that different readers—all striving for objectivity—will draw different conclusions from the very same letter. I remember one day in particular when I had finished reading Corinne Roosevelt's letters about her upcoming marriage to Douglas Robinson. At 5 P.M., when the Houghton Library closed its doors, I stopped by a Cambridge bookstore to see how Corinne's marriage was covered in the many biographies of Theodore. The typical interpretation was that she dreaded the marriage because she thought Douglas did not measure up to her brother, but I had seen no trace of that—even though the letters quoted in these books were the very same ones I had read a few hours earlier. To me it seemed obvious that it was her father whom she idolized, and it was her own independence that she feared losing by marriage. I concluded that books written after Theodore became famous suffered a time warp; they seemed to take for granted that he had always been admired—and even idolized—by his sisters.

My conclusions frequently clashed with the prevailing interpretation, even interpretations of scholars whose work I admire. Sylvia Morris's superb biography of Edith Kermit Roosevelt shows a more benevolent woman than I was able to see. My previous research on Mary Kingsbury Simkhovitch and the settlement house she founded, Greenwich House in Greenwich Village, turned up hints of a kinder, more interesting Sara Delano Roosevelt than I was able to find in the remarkable biographies of Eleanor by Joe Lash or Blanche Wiesen Cook. I was glad to follow David McCullough's leads to a shrewder Mittie Roosevelt than I found, for example, in Edmund Morris's excellent book on Theodore. And so it goes, the rich Roosevelt legacy continuing to provide the raw material for infinite reassessment and new conclusions.

༄

In the many years I have been at work on *The Roosevelt Women*, I have received help from more quarters than I can list here. Susan Rabiner, my editor for *First Ladies*, initially broached the subject of a book on the Roosevelt women, and she has continued for more than a decade, through many changes of hat, to promote it—as editor, agent, and friend. At Basic Books I have had excellent support from an enthusiastic team. Sarah Flynn came into the editing process at a very difficult time, and with her subtle nudging and frank queries, she pushed me to fill in a lot of the blanks. Working with her has been pure pleasure. Jo Ann Miller, executive editor, cheerfully kept us all on schedule, assisted ably by Libby Garland.

This book would not have been possible without the papers and the interviews, and I am grateful to many members of the Roosevelt family for their cooperation. They were unfailingly kind even though they must have tired long ago of answering the same questions over and over. Not only did they take time to talk with me, but they also took time to drive me to the station, make copies of rare photographs, and lend me old diaries and papers that had not yet made their way into the archives. Edith Williams and Sarah Alden Gannett opened up their mother's house in Vermont so that I could see that simple but cozy farmhouse where Ethel Roosevelt Derby spent her last years. The three daughters of Eleanor Roosevelt's brother Hall— Eleanor Roosevelt and her half sisters, Janet Katten and Diana Jaicks—gave me quite different pictures of their famous aunt and of their father. But they had explained in advance that they would. "You will not think," Diana Jaicks told me, "that Janet and I grew up in the same house."

Her observation raised a question that I had come up against before, especially in dealing with famous families: How much of it really happened, and how much seems to have happened because it has been written about so much? Eleanor Seagraves, Eleanor's oldest granddaughter, admitted that she could not be sure. For her the two merged in one seamless whole.

The Roosevelt archives are enormous, but I was fortunate to have superb assistance in sorting out the documents. Wallace Finley Dailey, at the Theodore Roosevelt Collection, Houghton Library, Harvard, has such a thorough knowledge of that rich archive and is so unfailingly helpful that I cannot imagine having done this book without him. Everyone with whom I dealt at the Franklin D. Roosevelt Library, Hyde Park; the Arizona Historical Society, Tucson; the Massachusetts Historical Society, Boston; and the Manuscript Division of the Library of Congress, Washington, D.C., cheerfully assisted me, bringing out dozens of boxes and pointing me to new sources. I am grateful to them all. Archivists at the Atlanta Public Library, Atlanta, Georgia, and the Oregon Historical Society, Portland, graciously filled my mail requests.

For the photos I have relied on the personal collections of John Alsop, Joseph Alsop VI, Evan Cowles, and Brie Quinby, and the postcard collection of Elizabeth Norris. At the libraries I have had the excellent assistance of Mark Renovitch at the Franklin D. Roosevelt Library, Allen Goodridge at the John F. Kennedy Library, and Wallace Dailey at the Houghton Library.

Grants from the Research Foundation of the City University of New York and released time from teaching at Kingsborough helped in the early stages. The Franklin and Eleanor Roosevelt Institute kindly provided me with two weeks of research at Hyde Park. I am grateful to both institutions.

New York City is rich in libraries, and I have used many of them. I am particularly thankful for the Research Division of the New York Public Library, where I work in the Wertheim Room, the Bobst Library at New York University, and the New-York Historical Society.

Many of my colleagues and friends have added to this project in ways that neither they nor I can remember precisely. But I want to acknowledge particularly the following: members of my two writing groups, especially Deborah Gardner, Carol Groneman, Dorothy Helly, Dona Munker, Carol Stanger, and Sydney Ladensohn Stern; friends and colleagues who offered suggestions or led me to sources—including Carol Cavallo, Blanche Wiesen Cook, Stacy Cordery, Mary Sue Hauck, Nora Mandel, Kristie Miller, and Dorothy Wick; Margaret Riddle, a distant relative of the Roosevelts through the Stobo branch, who helped me unravel Mittie's background; and the Washington Square crowd for daily encouragement and computer advice.

Since I often wrote and researched far from home, I depended on the hospitality of family and friends: Victoria Kirby in San Francisco; Eileen Moran in Boston; Ellinor and Peter Sokole in Tuscany; Flavia Miotti and Enzo Caroli in Posina and Vicenza, Italy; and Elena di Massimo and Pino Caroli on Lake Bracciano. My laptop adjusted admirably to all their homes, as it did to that special spot on the island of Bequia where, during the course of my writing this book, the little shrubs grew into trees that blocked my view of the sea.

In 1990 the Theodore Roosevelt Association, under the able direction of John Gable, published the Roosevelt genealogy, which I found invaluable. It would have been next to impossible to figure out just how everyone was related to everyone else without it. Kathleen Dalton and John Gable kindly read and commented on sections of the manuscript. The mistakes, of course, are mine.

To Livio Caroli, who would rather make music than books, I am forever grateful that he understands I see things differently.

BETTY BOYD CAROLI

New York City
May 1998

O N A COLD, RAW DAY IN JANUARY 1919, a huge crowd gathered at Christ Church in Oyster Bay, Long Island, for the
funeral of Theodore Roosevelt. The most popular man in America,
he would surely have been nominated for another term as president
if he had survived to the next election. Now many of the nation's
luminaries joined family and neighbors to pay their respects. He was
only sixty when he died, but his cocky heroism with his Rough Riders at San Juan Hill, his two terms as a "bully pulpit" President, his
exploits while hunting wild game in Africa and tracing a Brazilian
river to its source had rendered him larger than life to many Americans. His son Archie, home from Europe, where he had been
wounded in the war, cabled his two brothers who were still there:
"The old lion is dead."

Edith Roosevelt followed Victorian custom and did not attend her
husband's funeral—remaining at home where she read the Episco-
palian funeral service in private. But daughters Ethel Derby and
Alice Longworth were there, along with Theodore's sister, Corinne
Robinson, and her daughter, Corinney Alsop. His only other niece,
Eleanor Roosevelt, had just sailed to France with her husband,
Franklin, who was taking part in the peace talks at Versailles.

The heavy turnout of Roosevelt women at the funeral—while
their men were off on war business—might have tempted observers
to write them off as mere background figures, doing little more than
keeping the home fires burning while their men performed the
heroic, groundbreaking feats. But that judgment would be exposed
as wildly wrong.

Over the next few decades, the Roosevelt women emerged from
the shadows, breaking precedents and achieving national, even

international, reputations. Corinne Robinson stood up at the 1920 Republican National Convention to second a presidential nomination, the first woman ever to be so featured by a major party. Corinne Alsop was elected to the Connecticut House of Representatives three times and went on to be dubbed the "grand old lady" of the Republican Party in her state. Alice Longworth, Theodore's older daughter, never ran for office, but her sharp tongue and even sharper wit made her one of the most famous women in Washington for more than half a century. As presidents and potentates trooped over to her salon on Massachusetts Avenue, she heard herself described as "the *other* Washington monument." But, of course, it was Eleanor Roosevelt—who rose in the Democratic Party from local organizer to activist First Lady and then, after her husband's death, represented her country at the United Nations—who made the biggest headlines.

✑

It is not surprising that Anna Curtenius Roosevelt, one of Theodore's great-granddaughters and herself a brilliant anthropologist, once wondered aloud why everyone seemed so interested in the Roosevelt men. It was the women, she pointed out, who performed most remarkably while the men fought their wars and died young. Indeed, gender emerges as one of the main themes of this book. The reader cannot help but ask, as every thinking person is bound to ask more than once in a lifetime, what difference did it make to be born female? How did it affect choice and opportunity? How has that changed over the last century?

In thousands of letters that the Roosevelt women wrote and in interviews they gave me and other biographers, they have provided complex answers to those questions. As the men campaigned for high office and pinned on their war medals, the women shaped equally satisfying lives along parallel, sometimes intersecting, lines. They revealed few regrets; complaint has only a minuscule role in this story. Except for an occasional offhand remark, such as Corinne Alsop's point about her pregnant shape keeping her out of military training in 1915, the reader will find little evidence here that the women felt restrained by their sex. It is tantalizing to speculate that they kept their resentment mute, like many women of their time, and that resentment lies behind the scathing comments for which some of them became notorious. But that was never their conclusion.

In large part, the Roosevelts, regardless of their sex, held the same goals. Publishing articles and books, speaking to thousands of people, conversing with top political leaders, and traveling the world— all came as easily to most of the Roosevelt women as to most of the men. Although it is probably useless to assess who did better at any of these, it is, nevertheless, tempting. Eleanor evidently wrote with great facility, far more easily than Franklin did, and she turned out thousands of words—in articles and letters—with very little effort. So did her uncle Theodore and her aunt Corinne. But speaking to large audiences—something Eleanor's aunt Corinne and cousin Corinney tossed off easily—had to be painfully learned by Eleanor, and her cousin Alice never managed the feat.

In world travel there is hardly a laggard in the entire batch. They covered a staggering number of miles, often leaving behind very young children to be cared for by someone else. More than one prominent Roosevelt scholar has speculated that in this family, travel was seen as a cure and that the happiest times were those spent far from home. The women used long journeys for adventure, as the men did, but they also used them to recover from grief over a young son's death or to pick up the pieces of their lives after their husbands died. The mixture of emotions surrounding travel appears most poignantly in Edith Roosevelt's observation that women often had to wait until the "beloved shackles" of family obligation were removed before setting out to explore "the wide world."

Concentrating on one achieving family invites a warning: the temptation will be to overemphasize talent and under-report failure, resulting in a valentine of praise. This warning applies particularly to Americans. In the United States, where both monarchy and noble titles are banned by the Constitution, we have groped in odd corners for our heroes, looking to swashbuckling frontier folk (Davy Crockett and Annie Oakley) and colorful criminals (Bonnie and Clyde). Political families such as the Kennedys have emerged as icons, democratic versions of the king or queen (or Princess Diana) that Americans never had.

Besides the Kennedys, only two American families rank as political dynasties, exercising considerable power over several generations: the Adamses and the Roosevelts. But while the Kennedy and Adams women have had their chroniclers, the Roosevelts have not. The omission is regrettable. Long before anthropologist Anna Roosevelt made her observation about her female relatives inviting scrutiny, her great-aunt Ethel Derby offered a similar view. After a visit with her dynamic sister, Alice Longworth, Ethel lamented that no one had caught the unique energy in the female Roosevelts: "I wish Rebecca West or rather an American equivalent if there were one could write a book on Auntie Bye [Anna Roosevelt Cowles, also known as "Bamie"], Auntie Corinne [Corinne Roosevelt Robinson], Auntie Sister [Alice Roosevelt Longworth], Cousin Eleanor [Eleanor Roosevelt Roosevelt], with G[rand]Mother [Edith Carow Roosevelt] perhaps used as the liaison. What a study that would be."

Unfortunately, no American equivalent of Rebecca West has come forward to tell the story. Nor is one likely to do so, although excellent studies of individuals might be proposed for the Rebecca West league: Sylvia Morris's book on Edith Roosevelt, Blanche Wiesen Cook's biography of Eleanor Roosevelt, and Doris Kearns Goodwin's account of Franklin and Eleanor during the war years. By tracing these same subjects in a family context and looking at other, lesser-known Roosevelt women, I hope to add to our understanding of this much written about family and point to the rich material that remains unmined.

⁓

No one can write about the Roosevelts—or even think about them for very long—without running straight into the subject of class and how much it affected their lives. Even those Americans most adamant in believing that they live in a classless society will be struck by evidence to the contrary in this clan, part of that tiny fraction of the population perched at the privileged top, with the money and friends to make choices that were unavailable—even unknown—to others.

The Roosevelt name did not always wield great weight or wealth. Alice Longworth liked to quip that her Roosevelt forebears were just "upstart Dutch who made a couple of bucks." On another occasion she called them "peasants." Her father made nearly the same point when he reminded Franklin that the two of them were descended "from a common ancestor." Then, to underscore his point, he added jokingly, "*Very* common."

It took more than one hundred years after Claes Martenszen van Rosenvelt stepped ashore in New Amsterdam in the 1640s before this immigrant family, its name now changed to Roosevelt, made much of a mark in Manhattan. Two more centuries would pass before the family split into two branches—the Oyster Bay Republican "Theodores" and the Hyde Park Democratic "Franklins." By the time that division occurred in the twentieth century, hard work in a variety of enterprises had provided the Roosevelts with considerable wealth. In the nineteenth century they had rapidly increased their fortune through real estate deals and banking, and by 1868, Cornelius Van Schaack Roosevelt (a great-grandson of the immigrant Claes) was listed among New York's handful of millionaires. When he died three years later, his heirs came into a fortune. Although the exact total of Cornelius Van Schaack Roosevelt's estate has not been calculated, each of his five surviving sons inherited more than $1 million, a sum equivalent to more than $13 million in 1998.

Translating dollars into current equivalencies obscures the subtleties and may seriously mislead. One dollar in the late 1800s would buy a day of fieldwork from a man and nearly a week of laundering by a woman, but no amount of money could then purchase the washing machine or field equipment that would later substantially reduce the labor involved in those tasks. Ideas also changed. Virtually no Americans—even those with salaries in the six figures in the late twentieth century—would think of staffing their homes with the half-dozen live-in employees that merely prosperous Americans considered necessary a hundred years ago. If they tried to do so, they would find few applicants, for jobs involving menial labor and restricted living arrangements have become undesirable in our day.

Yet money figures in this family's history and needs an explanation that puts it in context. When Franklin and Eleanor Roosevelt married in 1905, their combined income from family investments amounted to $12,500, hardly remarkable until it is converted into its 1998 equivalent of $230,000. Except to the seasoned historian adept at deciphering spreadsheets of bygone eras, the $12,500 makes little impression, but almost every reader responds to the sound of $200,000, especially if it is yearly income that is not subject to income tax.

Eleanor (born in 1884) and Franklin (1882) grew up in a time when new names continually joined the list of big-spending American millionaires. Palatial mansions on upper Fifth Avenue, imported art treasures, and lavish entertaining inspired Mark Twain to proclaim the last decades of the nineteenth century the Gilded Age. "Old Guard" families like the Roosevelts, who had been quietly building their fortunes and spending prudently, frowned on such excesses and drew a protective circle around themselves. Dubbed the "nobs" to distinguish them from the more flamboyant "swells," they could afford, according to one of their chroniclers, "to live in tarnished magnificence on outmoded Second Avenue, while the 'swells' eddied like moths toward the luster of Fifth Avenue." Indeed, the Roosevelts, with one exception, avoided Fifth Avenue addresses, preferring Madison or the numbered streets in Murray Hill and the East Sixties. Franklin's much older half-brother, James Roosevelt Roosevelt, lived at 372 Fifth Avenue, but that choice probably owed more to the fact that his wife was an Astor than to his own connections.

These addresses became public record when the New York Social Register made its debut in 1887. With the population of Manhattan rapidly growing—more than doubling between 1850 and 1880—it was not always easy to pick out "our people." The *Social Register,* by selecting two thousand names out of more than one million New Yorkers, helped define exactly who constituted New York "society." Issued four times a year, the *Social Register* gave the names and addresses of "prominent families," their clubs and yacht rigs, as well as milestones such as marriages and deaths (but not births). In fact, children were excluded, not yet being part of people who mattered. Comings and goings of adults to summer houses and on trips abroad were duly recorded, at least those known to the compilers of the *Social Register* and deemed appropriate for inclusion.

From the very first issue of the *Social Register,* the Roosevelts claimed more than a dozen lines, although not in every issue and not for every move. What got into the *Register* (as well as what did not) reveals a great deal. When Theodore took a job in Washington or moved his family to Oyster Bay for the summer, the transfer went on record; when James and Sara Delano Roosevelt sailed abroad or returned home, the date and the name of the ship were reported. But Elliott's "drying out" trip to France was not mentioned, and his banishment to Virginia—a move to get him away from his wife and family until he got his life in order—was almost ignored. Corinne Roosevelt Robinson continued to merit inclusion even after she started spending most of the year out of town, either in Orange, New Jersey, or upstate New York. Her older sister, Bamie, listed only as "Miss Roosevelt" until she married at age forty, had to content herself with appearing as a subsidiary of her married brother, Theodore. Her name was listed beneath his, as though she were an appendage to the household, although she owned the house on Madison Avenue that he and his family used as their Manhattan residence.

Chances for getting into the *Social Register* were slim—no matter how large the bank account—if the skin color or the religion was not "right." Catholics, Jews, and the "wrong" Protestants usually found themselves corralled into the large pen of the excluded, along with Asians and African Americans. Changing one's religion, however, came more easily than changing one's race, and even the Roosevelts gradually made the switch from their forebears' Dutch church to the more socially prominent Presbyterian and then the elite Episcopalian. Theodore's generation mixed religions in their youth, but as they matured, their allegiance shifted. They all married in Presbyterian or Episcopalian ceremonies, and when they died, their coffins were all carried down Episcopalian aisles. When Corinne wed the Scottish-born Douglas Robinson in 1882, his family had already begun its own migration, one of the Robinsons having bought a pew at Grace (Episcopal) Church at Tenth Street and Broadway around 1840 "because all the better people go there."

Joseph Alsop, a grandson of Douglas and Corinne Robinson—as well as a famous columnist and friend of presidents—wrote amusingly about that small privileged few whom he called the WASP ascendancy. Being simply white, Anglo-Saxon, Protestant, and rich did not suffice to make it into the "ascendancy" category—the people who controlled power and claimed privilege in turn-of-the-century America. How one dressed and talked, where one studied and traveled, all had a place on the credentials list. Alsop listed "all sorts of do's and don'ts about clothes and shoes" in his autobiography, *I've Seen the Best of It,* but he limited himself to the rules for men since he admitted that he never could tell "what outward signs enabled my mother and her friends to choose the five or six other ladies who 'might be nice to know' from the scores of possibilities presented" aboard ship on a transatlantic crossing. Even a cursory inspection could detect impostors and weed out those who failed to measure up. What appeared to others an insignificant transgression—an inappropriate shoe color or wrong dress fabric—meant immediate expulsion from the list of people "worth" knowing.

Language also helped distinguish the WASP ascendancy from their imitators, according to Joe Alsop. In vocabulary, the rule required sticking to the earliest English version and rejecting all substitutions, especially those that aspired to "foreign" sophistication, had a "modern" slant, or showed the taint of euphemism. In the Roosevelts' circle, one was buried in a coffin, never a casket, and the person in charge was an undertaker, never a funeral director or mortician. At the window of one's house (never "home" unless it was an institution for the disabled or demented) one hung curtains (never drapes or draperies). People unfortunate enough to have their teeth pulled replaced them with false teeth rather than dentures until they died (never "passed away").

Not content to merely entertain in their large, comfortable houses (to call them "gracious homes" erred on two counts, since "gracious" was frowned on as an adjective), members of the WASP ascendancy had other responsibilities. They were expected to show a respect for culture by attending the opera and acquiring art. Just as surely they were expected to extend a helping hand to people stuck on the lower rungs of their society—not the rungs just below their own, which could lead to confusion and problems, or those at the very bottom, who were beyond helping, but those slightly above the bottom—what used to be called "the deserving poor." Franklin's mother, Sara Delano Roosevelt, became an early supporter of a New York settlement house serving Italian immigrants. Theodore's two sisters, Bamie and Corinne, regularly accompanied their father on his rounds to the newsboys' lodgings and to other charitable organizations that he supported. As adults they continued to donate time and money to a long list of organizations. Eleanor Roosevelt outdid them all by making her name synonymous with twentieth-century humanitarianism.

The Roosevelts adhered closely to some rules of the WASP ascendancy—although they would have shunned that designation as unseemly for themselves—while cheerfully breaking others. In speaking, Eleanor never lost the cadence of her class or made concessions in vocabulary to those who had not benefited from her kind of schooling and contacts. In "coming out" at eighteen (and scheduling a similar event for her only daughter when she reached that same age), Eleanor followed family tradition. But she also picked up hitchhikers as she drove herself between Washington and New York, and then sometimes impulsively invited them to her apartment for a hot meal. She saw no reason that labor leader Rose Schneiderman's Jewishness or her family's poverty which sent her out to work at age thirteen should render her an inappropriate friend for the wife of a Hudson River squire, even one who went on to become Governor of New York and President of the United States.

That some of the Roosevelts, whose southern forebears owned slaves, helped break down barriers between the races forms an important part of their story. Several generations put civil rights issues at the top of their list of needed reforms, although the sentiment was not equally shared among all the relatives. After Eleanor hired an African-American house staff in Washington, D.C., in 1913, her mother-in-law, Sara, objected loudly, underscoring her feeling on the matter by insisting that Eleanor's employees eat separately from hers whenever she brought them to Hyde Park. At the time, Eleanor could do nothing but comply. But later, after she moved into the White House in 1933, she spoke out forcefully for civil rights, becoming a special hero to many African Americans.

∽

To the old saw about the rich being "different from you and me" it is appropriate to add that wealthy women often play by rules unknown to poorer women. Those Roosevelt women with their own incomes enjoyed considerable independence in matters of the purse. At the time of her marriage, Eleanor's income was larger than Franklin's by about fifty percent, raising new questions about why she did not draw a firmer line between herself and her mother-in-law earlier. Especially in a time when few women worked for pay (and virtually none did in upper-class New York of the late nineteenth century), a woman with her own inheritance could make a trip to Europe or lavish gifts on her children without anyone's approval— as long as her money held out.

Other consequences of wealth merit attention. Upper-class women tended to marry earlier than their poorer contemporaries because parents were eager to get their daughters and the family fortune settled, and suitors gravitated to young ladies known to be rich. Henry James's *Washington Square* may have been fiction, but some version of it appeared all over New York as rich young women wrestled with the question of whether they were being courted for themselves or their inheritance.

The physical drudgery of housework (cooking, cleaning, and laundry) remained outside the experience of most women in the Roosevelts' circle before 1945. They would have more likely milked a cow or cleaned a stable (as part of their introduction to farm animals and pets) than put together a meal for guests. As First Lady, Eleanor was known to limit herself to scrambling eggs in a chafing dish for Sunday night dinners at the White House. Her female relatives were equally unfamiliar with kitchens. Her aunt Edith did not cook ever, and when her aunt Corinne happened to visit a friend who prepared a lunch in front of her guests, the result was viewed with amazement, almost as a miracle. That changed, of course, over time. When two of Theodore's granddaughters were asked in 1994 how their mother managed to accomplish so much, they immediately zeroed in on what they saw as the major difference between their lives and hers: she always had a cook.

Even the spacing of children differs with class. Breast-feeding, long recognized as an imperfect form of birth control (since breastfeeding may interfere with ovulation), stopped sooner among wealthy women than among their poorer counterparts. (Some immigrant women in turn-of-the-century New York nursed their babies until well after their first birthday, partly for economic reasons and partly because of family tradition.) Among the Roosevelts featured here, breast-feeding stopped after a few months, when a nurse took over, thus helping to explain how several of the Roosevelt women produced big families in a very short time.

Without the worry about supporting several children—a concern that would encourage limiting births by some form of contraception or sexual abstinence—wealthy women in good health sometimes out-produced poorer women. Eleanor's four deliveries in fifty-three months offer a case in point (after a respite, she gave birth to two more, only twenty-one months apart). Her cousin Corinney outdid that record, giving birth to three boys and one girl in less than five years. The timing no doubt helped confirm Corinney's view that "the romance of young motherhood is an overrated illusion."

A strong impetus to reproduce pervades the family history. Especially in the late nineteenth century when the popularity of Social Darwinism and talk of "natural superiority" permeated discussions in America, middle- and upper-class women connected maternity to patriotism. It is not clear whether Theodore Roosevelt affected behavior or was merely reflecting family sentiments when he wrote that he would not have his daughters shirk motherhood any more than he would have his sons shirk battle. Daughter Ethel conformed, producing four, as did nieces Eleanor and Corinne Alsop, but Theodore did not live to see his other daughter's only child.

In wealthy New York households, the mother played a largely managerial role. Reading to a child, choosing schools and clothes, leading a hike, arranging vacations and music lessons were all part of upper-class mothering—unlike changing diapers, cleaning up the play-room, or cooking the children's dinner, which were handled by servants. Some of the Roosevelts seem to have done better as manager-mothers than others. As a child, Eleanor suffered stoically through abuses from a cruel nanny until her grandmother finally intervened, but later, as a mother herself, she struggled to find just the right caregivers for her own children. Corinney recalled her own mother with great affection, although she saw her nowhere near as often as most middle-class children saw their schoolteachers. As a young girl, Corinney had a full-time nurse who managed her through the day and prepared her for bed at night. Then Corinne, dressed for an elegant dinner or dance, would sweep in to say good night, leaving a lasting (but loving) impression on the little girl.

With all its advantages, a place in upper-class New York had its own special problems. Exile—by the wrong marriage or some other breach of the rules—was one, and suffering the intense scrutiny of peers was another. The restraints on action and thinking, the brakes on change, the narrowness of dismissing much of the population as simply not worth knowing—all helped isolate this one segment of New York from the rest. Edith Wharton, a distant cousin of Edith Kermit Roosevelt, outlined these liabilities in her novels, especially *The House of Mirth* (1905) and *The Age of Innocence* (1920), but the Roosevelt women offer real-life examples. How they maneuvered over the hurdles and profited from their privilege figure equally in their story.

ళ.

An enormous cast of characters could claim a role in *The Roosevelt Women*. Because the first member of this prolific family (Claes Martenszen van Rosenvelt) arrived in America more than three hundred years ago, thousands of men and women can trace their ancestry back to him even though the Roosevelt name may have disappeared from their branch of the family tree many generations ago. For women the link is particularly difficult to establish, since those who were "born a Roosevelt" lost that identification at marriage, and their children almost always took their father's surname. (Eleanor Roosevelt is an obvious exception. By marrying her fifth cousin, she kept the name she was born with, and her children were Roosevelts.)

This book focuses on a few main characters—Martha "Mittie" Bulloch Roosevelt (1835–1884) and her female descendants. In addition to being the mother of the twenty-sixth President of the United States, Mittie was also the mother of two remarkable Roosevelt daughters, Bamie and Corinne, and the grandmother of four uncommonly prominent achievers: witty Alice Longworth, First Lady Eleanor Roosevelt, legislator Corinne Alsop, and the much-loved Ethel Derby, Theodore's younger daughter. Since tracing the Roosevelt women is difficult without mentioning those who married into the clan, wives' names pop up from time to time, and two of them—Edith Kermit Carow and Sara Delano—merit a chapter here as well. Each eventually headed opposing branches of the family, and each played a dominant role in the clan's story.

By the time Theodore died in 1919, Mittie had been dead for many years, but the family never quite forgot the quixotic mixture of feminine charm and cool confidence that defined this Georgian belle. As an eighteen-year-old bride from the rural South, she had to cope with living among the New York Roosevelts during the Civil War, thus offering a poignant, sad lesson in the price of adaptation.

Her elder daughter, Bamie, sixty-four when Theodore died, was too crippled by arthritis to attend his funeral. Her presence, however, must have been felt across the miles that separated her Connecticut home from the mourners at Oyster Bay. She was, it is generally agreed, one of those people whose personalities loom so large that they cannot translate to the printed page. Decades after she died, her niece, Alice Longworth, was asked by biographer Joseph Lash if Eleanor Roosevelt did not resemble their aunt Bamie in her energy and verve. Alice objected firmly: "There was no one like Auntie Bye."

Bamie's younger sister, Corinne, was the "baby" of their family, but birth order proved no handicap. It may even have helped propel her into the spotlight. Biographers of Theodore commonly write her off as the "adoring little sister," but her several volumes of published poetry, many articles, and hundreds of unpublished letters suggest that she would have made her mark even if she had a brother that nobody ever heard of.

Edith Carow Roosevelt, Theodore's second wife, started out in childhood as Corinne's best friend, but with time (and marriage to Theodore) the relationship soured. Two such opinionated women would have had trouble reconciling their views within any family, but a limelight family experienced special strains. The mystery surrounding Edith concerns why she is recorded in history as such a paragon of virtue, the perfect wife and mother, when she was viewed more warily within the family.

Edith's public relations feat is nothing, however, compared with the failure of Sara Delano Roosevelt to be known as anything more than an interfering mother-in-law. Mention her name—or identify her as Franklin's mother—to most Americans, and they hoot in derision. No fate could be worse, they volunteer, than having to contend with such a woman. Yet the family letters give a different picture, one that is underlined by evidence from other quarters, and the question emerges: how did that horrible, one-dimensional picture of Sara Delano Roosevelt develop?

Alice Longworth and Eleanor Roosevelt fall into that category tritely titled "needing no further introduction," because their public lives are entwined with so much of twentieth-century American history. Viewed in the family context, the pictures usually drawn of them gain a new dimension: Alice appears more kindly; Eleanor, more detached.

Mittie's other two granddaughters, however, are much less well known. Corinne Alsop, a leading Republican while First Lady Eleanor was making headlines as a Democrat, was not above lecturing her slightly older cousin. "I have been in politics," she would say to Eleanor, implying she knew more about the subject. Indeed, she was the only one of the four who ever won political office.

Of all the Roosevelt women considered here, none is more difficult to pin down than Ethel Roosevelt Derby. Of the four female cousins, Ethel remained the most private, her life defined by her husband, children, and the community in which she lived. In hundreds of letters she showed no sign that she would have wanted it any other way. While her sister, Alice, was making headlines in Washington, D.C., Ethel assured her own daughter that she wanted none of the limelight for herself. In any manual on how to negotiate the labyrinth of problems suffered by the offspring of famous parents, Ethel Derby could easily serve as model number one.

In comparison with Alice, who could never seem to get enough attention and had only derision for "do-gooders," Ethel had several advantages. She had not lost her mother at birth—as Alice had—and she had a more secure place in the birth order of that family. Alice was the oldest of six, and Ethel was the traditional middle child. Or perhaps it was schooling. Alice refused to enroll in any school outside her home, while Ethel happily attended the Cathedral School in Washington, D.C., where she became popular with other students.

It could also be argued that the seven-year age difference between the two sisters meant that Ethel grew up in a different time, when the family (as well as the nation) was shaped by different events. Much clearer is the fact that the next generations (Ethel's daughters and granddaughters) matured in a very different environment. None of Ethel's generation went to college, and only one of her three daughters did, but all of her granddaughters earned a B.A. In this respect the Roosevelts reflected changes felt all across the nation in the twentieth century as women's college enrollment caught up with men's.

✐

By the 1990s, Mittie's adult female progeny numbered sixty-four (twenty-one great-granddaughters and forty-three great-great-granddaughters), far too large a roster to be examined here except in the most cursory way. All born long after Mittie died, they reflect some of the changes that have affected all Americans, but at the same time they mirror peculiarly Roosevelt traditions and traits. Compared to the rest of the nation, they include an unusually high number of writers, academics, social service providers, and the politically engaged.

In a time of continuing debate over nurture versus nature, a book that focuses on a family of achievers will attract many critics. "What is innate and what is learned?" we constantly ask. If we suddenly discovered, for example, that Eleanor Roosevelt was adopted by the Roosevelts from an impoverished family in Wyoming, it would not change our evaluation of what she did. The fact remains, however, that she grew up among strong-minded female models. Her central educational experience came at a school run by an indomitable French woman with impeccable intellectual credentials. Nature and nurture are therefore as complexly mixed in this family as in any other.

It is impossible to prove exactly where Eleanor found her models, even after reading her many books and letters, just as it is difficult for most adults to clarify in their own minds who among their teachers, relatives, and friends affected them most. Nor can anyone really be sure why the four children of Theodore Sr. and Mittie turned out so differently—two outspoken daughters, one President of the United States, and one charming alcoholic who died at thirty-four. In that sense, this book is about all families and about questions that will remain unanswered.

Two traits that appear in Roosevelts of both sexes are their high energy and their intellectual curiosity. On just a few hours of sleep they confronted daunting physical feats and turned out thousands of written words. One of the Roosevelt women interviewed for this book warned against the "shoe-horn" approach, fitting all the subjects into a single tight shoe, and that advice bears heeding. But I was struck by how many times the answer to "What made them different?" could be partly explained by those two traits. Of course, class and privilege played a major role.

∽

The lengthy paper trail left by the Roosevelts raises the question of what we can trust. Some of Theodore's letters to his children, so carefully phrased and charmingly illustrated with his drawings, raise the suspicion that he wrote them partly for public consumption. In fact, his children, already well aware of their prominence in the nation's story, dubbed them his "posterity" letters. The women's letters, thousands of them, do not give the same sense of having been specially tailored. Their frank, often poignant communications about serious family problems, including alcoholism, drugs, delinquency, and money difficulties, suggest they wrote only for themselves. But the letters were screened, of course, before they were deposited in the archives where I looked at them. Only one unread letter, still pristinely sealed from 1895, turned up in hundreds of file boxes. Some of the letters survive in perfect sequence, week after week without interruption, but at other times the omissions are suspicious. Occasionally a word has been intentionally obliterated or a section of the page torn away, leaving the researcher to puzzle why.

For all their writing, the Roosevelts lacked consistency in spelling, using "Bamie," for example, along with "Bammie," and "aunti" as often as "auntie." In a variety of cases I have settled on one spelling and used it throughout, trying to stay with what seemed the most common. To avoid the constant repetition of one surname, I have resorted to first names, thus putting myself on what may appear an unwarranted level of familiarity. I could see no other solution. The frequent appearance of the same first names (especially Theodore, Anna, Corinne, and James) led to distinguishing many Roosevelts from one another through the generally objectionable method of nicknames. Corinne Robinson Alsop, for example, is "Corinney" in these pages, long after she matured beyond the childish name, but at least it distinguishes her from her mother, also named Corinne.

⁓

One shrewd Roosevelt objected, after reading yet another book on his family, that no one seemed to realize how much they were all "part of a clan." That observation is particularly apt for the women. In the thousands of letters they wrote to each other, exchanging advice and seeking consolation, the sense of family is very strong. When called upon to deal with yet another episode of alcoholism among their men, one of the women referred to their "sisterhood of pain." Even after the Democratic "Franklin" branch broke away from the Republican "Theodores" and feelings between the two sides became very bitter, Eleanor insisted they were all "family." This book attempts to isolate what made them "special" and, at the same time, show what they shared with other families facing similar challenges outside the public eye.

THE ROOSEVELT WOMEN

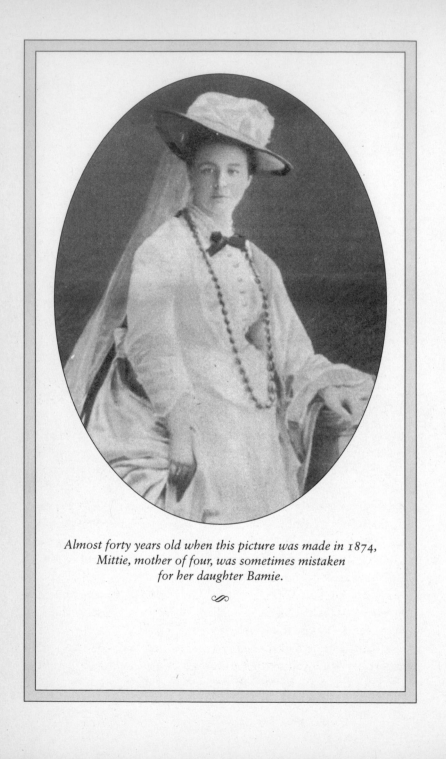

Almost forty years old when this picture was made in 1874, Mittie, mother of four, was sometimes mistaken for her daughter Bamie.

CHAPTER ONE

MARTHA "MITTIE" BULLOCH ROOSEVELT

(1835–1884)

 HE BRIDE WAS ONLY eighteen, and her slight figure and girlish face made her seem even younger as she stood in front of the dining room fireplace to take her vows. The bridegroom, at twenty-three, was solidly built, and his girth, combined with a ruddy, bewhiskered face, gave an impression more of protector than lover. As the groom stood close beside the bride, her face practically glowing from the light of the fire, they were both nearly upstaged by their surroundings. With Christmas only three days away, Bulloch Hall, the childhood home that the bride would remember fondly long after she had grown up, had been lavishly decorated with ribbons, candles, and green mistletoe and red holly berries that grew in abundance on the plantation just north of Atlanta. The entire household had worked for days to prepare for the Thursday evening in 1853 when Mittie Bulloch, the youngest daughter in the family, married Theodore Roosevelt of New York City.

At first the bride had wished for a small wedding, one that would not cost her widowed mother too much effort or money. But then, rethinking the matter, she had decided to splurge. A girl married only once, she reasoned, and she ought to make the most of it. When her parents built the house fewer than twenty years earlier, they had insisted on a fireplace in every room, and on this evening Mittie wanted every one of them blazing. And blaze they did.

She might be young, but the bride had already developed a strong will of her own. Before Theodore arrived in Georgia for the ceremony, she taunted him with the fact that she was receiving attention from other men. It was her right, she insisted, even as an engaged woman to dance with whomever she pleased. She even presumed to dictate his behavior, writing him careful instructions to arrive one day before the nuptials "and not a day sooner." Later it would be said that she possessed her own unique way of doing things, but even in her teens she showed a headstrong quality that set her apart from her contemporaries. For this occasion she had boasted to the bridegroom that she meant to show everyone in attendance how such celebrations should be staged.

Mittie's self-confidence showed in her choice of bridesmaids: she selected local women all slightly older than herself. Besides sister Anna, three girlhood friends stood beside the bride that evening: Evelyn King, from the impressive Barrington Hall a half mile down the road, and two others who came from only slightly farther away but from equally stately homes. All of them wore white, but Mittie's sanguine manner left no doubt about which one deserved center stage. It is sometimes said that every woman is beautiful on her wedding day, but Mittie was extraordinary. Barely five feet tall, she had the clear blue eyes and tiny hands and feet of a mannequin. But her most remarkable features were her complexion, described by her granddaughter as "more moonlight white than cream-white," and her mass of shiny black hair.

Definitely the bride's party, this celebration drew guests from all over that part of Georgia but only a remarkably small contingent of Roosevelts. None of Theodore's four brothers or their families had made the trip south for the ceremony; only his parents, the severe Cornelius Van Schaack Roosevelt, a prosperous New York merchant, and his Philadelphia-born wife, Margaret Barnhill, represented the clan. This marked the first time either Margaret or Cornelius had ventured into the Deep South. Evelyn King sensed some discomfort on their part, and many years later, as the last surviving bridesmaid, she told a young reporter, then known as Peggy Mitchell but later famous as the author of *Gone with the Wind*, what she thought of the Roosevelts: "Like most northern people of that time, they were very ignorant about the South. Goodness only knows what they expected us to be like."

Immediately following the ceremony, the celebration began. The bride's family had been preparing for weeks, and now tables throughout Bulloch Hall displayed an array of hams, turkeys, and cakes, alongside a huge assortment of salads and pickled vegetables. Most dazzling of all, the "frozen cream" attracted a string of gawkers. Ice cream, known in England since the mid-1600s, had been introduced in the colonies around the time of the Revolution, and Dolley Madison served the delicacy at her husband's second inaugural ball in 1813. But places like Roswell, Georgia, where temperatures rarely fell to freezing, had less acquaintance with the cold, creamy dessert. For Mittie's wedding the ice had to be shipped in from the North, and then, using the newly invented ice cream freezer, servants cranked several gallons of cream, sugar, and flavorings into a luscious concoction in just a few minutes.

In the style of the time, the festivities continued for one full week. For guests who had traveled too far to return home each night, the neighboring houses provided sleeping space, although hours for sleeping were short. During the day, luncheons and teas kept the older guests busy while the young people walked and rode horses. In the evening, all ages mingled in dancing and storytelling that filled the houses with song and laughter. Mittie's brother Dan provided the music the day of the ceremony by playing his flute "in perfect time" and thus making an indelible impression on the staid Roosevelts. In the days following the reception, hired musicians joined in, rotating with each other and the guests until it became impossible to distinguish who among them had come to work and who to dance. After seven days of fun, the wedding finally ended. As Evelyn King told Margaret Mitchell many years later: "Everybody packed up and went home for it was all over and we were very tired."

I

THE YOUNG Mrs. Roosevelt, who had written her fiancé just weeks earlier that he was the "only person who could so suit me and I put every confidence in you," now gamely set out with her new husband for the trip north. During the journey—partly in a carriage and partly by ship, Mittie Bulloch Roosevelt had plenty of time to think about what she was leaving behind. She may have had some doubts about the family she was marrying into, but not because of any feelings of inadequacy about her own family tree. Quite the contrary, she had reason to sense a slight edge on her part, especially if she ignored money and counted up the many achievements of her ancestors. An unbiased observer might have backed her up. Seven generations of Roosevelts had lived in America without achieving much fame, but their star rose quickly after she married into the clan.

By any standard, but certainly in comparison with the stodgy Roosevelts, the Bullochs were a colorful bunch. Family lore always included the story of the dramatic arrival in America of the family of Mittie's great-great-grandmother Jean Stobo. Had it not been for a remarkable chain of events, the Stobos might never have left Scotland or settled in the Carolinas.

The story begins in 1699 with Archibald Stobo. Then a young Presbyterian minister, he decided to join five other clergymen taking religion to a part of the world then known as Darien but later famous as Panama. Fresh out of the University of Edinburgh and newly married, he had enormous enthusiasm for the project, but unlike his fellow ministers, he wanted to take his bride with him, and she apparently wanted to go. Together the young couple sailed with several hundred Scots in early fall 1699. The trip must have seemed like a fairy tale adventure, especially when the travelers got their first glimpse of land—a tropical island.

But a very different picture met them when they reached their destination in late November. Instead of finding the thriving colony they expected, they found a settlement in ruins: the crude huts, built by the previous missionaries, had been burned down, and the surrounding area was overgrown with brush. The new arrivals had too much religious faith to give up immediately, but as they set to work trying to arrange for the minimum comforts, they were quickly weakened by tropical diseases.

As the months passed, the Stobos and their expedition faced a more ominous threat. The Spanish had not yet relinquished the idea of controlling that part of the Western Hemisphere, and the Scottish missionaries feared an attack. By February 1700 the young Mrs.

Stobo wanted to leave. But that required official permission from the church hierarchy that had financed the trip in the first place. On March 10, while the Stobos were still waiting for their request to be granted, the Spaniards landed ready for battle. Weakened by months of illness and a meager diet, many of the Scots had already died, and those who survived had little fight left in them. By the end of the month they surrendered. The Spaniards, however, raised no objection to their captives' leaving, and on April 11 the Presbyterians headed home on a ship called the *Rising Sun.*

On the way, the *Rising Sun* stopped at Charleston, South Carolina, the most important seaport in the South and home of many transplanted English nobles. During the ship's stay in Charleston harbor, Archibald Stobo, known as a magnetic speaker, agreed to preach to a local congregation. That day, while he and his wife were ashore, a violent storm came up suddenly, completely destroying the *Rising Sun* and killing everyone who had remained aboard. The Stobos took this as a clear signal that they should remain in Charleston. It was there, one year later, that their daughter, Jean, was born. It was her marriage to a local man, James Bulloch, that began the line that produced Mittie Bulloch and, later, Theodore Roosevelt and his remarkable sisters.

Neither her son Theodore nor her daughters made much of Mittie's early roots, but from the colonial period the Bullochs stood out as leaders and doers. Leaving the Carolinas in 1760 to take advantage of a two-thousand-acre land grant, they moved to Georgia where they quickly made names for themselves. Archibald Bulloch, a lawyer (and son of Jean Stobo Bulloch), served as speaker of the Georgia Royal Assembly, president of the Provincial Congress that took charge of the state in July 1775, and, later, as the state's commander-in-chief and one of its delegates to the First Continental Congress.

The Roosevelt women in Mittie's line never had any trouble establishing their credentials for membership in the Daughters of the American Revolution. On her father's side, Mittie was descended from James Bulloch, and on her mother's side, from Daniel Stewart. Both served courageously in the War for Independence, and Stewart also made a name for himself in the War of 1812.

The Bullochs' move to Georgia before the Revolution proved fortuitous. Savannah still struggled to survive when they first settled there, but it quickly grew in importance as cotton became the region's biggest crop. In 1793 the introduction of one simple machine, the cotton gin, changed the picture for cotton since the short staple variety, once deemed unusable because of its many seeds, could now be cheaply "combed out." As thousands of acres of cotton were planted across the South, Savannah became one of the central points for collection and shipment, and it was in this side of the business that the Bullochs prospered. By the time Mittie was born there in 1835, Savannah ranked among the top few cities in the amount of cotton it handled, and her father was one of the shippers.

By that time the Bulloch story had taken on elements of an Italian opera, with as many unlikely marriages as a farcical story line. Mittie was the child of one of these curious matches. Her parents, the handsome and charming James Bulloch (great-grandson of the original James Bulloch) and the beautiful Martha Stewart, grew up together in Savannah and courted each other, but for reasons never clear, they did not marry. Martha had other suitors, which may have irritated the self-confident James. One of the most ardent of her admirers was a widower, John Elliott, who came from a distinguished moneyed family and seemed headed for the U.S. Senate. The prospect of accompanying him to Washington, D.C., added glamour to his marriage offer and partly offset the fact that he was old enough to be her father. Still, Martha put him off, and while she dallied, weighing her options, James Bulloch married John Elliott's daughter, who at nineteen was just two years older than Martha. Within a week Martha had consented to marry the prospective senator, thus becoming, in 1818, the step-mother-in-law of her former suitor. Although the timing is curious, the motivation remains unclear. Her granddaughter Bamie later recalled hearing that Martha Stewart's hasty marriage to John Elliott occurred because her father was moving to Florida, a part of the frontier where he felt he could safely take his six sons but hesitated to take his only daughter.

The same year she married him, John Elliott did indeed win election to the U.S. Senate, and his young wife—on her first trip out of the Deep South—accompanied him to the capital. She did not go unnoticed. Extremely beautiful and very young for a legislator's wife, she called attention to herself by stylish clothing, often featuring an ostrich feather that "hung down to her belt." When she went on her husband's arm to church services at St. John's, just across Lafayette

Park from the President's House, she caused heads to turn, and when she held court at home, she attracted comment on her style and verve. John Elliott served only one term in the capital, and then he and his young wife moved back to Georgia. But a century later their great-granddaughter, Alice Roosevelt Longworth, attracted the same kind of attention as had the senator's wife.

The glamorous, young Mrs. Elliott might have anticipated returning to Washington, D.C., if her husband ever ran for and won a second term, but she never got the chance. Ten years after Martha married him, the senator died, and then, within a few months, his married daughter also died. Martha Elliott, now almost thirty years old, and her former suitor, James Bulloch, once again found themselves free to wed. They waited five years, perhaps concerned that some of the family found it strange that "Brother James" would marry "Mother Martha," and then they married in the Elliott house in Savannah on May 8, 1832. Americans, especially those of substantial wealth, frequently chose their mates from within the family circle in order to safeguard their property, but this union—involving not blood relatives but relatives by marriage—raised a few eyebrows.

More important to the story is the apparently joyful mixing of the several families, which was even more complicated than the proverbial "his," "hers," and "theirs." Martha brought two daughters and one son from her union with the senator; James Bulloch brought one son, who was already Martha's step-grandson by virtue of her previous marriage to the senator but now became her stepson as well. Martha and James Bulloch would eventually have four children of their own, but neither parent nor any of the children played favorites among the several batches. Mittie later recalled that she "never knew the difference" between her Bulloch half-brother and her own siblings. The next generation, more removed from the scene, had trouble getting everyone straight; and Mittie's daughter Corinne once wrote in a description of her first trip abroad, "My grandmother Roosevelt's family has always been most confusing in its relationships."

Martha's stepson, also called James, helped insert an interesting twist in the story. At the age of ten he was sent to boarding school in Connecticut, providing Martha with an excellent reason to make a trip north to visit him in the spring of 1835. Although several months pregnant, she made the journey from Savannah to Hartford accompanied by a female entourage that included her thirteen-year-old daughter from her first marriage and several slaves. Traveling in style, Martha settled in at Miss Oakes' Boarding House on Hartford's Main Street, a place so selective that the other guests had to preapprove all new lodgers. Once endorsed, Martha made friendships that lasted a lifetime, and after her death, her children and grandchildren sustained those friendships through generations. Nine decades after Martha left Connecticut, her granddaughter Bamie mused over the fact that an old friend of the family had died: "the one in whose grandmother's pew our grandmother always sat when at church during those months she spent in Hartford."

As summer temperatures rose in 1835, the pregnant Martha Bulloch deferred returning to Georgia, and on July 8 she gave birth to a baby girl. Whether the new mother had already conferred with her husband on a name or simply took it upon herself to choose one remains unclear. She already had two daughters (Susan and Georgia) by the senator and one (Anna) by James Bulloch, but now, several hundred miles away from the new baby's father, Martha named this child for herself. Dubbed "Mittie" from the start, the baby was introduced by that name to relatives and friends when she arrived in Georgia that fall. On the return trip, Martha had one less slave in her entourage, having granted freedom to a woman who requested it. According to family legend, Martha Bulloch even agreed to support the woman until she found work, thus showing a concern for others, whether slave or free, that her descendants liked to emphasize.

In 1838, while Mittie was still a toddler, her parents moved the family westward, away from the coast and into the hinterland. With six youngsters and two slave couples, the Bullochs followed an old Savannah friend to a place on the Chattahoochee River where a new settlement was under way at Roswell, thirteen miles north of Atlanta. High enough to be free of swampy patches, Roswell boasted a waterfall, which the settlers saw as furnishing power for the cotton mill they hoped to build.

In pioneer fashion the Bullochs lived in makeshift quarters (later transformed to slave dwellings) while construction began for the mansion that became Bulloch Hall. Mimosa Hall across the road and Barrington King's home, less than a mile away, were both far grander, but Bulloch Hall reflected its owners' wish for something elegant, yet practical and relatively unostentatious. Behind the tall Doric columns it featured a main hall with a grand staircase leading up to the second floor. Planned more with an eye to the region's oppressive summer heat than to the short but occasionally extremely cold winters, the house had huge windows to take advantage of the slightest breeze. The most whimsical feature of this stately house, visible not to the casual visitor but only to someone with the right vantage point, was the driveway. Shaped to form a valentine, it led from the road up to the wide front verandah (situated squarely at the top of the heart) and then, after another loop, back out to the road.

Every nook and cranny of Bulloch Hall remained imprinted in Mittie's mind long after she had left it, and she passed on that love and knowledge of the place to her children. In 1912, three decades after Mittie's death, her younger daughter, Corinne, went back to see Bulloch Hall as a grown woman. She could hardly believe that a place she had visited only briefly at age seven could remain so accurately recorded in her mind. Mittie's descriptions were so vivid and affectionate, her accounts of the Bulloch family so rich and complete, that Corinne felt "everything was just as I thought it would be—lovely old fireplace, splendid proportions and a beautiful view from the same back porch." In her mind's eye, Corinne saw them as clearly as though they stood before her, "and when I picked a piece of ivy from the same tree where my mother had gathered wet leaves for her lovely hair," she wrote, "my heart felt tender beyond words."

During the time that Mittie's family occupied Bulloch Hall, maintenance of the house and grounds depended on slave labor, a fact that her Roosevelt descendants would find "incredible" and, for the most part, avoid discussing. The evidence, however, is clear. Federal census takers in 1850 listed nineteen slaves at Bulloch Hall, including thirteen adults and six children.

It appears that each Bulloch child was assigned a personal slave, or "shadow," to act as companion. Mittie's "Lavinia," for example, went everywhere with her, stopping outside the classroom when Mittie went inside, and sleeping on a mat by her side at night. For the family, the stress was on the pleasure of the companionship rather than on the hostage implications in the arrangement or the grimmer side of slavery.

As a young child, Mittie's brother Irvine (always the "little brother" because he was seven years her junior) developed a close and mutually dependent relationship with his personal slave, Sarah.

The two became nearly inseparable for the very practical reason that they depended on each other for comfort and protection. Since she feared the darkness outside the house as much as he was terrified of the darkness inside, they huddled together on the back porch after the sun set, speculating on how the moon "crawled" and how thousands of fantastic creatures swarmed and swirled in the void just beyond what either of them could see or touch.

The sinister aspect to the slave system lay only slightly below the surface, even in the Bullochs' paternalistic accounts. One of Mittie's brothers shot and killed a slave in a fit of temper, and then in a not unusual rendering of "justice," he took a short vacation abroad rather than face the repercussions.

Mittie's children and grandchildren repeated her accounts of what it was like to grow up in the South. Since the "master" family had stressed the colorful personalities and individual strength of "the people" who worked the place, generations of Roosevelts passed on stories about "Daddy Luke," the accomplished and reliable coachman, and "Mom Charlotte," his handsome, elegant wife who left no doubt but that it was she who supervised the house. Much less was said about the murder of the young slave.

James and Martha Bulloch no doubt anticipated an easier, more relaxed life when they completed their spacious mansion, but it seemed tainted with bad luck almost from the beginning. Their first son, born at Bulloch Hall in 1837, died before his third birthday. In 1849 tragedy struck twice. First, daughter Georgia died at age twenty-seven, and then, less than five months later, James dropped dead while teaching a Sunday School class. Only fifty-five, he had enjoyed his new home for less than a decade. In his will he left his wife a considerable estate, including the plantation, a house in Savannah, and stock in a company that sent the first steamship across the Atlantic. Having served as president of the Savannah branch of the United States Bank, he had helped fund a textile factory that was still under construction at the time of his death but could be expected to produce income in the future.

Widowed at forty-nine, Martha Bulloch soon found that her life was being shaped more and more around her adult children. Daughter Susan's marriage to a Philadelphia physician, Hillbourne West, meant that she had moved north, but this union provided an important link in the Roosevelt story. To entertain her guests in Philadelphia, Susan would tell enchanting stories about growing up in the rural South. And because wealthy families of that era tended to socialize primarily with other family members, rather than neighbors or friends, among the frequent visitors to her home in Philadelphia were her sister-in-law from New York, Mary West, and Mary's husband, Silas Weir Roosevelt, occasionally accompanied by Silas's younger brother, Theodore Roosevelt. Here the plot thickens.

∽

Theodore, it seems, was smitten enough by Susan West's tales to want to see Bulloch Hall for himself, or at least that was how his family remembered the story. Susan may have harbored other thoughts when she described her loving family life and, in particular, her younger, extraordinarily beautiful sister, Mittie. Whether Theodore's thoughts ran in the same direction, family letters do not reveal. What is clear is that in 1850 the Wests invited nineteen-year-old Theodore to join them on their next trip home, and he accepted.

Love at first sight it was not—at least for the fifteen-year-old Mittie. For one thing, Theodore appeared so determinedly serious that she found him boring. He insisted on referring to plants by their Latin names and showed little appreciation of the frivolous activity and witty remarks so prized by the fun-loving Bullochs. Perhaps he was merely compensating for the insecurities of his childhood. As the fifth son of Cornelius Van Schaack and Margaret Roosevelt, he may have felt a bit neglected. Later he regaled his own children with stories of what it felt like to be the "fifth wheel to the coach" and unwilling recipient of his brothers' cast-off clothes. His mother evidently had her hands too full to give more than a distracted nod to her youngest, and she was routinely described around New York as "that lovely Mrs. Roosevelt" with "those five horrid boys."

One story, perhaps apocryphal, described Cornelius and Margaret Roosevelt, dressed in their Sunday best, walking out of church services one Sunday morning to face the spectacle of their youngest sons astride a pig and riding through the mud holes down the middle of Canal Street. Unfortunately, none of that mischievousness appears to have survived in the Theodore who visited the Bullochs in 1850.

But Mittie clearly made a permanent impression on him. With that creamy complexion that is so notable in person but cannot translate into words or pictures, she struck her contemporaries as "fascinating looking." She was relatively untutored, but Theodore apparently liked what he saw. According to family lore, he sent her a gold thimble after returning to New York.

Twelve months later, while traveling through Europe, he wrote a letter home in which he admitted he was seriously looking for a wife but did not mean to settle for less than the best. To his mind there were still plenty of fish in the sea "as were ever caught," and he wrote his aunt Lizzie that he had his eye on a young woman from Philadelphia by the name of "Stuart." As soon as he returned to the United States, he meant to look her up again. Although he had both her name and hometown incorrect, he surely meant Mittie Bulloch, daughter of Martha Stewart Bulloch of Roswell, Georgia, and half-sister of Susan West of Philadelphia. Perhaps he erred on purpose, aware that many of his family would be disappointed to hear that he had fallen for a southern girl.

Theodore's failure to court Mittie immediately (other than sending the thimble) is understandable in light of her age. Since she was only fifteen when he met her, he thought he had plenty of time to travel on his own, something that his four older brothers, who were married with families, rarely did. After a trip through the Midwest to look at family real estate, he sailed for Europe in June 1851. In London he saw the usual sights and then proceeded to hit all the cities traditionally part of the Grand Tour, including Paris, Florence, and Avignon. After eighteen months on the continent, he headed home, accompanied by a fellow bachelor from New York, John Carow. The two young men, very different in personality and goals, would cross paths many times, but only one of them would live long enough to see their children married to each other.

While Theodore was traveling in Europe, Mittie did what most wealthy young southern women did, and there is no evidence she gave much thought to him. Her mother had decided to send Mittie, along with her sister Anna, who was two years older, to a young ladies' academy in South Carolina. It is a remarkable decision because it meant that of all her children, only Irvine remained at home. After two years of studying at the academy, the sisters made their way to Philadelphia to visit Susan and Hillbourne West. As soon as Theodore learned that Mittie was a guest in the West household, he wasted no time in arranging an invitation to Philadelphia for himself. This time Mittie took more notice of him, if subsequent events are any indication, and the acquaintance of the two young people, renewed on neutral territory, quickly blossomed into romance. He invited her to New York City, where she stayed with Silas and Mary West Roosevelt, and had her first introduction to Theodore's parents.

Once in New York, Mittie evidently caught a glimpse of a special quality in Theodore that his children would later relish—a combination of spirit and goodness, of vitality and charity. They would call him the best man they ever knew, and they singled out the times with him as the most cherished of all their childhood memories. As Mittie got to know him better on that New York visit, she kept postponing her return to Georgia. Finally, sister Anna, who had gone on ahead, wrote back, inquiring into the causes for the delay, and the young couple, still in New York, had to decide what to do.

Mittie returned to Georgia, and days later, on May 15, 1853, Theodore wrote a letter asking her mother for permission to marry Mittie. Martha Bulloch must have had some misgivings about a second daughter marrying a northerner, but she kept them to herself. Replying immediately to "Mr Roosevelt Dear Sir," she recalled his previous visit with "much pleasure" but left the matter of marriage up to the principals: "I have never interfered with the matrimonial designs of my children and never will when the object chosen is a worthy one. Therefore I refer the matter back to Mittie and yourself." Theodore quickly arranged a trip to Georgia, and by the time he left Bulloch Hall a few weeks later, the engagement was official.

Now the tables turned a bit. The prospective bridegroom was nearly twenty-three, a typical age for men to marry at that time, but he may have had second thoughts once his fate seemed assured. In his correspondence with a friend, he jokingly referred to marriage as a "trap." Mittie, on the other hand, could hardly control her girlish exuberance. After her "Dearest Thee" left Georgia to attend to some business in New York, she wrote him that she loved him "tenderly." Try as she would, she could not help but cry when she saw him ride away. Tears came to her eyes with such force that she had to "rush away and be alone with myself. Everything now seems associated with you."

Mittie's tiny, regular script bespeaks a cautious, precise woman, and her vocabulary of carefully chosen, long words signals unusual intelligence. But she would soon have a chance to test how far that intelligence and self-confidence would take her. It was not a good time for a southern woman to marry a northerner, just when their respective regions of the nation moved toward civil war. Other eighteen-year-olds might have hesitated to move so far away from home, but it had already been demonstrated that Mittie did not do things like other people.

II

BEFORE HER wedding in December 1853, Mittie had spent little time above the Mason-Dixon line, but it was enough to show her that most northerners did not see slavery as her family did. Debate had recently sharpened over the extension of slavery into the territories, and by the time of Mittie's wedding, the Great Compromise of 1850—an attempt to draw a line across the United States, permanently separating the "slave" states from the "free"—showed little sign of holding. Some of her Georgia neighbors had talked of war, and even inside Bulloch Hall she had heard her two brothers' angry outbursts about what they would do if the U.S. Congress attempted to impose its will on the South in the matter of slavery. The right of individual states to decide important things for themselves had long been a tenet of southern political thought, and the Bullochs spoke as adamantly on the subject as anyone in Georgia.

To make matters worse for the young bride, she and Theodore had to reside with his parents when they reached New York—at least until their new house, a few blocks away, was ready for them. It was not a question of money. The family had plenty of that, but Margaret and Cornelius Van Schaack Roosevelt (known to history as CVS) made a point of keeping their children close to them, forming a kind of enclave protecting them from the rest of the world.

Their huge house on the southwest corner of Broadway and Fourteenth Street had been built in the 1830s specifically to accommodate their extended family after smaller residences proved inadequate. This mansion, less than an hour's walk from where the Roosevelt ancestors had started out in the mid 1600s, was one of the city's grand houses, but previous addresses had been more humble. The Roosevelts had added other enterprises to the mundane hardware business of the late 1700s, including real estate and a tannery, so that by the 1850s when Mittie joined the clan, her father-in-law was known as an important merchant, the founder and director of the Chemical National Bank, and one of the richest men in the city.

The rise in status had been relatively recent. CVS and Margaret had started out their married life in a modest house at the foot of Broadway, just above Bowling Green, when that part of New York still had the feel of a small town, and the family could sit on the back porch and watch ships come into the harbor. At 94 Maiden Lane they lived "above the store," before another move took them to Canal Street when it was still partly waterway. With each rise in their fortune they moved farther north, along with other successful New Yorkers.

When CVS and Margaret Roosevelt bought the huge plot at the corner of Broadway and Fourteenth Street, it faced what would later become an important gathering place and public park known as Union Square but at the time was still on the outskirts of city life. The Roosevelts were hardly facing the kind of risk that the Bullochs found in Roswell, but the site of their new home did seem an outpost in one respect—it lacked omnibus service. An older brother of CVS, James Roosevelt, a judge in the New York State Supreme Court, built an equally grand house on the opposite side of Broadway, and when the two men walked to work together in Lower Manhattan, they passed near Roosevelt Street. Their family had once owned large tracts of land in that part of the city, and the profits from the sales had provided a sizable chunk of the Roosevelt fortune. By the 1850s, however, the area around Roosevelt Street had taken on an unsavory reputation, replete with the crime and filth often associated with docks and overpopulated areas. As the brothers relished their success, they could, for the moment, overlook their differences, including their disagreements about social matters. The judge's wife, a daughter of the governor of Vermont, liked to entertain in what others described as "a foreign manner" because she had "evenings at home" for people who were not Roosevelts.

Though grand, the four-story house that CVS and Margaret built at Fourteenth Street was, relatively speaking, a simple house, later described by their granddaughter Bamie as "dignified." Built before the excesses of ornate Victorian furnishings gained favor, it included a ground floor study where their sons had their lessons. One cartoon of the time showed the boys' private tutor, John McMullen, looking helplessly out the window as his charges fled on horseback. During the summers, after the classes ended, the entire family moved out of the city for two months of country air, even though the plot on Broadway almost qualified as country. CVS had bought the entire block between Thirteenth and Fourteenth, as well as about 130 feet on Thirteenth Street, so that his wife could have a rose garden.

Guests at the Roosevelt house entered from Broadway, through a large door with two widely spaced windows on either side. Once inside the huge entry hall, visitors were immediately struck by the circular staircase that extended all the way to the top of the house, giving a majestic feeling, and the mahogany handrails and marble floor that provided a cool elegance. On the left side of the house, where lots of sun came through because the buildings to the south were still low, Margaret often sat beside a fireplace in the dining room, her sewing work basket and a pile of books close at hand. It was here that her five sons, who showed enormous devotion to her once they became adults, stopped to pay their respects each morning before they walked to work. Her grandchildren also expected to find her here, not far from a small closet in which she always kept a dish of perfectly polished apples and squares of rich pound cake to offer guests at any hour they happened to appear. On Saturday evenings the dining room bustled with activity as the whole extended family gathered there for dinner.

None of the other rooms on the first floor could compete with the sunny dining room because those on the right side of the hall all faced north. The big, stiffly furnished parlor seemed a little offputting, and the library beyond it, although lined with books and maps, lacked any chairs or other places to sit. It served more as a reference room where a book could be taken or some information looked up to use elsewhere.

Much as they liked to have their family around them, CVS and Margaret did not expect their married sons to remain with them indefinitely: each received his own brownstone as a gift. Two generations later, when Eleanor Roosevelt's mother-in-law bestowed a townhouse on her and Franklin (alongside one for herself), the act was viewed as unduly manipulative, but in fact the Roosevelts had a long tradition for such generosity and emphasis on proximity. CVS and Margaret built their sons' houses within a few blocks of each other and their own. Four of the houses were strung along Twentieth Street between Broadway and what was then Fourth Avenue but later became Park Avenue South, the one farthest east, Number 28, designated for Mittie and Theodore. When the young couple moved into the house in late 1854, Mittie was visibly pregnant, having conceived almost immediately after her wedding. Although she delighted in having her own place, she understood that she would still be expected to trek over to her in-laws several times a week.

On the only trip Mittie made to New York before her marriage, she sensed that her future mother-in-law did not like her, and she had relayed those doubts to Theodore, who tried to reassure her. Now, settled in New York, the young Georgian found Theodore's family polite and kind, but in one matter they frequently offended. Whenever the talk turned to slavery (and that was about the most important topic in the nation in the late 1850s), Mittie had to bite her tongue rather than come to the defense of southern slave owners like her family. Nineteen years old, pregnant, and hundreds of miles from Bulloch Hall, she would have to face such situations on her own.

When her first child was born on January 7, 1855, Mittie named her Anna for her favorite sister, but she called her "Bamie," from the Italian word *bambina* (little girl). None of the Bullochs had ever been to Italy, nor did they speak the language. But somehow Mittie approved of this delicate, soft-sounding Italian word as the nickname for her first daughter, and it stuck. No one in the family ever called her Anna, and historians have always favored the nickname.

For nearly four years Bamie was an only child, doted on by both parents, but Mittie understood that maternal responsibilities did not excuse her from all the family gatherings. The Roosevelts could be very severe and intolerant of views that differed from their own. After Bamie grew up, she admitted that her mother had shown remarkable fortitude, given the circumstances, and the daughter was not sure she could have performed as well. "I should hate to have married into [the Roosevelts] at that time," Bamie later wrote, "unless I had been one of them in thought. They think they are just, but they are hard."

It may have been partly a desire to escape the tensions in her situation that caused Mittie to take four-month-old Bamie on a trip home to Roswell in May 1855. During this, the first separation of husband and wife, their correspondence reveals a strong devotion to each other. Mittie repeatedly wrote of her love for "my darling husband" and of how she felt happy and protected when with him. Although this reunion with her mother and sister in Georgia reminded her of how much she loved them both, Mittie could not imagine living without Theodore. "I love you always and at all times but this afternoon I love you with so much tenderness," she wrote him on May 12, that "I cannot express half I feel."

Theodore responded in letters that mixed teasing with concern. After hinting that she seemed to be enjoying herself too much in Georgia, he vowed to join her as soon as possible, bringing with him the "enormous quart bottle" of the hair tonic that she had requested. As she prepared for his arrival, Mittie wrote him on May 17, "My own dearest Thee, I feel as tho I could not wait another minute to see you . . . I miss you in everything." She loved him "more than any other person," she assured him, and "I feel that you are everything to me . . . oh dearest, I hope we will be with each other a long long time" and never "be separated from each other again."

In conferring on plans for the summer, when both of them would be back in New York, Theodore sought his wife's approval. He hoped she would consent to renting a house in Orange, New Jersey, a fashionable spot at the time, so that he could go riding with her in the afternoons and the baby could have fresh country air. Joking about how much he missed her, he enclosed a dead insect in one of his letters, noting that it was "dedicated to the memory of his wife by Theo Roosevelt." Then he urged Mittie to delay getting her hair cut until after he arrived.

That trip to Georgia not only convinced Mittie how much she loved her husband and valued his companionship, it affected her mother's life, too. It had been nearly six years since her husband died, and Martha was finding Bulloch Hall a drain on her purse. The sight of little Bamie made her question her reasons for remaining in Georgia. With two of her married daughters now living in the North and her sons scattered, Martha had less reason to hold on to the family home, and during Mittie's visit she made up her mind to rent out Bulloch Hall, sell the furniture, and move north. Accompanied by Anna, twenty-two years old and still unmarried, Martha stayed for about a year with Susan and Hillborne West in Philadelphia, and then, in 1857, they moved to New York to reside with Mittie and Theodore.

Not long after Martha and Anna's arrival, Mittie began producing children again, and she did so at relatively short intervals: Theodore was born in October 1858; Elliott, sixteen months later; and then, nineteen months after that, another daughter, Corinne. In a pattern later repeated by her daughter and granddaughters, she had no more children after the age of thirty-six, suggesting the possibility that at least one of the parents decided that four were enough.

Mittie functioned as household manager, directing a full staff of "devoted servants," including a butler, gardener, cooks, cleaners, and children's nurses. While Martha provided some help, Mittie's most valued assistance came from Anna. The older sibling cheerfully tutored her nieces and nephews, who later agreed that she was "the most charming aunt . . . with whom children were ever blessed." In the beginning, she earned her keep as the children's teacher, since she had little income and did not wish to burden her brother-in-law, but her enthusiasm for the task soon outweighed any sense of obligation.

Aunt Anna, considered by the family "more spiritually minded [than Mittie] and very religious," regaled the children with stories about Georgia and what it had been like to grow up there. Mittie and Anna spurred each other to recount endless intrigues and adventures in graphic detail. When one of them forgot some small particular, the other prompted, and then, laughing together over the memory, they emphasized more than words ever could just how much fun they had had.

The stories about Georgia may have been delivered as much for the women's benefit as for the children's. Hundreds of miles away from Bulloch Hall, the two sisters relished every chance to mention it. Years later Bamie told a friend of hers in Washington, D.C., how she had come to know "everything about Georgia and Georgians that my mother knew. All the old jokes . . ." But what really made Bamie's "heart ache" was the realization that those stories were full of pain for her mother. "I could not know then," Bamie told her friend, "but I do now." Mittie was so homesick "for her own people [that] her heart bled." The stories were always of Georgia: "I never remember hearing her tell stories of any other part of the world; . . . and it was out of the very fullness of her heart that she used to tell us of home."

In recounting the games they had played or one of the Br'er Rabbit tales they liked, Mittie and Anna used words and phrases that the

New York–born children would not have otherwise heard, thus exposing them to special cadences and sounds. Bamie later showed a special fondness for the book *Porgy* (on which the musical *Porgy and Bess* was based) because the cadence of the language brought back stories from her youth. Combining humor, mystery, and adventure, Aunt Anna's accounts frequently received new twists in each telling. It is difficult to know how far Anna Bulloch's teaching and stories reached, but when President Theodore Roosevelt admonished his nation to "speak softly and carry a big stick," he echoed the "big stick" phrase he had first encountered in a McGuffey's reader that he studied with his aunt Anna.

During the two decades (1854–1873) that Mittie raised her children and hosted many parties on Twentieth Street, the surrounding blocks held a variety of little shops (along with lots of Roosevelt cousins). Bamie later recalled that whenever she walked to the house of her uncle James, she passed Badeau's grocery on the southwest corner of Broadway and Twentieth, and there would be "old Mrs. Badeau with a cap tied under her chin sitting in a window sewing." The Badeau name entered the Roosevelt lexicon, and a "Badeau secret" became code for any important secret that the children shared. The usage seemed natural enough—it originated when they concocted a joke, using a product from Badeau's grocery to pull it off. As Bamie told it, they hid a mouse "inside a partly used Dutchman's head cheese so when the cheese was past at table and Father took off the top, the mouse bounced out to the horror of everyone."

The house on Twentieth Street had a very special feeling about it that could never be reproduced. After the Roosevelts moved out, it was gutted to make a factory, but then, following the younger Theodore Roosevelt's death in 1919, it was rebuilt in 1923 to create a monument to the popular President. After it opened to the public, Bamie complained to her sister that the dimensions might be identical but the atmosphere was not: "I am so glad that the people at large really enjoy Roosevelt House but I never can get away from the feeling of how curiously different it is from the days of our childhood," when the street had boasted more than its share of exotic creatures. Bamie recalled "Mr. Goelet's birds of paradise [and his] pheasants." It was Goelet's magpie that gave the Roosevelts the most trouble—it would swoop over their outdoor "piazza" and pick up whatever shiny object caught its attention. Bamie recalled that

Aunt Anna once lost her watch in the middle of the winter and only "discovered it when the snow had melted" and she found it "in the gutter where the magpie had apparently dropped it."

Other fond memories concerned the outdoor exercise room that Theodore Sr. built for the children. For a family later known for physical prowess, these little Roosevelts looked like a sickly lot. Bamie had been born with a weakness in her spine, evident from the first time she tried to stand on her feet. Theodore was skinny, with weak eyesight and frequent and severe asthma attacks. Elliott, the only one of Mittie's children to inherit the good looks for which her side of the family was noted, began having mysterious headaches before he reached his teens. Corinne, the youngest, suffered from asthma (even more severely than Theodore) and hideous skin rashes that broke out all over her face and body for reasons unrelated to any identifiable cause. For each of these problems, Theodore Sr. counseled exercise, and the piazza that he built on the south side of his townhouse served as the exercise room.

Open to the weather, with a railing about nine feet high, the space faced south and was fitted with athletic equipment, including ladders, weights, and both parallel and swinging bars. About twenty-five feet long and twenty feet deep, the porch was warmed by the sun in the winter, and during the summer, wisteria sheltered it from excessive heat. Robert Roosevelt, an older brother of Theodore Sr., constructed a similar piazza on his adjoining house so that when the barrier between them was removed, one enormous, long porch provided a gymnasium large enough for the competitive little Roosevelts to run to their hearts' content.

Neither Mittie nor Robert's wife, Lizzie, would go near the exercise room, but Lizzie saw no reason that her many pets should not enjoy the space alongside the children. Her menagerie included guinea pigs, chickens, and a monkey that she sometimes dressed as a human being in little ruffled shirts and gold studs. Decked out in these clothes, the monkey could be very rambunctious, biting anyone who came within reach, and Bamie became one of its victims. One evening she was badly bitten—and carried the scars to prove it for the rest of her life— but while others chastised the offending monkey, its owner's sympathy was entirely on the monkey's side. Over and over again Aunt Lizzie kept soothing "poor Topsy" while Bamie shrieked with pain.

Aunt Lizzie was finally stymied when she insisted on installing a cow in the backyard. Since the only way to get it there was through the house, it was led down the stairs into the basement and then out to the yard. When the neighbors objected and threatened legal action, removing the cow proved more difficult because the animal, having once traversed the brownstone's basement, refused to repeat the experience. Finally, Bamie recalled, "it had to have its legs bound partly together and its eyes blindfolded" before it could be dragged out.

Weird as these episodes sound, Aunt Lizzie's real life was even more bizarre. She had married Robert Barnwell Roosevelt in 1850, but that marriage had never been as satisfactory as Mittie's. Robert had achieved a considerable reputation as a writer, lawyer, and conservationist, even getting himself elected to the U.S. Congress in 1870 and serving one term. But at the very time that he was representing his neighbors in Washington, he began keeping another family a few blocks away from Lizzie. While his wife raised their four children, the other woman, known in the neighborhood as the "Widow Fortescue," began raising the four born to her and Robert. Following Lizzie's death in 1887, Robert married the "widow" and the family regarded the four little "Fortescue children" as his stepchildren, but that open acceptance of them could not have occurred during Lizzie's lifetime. Bamie, old enough to sense the tensions in her uncle's house next door, could very well have connected her aunt's eccentric behavior with her unorthodox circumstances.

In recalling episodes from her youth, Bamie held a definite advantage over her younger siblings. Because of the unusually long interval between her birth and that of the next three, she always seemed to move easily among people of her parents' generation, almost as though she entered the world as a mature woman. Corinne explained later that Bamie, "though only four years older than my brother Theodore, was always mysteriously classed with the 'grown people,' [while] the 'nursery'" included Theodore, Elliott, and Corinne. The distinction seemed apparent to everyone, and even as a child, Theodore classified his slightly older sister as one of the grown-ups.

All four children took their classes at home, joined by various cousins and other young friends. This aristocratic version of what would later be called "home schooling" was a common arrangement at the time for wealthy New Yorkers. It kept control in the parents' hands—they hired the teachers, set the calendar, supervised the curriculum (if they chose to do so), and decided exactly who else would be in the class. In the case of the sickly Roosevelt children, there was another advantage: the parents could carefully monitor their health and make adjustments as they decided necessary or desirable.

Much of the learning for both sexes took place outside the formal lessons when they took nature walks with their father, visited a museum, or met a famous person. John Hay, President Lincoln's secretary who later became a statesman in his own right, stayed an entire summer with the Roosevelts, and Bamie later recalled that his "beautiful use of the English language" and love of reading made a big impression on her and her siblings.

At mealtime when the whole family gathered around the large mahogany dining table, discussion ran the gamut from the latest science news to the oldest classic. Occasionally, Theodore Sr. decreed that only French could be spoken at table—a rule that extended the class day considerably.

⁖

The children's lessons continued throughout the Civil War even though the war seriously complicated family life. For one thing, Martha and Anna Bulloch were cut off from their funds in Georgia and had to rely on family members for financial help. As strong supporters of the Confederacy, they could not help but feel that their actions were being closely watched in New York. In one letter to her daughter Susan in Philadelphia, Martha Bulloch apologized for mentioning "a little matter of business." The coupons due on some bonds would have to reach her through an intermediary since she could not depend on the mails. "Our letters are sometimes meddled with," she explained.

Mittie found herself caught in the middle, and to defend herself, she distanced herself from what went on around her. Bamie later remembered that Mittie "for a long time never came to the dinner table, but would have her dinner with us in the nursery, so that she would not be present during the discussions" of the war. With her southern accent, Mittie could hardly conceal her origins, but beyond that, she agreed with her mother and sister in their support of the Confederacy. Silence and low visibility seemed the best defense.

Out of regard for his wife's feelings, Theodore Roosevelt, Sr., thirty years old when the fighting started, decided not to volunteer for the Union forces—a decision that would later haunt and embarrass his intensely patriotic son. According to Bamie, her father recognized his wife's plight and, with her brothers "fighting on the southern side," he deemed it would be "almost unbearable to her" if he joined the Union forces. Not all of his brothers served either (although only one of them had a southern wife), but like Theodore, they found ways to assist in the Union cause. Theodore Sr. worked for the newly formed Union League Club and acted as allotment commissioner, charged with seeing that soldiers' wages not immediately needed by them were safely transferred to their families at home. In the process of signing up participants, he visited every regiment in the New York State Union forces, travel that involved considerable risk. While with the Army of the Potomac, he contracted typhoid fever and nearly died.

As allotment commissioner, Theodore Sr. often had to be away from home for weeks at a time, leaving Mittie in charge of their four children. He realized the weight of responsibility on her, and during one of his early trips he encouraged her to "enjoy yourself just as much as you can." Then, as though to underline the fact that he understood how difficult his young wife found this war and his part in it, he added, "I do not want you not to miss me, but remember that I would never have felt satisfied with myself after this war is over if I had done nothing, and that I do feel now that I am only doing my duty. I know you will not regret having me do what is right, and I do not believe you will love me any the less for it."

Mittie may not have loved Theodore less, but she worried about her three brothers. James, the older one, had assumed the visible but dangerous task of going to Liverpool, England, as purchasing agent for the Confederacy. Assigned to oversee the equipping of three important warships (the *Florida*, the *Alabama*, and the *Shenandoah*), he set upon the task with zeal. "Little brother" Irvine rushed to join the Confederates in November 1861 even though his mother was terrified that he would be killed. He later served on the ship *Savannah* and then on the *Alabama* as navigator and watch officer during the time it successfully captured sixty-three Union vessels in a two-year span. Daniel, who had played the flute at Mittie's wedding, did not go to sea but fought on land until his discharge in August 1862.

None of their worry about their men's safety caused the least weakening in the women's resolve or any diminishing of their fervent desire for a southern victory. Martha Bulloch, who had to hold her tongue in front of the Roosevelts, could write what she pleased to sympathetic relatives and friends still living below the Mason-Dixon line, and she did: "If I may judge at all of the embittered feeling of the South by myself, I would say they would rather be buried in one common grave than ever again live under the same government. I am confident I should."

Through friends who managed to visit Confederate soldiers being held prisoner in Baltimore, Martha Bulloch learned of their sorry state. To Susan she wrote that her friends had told her some of the soldiers were being held in prisons where food and clothing were both scarce and that living conditions were "squalid in the extreme." Forced to work without pay, the men suffered all kinds of indignities, causing Martha Bulloch to lament, "Oh it is hopeless and dreadful to think of."

Inside the Roosevelt household, the Bulloch women conspired to do all they could to help the southerners. They sent medicines and clothing to relatives still living in Georgia even though it meant shipping via Nassau. In October 1863, when it had become clear that the war would not end quickly, as both sides had predicted, Martha Bulloch attempted to persuade others to help her send packages of food and clothing, and she collected more than $200 for the cause.

Hearing one version of the war from the Bulloch women and another from their father's side, the four Roosevelt children began to reflect the division in their own contradictory ways. Echoing the pro-Union sentiment, they sometimes sounded more vehement than the grown-ups. In their bedtime prayers, apparently unaware of the agony they caused their mother, Bamie and young Theodore begged God to "grind the Southern troops to powder." At the same time, ten-year-old Bamie enthusiastically volunteered to help her grandmother sew a "drawerful" of clothing for southern girls, although neither of them knew where they would find the materials. All the talk of blockades and the covert sending of "well made up" packages inspired the Roosevelt children to invent war games of their own, which they played in the newly created Central Park. One child acted the part of a courier carrying contraband through enemy lines while the others tried to intercept. None of the players seemed concerned about the fact that in this game their mother's family was the "enemy."

When the war first began, it was common throughout the South to say that people's lives would never again be the same, but few of those who mouthed the words fully comprehended the enormity of what they said. Savannah, for example, suffered the destruction of six city blocks and its 104-mile-long rail link with Charleston. Roswell, only 13 miles north of Atlanta, sat squarely in the path of General Sherman's army, and Bulloch Hall was ransacked by the troops. The house itself remained unscathed, possibly because the soldiers noticed the Masonic symbols on each side and over the entrance, and, in deference to a fellow Mason, refrained from wrecking it—but they took what they could carry away. More than a decade after the war ended, when Theodore was a student at Harvard, a friend whose father had fought with General Sherman in Georgia showed him a leather pocket book taken from Roswell. It contained paper silhouettes of Mittie's family and a list of instructions for entertaining guests.

For Martha Bulloch the war's devastation went far beyond loss of property and mementos. It reached deep into her family as it did into most southern families. Irvine managed to survive the sinking of the *Alabama*, but as one of the conquered, he was barred from living in the land of his birth. James also had to remain abroad, although he used his time in exile to write two volumes detailing his role in outfitting the Confederate Navy. Daniel survived battle unscathed but then died of a pulmonary illness soon after his discharge in 1862. But Martha Bulloch never lived to see just how much the war had cost her. In August 1864, nearly nine months before the armistice was signed, she died at the age of sixty-five.

Deeply grieved by their mother's death, Mittie and Anna had even more reason to want to see their two surviving brothers. Fortunately, Irvine contrived a way to meet his sisters in New York three years after the war ended, but he had to enter the country clandestinely to do it. Newspapers at that time routinely gave all sorts of information, including who was visiting New York City, the hotels they were staying in, and the dates that ships docked and departed. Irvine could not reveal his identity, of course, but he placed in one newspaper a carefully worded announcement that he knew his sisters could not miss and would surely understand. The three of them had played too many games together at Bulloch Hall not to share a few coded words, and as soon as Mittie read it, she announced to Anna, "This must be from Irvine." By following his instructions to go to a specific tree in Central Park at a certain hour and date, the sisters were reunited with Irvine, and for an entire week they celebrated. Anna, who had married the year before but continued to teach her nieces and nephews, canceled classes for the week so that she could enjoy her time with Irvine.

After that brief reunion, Irvine returned to Liverpool, where he eventually became so successful in business that even an amnesty from the U.S. government could not entice him back. His story fascinated the young Roosevelts, however, and as long as he lived they made time for a visit to Uncle Irvine whenever they went to England. Eleanor Roosevelt, who usually showed limited interest in stories involving risk or adventure, would gleefully recount the saga of her great-uncle Irvine.

Mittie's short reunion with Irvine may have aroused some of her old sentiment for Roswell. Within months she arranged to visit Georgia, accompanied this time by Theodore Sr. and seven-year-old Corinne. Reunited with old friends that she had not seen since her trip with Bamie in 1855, Mittie was greeted warmly, and her hotel room was filled with flowers. Gratefully acknowledging the help she had given them during the fighting, the Georgians laughed and talked over the good times shared in their youth. But none of the conversation or the gratitude could convince Mittie that the rest of her life would have anything to do with Roswell.

Mittie's parents were dead; the plundered Bulloch Hall had been sold, and none of her siblings lived anywhere near it. At age thirty-three, she saw little reason to go back there again. Her own children had developed interests of their own, and for them rural Georgia seemed remote, almost as alien as Europe. Neither of her sons had yet visited the South, and Bamie went there only once—as a baby. With both of her brothers living in England, Mittie had more reasons to go there, and when she returned to New York in the early summer of 1868, she set about convincing her husband to take her and the whole family abroad. Less than sixteen years remained in her life, and Georgia figured in them hardly at all.

III

In May 1869, Mittie steamed out of New York Harbor with her husband and four children toward England for a year's stay abroad. Such a trip was not unusual for people of their class and time. Like other wealthy Americans, the Roosevelts had more than the money that made such long absences possible—they controlled other aspects of their lives as well. Since Theodore Sr. worked at the family business, he could arrange for one of his brothers to cover for him. The children's schooling was not a problem—they were accustomed to private tutors who could go along. It was another side of New York—Theodore's charitable organizations, Mittie's parties, and the children's friends—that they would miss the most.

Mittie had never been to Europe, and her husband's only tour of the Continent was sixteen years in the past when he was a bachelor. This trip promised to be very different. Bamie, age fourteen, could pretty much take care of herself, but the other three children would need lots of attention. Young Theodore, age ten, continued to suffer serious asthma attacks for which no cure seemed to work. His father tried everything—even urging him to smoke cigars and go for fast nighttime carriage rides. At nine, Elliott appeared healthier, the better coordinated of the two boys; his jaunty good looks made him popular with people of all ages, but his inability to concentrate or focus rendered him undependable. At seven, Corinne showed a lot of spark, sometimes stepping forward to try to outdo her older brothers in some physical contest.

Traveling with her tight-knit little family, Mittie regretted leaving her sister behind. Since her marriage to James Gracie in 1866, Anna had moved a few blocks away from the Roosevelt house on Twentieth Street, but she continued to teach the children and see a lot of Mittie. Now, for the first time in their lives, the sisters would be separated for more than a few weeks, and Mittie wrote her most detailed letters back to Anna.

More than simply a chronicle of her travels, these letters reveal considerable wit. A steward, who served passengers who remained on deck at mealtimes, soon caught Mittie's eye, and she described him as "a wonderfully constructed creature having amiable knobs all over his body, upon which he supports more bowls of soup and plates of eatables than you can imagine." He had a habit of standing "panting over you while you take your plate, with such wide extended nostrils that they take in the Irish coast, and the draught from them cools the soup!"

Mittie's stateroom on the paddle-wheel steamer *Scotia* came in for similar scrutiny. The ship, although steam powered, featured paddles that facilitated movement by churning the water, and Mittie found it cleaner than she had expected. But her quarters did not measure up in one respect. "The carpet," she informed her sister, "is filled with organic matter which, if distilled, would make a kind of anchovy paste, only fit to be the appetizer before the famous 'witches' broth,' the [recipe] for which Shakespeare gives in 'Macbeth'."

Arriving in Liverpool in mid-May, Mittie was immediately reunited with Irvine and James, who showed her family around the city. Her husband, who might have hesitated to spend much time with his brothers-in-law, given their role in the Civil War, evidently enjoyed their company, and the children accepted these Bulloch uncles as exciting figures. Irvine, especially, had more war stories than seemed possible given that he was not yet thirty years old. Both men had married Englishwomen, and young Theodore thought the aunts too quick to plant big kisses on him and his siblings. Otherwise, they were fun to observe, with their English accents and different ways of doing things.

Following that stop, the Roosevelts traveled to both Scotland and London, then crossed the channel and visited Holland and France before making their way to Italy. Although thousands of miles from home, they struggled to recreate the important rituals celebrated in New York. Christmas in a Rome hotel featured the same mysterious bulging stockings that the children had gleefully unpacked in the brownstone on Twentieth Street. Scores of letters flowed between the children and their friends and cousins at home.

When the rest of the family returned with a "Hip! Hurrah" to New York on May 25, 1870, Bamie remained at Versailles to enroll in a school then popular with wealthy Europeans called Les Ruches. She had just turned fifteen, the same age at which Mittie enrolled in the girls' academy in South Carolina, and it was probably Mittie's idea that her elder daughter have this opportunity. The school was run by an agnostic freethinker named Marie Souvestre, who among other eccentricities considered sports a waste of time—hardly the sort of teacher who would have appealed to the athletic-minded Theodore Sr., but she had enough of the exotic about her to make a fan of Mittie.

For the Roosevelts who returned to New York, life resumed where it had been interrupted twelve months earlier. After summer in the country, the three younger children took up their studies again. The boys' lessons gradually became more rigorous to prepare them for college entrance exams, but Corinne, who had no such goal, stuck to literature and language as her mother and Aunt Anna had done.

Mittie's social schedule, increasingly gayer after the war ended, made her a prominent New York figure. Her ebony hair and ivory complexion, enhanced by a fragile figure always expensively dressed, made her stand out wherever she went. Bamie, in recalling her mother's "exquisite beauty" long after her death, gave a precise description of the outfit she had chosen many years earlier for the wedding of a friend's daughter in Westchester: Over "an enormous crinoline" Mittie donned "a white muslin dress [with] a pink silk lining . . . all the little ruffles at the bottom edged with real lace" and a matching long cape. Her bonnet was tied under her chin "with great pink ribbons," and on the brim was "a big pink rose with perfectly realistic little green dragon flies." Her parasol featured an ivory handle and pink lining, trimmed with lace. It was only natural, her daughter concluded, that at the wedding where guests came from the most fashionable New York families, Mittie distinguished herself as "one of the beauties."

Constance Harrison, a contemporary of Mittie's and one of New York's social leaders, stressed Mittie's competence at her perfectly managed afternoon teas. According to Harrison, the entire house on Twentieth Street "seemed somehow to convey a waft of violets, of which blossoms she had many surrounding her and the service to her door and tea-table was performed by neat little maids dressed in lilac print gowns."

The gay round of partying was interrupted in October 1872 when Mittie and Theodore Sr. decided to pack everyone up and return to Europe for another extended stay. The time seemed right. Bamie had returned to New York after only a few months at Souvestre's school, and now, a less than attractive seventeen-year-old, she could gain sophistication from travel. The other three, now that they were older, would presumably get more out of this trip than the previous one when they had complained a lot about what they were missing in New York.

In some ways this was a pivotal time for the family. CVS had died in August 1871, leaving his considerable estate to his five sons, and Theodore and Mittie had decided to use some of their money to build a larger house in an area that was becoming more fashionable—Fifty-seventh Street near Fifth Avenue. Construction would not be finished for a year, but there was good reason to get away from the house on Twentieth Street. Theodore Sr.'s brother Robert, in the adjoining brownstone, was attracting attention as a U.S. congressman, and it was just a matter of time before people noticed his second family—with the Widow Fortescue—on the side. Going abroad would also give Mittie a chance to buy furnishings for the new house and update her wardrobe. She had always liked pretty clothes, and now with a much bigger budget, she could really enjoy herself.

First on the agenda was another visit to the exiled uncles in England, and then the Roosevelts journeyed to Brindisi, Italy, and from there to Alexandria, Egypt. After a few weeks in Cairo, they boarded a *dahabeah*, or houseboat, and spent the next three months on the Nile. Bamie assumed the task of tutoring her siblings in French and English, although she admitted that she knew little more than they did and had to struggle to get them to work in regular sessions.

Many of the lessons came from their surroundings—the museums and sites they visited and the people their parents introduced them to along the way. Corinne recalled meeting the revered American poet Ralph Waldo Emerson, eighty years old and seeing the Nile from another *dahabeah*. The high point of the trip for Bamie came on her eighteenth birthday in January when the whole family celebrated with a moonlight ride to the temple of Karnack.

Following the Nile excursion and a short stop in Vienna, the Roosevelts split up. Theodore Sr. returned to New York to look after business, supervise construction of the new house, and begin negotiations for a country place on Long Island. The three younger children went to Dresden, where they would board with families and study German, while Bamie, in what was clearly becoming a companion role, accompanied her mother to take the waters near Carlsbad.

The spa was not far from Dresden, so Mittie could keep a careful watch on the children. When cholera broke out in Dresden, she had no time to consult her husband three thousand miles away, but she acted quickly and decisively, packing up everyone, including Bamie, and taking them to Samaden in Switzerland. From there she wrote Theodore Sr. that she hoped he approved. She disliked interrupting the children's studies just when they had begun making progress in German, but she feared cholera much more.

In the accounts that Mittie's children later wrote of their family, their father always took center stage, leaving Mittie a place in the wings. As he grew older, his personality rounded out beyond the bookish, serious youth, and he became, in Corinne's words, "one of the most enchanting characters with whom I, personally, have ever come in contact: sunny, gay, dominant, unselfish, forceful and versatile . . . an 'all-round' man." High spirited as well as earnest, he liked to drive his coach fast during the day and then go out dancing late into the night. To all of his children he passed on his encyclopedic knowledge of flora and fauna, patiently teaching them the Latin names for every plant they might encounter and the distinctive sound of every bird. But he also found ways to make each child feel specially loved. On each of their birthdays he routinely canceled all other appointments, both personal and business, and devoted the entire day to whatever the celebrating child wanted to do. "To be with [him was] the most valued possession of the children's lives," one of his grandsons later wrote.

As much as he was a devoted father, Theodore Roosevelt, Sr., was a devoted citizen of New York. Although still involved in the family business, he took one day off each week to help the poor, visiting them in their homes and arranging for their assistance. He also helped found an extraordinary number of charitable and educational organizations, including the Children's Aid Society, the Museum of Natural History, and the Orthopedic Hospital. This last institution carried special poignancy for him and his family because of Bamie's slightly curved spine, and he never lost hope of healing her completely. When one treatment or another offered promise, he arranged it for her, but he did not stop there. Convinced that other families less wealthy than his could profit from the same treatment, he solicited money from rich friends to pay the bills. His charitable work caused some amusement among his business associates, and they insisted that whenever they saw him coming, they would take out their wallets and inquire, "How much this time?"

The entire Roosevelt household joined in the fund-raising. Mittie would invite her well-heeled friends to an afternoon reception, and on arrival at her brownstone, they would find crippled children lying on tables or easy chairs. Corinne, at the age of seven, began assisting at these receptions by demonstrating how a particular appliance worked on a crippled child. Years later Corinne recalled, "I can still hear the voice of the first Mrs. John Jacob Astor as she leaned over one fragile-looking child and, turning to my father, said, 'Theodore, you are right; these children must be restored and made into active citizens again, and I for one will help you in your work.'"

Only an incredible energy and a strong desire to help the less fortunate prevented Theodore Sr. from neglecting his own children. Every Sunday evening after supper at home he walked a few blocks to the Newboys' Lodging House that the Children's Aid Society had started on Eighteenth Street. There the youngsters, sometimes as young as ten, found a bed and a meager meal after hawking newspapers on street corners. For a day's work, beginning before dawn and ending well after dark, they earned only a pittance, but most of them had little choice but to continue. Many were orphaned and others were immigrants, having come to New York because their parents had fallen for the outlandish promises of unscrupulous labor recruiters. Thousands of miles from home, the boys became virtual slaves, cut off from family and too young to work legally. Their tragic circumstances inspired many people to help them, but Theodore Sr. became one of their most cherished and dependable supporters. Because he took time to know many of them personally, they remembered him with special affection. Years after his death, his very famous son met one of those newsboys—who also had made a brilliant career for himself—and was pleased to hear that the man was thrilled to make his acquaintance, not for any of his own accomplishments but "as the son of your father."

∾

How could any mother compete with a father who inspired such adoration? Mittie did not even try, preferring to withdraw into her own little world, surrounded by beauty both imagined and real. The retreat that she had begun during the war years, when she took her meals in the nursery rather than face adult discussions, now broadened in a curious way. Never a recluse—she liked partying too much for that—she distanced herself psychologically from her children as they matured. Her husband, by focusing so much of his attention on them, added to their sense that she was cut off from them. Instead of talk about the minutiae of ornithology, she preferred witty conversation about people she knew. She could still out-walk the others (if she fancied doing so) and was rarely sick (although her children later remembered her as "delicate"), but the confident gaiety so apparent in her youth was now reserved for people outside her immediate household. Her descendants tended to describe her as "vague" and "nebulous."

Sometimes this detachment seemed like stupidity, and Mittie's children began emphasizing that side of her. They laughed about the time that her pet parrot flew out of the house and perched on a tree nearby. Her solution was to summon the butler and instruct him to stand under the tree and make sure the bird did not fly away. Another story concerned the coachmen's uniforms. Since Mittie insisted that they be made of a specific kind of fabric, she bought up bolts of it to prepare for the day when it was no longer available. But before she ever got the chance to use it all, moths ruined it and she had to scrap the entire batch.

Some of Mittie's personal habits annoyed her more punctual relatives. Helen Roosevelt Robinson, a Roosevelt by both birth and marriage, recalled hearing from her elders that Mittie was a "nebulous figure . . . beautiful and very Southern in her ways. She never cared whether she was three hours late for a meal or half an hour." But when she appeared, she would be "perfectly beautiful" in her "lovely white muslin clothes."

With her southern roots and her preference for the slow pace, Mittie had little use for the frantic activity level that pleased her husband, and she characterized his Saturdays, when he scheduled a whirl of appointments, as "butchered to make a Roman holiday." She preferred spending time with the socially prominent, and she became a close friend of Ward McAllister, the social entrepreneur who coined the term "the Four Hundred" in the 1870s. Like Mittie, he came from an old Savannah family, and the two transplanted southerners took an immediate liking to each other when they met in New York. Unlike Mittie, McAllister harbored social ambitions far too expensive for his purse.

Just how McAllister viewed money is suggested by his statement that a million dollars amounted to only "respectable poverty." Since one million dollars at that time equaled about thirteen million 1998 dollars, he clearly needed some help, and when his one hope, a wealthy relative, died and left him very little, he set out to make his way on his own. Fortunately for him, Caroline Schermerhorn Astor, a woman with virtually unlimited funds, needed a social adviser at the same time that he needed cash, and the two of them hooked up in a mutually beneficial partnership.

Although Caroline Astor came from an old New York family and spoke with such authority that people tended to accept her pronouncements as truth, she had a squat, square figure and considered herself unattractive. Her marriage to an Astor might have conferred the confidence she coveted, but her husband, William Backhouse Astor, Jr., was a "second son" and thus less favored. Adding to her sense of social disadvantage, she gave birth to four daughters (before finally producing a son in 1864) and felt the need to place them in advantageous unions. Fortuitously, she met Ward McAllister (who also had a marriageable daughter) in 1872, just when the oldest Astor daughter was preparing for the husband hunt.

McAllister, who had traveled in England and formed some ideas about the value of limiting access to a social circle, came up with his own formula for New York. By funneling tidbits to newspaper gossip columnists, especially the author of "Town Talk," he flaunted the list of invitees, thus tantalizing and shaming all those who had been excluded. Caroline Astor did her part by giving extravagant parties with costly flower arrangements and menus written pretentiously in French. Each January she hosted a ball at her mansion at 360 Fifth Avenue, near Thirty-fourth Street. Twentieth-century New Yorkers, familiar with brownstones twenty feet wide, have trouble visualizing the mansions of Mrs. Astor's time. Some boasted their own gymnasiums, mammoth libraries, and botanical gardens. Mrs. Astor's was one of the most luxurious in the Gilded Age, though she replaced it in the 1890s with an even grander one at Fifth Avenue and Sixty-fifth Street. The plot she abandoned at Thirty-fourth Street had a

penchant for attracting excess: the Empire State Building later tow-
ered over the space where an Astor mansion once stood.

It is sometimes suggested that the term "the Four Hundred" originated because it was the maximum that Mrs. Astor could comfortably accommodate at home, but in fact she entertained twice that
number. Dozens of servants passed among the guests, and the most
talented musicians in town provided the music. McAllister never
explained his reason for setting the number at four hundred, but
when he published his memoir in 1890, he printed only four hundred copies. As McAllister helped include people on the most coveted invitation lists (or exclude them), getting his attention was no
small feat, but Mittie managed to do so.

By the time Bamie was eighteen, she had developed contempt for
some of her mother's friends, including McAllister, whom she
viewed as unattractively calculating and shrewd, acting solely for his
own advantage. By insinuating himself in among moneyed New
Yorkers, McAllister introduced his daughter, whom Bamie described
as "witty but very ugly," at very little cost to himself.

Bamie also zeroed in on her mother's southern roots and blamed
them for setting the children apart from others of their age. All the
Roosevelts were famous for sticking with family, and it was once
suggested that so many of them married their cousins because they
rarely met anyone else. But Bamie laid the onus on Mittie for isolat-
ing the children from others their own age. For Theodore Roosevelt,
Sr., Bamie had only praise, and she credited him with bringing gaiety into their household.

Outside the family, Mittie had many admirers, and they singled
her out as one of the most winsome, delightful women they had ever
met. Constance Harrison, her contemporary, described Mittie as in
a class of her own. Only a handful of women qualified in the 1870s,
Harrison wrote, by "birth, breeding and tact" to be considered the
leaders in Gotham, and of the five that she named, "Mrs. Theodore
Roosevelt . . . seemed . . . easily the most beautiful, and in the graciousness of her manner and that inherent talent for winning and
holding the sympathetic interest of those around her, I have seen
none to surpass her."

Unfortunately, that exceptional beauty failed to reappear in Mittie's daughters, and Harrison did not pretend otherwise. "One asks

oneself," she wrote with telling cruelty, "why such loveliness of line and tinting, why such sweet courtesy of manner cannot be passed down the years instead of dying upon the stem like a single perfect flower. Why nature, having formed such a combination, should not be content with repeating it."

The contrast between their own appearance and that of their mother surely colored Mittie's daughters' accounts of her. By dwelling on her failings, they diminished her, rendering her eccentric or, even worse, childish. They made fun of her hygiene standards, noting that she always required two tubs for bathing—one for washing and one for rinsing. She wore white, whatever the season or temperature, as though to protect herself from all impurities. Even the children's nickname for her, "Little Motherling," suggested the need for protection, and they often spoke of her as a younger, underdeveloped sibling rather than a parent.

Other evidence shows Mittie a far more complex figure than her children ever acknowledged. Sara Delano Roosevelt, who became Bamie's friend while both were in their teens, recalled that Mittie made a remarkably strong and favorable impression on her because she "had fascinating little ways which kept even her children charmed." A remarkable mimic and storyteller, she entertained at a phenomenal rate, hosting dinner parties, afternoon teas, and both daughters' lavish debuts. Since she and Theodore fled Manhattan during the summer months, she had to open and close a house every few months, supervising all the packing and arranging entailed in the task.

When her family grudgingly gave Mittie any credit, it was for the high spirits and the taste that she brought to the family. Her granddaughter Corinne Alsop pointed out that one could scrutinize all the Roosevelts and never match the sense of "bon vivre" that you found in the Bulloch women. The men had their strong points, they were solid and good, but in the ability to enjoy, they just "didn't have it." Mittie and Anna "both had it, to the nth degree. And they gave it to the next generation." Bamie acknowledged that none of the Bullochs had much formal education, but they made up for it in many ways, with their good looks and "stormy love affairs," which "we adored hearing about."

It was Mittie's people who nourished an interest in art and elegant style. Her husband never bought wine without having her sample

and approve the choice, and her friends frequently sought her opinion on matters of taste. She had an unusually discerning eye and
tried to pass it on to her children. On their first trip to Rome she
wanted to initiate eight-year-old Corinne into the beauties of Vatican sculpture. Mittie led the girl into a room exhibiting only a torso
by Michelangelo and, seating the girl in front of it, told her, "This is
one of the greatest works of art in the world, and I am going to leave
you here alone for five minutes, because I want you to sit very quietly and look at it, and perhaps when I come back . . . you will be
able to realize how beautiful it is."

Young Corinne, accustomed to obeying, kept her eyes glued to the
armless torso for the allotted time, and when her mother returned
and inquired what she thought, Corinne burst out, "Well, mamma,
it seems to me a little 'chumpy.'" Mittie erupted in laughter, but the
judgment would haunt Corinne for years while other members of
the family taunted her with her evaluation of "chumpy" art. But
that encounter prodded an interest in art, and later, as an adult,
Corinne felt comfortable enough about her opinions to write articles
and speak publicly about her favorite Italian painters.

Beautiful things often carried a high price, and Mittie willingly
paid. In her children's opinion, she spent too much, especially when
furnishing the house on Fifty-seventh Street. Unfortunately, the family returned home from their second trip abroad to find a house not
exactly as they had ordered, and they had to pay for adjustments.
According to Bamie, the hand-carved staircase had to be remade.
Measurements for several of the rooms did not correspond to those
that Mittie had used in purchasing Persian rugs abroad, and costly
alterations were required.

While much of the additional expense and inconvenience resulted
from the builder's error, it was Mittie who got blamed for over-
spending. Years later Corinne Alsop recalled that her grandmother had
been "terribly, terribly extravagant" during that European sojourn and
wanted to buy "everything that was beautiful." But historian David
McCullough found no evidence that Mittie exceeded her budget.
With the recent inheritance from CVS Roosevelt, Mittie hardly had
to deprive herself of furnishings that struck her fancy.

The summer after they moved to Fifty-seventh Street, the Roosevelts rented a vacation home at Oyster Bay, where many of their

relatives had been going for years. The family's association with that Long Island community about thirty miles east of New York City would extend over generations, but that first year stood as the one the children remembered as the happiest of their lives. Little about the place ever suggested repose, and their friends hooted at its name, "Tranquillity." Both parents encouraged their daughters as well as their sons in all manner of activities—picnic lunches at a spot called Cooper's Bluff, poetry-writing contests, sailing, riding, and an infinite variety of games. Corinne later traced her early interest in poetry back to those fun-filled days at Tranquillity.

Unfortunately, the Roosevelt family had little time to enjoy either house together because its members began to scatter. Theodore Jr. entered Harvard in 1876, and Elliott, whose headaches had become worse and more incapacitating, opted for travel in the western states rather than college. By late 1877, Theodore Sr., not yet forty-six, began to fail in health as stomach cancer, not yet diagnosed, sapped his strength. When the family gathered that Christmas, he showed little of his usual vigor, and by February 9, 1878, he was dead.

Mittie found herself—like her mother before her—widowed while still in her forties. But unlike the outspoken Martha Bulloch, the daughter showed less determination in how she wanted to spend her remaining years. Her husband's will provided that she be permitted use of the Fifty-seventh Street house for as long as she lived, and even though her children found it expensive, they complied. Bamie, now twenty-three, took over management of the house while her brother Theodore wrote encouraging long letters from Harvard to "Darling Motherling."

Their father's death altered everything for his children; as Bamie wrote, "Life was completely changed for us." In short order, three of them married. Theodore brought the wispy, blond Alice Lee of Boston to meet his mother, and soon after, on October 27, 1880, he married her and brought her to live at the Fifty-seventh Street house. Corinne did not wed quite as young as her mother, but in April 1882, at age twenty-one, she married a friend of Elliott's. A year later she produced Mittie's first grandchild (the only one Mittie lived to see). Even the unpredictable Elliott seemed to have settled down by December 1883 when he married the beautiful Anna Hall from Tivoli on the Hudson. This last marriage was particularly welcome to Mittie because her younger son, named for her side of the family and always a favorite of hers and Anna's, had become even less focused as he matured. In contrast with Theodore, who had built his physical strength, graduated from Harvard, and was making a place for himself in Republican circles, Elliott looked aimless. Now, with a wife, he might do better.

Only Bamie remained single—continuing to serve as competent companion to her mother. With her square, slightly drooping body and serious face, Bamie looked more like a contemporary of her mother's than a daughter, and the correspondence between the two women is that of equals. Mittie wrote to "Dearest Bamie" or "Dearest Bambie" in an elegant hand whenever the two were separated, often to outline details about travel arrangements or the sending of trunks. The older woman always made a point of crediting the assistance she received from her level-headed daughter, and on one occasion she insisted that she could not have managed without her. In affectionate terms Mittie confided in Bamie, who carefully tended her "little mother" with bouquets of violets and carefully chosen gifts.

By 1884, after half a dozen years of widowhood, Mittie had settled into her role. All three married children lived with her or nearby, and her sister Anna resided only a short carriage ride away. When the bustle of Gotham became too much, Mittie and Anna could chat about the virtues of pastoral Georgia and console each other with talk about their childhood memories.

But this idyllic family scene dissolved quickly in February of that year. Mittie, so meticulous about every aspect of personal hygiene, came down with the "dirty water disease," typhoid fever, while Theodore's pregnant wife lay gravely ill in the same house with Bright's disease, a kidney ailment. On February 12, hours after Alice gave birth to a baby girl, Alice's condition worsened. By the time Theodore, now a state assemblyman, returned from Albany on February 13, he was confronted with two dying women to comfort. In grieved astonishment he watched his mother die first in the early hours of the fourteenth and then, that same afternoon, his twenty-three-year-old wife. It is no wonder that when Corinne and her husband rushed back from a short trip out of town, they met a grieving Elliott who pronounced the house "cursed." After a double funeral, Mittie and her daughter-in-law were buried at the then fashionable Greenwood Cemetery in Brooklyn.

In addition to the extreme emotional stress surrounding these two sudden, unlikely deaths, the Roosevelt children had to deal with the financial impact. They had never had much reason to think about money because their father's brother James had been overseeing the family's investments. Now, without consulting them or making any provision for their needs, he put the Fifty-seventh Street house up for sale, and within a week of her mother's death, Bamie had to start moving out. In addition to overseeing the care of the new baby, she had to divide up household goods and buy a place for herself. No wonder she remembered that year as one of the worst of her life.

∽

Aunt Anna tried to fill some of the void left by her sister's death. Her marriage to James K. Gracie (whose family built the mansion later famous as the mayor's home) had not distanced her from her nieces and nephews, for the Gracies, who never had children, virtually adopted Mittie's as their own. For their part, the children reserved a special place in their affections for their aunt. Soon after their marriage, when James Gracie was "barely beginning to earn his living," the couple lived in cramped quarters on Fourth Avenue, around the corner from the brownstone on Twentieth Street. Everything about the modest accommodations intrigued the young Roosevelts, and one of them recalled, "There was no dissipation in the world that so appealed to our fancy as lunching with Aunt Annie in those rooms," even though the food was often overcooked lamb and large green pickles.

As the Roosevelt children grew up and formed families of their own, Aunt Anna continued to play an important part in their lives. She had her favorites and felt especially fond of Theodore's bride, Alice, whom she confessed to loving "as my own child." As soon as Theodore brought the Bostonian to New York, Aunt Anna formed a special bond with her, and she later wrote that from that minute "I never felt that I was childless." Alice's death hit hard, as, of course did Mittie's, and Anna could hardly control her grief. But she knew that the baby, also called Alice, would someday want to know the details of her birth, so she wrote them down to assure the little girl how much she had been loved. Some of the details were purely factual: the exact hour, "8:30 p.m.," the date, "Feb 12," the place, "6 W 57th" and the weight of the newborn "8 and 3/4 pounds." But the rest could be reported only by someone who was there. One member of the household had evidently grumbled that the child "should have been a boy," to which the dying mother responded with as much enthusiasm as her weakened state permitted: "I *love* a little *girl*."

As the next generation of great-nieces and great-nephews increased in number, Aunt Anna Gracie cheerfully helped oversee their training, as she had done with their parents. After Theodore remarried, this time to his childhood friend Edith Carow, and had a daughter, Aunt Anna was chosen as the baby's godmother. Corinne, who liked to travel as much as any of the Roosevelts, relied heavily on Aunt Anna to oversee her young children. Corinne's oldest son, Teddy, spent so much time with his great-aunt that, after he was grown, his wife insisted that he had been "almost brought up by Aunt Anna and Uncle Gracie," who acted "like an extra set of parents."

At the same time the Gracies were looking after "little Teddy," they invited his two girl cousins, both of whom would become far better known than he, to their house on Long Island. The Gracies reported that "sweet little Eleanor" (age two) seemed to get "along well with Teddy," but who knows what future they saw for any of the children? Motherless Alice was already showing herself to be a spirited child. At twenty-eight months of age, she was prone to laughing until "her little sides shook."

For all her nurturing spirit, Aunt Anna held strong opinions, a trait that her young nieces and nephews could not help but notice. In October 1890 she confessed that she hated the newly published *Hedda Gabler* "and anything Ibsen writes." As she saw it, nothing could possibly justify Hedda's conduct. It was her fault that she "married the dolt."

But Anna was remembered best for her strong support in time of crisis. Mittie died before it became clear that Elliott was an alcoholic, but Aunt Anna, who lived nearly a decade longer, had plenty of time to see what was happening. She had watched his marriage fall apart and his siblings struggle with how to help him. When it finally became clear even to the forgiving Aunt Anna that disaster lay ahead, she wrote his sister Corinne a long letter, ending, "Child of the house, child of the heart. Do you not hear in all this letter the sob which will not be restrained?"

Anna Gracie died of diphtheria in 1893 at the age of sixty, cutting off the strongest surviving tie between the Roosevelts in New York and their mother's Georgia roots. Mittie's children tended to treat the Bulloch ancestors lightly, as little more than an embellishment on the family tree, but the evidence points to something more. With her marriage into the Roosevelt clan, this complicated southerner brought a change in fortune. After more than two centuries in America, during which the Roosevelts produced nothing more remarkable than a minor inventor, an even more minor organist, and quite a lot of money, their star suddenly rose. One of Mittie's sons climbed to the top of the nation's political ladder, becoming President of the United States. Her granddaughter Eleanor made an equally impressive career for herself, becoming a precedent-breaking First Lady of the United States and then, in many people's books, "First Lady of the World." Another granddaughter of Mittie's, Ethel Derby (daughter of Theodore and Edith), admitted that she sometimes felt closer to the Bullochs than to the Dutch Roosevelts, whom she pronounced lacking in color: "Nothing romantic there." Then she pointed with pride to Georgia: "Our southern blood runs strong."

Mittie, who never lived to see any of her four granddaughters, had no way of knowing how they credited her. Ethel Derby pointed to her rich use of words. In informing her own daughter about a relative whose husband had left her, Ethel wrote, "Just whisked himself away. 'Sweeted himself away' as the family saying goes." Then she stopped to reflect that the latter expression had probably come from Mittie, though she was unsure how it got passed on. Granddaughter Corinne Alsop held up Mittie as a model for women. In an interview with the authors Hermann and Mary Hagedorn, Corinney pointed out that Mittie was "practical in her own strange way. She had everything she wanted, and I call that quite practical!"

Most writers on the Roosevelt family have concentrated on the frivolous side of Mittie and ignored the rest. Biographer Edmund Morris described her as "small, vague and feminine to the point of caricature." By focusing on her extravagance, it is easy to treat her as a spoiled child who never grew up. But this complex woman could be a caring mother and a patient teacher. She cultivated the social contacts that supported her husband's charities and supplied her children's spouses. In another era or if she had married into a different family, she might have also directed her energies to painting or opening a gallery, but among the Roosevelts of her generation that would have been seen as silly.

In writing about the Roosevelts, David McCullough singled Mittie out as "the most fascinating of them all." Indeed, her life has puzzling aspects. Starting out as a confident young woman, sure of her opinions, she became a wife and mother whom her family treated as a detached "little one." During the years of their courtship and the first part of their marriage, Theodore addressed her in his letters as "Dearest" or "Darling" or "My own dearest Mittie."

With time, however, his tone changed, and after two decades of marriage, he almost always used a diminutive form of salutation. In June 1873 he wrote from a London hotel to "My own Darling Little Mittie" to lament the fact that he was headed back to America, leaving her "to try to take care of yourself for the first time in your life." He admitted she was up to the task but hesitated to see her undertake it since "I have always been accustomed to think of you as one of my little babies." He began a subsequent letter to his wife, "Darling Little Girl," and another to "My own little Girl." In 1874 he closed a letter to his forty-year-old wife in terms more appropriate for a young daughter, "I wish I could kiss you good night my own little baby." During their courtship, when she was a petite teenager, the diminutives might have seemed appropriate, but how to explain his beginning to use them when she was a matron in her forties?

Since it was not only Theodore but also their four children who stressed the fragile side of Mittie, it is interesting that her letters do not support such a view. She wrote remarkably intelligent and insightful descriptions of her travels, including an account of Venice in 1869 that helps explain why her son Theodore favored Venice above all foreign cities. Her handwriting became far bolder after her marriage, the tiny controlled calligraphy growing into large strokes and flourishes. Her actions were just as resolute. When she had to deal with suppliers and employees, she was both definite and determined. Her letters on many subjects, including her daughter's marriage, the decoration of her houses, and the intricacies of entertaining, show her as anything but ineffectual or feeble.

On the matter of spending, Mittie conducted herself responsibly, and on her trips abroad she kept her husband informed of what she was buying. When she wanted to invite two friends to spend a week with her in Paris (a common generosity among women of her class and time), she sought Theodore's opinion, writing him in July 1873 that if "the *money matters are going on well* and you think it *wise,*" she would proceed with the invitations. Preoccupied with the new house they were building at the time, she sent him "a long list of questions, directions and suggestions," urging him to "look them over very carefully and act upon them where you think it best." She confidently made purchases herself, pointing out in one of her messages to her husband that "Mr F was in doubt about furniture, [but] of course my letter settles that." When necessary she willingly made concessions, accepting "temporary carpet for my own room," hardly the sign of a capricious or spendthrift wife.

The contradiction between the "little" Mittie that her husband and children described and the decisive woman of her letters and actions may very well have resulted from a conscious effort on her part. In this high-energy family where competition was the name of the game, she preferred the role of spectator. As a southerner transplanted to New York, she always felt herself peripheral, and by playing up her frailties, she preserved her outsider's status.

Her withdrawal from family competition, whether conscious or not, served another useful purpose: it permitted her daughters to feel superior to her, to develop both wit and charm sufficient to outshine her inordinately good looks. Plain daughters of exquisite mothers are not always so lucky, as Mittie's granddaughter Eleanor Roosevelt would later demonstrate. Prodded and pitied by her glamorous mother, Eleanor as a child became dejected and unsure of herself. Mittie's daughters were far more fortunate, and if she lost out in the bargain, becoming a caricature of the vague female, she never showed that she minded the sacrifice.

With her two sons, Mittie batted only .500—one of them becoming an outstanding President of the United States and the other a failure—but she did much better with her two daughters. Neither of them had her beauty, but their strong personalities enabled them to fascinate almost everyone who met them. The elder, Bamie, developed into one of the most magnetic figures of her time, though she never seemed to think that her "little motherling" had anything to do with it.

Many of those people who knew her best insisted
that Bamie, instead of her brother Theodore, would have been
President of the United States—had she been born a man.

CHAPTER TWO

ANNA "BAMIE" ROOSEVELT COWLES

(1855–1931)

n March 1894 an unusual presentation occurred at Buckingham Palace. A plain, rather odd-shaped spinster of thirty-nine approached Queen Victoria, flung her arms wide, as required for royalty, and held her shoulders stiffly straight so as to conceal the curve in her spine and the slight hunch in her back. She understood that others going through this ceremony had succumbed to nerves, and it was even rumored that one young woman had become so upset that she had removed her shoe and promptly vomited into it. Chamberlains stood ready to whisk away anyone who fainted, but Bamie, presented that evening as "Miss Anna E. Roosevelt," required no such assistance.

As a single woman in her middle years, Bamie had no right to expect an introduction to the Queen, and she understood that this one was quite unorthodox. Twenty years earlier the presentation would have been appropriate as her "coming out," but then she would have worn a wispy white chiffon gown and ostrich feathers in her hair. Middle-aged women were supposed to approach the Queen on their husband's arm, but Bamie rarely thought of rules as applying to herself. She needed this introduction in order to move in her own right in London society—to entertain and be entertained at the most important parties in town. While living with her cousin Rosy, who held a high position at the American embassy, she had attended parties as his guest, but now she could act on her own.

In London as in New York, almost no one who knew her well called her by her given name. "Bamie" had suited her when she was a fragile, little person, but that name had gradually been replaced by another one. As she matured and her phenomenal energy level became apparent to everyone who met her, she was called "Bye," as in "bye, bye." The nickname she had chosen for herself as a toddler seemed particularly appropriate as she matured because she was forever on the go. Both names followed her through life, with most of her contemporaries preferring "Bamie" while the next generation called her "Bye."

Whatever she was called, she had enough energy for several people. Her brother Theodore, away at Harvard, once wrote her a letter in which he marveled at how much she accomplished, then concluded, "Oh Energy, Thy name is Bamie." More than a century later, another Roosevelt with unusual zest was described as having "the energy" of Bye.

That a slightly crippled woman should be singled out for her high energy level, especially in a family that included the super active President Theodore Roosevelt, might strike some people as strange. But their contemporaries who compared these two siblings often maintained that Bamie was the superior one. A cousin, Nicholas Roosevelt, later argued that it was difficult to do justice to her "extraordinary personality" and that her sole biographer had failed to capture the "richness" of Bamie, who possessed the best mind in the family and the most varied and fascinating character. In his own book, *A Front Row Seat*, he hypothesized that had "she been a man in seventeenth-century Europe, it would be easy to imagine her as a successful and highly capable minister of state or perhaps a cardinal, unquenchable in zeal and effective in guile." Theodore's daughter, Alice Longworth, who had been raised by Bamie until the age of four, told a biographer: "I always believed that if she had been a man, she, rather than my father, would have been President."

But of course she was not a man, and that made all the difference. In nineteenth-century America, brains and shrewdness, even when buttressed by enormous self-discipline and ambition, played themselves out under rules defined by sex. A smart young female, even one possessing the money and contacts of Anna E. Roosevelt, had no chance at the offices and honors that her brother Theodore sought and won. Amazingly enough, she seems not to have minded. Nor did she ever complain that she felt limited by the rules of her time.

I

EVEN AS A CHILD, Bamie seemed satisfied with (and in command of) her life. Described as "too smart by half" and remarkably disciplined, she acted like a much older person. Family lore had it that she had been headstrong from the start and that as a youngster she resisted all help from her nurse, Dora, to pack. The little girl announced: "Doh pack Doh trunk, Bye pack Bye trunk." At age fourteen, on that first family trip to Europe, she wrote a complete accounting back to relatives and friends in New York. In the style of an elderly aunt or a social secretary employed to keep the records straight, she described each sight the family had seen and with whom her parents had dined. Then the precocious young woman signed herself with a businesslike "Anna E. Roosevelt." The "E" she had added herself just because she liked the sound of it, and no one would have dared to object.

Behind the competent exterior, Bamie harbored a witty appreciation of the offbeat—a trait much prized by Mittie's side of the family. Her aunt Anna referred to this side of her personality in August 1890 when writing to her sister-in-law about various great-nieces and -nephews she had in her care while their parents traveled. She noted that she had escorted the youngsters to see some animals, and they had preferred "four great and hideous swine" over anything else they saw that day. "I surmise the taste [is] inherited from [their] Aunty Bye," she wrote, "as I spent many a weary time looking at such sights with her when she was as small as they are."

Photographs taken of Bamie while she was still in her teens show an eerily serious young woman, her deep-set eyes hooded as though in great pain or sadness. The demeanor, the posture, and the rich fabric in her clothing all suggest a woman decades older. It is no wonder that she later described herself as skipping youth entirely. An acquaintance put it more cruelly, recalling that Bamie "had no particular girlhood because she was frightfully ugly, very badly made and a very curious, dark color . . . so brown."

Part of her unfortunate appearance resulted from the weakness in her spine that made her appear, even as an infant, slightly crippled. Grandmother Bulloch had noticed that something was wrong with Bamie almost as soon as she started to walk, but the cause was never clear. Bamie always maintained that she had been dropped by a nurse, but historians speculate that she had polio or Pott's disease, a deformity of the spine caused by tuberculosis.

Whatever its origin, her condition required treatment. Mittie and Theodore turned first to a doctor who put her in a heavy steel brace that encased her body and weighed so much that she could not maneuver on her own and had to be carried from room to room. In other wealthy families such a problem might have earned her pity and encouraged her to recede into a sedentary, spectator's existence, but the Roosevelts, who eventually had to struggle with many serious illnesses, never had much use for pampering. Bamie's father brought her goodies—she remembered especially the fresh fruit and ice cream—but he also encouraged her to be active, and she treasured above all else an invitation to accompany him on a fast carriage ride through Central Park, landscaped and opened to the public soon after she was born.

When she was about five, Bamie's therapy changed after her parents decided to switch doctors. Instead of the heavy brace designed to keep her immobile and thus strengthen her weak and wobbly spine, she wore a much lighter harness that permitted movement. Dr. Charles Fayette Taylor, the new physician, received high marks from Bamie. "Instead of the terrible instrument that I had formerly had to wear," she explained, he prescribed one "which allowed of my being up and about all the time." She immediately felt much better and, according to her own recollection, "became very strong and well." But the slight deformity remained for life, and as she aged and put on weight, it was magnified.

Besides the physical problem that helped catapult Bamie out of childhood, the effects of the Civil War also pushed her into adulthood. Six years old when the fighting started (her brother Theodore was only three), Bamie was the only one of the four Roosevelt children mature enough to comprehend the tensions resulting from the southern, pro-Confederate Bulloch women living among loudly anti-Confederate Roosevelts. She quickly learned to accommodate both sides, going merrily to her paternal grandparents' house at Broadway and Fourteenth Street, where much of the adult conversation centered on decimating the hated "rebels," and then returning to her own home a few blocks away and listening to Grandmother Bulloch talk about how much the southerners needed help. It is no wonder that a diplomat who met the adult Bamie commented on her "possessing an immense capacity for getting on with all sorts of people."

Like all the Roosevelt women of her generation, Bamie's formal education was negligible. Not until age fifteen did Bamie enroll in classes outside the home, and then it was at Les Ruches, the girls school in Versailles, France, run by Marie Souvestre. Daughter of Emil Souvestre, author of *Le Philosophe sous les Toits*, Marie Souvestre was well acquainted with French intellectuals, and she counted many of them among her close friends. With her large collection of art and books and her insatiable interest in matters of the mind, she reached out to all her students but chose some as her protégées. Never boring, she could erupt in tantrums on little warning, but she challenged her students to think outside the usual frames. Paying absolutely no attention to the then commonly held view that girls' minds were limited and that stretching them put them at risk of physical impairment, Souvestre insisted on a rigorous curriculum. Students conversed in French, Italian, and German, inside the classroom and outside, and discussion of the classics formed as much a part of every meal as did bread and water.

Because she taught two generations of Roosevelt women (Bamie and two of her nieces, Eleanor and Corinney), Souvestre played a significant role in their story, but their judgment of her was mixed. Eleanor singled her out as an important influence on her life while Corinney was more restrained. She appreciated Mademoiselle's intellectual prowess but disliked her tantrums and her favoring one girl over another. Bamie, neither as critical as Corinney nor as awed as Eleanor, remembered her few months at Souvestre's school with mixed emotions. Two decades later, while in Paris, Bamie arranged

JOHNSTON PUBLIC LIBRARY
JOHNSTON, IOWA 50131

a reunion with Souvestre. Anticipating a "charming afternoon," Bamie could not help but remember that the time under Mademoiselle had been "a very crude period of girlhood. . . . Not a period to which many of my happiest and most amusing memories cling."

Some of the circumstances blighting that period lay entirely beyond the control of either the headmistress or the student. Bamie happened to enroll at Les Ruches just as the Franco-Prussian War was starting, and she wrote her worried parents about watching troops march past the school. Bamie missed her family even though they all wrote her long letters about what they were doing. But she did not miss them for long. Her parents, concerned that she might be caught up in the war, arranged for her to go to her Bulloch uncles in Liverpool and then sail for home.

Bamie's second trip to Europe with the family, in 1872, had far larger repercussions. Nearly eighteen years old, she had settled into her role as tutor to her siblings, apparently resigned to looking like the spinster governess while her thirty-eight-year-old mother continued to attract the attention of men who were half her age. As the Roosevelt entourage drifted along the Nile in their dahabeah, they met a quartet of young Harvard graduates living on their own houseboat. Eventually, the two groups spent a lot of time together, combining forces for land excursions and evening parties, but in the beginning the Harvard men had mistaken Bamie and Mittie for sisters. Only slowly did the daughter realize that they had assumed she was the older of the two. Whatever anger or jealousy Bamie felt, she failed to record it—at least in letters that have survived. A subsequent stop in Vienna confirmed Bamie's plight. At a ball at the Opera House she was relegated for much of the evening to a side room where the young women guests sat waiting for invitations to dance. Bamie was more accustomed to chatting with her dance partners rather than being dropped abruptly to wait in isolation, and she found this evening very long.

On that second trip Bamie acted the part of protective parent to her younger siblings, especially after Theodore Sr. returned to America. When Theodore Jr. went off with Elliott and Corinne to study in Dresden, Bamie wrote him from Carlsbad in very fine adult hand—almost the hand of an elderly matron—but in a hearty "old boy" style. Referring to walks they would soon be taking together, she scolded him for not writing often enough and then commiserated about his asthma. Most important, she indicated that there was no problem he faced that she could not help him solve: "When we reach Dresden, we will settle it all." Even at that age she had perfected her crisp, managerial style. As her niece Alice later explained: "There is always someone in every family who keeps it together. In ours, it was Auntie Bye."

As soon as she returned to New York in October 1873, Bamie was slated for her own coming out, but the new house on Fifty-seventh Street, the designated site of the celebration, had not yet been completed. That was the official explanation, at least, for holding Bamie's debut out of town. In hindsight the solution has a fishy taint about it, as though her parents understood that Bamie's limited circle of friends in New York would not provide much fun. Even she found trouble explaining the decision when, decades later, she wrote, "It all seems utterly unaccountable as I look back upon it."

Philadelphia friends of her father, the Lippincotts, invited Bamie to spend a few weeks with them that winter, and it was there, in the foyer of the Academy of Music, that she officially "came out." Bamie's recollection of that evening is telling. "It was the fashion," she later wrote, although she deemed it "perfectly idiotic," to send each debutante large flower arrangements, and she was "immensely pleased" when two chairs next to hers were stacked high with the extravagant bouquets that friends of her parents sent her.

Once the new Roosevelt house was completed, Bamie's parents gave her a party there, but it proved an ordeal and not nearly as pleasant as the one in Philadelphia. She had lived her entire life in New York (except for the trips abroad), but because she was always classed as a grown-up, she moved more easily among her parents' generation than her own. A brother might have helped, but the four-year difference between her and Theodore put him in what sometimes seemed like a subsequent generation. She remembered that winter of her debut "with mingled feelings of pleasure and disappointment. Not knowing many young people made it very hard."

At least she could congratulate herself that she was not wearing glasses. One of her friends recalled that just before the big event, Bamie had some trouble with her eyes and a doctor prescribed glasses. Then her father, who had already coaxed his son to "make" his body, announced that he would "not bring out in New York society any young girl who wears glasses all the time." Bamie, who was every bit as desirous of her father's approval as Theodore was, promptly removed the glasses, and except for reading, she never put them on again.

That same determination—some might call it vanity—showed up in her strong self-confidence that seemed to attract people of all ages. Young men, including her debut escort, formed a coterie of admirers, and others sought her company for conversation and wit. As she matured, she seemed to collect men several years her junior, and her family, alluding to the fact that some were obviously younger than she, dubbed them her "Joe-Bobs" after two of the most persistent.

Amazingly, she continued to attract them until she was very old. Not long before her death, a friend who knew her well searched in vain for the source of Bamie's magnetism: "She is a woman no longer young. She is very deaf; she is badly crippled with arthritis; from all ordinary standards she is very plain. And yet when she is in a room, every man in the room, old and young, wants to sit beside her, listen to her, and will desert the younger, more beautiful ladies." It was a trait that her nieces would copy for themselves.

Southern precedents helped, although Bamie rarely conceded that. Her mother and her aunt Anna had perfected a combination of competence and feminine fragility, and it served them well. Their smiles could wilt all but the most hostile audience, and their accents, retaining the long vowels of their native Georgia, underlined their easy, relaxed approach to life and their insistence on seeing the pleasures and not the pain. Although they suffered at least their share of death and loss, they maintained an upbeat, cheerful countenance that expressed itself in what became a common family saying, "Live for the living, not the dead." This attitude would be a distinctive characteristic of all the Roosevelt children.

Her "can-do" attitude marked Bamie through family tragedies and great personal pain. Within a year of the disappointing debut, she found her stride and began to make friends, or as she later wrote, "From then on, [I] thoroughly enjoyed what I had of life in New York." Her mother turned over much of the management of the family home to her, and when Theodore entered Harvard in September 1876, it was twenty-one-year-old Bamie who journeyed up to Cambridge to locate living quarters for him. Harvard had not yet set up its Women's Annex (which later became Radcliffe College), but Bamie would have taken no note of it anyway. In late nineteenth-century America, women of her class saw college as something that others who lacked their own portfolios or family income might think they wanted or needed to do.

In Cambridge, Bamie looked after every detail of furnishing her brother's apartment, which she insisted had to be on the second floor because of his asthma. He thoroughly appreciated her efforts, writing her as soon as he settled in at 16 Winthrop Street that he did not know how he would have managed without her. "The curtains, carpet, furniture, in short everything is really beautiful; I have never seen prettier or more tasteful wall paper."

Theodore owed more than his college quarters to his older sister. In Cambridge, he met the beautiful young Alice Lee from nearby Chestnut Hill, and he courted her with a passion that exceeded hers. When she finally agreed to marry him, her parents objected, insisting that Alice was still much too young. Only after hearing that the newlyweds would be residing with Bamie and Mittie did the Lees change their minds. According to Theodore, Bamie's competence was well established even in the Boston area, where she was spoken of so highly that Theodore could not resist passing the compliment along to her: " It has really made me feel proud to hear the way you are spoken of by your friends."

Bamie also encouraged Theodore's political aspirations. Soon after he married, in October 1880, and moved back to New York, Theodore began showing an interest in politics. He attended Republican district meetings one evening a week and was elected to the state assembly in November 1881. Their uncle Robert, a Democrat, had served in the U.S. Congress a decade earlier, but few of the Roosevelts' friends wanted to run for office. Bamie disagreed. For her, government offered a chance to make a difference, and she thought it a "peculiar attitude" to want to ignore that possibility. She could thank her father for initiating her in the subject. Having aligned with the Republican Party from the time of its formation in the 1850s, he shared his opinions with his eldest child, and while she attended school in France, he wrote her on the stationery of the Republican

Reform Club at 39 Union Square. After his death in 1878, when she was twenty-three, she did not jettison that interest—but she moved her brother to center stage.

Further encouragement from Bamie came when Theodore's interest in politics waned and he seemed about to abandon it. Alice Lee's death in February 1884, after she and Theodore had been married only three and a half years, left him listless and depressed. The short tribute he wrote to her shows something of Theodore's grief. "For joy or for sorrow," he concluded the homage, "my life has now been lived out."

But a young man in his mid-twenties still had much of his life ahead of him, and he turned to a part of the country that held for him almost no association with his dead wife. In the fall of 1883 he had traveled to the Dakota Territory, hoping to invest there and take part in both the adventure and the profit that the area offered. Now, with Alice's death, he fled to that flat, open plain as though it would blot out his grief. Cut off from political news in the East, he relied on his sister to read the newspapers and forward important articles to him. Then he shared his reactions with her. He did attend the Republican National Convention, held just months after his wife's death, and he wrote Bamie what he thought of the candidates and their messages. As for the speech he made, he judged it was "listened to very attentively and was very well received" by the delegates, but he still considered his political career finished.

Unwilling to let him give up so easily, Bamie had plenty of worries of her own that year. After Mittie and Alice died, she oversaw clearing out the Fifty-seventh Street house as well as another one on Forty-fifth Street that Theodore and Elliott had briefly occupied with their young wives. She remembered that spring as "a perfect nightmare" because it meant "parting with all the places that we had cared for, dividing everything that had always meant home and deciding how to recommence life."

One of the few bright spots in an otherwise dismal period occurred that spring while she was still moving out. During a brief trip to Washington, Theodore had telegraphed her that he would be bringing a friend to New York for her to meet. In her usual accommodating manner, she quickly rearranged the little furniture left in the house and prepared to welcome her brother's guest, the young senator from

Massachusetts, Henry Cabot Lodge. Bamie and the senator took an immediate liking to each other (although they never had the intense relationship that Corinne later had with him), and they soon depended on each other for advice and insight. With Bamie, Cabot liked to range over a host of topics, skipping from foreign policy to Republican tactics without missing a beat. When separated, they wrote each other, and after she moved to London in 1893, he sought her judgment and help on a variety of foreign policy matters.

✑

The other bright spot in Bamie's life in the 1880s was Theodore's infant daughter, Alice, whom she accepted the responsibility for raising. The baby might have been bundled off to her maternal grandparents in Boston—but "Baba," as she was then called, was the first granddaughter for this branch of Roosevelts. The capable Bamie saw no reason to relinquish her to anyone else, although the wealthy Lees, who lived more than a day's journey away, remained devoted to the child and contributed substantial sums to her upkeep throughout her youth.

At twenty-nine, with no marriage prospect in sight, Bamie saw a very special place in her life for this child. By May 1884, just three months after the double funeral of Mittie and her daughter-in-law, Bamie had bought herself a brownstone at 422 Madison Avenue and moved there with baby Alice. Corinne and Elliott, with their respective spouses, lived only a few blocks away.

That summer the Lee grandparents took Alice to Chestnut Hill, leaving Bamie free to spend the hot months with Aunt Anna and her husband at Oyster Bay. That turned into Bamie's routine for the next few years: summers on Long Island and winters in Manhattan, where Theodore frequently joined her. "I always insisted that we did not live together," Bamie later wrote, "that we only visited one another, realizing beforehand that that would be a much easier relationship to break than had we made a mutual home. And this proved the case when he married his second wife."

While Theodore continued to try to assuage his grief over Alice Lee's death by living a cowboy's life in the Dakota Badlands, he kept up a full correspondence with Bamie. They liked the same kind of people, and in April 1886 he approved some new acquaintances of hers, whom he judged potential "additions to our limited list of intellec-

tual acquaintances and further material for that far distant salon."
Both sister and brother felt comfortable casting a wide net, including
people in "politics, literature . . . art" as long as those "politicians,
authors and artists" have "personal habits [that] do not disqualify
them for society." To enter this charmed circle, the women had to be
"clever" and not dress "primatically, nor," Theodore continued in
what might be seen as a veiled reference to Corinne's husband, "yet
have committed the still graver crime of marrying dull husbands."

To his shrewd and witty sister Theodore felt comfortable complaining about some of "our friends [who] do things that sound
interesting [but] do them in a way that makes them very dull."
Henry Cabot Lodge and his wife, Nannie, were among the few who
met their high standards, and Theodore confided to his sister: "I am
delighted you enjoyed the Lodges so much; it is the only place outside of the family that I really care to visit."

Theodore and Bamie passed advice and information back and
forth in the manner of equals, without any suggestion that she possessed a lesser mind. From the small ranchers' town of Medora, near
the western boundary of the Dakota Territory, he wrote her in June
1886 about a political offer "which I suppose you know all about."
When she advised him not to send "the horse thief piece" he had written to *Century* magazine, he reluctantly agreed. He conferred with her
on his job offers, including one from the Reverend Endicott Peabody
"to become a teacher in his school." Most significant, Theodore
showed no qualms about endorsing Bamie's financial decisions even
when he was too far away to know exactly what was at stake. In one
letter he assured her that whatever position she took on a particular
"railroad scheme," he wanted her to know, "I will back you."

In some ways Theodore treated Bamie as if they were brothers,
especially when he described some of the attractive women he met
in the Dakotas. One of the ranchers' wives, Patty Selmes, was, he
wrote, "really to my mind a singularly attractive woman . . . very
handsome . . . and," as one of his neighbors put it, "very 'séduisante'
like most Kentucky girls." In extending his list of what made Patty
Selmes interesting, Theodore added details that sounded more like
Bamie: "She is very well read, has a delicious sense of humor and is
extremely fond of poetry, including that of my new favorite Brown-
ing as well as my old one Swinburne." Patty Selmes and her daugh-

ter, Isabella, remained part of the Roosevelt story for several generations, but they had first entered it through Theodore and Bamie.

Her brother's descriptions of the West whetted Bamie's appetite to see the Badlands for herself, but Theodore encouraged her to wait. In April 1886, while he was secretly proceeding with his courtship of Edith Carow, even arranging through Bamie for some flowers to be sent to her, he gently dissuaded Bamie from visiting. His cabin was not comfortable enough for her and Corinne, he wrote, but in another year or so he hoped to offer something better.

Then he added, as he often did in referring to the daughter that he had left in Bamie's care, "best love to stony hearted Baby Lee." This was a slight variation on his usual "cunning little yellow headed baby Lee," but it was about as close as Theodore came to accepting responsibility for his child. All decisions about her care and upbringing remained with Bamie—at least for now.

Living on her own in New York, Bamie had enough money to do pretty much as she pleased. She owned considerable real estate, and various stocks and bonds inherited from her parents yielded a comfortable annual income of $2,600. In a later memoir she described her life during those years after her mother's death as coming right out of Edith Wharton: "It was very much [like *The*] *Age of Innocence*, though naturally I did not realize it at the time, and we had a very interesting life."

As Wharton described it, upper-class life in New York City in the late nineteenth century included a brownstone with several servants, a summer house in some tranquil spot outside the urban grit, and a coterie of friends who frequently entertained one another in their homes and traveled together abroad. For her country retreat Bamie still chose Oyster Bay, Long Island, where her family had been summering since 1874. Even before little Alice's birth, Bamie paid Theodore $7,000 for thirty acres of harborfront there and started building a house for herself. But she abandoned the project and went to manage his house after the elder Alice died. Following the "season" in Manhattan, full of theater dates and fashionable parties, she could remove herself to Long Island for restful summer days punctuated by visits from her nieces and nephews.

In spite of her description of her life as interesting, Bamie appeared not entirely satisfied. Restlessly, she continued to look for change. In

1886, shortly after Alice turned two, Bamie spent $50,000 on a new house, 689 Madison Avenue, near Sixty-second Street. Just before the transfer she left her niece with the Lee grandparents and set off for Mexico in the company of her girlhood friend Sara Delano, who had married Bamie's distant cousin James Roosevelt. Bamie conferred equivalent status on them, referring to them as "Cousin Sally and Cousin James." Their little boy, Franklin Delano, age four, remained behind as his parents' undertook the journey. Theodore heartily approved of the trip, describing it as "pretty nearly ideal," adding, "hardly any European trip would be as fascinating."

James Roosevelt's private railroad car, "Monon," earned high marks from Bamie, who referred to the plush accommodations as "the most ideal way of traveling." With their meals prepared by a superb cook, the party soaked up the sights as their train wound its way through the United States and across the Rio Grande into Mexico. Bamie, who wondered why more wealthy people did not travel in similar style, admitted this trip involved some danger. In Mexico the "Monon" parked overnight in train stations so as to thwart bandits who might rob the passengers on a night journey. During the day, when a luxurious private car might attract unwelcome attention as it moved through the countryside, local men were hired as guards, but Bamie viewed them with some misgivings. The best applicants for the job were those who had formerly been bandits themselves and presumably knew the most vulnerable spots.

After seeing enough of Mexico, the Roosevelt party traveled through Arizona and southern California, which they found "a mass of bloom." Following a stop in San Francisco they headed east, and Bamie, who had been tired when she left, arrived back in New York seven weeks later feeling enormously refreshed.

All the benefits of that relaxing trip fell away quickly in the face of a family crisis. To her surprise, Bamie found a gossip item in one of the New York newspapers saying that Theodore would soon marry Edith Carow, a woman Bamie knew well. She had been a friend of the family since she was a toddler, and a youthful romance had developed between her and Theodore. But that had presumably ended before he met Alice Lee, and his grief over Alice's death, combined with strong feelings that a widower who was properly loyal to his deceased wife would never remarry, made the announcement outlandish—at least to Bamie. She also knew that Edith was abroad, having moved with her mother and sister to Europe the previous spring to live more cheaply after her father's death.

So sure of herself that she did not bother to check with either of the principals, Bamie rushed to place a sharply worded denial in the newspaper, noting that "nothing is more common in society than to hear positive assertions constantly made regarding the engagement of persons who have been at all in each other's company, and no practice is more reprehensible." But Bamie might have taken the time to check at least with Theodore. That she proceeded so quickly and forcefully underlines how confident she felt that her brother kept no secrets from her.

Theodore's reply must have dumbfounded her. In a long apologetic letter he confessed that the newspaper report was substantially correct and that he would go to London within a few months to marry Edith. He had meant to tell Bamie sooner but never seemed to find the right moment. Although he was "savagely irritated" to see the newspaper account, he had no idea how it had leaked unless some servant of his or of Edith's household had spied on their correspondence. He had told no one, he assured his sister, and the final decision about the date had been made after he had last seen Bamie in New York. He had hesitated to write her, he explained, "because a letter is such a miserably poor substitute for talking face to face."

Perhaps his biggest deterrent came from his own misgivings about what he was doing. Admitting that he "utterly disbelieve[d] in and disapprove[d] of second marriages," he said he had viewed them as a sign of "weakness in a man's character," of "inconstancy and unfaithfulness" to the deceased spouse. Now, having put himself in a predicament by agreeing to marry a second time, he insisted that all the blame be heaped on him, and he did "earnestly ask" that Bamie not blame "poor little Edith. It is certainly not her fault and the entire blame rests on my shoulders."

Theodore went on to give more detail than his sister probably needed: "Eight years ago [Edith] and I had very intimate relations; one day there came a break for we both of us had, and I suppose have, tempers that were far from being of the best. To no soul now living have either of us ever since spoken a word of this."

Then Theodore came to the part that involved Bamie most directly. Referring to the fact that he stayed with her whenever he returned from the Dakotas, he wrote: "As regards yourself, my dearest sister, I can only say you will be giving me the greatest happiness in your power if you will continue to pass your summers with me." He predicted that he and his new wife would "have to live in the country almost the entire year" and that this marriage would make substantial changes in his own life. But he insisted he had no intention of taking his daughter from Bamie: "If you wish to, you shall keep Baby Lee, I of course paying the expense." That apparently offhand renunciation of his daughter later fueled Alice's fury, and when she grew up, she quoted it as evidence that her father had never taken the least interest in her or what happened to her.

Although hurt by Theodore's secretiveness on such an important point as his remarriage, Bamie quickly gathered her resources and moved on. She might have felt more left out if Corinne had been in on the plans, but her sister, who had always considered Edith Carow her closest friend, was as completely in the dark as Bamie. That summer while Bamie was off seeing Mexico, Corinne had given birth to her second child, a daughter. Elliott, who was busy with his own family, his plan to build a new house on Long Island, and his own playboy schedule, had little time for Theodore. In fact, the brothers, once so close, were seeing less and less of each other.

It was fortunate that Theodore had Bamie to depend on that fall—she was the only one of his siblings who could devote full time to him. When he returned to New York a few weeks after the newspaper item concerning his forthcoming marriage, he had agreed to run as the Republican candidate for mayor of the city, a job no one (including himself) thought he could win. Both the Democratic candidate, Abram Hewitt, and the Independent, the single-tax advocate Henry George, appeared far more popular—and, in the end, both outran Theodore. His underdog status did not deter his relatives, either in enthusiasm or action. Bamie, who proudly noted the "hold" that her brother had on the public, hosted him during the short campaign, and Corinne's husband, Douglas Robinson, organized the Roosevelt Campaign Club of Business Men.

The day after the votes were counted, Bamie sailed with Theodore to England. If she had been really miffed with him about Edith, she could have refused to accompany him. The two booked space as "Mr. and Miss Merrifield" to get by the prying eyes of the gossip columnists who read passenger lists and even published names. Bamie later wrote of the night before they left: "I will never forget [it] . . . Theodore and I sat up until almost morning" to write notes telling friends of his engagement.

It was on that ocean crossing that Bamie first met an Englishman named Cecil Spring-Rice, who later became a distinguished diplomat but was then just starting out in his career. The same age as Theodore, Spring-Rice had graduated from Oxford, gone immediately into the Foreign Office as a clerk, and when he met Bamie in late 1886, was just beginning what turned out to be nearly a decade at the British embassy in Washington, D.C.

The few months he had already spent there had served him well, however, and he immediately saw through the "Miss Merrifield" disguise. Well out of sight of land, Bamie admitted her identity, and together with him and two of his friends, she and Theodore partied for the remainder of the voyage. Spring-Rice, whose spirited approach to life showed up in his nickname, "Springy," delighted everyone who met him with his amusing banter and his whimsical drawings, and this oceanic crossing sealed his friendship with both Roosevelts. Theodore asked him to serve as best man at his wedding a few weeks later.

On the date set for the wedding, December 2, 1886, the fog was so thick in London that Bamie could barely make her way from Brown's Hotel, where she was staying, to St. George's Church on Hanover Square. Once inside, she could not clearly distinguish the wedding party gathered in front of the altar because, she maintained, the place was so dimly lit—but more likely it was because she still refused to wear glasses. She later boasted that she proceeded "undauntedly" forward, and "they gradually developed," including the face of Springy. Just how much courage she had to muster to make that trip and watch her brother marry for a second time (and thus exclude her from much of his life) Bamie never revealed. At the time of the wedding she did not yet know. For his part, Theodore showed gratitude that she had made the trip, and afterward he wrote her: "You dearest sister, I cannot say how much I appreciated your coming over; it has been everything for both Edith and myself."

Bamie tarried in England only briefly after the ceremony to visit friends in Shropshire before starting home to the person most important in her life—young Alice, who was almost three. It turned out to be a short reunion, however, because Theodore wrote from Italy, where he and Edith were honeymooning, that he wanted to reclaim his daughter—or, rather his new wife did: "I hardly know what to say about Baby Lee, Edith feels more strongly about her than I could have imagined possible." Still, he put off the final decision, hoping to "decide it all when we meet." In the meantime, he sent "my best love to the darling, and many kisses."

Bamie doted on the blond, curly-haired niece whose dark complexion and languid eyes resembled her own, but she knew Edith Carow well enough to know that she usually got what she wanted. When the honeymooners arrived in New York in March, Bamie had Alice ready, dressed in her Sunday best and holding a bouquet of flowers for "Mother." As the child went off with Theodore and Edith to live in Theodore's Long Island house, soon to be renamed Sagamore Hill, Bamie could only remind her that she could always come back. At that age the little girl could hardly object to the new arrangement, but she must have sensed an enormous contrast between the two women. Later, Alice recalled that when Auntie Bye had entertained at Sagamore Hill for Theodore, "there was a wonderful feeling of warmth and ease and hospitality . . . which was never quite the case with my stepmother."

After the fact, Bamie explained why she had agreed to let Alice go. Bamie's own father had played such a central role in her childhood that she could not imagine denying a similar pleasure to her niece: "It almost broke my heart to give her up. Still I felt perfectly sure that it was for her good, and that unless she lived with her father she would never see much of him, and as my father and I had had such a close relationship, this would have been a terrible wrong to her, all of which fortunately proved true, as she adored her father, and was really more like him than any of his other children."

Other evidence suggests that Bamie suffered far more from the separation than she revealed in that account. She once wrote to a close friend that losing the child had permanently crippled her emotionally: "Since my little Alice had to leave me I have never allowed myself to take even the just transient interest in any one old [or] young." Although she was perceptive enough to recognize her reaction as one of "great cowardliness" that was bound to lead her to "despair," she could not help herself.

Besides the loss of Alice, Bamie had other reasons to regret Theodore's marriage to Edith Carow. Since childhood, Edith had been in and out of the Roosevelt house, studying alongside Corinne, who was almost exactly her age. The two girls had exchanged poetry and their thoughts about the future. But as she matured, Edith showed a strong will that could easily come between her husband and his sisters.

Alice Lee had been a sweet, malleable creature, willing to bend to the wishes of all the Roosevelts, but Edith was, even in her twenties, steely strong. Something about Alice Lee obviously impressed the Roosevelts as fragile and helpless; they constantly referred to her as "little Alice" although she was five feet seven inches, nearly as tall as Theodore. It was hard to think of Edith as "little," at least after she reached her teens, and she would have aimed a scathing stare at anyone who addressed her as "Baby."

In addition, Edith showed less enthusiasm for politics than either of her husband's sisters. Bamie had always matched Theodore's interest in campaigns, and after the lull in his political life following Alice's death, she jubilantly watched him come to life in the recent mayoral race. At the time she had written Edith in London that she was thrilled to see him "at his very best once more." The years "out of politics in any active form" had been sad ones, "a real heart sorrow to me." He had hardly frittered away his time ("He always made more of his life than any other man I knew"), but he had lost out on some important years: "It was a permanent source of poignant regret that even at this early age he should lose these years without the possibility of doing his best and most telling work." Bamie had feared, she wrote in that same letter, that too long out of the political arena would cripple him, and "he might find his hold over the public gone when he once more came before them." But his run for mayor renewed her faith that he "has enough work to keep him exerting all his powers." Bamie, wary of Edith's taste for politics, could hardly have signaled more strongly how vital she saw government service as a part of Theodore's life.

As soon as Edith had replaced her as the central woman in Theodore's life, Bamie sought consolation in the old family medicine—travel. The first summer after losing Alice, she visited a variety of friends and relatives, and the second summer she went abroad with the Lippincotts, the Philadelphia friends who had arranged her debut there. As Edith Wharton described so well in her novels, wealthy New Yorkers composed their own travel parties for their sojourns abroad—a variation on their house parties in the country. Bamie's trip with the Lippincotts was "perfectly enchanting," she later wrote, because she took full charge of the itinerary. For some reason her mind "turned to west coasts, and we got off at Cork" and traveled to the west coast of Ireland, up through Galway, then to Connemara, across to Norway and Sweden, and down to Denmark.

After leaving the Lippincotts, Bamie proceeded on her own to Bremen, where she met an old friend, Kate Marquand, and together the women started south to Vienna, where they visited James Roosevelt Roosevelt, then serving as first secretary at the American embassy, located in an old Austrian palace. Bamie would have had trouble saying just what her connection was to the man everyone in the family called Rosy, who was about her age. The son of her distant cousin James and his first wife, Rosy was now the stepson of Sara Delano, Bamie's girlhood friend. When Rosy had married Helen Astor, a daughter of Caroline Astor, Bamie was a bridesmaid, and when their daughter was born, she was the godmother. For now, Rosy's diplomatic career provided her with her first chance to stay in a real palace, but later she would have to disrupt her life to help him out.

Wherever she went on that European trip, Bamie thrived on adventure. Her looks had not improved since the days when young men overlooked her in favor of her mother, but she had apparently already developed a magnetic personality. She received many invitations, including one from a man she met on a train who turned out to be "one of the most exclusively aristocratic Hungarians."

Back in New York by the fall of 1888, Bamie returned to her "Edith Wharton life," punctuated, as Wharton's characters' lives were not, by a strong injection of politics. Bamie always insisted that Wharton's characters acted as though they were living in the wrong time, but whatever the period, they seemed caught in the web of social jousting and oblivious to political currents. Bamie could hardly isolate herself from current events even if she wished to. As the 1888 presidential election approached, she and Theodore conferred on the Republicans' prospects for victory. He volunteered that "there is really some chance" of winning, although "I am by no means as hopeful as Cabot [Lodge]." Theodore judged the Republican ticket "first class" and thought the presidential nominee, Benjamin Harrison, a "clean, able man, with a good record—as a soldier and a senator." The Republican platform in its entirety did not please Theodore, but "on important issues, such as civil service reforms and on the admission of the northwestern territories as states . . . it is sound while the Democratic platform is not."

While Bamie's intellectual relationship with her brother remained strong and vital, the personal contacts between them showed small strains. Theodore was not at all sensitive to the fact that Bamie might feel some embarrassment about her figure, especially in comparison to the lithe Edith Carow. Even as a teenager Bamie had begun to put on weight, and by the late 1880s, when she was in her thirties, she had become what her niece Alice called "a big man of a woman." Edith, who easily kept her weight in the 120-pound range all her life (except for her seven pregnancies), never seemed to understand why other women could not. She and Bamie had already vied with each other to see who would get to ride one of their favorite horses, Caution, and Theodore had settled the matter in a letter to Bamie: "I wish Caution were big enough for you to ride but I am afraid she is much too light."

Events the next summer further underlined how Edith Carow's marriage into the family had altered Bamie's role. Edith was already pregnant again, having delivered her first son in October 1887, and Theodore informed his sister that they would like to use Bamie's Manhattan house for the confinement that winter: "Alice's wish for another brother or sister will, I rather regret to say, probably be gratified about the end of next January." Edith's desire to remain at Sagamore Hill for the delivery had been vetoed by their doctor, who thought that plan "outrageous folly" given the severity of Long Island winters. Theodore admitted that his sister would be inconvenienced, "but at the same time I told [Edith] I was sure you would not be willing to have her go to a hotel—or anywhere else. Now, you darling Bysie, you must write perfectly frankly about it."

Such requests underlined the accommodating role that Bamie filled for the entire family. Whether it was a sick child or an ailing adult, she was expected to perform as what she revealingly called "an odd-job man." She apparently acquiesced to each plea for help, and in the case of Edith's "lying in" she did not refuse hospitality. Just a few days later, however, the matter was taken out of her hands. On August 8, Theodore explained that "Edith has just had a miscarriage." He attributed her losing the baby to a small accident he had while playing polo. When he fell, he "looked bad," and seeing him "limp and senseless" had so upset Edith that she had miscarried, "though we did not know it for over a week."

Now free to claim her entire house for herself, Bamie could go about her own life. She settled in to a winter of entertaining and being entertained, much of it centering on a young man who almost filled the vacuum left when Alice was taken from her. Coincidentally, Bamie first met the handsome Robert Ferguson through Cecil Spring-Rice when she was in London for Theodore's wedding, just weeks before she learned she would lose Alice. The Ferguson family came from a distinguished old Scottish line, and as soon as they met Bamie, all of them, including Bob's brothers, sisters and widowed mother, took an immediate liking to her. But it was Bob who became her very special friend. Unlike his older brother, who was already in the diplomatic service, Bob had not decided what to do with his life. A charming and witty raconteur, he immediately became a favorite of all the Roosevelts, but to Bamie he was much more than that. For the next few years after she met him, he replaced Theodore as the central focus in her life—at least until she got to London and met someone to replace him.

II

BAMIE SEALED HER friendship with Bob Ferguson on a trip they took together in the fall of 1889, nearly three years after they first met. Theodore, newly appointed as Civil Service Commissioner by President Harrison in Washington, D.C., had finally agreed to show his sisters around the Dakota Badlands. He had expanded his investment there, buying a large ranch, Elkhorn, about forty miles north of Chimney Butte, and he was eager to show it off to his entire family. Elliott's wife, Anna, was due to deliver their second child in September, so there was no question about his joining the excursion, but Corinne and her husband went. Theodore and Edith started out

ahead of the others so they could accompany the Minnesota governor to the opening of a new opera house in St. Paul. Corinne and
Bamie went by train directly from New York, and by the time they
arrived in Minnesota, everyone was eager to see this part of the
nation that Theodore had praised so highly. As their train moved
across the flat, treeless plains of North Dakota and the red, odd-
shaped Badlands finally emerged, his sisters knew why Theodore
had been so drawn to this part of the country.

Bamie had considerable travel experience by now, but she had
never seen anything like Medora, the little town where they got off
the train. The name itself was quite a story. The French Marquis de
Mores had called it Medora in honor of his American-born wife,
perhaps because her wealthy father was footing the bill for the
count's investment there. Along with a roomy chateau (his name for
it), Mores planned to build a meat-processing plant where he would
butcher cattle and then send the iced meat back east. The meat-
packing part ended in fiasco when Mores's competitors schemed
against him and made sure a big shipment got slowed down until the
meat spoiled, but his house stood as an odd testament to a French-
man transplanted to the plains. Mores imported the most costly
wines from a New York merchant—until his father-in-law cut off
funds, and he eventually returned to France.

The Roosevelt party's accommodations were not as luxurious as
the chateau. Bamie found herself in a two-story cabin that served as
both grocery store and sleeping facility. In the casual camaraderie of
the frontier, where little attention was paid to matters of privacy and
who slept where, she ended up sharing the ground floor with two
men in her party—Cabot Lodge's son, Bay, and Bob Ferguson—
while the two married couples took over the second floor. Accustomed to having not only her own bedroom but also her own
personal maid, Bamie was delighted with these "make-do" arrangements. This was exactly the kind of situation she liked to recount in
great detail, each discomfort carefully embroidered to illustrate the
adventure and underline the incongruity it represented in her life.

Among the colorful characters that she met on that trip, one left
an indelible impression. "Hell-roaring Bill" was a "tall, typically
Western man . . . exactly like the Remington illustrations," Bamie
wrote, and he spat tobacco juice with such unerring aim that every-

one around him "felt perfectly safe." Several others were just as extraordinary, and she concluded: "There never was a place where one saw such a flotsam and jetsam of life as the West in those days." Bamie rode the thirty-eight miles from the town to the ranch in a makeshift carriage with seats that rattled around as though they could come loose at any moment. Among the many surprises, she saw more scrawny prairie dogs than she could count, and after one man told her that he had killed more than two hundred rattlesnakes, she decided to do her sightseeing from horseback.

After inspecting the Elkhorn ranch, with its cattle roundups and calf branding, and watching Corinne dazzle the local cowhands with her horse-riding prowess, the Roosevelt party boarded a train for the Pacific Coast, and Bamie recognized what a "perfectly disreputable looking party we were." She rode horseback in Yellowstone, although she insisted that some of the horses "had never been used by ladies before." Edith's horse appeared particularly hostile, but perhaps because she did not want to look like a coward in comparison with Corinne, Edith refused to dismount even when the groom insisted that he was helpless to control it. After two weeks of sleeping in tents, the party moved on to Seattle, where they presented letters of introduction to some of the city's leaders. Leaving Washington State, the entourage moved south to San Francisco and then returned to New York via Kansas City, arriving home in October.

Whatever Bamie said about the sites and the adventures, the most enduring part of that trip was the time she spent with the charismatic Bob Ferguson. The two had not previously been together for more than a few hours at a time, and now, with the arranging and the adventure that accompanies travel to new places, they saw each other in a new light. He appreciated her wit, and she, like many others, was drawn to his sensitivity and charm. Exactly what made him unsuitable for marriage to Bamie remains unclear. He was thirteen years her junior, a considerable difference, and even in his twenties, he was not entirely healthy. But probably his biggest disability was lack of a future. He showed no signs of making a career, either in government or business, that Bamie could point to with pride. She liked his good stories and appreciated his attentions to her, but when it came time to marry, she looked for a more substantial man with a pedigree to match her own.

Still addressing him as "My dear Mr. Ferguson" in October 1890, a year after their western sojourn, she invited him to visit her at 689 Madison Avenue whenever he chose to come, even without warning. As additional enticement she dangled the prospect that Theodore might possibly visit at the same time. Over the next three years the young Scotsman went to her Manhattan house so often that it became associated with him in her mind. Faced with returning there after spending time with him at Corinne's upstate New York country house, Bamie complained that she would "hate to think" of going home without him. Always mindful of his frail health, she reminded him not to "overfatigue" himself "more than absolutely necessary" and that he could always come to her. "Your room will always be waiting," she wrote him in one letter, and then a few weeks later, "Bob if ever you are ill or, *anything* is the matter you must come directly home to me."

With him more than any other person she knew, Bamie could share her thoughts about her family, including their money problems. After lamenting that "business is really in a terrible state," making "Uncle Gracie terribly nervous," she fretted that Corinne was having her own difficulties. With four young children, all under the age of ten, she found herself exhausted by the many demands her family put on her. To make matters worse, the Robinsons' scheme to make some money by renting out their city house had not produced the gains anticipated.

Bamie's other sibling, too, was causing her much anxiety. It had become clear to Bamie that Elliott was an alcoholic (although she would have shunned that term). Better natured than Theodore, Elliott was always erratic, but he got away with a lot because of his charisma. Both Mittie and Aunt Anna had doted on him when he was young, and they saw his easy-going ways and his appreciation of fun and laughter as an echo of Bulloch Hall. The mysterious headaches and frequent lapses in attention had troubled the family during his teen years, and by the time he turned twenty, it was clear that Elliott would not be following his older brother to Harvard. After standing up as Theodore's best man, Elliott set out to travel the world. Sailing on the same ship as James and Sara Delano Roosevelt, he went first to Europe and then, on his own, he continued to India where he amused himself by shooting elephants and tigers for several months. By the time he returned in early 1882, he seemed inordinately fond of

partying and did little else, but his marriage to Anna Hall the following year signaled to his family that he had entered a more serious
phase. Sometime in the next half-dozen years—no one seems to have
pinpointed the precise date—it became obvious that this was not the
case and that he was far too dependent on alcohol.

By the time Elliott turned thirty, Bamie recognized that her bon
vivant brother had become a difficult drunk. Corinne was slower to
admit what had happened, perhaps because her personality was
more tolerant and less willing to judge. But Theodore and Bamie
knew they had a problem. Elliott tried different cures, including a
clinic in Michigan, but in 1890 he took Anna and their two young
children (Eleanor was six and Elliott Jr. was one) and went to
Europe for treatment.

Weeks later Bamie joined them. After consulting with doctors in
Vienna, she transferred Elliott to a sanitarium located in an old
palace in Graz and insisted on staying herself to monitor his
progress even though "it was against the rules." Since the clinic had
no rooms set aside for relatives, she was shunted from place to place,
ending up in a huge room on the third floor that had been used by
the ladies-in-waiting to the empress who had once lived there. Each
corner provided a separate sleeping nook, its tiny bedroom furniture
reminiscent of a dollhouse, and one corner also had a desk, linked
to the door by a large strip of carpet that ran diagonally across the
room. That desk, Bamie recalled, "became my home." She engaged
a young male high school teacher to instruct her in German,
although he was, she admitted, shocked by the impropriety of a
young unmarried woman taking language instruction in what
looked like multiple bedrooms.

Just as the snow began to melt in Graz, Bamie moved Elliott and
family to Paris. Anna had conceived during the winter, and Bamie
decided that the birth should occur in France. She located the best
doctor she could find, took his recommendation, and rented a house
in Neuilly, a suburb, and then was startled when the doctor
announced that he would never attend a patient at night in such a
remote location. She would have to find herself another doctor.

Bamie rarely let herself be sidetracked by cantankerous employees, among whom she included the doctor, and in this case she acted
true to form. Aware that he was fascinated by the exceptionally

beautiful Anna, Bamie encouraged him to visit, which he did regularly, driving out in the evening with a friend "in a strange little one-horse fiacre, wearing a high hat with a strange, flat brim which apparently marked the medical profession." One evening in June when Bamie judged the delivery imminent, she and Elliott managed to detain the doctor "and by those measures succeeded in having him present for the birth of Hall Roosevelt."

Bits and pieces of that trip remained with Bamie as pleasant memories of things she "loved," such as "sitting in the Luxemburg Gardens reading and feeding the birds" and becoming reacquainted with Tom Reed, whom she had met years earlier through Theodore. Fifteen years Bamie's senior, Thomas Reed, a Republican congressman, had grown up in Maine, but he nurtured a flair for the continental and kept his personal diary in French just for practice. From the time he first entered the U.S. House of Representatives in 1877, he was popular with other members, and in 1889 his Republican colleagues chose him as Speaker. By the time he and Bamie were reunited in Paris in 1891, the Democrats held a majority in the House, so Reed was relegated to minority leader, but he still wielded considerable clout. Exactly the kind of intelligent but unpredictable man that Bamie liked, Reed returned her appreciation, and following their visit in Paris, he wrote Theodore about how "heartily" he enjoyed seeing Bamie.

But much of that year, which Bamie insisted on referring to as "the year that Elliott was ill," turned into pure frustration. She found her days filled with looking after her brother's family and trying to get him to follow the doctor's advice on exercise and diet—especially the liquid part of his diet. By the summer of 1891 he showed so little improvement that she gave up on ever getting him to change, and leaving him behind, she packed up Anna and the three children and returned to New York. Up to that time Bamie had been a patient sister, generous with her time, but now something snapped and she accepted the fact that Elliott would have to help himself. Corinne would continue to admonish and cajole Elliott, but Bamie had had enough.

In Bamie's absence from New York, Bob Ferguson moved into her New York house. In her frequent letters (now written to "Dear Bob" rather than "Mr. Ferguson,") she vaguely teased him, as though to conceal how much she cared for him. She remembered every birthday and other special days as well, each of them an occasion for reminding him how much she treasured his friendship. During that otherwise draining European stay, she did manage to sandwich in a detour to Scotland to visit Bob's family. From her Paris hotel she assured him that his relatives had treated her very kindly, especially his sister, Edie. Speculating on how the Fergusons might find him changed when he returned to Scotland, Bamie settled on "decidedly older." Then, in an oblique reference to how much had happened in Bob's life during his time in America and his friendship with her, she continued: "I think with trembling of all that may be written!"

By late 1892, after Bob had left New York and she was back in her own house, she was warning him that he had the power to make some woman very happy while remaining very unhappy himself. Her letters avoided flirtation, but only barely, and they showed a lot of concern. Whenever he became ill, she wanted him to come back and stay with her so that she could nurse him to health.

Wherever she went, Bamie most desired the company of Bob Ferguson. When she described an especially beautiful sight, such as a drive through Massachusetts on a "glittering autumn day! with the green quivering birches and the dark pines," he was the one she wished to have at her side. Letters served as a poor substitute for a conversation: "There is very very much I wish to know and hear that I will never really understand until we meet though your letters are a great satisfaction and pleasure," she wrote him.

In the summer of 1893, when she attended the World's Columbian Exposition in Chicago, Bamie composed her fullest descriptions of the extravagant fair to Bob. Chicago, then at the forefront of American cities in introducing new architectural forms incorporating the steel skeleton and the elevator, had won the honor of hosting the exposition, which lasted from May to November. Hopes ran high among Americans that the largest city in the Midwest would make them proud, putting on a show to outshine the 1889 World's Fair in Paris. Among the numerous remarkable structures put up on the Seine for that celebration, one became the city's signature—the Eiffel Tower—and Chicagoans anticipated making an even grander gesture themselves.

By some measures the Columbian Exposition did surpass the Paris extravaganza. In size of the grounds, Chicago dwarfed what the French capital had offered, boasting nearly ten times the seventy-two acres that had sufficed in Paris. No one structure equaled the unique Eiffel Tower, although the abundance of ornate white buildings in Chicago led to the fairgrounds being dubbed the "White City." Thirty-nine states and eighteen foreign nations erected their own temples to progress, and more than twenty million people paid admission to visit them—at a time when the entire population of the United States stood at about fifty-two million.

Exhibitions on work and leisure and on art and science all drew crowds, but the biggest magnet of all was the Ferris wheel, invented and installed for the occasion. The 264-foot-high revolving wheel, centrally located on the grounds so that virtually every visitor walked in its shadow, could carry more than two thousand people when all thirty-six cars were filled, and lines formed for the chance to pay fifty cents (about half a day's wage for a workingman) and view the fair from atop the wheel. Bamie showed little interest in the Ferris wheel, but she waxed enthusiastically about the exhibits. Many years later she described the fair as "perfectly wonderful."

Bamie was not merely a spectator at the fair, however. She had gone as a member of the New York State Women's Board to help with the "Women's Building," a display of the accomplishments of American women. Theodore had arranged for her appointment to the board and she accepted the task against her better judgment since she disliked working with women's groups—or, indeed, groups of any kind. Although she had not yet spoken out publicly on the subject, she disapproved of giving women the vote, and the prospect of singling out women's achievements in a separate building struck her as odd. After meeting with other board members, she changed her mind, however, and wrote Bob that she was looking forward to working on the project.

The controversy that had grown up around the idea of a women's building evidently did not deter her. A group of dissidents, led by Susan B. Anthony and calling themselves "Isabellas" after the strong Spanish queen, began urging other American women to boycott the fair until distinctions on the basis of sex were eliminated. The chair of the national board, Bertha Palmer, wife of the wealthy Chicago businessman, tried to accommodate the "Isabellas" and arrange for displaying some women's achievements alongside men's, but in the end she pretty much gave up and concentrated on constructing an outstanding Women's Building. In the process she called attention to women whose careers could use some publicity, including the building's architect, Sophia Hayden, the first female graduate in architecture from the Massachusetts Institute of Technology, and Alice Redout, the nineteen-year-old who triumphed over all competition to become the official sculptor. One of the tasks that Bamie undertook for herself was arranging loans for various exhibits. When the celebration ended, she made a point of going every morning at seven to supervise the workers. Later she wrote, "I never will forget our pride when we found that every single thing had reached its owner without harm."

Unfortunately, Bamie's time at the exposition was interrupted by several family crises. In May, soon after she arrived in Chicago for the opening, she learned that Elliott's older son and namesake had died of diphtheria just short of his fourth birthday. Then Aunt Anna Gracie died of the same disease. Bob Ferguson, who had volunteered to help nurse Bamie's nephew, got sick himself, and Bamie had to return again to New York. Back in Chicago for the closing ceremonies, as she sat in a gondola in the large pool in front of the Court of Honor and listened to the guns signaling the end of the extravaganza, she had the sensation, she later wrote, that "life would not be worth living without that exquisite spot to go to."

Her work on the exposition gave Bamie a chance to make new friends. She had traveled to Chicago with the party of architect Charles McKim, the same man who would a decade later respond to Theodore's request for help in renovating the White House. They had moved across the eastern United States in two special cars carrying a party of some of the most outstanding architects and artists of the time. Once in Chicago, Bamie got a chance to visit Hull House, barely four years old and still struggling to find sound financial footing. The settlement house's founder, Jane Addams, had not yet gained the enormous national reputation that she achieved a decade later, but Bamie was impressed with what she had done and wrote Bob about her visit to the "wonderful college settlement of which I had heard so much."

Theodore praised his sister's work on the exposition and passed on compliments that he had heard from others. In Washington he had met an accomplished and much-published woman—the type he liked because she "knew every foot of ground she had covered, and yet was, as became her blood, a thorough lady." This woman had singled Bamie out, saying she had heard from members of the Women's Board of Bamie's outstanding performance and that "you were really a wonder and worth all the rest of [them] put together." Then he added ruefully, "If I had your capacity, *what* a civil service commissioner I should be!"

∽

No one can say what other assignments might have come to Bamie had family duty not called once again. A few weeks after returning to New York, she accepted an invitation that changed her life, although she later admitted that she "did not recognize it as such at the time." The same distant cousin, Rosy Roosevelt, whom she had last visited in Vienna, now held the assignment of assistant secretary at the American embassy in London, but his wife, Helen, was seriously ill; he found himself unable to cope, either with the official entertaining expected of him or with the supervision of their two young children. Helen had already extracted a promise from him to consult with Bamie before making any decisions, and now he suggested that she come to his family's rescue.

Before Bamie agreed to go, Helen died, adding urgency to his requests. Late in November, soon after Bamie wired Rosy her acceptance, she informed Bob Ferguson that she expected to sail in early January, though at the moment she felt "unequal to facing trunks even for others." She understood "it is selfish to feel as I do" and that Rosy badly needed her. His wife's death had left him "completely broken up," and "his cables have been despairing." She foresaw only a brief stay in London and hoped she would find a "pleasant side" to it, but she felt she had to go.

Some historians later attributed Bamie's trip to her romantic interest in Rosy—even perhaps a desire to marry him. Nothing in her correspondence supports such a view. It was Bob Ferguson who interested her: "Bob dear, I hate to lose any chances of seeing you but remember the house here will be . . . entirely in order . . . whenever you wish to come." If she harbored any hope of marrying Rosy, she would not have promised Bob to be back in New York "by the end of March" even though "it will be difficult to leave Rosy at that time."

She shared another family secret, one that would serve as the excuse for leaving London if all else failed. Edith and Theodore were expecting another baby in April, and they had already prevailed on her to take their older children for a few weeks during the confinement.

Although dreading the London trip, she struggled to remain optimistic. The New York Republicans had done much better than expected in the November off-year election, achieving what Bamie called a "marvelous and overwhelming . . . victory," and thus adding to her reluctance to move away from the center of political action. Struggling to find the bright side, she wrote Bob on December 1, "I feel today that I detest going abroad but it will no doubt be good for me and it will not be long to. the middle of March when I return." Bob had gone into real estate with Corinne's husband, requiring many trips to Virginia and other parts of the country. Before she sailed, Bamie wrote that she hoped that he would take some time out and visit her "for as many days as you could be spared." As the date to board her ship approached, she admitted it was "a pleasure I will postpone as late as possible."

When she had to move up her sailing to a few days before Christmas, Bamie grew even more distraught. She hated saying good-bye to Theodore ("it is dreadful"), and she explained that in her own home she felt "protected [but] away it is different." The short visit with Bob that had been arranged gave her pleasure, and she reminded him again of her affection: "I cannot tell you what a real difference it made seeing you again dear young gentleman. [T]here was only the parting to come that was bad." Bob gave her a Christmas gift before she sailed, and she thanked him for "the exquisite pocket book" and promised to open it again on December 25 and "pretend to receive it all over again." Nine-year-old Alice, whom she still referred to as "my Alice," had come to the ship to say good-bye but then became so overwrought at the idea of separation that she broke down in tears and "had a sad time of crying."

As soon as Bamie landed in London and settled in at Rosy's house at 2 Upper Belgrave Street, she had her work cut out for her. It was holiday time, and she knew the children, Helen and James, would find it a time of sad memories so soon after their mother's death. In addition to her feelings of responsibility to Rosy, she also felt an obligation to his deceased wife. Bamie had served as bridesmaid at their wedding years earlier, and she had been named godmother to young Helen. Now, in sizing up the household, she saw a need to make immediate changes in the staff. She fired the "very pretty French governess" who had been with the household for several years, explaining that a widower should not employ an attractive young woman in his house unless he wanted gossip. The replacement, an English-woman with snow-white hair, struck Bamie as far more "proper."

Although she had never lived in London, Bamie took over Rosy's home as though she had run it in a former life. Twelve-year-old Helen was still deeply troubled by her mother's death, but she was enormously pleased by her godmother's presence. Bamie, she later recalled, transformed the place almost overnight and made a big difference in her life. Friends and acquaintances who had shied away after the death now returned in droves, and Bamie somehow located young people to call on Helen and fourteen-year-old James "so that everything became very happy in the house."

Bamie "immediately caught on to the English ways and English people," her young charge remembered, and "she ran everything in the most absolutely superb fashion." Bamie even became the "right hand man" to the wife of Thomas Bayard, the American minister to the Court of St. James's. "I think she ran all of Mrs. Bayard's parties, told her just how many feathers to put on her head when she was presented, what kind of gloves to wear and everything. Auntie Bye always seemed to know just what to do."

Where Bamie picked up such information remains unclear, but Helen speculated that she "knew instinctively . . . she grasped everything immediately and she knew just what should be done and what the English expected of the Ambassadress." Because Bamie had such a lively mind, she was much in demand as a guest and "was very often dashing off to the country for weekends with all her new-made friends who adored her." Among those friends were, of course, Bob Ferguson's relatives in Scotland.

The young Helen Roosevelt, who later married Corinne's son Teddy and thus became Bamie's niece by marriage as well as her goddaughter and distant cousin, saw a lot of Bamie during the London period and knew that she had already begun to lose her hearing. She covered it up so cleverly, however, that few of the people she met had any inkling. Like many others who find themselves in the same predicament, Bamie concentrated on a few key words in any discussion and then made some general reply that gave little hint of what she had missed.

Anyone who sized up Bamie simply on appearance was not impressed. Helen described her this way: "No good looks, whatever . . . really plain. Even her figure was bad . . . dumpy looking." But Bamie had mastered a skill that her niece Eleanor and other Roosevelt women also perfected—they projected such a keen interest, such an animated intelligence and curiosity, that people who met them saw only beauty. Helen remembered: "[W]hen her face was animated it was extraordinary. She gave out a light and an animation . . . very, very rare. It was contagious."

Bamie also seemed to have an innate ability to make other people appear at their best, a skill particularly useful among the English, whom Helen considered "a curiously stiff sort of people." After only a few months among them, Bamie broke through the reserve and converted many acquaintances into loyal friends.

Her success may have helped reconcile Bamie to her stay, which was extending beyond the three or four months she had predicted. Theodore consoled her in letters, and like an overzealous debater, he piled up the reasons why she should feel good about being in London: "You are doing the wisest thing and you are performing a real service and it will be good for you and in the end you will enjoy it." Bamie recognized the compensations: she found her goddaughter a "dear," and she enjoyed the luxury of Rosy's home with its two "beautiful drawing rooms" and spacious quarters for herself. As she met more and more important people through the embassy and they showed their respect for her intelligence by including her in their discussions, she liked her situation even better. The presentation to the Queen on that March day in 1894 sealed her future: she was now fully recognized as a person in her own right—her name, even without a husband, would routinely appear on all the invitation lists that mattered.

By the end of April, Bamie had agreed to remain in London until early September when she would take James, just turned fifteen, "back with me after his summer vacation." In the meantime she urged Bob Ferguson to come and see her in England. Their correspondence had never stopped, touching on her family problems and his financial matters (with her pointing out that she had done everything she could to help him), but he could not manage the face-to-face visit that Bamie longed for.

Theodore continued to imply that she did her country a favor by staying in London. A rumor had reached him indicating that Minister Bayard disapproved of an agreement made in 1889 which provided that the United States share with Germany and Great Britain the responsibility for the Samoan Islands. Theodore strongly supported the agreement, and he turned to Bamie to relay his view to the minister. Since she saw most of the diplomatic corps frequently, this was no insignificant request.

On other matters Bamie performed even more valuable services. She well knew that the U.S. economy was in trouble by the spring of 1894, though she had no way of knowing that the depression would continue for four years, making it the worst in the nation's history up to that time. Many of the men and women who lost their jobs and their investments laid the blame for their plight on the monetary system. The United States had used both gold and silver as its monetary basis, but now the system was in disarray as newly opened mines produced so much silver that it lost its value in relation to gold. As Americans began to panic, they withdrew their gold deposits, thus depleting the government's reserves. But creditors, just as worried about silver's loss of value, began demanding payment in gold, making matters even worse. Finally, President Cleveland decided to restore government reserves by floating a large bond issue, and eventually the economy got back on track.

Although no one single explanation sufficed for what rocked the financial world, many Americans blamed Great Britain for not helping to boost silver's value. Theodore joined the chorus, assuring Bamie that he had spoken with several of "our economic thinkers" who agreed with him: they pointed to England as the "great obstacle in the way of an international agreement to restore silver to its place in currency." On May 6, 1894, after admitting that he found the whole debate confusing ("I know nothing of currency myself"), he insisted that someone had to help change English thinking and force it "out of its present attitude before the finances of the world can stand on a sound or stable basis." Although he did not actually ask for Bamie's direct intervention, he took time to share with her the gravity of the situation.

The sagging American economy did have one bright spot for the Republican Roosevelts: the current Democratic administration stood to get the blame, thus easing the way for a Republican victory in the next election. Theodore described the opposition party as in "a hopeless snarl" in 1894, leaving it "probable" that his own party could win a majority in the House of Representatives at the next election. In that case Bamie's old friend Tom Reed stood in line for the speakership, a position that would "give him a fighting chance for the Presidential nomination" in 1896.

After Theodore's death, when Bamie published his letters to her, she edited them heavily, cutting out most of the references to her political insight or influence. Nevertheless, her short, factual notes on the letters hint at how many important people she knew well. Names of several dot the pages, including John Hay, the diplomat, and Captain Alfred Mahan, the naval expert. It is unlikely that Theodore would have corresponded with her on so many weighty matters had he not valued her judgment and trusted her intelligence.

Other family members besides Theodore wrote Bamie that first London winter, although she hardly rated them equally. She confided to Bob Ferguson: "Theodore is so good, writes me with clock like regularity letters that contain any amount of news cramped into a tiny space." His wife, Edith, had "done the same," but as for Corinne, the "letters have been dear but very hurried, irregular."

The relationship between Bamie and Corinne had been complicated by the fact that the latter occasionally used her sister's New York house without being completely open about it. Bamie confessed to Bob—as she could not have told Theodore—just how the letters of Corinne and the trusted butler, Chamberlain, differed on what went on at 689 Madison Avenue: "Corinne in a vague way says she has been there occasionally ... whereas Chamberlain, being methodical, promptly every week tells me when and with whom she has been there."

Bamie returned to New York for a few weeks that fall, but by January 1895 she was back in London. Her letters communicated such a cheerfulness that Edith attributed the "very good spirits" to the fact that she had settled in and acquired "many friends." In fact, it was one specific friend: forty-nine-year-old William Sheffield Cowles—a naval attaché at the American embassy, whom she had met soon after arriving in London—and that friendship gradually evolved into romance.

What these two middle-aged Americans saw in each other remained something of an enigma to almost everyone who knew them. He was no Don Juan, and his rather fleshy body conveyed a kind of lethargy not frequently connected to romance. Helen Roosevelt later recalled him as "a darling . . . but not a ball of fire by any means . . . rather stout and calm and quiet." He left no doubt about his feelings for Bamie, though. According to Helen, "He simply adored her . . . I've never seen such adoration!"

Bamie gave conflicting signals about her feelings for Will, as she always called him. According to her goddaughter: "I don't think she was in love with him, really. . . . Both Auntie Bye and [Corinne] were [never] in love with any man, including their husbands. But I think Auntie Bye began to feel that her position in London at that time was drawing to an end as regards being my father's hostess, and I think she felt that it would be very pleasant to be still a part of the Embassy and to continue living in London near Father and me, but not any longer a part of our household."

Her family might have guessed that if she married at all, Bamie would choose a man like Will Cowles. The Cowleses (using many spelling variations on the family name) had a long, illustrious record in America, heavily marked by intellectual and political achievement. They had arrived in Connecticut in the 1630s (at least a decade before the Roosevelts landed in New York) and almost immediately settled in Farmington, not far from Hartford, where they produced community leaders and strong-minded women. Will's father, Thomas Cowles, a Yale graduate, had first married his cousin, but when she died in childbirth, he married Elizabeth Ells Sheffield, a woman described in family records as "remarkably intellectual and accomplished." During that second marriage, Thomas Cowles served in the state assembly (first as a Democrat and then as a Republican), in the state senate, and as Farmington deputy sheriff and justice of the peace. None of the four sons of that second marriage ever quite matched their father's accomplishments, but one of them earned a doctorate from Yale and two of them, including Will, the eldest, graduated from the U.S. Naval Academy. After an active career at sea, he had arrived in London just a few months ahead of Bamie, bringing with him his genealogical credentials, acquaintance with public service, and a genuine interest in women who thought for themselves.

By the spring of 1895, Bamie and Will were meeting frequently at various embassy receptions and dinners, but no precise record of the courtship survives because they kept the news about it to themselves. When Corinne came through London in early July, she met Will, but only as one of Bamie's many friends. Yet it is clear that Bamie had already made up her mind to marry Will. Later she tossed off the fact that she married so late by saying, "It took the solitude of a London season to give me time to become engaged." More likely she was aware of the reality of the biological time clock (although she used no such term) and wanted to marry and produce a child while she still could.

The news of her engagement struck Bamie's relatives like a bombshell. Theodore, in New York for the summer, spoke for the entire family when he wired her in early July: "To say that your cable and letter surprised us is a hopelessly inadequate way of saying what we felt. We were dumbfounded." But he declared that he was delighted to welcome into the family "an officer in our navy" and "glad it wasn't an Englishman!" On one matter he requested particulars: "By the way, tell me his exact rank; is he a captain or a commander?" He was, in fact, a lieutenant commander, though many family members always referred to him as captain.

Theodore implied that the decision to marry was long overdue. "I have always felt it a shame that you, one of the two or three finest women whom I have met or known of, that you, a really noble woman, should not marry." Cabot Lodge was less enthusiastic and asked her, "Why on earth should you get married? You have Theodore and myself."

Before she told Bob Ferguson of her relationship with Will, Bamie had to settle another matter: the validity of Will's divorce from his first wife. More than twenty years earlier Will had married Mary Thurman, who came from an Ohio family more prominent in politics than Bamie's (although from the opposing political party). In fact, Will's first wife claimed two generations of government leaders in Ohio. Her grandfather served as governor, and her father, Allen Thurman, was nominated for (and frequently elected to) every high office in the state—congressman, senator, and governor. Some of his backers even put his name forward for the presidency in 1884, but he supported his good friend Grover Cleveland. By the time Will courted Bamie in 1895, Allen Thurman was dead, but he was still remembered by many loyal friends, including President Cleveland.

Whatever any of her family and friends thought about Will's marriage to Miss Thurman, it had not lasted. Will was frequently absent on naval assignment, sometimes for several months at a time, and after the two drifted apart, he had obtained a divorce in California. But dissolving marriages in late-nineteenth-century America was rarely a neat matter, and it was generally conceded that this divorce had been granted on "flimsy" grounds. Bamie turned to Theodore for legal advice and some assessment of the risks she ran by marrying Will. As soon as she confided in Theodore, letters and wires began to fly between brother and sister as Theodore delivered one dire warning after another, and she frantically kept looking for a signal that she could proceed.

On the surface, Theodore's attempts to help his sister appear genuine. While he waited for a "full written report [from] the clerk in California," he urged "my own darling Bye" to proceed with caution. The American attorney he consulted had begged Theodore, "in the most urgent terms . . . and with more feeling than I had supposed it possible he would show, to insist that you must do *Nothing* now, but wait." Theodore admitted that he would have been tempted to take the risk, in the face of a "law [that] seemed so monstrous and foolish," but that when he proposed just that to the attorney, he seemed "frightened" and "made me promise to state the case very plainly to you, and tell you that you must not for any consideration marry. . . . He is confident the divorce is a nullity even in California." Even if found valid on the West Coast, other states, including New Jersey and New York where the Cowleses might prefer to reside, could refuse to recognize the divorce.

In hindsight, Theodore's warnings seem shrill and overcautious. He pointed out that if Bamie and Will decided to risk living in a state where their marriage was considered "bigamous," any children born to them would be illegitimate. Then Theodore, with perhaps his own political future in mind as much as his sister's happiness, brought up another possibility: any unscrupulous "person who wished to annoy or blackmail either of you—or who chose to strike at me through you or who wished to prevent your property from descending as you wished, could bring suit against you." Who won was not the point: "As soon as [the suit] was brought, all would be at an end."

Bamie wrestled with the alternatives that Theodore's attorney presented. She could take her chances and go ahead and marry, especially if she planned to remain in England. Or she could appeal to the New York State legislature to pass a special law for her, but that would take at least a year. One attorney suggested that Will could "*probably* get relief by returning to his domicile and suing his wife for adultery," but that would take time and no one could guarantee the result. Theodore, always so action oriented, appeared stymied: "I am at my wits end; it is inhuman, infamous; I do not know what to write you, my darling sister, and yet I fear that some more and more terrible wrong may follow if I do not write as plainly" as the lawyer advised. He recommended that she and Will come back to New York and get the attorney's advice firsthand.

A few days later Theodore's attorney became a "little more hopeful" and suggested that if Bamie and Will wanted to go ahead and marry, they should plan to live in California and take all their property there. As long as Bamie (and any children born to her) remained in California, coming to New York only "for short times," the property should be safe. But Theodore cautioned: "Any person interested in Father's will—any one of our children who turned out to be a sneak, for instance—or any overconscientious lawyer who had a client who was about to purchase property held under the will, might bring suit, and have your marriage declared illegal, in which case all your property here in New York would go."

Bamie realized that she and Will could not reasonably expect to spend the rest of their lives in California. He was too young to retire from the navy and too old to change careers. If he remained in the service, he needed flexibility to accept the best assignments in the future and not confine himself to one state.

With so many questions, Theodore continued to counsel caution. On August 5 he wrote Bamie that his attorney "insisted on my writing that under no consideration should the marriage take place at present; and he nearly had a fit when I suggested that you should 'go ahead and chance it.'" Perhaps the whole thing could be worked out in a few months, he advised her. "In so vital a matter, six months delay is better than a blunder which, by some remote chance, MIGHT wreck your life."

Never one to sit around and wait for others to tell her what to do, Bamie made her own inquiries, seeking legal advice from another New York attorney whom Theodore admitted was "better" than his own. When her lawyer pronounced the risk "literally infinitesimal," she decided to proceed with the marriage in London. Now, suddenly, Theodore dropped his objections and dire warnings, merely inquiring if she planned to stay in England or return to New York the following winter. This was a matter of some personal urgency since he had resigned as civil service commissioner in May and accepted an appointment to the New York City Police Commission. Her house on Madison Avenue would be very convenient for him and his family.

By the end of August the decision to marry was firm, although the couple had not decided where to live. Theodore pushed for England. "I have devoted much thought to next winter, and hope you two will stay over in London if you possibly can! I feel it would give you such a good start to have your first winter with an official position of the kind for which you both are so well fitted." Then he pulled out all the stops, writing her that Cabot Lodge had singled out Bamie and Commander Cowles as the "real mainstays of the Embassy!" With a house of their own in London, Theodore continued, "you would at once take a position with all our countrymen which would always be remembered."

As for her house in New York, Theodore suggested that she rent it to the highest bidder "without regard to us." Then he bargained a bit. He had discussed the matter with Edith, he wrote on September 15, and since they would be in New York only three or four months a year, they did not "wish to give more than a couple of thousand." When his sister accepted that offer, he suddenly became enthusiastic about the many virtues of her house: his family liked it, and it kept him "in the district" for political purposes and the children near the park.

By October, Bamie had chosen the twenty-fifth of November for her wedding. Most of the family remained unaware of all these negotiations until they were well under way, and now an updating was necessary. Theodore reminded her that everyone would be "dumbfounded" and admonished, "I hope you have written Alice." Few of her relatives seemed prepared to hear that Bamie, who had bailed out one brother, then another, and then her cousin, was finally making a family of her own. Eleven-year-old Eleanor Roosevelt hardly knew what to make of it, and she wrote her aunt on November 15 from Tivoli on the Hudson, where she was staying with her maternal grandmother: "It seems so funny to think that you are engaged."

Although Bamie had accompanied Theodore to London for his marriage to Edith Carow almost exactly nine years earlier, he had already decided that he could not possibly absent himself from New York at election time—it would be "dishonorable." Corinne, already traveling in Europe with her children, would represent the entire family. Edith had suggested a Sagamore Hill ceremony, but when Bamie demurred, Edith agreed: "I see the wisdom of your plans."

One person required a special notice concerning Bamie's plans, but she wanted to make her announcement face-to-face. Bob Ferguson had been absent during her most recent trip to New York, and she had not seen him for more than eighteen months, although they had corresponded. Without explaining exactly why, she wrote him a letter in August practically begging him to come to London "this autumn somewhere somehow *surely* for life is not worth living never seeing those we care for." Then Bamie chose such a remarkably melancholy closing for that letter that it suggests she had mixed feelings about her marriage: "It has poured [rain here in London] until I feel there simply will be a deluge which washing us all into eternity will completely arrange many minor difficulties."

Bob did make the trip to London, and after he left, Bamie wrote him that the visit "did me a world of good," because "except Theodore you were the only person I could, no, would have cared to speak of my engagement to." She hoped that Bob and Will would become friends, while recognizing that it was "useless to try and force people on one another." Insisting that Will genuinely cared for everyone important to her, she reassured Bob where he stood with her: "for always your interests and advantages will be my desire and your affection and interest really important in my life." Bamie admitted to Bob a rather bizarre quality about her engagement, which "has been so terribly strange and all . . . feelings so strained." But as soon as the date and place were set, she informed him: "You will be expected to assist at least."

As the date drew closer, the surreal quality did not evaporate. Bamie later wrote in her memoir that nearly everything surrounding the wedding was "ridiculous." Cousin Rosy hardly knew what to make of it, and in his confusion he left town for ten days before the ceremony, then returned in time to give the bride away. Among the gifts that poured in were nine tea caddies and several cigarette cases. Rather than going directly to London, Corinne took her time, stopping first in Rome, then in Paris to buy her children their winter wardrobes. By the time she reached England, leaving her children behind in Paris so as to avoid multiple channel crossings, she described herself as "so excited" about the wedding that she could hardly contain herself. She put off purchasing a gift, assuming her sister would welcome "a jewel" but not knowing for sure, and she hesitated to mention the wedding in her letters back home because she remained unsure who among her American friends had been informed of it.

As soon as she was reunited with Bamie, Corinne gave the union her blessing. She had worried about how Bamie would act around Bob Ferguson, who, accompanied by his older brother, had returned to London for the nuptials. Now Corinne reported: "She is wonderfully natural with Bob and Hector who arrived yesterday for the wedding. *They* moved all the furniture for her yesterday." As for the bridegroom, he seemed to take everything in stride: "Captain Cowles accepts [the Fergusons] very sweetly and *certainly appears* very well under these rather trying circumstances." As for Will's attention to Bamie, Corinne endorsed what others had said: "He simply adores her, and cannot take his eyes off her."

In her usual managerial style, the bride took charge, and at dinner the night before the wedding, she was, her sister reported, "as executive as usual about lists and where people should sit." However, Corinne could not be absolutely certain how the bride really felt about the marriage, and she detected "for the first time the little shade of apprehension" on Bamie's face and found it "very pathetic. Still I think she is really happy."

The ceremony itself went "beautifully," according to Corinne. Cousin Rosy composed himself sufficiently to return to London to give the bride away, and Corinne thought he looked "very blue but very refined." The "*poor* Capt Cowles was, I think, frightened to death." The bride had requested that there be "no rice and no slipper but somehow or other she was deluged." Bamie missed having Theodore with her for this occasion, and just before going to the church she wrote him a letter telling him so. Even his generous gift of a diamond necklace, although "lovely," could not compensate for his absence.

For their wedding trip the Cowleses traveled first to Bonn and then to Paris, where they met up with Corinne and her children. Corinne, worried about her own health and not fully attuned to the newlyweds' wish for privacy, signed herself into a spa in the Loire valley, leaving her four children, ranging in age from six to twelve, for the Cowleses to look after. Bamie later recalled that Will was stuck reading fairy tales and being interrupted several times a day by the Robinson children.

Back in London, Bamie and Will set up their own cozy home. Friends who visited them there remembered that she usually had a fire burning in the fireplace, fresh flowers in every room, and stacks of books on tables and chairs. With the help of an excellent French chef and a superb wine cellar, she entertained often, and when the opportunity arose, she presented the American side of any issue in terms as persuasive as possible.

Just about the time of her marriage, Cabot Lodge, in his role as senator, had confided in her and asked for help on a matter of international importance. For decades a disagreement had been brewing over the boundary between Venezuela and British Guyana, but with the discovery of gold in the disputed area, the stakes rose. When Great Britain showed signs of using its military superiority to gain control, war looked like a real possibility. As Cabot wrote Bamie: "A spark would kindle a blaze. . . . Try to make some of the people you see, who are sensible, understand it, for we don't want war." It was hardly the sort of request that a newly married woman wants to receive just as she is leaving on her honeymoon, but it is indicative of the esteem in which she was held by more than one powerful man. Fortunately for everyone, the British agreed to arbitrate the boundary, and by the time the Cowleses returned from their trip on the Continent, the matter had been resolved.

Bamie's association with the American embassy, first through Rosy and then Will, gave her a window on important events around the world. When the Italians invaded Ethiopia, often referred to at that time as Abyssinia, and then had to withdraw after a bloody battle at Aduwa, most people read about the debacle in their newspapers. But Bamie got her news from diplomats. To Bob Ferguson she wrote that the Italian ambassador and naval attaché were "simply pathetic" in their reaction "to the terrible calamity they have suffered in Abyssinia." For information about what was happening in Washington, she depended on Theodore to enclose the latest issues of the *Congressional Record* along with his letters.

Will's official duties at the embassy were largely social, but as a dedicated navy man, he maintained a keen interest in ship construction, new equipment, and performance records. Bamie insisted that she enjoyed his friends, even though their interests rarely overlapped with hers. Writing to Bob in terms that sounded nothing like the exuberance with which she discussed politics, she described how Will kept busy "with all his naval matters and I see much of his various people, makers of armor plate, torpedoes, etc and all the naval people."

Bamie still missed her Scotsman: "Bob dear, if you only began to know how I wish to see you and how always and constantly my thoughts turn to you wondering when you will ever be with us satisfactorily again. We all seem to be scattered now." She insisted that her husband joined her in extending the invitation. He "told me to fondly say when I wrote that he is as anxious as I am to have you with us."

But when Bob had to go to London in August 1896, as part of his business arrangement with Douglas Robinson, he stayed at a nearby hotel rather than in the Cowleses' house. His feelings about Will remained unclear, although he received some bantering letters concerning Will's weight from Douglas, who wrote in September that he had heard Bamie was looking well and that the Captain (as the family insisted on calling the lieutenant commander) was "bursting with pride or with too much Captain. I would give worlds to see him in a kilt. I hope you have one large enough to go around."

No matter how attached Bamie may have been to Bob emotionally, everyone agreed that she thrived in the marriage. Helen Roosevelt Robinson, who saw a lot of her during those years, insisted that she developed a love for Will after her marriage, and the union "turned out to be ... very happy" partly because they were such opposites. "He was a dear, humdrum sort of person [and] she felt the security of being married to somebody like that. . . . She much preferred that to being married to a more exciting type of man." He was her "dear old Bear" and she called him "Bearo," though, interestingly, she never allowed him to call her anything but Anna. She permitted the use of Bamie or Bye by relatives and friends, but for him (and for Bob Ferguson) she was always "Anna."

Much as some of her family poked fun at the rotund lieutenant commander, Bamie saw a side that they did not—one that mixed intelligence and charm with a touch of the risqué. To illustrate that aspect of him, she occasionally talked about his adventures before he became an overweight, middle-aged naval aide. In his early days in the navy, he and a buddy had spent "a merry couple of weeks" on the Continent with two young Englishwomen—before "traveling without a chaperone" was "usual." To clarify how vivacious the women were, Bamie recalled a time when Will had taken her to meet one of them. Always appearing "the most respectable of people," he had not prepared her "for his curious choice of friends." They arrived at a house outside London, where Bamie met the woman, now married to the Earl of Limerick. A Major Elliot lived with them. But "it was rather a shock," Bamie explained later, "to find that the so-called Limerick children were equally divided as to looks in their resemblance to the Earl and to Major Elliott."

Such friends show another side of Will Cowles. His social success in London, his popularity as a dancer and dinner companion throughout his life, and his unorthodox collection of friends all suggest that he was a far more interesting life partner than most of Bamie's contemporaries recognized. She must have seen something in him. She could be disparaging about him, as when she said he looked like a "cloth doll," but she shaped the final third of her life around him, and apparently without regrets.

III

BY THE SPRING OF 1897, Will and Bamie were ready to move back to the United States. A variety of reasons no doubt contributed to their decision. With a Republican, William McKinley, in the presidency, the political game became a lot more interesting. Theodore's prospects improved, and after two years in New York,

Transplanted to New York City from her native Georgia, Mittie Bulloch Roosevelt (shown here about 1855) soon established herself as a fashion and social leader.

No aunt ever earned higher accolades from her nieces and nephews than Mittie's older sister, Anna Bulloch Gracie, who moved to New York to be near her sister and provided Mittie's children with much of their early schooling.

Bulloch Hall, [top], in Roswell, Georgia, where Mittie grew up, bore a striking resemblance to Tranquillity, [bottom], the house that she and Theodore began renting on Long Island in 1874.

While still in her teens, Bamie (shown here with her father, Theodore Sr.) looked very mature because, she said, she never gave herself the chance to be young.

Bamie raised her brother Theodore's daughter Alice until she was three and a half, when the little girl went to live with Theodore and his second wife, Edith.

In one of the very few photos ever made of Bamie and her family, this one, taken at a neighbor's house in Farmington about 1920, shows Will at his favorite pastime— solitaire—and their son, Shef, staring straight at the camera.

At age seven, Corinne Roosevelt posed with a doll, but she had already shown herself to be a daredevil with ponies.

In spite of its name, P.O.R.E. (for Paradise of Ravenous Eaters) was a literary group that included Edith Carow (far left) and Corinne Roosevelt (standing center), who at this point in their lives still considered each other a "best" friend.

Before she married at age twenty, Corinne Roosevelt raised many objections to becoming Mrs. Douglas Robinson.

As a poet and public speaker, Corinne Roosevelt Robinson earned a reputation in her own right, quite apart from being the President's "little sister."

At Henderson House, the Robinsons' summer place in Herkimer County, New York, Hyde Park Roosevelts mingled with those from Oyster Bay—at least before 1933.

Labeled "Corinne's New Year's Party, 1882, Montreal," this studio photo shows Bamie (second woman standing from left), Alice Lee Roosevelt (standing center), Corinne (to Alice's left), and Edith Carow (standing far right) in what was apparently the only picture ever taken of them together. Douglas Robinson stands in top row center, to Corinne's right.

As a First Lady who is said to have "never made a mistake," Edith Roosevelt set precedents that niece Eleanor Roosevelt later followed. On the desk at right is a picture of her mother, Gertrude Carow.

Before word reached Oyster Bay of son Quentin's death in World War I, Edith and Theodore (holding grandson Archie Jr.) posed with daughter-in-law Belle (standing) and daughter Ethel (sitting right and holding her daughter Edith). Richard Derby sits on his grandmother's lap.

In 1932, when Franklin Roosevelt first ran for president, Theodore's widow, Edith Roosevelt, spoke for his opponent, Herbert Hoover, at a Madison Square Garden rally.

On one of her many trips abroad, Edith Kermit Roosevelt stopped in Lisbon in 1934.

where he served as police commissioner and used Bamie's house as his city residence, he would be returning to Washington as assistant Secretary of the Navy. That move would not only free up Bamie's house, but it would also put Theodore in a position to have some influence on Will's naval career. Will actually returned first, and Bamie, who had not yet conceived after nearly two years of marriage, followed just a few weeks later.

On the subject of wanting a child of her own, Bamie's letters are mute, at least those letters that survive. But family lore is very clear on the subject: she was dead set on the idea (although it is not clear at what point in her life she made this decision), and she married for the definite purpose of having a child. John Alsop, a grandson of her sister Corinne, called it sheer "determination," and he marveled: "Think of that . . . if you have the kind of back she had. Of deciding to get married and have a child." Such observations underline the view that Will served as a biological necessity as much as affectionate partner.

That first year in New York gave Bamie the chance to introduce Will to her friends, see more of Corinne, whom she loved dearly in spite of occasional objections to her lack of consideration, and try to get reacquainted with Elliott's orphaned children: Eleanor, now thirteen, and Hall, who was six. Grandmother Hall, with whom they lived, kept Eleanor and Hall out of the Roosevelt orbit, and although Bamie had once considered the possibility of legal action to take them away, she had abandoned the idea. On her deathbed in 1892, the children's mother had consigned them to her mother, and nothing that Elliott did after her death altered that arrangement.

By late 1897, Bamie had other worries besides her brother's children: America's growing fervor for war with Spain. For many years the United States had toyed with the idea of annexing Cuba, and by the 1890s, when the worldwide depression rocked the island economy and endangered American investments there, the time seemed right. A Cuban uprising against Spanish rule added to the sense of urgency. First President Cleveland and then President McKinley held off, until reports of Spanish atrocities moved public opinion beyond the point of turning back. Two New York newspapers, Joseph Pulitzer's *World* and William Randolph Hearst's *Journal*, engaged in their own circulation war, vied with each other to report the most barbarous deed. Hearst even hired a famous artist, Frederic Remington, to go to Cuba and send back drawings. After investigating the situation, Remington demurred, arguing that conditions in Cuba did not warrant war, but Hearst reportedly instructed him, "You furnish the pictures and I'll furnish the war."

When the American battleship *Maine* exploded in Havana harbor in February 1898, the effect on Bamie's life was immediate. Historians would debate the causes and culpability for decades, but to Bamie it made little difference. Will left almost immediately aboard the *Fern* to help investigate the incident, and the two other important men in her life—Theodore and Bob Ferguson—joined volunteers rushing to get to Cuba. Theodore, whose eyesight was as poor as Bamie's hearing, resigned from the Navy Department and took the title of lieutenant colonel in order to go with the Rough Riders, a motley crew later described by one historian as "cowboys, ex-polo players and ex-convicts" who were "short on discipline but long on dash."

On a personal level, Bamie had other concerns. Soon after Will left, she realized she was pregnant. Corinne had four children, the youngest of them ten years old, and Theodore had six. Now Bamie, age forty-three and the oldest in her family, was finally going to produce a child of her own. By the time Theodore and his Rough Riders shipped out of San Antonio in May, Bamie had been called on to help out his family, too. Edith had been seriously ill following the birth of Quentin in November, and Theodore, who had no intention of remaining in the country to look after her, sent his two older children, Alice and Ted, to stay with Bamie in New York. By June she must have felt deserted and overwhelmed: her men had all shipped out, and she waited out that long, hot summer on her own.

In hindsight the Spanish-American War of 1898 looks like a minor skirmish, more a sign of imperialistic intentions than a true war. By mid-August it was over, and ten times as many men had died of disease (malaria, typhoid, dysentery, and yellow fever) and tainted food as from bullets. During the actual fighting, Bamie had no way of knowing how it would turn out, and afterward she admitted that she had been almost "petrified" with "the weeks of vital anxiety." With Will, Theodore, and Bob all in uniform, it seemed impossible that all three could come "home safely to us." Each letter from Cuba was passed around among Edith, Corinne, and Bamie. Of their men, only Douglas

Robinson had opted not to volunteer, but he did take over payment of Theodore's life insurance, which otherwise would have lapsed.

By late August the men all began making their way back to the United States. Theodore's ship landed at Montauk, at the tip of Long Island, but the men did not have permission to disembark immediately. Edith, so eager to see Theodore that she could not wait for his release, rode in the rain in an open carriage just to catch a glimpse of him. Bamie, now in her seventh month of pregnancy, had the chance to confer with Will when he stopped in New York on his way to Boston. He returned in time for the birth of their son but had to spend the intervening weeks aboard ship. Bob Ferguson also came for a quick visit during her pregnancy, and after he left, she wrote him: "Bob dear, you do not know the real deep unspeakable joy it was to see you again and well."

Her letters to Will during their separation underlined her own apprehensions at the same time they reiterated her love for him. She understood that her age could complicate the delivery and lots could go wrong. Patiently, lovingly, she tried to prepare her husband for the worst. If he needed help, he should turn to her people because they were "good people." Then, in October, as the delivery loomed nearer, she reassured Will: he should not mind if things went wrong because she had been "so happy." And she closed even this poignant, loving letter, as she always did after her marriage, with the businesslike initials "ARC."

Two days after writing that letter, on October 18, 1898, Bamie delivered a healthy baby boy and named him not for any of the Roosevelts (who typically put considerable importance on such things) but for his father, adding the requisite Jr. To distinguish her son from Will, she always called him "Sheffield" or "Shef." His godfather was Bob Ferguson.

No mother ever lavished more loving attention on a child than the middle-aged Bamie bestowed on that little boy. His every achievement became a feather in her cap, and when she forwarded his childish scrawls to relatives, she admitted that they caused her "to fairly smirk with pride." Not until he celebrated his fourth birthday did she cut his hair. The haircut caused Edith Roosevelt to comment approvingly in a letter to her teenage son Kermit that Sheffield "is much more boyish looking." In the manner of so many overprotective parents, Bamie took her son everywhere, and when she visited Theodore and his family at Oyster Bay in July 1904, Edith complained to her sister that the little boy's presence would make "a little difference and naturally one can't be quite as independent." Each childhood illness became a major catastrophe, calling for the services of a specialist.

Still, having a child did not divert Bamie from the subjects that had always fascinated her—politics and government. And what better place to satisfy that fascination than Washington, D.C.? In October 1899, when Shef was just one year old, Bamie and Will bought a house there at 1733 N Street, N.W., near Dupont Circle. Theodore had suggested the move even before they returned from England, and he had written her that the Lodges joined him and Edith in hoping she would choose to live in the capital. By the time Bamie bought the house, Theodore had been elected governor of New York and moved his family to Albany. But Will's work at the Navy Department gave Bamie a reason to spend time in the capital—and the move put her where she could observe developments and report them to her brother.

For the two years that Theodore lived in Albany (1899–1901), letters between him and Bamie touched on many subjects: whether or not he should run for vice president, how to regulate corporations, and the details of the war in South Africa. Bamie and Will also resided part-time at Oldgate, his ancestral home in Farmington, Connecticut, a large Georgian mansion that he had inherited. But she preferred Washington for the "season." There on the Potomac she was perfectly situated to manage Theodore's arrival in the capital when he came for his inauguration as William McKinley's second-term vice president in March 1901.

On the train trip from New York, Theodore and Edith added numbers along the way. Corinne and Douglas and their four children got on board in New Jersey, joined later by Uncle James Gracie (Aunt Anna's widower) and Bob Ferguson. As soon as they pulled into Union Station, Bamie took charge—or, as Edith described it, "Bamie met us at the train and hurried Theodore off before enough people recognized him to make a crush."

At age forty-two Theodore had already gained more attention than many people—but not his family—thought he merited. His two years as police commissioner in New York (1895–97) put him in the news, and his charge up San Juan Hill added to his popularity, but many of his fellow Republicans saw him as mostly talk. Senator Mark Hanna's reaction to the idea of Theodore becoming vice president is typical of opinion in some quarters. The powerful politician from Ohio reportedly warned that there would be only one heartbeat between that "damned cowboy" and the White House.

Within the family, Theodore was seen as deserving every promotion that came his way. For twenty years, since he first engaged in politics in New York City, Bamie had pushed him, applauding each victory and boasting of his competence and goodness. Edith, who had discouraged him from a second run for mayor in 1894 and then chastised herself for holding him back, now got into the role of political wife. During the summer of 1901, while Theodore was still vice president, Edith hired a social secretary to handle the mail that came to her because of her husband's job. In early September, after President McKinley had been shot in Buffalo, New York, but showed every sign of surviving, Theodore left it to Bamie to decide on what guests to invite during an upcoming visit to her: "I shall have to trust to your own knowledge. You will ask both the Senators and the Governor, will you not?"

Suddenly, President McKinley's condition worsened, and after he died on September 14, Theodore Roosevelt became the youngest president in history. While a frail Ida McKinley needed time to move out of the White House, Bamie's house on N Street served as headquarters for the new administration. It was only a twenty-minute walk from 1600 Pennsylvania Avenue, and Theodore continued to use it as a hideaway after he moved into the White House. Alice Longworth, who was seventeen in 1901, recalled that Auntie Bye's house offered many advantages. The food was always good (with hot chocolate and champagne on Sundays), and since all sorts of interesting people converged on it, Theodore went there often. In addition to comfort, Bamie's house provided privacy, and he held his first cabinet meetings there.

Bamie and Corinne exchanged so many letters on the subject of how a president's siblings should behave, they could have written a book. Bamie cautioned Corinne that both of them would have to walk a narrow line if they hoped to escape criticism. Theodore had added his own warning. He was *"very* emphatic," Bamie wrote Corinne, that under *"no* circumstances" should either sister request "anything for anyone but ourselves." In April 1902, Bamie instructed Corinne that the two of them ought not to expect anything as the President's sisters and should "in no way" think of themselves as representing Theodore. As for favors offered them because of him, they might accept those that came to them "as private citizens," but they should stay on guard. Bamie, who of course knew her way around the American embassy in London, explained: "[W]ith diplomatic matters, one little false step involves so much."

But on one matter Bamie bent her rule about asking Theodore for favors, and it was a move she soon regretted. In response to her request, the President had arranged for Will to take command of the ship *Missouri,* and when it collided with the battleship *Illinois* in April 1904, she knew her husband would be blamed. To make matters worse, the *Missouri* was involved in an even more disastrous accident a few weeks later. Ammunition stored on board exploded, transforming crew members unlucky enough to be in the vicinity into human targets. Five officers and twenty-four seamen were killed, making it, as one newspaper noted, "the worst disaster that has befallen the American navy since the blowing up of the *Maine* in Havana harbor."

Dozens of friends and acquaintances wrote to Will, wishing him well and congratulating him on his role in making the accident less serious than it might have been. But Bamie continued to worry about the consequences, and the fact that her brother was President of the United States complicated matters. When one story spread that Theodore had somehow manipulated an investigation of the accident as a favor to her and Will, she called it "an outrage" and then, with an eye on the upcoming election, she warned Corinne, "The next six months will be fraught with such pleasures for us all."

Before the unfortunate events of April 1904, Will had enjoyed special assignments as a result of his relationship with Theodore. He had even been promoted to rear admiral. In 1902 he accompanied Prince Henry of Prussia across the United States, and later that year as the American naval representative he attended the coronation of King Edward VII. As chief of the Naval Bureau of Equipment and a member of the Board of Construction, offices that Theodore appointed him to, he performed well and might have stayed on into the Taft presidency (Theodore insisted that he had arranged it with his successor). But Will chose to retire instead. When he left the navy on his sixty-second birthday—August 1, 1908, just months before Theodore's presidency ended—he had spent forty-five years in the service.

Throughout her brother's White House years, Bamie thought he saw too much of others and not enough of her. A few weeks after he took office, she wrote Corinne, "Theodore I see very seldom and almost always with outsiders and of course of necessity except when by some *rare* chance we are entirely alone." The situation was, she added, "not absolutely satisfying," and she sometimes felt "rather terrified" that her entree would be shut off. "The dignity" of the office had its requisites, but the whole situation had become "rather absurd." Casual friends blithely called him by his first name "when I cannot, unless entirely alone" with him.

Though she might have seen Theodore less frequently than she liked, Bamie was hardly a stranger to the presidential family. After Eleanor returned from boarding school in England in the summer of 1902, Bamie invited her niece to stay several weeks in Washington and see the White House firsthand. Bamie's list of activities during the winter of 1902–03 included teas with Eleanor, drives with her sister-in-law, First Lady Edith, and birthday parties for several young Roosevelts at the White House, newly renovated under the direction of Charles McKim. On New Year's Day 1903, Bamie assisted at the President's open house, which Eleanor also attended. Each year on January 1 he (like his predecessors) welcomed several thousand people and shook hands with every one of them. Bamie stoically stood in the reception line, and afterward she wrote Corinne that the event was "the best I have seen as to management" but "hard on us all receiving so many times."

Bamie's exact role in her brother's presidency is not easily documented. The fact that Theodore could enter her house without anyone knowing—or indeed realizing that he had left the White House—obscures the record. Bamie showed no interest in flaunting her importance, generally playing down her role. Her relatives noted, however, that he made 1733 N Street his favorite hideaway, and Eleanor recalled that her uncle Theodore never made an important decision without talking it over first with Bamie. Among the letters between Theodore and Bamie that do survive, several indicate that they conferred on many subjects, including the Democratic candidates for president and vice president in 1904, her attempt to influence the *New York Tribune* (through her good friend, the publisher's wife, Elisabeth Reid), and appointments of important officials.

By the time Theodore's presidency ended in March 1909, the Cowles family had several reasons for spending more time in Connecticut. Will's retirement from the navy freed him to become more involved in the community of Farmington; Sheffield, now ten, would soon be entering Groton, the Massachusetts preparatory school, so they would be closer to him; and Bamie's health was declining. Oldgate, in a rural setting, seemed more congenial for all these reasons. They retained the Washington house, renting it out, and Farmington became their primary residence.

Bamie's back problems had largely disappeared during her twenties and thirties (except for the slightly curved spine), but in her late forties she became increasingly crippled by arthritis. Although she played down the pain and suffering, over the next few years her relatives noticed a gradual decline in her ability to move around. In the summer of 1909, scoffing at reports that a nephew had described her "in the last stages of decrepitude," she insisted, "I do not know when I have been so well as this summer." A year later, at age fifty-five, she could no longer hide the fact that she was unable to write her own letters and had to dictate them to an employee, though she still tried to keep them personal and avoid what she had ridiculed, many years earlier, as a "machine-made sensation" in some of the letters she received. If she had any idea of this disability being temporary, a new physician she consulted in October 1910 set her straight. He diagnosed her condition as chronic and said it "*cannot* be cured only ameliorated at best."

Bamie continued to search for some relief. During the summer of 1911 she checked herself into a luxurious hotel in Mount Clemens, Michigan, then known as "Bath City" because of its health-giving baths. How much she improved or enjoyed herself remains uncertain. She complained to Corinne that she had forgotten "what solitary confinement meant!" Accommodations were comfortable enough, but "my only recreations are French lessons." In the face of a family code that prohibited complaints about physical ailments,

Bamie apologized for breaking the rules, saying she had talked "far too much about my stupid knees and I am sorry." She found her pleasures where she could, continuing to try to play golf until nearly sixty and occasionally traveling, even though her sister worried about how she could negotiate stairs.

Will immersed himself in a variety of activities, becoming, in Bamie's words, "the busiest person in the house, leading Bible class, looking after the schools, playing bridge, calling on all the oldest as well as the youngest ladies." On the more serious side, he lectured occasionally on naval topics (with what Bamie proudly described to a friend as "great success") and reported to Congress on how to extend wireless service on U.S. Navy vessels. After trying to run for the Connecticut assembly (and being rejected because he failed to meet the residency requirement), he finally won a seat in 1917, just in time to vote against woman suffrage when it came up for consideration in a special session. After a hiatus in which no new states granted women the vote, several legislatures were moving to enfranchise women before the Nineteenth Amendment made it the law of the land. As the Connecticut legislature began to consider the measure, the only copy of the bill somehow ended up in Will Cowles's hands, and he managed to lose it, thus fueling a rumor that he had "absconded with the suffrage bill."

Bamie certainly lost no sleep on the subject of the vote for women. She typically ridiculed the suffragists as dowdy, overzealous, and misguided. Carrie Chapman Catt, the midwesterner who emerged as the foremost suffrage leader after 1914, aroused Bamie's ire by making "taxation without representation" a slogan of the movement. Bamie noted that Catt and her colleagues paid very little in taxes while Bamie and her friends paid far more but thought the vote irrelevant. She agreed with Corinne, who had long ago noted that "the people one would expect to be for" suffrage are "strongly against it, and all the little domestic fair haired women are crazy to vote!"

Much as she disliked the idea of woman suffrage, Bamie had kept quiet on the subject, but her views were well known to anyone who cared to look at her record. In 1917 she explained to Eleanor that she had been put on a committee for the sole reason of giving it "the faint aroma of non-suffragism." Theodore had already gone on record as favoring suffrage, though he sometimes took a lukewarm stand. In 1911 he admitted he did "not regard it as a reform of much consequence, nothing like as important as any number of others." In his opinion it might do "only the tiniest fraction of the good that is anticipated" but none "of the harm that is anticipated." In 1913 when he prepared to address a "huge woman suffrage meeting," he admitted in a letter to his daughter Ethel, "Ugh! How I loathe these speeches!" To emphasize his point, he enclosed a cartoon entitled "Father addressing the woman suffragists." Standing on a platform, bent over a pitcher labeled "Nothing but ice water," he faces three women, one labeled "lady with genteel figure," another a dumpy woman in an ugly hat, labeled "sympathizer with militancy," and behind her a fierce-looking woman leaning on something labeled "umbrella" that looks more like a weapon.

Bamie was even more dismissive of the suffragists than Theodore—she insisted that giving women a place at the polls would only multiply the "stupid vote." Her goddaughter, Helen Roosevelt Robinson, recalled that Bamie "just wasn't attuned to the thought of women voting and taking any active part in politics." Many of her Connecticut neighbors agreed with her, and that state—where woman suffrage was often touted as a way to deprive political bosses of their power—did not ratify the Nineteenth Amendment until after it had become law throughout the nation. Bamie disliked autocratic political bosses as much as anyone, but she correctly discounted women's votes as a remedy for them.

For a woman so interested in politics and government, it might seem odd in hindsight that Bamie would be against suffrage for women. In her day and in her circle, though, intelligent women like herself would always find ways to act behind the scenes in politics, away from public scrutiny. Her niece Alice assessed this preference correctly when she admitted that Auntie Bye might have preferred the role of political boss, acting behind the scenes, rather than presidential candidate. Another niece, Corinne Alsop, described Bamie's political role as "just exactly the kind of part that she thought the women should take—an indirect part." Senators and governors dropped by her house so that she "always knew everybody and knew what was happening," and her name appeared as an endorsement of one candidate or another "because she was a person who was important in Connecticut."

By the time women won the vote in 1920, both Bamie and Will were showing their age. Always absentminded, Will seemed to forget much more, and his general health declined. He moved with difficulty, and his hearing and eyesight both deteriorated. Somehow the United States' 1917 entry into the war underlined his age—it was the first war in his adult lifetime that he was too old to fight, and like Theodore, he took it hard. When Shef volunteered, Bamie saw "a wistful look" in Will's eyes, and it made her "sad. The man is heavy in his soul as I suppose we all don't quite realize who have missed active military lives. In him it is so vivid and clear." He still managed to appear "gay as a bird and as the most inveterate dancer" at a New Year's party in 1919, but it was only a temporary burst of energy.

When Theodore died in January 1919, Bamie, devastated as she was by the death, was too crippled to attend his funeral. In fact, she rarely left her husband's side, though she would have been hard put to define exactly what ailed him. By February 1921, when Corinne offered to stay with him while Bamie went to New York, she refused the offer: "A visit to New York this year has no attraction for me, and unless my health really requires it, which it does not, I could not bear to leave my old Admiral." She had always tended to manage their household, and he had gladly accepted her help. But now a defenseless quality marked him, and he played on it, even getting some jeers out of his young Roosevelt nephews when they were sick and he refused to go near them (although Bamie did). Each minor stroke, which Bamie called his "tukee," left him in worse condition and increasing incoherency.

Will died at Oldgate on May 1, 1923, three months short of his seventy-seventh birthday. Funeral services three days later at the Congregational Church in Farmington included "full honors accorded his naval rank":the flag-draped coffin was carried from the church by sailors from the New London submarine base. Among the mourners was Ted Roosevelt, now being called Theodore and serving as assistant secretary of the Navy, as his father and cousin Franklin had done before him. It was young Theodore who furnished Bamie with a copy of the admiral's insignia so that she could have it reproduced on Will's tombstone. After twenty-eight years of marriage to Will, Bamie knew him well enough to know he would have wanted his naval rank recorded.

Within weeks of Will's death, Bamie also lost Bob Ferguson. In some ways she had lost him much earlier. In 1906 he had married eighteen-year-old Isabella Selmes, daughter of Patty Selmes, the woman Theodore had found so attractive when he met her in the Dakota Territory. After his marriage, he and Bamie had seen less and less of each other, although he and Isabella had asked her to be godmother to their daughter. She had declined on the grounds of age: "I truly think it would be better to have some younger Godmother for the precious little girl." When Bob's poor health led the Fergusons to move to the Southwest in 1909, the physical distance multiplied the emotional span. Sometimes it seemed that the man once so close to Bamie had forgotten her.

Occasional letters came east, always written in the most endearing terms to "Mrs. Anna." The Fergusons sent carefully chosen gifts, ranging from the exotic to the most practical. One Christmas it was a pink silk jacket with ostrich feathers and another, a jar of honey. But the magic between Bob and Bamie had broken with his marriage, and the feeling between them was never quite the same. In her circle of friends he had been replaced by other charmers, especially the appealing bachelor Joseph Alsop, who bought a tobacco farm near the town of Avon, not far from Oldgate, in 1905. Bamie took him under her patronage immediately, and the thirtyish gentleman and the fiftyish matron were soon spending a lot of time together, each of them impressed by the other's wit and intellect. After Joe visited the Cowleses in Washington, she wrote him, "I feel quite like a proud hen with a refracting duckling and you are the duckling. EVERY ONE asked for you and said such nice things."

Other Roosevelt women formed strong friendships with younger men and continued them after the men formed romantic attachments elsewhere and married. Eleanor Roosevelt's association with the student activist (and later her biographer) Joe Lash is one of the most documented, but there were many others, all following Bamie's model. Perhaps the women delighted in the youthful intensity of the men; they may have reveled in the attention they received. Certainly they had enough self-confidence to disregard any suggestion that such liaisons were inappropriate or odd.

∽

Bamie's son had always been an important source of joy in her life, and she took particular pride in his achievements as he grew older.

When he passed exams for admission to Groton, her niece Corinney described her as "naturally bursting with pride." He remained there, in spite of bouts of homesickness. As Shef reached his teens and began to look a lot like his portly father, Eleanor Roosevelt, now more attuned to such matters since she had four sons of her own, worried that he was growing too fast. In 1914, Eleanor wrote to Isabella Selmes Ferguson, whom she had known for about as long as she could remember: "Poor Sheffield has strained his heart and had to give up his hunting trip." Eleanor felt sure it was "only a temporary thing caused partly by overgrowth."

After Groton, Shef chose Yale, where his paternal grandfather had gone, rather than Harvard, favored by most of the Roosevelt men. But as soon as the United States entered the war in April 1917, he dropped out to enlist in the navy. When time came to ship out to France, his managerial mother, moving now increasingly by wheelchair, acted true to form. Rather than dwelling on the subject of his safety, she polled her friends and her sister for people in Paris whom he might contact when he got there. Eleanor Roosevelt thought a little time away from his mother would do him good. "If he comes back, it will be the making of him," she wrote Isabella.

After the fighting ended, Shef was chosen by Franklin to accompany him and Eleanor back from the peace talks in France. By early 1919 he was back at Yale, and Bamie wrote to Bob Ferguson that he was "working hard at New Haven tutoring and rowing, so as to get back in his own class, if possible on the first of April. . . . He is very darling and I long for him to know you. I mean by knowing you to be with you after all the years not having seen you." But Robert Ferguson never had the chance.

Like most of the Roosevelt men, Shef married young—at twenty-one—in a ceremony his mother must have approved because *The New York Times* singled it out as "one of the most notable [social events] of the Summer." Newspaper accounts predicted that Shef and his bride, Margaret A. Krech, known as Bobbie, would reside in New York after their honeymoon, but they were wrong. The young couple took up residence in a little cottage on the grounds of Oldgate. The big house, constructed during the American Revolution, would have accommodated all of them, but they maintained separate households. To Corinne, Bamie confided, "I feel as though Bobbie and Sheffield were moving into a very dainty poorhouse. Everything costs so much, and they have the same unerring eye that I have for the most expensive things." Shef, just starting out in banking, was glad to accept a used kitchen stove from a neighbor who was no longer using it, his mother reported.

When her "children," as Bamie called them, produced a child of their own in March 1923, they named him after his grandfather, who was by then gravely ill. Bamie rejoiced in her "beloved grandson, who I am firmly going to call Will, for my private delectation." The baby's birth no doubt cheered the entire household because Bamie's letters, even those on black-bordered paper after Will's death, show an upbeat quality. At just a few months of age the baby fascinated her, and she described him as "too adorable for words . . . [it] curdles my blood. . . . When he finds he cannot stand up on his feet, [he tries] to stand up on his head." Bamie could not see enough of her grandson. Even while complaining to her sister that he had "ruined every pretty sofa pillow I have," she still insisted "he is perfectly adorable."

The proud but aging mother followed her son's every job move, and when Shef considered a transfer to London in September 1926, she encouraged him to go in spite of the distance it would put between them. "I have felt sure he ought either to have a move upward [in his firm] or he ought to go elsewhere," she wrote Corinne.

᷾

In that final decade of her life a colorful cast of guests moved through Bamie's Connecticut home—writers and actresses, including Vita Sackville West and Anne Meredith, as well as governors and teachers. If she feared that any one of them might stay too long, she simply announced that two nights was "the limit I could stand my greatest pleasures." She gleefully recounted how one of her tea hours—when she entertained guests who passed through Oldgate—had turned into a disaster. One widow, who looked "withered away, like a very faded little autumn leaf," had a shock when Bamie's son mistook her for somebody else. In showing her to her car, he mentioned that he was sorry that the woman's husband "had not gotten the nomination for Senator." His concern must have "puzzled the lady in question," Bamie added gleefully, "with her husband long since in higher regions than even our Senate."

Her descriptive powers did not desert her even when her sight and hearing continued to fail. In May 1926 when an actor friend visited her, she gave such a vivid description of the Indians that had once inhabited the Connecticut valley that he "felt absolutely creepy and hated to go out of the house." She delighted in fooling her friends, especially at bridge, in which she continued to take instruction long after she mastered the game. The teacher (with the unlikely name of "Mr. Work") evidently served her purposes. Bamie cheerfully informed Corinne that she liked to play her cards all wrong until the instructor left. But as soon as "a pleasant bridge table is arranged, I win all their money, which is quite a satisfactory result of the lesson."

No one saw Bamie with greater clarity than she saw herself. When a maid insisted on fixing Bamie's hair in an ornate style she disliked, she wrote Corinne that she ended up looking like "a very worn out, decrepit German lady of some past dynasty." When an old friend scheduled a visit, Bamie joked: "I think that she combines [a visit to] me with preserving peaches. I hope so, for to look me over will hardly pay her for the trip down." When another friend sent a note typed in red (but with one big black exception), Bamie laughed at the delicate language and showed her disdain for those who went to great lengths to avoid four-letter words: "[the] one black word . . . for a moment staggered me. It was 'helova.' You might not expect it made Hell of a, but that was the word."

Like many competent women of her time, she preferred the company of men, especially powerful, smart, and witty men. In the large correspondence that survives, males predominate, and as for women, most are relatives. Among her favorites, nieces Alice and Eleanor head the list, possibly because their orphaned state engaged her sympathy. More probably their strong personalities tickled her. Each of them, like her, hankered to do things "against the rules," and all three invented remarkable adult lives for themselves after sad and troubled childhoods.

Corinne was probably closest to Bamie of all her relatives. The seven-year difference in their ages meant that they never operated as true equals, and their personalities also divided them. Bamie thought Corinne operated at too high an energy level and showed far too much attention to money and travel, but she delighted in Corinne's accomplishments as a public speaker and writer. The sisters stood united in their admiration for their brother, Theodore. Helen Roosevelt Robinson recalled in an interview long after both Bamie and Corinne had died: "[There was never] one bit of jealousy between them about him. . . . [I]t was just give, give, give . . . to further his interests."

Much of the correspondence between the sisters dealt with the humdrum details of life—arranging travel, conferring on birthday and Christmas gifts, dealing with servants. But when Bamie read a book that she especially liked, such as the autobiography of Ulysses S. Grant, she passed it on to Corinne. They had always exchanged views on art and travel. When the younger sister wrote from Europe that she would be seeing "Parsifal" at Beyreuth, Bamie replied enthusiastically: "The first time I heard it was one of the absolute sensations of my life."

It is difficult to overestimate Bamie's lack of interest in achieving fame for herself. To her mind, actions counted in a person's life—not the publicity surrounding them. Late in her life, in discussing Grace Dodge, an educator, philanthropist, and fellow New Yorker whom she had known since childhood, Bamie noted approvingly: "She certainly accomplished the most enormous amount without ever having her name come before the public." Of course many people knew Dodge as a founder of Columbia Teachers College and a leader of the YWCA, but she never aspired to the title of public heroine that Bamie found so distasteful.

By September 1929, Bamie, always so confident of her own judgment, began to distrust herself. She confided to Corinne that in the process of interviewing prospective servants, she often forgot what each of the applicants had said. Her voice was failing her, too, and although others kindly attributed her hoarseness to a cold, she knew it was not. The time had come to "live on bitter tonics and plenty of food."

The energy was no longer there to play the kinds of jokes that Bamie liked, but she retained memories of the most outlandish. One story she sometimes told involved a wealthy friend who planned a party for her granddaughter at her Fifth Avenue mansion and arranged for trained seals to perform. Unfortunately, the appointed room was on the second floor, and the seals had to be fed fish all the way up the stairs to entice them into their places. The hostess, horrified at the prospect of all that fish being thrown to the seals on her beautiful antique rugs, still managed to see the amusing side of the event and, although rueful about possible damage, giggled at what she had done. It was exactly the kind of gesture that Bamie applauded.

Her closest woman friend outside the family still lived: Elisabeth Reid, widow of Whitelaw Reid, diplomat and publisher of the *New York Tribune*. When Bamie and Elisabeth first met, they were in their late teens and unattractive daughters of wealthy, powerful fathers. But both went on to shape interesting lives for themselves. According to Sheffield Cowles, Elisabeth Reid had "rather a man's mind, a man's turn of thinking." She thought "on a very large scale" and concentrated her energies on the Republican Party, the family newspaper, and various "charitable and financial interests."

Stories abounded of how the wealthy, strong-minded Mrs. Reid shaped her environment and dealt with obstacles. One of the Roosevelts recalled that if she tired of the conversation, she simply turned off the speaker by shifting her eyes away from whoever was talking. She was bluntly honest about her own son, and when her good friend Mary Harriman, widow of railroad magnate Edward Henry Harriman, boasted of having lost more than a million dollars on her son Averell's shipping business, Elisabeth Reid countered with: "That is nothing. Let me tell you what I've lost on Ogden." In other words, she was precisely the kind of woman who appealed to Bamie—one who never doubted that she held the reins to the important things in life.

That presence or sense of self tended to daunt some of Bamie's relatives. Helen Roosevelt Robinson pointed to a sharpness in her manner. Niece Ethel Roosevelt Derby attributed to Bamie "a certain quality of significance, of being important," traits that Ethel never would have wished for herself even though she thought them "fine for others."

Preserving her dignity required more effort after Bamie's stamina declined and she became increasingly crippled. She had long ago admitted to her sister that she could understand how one would want to "leave a life where one seems so cramped and, as I do, useless and yet for some inexplicable [reason] one has to go on . . . [even though] one can only be a burden every year."

Bamie recognized that she was not alone in her predicament. In September 1922 when she was preparing to entertain her nephew

Franklin, recently crippled by polio, and another friend, Amory Gardiner, who also had limited mobility, she joked to Corinne: "I have rather an odd sensation as to the end of the week. As you know, I always say that to be in a home for incurables kept by an incurable is not a wise plan, to which I am going to add a convalescent hospital department." She thought it "heavenly" to host Franklin, always a favorite of hers, but she continued, "I would much prefer having my invalids one by one, as having so many at the same time seems to give a choice of painful possibilities."

When Corinne's health worsened, too, Bamie concluded that the problem must lie in their genes. In March 1926, while Corinne was hospitalized for eye surgery, Bamie inquired of her: "Blessed Corinne, what crimes do you suppose you and I ever perpetrated to have had such curious punishments? I feel as though somehow one ought to be able to study heredity backward from us." She had never heard of any one of their ancestors suffering with eye problems or arthritis, although she pointed to Mittie and several others on that side who had become quite deaf, including Aunt Anna and several cousins.

In 1928 the downward spiral of Bamie's life gathered speed. Her house caught fire in March for reasons never fully understood. Like most people unable to move on their own (including Franklin), she had an inordinate fear of burning houses, and although she was carried to safety, the experience unnerved her and seemed to hasten her decline. Her eyesight deteriorated, and she suffered circulatory problems. In June 1929, Edith visited her but confessed that she doubted Bamie took much pleasure in the meeting. "She . . . seems to have gone away," Edith wrote Corinne, "from all except the circle of Farmington friends and continual pain."

By the summer of 1931, Bamie's pleasures were few. She viewed much of what happened to her as from afar—as though it did not concern her. The intense summer heat made "perspiration run down my face continually," she wrote in a dictated letter to Corinne, "and when Billy Smith is here on Sundays and we play bridge after lunch, I have a very hard time preventing him from taking a very sweet smelling handkerchief and wiping my face." She still had some good days, but now her mind began to fail her. She repeated the same story over and over, and one visitor noted: "Of course every thing was more or less hung around Theodore!" Her niece Corinne Alsop, who lived nearby and visited often, feared that Bamie had very little time left. The prospect of losing her was daunting, but so was the prospect of watching her endure so much pain. Corinne, who had married Bamie's friend Joe Alsop, wrote her mother: "I cannot face our lives in one way without her—Oldgate is such an important thread in the fabric of our lives but I can think of nothing but the elimination of her agony."

In the end, Bamie orchestrated a thoroughly fitting death for herself. On an August afternoon in 1931, about half a dozen young people, including Shef, Bobbie, and Corinney, had come to visit her and then gone out to play golf on a nearby course. Suddenly they were summoned by a servant who explained that Bamie insisted on being wheeled into the parlor for tea. They all went inside, knowing that Bamie was dying, but they proceeded with the charade that this was just an ordinary tea. Of course Bamie could neither pour tea nor drink it, and very quickly she had to be wheeled out of the room. The next day she died.

The enormous determination, vitality, and style that characterized Bamie's last tea defined her entire life. Even while confined to a wheelchair and dependent on others to see to every physical need, she retained command. One of her friends at the end emphasized the monumental spirit that sustained her through those pain-filled years: "I always had the feeling, especially during the last years, that she was like a ship, a battleship, that might be going down, but every flag was flying and the band playing."

With a long list of male admirers, Corinne (shown here in her mid-thirties) was always the height of elegance.

CHAPTER THREE

CORINNE ROOSEVELT ROBINSON

(1861–1933)

N A MUGGY Friday morning in June 1920, while Bamie
sat in her wheelchair in Connecticut, Corinne entered
the huge Coliseum in Chicago, apparently oblivious to
the fact that she was about to make history. Nearly
fourteen thousand Republicans had gathered from all
over the nation to choose their party's candidate for president, and Corinne
Roosevelt Robinson had agreed to give one of the nominating
speeches. No woman had ever given a major address at a convention
of either of the two major parties, and the size of this audience would
have daunted many seasoned speakers of either sex. But Corinne, trim
at fifty-nine and dressed entirely in black, showed not a hint of nerves.

Like a true politician, before entering the Coliseum she stopped outside to chat with protesters. Several dozen members of the National
Woman's Party had come to Chicago to remind delegates that their
leaders had done little to help enfranchise women. "Vote against the
Republican Party as long as it blocks suffrage" one of their signs read,
and several others were just as blunt. Twenty-eight states had already
acted on their own and enfranchised women, some of whom were
attending this convention as delegates, but in other parts of the
nation, females were legally barred from voting booths.

Like Bamie, Corinne had never had much use for the suffragists and their fight, but she knew enough to greet the demonstrators amicably and remind them that her brother had once called them heroes. By adding that she also admired their courage, she gave the erroneous impression that she supported their cause more than she did. After all, the Nineteenth Amendment might actually get ratified in the requisite number of states before the November election, and then *all* those women would have a vote. She saw no need to antagonize or slight them now.

Massachusetts senator Henry Cabot Lodge, who had long ago become closer to Corinne than he was to Bamie, presided over the Republican convention that year, but his reputation as elder statesman carried limited weight with the rambunctious crowd. Try as he might, he could not get the huge assembly quiet enough to begin deliberations. Finally, after nearly half an hour of banging the gavel, he achieved some order, and the roll call of states began. In alphabetical order, each one yielded, until Kansas, where sentiment ran very strong, came up, and a delegate placed in nomination the name of General Leonard Wood.

Corinne had known Wood almost as long as she could remember, and she had come to Chicago to try to convince other Republicans that he would make the strongest candidate. He had entered the Roosevelt circle when he began studying medicine at Harvard, three years behind Theodore. In the Spanish-American War, Wood commanded Theodore and his Rough Riders in Cuba, and after the war ended, Wood returned to the island to serve as governor.

A popular war hero to many Americans, Wood did not appeal to the party bosses. The delegates liked his "outsider" image and the fact that he showed integrity and independence. His ideas on government helped, too. In this first election after the Great War, when prosperity stood high on people's wish list, his statement that government should be run like business sounded particularly appealing. Party leaders, looking for a way to squelch a man they could not be sure of controlling, argued against choosing a military hero. Harry Daugherty, the Republican boss from Ohio, announced with conviction: "There's not enough money in the world to buy the nomination for a man with epaulettes on his shoulders."

After the first nominating speech for Wood, an outburst of shouts and band music mixed in a cacophonous roar, and thousands of feathers, painted in the brilliant blue, red, and green that had already been identified as General Wood's colors, showered down on the delegates. The deluge of plumes descending out of rafters bedecked in American flags and colorful bunting added a chaotic, frenzied feeling and helped push the noise volume a notch louder. Senator Lodge's repeated pleas for order went virtually ignored (although this time he cared less since the demonstration honored his own personal favorite), so he retreated to his chair on the speakers' dais to await calm.

Thirty-eight minutes later, when chants of "Wood, Wood, we want Wood" finally waned, Corinne Robinson was, according to *The New York Times,* "deferentially escorted" to the podium. As soon as people recognized her but well before anyone mentioned her name, a "roar of welcome" rose in the hall. Then, the newspaper continued, "the convention was due for its first real thrill." Senator Lodge announced: "Corinne Roosevelt Robinson, the sister of Theodore Roosevelt."

An earlier mention of the former President's name had produced only a muted response, far less exuberant than some reporters expected a little more than a year after his death. But the sight of a living Roosevelt caused a spontaneous eruption of enthusiasm, and as soon as Corinne opened her mouth, anyone who had ever heard Colonel Roosevelt (as Theodore preferred to be called in his post-presidential years) had no doubt of the relationship between them. "Her gestures, her mannerisms, the intonation of her sentences all must have recalled to the convention the man who might have been its unrivaled candidate for the Presidential nomination had he lived long enough," the *Times* reported.

Corinne spoke so loudly and clearly that her voice reached the very last row, and her carefully chosen words made an immediate impact. Beginning with a reference to the recent war, she pointed out how her choice for the nomination had acted forcefully in that conflict: "I can voice the feelings of thousands of American mothers when I say that the foresight of Leonard Wood made of their sons fighting machines instead of cannon fodder. . . ." Then she attacked the incumbent Democratic President (although not by name) for delaying the entry of the United States' into the war. Making a not too subtle contrast between Woodrow Wilson and Leonard Wood, she continued: "We want *not* the man who waits for the psychological moment; we want the man who *makes* the psychological moment." Continuing in short snappy phrases, Corinne reminded the delegates that General Wood was a good friend of her brother's and a good friend of hers, but friendship was not the point: Leonard Wood was a Roosevelt "type" of candidate with a long record of achievement and a solid reputation for doing right.

The following day, newspapers across the country singled out Corinne Robinson as the outstanding orator of the day and reminded women readers that although they would not see one of their own nominated that year, they could find satisfaction in Mrs. Robinson's performance. Over the next few weeks, magazines applauded her ability. Frederick M. Davenport, who covered the convention for the magazine *Outlook,* noted that most of the speeches in Chicago lacked color, and there were "few in real quality . . . [but] incomparably the finest [was] the gem of a speech by Theodore Roosevelt's sister." Senator Lodge said afterward that it was the only convention speech he ever heard that "might have changed votes." To Bamie he wrote, "You can imagine my pride in her."

Corinne Roosevelt Robinson did not suddenly burst into national prominence that June day in 1920. She had already achieved a considerable reputation as a lecturer and author, with three volumes to her credit. For the last half-dozen years she had been addressing audiences across the nation, from high schools in Brooklyn to Republican gatherings on the West Coast, on subjects ranging from civic duty to world travel.

But there was another reason—besides her competence—that explained her selection to speak at the Republican convention. By the summer of 1920, leaders in both major parties understood that in the upcoming November election, twenty-six million women would more than likely have the right to cast a vote worth every bit as much as that cast by their husbands or brothers. Republicans and Democrats alike stretched to look inclusive, and when the Chicago convention ended, with the photogenic Senator Warren G. Harding from Ohio as its candidate, Republican National Chairman Will Hays named an Executive Committee that included seven women, Corinne Robinson among them.

Often introduced as a sister of the popular President, Corinne had now emerged as the most prominent of all the Roosevelt women.

Bamie, probably the most astute politically, was tied to her Connecticut home. Corinne's daughter, Corinne Alsop, although already initiated into politics, had four children under the age of ten and little time for public appearances. Eleanor Roosevelt, still more famous as Theodore's niece than as Franklin's wife, was beginning to move tentatively in Democratic circles (especially after her husband was nominated for vice president later that summer), but she had not yet gained the self-confidence to act on her own. Alice Longworth, Theodore's daughter and now the wife of a powerful congressman, could be witty and outspoken in the safety of her own salon, but she disliked addressing large groups and would have blanched at the prospect of talking to fourteen thousand people.

Of course the Republicans could have capitalized on the Roosevelt name by putting one of the next generation of men on the podium. Theodore's sons had all distinguished themselves in the war, and the eldest, Theodore, had won his first elective office, to the New York State Assembly. Corinne's eldest son, Ted Robinson, began serving in the New York State Assembly in 1916. But all were passed over in favor of the popular, seasoned speaker—Corinne.

I

EXACTLY WHERE Corinne gained her confidence remains unclear, but from childhood she was encouraged to speak up. In the first years of schooling, Aunt Anna had taught Corinne (and her good friend Edith Carow) alongside Theodore and Elliott, and nothing indicates she required less of the girls than the boys. From the time she was ten, Corinne thrived on forming groups for reading and discussion, and she was not shy about taking charge of the meetings. Later, when faced with audiences of hundreds or even thousands, they seemed no more daunting to her than an assembly of five or ten. She probably could not have given the date of her first "public speech" since for as long as she could remember she had been talking to gatherings of newsboys, one of her father's favorite charities, and to her parents' guests. Speaking was just something she did, and if asked why she did it, she would have likely replied that no one ever told her not to.

Corinne's formal education was even less impressive than Bamie's. After Aunt Anna's classes and the sporadic classes at neighboring families' homes, Corinne had nothing but family discussions and the long excursions abroad. Mlle. Souvestre had transferred her school from France to England by the time Corinne was old enough to enroll, and she chose to remain in New York, where she had more friends than Bamie had had. Theodore and Elliott began receiving extra instruction in science and history, especially Theodore after he set his sights on Harvard, but Corinne was not included since college was not even a consideration. Exceptionally well read in the classics, she picked up what she knew about science and math where she could. Although she made no complaints at the time, twenty years later, as a young wife and mother, she prevailed on Theodore to tutor her in American history. She "longed" to learn everything that he knew, she told him.

At the end of the family's second trip abroad, when Corinne was twelve, she managed to share her brothers' tutors. The parents initially split up the three siblings, putting Theodore and Elliott to board with one family in Dresden while Corinne went to stay in another household several miles away. The explanation Mittie and Theodore offered at the time—that they wanted to discourage their children from speaking English with each other—does not ring entirely true since the two boys were allowed to live together from the start. Whatever the reasons for the separation, Corinne hated it. She had never before been apart from her brothers for any length of time, and she was homesick and lonely. She later singled out that experience as leading her to write her first poem, "The Lament of an American Child in a German Family."

Poetry offered solace but no rescue, and Corinne appealed for help. After realizing how miserable she was, Mittie and Bamie interrupted their relaxing stay at the spa in Carlsbad and went to Dresden, where they moved Corinne into the same family where Theodore and Elliott were living.

Corinne found the next few months idyllic in spite of Elliott's complaints about learning from "two young ladies, . . . a rather fat 'Mama' and a 'Herr Papa.'" One hour of French and another of music followed two hours of German every morning. Then in the afternoon, after more study, the three siblings went for a ride or "excursion," often a hike in the hills outside town.

Struggling to compete with her older brothers, Corinne worked hard at language lessons. Very quickly her letters in German to "Darling Father" looked very good, especially for a girl who had not yet celebrated her thirteenth birthday. Within weeks of coming to Dresden, she had apparently mastered the grammar and was writing an elegant, ornate German script. Perhaps she feared that her father might suspect that she had some assistance because she pointedly assured him: "I have written this letter all alone." Her claim stretches credulity, partly because the script is so different from her usual writing and the content so advanced for someone with so little instruction. But perhaps the claim was accurate. As though to underscore her assertion about her progress, she followed up with four more letters in German the following month.

Not all of her brothers' activities were open to their "little sister." When Elliott and Theodore, who now considered boxing their "favorite amusement," received boxing gloves from their father, there were none, of course, for Corinne. But when time came for the children to form a club, partly to mitigate the loneliness they felt in a foreign country, they rather pretentiously named it the Dresden Literary–American Club, and Corinne became a full-fledged member. Along with two of their cousins, Maud and John Elliott, who happened to be studying in Germany at the same time, they settled on an acronym to unite them. Only later would Corinne admit that "W.A.N.A" stood for a defiant: "We are No Asses."

Something of the daredevil characterized Corinne from her youngest years. At age eight, for instance, she surprised her father by taking him up on a challenge before either of her brothers had the courage to act. Theodore Sr. had brought home an unbroken pony and announced that he would give it to the first child who attempted to ride it. The boys hung back, sizing up their risks, while the younger Corinne rushed forward to volunteer—and won the pony.

That adventuresome spirit continued to characterize Corinne as she matured, and although her "body building" took a different shape from Theodore's, it was no less zealously pursued. In his later years Theodore's excessive adventuring proved foolhardy, and he nearly killed himself on a trip he took through the Brazil jungle with his son Kermit. Corinne avoided forays into the jungle, but she was as adamant as Theodore about adhering to a family motto concerning how to confront obstacles. "Over or under, but never around," the motto exhorted, and on hikes with her brothers, she struggled to outdo them, crossing rough terrain or difficult waterways rather than give in to an easier route.

The high energy level, so characteristic of Bamie until arthritis crippled her, remained Corinne's hallmark. Almost nothing seemed to slow her down, and as a middle-aged woman she exasperated her adult children who had trouble keeping up with her. Her son Monroe remembered going out with her for a walk one day and being nonplused by her determination. When the two of them came to a large barn, she muttered something about "over or under but never around" and then laboriously climbed up across the roof of the barn and down on the other side rather than take the infinitely less difficult route around.

Part of her zeal may have grown out of her desire to compete with her brothers. She was only eighteen months younger than Elliott and three years younger than Theodore, but by the time they were in their teens, the boys treated the difference in age as a considerable gulf. In 1873 when the family returned from their stay in Europe, Elliott wrote his older sister as "Dear Bamie" but Corinne was still "My Baby Sister" or "My Dear Little One."

Through her early years Corinne's closest friend was Edith Carow. Born less than two months apart (with Corinne the younger) the girls met when they were barely toddlers. Their fathers, who had been boyhood friends, both married out-of-town women and then settled into houses just a few minutes' walk from each other. The Carow family fortunes fell just as the Roosevelts' wealth grew, and Edith never got to explore Europe on long, luxurious trips with her parents. But even when separated from the Roosevelt children during their trips abroad, she wrote detailed letters about what was going on at home.

As Corinne and Edith matured, they mused on many topics in their letters. About the time Edith prepared to celebrate her seventeenth birthday, Corinne reminded her "how very old we are getting, quite grown up, one short year more, and the brook will be past, and that mysterious eighteen years reached." The death of Corinne's father a few months earlier may have added to her melancholy on this occasion. In an allusion to Edith's troubled home life that included an alcoholic father and a precarious financial situation,

Corinne continued that she hoped "the next seventeen years of your life will be as peaceful and sheltered (I know they have not been untroubled) as those past." Corinne admitted that she often pondered what the future might bring for them both "and whether we will always be so placed as to see much of each other." But she relished the prospect of surprise, pointing out to her friend that "the future is very secretive and on the whole I am glad."

∞

Within two years of writing that letter, Corinne's life underwent a major change. Through her brother Elliott she met Douglas Robinson, six years her senior. On one side of his family, Douglas had American roots (President James Monroe was his great-uncle, and some of his relatives had established a foothold in upstate New York). But he considered himself Scottish, having been born in Scotland to a distinguished family and having graduated from Oxford University. By the time she met him, he had already begun making his fortune in American real estate, although he had lived in the United States only a few years.

On his part, Douglas fell in love with Corinne the day he first met her, and with his credentials it is no surprise that her family immediately decided this was the man she should marry. Tradition—some might call it a family rule—dictated that daughters should marry as soon as they "came out" at eighteen, and Corinne had passed the magic age. So had Bamie, of course, but with her slightly odd-shaped body and managerial manner, she somehow seemed to have skipped right over the "marriageable" category. Now the family turned its attention to Corinne, athletic and smart, passably pretty, and already heir to part of her father's estate.

Douglas Robinson quickly enlisted the Roosevelts on his side in winning Corinne. Family legend had it that whenever she expressed an objection to marrying him, Bamie would brandish "a sword of Damocles in her hand" and admonish: "You must not retreat." Mittie also favored her daughter's marriage to the bland Scotsman, and after enumerating his virtues she summed him up as only she could do. "I think you will be able to stand him," she told Corinne. "He's a very fine man but he is very, very plain. But not a bad plainness. It's like quinine. It's a clean plainness."

To say that Corinne remained reluctant understates the case: her letters to Douglas on the subject of marriage sound tortured. For two years while her family considered her engaged to Douglas, she put off setting a date. Apologizing for hurting his feelings, she suggested that Bamie, who was closer to his age, would have been a better match. While admitting that Douglas loved her, she could not bring herself to marry him.

Some historians attributed Corinne's reservations to her judgment that Douglas did not measure up to her brother Theodore, but there is little evidence for such a conclusion. At the time she was putting off Douglas, he certainly measured up to Theodore, who had not yet done anything particularly noteworthy or impressive. More probably it was the senior Theodore who served as the real model to emulate. Corinne wrote Douglas: "Sometimes I think if I could have one talk with [my father] it would be all right." In another letter she assured Douglas that she found him "strong and tender," much like her father.

Corinne may have suffered some anxieties about the sexual side of matrimony. She discussed the subject with Douglas's sister, who was also reluctant about marrying, and then reported to him: We "both say we would like to be suddenly married a year without knowing anything about it and then things would not look so hard." In a moment of panic, Corinne confessed to Douglas that perhaps it was not meant for her to marry "or I would not have the horror of it that I have."

While the rest of the family puzzled over her reluctance and her mood swings (one of them described by Theodore as "bluer than indigo"), Corinne stonewalled. She seemed to like Douglas, frequently calling him a "dear old fellow" and signing her letters to him, "your little girl," but she would not walk down the aisle. While Douglas patiently bided his time, moving between New York and Virginia, where he already owned a large parcel of real estate, she kept up a full social schedule in New York. Mornings were often spent reading with Edith Carow, and in the afternoons they rode or walked or met with other women friends to discuss books. During that time they formed a group, the Fortnightly Club, and regularly engaged in what Corinne described as discussions of such subjects as "Nihilism (deep) and deportment (less deep)." Asserting her own independence in excursions around the city, Corinne related to Douglas that she and Edith had been in vehicles involved in a "tremendous collision" on Broadway, but both women took it in stride, remaining calm even when other people panicked.

Whether she could express herself on the subject or not, Corinne had valid reasons for not marrying Douglas Robinson. His mother, authoritarian and self-centered, had chosen to live in New York since her husband's death, dividing her time between Manhattan and a large summer home in the Adirondacks. Douglas had not proposed that he and Corinne reside with his mother, who clearly spelled trouble for any daughter-in-law, but Corinne viewed her as a problem and saw through several attempts to reassure her on that subject. Although "fascinating" and "intelligent," Douglas's mother had a reputation for treating her servants "like pieces of dirt," screaming and yelling at them at the slightest lapse or provocation. Not an isolated case in the Robinson family, she had other relatives just as bad-tempered. One reportedly dropped dead in a tantrum after he became agitated at the ringing of church bells.

But Corinne's real reasons went beyond such peripheral concerns to something far more important. Walking down the aisle meant renouncing her own autonomy, an idea she did not like. During her courtship she informed Douglas that she had decided to miss the wedding of one of his relatives in order to attend the marriage of an old friend of hers. The bride had belonged to a club Corinne had started and presided over at the age of fourteen. In spite of its name, P.O.R.E., which stood for Paradise of Ravenous Eaters, it had been, she boasted to Douglas, "a literary society of great renown" and had "flourished two years." She signed that letter "Yours" and then crossed it out, adding tellingly, "I do not like the idea of being anybody's except my own." When Douglas did not take to one of her friends, she defended the woman as "true and strong," insisting that these were the traits "I most admire."

Corinne Roosevelt liked her life exactly as it was, and she understood that marriage would alter it entirely. Even though she had the money inherited from her father, she knew it would probably come under her husband's control. With undependable contraception available, she faced the prospect of one pregnancy after another and the limitations on her movement and freedom that those pregnancies (and babies) carried with them. Even without children she somehow saw herself as doomed to operate in her husband's shadow, an unappealing prospect. A visit to Mittie's aging sister in Philadelphia underlined in Corinne's mind how much a husband shaped a woman's happiness. Aunt Susan West, the same woman whose stories about Georgia had inspired Theodore to visit Bulloch Hall in the first place, was "a real saint of a woman," Corinne wrote Douglas, but she had to "put up with a husband who's never accomplished much and with his 88-year-old mother who's lost her mind and her memory." It all seemed "sad and dull," Corinne concluded, and she wanted none of that for herself.

Corinne also harbored a suspicion that Douglas's interest in politics fell short of hers. He showed too little regard for American leaders, an attitude she attributed to his being born in Scotland. She got as excited about Theodore's election to the state legislature as she did about Elliott's polo victories, and she wanted a husband who was just as involved. "You *must* be naturalized," she wrote him, and then continued: "I hope you take a great deal of interest in politics. I mean our politics, not only foreign affairs such as would naturally interest you after a foreign education. If there is one thing I like particularly, it is public spirit." When a political opponent shot and wounded President Garfield in July 1881, she informed Douglas that both she and Bamie were "much excited. . . . Is it not fearful? I hope you are properly excited and infuriated by it!!" Having first gotten a whiff of the fun of political intrigue when Theodore started attending Republican meetings right after college, she had no intention of being cut off from that excitement by a husband whose only interest was real estate and making money.

Finally, however, for reasons that she kept to herself, she capitulated to the pressure of Douglas and her family. On April 29, 1882, she and Douglas were married at the Fifth Avenue Presbyterian Church in New York City. Just months short of her twenty-first birthday, and a long way from her speaking triumph at the Republican convention in 1920, Corinne spent most of that day crying.

Their children later pondered why Corinne ever married Douglas. Their son Monroe explained that "the true spark" was missing in that union and that his mother was wont to say, "I married your father when I was too young." Corinney also questioned why her mother proceeded with the marriage, especially since she had other options in the form of "two or three men who were madly in love with her." A granddaughter may have come up with the correct answer. She discounted Douglas as merely "convenient," a man who fit his wife's purposes perfectly, supplying the money so that she could go her own way, living her life pretty much as she wanted.

That description of Douglas Robinson does not really do him justice. Aside from his business pursuits, he had leisure interests that he shared with Corinne. He loved horses, rode well, played polo, and liked to be the first one out on the dance floor. Most important, he was on the best of terms with both of Corinne's brothers, especially Elliott who in her eyes could do no wrong.

II

CORINNE UNDERSTOOD all too well the immediate, enormous change that her marriage would make in her life. The youngest daughter in a well-run household, she now took over management of her own home in Manhattan, and within a year she had a son to look after. Teddy, as he was always called, was named for his much admired grandfather. Unlikely as it might have seemed, Mittie's youngest child produced her first grandson, and at forty-seven years of age, Mittie thought it was high time she was a grandmother. Theodore and Alice, married for more than two years, had not managed to conceive, and so all the attention focused on little Teddy Robinson.

For nearly three years after Teddy's birth, Corinne had no more children, and then, at roughly eighteen-month intervals, she gave birth to three: Corinne, known as Corinney, in July 1886; Monroe in December 1887; and Stewart in March 1889. The spacing of their births is so remarkably like that of Mittie's a generation earlier that it raises the possibility that mother and daughter had the same physical problem in conceiving a second child.

Over the first few years of her marriage, Corinne busied herself with her young family while Douglas focused on business—a little too much so for her taste. She once composed a ditty for her children, emphasizing how important his work was to him. "He loves you dears / he loves you / He roars it in your ear / But a real estate transaction / Is a thousand times more dear!"

With his success, her own responsibilities increased, especially after the family began spending part of each year at their seventy-two-acre estate in Orange, New Jersey. Perched on a hilltop, and with its own pond and stables, the Orange property became the children's favorite—at least for the time they could not be at the even larger estate, Henderson House, that Douglas's family kept in Herkimer County, New York, on the western edge of the Adirondacks.

The logistics of moving among the various houses was definitely "woman's work," although it involved considerable executive ability. Corinne had watched Mittie supervise the opening and closing of the "summer" house and the "winter" house, the shipping of trunks (both in New York and abroad), and the hiring and supervising of a staff that numbered at least six. Now she faced the same list of tasks herself—but with one extra complication: Henderson House, a replica of a Scottish castle, was two hundred miles north of New York City and far more difficult to reach and administer than the Long Island homes favored by so many of the Roosevelts. Henderson House had been in the Robinson family since the 1740s, but it came under Corinne's full control after her mother-in-law's death in 1906.

Arranging for the children's lessons, clothing, and medical care was Corinne's responsibility, although she soon hired a Frenchwoman, Josephine Poirot, to assist her. More than a nanny, Josephine functioned as chief assistant to Corinne. After the children were all grown and had left home, Josephine stayed on as traveling companion and confidante. Douglas Robinson attended to household matters only in a pinch. During one of Corinne's absences from the city, she asked him to interview a prospective butler, but he treated it as a joke. After putting the applicant through "the catechism as far as I know it," Douglas hired him, not because he seemed particularly qualified but because he had a "large, good ample figure like mine."

In 1894, a dozen years into their marriage, Corinne persuaded Douglas to give up the house in Manhattan and make Orange their principal home. Economy was offered as the main reason—since they could rent out the city house—but Douglas was making more money than ever before, so that hardly explains the change. More likely it was Corinne's preference. Elliott had just died, leaving Corinne with many bad memories of his last weeks, and Aunt Anna Gracie had also died. With Bamie living in London, and Theodore and Edith in Washington, Corinne had little reason to spend much time in Manhattan.

The area surrounding the Robinson estate was still rural enough to offer a restful oasis in the mid-1890s. Yet it was close enough to New York for easy commuting. Douglas could take a short train ride and then a ferry across the Hudson to his office in lower Manhattan. The four Robinson children thrived in the country, and they later tied some of their best childhood memories to the New Jersey house and grounds. When the pond froze, they skated (but never as well as their mother), and after they tired themselves out gliding across the ice, they gathered in the house's great hall, where Corinne poured tea and provided everyone present with a copy of whatever Shakespeare play she happened to be reading at the time. In milder seasons the big stable furnished horses for everyone who wanted to ride. Douglas and Corinne, both extraordinarily good riders, often led the pack and instructed their children about horses.

A tireless and dramatic teacher, Corinne devised rigorous lessons for her children. Map in hand, she would lead them up a very small ladder on the third floor of the house and out onto a flat roof where she instructed them to lie on their stomachs and study the stars. On Sunday mornings she permitted no activities to interfere with church. The whole family piled into a large yellow wagon, called a "Democrat," to go to services. Afterward they walked home so that James, the driver, could have the day off. Corinne, who was as devout as her aunt Anna Gracie had been, taught Sunday school, telling the Bible stories in such graphic detail that Corinney later admitted she could not even bear to hear about the crucifixion. Other biblical accounts caused considerable anxiety as well. One Sunday night, when Corinney could not seem to stop crying, her mother inquired the cause, and the girl sobbed, "Moses, poor Moses never saw the Promised Land!"

The children soon learned to recognize how Corinne played both sides of the fence as far as Douglas was concerned. She fueled his jealousy one minute and then swore her devotion to him the next. To illustrate how she sometimes taunted him, Corinney passed on her mother's account of a New Jersey neighbor who was "madly in love" with Corinne and wanted to leave his wife for her. At first Corinne showed no interest in him, but one evening (without a thought to the consequences, she maintained), she agreed to let him drive her home in his buggy after a party. Douglas, who had escorted her that evening, was understandably annoyed, and Corinne impishly told her daughter how she had dealt with him. Arriving home first and undoing her long braids, she "got down on [her] knees and prayed." When Douglas arrived, he did not dare interrupt her nightly religious ritual, and she prolonged her prayers until at last he got into bed, so furious that the bed shook. She remained kneeling and praying, hoping he'd go to sleep, but she had no such luck. Finally, in a big stentorian voice, he said, "Get up from your knees. This is nothing but subterfuge." And she did, to face what she called "the dire wrath of . . . Mars ready to kill."

In spite of such dallying, Corinne went to great lengths to assure Douglas that she wanted to please him. Sometimes she reminded him that she wore a particular bracelet that he had given her because it caused her to think of him. She apologized for being difficult, writing him one spring: "I know that I am very trying at times and irritable too and I too will do my best to be my very best in my own dear home." Too often people are "careless with those who are nearest them," she continued, but she meant to do better: "I value your love deeply and want you to value mine." She begged him to spend more time at home, saying that without him she had little heart to entertain. Then, in a sentence that underlined her enthusiasm and free spirit, she added that she had just given two of her children a driving lesson. They were both under six at the time.

Her honey-coated words and simpering tones camouflaged a strong penchant to go off and do what she wanted. As wife and mother of four, she continued to learn and travel on her own. Music lessons could be taken at home, but art study required trips abroad. During her many trips, she often wrote letters back to Douglas that seemed calculated to arouse his suspicions. While in Italy in 1895, she cautioned her husband not to forget her: "If you do, I will have my revenge by running off with the next archeologist I meet." She had already regaled him with accounts of being shown around the Eternal City by "Mr. Briggs, my attractive, young architect." In guessing the origin of some paintings, she boasted that she was correct more often than he. While her guide tried to "impress deeply upon my mind the beautiful 'sleeping Ariadne,' the 'genius of the

Vatican,' the 'Hermes,' 'Apollo Bevedere,' etc., . . . they really all seemed like old friends any way."

How completely serene Corinne was on that trip remains unclear because she confessed to her husband that she slept through a serious earthquake that shook central Italy. When the quake hit on a Sunday evening, Florence suffered the worst damage, and many people fled their homes for safety. But even in Rome where Corinne was staying, the tremors were felt—but not by her. She had taken a sleeping medication after dinner (fearing that the strong coffee she drank would keep her awake) and only heard about the quake the next day. An acquaintance teased her that he was surprised because he had understood that the "Roosevelts [always remained] wide awake."

Most of Corinne's letters abounded in assurances that she missed Douglas and wished to be with him. During an extended trip to England she complained about her asthma and eczema, especially the latter because, she wrote in words calculated to massage her husband's ego, she feared he would "not find me attractive . . . [and] I love to be attractive to you."

A hard-driving businessman such as Douglas Robinson had little use for such sentimental phrases. For him, money was the name of the game, and he was making plenty of it by the 1890s, even after the nation's economy plunged into a depression beginning in 1893. Operating his real estate agency, Douglas Robinson and Company, out of two offices, he bought and sold some of the city's largest, most prestigious buildings. In discussing his business with Bamie's friend Bob Ferguson, who eventually worked with him for several years, Douglas insisted he would deal only in those buildings in the best locations. He wanted "nothing second cut."

This preoccupation with business is only one explanation as to why Douglas remained on the periphery of Corinne's life. Although they stayed married for thirty-six years, until his death in 1918, she focused most of her emotional energy elsewhere. At least three of the other men who were important in her life entered it before she was forty, and they stayed central for decades. The aesthete Charles Allen Munn, a New Jersey neighbor, gave her priceless art; Henry Cabot Lodge, the Massachusetts senator who was also Bamie's friend, critiqued her writing and took her into his confidence on other matters; Charles Erskine Scott Wood, a Seattle attorney and poet, wrote her long letters and visited her whenever he came east. According to her daughter, Corinne always set aside Wednesday afternoon "whether in Orange or New York" for one man who "loved her all his life." While the children felt a little jealous when their mother's "door was shut," keeping them out, Douglas seems to have tolerated all her male friends.

For other Roosevelts as well, Douglas stayed on the sidelines, called in only on money matters. Bamie sought financial advice from him, both before her marriage in 1895 and afterward. Theodore turned to him on business matters as well as campaign funding. Corinne deferred to him whenever the subject of finances came up. In the early 1900s the Robinsons had toyed with the idea of building a new home at Seventy-first Street and Madison Avenue, but by February 1903, Douglas decided that they could not afford it. Corinne went along with the decision, noting that she much preferred a country home, as she called the New Jersey estate, since she thought the "really best times" were there. In Manhattan they would make do with something already built.

∾

By the beginning of the twentieth century Corinne was entering her mid-years (she turned forty in September 1901) and preparing to remake herself into the confident woman who spoke at the 1920 convention. That decade between 1900 and 1910 actually transformed her life. Theodore's eight years as president pulled her into Washington activities more than ever before, although not so much as they did Bamie who had her own house on N Street. The four Robinson children, all under eighteen in 1900, gradually began going their separate ways, with disappointing and even tragic results, making it all the more imperative that Corinne define a life for herself.

Mothering still took up considerable time, especially since her three sons revealed such different personalities. The eldest, Teddy, who enrolled at Harvard in the same class as Franklin Delano Roosevelt, seemed to think he held the edge on his distant cousin. At least he thought he married better. In 1902, while still a student, he became engaged to Helen Roosevelt, who had matured into a confident young woman since Bamie had looked after her in London.

Helen's wealth, inherited from her mother's family, the Astors, opened many doors for Teddy, but it did little to soften his abrasive personality, and he was never a favorite of his mother.

That spot was reserved for Stewart, her youngest, whom she had named for Mittie's side of the family. With his "very sunny character" and innocent good looks, his "blue eyes and kind of thatched yellow hair," he was already winning more friends than he knew what to do with. Open and generous, he collected homeless dogs around his New Jersey neighborhood, and at one time he admitted to keeping seventeen. At age twelve, when he entered boarding school at St. Paul's, he transferred his recklessness and gaiety to the hockey field, and classmates remembered him as one of the best goalies the school ever had. His parents assumed that he would follow Teddy to Harvard.

The middle two, Corinney and Monroe, presented problems of different kinds, and in March 1902 their mother took an extended trip to England to enroll them in schools there. Corinney would be joining her cousin Eleanor, who was just finishing her third year at Mlle. Souvestre's school, now located just outside London and called Allenswood. Although Corinne had never studied with the formidable Frenchwoman, she knew her and had corresponded with her. The fact that Eleanor seemed to thrive at the school (and would presumably help orient her cousin) added to the attraction of Allenswood.

Monroe, however, would be more difficult to place. Named for Douglas's side, he was now fourteen and showing all the failings that his uncle Elliott had exhibited at the same age. Teachers objected that Monroe had trouble concentrating, and although "very able in his studies," he was "very fractious and short of temper." Corinne understood that he could be difficult, but she wrote to Douglas, "I am filled with yearning tenderness for my boy, yet so anxious, distressed and apprehensive."

Perhaps a fresh start at a British boarding school would do him good, and Corinne selected Harrow. When she arrived there, the headmaster received her warmly, insisting he was pleased to enroll a relative of two American presidents. Although she found the school's sleeping arrangements unhealthy—with three folding beds to a room—she held her tongue, writing to her husband, "Of course I said nothing."

Other aspects of the arrangement concerned her more. Monroe would be with boys much younger than himself "because that's how he tested on paper," and she described herself as "dreadfully afraid" he would not get moved to a higher grade. "Boys he's with are too young to make friends with," she reported. But she had done all she could for him, going into great detail with school authorities about his various health problems, including "his eyes, his tendency to bronchitis, our wishes in case of diphtheria." Even the headmaster, experienced at dealing with concerned parents, was "a little amused—said he had never received such a thorough medical document before."

From Scotland, where she was visiting Douglas's sister after parting from Monroe, Corinne wrote of a conversation where everybody present joined in fantasizing how each of the famous guests might perform at Teddy's wedding. The ceremony would not take place until Teddy graduated from Harvard nearly two years later, but since he was the first in that generation to marry, talk had already started about the event. "The President of the U.S. will be train-bearer to Auntie Bye," Corinne reported. "All the children of the White House headed by Grandmother Robinson as great niece of President Monroe will take the cake! . . . As the bridal couple drive away, Grandma Astor, clad in auburn hair and ropes of pearls, will hurl a heavily jeweled slipper at the bridegroom's head. Stunned by the blow (the slipper was so stunning) he falls into the arms of his beloved and sleeps heavily as is his wont." Corinne had to admit it was all "such nonsense but we had fun over it."

Theodore's prominence as President of the United States opened many doors for Corinne on that six-month trip to England. In London the American minister Henry White arranged for her to meet King Edward, whom Corinne described as "looking very much like Humpty Dumpty" and giving her "Alice in Wonderland's confused feeling about his belt and cravat." Corinne had not yet become used to the fact that her brother was a world figure, and she found it "all so funny" that the King of England inquired about him. To her he was just Theodore.

On her trip home in October, Corinne found that, as sister of the president, she could no longer travel unnoticed. When she had to have a small growth removed from her head, newspapers ran sensational headlines: "The President's Sister in Peril! Since Under the

Knife during her passage!" Much as she disliked the embarrassing publicity, she admitted to her daughter that she enjoyed the flowers that people sent. After landing in New York, she resumed a full schedule at once, covering the bald spot on the back of her head with a big black velvet bow.

Douglas Robinson had already gotten a taste of what it meant to be married to the sister of the President. A few months after taking office, Theodore warned him to stay away from a certain business deal involving government property: "This is one of the penalties that you have to pay for being so unfortunate as to have a brother-in-law in the Presidency." Douglas did not always cheerfully accept the prominence in which his wife's brother placed him. When summoned to Washington to testify as a witness in a libel suit against Joseph Pulitzer, Douglas was described by Corinne as "*very* mad."

Frequent invitations to 1600 Pennsylvania Avenue helped smooth over some of the objections. By November 1902, just weeks after she had returned from England, Corinne and Douglas participated in their first real White House Thanksgiving. Theodore's family had not fully settled in the previous year, so this called for special celebration. The Executive Mansion (now officially renamed the White House) had just reopened after its thorough renovation, and the offices that had taken up half of the second floor had been moved to a new structure just to the west of the residence, freeing up rooms on the second floor for guests.

That holiday stood out in Corinne's memory as exceptionally pleasant despite the fact that two of her children were in England. Nearly two dozen of the clan gathered in Washington, D.C., and the Robinsons stayed at the White House. Even 'Teddy Robinson attended, along with Helen, though it took a special concession from the dean of Harvard to let him leave Cambridge for the weekend, and Stewart made the trip from St. Paul's.

Automobiles had not yet been introduced into the presidential household, and White House residents relied on their own large stable of horses, both for recreational riding and for pulling their carriages. Edith and Theodore made horseback jaunts to Rock Creek Park their favorite afternoon exercise (a habit that Eleanor would also adopt during her White House tenure). During the 1902 visit, Corinne, who was not quite up to her usual energy level after the shipboard surgery, wrote her daughter that she often "stayed in bed till about eleven," while the others went horseback riding: "Such a cavalcade! Uncle Ted, Aunt Edith, Father, . . . Ethel and Archie and Ted." Then the entire party convened at Bamie's house on N Street, and the riders joined them "just as they were, liberally sprinkled with mud."

Thanksgiving dinner in the new State Dining Room was the highlight of the visit. Theodore had imposed his own personal taste by making it look like a hunting lodge, and Corinne approved of the change. She described it as "really a magnificent room, done in superb oak paneling, of fine old tapestries and magnificent moose and deer heads on the walls." At the end of the meal, Cabot Lodge, such a close friend of the family that he and Nannie had been invited to join them, proposed a toast to the President's health. Then, as Corinne described the event to her daughter two thousand miles away, "Aunt Edith proposed [a toast to] 'our absentees' which I drank with a sharp pain in my heart and then Uncle Ted proposed Aunt Edith's health in a pretty little speech." Afterward, the entire group adjourned to the hall for dancing, and "Mr. Bob Fergussy [Ferguson] and Ethel [his goddaughter] cavorted."

As soon as the party ended, Corinne returned to her own responsibilities. Besides the normal family matters associated with Christmas, she had the annual newsboys' dinner to oversee. The event had grown since her father started it decades earlier—an annual celebration to top off his weekly dinners with the orphaned boys. Theodore Sr. became a hero to the newsboys, but in the next generation it was the women who oversaw the part of the Children's Aid Society that helped the "newsies." After 1900, hawking newspapers would gradually change in personnel and fewer of the boys who did that work were orphans, but in 1902 the party was still a big event. More than one hundred boys attended, prompting Corinne to write her daughter that it was "the largest dinner we have ever had, and oh! how they ate!" Twenty-year-old Eleanor "gave out the candy."

After New Year's, Corinne returned to Washington and attended the various White House receptions typically given during that season to honor various government leaders. Through the ritual and protocol she picked up amusing details and recounted them to her daughter. One letter described the effect of seeing the wife of newly appointed Secretary of the Treasury Leslie Mortier Shaw from

Iowa—"the most enormous creature you have ever seen"—standing between "lovely, refined looking Aunt Edith and . . . tiny little Mrs. Knox," wife of Attorney General Philander Chase Knox. "She looked like a vulgar elephant," Corinne reported. Mrs. Shaw's unfortunate appearance, enough to render her "perfectly impossible," was underlined by poor social skills. When the President introduced her to Owen Wister, whose novel *The Virginian* had just come out and who, Corinne explained, "naturally thinks his name rather well known at the moment," Mrs. Shaw blurted out: " 'I don't remember names very well, Mr. Worcester, but I shan't forget yours on account of the sauce!' " Corinne judged the gaffe "good enough for inclusion in *Punch*," the popular magazine.

One story that Corinne did not relay concerned herself. While standing in the receiving line greeting guests, a man approached who had first met her in the Dakotas more than a dozen years earlier when she went there with Bamie and Theodore. He could hardly believe that this elegant matron was the same woman he had seen on the ranch, and he blurted out: "I'll never forget how you wrestled that calf to the ground."

White House parties had a special excitement about them, even for a seasoned hostess such as Corinne Robinson, and she described for Corinney a "brilliant evening" that included dancing in the East Room. Edith came in for some high praise, both as First Lady and as energetic pacesetter. It is true that Corinne was not yet her normally rigorous self, but she marveled at Edith's stamina. The two women had taken a French lesson and then gone for a walk that triggered an asthma attack in Corinne. Trying to hide her discomfort and fatigue during this one time that she lagged behind Edith, Corinne struggled to keep up but found Edith "strong as a horse." Finally, after three hours of steady walking, the marathon session ended, with Corinne completely exhausted. "I sank on my sofa and had to take whiskey," she admitted to Corinney, "and could hardly drag myself later into my clothes to go to a dinner." She could console herself that the dynamic Bamie was also slowing down. Although still holding forth in her salon on N Street, she appeared "pretty official, but not," Corinne added perceptively, "as much so . . . as usual."

Corinne's extended visits to Washington revealed how tiring high political office could be. After observing her brother in the presidency, she concluded that he had been "very bright and well when I first arrived," but then the responsibilities of the job weighed on him; by the time she left ten days later, "he seemed pretty well hectored and tired." Even so, he never wavered on wanting a second term—or, in this case, an entire term of his own since he had come into the White House to complete the term of the murdered William McKinley.

Part of Theodore's popularity with the common folk resulted from his firm stand on big corporations. At the time he took office, more and more American businesses were merging, forming giant corporations that Congress had not yet found a way to regulate. In 1902 he ordered the Justice Department to bring suit against one of the largest, the Northern Securities Company, which the previous year had put the Great Northern, the Northern Pacific, and other smaller railroads under one umbrella of control. The merger itself had been accompanied by considerable anxiety—even panic—among shareholders and the general public alike, and the President's strike against the railroad giant got him plenty of attention. Just how deep Theodore's anti-business streak went remained the subject of debate for generations of historians, but he received good press at the time. In 1904 he was a shoo-in for reelection, winning 56 percent of the popular vote and more than double his opponent's vote in the electoral college.

When time came to plan the March 1905 inauguration, he insisted on making it a family celebration. Months in advance, Edith wrote Corinne that the President wanted her to stay at the White House during the festivities. Mindful that Bamie might expect to host the Robinsons on N Street, Edith prepared the ground carefully and then informed Corinne: "I have just seen Bamie and she has waived her claim." What Edith failed to do was secure enough tickets so that all the Robinson children got seats, too, and Corinne was so bitter about the oversight that she lashed out at everyone—even Bamie. Only through the intervention of Nannie Lodge did Corinne manage to accommodate everyone. Even then, she did not forget the episode, and years later she still smarted from the oversight. Why Franklin and Eleanor, now happily engaged and slated to marry a few days later in New York, got prized seats while her own boys did not remained inexplicable to her.

Corinne's pique never seems to have been directed at Theodore. Indeed, throughout his presidency she supported him in ways that most people had no way of knowing. For instance, in one small but revealing gesture she endorsed Theodore's 1901 invitation to the noted educator Booker T. Washington to dine at the White House, the first person of color to be so honored since Reconstruction. A furor erupted immediately, with several southern newspapers excoriating the President for "defiling" the White House. One especially irate southerner charged that 1600 Pennsylvania Avenue was so cheapened that even "the rats have taken refuge in the stable." Corinne, whose views on race were doubtless as complicated as her brother's, later entertained Washington in her New York home. Whether the subject of Roswell, Georgia, came up that day has not been recorded, but Corinne clearly underlined Theodore's strike against bigotry.

As for any influence on important questions that Theodore faced, Corinne's record is difficult to document. Like Bamie, she refused to flaunt her access to the President, and she seemed determined to obscure any part in his administration. But the evidence mounts bit by bit that she helped sway him on some matters. Both sisters had enthusiastically supported his political career from the beginning, and by the time he became governor of New York, he used their homes as his headquarters in the city. When he left Albany to go to Washington, D.C., as vice president in 1901, he wrote Corinne, "Haven't *we* had fun being Governor of New York State?"

Corinne and Douglas had accompanied Theodore to the nominating convention in 1900 when he agreed to run on the Republican national ticket. On September 22, 1901, Corinne and Bamie went with their husbands to dine with him the very first night after he moved into the White House. The date would have been the seventieth birthday of the elder Theodore Roosevelt, and it seemed appropriate that his only surviving children would make a special effort to join together on a day that mixed personal celebration with fond memories.

During Theodore's presidency, Corinne frequently visited Washington, but most of her contacts with him were informal and unrecorded. No one could hear what they discussed as they toured the gardens or went horseback riding in Rock Creek Park. Her relationship with her brother was so easy and comfortable that she showed little awe of him, whether she saw him in the White House or elsewhere. In the letters she wrote him, she blithely mixed personal news with politics, aesthetic judgment with foreign affairs, as though they all weighed equally on her mind.

After his death, when she wrote a biography called *My Brother Theodore Roosevelt*, she did admit that she had suggested names of people he might wish to invite to the White House, "or at least I ask[ed] him to see them." On one matter she confessed to direct intervention. During a trip to Puerto Rico, which had been administered by the United States since the Spanish-American War, she became convinced that one of the American officials there should be removed. On her return to New York she telegraphed her brother for an appointment, and he set one up for a few days later in his office in the West Wing. After listening carefully to her arguments, he acted, she reported with satisfaction, and "with one strong stroke effaced that name from official connection with Puerto Rico forever."

The final months of Theodore's presidency began well enough in 1909. As usual, Corinne went to Washington for the round of parties in January, which she found all the more exciting that year since it would presumably be the last. Her brother's term ended on March 4, and he had already announced plans for a long hunting trip in Africa with his son Kermit, to be followed by a grand tour of European capitals with Edith. But the last days of Theodore's presidency were suddenly marred by news that would permanently change Corinne's life.

∽

On Sunday morning, February 23, Corinne received a message from officials at Harvard. Her son Stewart was dead. He had attended a party on Saturday night and then returned to his dormitory near Harvard Square at about 2 A.M., but a few hours later he had fallen from his fourth-floor room to the street below. His body was mangled so badly that his mother would not be permitted to view it.

The college officials treated the death as entirely accidental, and his mother apparently accepted that verdict. Many people could not help but wonder, though, how a young man could fall out of a window if he was both sober and healthy. Years later, in an interview she gave authors Hermann and Mary Hagedorn, Stewart's sister Corinney repeated the sanitized version: Stewart had simply hit his head in his room, become dizzy or lightheaded, and then, losing his balance, toppled from the wide ledge that rimmed the fourth floor. There was "no problem, no difficulties, no anything."

Corinney's son, the columnist Joe Alsop, gave a more credible account, conjecturing that the fall resulted from an attempt to duplicate the opening scene in *War and Peace*. In Tolstoy's novel, several wealthy young men gathered together and bet each other on who among them could out-drink the others. The special challenge they set for themselves involved drinking an entire bottle of rum while seated precariously on a high window ledge, legs dangling over the side. In the book, the young man who tries it actually succeeds and no one is hurt, perhaps an incentive to fun-loving Stewart to try to equal the feat.

Whatever happened that night, Stewart fell to his death just days before he would have celebrated his twentieth birthday. Like most of the women in her family, Corinney had trouble recognizing the signs of alcohol abuse, especially in someone she loved. Stewart had been a favorite, his life full of promise, and his engagement was imminent to a young woman with whom he "was very much in love." She could not imagine why he would want to risk his life in such a manner.

His mother's reserve of strength shattered at Stewart's death. For months afterward she would burst into tears at mealtimes or whenever some object or comment brought him to mind. Bamie's daughter-in-law, who met Corinne a dozen years after Stewart's death, recalled that her eyes still welled up at the sight of Bamie's son because he reminded her so much of her own. Corinne looked for solace in writing poetry, a source of comfort ever since she had penned her first poem in Dresden, but she failed to refocus on life. The oft-quoted family motto "Live for the living and not the dead" seemed utterly inadequate in the face of this tragedy, and she found herself powerless to muster the energy to move on. In late November 1909, after overseeing Corinney's wedding, she reluctantly started out on a trip around the world, escorted by Douglas and Monroe. Before sailing, she picked out Stewart's headstone, but the chore so depleted her spirit that she confessed to her daughter: "Everything seems to have gone out of my life." Nothing seemed to matter, and even the prospect of a trip to the Orient failed to distract her.

Sailing out of New York on the *Dampfer Konig Albert*, the person whom Corinne most wanted as her companion—Corinney—

could not join her. Soon after she went aboard, Corinne wrote her, "To part with you was laceration. I could hardly stand it, but I am going to come home to you strong and well." Corinne reminded her daughter that she had not wanted to make the trip, scheduled to take more than six months, but she hoped that Douglas and Monroe would benefit from it even if she did not. Her family had always found refuge in travel, partly because it exposed them to new people, and this crossing offered the chance to be with "pleasant people with whom I had no aching memories in common." More important, she got away for the holidays: "I do not think I could have stood Christmas at home. We always made so much of it and every tender association with my 'Beloved' is particularly strong."

Corinne's thoughts inevitably turned toward home, especially to her newly married daughter. If Corinney suspected she might be pregnant, she should avoid long rides, her mother warned, because "a motor trip might not be the right thing for you." In case of doubts she should "consult Auntie Bye, [because] she is very wise and not too nervous, except," Corinne added pointedly, "about Sheffield."

During the first stop in Italy, Corinne compared this trip, in the company of her dull husband and son, to other trips she had made on her own. Neither of the men cared "about art or the kind of things that other people might make a study of to pass time away," she complained. When Douglas did accompany his wife on her art expeditions, he made perfectly clear that he would have preferred being elsewhere. "You know how he is when he gets on land!" Corinne explained. Monroe was little help. He went off to Capri with a young woman he had just met, not even stopping to pack an overnight bag: "Wasn't that exactly like him?"

In the early stages of the trip, Corinne feared she would have to turn back because of a skin problem. What started out as a "horrid spot" on her face developed into a "thick lump," and she had it "burned" off while on board ship. In Naples she followed up with minor surgery, but she feared "permanent disfigurement." Only when doctors assured her that she ran no serious risk did she proceed, and she was soon convinced she had made the right decision. Sailing past Port Said on December 20, Corinne wrote: "This boat is like a yacht, beautifully kept. . . . Our apartments are deliciously luxurious."

She saw Mt. Sinai, "with its three peaks . . . like a chameleon as it reflected each color of the sunset," and she persuaded Monroe to accompany her up to the bridge, where she read Omar Khayyam, the Persian poet, aloud to him "and he loved it."

In India her spirits picked up a bit as well. She remembered her brother Elliott and the thrill he found traveling there three decades earlier. "Many of his interesting letters came back to me with full force," she wrote Eleanor, his daughter. "India has interested me more than I can say. Its myriad nationalities, its varied religions, its beautiful tombs and temples and at Darjuling, its grand impressive scenery have all inspired one's imagination." The Taj Mahal so impressed her that she could not see enough of it. Some days she made more than one pilgrimage: "I saw it early in the morning, at noon, at sunset, at the full moon and each time it seemed more beautiful." For hours at a time, she sat in the garden "drinking it in and absorbing it."

In Calcutta the Robinsons enjoyed the luxury of the Government House, since the British were only too happy to host the sister of the former president. But Corinne felt detached from what went on around her. She had the same impersonal feeling, she wrote home, that she had experienced at the White House. It always felt as though one were lodging in a luxurious hotel. Finally, she caught sight of the Himalayas, which had been covered in clouds for days but then came out of the mist for the two days that Corinne was able to see them.

Toward the end of February, Corinne's spirits began to sag. Part of her weariness no doubt resulted from her health because, at nearly forty-nine, she was menopausal. To her daughter she wrote a few months later: "I know I am nervous and restless and irritable but you must forgive me darling. . . . I would gladly be more satisfactory if I had more self-control. I am trying to have it, but all doctors agree that just at this special moment in a woman's life it is the one thing one loses."

Monroe also gave her reason to worry. The staid entertainment of his parents' generation did not satisfy him, and he sought out the younger crowds in each of the cities they visited. Cut off from the restraining influences of his home base and people who knew him, he overindulged in alcohol and then behaved badly. In Calcutta he ended up in an incident that embarrassed his parents more than they cared to admit or ever fully describe. Such behavior continued throughout the trip, much to Corinne's disappointment.

In China, President William Howard Taft's letter of introduction got the Robinsons more VIP treatment. Corinne wrote from Peking on March 28 that her party had received a "semi official" welcome, including a private audience at the Winter Palace and a full day's use of the Summer Palace: "All the high muck a mucks of the Foreign Office with their lovely pigtails and beautiful tasseled caps and brocaded gowns received us there while a special regiment (brought out for the occasion, I think) saluted and everything was very elegant indeed!!" In the Chinese capital she saw a newspaper article about the engagement of Ted Roosevelt, Theodore's eldest, but "disbelieved" it until a friend of the family showed her a letter Edith had written him, confirming the engagement and describing a "pink cloud of happiness for the two young people."

Corinne's spirits continued to yo-yo. During one portion of the trip she met a group of "able, agreeable Englishmen" who brightened her days considerably. They offered intellectual stimulation that neither Douglas nor Monroe could manage, and Corinne felt more alive: "I am more vital again—for my dormant intellect has been aroused." Then signs of a new season brought back the old sadness in full force. The spring leaves and flowers reminded her of Stewart, the "incarnation of youth and Spring to me, and I cannot believe that there will never be Spring for me again."

Corinne mused about how Stewart would have responded to the new sights and people she was seeing. She wrote from Japan that she felt sure he would have seen right through Douglas's flowery ovations to Chinese and Japanese officials. The boy would probably have imitated his father and her own "perpetual Cheshire cat smile! I can see him do it." Such thoughts no doubt compounded her grief, and sometimes she judged the trip too exhausting to continue. Sightseeing she could manage, but the social events included reminiscence. They made "the happy days at Washington, before the sunshine went, too clear to me again. [They] made me ill." She might have buried her grief if she had attended more cultural events, such as the plays she enjoyed seeing in Japan, but Douglas and Monroe were both bored by such events, and their reluctance deterred her from going.

By the time the Robinsons reached Korea, all three of them were ready to head home. Corinne got the flu in Seoul and saw little of the city. Monroe's drunken bouts had left him ill, and he suffered recurring sore throats and other ailments that Corinne continued to attribute vaguely to his "poisoned" system. Douglas, who had maintained his usual robust appearance, was disgusted with descriptions of himself in local newspapers as a " 'very large man with a red face.' "

Their original plans left open the exact route of return to America. One version had them traveling through Europe, spending Holy Week in Rome, where they would meet the King and Queen of Italy at the Quirinale and the Pope at the Vatican. The alternate plan had them sailing across the Pacific to California. From there they would proceed to the East Coast. Fatigued and weary of sightseeing, Corinne wanted to get back as quickly as possible to New Jersey, where she hoped the whole clan, including Bamie and her family, would be waiting to welcome them. At the same time she dreaded the idea of returning to the house, full as it was of so many memories of Stewart. Since she had been gone more than six months, she would have to employ and train a new roster of servants—or, as she put it, "have a new household." To her friend Cabot Lodge she wrote, "I both long and dread to get home, the home which can never again be what it was. Oh! Cabot, the pain!"

The Robinsons opted to miss the pomp of Rome and take the quickest journey home, across the Pacific and over land to the East Coast. Back in New Jersey by early June 1910, Corinne set about the tasks that her long absence had piled up for her, and she tried to be strong. It had now been more than a year since Stewart's death, and she understood that her friends expected her to resume a full schedule. She accepted their invitations, and after one party she confided to her daughter: "I longed for you and for Stewart . . . but I danced . . . and tried to give them the feeling that I was happy too."

In addition to her grief, Corinne had increasing problems with her health. Arthritis had begun to cripple her right hand ten years earlier, but now it reappeared, and she had to scratch out letters with her left hand. A dedicated letter writer and poet, she had to face up to the fact that most people could not decipher her scrawl even when she struggled hard to make the letters clear. Her eyes bothered her, too, and she began to fear that she would lose her vision.

Yet the next few years turned into some of the most productive in her life. Gradually, she worked her way out of the initial period of deep, incapacitating grief. Stewart's death still carried its ache, but neither the trauma nor the health problems could silence her. In fact, she came back stronger than ever before, regrouping her energies to publish and speak herself into national celebrity status.

III

B ALANCING ALL THE parts of her life did not come easily, even to someone with the money, stamina, and contacts of Corinne Roosevelt Robinson. She had to find time for Douglas as well as her many friends—and keep some energy for herself, especially her speaking and writing. Not all of it would have been possible, Corinney joked, had her mother not been superbly organized—and she had, of course, the very best paid help.

Theodore still claimed his share of lively attention, and the fact that he continued to play an important political role after his presidency ended in 1909 drew her into politics, too. She joked with Corinney about going to Oyster Bay "to consult the 'Big Stick.'" Whenever she could, she lunched with Theodore, and after one such meeting in 1911, she called it the "kind I like best in the world." He had talked frankly with her about an article he had written on the harmful effect of business monopolies and trusts, even admitting that he would be loudly criticized for his stand, but he insisted on expressing his convictions. In spite of everything he was, Corinne wrote Corinney, "as full of that wonderful vigor and life as ever, and so loving and dear."

As the election of 1912 approached, Corinne followed events closely. Theodore had never really reconciled himself to the fact that he would never be president again, and now that his party was in disarray, many of his fellow Republicans began turning to him as their best hope. In January, several months before the nominating convention, Corinne and Douglas were guests of Cabot and Nannie Lodge in Washington, where the talk inevitably turned to the upcoming race. As Corinne explained to her daughter, the four of them "sat by the Library fire and talked of many things. Mr. Lodge feels that the great sentiment for Uncle Ted is like a river at present, held in by its banks but that if an extra hard rain (any open move in other words) came that it would flood the whole country and become unmanageable."

Corinne weighed that prediction against what Theodore had told her about his availability: "I am not a candidate, I don't want to be a candidate. I *won't* be a candidate, but I also *won't* say anything which would make it impossible for me to serve my country, if a situation arose which seemed to demand my services." In other words, he would accept a draft. Apparently the presidency had lost a bit of its glamour for him—or, as she described it, "he had had it."

As the spring progressed and Theodore came closer to running, Corinne stayed very involved, and the decision to run as a candidate for the splinter Progressives, the Bull Moose Party, was made at her Manhattan house. Theodore had been there "constantly," she wrote Corinney. One day she gave both a tea and a dinner for him, describing the tea as "very amusing and quite like Washington—scientists, artists, and literateurs were cheek by jowl with hobble skirts and headless fashion . . . each much flattered by being with the other." The former President had gotten into a "delicious discussion" on the subject of art with the noted painter George de Forest Brush. As Corinne described it: "The latter darling and irrelevant elderly child of the paint pot had . . . combated Uncle Ted to the last ditch."

The tea served as prelude to the dinner that followed: "I had to sweep out the last guests and hurry to dress for my dinner [where] we had good political talk [and] some story telling." A less energetic person might have called it quits after such a hectic evening, choosing to sleep late the next morning, but Corinne was up early, ready to hold forth at the breakfast table. Guests included her childhood friend Frances Parsons and a history professor who led all those present, including Theodore and Corinne, in a lively discussion of "Serb poetry and intricate details of Balkan character and history." In the afternoon she accompanied Theodore to the Three Acts Club, where he spoke, and then she "took him to a wonderful loan exhibition of paintings at [the gallery] Knoedlers and we spent a quiet evening together." With difficulty she limited herself to four evenings out each week.

It would be tempting to read these exuberant accounts of moving in Theodore's world as evidence that Corinne's life otherwise lacked color and interest. But that would be wrong. In one of her regular letters to her daughter, she reported that she had done the usual charity work, visited a new grand nephew (the baby of the Ted Roosevelts, whom she had found "just a bundle of energy"), heard Enrico Caruso perform in the opera *Pagliacci,* and lectured on her travels. Another dinner for Theodore was just part of the week.

Corinne's circle of friends reached beyond Theodore to people she cultivated on her own. One of the most persistent was her friend from Seattle, Charles Erskine Scott Wood, a man who defies categories (or easy description) because he combined such disparate interests. Nine years her senior, Wood had graduated from West Point and served a brief stint in the army before settling down to a successful career as an attorney in Portland, Oregon. On September 24, 1890, when Corinne first met him, she was twenty-nine, the mother of four, and traveling through the West with a small party that included her sister and her husband. Charles Wood was equally settled into an apparently proper, stable family, with wife and children, but his debonair style and dark, good looks (his son credited him with being both "handsome and brilliant") made him attractive to many women.

Like Corinne, Charles Wood's interests ran a wide gamut. Successful as an attorney, he took time out to paint and write poetry, even keeping a little hideaway studio across the street from his law office so he could escape for a few minutes of writing or art. Not that he needed solitude to work; he had a reputation for being able to compose just about anywhere—on horseback, in a rough tent, or driving across the country. He loved the desert, and his long poem "The Poet in the Desert" makes clear why: the flat, empty landscape gave him peace while it highlighted a favorite subject of Wood's: man's misuse of land and water around the globe.

An original in many ways, Charles Wood railed against the restrictions that government put on human freedom, and he chose inventive, satiric forms in which to vent his wrath. His irreverent attitude is best revealed in a book he wrote toward the end of his life, *Heavenly Discourse* (1927). In invented conversations between God and others (including Jesus, Hitler, and the transcendentalist author Margaret Fuller), Wood makes clear what he thinks about mankind's pathetic attempts to improve on what began (and should have remained, in his opinion) a beautifully simple and infinitely open universe. One after another Wood takes on prohibition, marriage, censorship, and other topics, making each one a ridiculously wrongful intrusion on human freedom.

That people as different as Charles Wood and Corinne Robinson could have connected in a significant way supports his claim that some relationships elude explanation. In July 1913, after she told him how much she valued his comments on her poetry, he replied that words are "perfectly inadequate to express the subtle understanding of what, for lack of a better word, we call 'SOULS.'" Something happens between people, "between souls that understand; not knowing why they understand, and not able to express what they understand."

Moving on to a subject that evidently concerned him a great deal, considering the vehemence with which he attacked it, Wood defended the idea of "free love." To his way of thinking, "really and truly down in the essence of things, love always is free," and "neither church, nor state, nor marriage, nor society has ever succeeded in chaining or controlling love." This particular letter was dictated to the train stenographer on a cross-country trip, one of the few instances where the motion made writing difficult for Wood, and he could not resist having a little fun with one of the stenographer's spelling errors. The word "mistressicies" (for what should have been "mysteries") was a "good word," Wood penned in using his trademark green ink, "but not mine."

Leaving no doubt how misguided he judged those people who tied themselves to marriage vows under the misapprehension that they were acting morally, Wood pronounced such conduct "infinitely shocking and immoral." People should not go through life "rigidly stifling the most tremendous call in them" in order to obey what they considered "a higher duty to home and children." Physical love was "everywhere transitory," from the smallest creature to human beings, because "nature made it fickle." To pretend otherwise was naïve and could lead only to disappointment.

How much Corinne Robinson and Charles Wood saw of each other, and exactly how intimate their relationship was, remains unclear. His son described their relationship, which lasted four decades, as a "literary and poetical love affair." Charles's penciled note of February 14, 1899, making some disparaging comments about Corinne's husband and then asking her to be his "Valentine," suggests that the two communicated easily across the twenty-five hundred miles that separated them. He sometimes came east to argue cases before the Supreme Court, to handle other business, or to see his son who went to school in the East, and he always made a point of seeing Corinne. On one occasion Douglas Robinson returned home to find them reading romantic poetry to each other, but rather than object, he erupted in loud laughter at their sentimental tones.

When Wood was detained in Minnesota and could not join her at her summer retreat, he wrote how much he would prefer to be with her, then added, "but I do not remember that I have ever done anything in my life that I wanted to do. . . . I am tenaciously cherishing the hope of a few days with you when we can really talk." He addressed her as "Sappho," "Dearest Sappho," or "Friend of my Heart" and asked her repeatedly to be his "Valentine." He thought so highly of her that, invited to one of her dinner parties and warned that other guests would look askance at the ruffled shirt he always wore, he went out and bought a starched one, the only one he ever owned.

∞

Besides the "poetic and literary love affair" with Wood, Corinne had other reasons to write poetry. She had always enjoyed stringing words together, at least since the days on Cooper's Bluff when her family had vied among themselves for the cleverest verse, and now she turned seriously to the idea of publishing her work. Like the cartoons that her father and brother sketched to delight friends and relatives, her verse was often light and witty, zeroing in on what made an individual special or unique. In 1907, while visiting Edith Wharton's home, The Mount, in Lenox, Massachusetts, Corinne tried out some of her poems on the other guests, a group the hostess praised as being "a discriminating public." Wharton, then at the peak of her success, having just published *House of Mirth* in 1905, cheered Corinne on, assuring her that she saw "elements of popular success" in what she heard.

With that encouragement, Corinne continued writing poetry, and in August 1911, *Scribner's* published "The Call of Brotherhood." She sent a copy of the magazine to Wharton, who wrote back that the "verses have a fine militant ring and swing, a good marching rhythm, not always an easy thing to achieve in irregular metre." At one point Wharton commented, "The movement seems to me particularly good." But Wharton respected Corinne enough to go beyond simple praise. Some of the words seemed "rather flat and anti-climaxy." Where Corinne had written "The baby who pulls at the breast," Wharton objected: "The milkless, feared pampered baby has had more done for him in literature than in life, and I think the poem would have gained if he had been suggested rather than described in detail."

Corinne's first volume of poetry, *The Call of Brotherhood,* was published in 1912, only three years after Stewart's death, so it is not surprising that it included several poems about that tragic event. When she wrote about the day he died, she titled the poem "Feb. 21, 1909," and began it: "This was the day I died, when all Life's sun / Was blotted out in dark and dreadful night." On the third anniversary of his death she mused: "Can it be true the triple years have passed / With dull and laggard steps above your head. . . ." In one poem she begged for the chance to look into his blue eyes once more, and in another she admitted how much she had suffered: "Pain, the Interpreter, has seared my soul."

One friend who helped her through that painful period was Cabot Lodge, whose own son, Bay, died just seven months after Stewart, following a winter that was, Corinne later wrote Cabot, the "last of our lives." Only twenty-seven years old and apparently healthy, Bay Lodge had become ill while vacationing with his father at the family's summer home in Massachusetts and died within hours. In shock and grief, Cabot wrote to Corinne on September 3, 1909, that he felt as though "a portion of my life has been torn away." He had written hardly anyone, but a letter from her encouraged him to write back. In signing the long handwritten letter, he eschewed his usual reserve. To "Ever, dear Corinne," he was "Yrs, H C Lodge."

When the two first met, through Theodore and Bamie, Corinne was a young wife and mother, but Cabot, eleven years her senior, had already racked up the kind of wunderkind achievements that so appealed to the Roosevelts. After graduating from Harvard, he earned a law degree there and then one of the first doctorates ever granted by the college in political science—all by the age of thirty. While writing heavy tomes of history, Cabot also taught Harvard undergraduates, including Theodore who did not immediately take a liking to the brilliant instructor only eight years older than himself. The relationship between the two men eventually warmed as their positions in life evened out, and their correspondence provided material for two volumes, which Cabot published after Theodore's death.

Since Corinne and Douglas began seeing the Lodges socially in the early 1890s, she had engaged in her own correspondence with the senator, frequently about Theodore. Cabot had warned her then that Theodore needed loyal friends because "his public friends abuse him." In 1912, when the relationship between the two men soured after Cabot chaired the Republican convention that ruled against Theodore's delegates, she stayed close to them both. Later, she worked hard to restore the friendship between them.

But Cabot was far more to her than her brother's friend. Although never a resident of the state Cabot represented, Corinne followed his career as avidly as anyone from Massachusetts. She clipped newspaper articles on his speeches and sent them to him, and he responded with full manuscripts of his talks, noting those too lengthy to get into the newspapers in their entirety. He was pleased when she complimented him or recognized the source of some obscure quotation. The normally aloof senator did not reveal his emotional side to very many people, but when his mother died in 1900, he shared the enormity of the loss with Corinne, admitting, "It is a heavy blow to bear. A great loyal unquestioning love has gone out of my life and there is blankness and silence in its place."

During Theodore's presidency, Cabot and Nannie Lodge moved among the Roosevelts almost as though they were family. In the U.S. Senate since 1893, Cabot had long been one of the most important Republicans in the capital, and Nannie was one of the most popular hostesses. Theodore and Bamie had agreed long before that this was one couple in which both parties merited inclusion in their "salon" of witty, bright people.

As with Charles Wood, just how intimate Corinne became with Cabot remains unclear, the details muddied by time and by the discretion of the principals and the people closest to them. But their letters show that this friendship matured into one of the most important of Corinne's life, especially after each had suffered the death of a son. Cabot could drown himself in Senate work while Corinne started on her trip around the world, but the correspondence between them never stopped. She let him know that her spirits had picked up in India, where the sights "seemed to wake up my dormant brain and I was able to read and study a little again, an effort which, for a year, had been impossible." He filled her in on enough political news for her to realize what a difficult time he was having. Lacking information from "behind the scenes," she hesitated to criticize but did volunteer that things looked "very unsatisfactory just from a party outlook" for the Republicans in 1910. President Taft, handpicked for candidacy by Theodore, had been a disappointment, and Theodore, off hunting wild game in Africa, would have to come home and shape things up. Corinne sympathized with her brother's desire to stay away as long as possible but admitted that Edith Roosevelt had a point when she "aptly" remarked to Corinne, "He cannot remain permanently in exile on account of political reasons."

After Corinne started writing serious poetry, she sent the results to Cabot for comment and criticism, just as she had to Wood. Cabot encouraged her but regretted that the same outlet for grief did not serve him. In January 1911 he complimented her on having "a gift of saying what is in your heart. . . . I often have so much in my heart and then I cannot say it. The right words will not come." The mighty senator, whom historians have judged erudite and egotistical, showed a pathetic vulnerability to Corinne. He insisted to her that while he cared little for what the general public thought of him, he needed the approval of people who counted—like herself: "Your love, your sympathy I know are mine whatever may befall but it means more to me than you realize to find that you approve me, that you are proud of me for you would not say it unless you were." He shared family disappointments with her, including the fact that he did not care much for the woman that his second son had just married.

Corinne sought very specific advice from Cabot. In the summer of 1913 she wrote a poem, "One Woman to Another," that was really directed to her daughter, Corinney. It dealt with how both mother and daughter had been unable to intervene in their brothers' deaths—Elliott's in 1894 and Stewart's fifteen years later—although it completely sidestepped the role of alcohol in each instance. Corinne solicited Cabot's impression of the poem, saying she "would be glad of any criticism or suggestion. Do you like 'years' or 'days' in the first line?"

In May 1916 she wrote Cabot a long letter, enclosing one poem, "Uriel," which had already been accepted by *Scribner's,* and another one, "The Last Leaf in Spring," which she had not yet submitted for publication. A bit tentative about whether or not any magazine would want it, she predicted it was "too long for their favor," but she hoped Cabot approved: "Tell me frankly if you do or not." When he encouraged her, she was "emboldened" to submit it to *Scribner's,* and "they took it at once."

Besides Cabot and Charles Wood, Corinne continued to seek help from other critics, including Edith Wharton who went over Corinne's poems, suggesting word changes and commenting on cadence. Wharton never sugarcoated her judgments, and in one letter she reminded "O Poetess" that "it is not permitted to split an infinitive, and I have ventured to put a faint protesting pencil mark against a dismembered one."

For all their sharpness, Wharton's comments could not help but encourage Corinne to write. It gave too much pleasure to stop. As Wharton wrote on June 9, 1912, "I hope you are still writing and writing more and more. . . . Every writer will corroborate . . . that nothing is more blessed. . . . [Writing] is the surest of refuges, and much more than a refuge, and the more one does of it the more absorbing it is."

Much as she enjoyed writing, Corinne continued to take a keen interest in politics and to share that interest with Cabot. The unexpected death of Nannie Lodge in 1915 drew Cabot and Corinne closer together. His wife had suffered some heart problems but seemed well enough during the summer. Then, on an October evening, after dining with her family, she went to her bedroom and died. Cabot and Nannie had been married more than forty years, and although it was common gossip in Washington that she had once had a long, ardent relationship with John Hay, the diplomat and editor, she held her own in her marriage to Cabot. Extremely beautiful and knowledgeable about art and literature, she was one of the few people who could deflate the pompous senator. As he held forth on some topic or another, she sweetly addressed him as "Pinky." Of course Corinne left out most of these details when she wrote a memorial tribute to Nannie for the *Boston Transcript.*

In 1916, Corinne and Cabot joined forces to help defeat their arch-enemy Woodrow Wilson for reelection to the presidency. It is difficult to find a word strong enough to convey the full antipathy that Cabot Lodge felt for the Democratic president. Political differences separated them, of course, but their personalities and approaches to problems were so far apart that civil conversation between them sometimes seemed an impossible goal. After one meeting with Wilson, Cabot's description showed how much he detested him: "I never saw such a spectacle of incompetency, insincerity and utter timidity." Corinne had her own put-down for the "preacher in the White House." She quoted Theodore as saying Wilson's "'ultimatums' do not 'ultimate.'"

At the Republican nominating convention in Chicago that year, Corinne and Cabot spent time together, and afterward he wrote her what a "happiness and a comfort" her company brought him. "You are almost the only person in the world to whom I dare to break down. I think you know what that means to me." But the November election brought a long list of disappointments. The Republican nominee, Charles Evans Hughes, no great hero with either of them but far superior to Wilson in their eyes, lost narrowly. When it looked as though Teddy Robinson, Corinne's eldest, had also failed in his bid for a seat in the New York State Senate (despite Cabot Lodge's having campaigned for him), Corinne wrote Cabot: "Apparently the only certain thing in this strange and disappointing . . . election is the fact that at least you will return to the Senate." She confessed she felt "utterly at sea" until word came that Teddy had also won.

It was a combination of politics and Cabot that pushed Corinne's public speaking career. Her speechmaking grew quickly after 1912, especially during presidential campaigns. Corinne seemed unable to refuse any request, no matter how humble the audience or how distant the location. In November 1916, for example, she made several appearances for Charles Evans Hughes, despite her rather lukewarm feelings about his ability to serve. In just one week she spoke near her home in Orange, took charge of several meetings in Manhattan, and participated in a large rally in Madison Square Garden.

Four years later when she became even more involved in Warren Harding's campaign, she traveled all over the country. Alongside a U.S. senator she spoke at Montclair, New Jersey, and then traveled to upstate New York to address a Women's State Committee luncheon and a rally in Utica, near her summer home. By now she was scheduled by a speakers' bureau, and she boasted to Corinney that she was being sent to "Chicago on Thursday evening." After a week of speaking in "that part of the world," she expected to end up in Ohio at the [candidate's] Front Porch."

In addition to politics, Corinne lectured on other topics. Following her extended trip in 1909–10, she started giving speeches, and gradually her topics grew to include her favorite authors, women in politics, the problems of divorce, her love for her country, and, of course, her brother, Theodore. Nothing seemed to slow her down— not her illnesses, her worries over her son Monroe, or even the death of her husband.

The long, successful speaking career is a significant part of Corinne's achievement for many reasons. She inherited part of her wealth (and married the rest), but the speaking was all her own doing. Perhaps it was just Mittie's independence showing up in a slightly different form. Like her mother, Corinne "talked the talk" of the idealized female standing helpless on the "lady" pedestal, but she showed enormous strength of her own. When she blithely walked to the front of an auditorium or took a radio microphone to address thousands of people, she was on her own, and she was performing in a way that most of her contemporaries—male or female—would have feared trying.

⌒

As much as Corinne considered herself in control of her own life, she must have reeled from the series of deaths that she faced within a few months. In July 1918, Theodore's youngest son, Quentin, was shot down and killed while fighting in France—the first of that generation (except for Stewart) to die. By the fall a huge influenza epidemic was spreading rapidly, and several members of Corinne's family took ill. Although none of them died, the seriousness of the epidemic was underlined by the number of deaths reported all over the nation—far more than had died in the war.

Douglas Robinson did not get the flu, but on September 12, 1918, he died of a heart attack while on the way to join Corinne at Henderson House. The death came as a complete surprise to his family. Douglas had just spent the previous evening with their son-in-law, Joseph Alsop. After dinner at Robinson's club, the two men spent the night at the Robinson house on Sixty-first Street, and the next morning Douglas insisted on accompanying his son-in-law to the station to get his train back to Connecticut. Joe remembered: "He even went through the gates up to my car with me [and] I remember thinking how well he looked." Corinne, whose two remaining sons were fighting in France, had to manage the funeral details herself, assisted, of course, by Corinney. Four months later Theodore, the brother for whom she could never quite find words of adequate praise, died.

Other women might have been silenced by these rapid-fire losses, but Corinne appeared to acquire new resolve. She signed a contract to write a book, *My Brother Theodore Roosevelt*, and the publisher, Scribner's, serialized it in the popular magazine by the same name. Since the total manuscript was written in less than nine months, at a time when the subject's hero halo was still very strong, the book suffers from an overabundance of favorable adjectives and a dearth of realistic appraisal. *The New York Times* reviewer objected that she showed an addiction to "the adjective, especially the adjective of admiration." Another review noted, "Mrs. Robinson loved her brother too well to be a perfect biographer." Most critics admitted that the book's major value was its description of the childhood that Corinne and Theodore shared.

Two years earlier the critics had been kinder. In reviewing her third volume of poetry, *Service and Sacrifice* (a second volume, *One Woman to Another*, appeared in 1914), *Literary Digest* praised her in its monthly column, "Current Poetry." Her writing showed a "distinguished and spirited personality," the *Digest* noted, especially evident in the poems suggested by war occasions. Two of the poems that the *Digest* singled out were hymns of praise for Theodore: "To My Brother" and "Valiant for Truth."

The other two poems of Corinne's that the *Digest* chose to reprint had nothing at all to do with Theodore. "In Bed," which the magazine described as "happily" conveying the "sympathy and imagination of a child's mind," was written in 1917 for the Enfants de la Frontiere, a war relief organization. From a child's point of view, it talks about hearing that other children are cold and hungry—and how a mother's voice at bedtime soothes a child's mind into sleep. The other short poem, "The Old House," was as close as Corinne ever came to acknowledging the impact of her husband's death—or her marriage of thirty-six years. It talks of an "old house on the Hill" that "Has Harbored many a fire / Keen heart and young desire, / All silent now and still."

Literary Digest had already focused on Corinne in its "Current Poetry Section" in 1914. She had always shown charm, the *Digest* noted, but "charm alone never insured a poem's place in literature." Her recent work had gained in "sincerity and power." Most remarkable was the company in which Corinne found herself. She was being included alongside some of the nation's most prominent women writers, including Amy Lowell, Katharine Lee Bates, and Harriet Monroe. The same month that Corinne gave her speech at the Republican convention in Chicago, she was also featured in the magazine *Mentor* in a special issue on "Makers of Modern American Poetry (Women)."

At the same time Corinne's writing was gaining public attention, her friendship with Cabot Lodge intensified. In fact, the relationship warmed considerably following Douglas's death. The tone of their letters changed, becoming more intimate, even though the Senator struggled to explain how his own reserve made it difficult to put into words his feelings for her: "You must know how much you have been to me for a long time, and especially in these later years. My work was simply an expression, not to be avoided, of very strong feeling seldom uttered because I suffer from the reserve of my race very strong—as a New Englander." He had been depressed recently, aware that "one may go over the edge with helplessness and suffering or with the great silence at any moment," and his recent visit with her in New York had given him a boost: "[B]eing with you cleared the clouds, soothed and comforted me.... When I came away and sat in the train, I felt exhilaration, very different from when I came on." He regretted that his Senate work kept them apart: "It is hard that fate should compel me to dwell in a town where you are not and see you only at intervals when I have no time to spare for intervals and so little time remains." A few days later he came back to the same theme in another letter: "I long to see you, to be with you, to talk with you and the Fate which keeps us apart is unkind indeed."

The correspondence between them increased in frequency, as did their visits. In April 1919, Cabot traveled to New York again to spend several days with Corinne, now widowed for six months.

When she went to Washington, she often stayed at his house, and before one of these visits, she wrote Corinney how much she looked forward to the stay. In going "to Cabot for several days," she wrote, "I think that will do me real good."

These visits continued through early 1923, but then something seems to have strained the closeness, though it is not clear exactly what. Perhaps the change resulted from their own physical deterioration. She underwent eye surgery; his health declined. They may have been busier. Cabot was preparing the book of his correspondence with Theodore (which may have caused its own problems between them), and she persisted in requesting favors that he thought she should seek elsewhere. On one occasion when she asked for tickets to a ceremony at the Tomb of the Unknown Soldier, he replied curtly that she should go to her "distinguished nephew," Ted Roosevelt, for such help. He still complied with some requests, sending letters of recommendation for her son Teddy when he went to Mexico and for Corinney when she traveled abroad, but the favors were delivered more in the manner of a responsible senator replying to a constituent than to an old, much loved friend. Still, when he died in November 1924, Corinne wrote a glowing tribute to him that was published in the national magazine *Outlook*.

Cabot Lodge's death came at a particularly low point in Corinne's life because just months earlier she had lost another old friend, Charles Allen Munn. A bachelor whom she had known for years and sometimes traveled with in Europe, he lived just a few minutes' walk from the house at 9 East Sixty-third Street that she moved into after Douglas's death. A year older than Corinne, Munn had been educated in New York and Paris before entering Princeton and then the family business, Munn & Company, that made huge profits in a variety of enterprises. The family's millions permitted him to do just about anything he chose with his life, and he chose to mix erudition and aesthetics. He filled his Manhattan brownstone with valuable Americana, including priceless antiques and portraits by Gilbert Stuart and John Singleton Copley. His father had founded *Scientific American* magazine as a side interest, and Charles Munn spent his professional life editing that highly respected publication. He excelled at tennis, polo, and other outdoor sports, and was on a fishing trip to Scotland in April 1924 when he collapsed and died.

How deeply that death was felt can only be guessed from evidence pieced together later. Among the mourners attending his funeral services in New York, "Mrs. Douglas Robinson" headed the list. An admiring tribute later appeared in *The New York Times* (signed only "C.R.R.") citing his generous spirit and sound judgment in art. Corinne wrote more revealingly to her daughter of the "pain in the loss of a great love."

By the time of Munn's funeral, Charles Wood had already retreated from Corinne, staying in touch with her only sporadically. After he met Sara Field, the woman who became his second wife, his letters to Corinne changed in tone and number. All flirtation gone, as far as Mrs. Robinson was concerned, he referred to his new love as "Sara," in contrast to the "Mrs. Wood" that he had used for his first wife. After discussing his own new book, *Too Much Government*, he boasted of what Sara was writing. When he and Sara traveled abroad—with her sporting documents that identified her as his wife although she was not yet— Corinne sent a strong reprimand, and the bond between her and Charles was weakened.

Even as she lost many of those closest to her, Corinne kept up her public speaking. Following her appearance at the Republican convention, she received more offers than she could accept. During one marathon session in Boston in November 1921, she spoke in the morning to an audience of eighteen thousand and in the afternoon to a teachers' convention. She took time, however, to taxi out to Cambridge for lunch with Bamie's new daughter-in-law, Bobbie. By the time Corinne returned to her hotel, she found Monroe's four-year-old daughter, Dorothy, who greeted her: "Where's your platform, Grandmother?" Corinne could only respond, "Little rogue!"

As long as her health held out, Corinne thrived on public speaking; she found it exhilarating to stand up in front of people and tell them what she thought. She also liked the idea of earning some money on her own. In October 1922, explaining that she had accepted an invitation from Mt. Holyoke College "as it was a paying one," she speculated: "I could make my living (modestly!) if I could accept all the demands." She had inherited $300,000 from Douglas in 1918, but money she earned herself came in a category all its own, an attitude she shared with Eleanor.

Corinne liked being the trailblazer among the Roosevelt women. Edith, her contemporary, had always shown enormous self-confidence in most matters and had compiled an impressive record as First Lady, but she had shied away from speechmaking. So it gave Corinne some satisfaction to have her sister-in-law come to hear her on one occasion and see "the mass of women with their eager faces and quick responses. . . . I think she really liked my speech."

Some appearances were tiring, and in 1923, Corinne admitted to needing a rest on the sofa after speaking at a public school in Brooklyn. Nevertheless, she came away "as usual after about two hours and a half . . . thrilled." The school, located in what Corinne described as the "largest Jewish community in the world," enrolled five thousand children. "Think of that," she boasted. Later that year she set off on a speaking trip to Cleveland and Chicago. In one place she reported that "hundreds were turned away and the line of people stretched for two blocks." She acquitted herself well, she insisted. "In the forum [question and answer] section, I am conceited enough to think I got the best of some of my questioners."

But even the famous Roosevelt energy had its limits. By the mid-1920s, Corinne was in her seventies, and she recognized that she had less stamina. After 1922, when she lost most of the vision in one eye, she made numerous trips to Baltimore for surgery by a trusted Johns Hopkins ophthalmologist in an attempt to retain some use of the other eye. Even with the prospect of blindness, though, she maintained an upbeat attitude. During the preparation for her ninth eye operation, Corinne focused on poetry, later insisting that the words of one verse came to her in the form of writing on the operating room wall. It began, "Let there be light."

By 1930, Corinne's normally sunny disposition was tested on many fronts. Her arthritis had worsened, and she could not help but notice that Bamie's suffering had also increased. Twenty-year-old Joe Alsop broke his ankle and chose his grandmother's summer place to convalesce. But it was Monroe who gave Corinne the most worry. After a brief marriage in 1916 and the birth of a daughter, he had been on his own again since the divorce in 1925. He showed writing talent, and his letters from France, where he fought in the war, inspired Bamie to write to his mother that she thought them "perfectly splendid. . . . They are by far the best letters I have seen from any of the young men who have gone over." After he returned to the States, he took a position at the Chemical Bank, but he did not hold it for long. He flirted with different cures for his alcoholism, including American treatment centers and European spas, much in the pattern of his uncle Elliott, but nothing seemed to work. He even changed religious affiliation, and for a while his mother hoped that regular meetings with his Christian Science colleagues might reform him. Bouncing from one job to another, without a fixed address, he showed little sign that he would change. Corinney later recalled that it had been "the tragedy of drink [that] really destroyed" him. His mother, who recognized the problem, continued to serve alcohol in his presence because, according to Corinney, she never "thought of not doing so. She understood that if he wanted to drink he was going to find a way to do it." The drinking bouts came in spurts, as Corinney recalled: "It was just like a bowl filling up . . . you knew perfectly well that it was coming on."

∽

These failings all around her made Corinne feel more and more the weight of her own mortality. After a visit to a friend who was dying slowly, Corinne instructed her daughter: "Darling, if I get to the age of 84 and am a great sufferer and yet cannot die, please help to let me pass away." Bamie's death in August 1931 added a certain urgency to this request. Now all three of Corinne's siblings were dead, and for the second time in her life, Corinne dreaded the end-of-the-year holidays. In mid-November she wrote her daughter that Thanksgiving would not be the same: "I cannot realize that [Bamie] is gone and [I] see her so clearly all the time."

In 1932, Corinne tried to pull herself together for the presidential campaign. Franklin, who had been governor of New York State since 1929 and candidate for vice president in 1920, received his party's nomination for the top spot, thus pitting him against the Republican incumbent, Herbert Hoover. Corinne had given a string of speeches for Hoover in the 1928 election, but now she decided she could not work against Franklin. Even when Hoover asked for her help, she refused, although she did not actively campaign for Franklin, either. Edith Roosevelt was not so cautious—she gave speeches for Hoover and even sent out letters in bright pink envelopes with her preference for Hoover printed in large letters on the outside. Such actions underlined the break between the "Theodores" and the "Franklins" that had become very clear in the 1920s.

By the time of the voting in November 1932, the nation was in the trough of the Great Depression, with more people out of work than ever before. Franklin Roosevelt did not offer a specific program for recovery, but his jaunty attitude convinced voters that he would find a way to make things better. They sent him to the White House by a landslide, giving him 57 percent of the popular vote and 472 votes in the electoral college. When word reached Hyde Park that Corinne had crossed party lines to vote for Franklin, Sara Delano could hardly find words to express her gratitude. She had already written to her in 1928, upon learning that Corinne had voted for Franklin for governor: "There is no one on earth like [you]. I think it is wonderful your voting for [Franklin]. I never expected it dear. . . . Some people have fine *minds*, others have warm *hearts*, but you have both."

Among the parties given for First Lady–elect Eleanor Roosevelt was one at the Waldorf-Astoria on January 17, 1933. It was a frigid, wintry night, and Corinne, who had been suffering from a respiratory infection, refused all advice to stay home. She had taken great satisfaction in Franklin's victory (the last letter she ever wrote had been about him), and now nothing could keep her from this celebration for her favorite brother's favorite child. It was not a late party, but Corinne's condition immediately worsened after she attended, and on February 17, surrounded by her family, she died. A few months earlier, her old friend Charles Wood had sent her "all wishes for happiness and health and a hope for a meeting sometime in this circus ring—before the exit trumpet blows." But for Corinne, the circus was over. She would leave to others the judgment of her part in it.

Sometimes called "the goddess" picture of Edith, this is the only one of her that her husband, Theodore, professed to like.

At age twenty-two, Sara Delano had already traveled the world and was considered among the most beautiful women in New York.

CHAPTER FOUR

EDITH KERMIT CAROW ROOSEVELT

(1861–1948)

AND

SARA DELANO ROOSEVELT

(1854–1941)

N A NOVEMBER EVENING IN 1904, Corinne Robinson returned to the President's private railcar,
exhausted after two hectic days at the St. Louis
World's Fair. Theodore's recent election to a second
term rendered his appearance at the fair a kind of tri-
umphal celebration, and Corinne had not wanted to miss any of it—
the many receptions, luncheons and banquets that merged into one
"perpetual jog-trot." Now, well past midnight and eager to get some
rest on the trip back East, she could not resist Theodore's invitation
to talk over the review he was writing of James Rhodes's last two
volumes of *History of the United States*. Theodore and Corinne discussed the book until five in the morning while he wrote, and then
he turned to an article on the "Irish Question," keeping his sister up
until seven. His wife had retired at midnight, but as Corinne
explained years later when she wrote about that marathon session
of talking and writing, "She was not born a Roosevelt."

In throwing down the gauntlet of family energy, Corinne had a
point. But Edith could have countered that the men in that family frequently chose women more Rooseveltian than themselves—women

who managed to seem larger than life. Edith could also have noted that marrying into the Roosevelt family carried its own caveat: dealing with such strong-minded relatives was not always easy.

That trip to St. Louis occurred before the most significant breach in the relationship between Edith and Corinne, but evidence of a rift had been mounting for years. Edith's self-contained personality permitted few really close friendships, while Corinne was always reaching out to people. When she and Theodore rekindled their romance in secret, Edith gave a clear signal that she did not mean to include his sisters in everything she did, and that exclusion became the pattern. After Edith's miscarriage in 1888, Corinne speculated to Bamie that "the whole thing has been most mysterious and neither Anna nor I think there would have been any mishap had not the tendency to it been rather acquiesced in by all parties."

While Theodore and Edith were living in Washington, during his years as a civil service commissioner, the two women's paths crossed less frequently, and each of them made new friends. But the misunderstanding at the time of the 1905 inauguration showed how much their old friendship had deteriorated. Considering Edith's reputation for careful planning, it is difficult to imagine that her failure to provide enough tickets for Corinne's family to attend the various events was an unintentional oversight or that, as wife of the President, she could not rectify any error that Bamie had made. For public consumption, Corinne put a good face on the event, and in *My Brother Theodore Roosevelt*, she described the inauguration as pure joy for her: "The atmosphere was one of great family gaiety. . . . What a day it was! . . . Dinner was . . . very merry. . . . We felt so gay, so full of life and fun." Corinne even made a point of crediting Edith with the special kindness of inviting Corinney to stay on a few extra days at the White House.

But Corinne's letters to Bamie, written at the time, show a very different picture. On Sunday, March 5, after her sons' exclusion from the festivities on Saturday had caused her to lash out at everyone around her, Corinne wrote, "I know I was very wrong to speak as excitedly as I spoke but I had been much wrought up at lunch by everybody asking me why my boys were not in the Senate Chamber when everyone else was there and I felt hurt to the quick that they had been so unnecessarily excluded." Begging Bamie for understanding, she regretted that the old sisterly feeling between them had been so tested. But if Corinne ever wrote such sentiments to Edith, the letters have not survived. The two women continued to see each other occasionally and correspond, but the relationship definitely cooled, giving the lie to Corinne's claim that they had been "pledged friends from birth."

∽

Edith was not the only in-law to leave a strong imprint on the Roosevelt record. Sara Delano, Franklin's mother, was another, and the two women's lives provide a vivid counterpoint. They started out as youthful friends but had become, by the time they died, bitter enemies—one the matriarch of the Oyster Bay "Theodores" and the other in the same role for the Hyde Park "Franklins." At the time of Eleanor's marriage in 1905, they could all joke about keeping the name in the family, but feelings gradually soured among them. As Franklin's stature grew, ideas about who outranked whom had to be revised.

Between 1910 and 1920 a new generation lined up to follow in Theodore's footsteps to fame, but no one in the family (except Sara, of course) would have predicted that Franklin would outrun them all. He won his first election in 1910, but other men in the family were also waging victorious campaigns that same year. After serving two years in the New York State Senate, he went to Washington as Assistant Secretary of the Navy in 1913, a job that Theodore had held fourteen years earlier. Franklin lost a 1914 race for the U.S. Senate but then won the number two spot on the Democrats' national presidential ticket in 1920.

Now the stakes were higher, and suddenly hostility between the Franklins and the Theodores became more obvious. Alice Longworth later insisted that Franklin had voted for Theodore in the presidential election of 1904 (even though he had to split his ticket to do so), but she adamantly contended that no one in her branch returned the favor. To them, he seemed like an upstart in 1920, or as she put it: "There we were—THE Roosevelts—hubris up to the eyebrows, *beyond* the eyebrows, and then who should come sailing down the river but Nemesis in the person of Franklin. We were out. Run over." Young Ted Roosevelt, Theodore's son, campaigned against Franklin in 1920, calling him a maverick and accusing him of grasping at the coattails of Ted's popular father who had died just a year earlier. Sara was taken aback by what she perceived as the family's unfriendly treatment of her son. When asked what accounted for the hard feelings in the Theodore branch, she retorted, "I can't possibly imagine unless it's that our side is better looking."

The rift widened through the 1920s. Eleanor campaigned for Al Smith in his race for governor of New York in 1924 when he ran against her cousin Ted Roosevelt. By the time Franklin won the White House in 1933, Ted had finally gotten a plush appointment from President Hoover—as governor of the Philippines—but he was no sooner on the job than he faced the prospect that Franklin would call him home and appoint someone else. When asked exactly what his relationship was to the new president, Ted Roosevelt joked, "Fifth cousin, about to be removed." That same reporter inquired why Kermit appeared to be on such friendly terms with Franklin, sailing and socializing very publicly with him. While Ted paused, searching for a diplomatic reply, Edith, who was visiting him at the time, spoke up: "Because his mother wasn't there." If there had been any doubt about feelings between Edith's "side" and Sara's, the events of 1933 made the division very clear.

In the retelling of their stories, both Edith Kermit Roosevelt and Sara Delano Roosevelt became caricatures of the extremes in American womanhood—Edith, the devoted wife and model First Lady; Sara, the epitome of the shrewish mother-in-law. Few women deserve such a flat, one-dimensional depiction, but for Sara and Edith the oversimplification is particularly unfair. Edith could be scathing in her judgments, difficult with her children, and unreasonable in her demands; Sara could show a political awareness and concern for others that made her more than just a manipulative egotist.

In the outline of their lives, the two resemble each other. Born in that turbulent time just before the Civil War ripped the nation apart (Sara in 1854 and Edith in 1861), they married in their mid-twenties, relatively late for women of their time. Both wed widowers, thus earning the "second choice" label, but nothing about them suggests a lack of self-confidence. Each one had enough determination for both, and they frequently acted with an intrepidity that discounted the possibility of error. Since they both lived to the age of eighty-seven, surviving their husbands by several decades (twenty-nine years in Edith's case, forty in Sara's), they had ample time to write their own names in the nation's history. Edith wrote hers large, as attentive mother to a large family, much-praised Washington wife, and, according to one historian, a First Lady who "never made a mistake."

I

CHARLES CAROW (1825–1883), Edith's father, worked in the family's shipping company, but much less successfully than some of his colleagues. In that volatile business, a fortune could be lost in a flash in the nineteenth century. Storms at sea wrecked ships; fickle consumers turned away from a product just when the stock-piles were highest; unreliable suppliers failed to deliver as promised. Charles Carow seemed to attract bad luck, and while others in the shipping business (such as Sara Delano's father) managed to negotiate through the bad patches without permanent damage, Charles Carow could not. Rumor had it that by the time he reached his thirties, he preferred to drink and forget his problems rather than struggle to re-earn the fortune that got away.

The family name, Carow, derived from the French Quereau, Protestants who fled to America in the 1680s when Catholic France left them little choice. In New York they not only anglicized their name but they also joined the English stronghold church—Trinity, down near Wall Street—thus assuring themselves a pew among the city's elite. By the early 1800s the shipping firm of Kermit & Carow had prospered, specializing in moving a whole range of lowly items and costly merchandise between Liverpool, the West Indies, and New York.

In 1859 when he was thirty-three and still relatively successful, Charles Carow married Gertrude Tyler, a young Connecticut woman who had just completed finishing school in France. On both sides of her family she matched—even surpassed—the Carow prominence. Gertrude claimed two British prime ministers on her mother's side of the family tree, and among her father's forebears was the renowned Puritan leader Jonathan Edwards. After Charles and Gertrude were married (in Norwich's Christ Episcopal Church, a short distance from the bride's family mansion), they traveled in their own launch to Manhattan, where they would reside and start their family, just a few blocks from the bridegroom's boyhood friend, Theodore Roosevelt, Sr., and his wife, Mittie.

In 1861 a daughter, Edith, was born to the Carows, and in two years Emily, her only sibling to survive infancy, was born. All through her long life Edith would pick and choose which parts of her family history to use and which to ignore. For example, as an adult she rarely mentioned her parents, and sometimes seemed intent on disassociating herself from them. After her marriage to Theodore, she discarded her family name, becoming Edith Kermit Roosevelt (Kermit being the middle name her parents had given her in honor of a paternal uncle). But late in life when she teamed up with her son Kermit to write a book, she chose her ancestors, especially her mother, as the main subject. The title left no doubt about the focus: *American Backlogs: The Story of Gertrude Tyler and Her Family, 1660–1860.*

As the elder of two daughters, Edith developed close ties with her father—at least closer than those she had with her remote mother—despite his alcoholism and his long absences on business trips. Charles Carow liked good books and learning, and he passed his passion for both along to Edith. Unlike his friend Theodore, Charles had no sons, but both men taught their daughters sports and the intricacies of flora and fauna. Edith, who shared an interest in theater with her father, was left with a store of fond memories when he died. Perhaps it was her embarrassment over his mixed record that kept her from talking about him very much, but when she did, it was with affection. Decades after he died, she named her riding horse for his, and in describing him to a relative who had never met him, she called him "an angel."

Charles Carow's docile, intellectual bent no doubt added to his difficulties in business, and by the mid-1860s when Edith was still a child, the Carows had to adjust to what were then politely called "diminished circumstances." From that time on, his daughter recalled, the family had to rely on relatives for funds and a place to live. For a while they stayed with some of Gertrude's relatives who maintained a large house near the C.V.S. Roosevelt mansion at Fourteenth and Broadway.

The Carows were not out-on-the-street poor. Little Edith could still write letters to the Roosevelt children about receiving a pet pig that had "been all around the world in one of Papa's ships." But she and Emily grew up having less than their friends and trying to conceal that fact from others. Their Irish nurse, Mame, who later cared for Edith's children, encouraged the Carow girls to make the best of what they had. Edith remembered that when the Roosevelt children first came to her house to play, she had started putting away her shabbiest toys, but then Mame had wisely suggested that those well-loved toys might be the very ones that her guests would most enjoy.

Bounced from one house to another, supported by her mother's relatives, Edith learned at a very young age how to maintain an invisible wall around herself, protecting her from whatever went on outside. She perfected the knack of standing apart, even from her own immediate family, as Alice Roosevelt Longworth later noted when she said that her stepmother had "almost a gift for making her own people uncomfortable." To outsiders, Edith appeared "inscrutable," and after she became First Lady in 1901, observers described her as "almost Oriental" in her detachment. Margaret Chanler, who lived near the Roosevelts in Washington and often visited them in New York, found Edith difficult to describe. "While Theodore's personality invites description," Chanler wrote, "Mrs. Roosevelt is more difficult of access; praise does not reach or define her. Just as the camera is focused, she steps aside to avoid the click of the shutter." Alice traced that detachment to her youth, observing that Edith's early years "had been unhappy, which could account for her withdrawn, rather parched quality."

Edith's sister, Emily, cut herself off even more, both physically and psychologically, until her eccentricities—nonstop talk and outlandish clothes—went beyond normal limits. For her entire adult life she resided in Europe, most of that time on the Italian Riviera, where she took advantage of her expatriate status to disassociate herself from things both American and Italian. Whenever she returned to the United States to visit relatives, she made life so unpleasant for them that they began dreading every arrival. Her nieces and nephews invented cruel but apt nicknames for her, such as "the Mediterranean menace"; and in a reference to her skinny frame, Alice called her pet snake "Spinach Emily." In her later years when she grew abundant facial hair, she was dubbed the "whiskered brigand." Never married—though much courted, she insisted—Emily Carow lavished her attention on a succession of very pampered dogs, and when she died in 1939, about the only positive thing that her nieces and nephews could find to say about her was that she left her entire estate to them.

Edith had a big advantage over her younger sister: she latched on to the Roosevelts at a young age, and no matter what happened, she never let go. Only seven weeks older than Corinne, Edith became her friend as soon as their parents brought them together as toddlers. Through the classes taught at the Roosevelt home by Aunt Anna and the parties they attended together, the girls nurtured that friendship even though the Roosevelt money provided Corinne indulgences that Edith experienced only as a spectator.

Both girls loved poetry, and Edith was one of the mainstays in P.O.R.E, the literary club that Corinne founded when they were in their teens. In her verses for P.O.R.E., Edith revealed about as much about herself as she ever permitted anyone to see. One of her efforts, singled out as significant by her biographer Sylvia Morris, described her "dream castles" where "none may enter / But the few." The innermost sanctum was reserved for herself: "Only one, one tiny room / Locked they find," the place where she alone could go "When my heart all worn by grief / Sinketh low."

Something about the introspective, reserved Edith Carow appealed to the young Theodore Roosevelt, only three years her senior, and the two began pairing off while still in their early teens. Neither of them could boast particularly good looks, but looks rarely appeared on the Roosevelt "want" list. Before he left for Harvard, Theodore spent a good deal of time with Edith, and later he bragged that she was the "most cultivated, best-read girl I know." He may have proposed and Edith turned him down, as she later insisted, but the specifics are missing as to time and place. Then, just before Theodore left to go to Harvard, something happened that snapped the tie between them, at least temporarily.

Neither of the principals ever explained exactly what occurred at the Roosevelts' summer house on August 22, 1876, but Theodore later admitted that they had disagreed so sharply on some matter that it had caused the breach. In his second year at Harvard, he had rearranged his affections so that Edith was replaced by the wispy

Alice Lee, who became his wife just months after he graduated in 1880.

Another woman, less determined than Edith Kermit Carow, might have exited the Roosevelt circle at that point, embarrassed by her rejection and intent on finding friends and a mate elsewhere. But Edith did anything but exit. She attended Theodore's wedding (nearly dancing the soles of her shoes off, according to one report) and gave a party for him in 1882 when he won election to the New York State Assembly. As a friend of Bamie's and Corinne's, she had ample opportunity to encounter him and his wife, even joining them for an excursion to Montreal for New Year's day 1882.

After Alice's death in February 1884, Theodore asked his sisters to see that his path did not cross Edith's, and for a while that kept them from meeting. The grieving widower escaped to the Badlands, but on his visits back to New York, unbeknownst to Bamie and Corinne, he resumed the courtship that he and Edith had broken off nearly a decade earlier. By November 1885, less than two years after Alice's death, they had agreed to marry.

The engagement marked a definite upward turn in Edith's life, since the last few years had not been easy. Her father, whose fortunes had continued to decline along with his health, died in March 1883, leaving such a small estate that his wife and daughters scrambled to make ends meet. By early spring 1886 they decided to move to Europe. It was common knowledge at the time that living abroad cost a fraction of what it cost in the United States. Perhaps more important, the distance between the continents permitted cutting corners on wardrobes and entertaining without needing to make excuses or attracting pity. With two unmarried daughters in their early twenties, Gertrude Carow would have seen the advantages of such a move, and Edith had her own reasons. Until her mother and sister were settled where they could live on their income, she could hardly leave them. The move to London solved that problem, and by the end of the summer she informed Theodore that the two of them could go ahead with their plans to marry.

Bamie and Corinne both recovered from their surprise upon learning through the newspaper, rather than from Theodore, about the impending marriage, and Bamie even attended the December 2 ceremony. But Edith's lifelong friend Corinne decided not to make the trip. Now the mother of a three-year-old son and a five-month-old girl, she hardly had to offer an excuse for staying home, but her letters to Edith are curiously missing for this period.

Whatever his sisters may have thought about Theodore's marrying a second time, Edith gave no indication that Alice Lee's ghost would disturb her. In fact, she later made very clear her contempt for Alice. Theodore would have soon tired of her, Edith insisted, because she would "have bored [him] to death." In Edith's view, Alice had beauty but lacked depth, and she had the impracticality of a featherbrain. This confidence in her own superiority as Theodore's wife no doubt helped Edith adjust to her circumstances. Upon their return to the United States she went to live in the house in Oyster Bay that Theodore had built for his first wife (wisely, he changed its name from Lee-Holm to Sagamore Hill). As it turned out, it would be her principal home until the day she died. Enlarged and changed during more than half a century, the twenty-two-room house never had much style on the outside, but Edith more than made up for that with her own personal touch inside.

A woman as determined and confident as Edith could cause even strong women to step aside. Alice Longworth recalled hearing from her aunt Corinne that she and Bamie "were rather concerned" when Edith married Theodore because they feared she would monopolize him and come between him and his sisters. Everyone seemed to accept the fact that it was not easy to bargain with Edith, and her nephew, Sheffield Cowles, recalled hearing from one of her children: "Mother never took any prisoners."

Theodore's sisters may have been "concerned" about Edith marrying their brother because they suspected she had little taste for politics. In fact, she took little pleasure in most of the political game, especially the glad-handing side of campaigning, and she detested the public's scrutiny of leaders' private lives. Literary topics interested her far more than any legislation. Yet she had an uncanny ability to make the right judgment behind the scenes, and in the family it was acknowledged that she had "the long head in politics."

The determined, intellectual Edith also had a passionate side—at least if Theodore's words on the subject can be accepted as truth. She destroyed many of the letters that would have substantiated that view, but those that survive underline a mutual devotion. He often signed himself "Your own Lover" or some variation on that theme. In letters to friends or family, he often boasted of how his love for Edith had endured over the years. In writing to congratulate a friend on his engagement, Theodore insisted that "nothing in the world—no possible success, military or political" could equal the "happiness that comes to those fortunate enough to make a real love-match—a match in which lover and sweetheart will never be lost in husband or wife." For her part, Edith treasured the sexual part of marriage—unlike many of her female in-laws who tended to talk of sex as "duty." Sylvia Morris reported that, in her old age, Edith shocked a granddaughter by referring to that "wonderful silky private part of woman."

⁂

During the first decade of her marriage, Edith followed Roosevelt tradition by having a large family in a short time. Although she had been one of only two children, she gave birth to five (and had at least one miscarriage) in just over ten years: Theodore Jr. (Ted) in September 1887; Kermit in October 1889; Ethel in August 1891; Archibald in April 1894; and Quentin in November 1897. Two more miscarriages followed during Theodore's presidency. But it was also family tradition to have a large household staff, and in addition to Mame, the Irish nanny who looked after the children, Edith had several servants to cook, clean, launder, and chauffeur her around.

As a young mother, Edith tended her children lovingly, though she could be a strict disciplinarian and set high standards. The long descriptions written to her sister in Europe indicate a mixture of the eye of a doting parent and the cool detachment of a presiding judge. In 1894, Edith observed that the new baby, Archie, looked much older than three months, and although "perfectly strong and healthy," he had such "a Heavenly little face that I cannot feel he will live to grow up." Edith associated the "divine expression in his eyes" with "some of the pictures of the Christ child." Daughter Ethel, three years old, was a "bustling person, a born manager and orders [her brothers] about constantly." Something about the daughter's sturdiness caused a mixture of pride and fear: "She is a splendid specimen but so strong and rough that I am almost afraid when she comes near me." In one letter Edith described her as "fat." When searching for attractive clothing for the little girl, Edith complained that she looked "like a little guttersnipe in dark colours so I have to bend to fate."

Later, it would be said that Edith had been unkind to her stepdaughter, but her letters do not show that Alice received harsher judgments than Edith's birth children. When Gertrude Carow, still living in Europe, complained that a recent photo of her grandchildren had not done them justice, Edith responded rather crossly that "none of them [is] in the least picturesque, except occasionally Ted. . . . None . . . are really pretty except Kermit who is an unusual looking child." The children had their good points: "Alice has pretty blue eyes, a good honest face and carries herself well. . . . Ethel a great jolly, rollicking baby. . . . Nothing can make them picturesque."

With Theodore often absent on political business or overseeing his investments in the West, Edith did most of the parenting—no small task since serious health problems plagued the little Roosevelts. Kermit, at age five, had "water on the knee," requiring that he wear a brace during his waking hours, and Alice, although she had a different problem, also wore braces. A heel tendon turned her foot to one side, and the doctor prescribed strapping her foot and leg to "an instrument," then turning a key to lengthen or stretch the tendon and force the foot into proper position. To Edith fell the job of doing the stretching, which was, she admitted, "most appalling looking." It reminded her of an "instrument of torture" she had once seen in a museum.

Cool and detached as she was, Edith had a far warmer relationship with her children when they were young than later. She enjoyed them then, they later maintained, but as they matured, she found them less interesting. What they saw as a turning away may really have been her expression of her own independence—an insistence on some time for herself—but she could be rather harsh on the subject. If she had to choose between her children's respect and their love, she preferred their respect, she insisted. One of the family (who had plenty of information on which to base the judgment) said that Edith could be as "mean as a snake" with her own children. About her grandchildren, Edith was known to say, "I like to see their little faces, but I prefer to see their backs [when they go]."

Alice Longworth recalled a kind of rapprochement near the end of Edith's life when the two of them were able to laugh at the same things. It was at that stage of their lives, when Edith had confessed to Alice that she thought she had been very unkind to her, that Alice disagreed. In many respects she had treated her better than she had treated her own children. But that was not saying a great deal. Only Edith's second-born son, Kermit, seemed to do no wrong, and he remained her clear favorite as long as he lived. This brilliant, introspective son started out to explore the world but ended up an alcoholic and a disappointment to his family. Yet Edith never gave up on him, and during their last visit, just months before his death in 1943, she mused over how much he meant to her.

The Carows' uncertain finances during Edith's youth left her nervous about money. In contrast to Theodore's sisters, who rarely spoke about such things, Edith never seemed satisfied that she had sufficient funds, and she frequently complained about the high cost of household help and medical care. Even with the substantial salary that Theodore earned as a civil service commissioner in the 1890s, she did not relax, and the extra money he earned from writing articles, although it could be considerable, was not the kind of money to ease Edith's worries. She could not count on its continuing every year. In early 1895 she complained to her sister that the doctor's current bill for Kermit alone amounted to $294, a sum that "depressed" her. Fortunately, Alice's grandmother paid her medical bills, prompting Edith to revive an old childhood saying: "I think she 'done' noble." Still, this was no time to worry about the cost: "I feel I owe Kermit's life to Dr. Shaffer," Edith wrote Emily, "and would cheerfully give him the clothes off my back if they happened to be worth anything!"

Edith's complaints should be taken in context (and her attempt to economize by once trying to make her own toothpaste should be seen as merely a gesture). At the time, she had far more than Theodore's $3,500 salary to spend. His sizable inheritance from his parents, although greatly depleted by the heavy losses his cattle ranching cost him, still yielded some income. Edith herself inherited from a maternal uncle in the early 1890s, and although the principal had to remain invested, the annual income was about $1,200. Her maternal grandfather left a sizable estate, and Edith received half of her mother's share in 1898. When Edith's daughter Ethel later went through the household account books from the 1890s, she estimated that her mother was spending about $17,000 a year—$325,000 in 1998 dollars. It was enough, Ethel confided to her own daughter, to make her think that Edith "liked the butter spread pretty thick!"

In a family where wry comments and sarcastic observations were routine, Edith could outdo almost anyone. Why stepdaughter Alice picked up this tartness while daughter Ethel did not is a question only they could have answered. Edith did confine her remarks to a sympathetic audience, either family or friends whom she could trust, while Alice was less careful about who heard her. After attending a dinner in Washington at the home of her and Theodore's good friends Senator Henry Cabot Lodge and his wife, Nannie, Edith informed her sister that the other guests had been "deadly dull" and two of them were "dead heads." About one guest whom Edith particularly disliked, she wrote that he was "so oily and cat like" that he could "walk over a corduroy road in wooden shoes without any clatter." In that same letter she wrote of one southern senator: "I do not think he has left a bottle of hair dye in the state of Virginia."

Even relatives did not escape Edith's unflattering description. She informed Emily that she had attended a "crush" at the British embassy and encountered an uncle of theirs—who looked "very blowsy and like an over blown peony, and I regret to say his wig gave him rather an actor's look." When someone mustered the temerity to comment on Edith's sharp tongue, she retorted that she would do as she pleased, and, if necessary, she would ask for the privilege "of losing my temper for a Christmas gift." It is no wonder that Bamie once referred to Edith's "snarkish mood."

✆

The public held a far more positive image of Edith than did some of her relatives, although both camps agreed that she had enormous confidence in her own taste. Like Bamie, she seemed to have innate good sense about what was appropriate or fitting—a trait particularly evident during her nearly eight years as First Lady (1901–09). As the most prominent woman in the United States, Edith was the subject of many articles in newspapers and magazines, most of them very flattering. But when one fashion-conscious reporter commented a bit snidely on how small a wardrobe Edith kept, she proudly clipped the item and pasted it in her scrapbook.

The confidence that she took to the job of First Lady was based partly on experience because even though only forty years old when Theodore became president, she had been in the public eye for some time. As a Washington wife during his years as a civil service commissioner, she had made friends there, and during his two years as governor of New York, she drew up her own rules for how to deal with long reception lines and prying eyes. To avoid shaking hands with all the guests who showed up at receptions in Albany, she clutched a bouquet of flowers, and the tactic worked so well that she took it with her to the White House.

Even before President McKinley was assassinated, she hired a social secretary, Isabella Hagner (who had previously worked for Bamie), to pass out information about herself, her entertaining, and her children. As First Lady she continued to rely heavily on Hagner, thus setting a precedent for women who followed her into the White House to name their own secretaries. Previous residents' wives had found trouble shielding youngsters from a curious public, and with the popularity of personal cameras around the turn of the century, curiosity ran rampant. Edith decided to pass out formal photographs of herself and the children and then request that photographers keep their distance. Somehow she managed all this without the criticism that had met her predecessors, especially Frances Cleveland and Julia Grant who were called elitist or rumored to have deformed children when they tried to shield them from the public.

Soon after her arrival in the White House, Edith began holding regular meetings with the wives of cabinet members to help set social rules. One wife reportedly ended an adulterous affair after the other cabinet wives made their disapproval known. Edith used the gatherings to discuss many topics, including just how much was being spent on entertaining, thus subtly warning women with large budgets that they should not outshine the President's wife in staging their parties. To cut costs on year-round staff, Edith engaged a caterer and paid a hefty $7.50 per plate, but because her invitations went out R.S.V.P., she had an accurate count of guests in advance.

One big problem that had perplexed previous presidents' wives was neatly solved by Edith. Like them, she realized that the Executive Mansion, as it was still officially called, could no longer accommodate the President's staff and family. Proposals for a new office wing had been abandoned in the past because of objections that another building would mar the beauty of the residence, but the Roosevelts' popularity helped overcome resistance.

Theodore called in his old friend Charles McKim, the most famous architect in America, and his firm, McKim, Mead and White, began an extensive remodeling in 1902. The large glass conservatories came down, the West Wing went up, and the residence underwent major changes to allow for more sleeping quarters for both family and guests. By then more than a century old, the main building had developed some dangerously weak spots, and whenever large crowds were expected, the first floor had to be reinforced with extra beams. Those problems were solved and a stairway was removed, resulting in a much larger State Dining Room. The velvety, fringed, potted palm look of the East Room was replaced by elegant yellow and gold. Edith was always very guarded about her role in the renovation, but the record shows that she met privately with McKim and expressed her opinions to him. The renovated White House, as it was now officially renamed, reopened in the autumn of 1902 to widespread approval. During the next century it required much more reinforcing and additional space, but the sparse elegance that Edith had dictated for the East Room endured.

In her effort to make the White House a dignified place that all Americans could take pride in, Edith instituted several changes. Her predecessors had held musicales, but she upgraded the level of performance. Formerly any congressman wanting one of his constituents or friends to have the honor of performing for the President and his guests would pressure the First Lady until an appearance was arranged. Edith turned the selection process over to others more qualified than she, thus freeing herself from the unpleasant and time-consuming task of turning down requests. A delegate of Steinway & Brothers in New York auditioned and chose the musicians. It was a change much appreciated by her niece Eleanor who, when she became First Lady in 1933, found herself inundated with requests to perform.

During her years in Washington as a commissioner's wife, Edith had chafed at how old White House china and glassware were doled out. Chipped pieces or odd bits from depleted sets would turn up at auctions and go on sale, touted as "from the President's House." Edith thought this unseemly, almost an indication that the nation's highest official lacked funds, and she arranged a more dignified demise for the castoffs. When she decreed that they be broken and the pieces thrown into the Potomac, one of her aides conceded that he saw her point. But he admitted that it nearly broke his heart to follow the order—he knew that many Americans, including himself, hankered for a plate from the President's table.

The fact that Edith managed a large family in the White House with such ease and success could not have escaped her relatives. Eleanor visited her there more than once after returning from Allenswood in the summer of 1902. When Eleanor took on the same job herself, she handled it very differently, giving interviews and speeches rather than trying to remain out of the public eye. But Edith's example was very important. Simply moving around that famous house at 1600 Pennsylvania Avenue and seeing someone she had known all her life administer it with such confidence and ease had an impact.

Eleanor well knew the inconveniences associated with the job, and her own youthful experiences in Washington may have led her to insist many times that she had never wanted to live in the White House. But those same experiences helped buoy her confidence to handle tasks that other presidents' wives found daunting. She also absorbed some of her aunt's insistence that the national spotlight need not change her. Edith once wrote a friend: "Being the centre of things is very interesting, yet the same proportions remain." When she heard an old hymn or read a familiar poem, "they mean just what they did [before] so I don't believe I have been forced into the 'first lady of the land' model of my predecessors."

Eleanor also learned from her aunt Edith that a wife did not have to move in her husband's shadow. Franklin Roosevelt once observed that Edith managed Theodore "very cleverly without his being conscious of it." Margaret Chanler wrote, "We used to think that Theodore, whom she adored, was a little afraid of his 'Edie.'" Henry Adams concurred, writing that Theodore "stands in abject terror of Edith." When Theodore brashly announced in 1904 that he would not run again in 1908, Edith told an aide that he should have waited to show his hand. After leaving the presidency, Theodore scheduled a triumphant tour of Europe and considered wearing military attire; but Edith objected that such an outfit would be considered "ridiculous," and he altered his plans.

When Edith and Theodore left the White House in March 1909, she had compiled an impressive public record. Her picture had frequently appeared in popular national magazines, and when she left Washington, *The Delineator* published an admiring article, "Mrs. Roosevelt: The Woman in the Background"; and *Ladies Home Journal* marveled, "Why Mrs. Roosevelt Has Not Broken Down." Historians would later rank her in the top ten of the first forty-two women to hold the job.

∽

Edith's family and close friends had a mixed picture of her. Her only formal schooling was at Miss Comstock's, but it was generally agreed that her taste in literature was superb. Henry Cabot Lodge and Henry Adams—who both adhered to the highest standards in matters related to the mind—declared Edith their equal, and Theodore agreed, writing in 1893 when she was just about to give birth to their fourth child: "[Cabot] is one of the few men I know who is as well read as [Edith] in English literature and she delights to talk with him." Alice Longworth later underscored Edith's intellectual superiority, noting that she "had great literary taste and CARED for things. I think she thought my father's family were all uneducated Dutch peasants."

No matter what her judgment of Theodore's ancestors, Edith wore his family name proudly, both before his death and afterward—no small undertaking when it was the most famous name in America. In 1924 she traveled to the Far East and spoke at a girls' school in Japan. Local newspapers reported her success as she stood, dressed entirely in widow's black, alongside an interpreter wearing a white kimono. Her topic was "Social Service," and in "pithy and cogent phrases," Edith charmed the audience, telling them how hospitals, schools, and other public institutions in the United States had recently established a "social service" department. The spirit behind this change was the same one, Edith explained, that inspired one of her husband's mottoes: "Spend and be Spent."

Back in the United States, Edith continued speaking in public, even appearing on national radio in September 1935 in a program celebrating an anniversary of the U.S. Constitution. According to Sylvia Morris, who heard a recording of the speech, Edith was a "born public speaker, able to manipulate emotions without being moved herself." Not unaware of her skill, Edith confidently inquired before each speech, "Shall I make them laugh or shall I make them cry?"

Like most Roosevelts, Edith thrived on travel. While her children were still young, she found few opportunities to go abroad and later wrote that she had felt restrained those years. In the 1920s, when Kermit, his wife, Belle, and Ethel's husband, Richard Derby, decided to write a book on travel, Edith contributed a chapter. Her "Odyssey of a Grandmother" explained that many women, including herself, have to forgo travel while their children are young. "Women who marry pass their best and happiest years," Edith wrote, "in giving life and fostering it, meeting and facing the problems of the next generation and helping the universe to move, and those born with the wanderfoot are sometimes irked by the weight of the always beloved shackles. Then the birds fly, the nest is empty, and at the feet of the knitters in the sun lies the wide world." By the 1920s, Edith's "beloved shackles" had been removed, and she cheerfully put down her knitting to travel the "wide world."

Travel was certainly not unknown to Edith—after all, she had lived abroad briefly before her marriage and had taken numerous trips since then. In March 1900, accompanied by her sister, she visited Cuba to see, she joked, what San Juan Hill looked like. During her White House years she accompanied Theodore on a 1906 trip to Panama to investigate progress on the canal, marking the first time a president and his wife ever traveled together outside the nation. While Theodore hunted wild game with Kermit in Africa in 1909–10, Edith and Ethel journeyed through Europe on their own. In February 1912, when Theodore showed signs of announcing that he would run again for president, Edith set sail for South America, accompanied again by Ethel. In 1913, when Theodore set out with Kermit on what he called his "last chance to be a boy" and explore a Brazilian wilderness, Edith accompanied them through several South American countries, parting ways only when the dangerous portion of the exploration began. In 1916 she and Theodore traveled in the Caribbean; they had planned to return the following year and then continue to the Polynesian islands, but the war intervened and they had to cancel.

As a widow, though, Edith came into her own as a traveler, circling the globe many times. Her time away from home soothed and restored her, she insisted. In January 1919, two days after Theodore was buried, she left Sagamore Hill to visit Bamie at Oldgate, a poignant gesture since Theodore's sister had been too crippled to attend the funeral. That was hardly the kind of travel that Edith found soothing, however, and on February 5 she sailed with her maid to France. After only two days at sea, she felt rejuvenated. The solitude of simple tasks—arranging her clothing, walking on deck, reading, and crocheting—calmed her. She wrote to her daughter: "Last night I began to feel rested and by the time I meet the boys I shall be quite able to face everything."

Everything included visiting her youngest son's grave. Twenty-year-old aviator Quentin had been shot down eight months earlier behind enemy lines in northeastern France. Now Ted and Kermit, along with Belle, met her when she landed, and together the saddened family made its way to his grave site. The Roosevelts had a long tradition of burying wherever death came—"Let the tree lie where it falls"—and Edith followed it even though it meant her youngest son's grave was thousands of miles from Sagamore Hill.

In spite of her enormous grief, Edith left again within months of returning to the States, sailing to South America in December with Kermit. She explored the sights while he attended to business matters in Argentina, Chile, and Brazil, and when she returned to New York in mid-January, the sad anniversary of Theodore's death had passed. Winter trips had the advantage of taking her away from Oyster Bay during the bleakest part of the year when snow and ice sometimes marooned her in the "house on the hill" for days or even weeks at a time, and she made it a point to go to sunnier climates, often the Caribbean, at that time of year.

In January 1922 she accompanied her son Archie while he conducted business in France, but she hardly tied herself to his activities. After wandering around Paris, she took her first airplane trip, and although the flight had to be aborted short of its destination because of a storm, she seemed unfazed by the adventure. From England, Edith sailed to South Africa, where she thrilled at the sight of the "jade green ocean" and the "porcelain beauty" of her surroundings.

During all those times when Theodore went west to the Badlands, hunted wild game, or campaigned across the country, Edith almost always remained at home. Now she seemed determined to make up for lost time, and rather than choosing familiar places, she sought new spots where she knew no one. A sense of duty did occasionally dictate a visit with Emily in Italy, but Edith preferred more exotic destinations. In early 1923 she returned again to Brazil, nine years after Theodore had become a popular hero there with his and Kermit's exploration of the source of the River of Doubt.

No one has added up the miles Edith covered, but the total was remarkable. In December 1923 just before the Christmas holidays would have weighed her down, she set out with Kermit for her most ambitious journey: a two-month trip around the world. Leaving the California coast, they stopped in Hawaii and then Japan, where the effects of the recent great earthquake were still visible. Fortunately, she stayed in the new Imperial Hotel, designed by the American Frank Lloyd Wright to withstand such quakes, because more tremors followed.

The visit to China was a disappointment. Alice had reveled in her own tour of Peking in 1905 when she was treated like a princess and entertained by the empress in the Summer Palace. But the revolution of 1911 had changed the face of the city, and Edith objected to the unsettled, military feeling that surrounded her there. She was glad to leave China for the next leg of the trip—six thousand miles on the Trans-Siberian Express to Moscow.

For a sixty-two-year-old woman like Edith, accustomed to traveling with at least one maid, this winter journey through Siberia must have been grueling. Food supplies were unpredictable, and the washroom water froze solid. During the short days she saw magnificent stretches of snow-covered plains, but the winter nights were long. When Edith and Kermit finally reached Moscow in February 1924, they found another city changed by revolution. According to Sylvia Morris, Edith perceived in the people "an ever-present fear." Rather than complain about problems that inevitably arise on such a long, arduous journey, especially one in that part of the world during the coldest months, she insisted on making do, saying only, "Travelers must be content."

Edith still spent enough time in the States to make her presence felt. When historian William Thayer started his book *Theodore*

Roosevelt: An Intimate Biography in 1919, he had trouble getting permission from Edith and others to quote from family letters, so he turned to Corinne for assistance. But she hardly knew what to make of the situation. "I still cannot understand," she wrote Thayer in dismay, "how anyone, Mrs. Roosevelt or anyone else, has the right to object." She decided there must be a "screw loose somewhere" and urged Thayer to contact Edith again. As for "the nice sentence about Theodore's sisters," Corinne thought it preferable to play down any idea that they had influenced him. She humbly substituted a line about how Theodore "with his wonderful generosity . . . listened with unfailing respect" to his sisters' views.

Family letters deposited in archives give a less clear picture of the strained relationship that had developed between Corinne and Edith than does some of their correspondence with others. The tension had arisen almost as soon as Edith married Theodore. It grew into conscious competition during the White House years, and after his death, the two women saw much less of each other. Even so, Corinne was careful not to antagonize Edith, especially when it came to communications with historians.

When biographer Henry Pringle began his book on Theodore in the late 1920s, he delved into the courtship of Alice Lee and sent his manuscript to Corinne for comment. She counseled caution. Although she would cooperate with his research, even giving information about Alice, she did not want to be listed as a source. "During my present sister-in-law's life time," Corinne wrote Pringle, "I must be very careful, and I prefer not to have my name actually mentioned. You can say 'from those close to the family' or something of that sort." As for Pringle's writing that Theodore was "half out of his mind" over the prospect that Alice was going to turn him down, Corinne suggested that it might better be described as "youthful despair."

✣ ❧

Feeling the aches of her years more and more, Edith decreased her travel, but with great reluctance. After turning seventy in 1931, she returned to South America, toured Greece with Ethel, and visited Ted in Puerto Rico, but the trips were now shorter and tied more often to family. By the 1940s she rarely ventured far from the East Coast. In early summer she would leave Sagamore Hill, and with a maid, a cook, and a chauffeur in attendance, she made her way to the house in Brooklyn, Connecticut, that she had bought for herself in 1927. It was only about twenty miles from where her mother had grown up in Norwich. There, Edith could muse over her own roots and the turns her life had taken.

Theodore's death had ended the most remarkable love story in the Roosevelt clan. Unlike Bamie and Corinne, who married men they could dangle, Edith's relationship with Theodore showed evidence of far more passion. Throughout the thirty-two years of their marriage, their love remained strong and evident to almost anyone who saw them together as they rowed across the pond while reading poetry to each other or rode their horses through the park. Journalist Jacob Riis once described the poignant scene as Edith made her way in the rain out to Montauk, riding hours in a rickety wagon so that she could be briefly reunited with Theodore after he returned from the Spanish-American War.

That love for her husband led Edith into a political life she would never have chosen herself. In 1894 when Theodore hankered to run for mayor of New York, she had discouraged him, partly because she feared the job would reign her in financially. But like a woman very much in love, she soon understood how disappointed Theodore was at not running, and she rushed to change course. She wrote to Bamie that she felt "terribly" and realized that Theodore "never should have married me, and then he would have been free to take his own course." Having failed Theodore, she was "utterly unnerved and a prey to the deepest despair," but she resolved never to repeat her error: "This is a lesson that will last my life, never to give [my opinion] for it is utterly worthless when given, worse than that in this case for it has helped to spoil some years of a life which I would have given my own for."

Edith had twenty-five more years after she wrote that letter to make up for her mistake, and she put her heart into it. During Theodore's nearly eight years as president, his run for a third term in 1912, and his continued interest in the political game, she kept very quiet about any objections she may have had and encouraged him to do what he thought right. Her devotion to him was such that when he died in 1919, Ethel feared the effect on her mother. "She has so lived for Father," Ethel wrote her husband, "that I almost believe she will die too."

Corinne's husband had died just three months before Theodore, and Edith may have taken her sister-in-law as a model, becoming more active in politics than she had ever been before. In September 1920, a month after the Nineteenth Amendment was finally ratified by the last of the required thirty-six states, Edith wrote for *The Woman-Republican* how important it was to vote for Warren Harding. After the 1928 election she was exuberant about the turnout and the results—Herbert Hoover's landslide over New York governor Al Smith. She gloated to Ethel: "Every enrolled Republican on Cove Neck voted, except one lady who is dying."

Edith had also been pulled into the political game by the rift within the family. Her eldest son, Ted, rose temporarily to the top of the Republican lists in New York State while Franklin and Eleanor were actively promoting his Democratic opponents. In 1932, while Franklin was campaigning hard for the White House, Edith took advantage of her position as the "Chieftess of the Roosevelt Clan" (the term used by *The New York Times)* to speak for his opponent, incumbent President Hoover, at Madison Square Garden. She had never had much regard for Franklin's leadership abilities, and she had no qualms about opposing his election.

Like most of the Roosevelt women, Edith tried her hand at writing. Besides the chapter in the family travel book and the book on her ancestors (written with Kermit), she contributed travel articles to *Scribner's,* the same magazine that had handsomely paid Theodore for many articles over the years. Correcting proofs for one piece, she expressed doubts that it was "worth publishing," but she was still "glad" that she wrote it "for it will amuse the grandchildren some day." The style, rather than the content, dissatisfied her—she found it "too staccato for the world."

Edith's more interesting compositions turned up in her letters. In 1927, the same year that she wrote for *Scribner's,* she explored with her daughter the nature of happiness. It had been eight years since Theodore's death, and when Ethel brought up the subject of happiness, Edith replied that it had "been much in my mind lately, not just happiness but the state of being happy which I had been for so long that I thought no more of it than the air I breathed." Even with all her travels, Edith realized that she had felt happy only "twice since Father died." One occasion was during a dream about a place where the family vacationed in Vermont, and the other was after taking gas to have some teeth extracted. In the latter case, Edith had visions of herself "walking down Madison Avenue and the world was right again and I was happy. Which shows that with me, while I can have pleasure and enjoyment, interest and amusement . . . being happy is a state of unconscious mind. I think 'content' would be but a poor substitute, at least I find it so."

Happiness became even more elusive as Edith began to fail physically. In her eighties, she found travel ever more difficult; public speaking, out of reach. She grieved over the deaths of Kermit in Alaska in 1943 and Ted in France in 1944, and although she never knew that Kermit's was a suicide (having been told that he died of heart failure), she took it very hard. To her niece Eleanor, who sent a typed note of condolence, Edith replied in her own, now shaky hand: "In these days all we can do is brace ourselves to meet whatever comes. Kermit would not have shirked . . . and I who loved him so dearly must be strong to meet whatever the future brings."

For Edith Kermit Roosevelt, little future remained. On September 30, 1948, she died at Sagamore Hill at age eighty-seven, having outlived her husband, three of her sons, and Bamie and Corinne. She had every reason to believe that historians would treat her kindly, and she was right. But within the family ranks she left a more nuanced picture, one that showed some knobby spots under a polished exterior.

II

SARA DELANO COULD trace her American roots even further back than Edith Carow. The first Delano, spelling the name "De la Noye," landed at Plymouth the year after the *Mayflower*, and other relatives of Sara's sailed on that illustrious little ship under different names. Her most famous ancestor, the religious rebel Anne Hutchinson, headed up a list of frank, risk-taking female forebears. The men were also attracted to leadership and government service, and Sara's maternal grandfather served as Speaker of the Massachusetts House of Representatives.

Warren Delano, Sara's father, showed less interest in politics than in making money, and by the time she was born in 1854, he had piled up considerable wealth. Fortunes could be made quickly in the mid–nineteenth century by moving high-priced goods between the Orient and the Americas, and Warren Delano set out as a young man to learn that business. In 1824, when he was fifteen, he graduated from Fairhaven Academy, one of the many schools that completed the formal education of men not bound for college, and immediately apprenticed to a Boston importer. A job in New York followed, but he had his sights set on something a little more adventurous. When he was twenty-four, he got his chance—an offer to become a junior partner in the Boston-based Russell, Sturgis and Company—and he sailed to China to take it. Seven years later he became a senior partner with that firm, the largest American shipper on the Far East route at that time.

Promotion and compensation may have come quickly, but Warren's apprenticeship in China was hard, lonely work. The entirely male compound where he lived in Canton (no foreign women permitted) was a rough and scrappy place. Deals made there required quick thinking and shrewd bargaining. Each one carried risks, some of them enormous and with the potential for gaining a fortune or losing everything. In this environment Warren Delano developed some of the machismo that later set him apart from other Hudson River squires; even his big burly mustache was a symbol of his acquaintance with the rough-and-ready world of commerce in exotic, distant places. Even after a younger brother joined him in Canton midway through his stint, Warren led an uprooted, unsettled life.

Foreign shippers such as Delano made arrangements via a man known simply as the Houqua, an agent who served as go-between for local merchants and their foreign suppliers. Later, historians could only guess at the percentage that the Houqua kept for himself. One estimate titled him "the wealthiest merchant on earth" by the time Warren Delano first did business with him. The exact size of that fortune was less important than how the Houqua lived: he was pampered by an endless number of servants in a palace with marble-floored banquet rooms and walled gardens that protected him from the bustle of the city outside. Whether the Houqua dazzled Warren Delano more because of his wealth or his business skills is unclear, but he definitely made an impression. Warren Delano always kept a portrait of the Chinese businessman in his parlor, and he even offered to assist him in coming to visit America.

Warren Delano was in China during the Opium War (1839–42), when the British traders opened their guns on the Chinese rulers and forced them to accept importation of a product the rulers had previously banned. The local population might be willing to purchase opium at almost any price, but they required foreign suppliers to bring it to them; British traders, looking for a product to take into China (in exchange for the silks, tea, and spices they took out), were happy to oblige. The poppy fields of India, then under British rule, provided them with a source of opium. American traders had to buy in Turkey, but few of them (except the Quakers) showed any qualms about ignoring Chinese laws and delivering opium to China. Warren Delano, who considered his part in the opium trade no worse than if he had been delivering rum, wrote one of his brothers: "I do not pretend to justify . . . the opium trade in a moral and philanthropic point of view but as a merchant I insist that it has been . . . fair, honorable and legitimate . . . liable to no further or weightier objections than is the importation of Wines, Brandies and Spirit into the U. States."

By 1843, Warren Delano left Canton and returned to America to find a wife. While visiting friends in Massachusetts, the thirty-three-year-old bachelor met eighteen-year-old Catherine Lyman, the youngest daughter of an intellectual and dignified, but never wealthy, family. What the Lymans lacked in money, they made up in connections, and Catherine's father, a judge, counted among his friends some of the most luminous names of the day—including the Adamses and Websters. The courtship was swift, and within months of meeting, Warren and Catherine married and left for China. How his young bride viewed that rapid transformation in her life remains mostly speculation, although she wrote some letters indicating she found the prospect a bit daunting. After a voyage of 104 days, the newlyweds arrived in China. They lived there for the next three years, and Catherine gave birth to two children, one of whom died at age one.

When the Delanos moved back to New York in 1846, Warren thought he had a big enough fortune to cushion him for the rest of his life; they would live off his investments in American businesses such as railroads and mining. The couple bought a house at 39 Lafayette Place in what was then the most fashionable neighborhood in Manhattan, just east of Washington Square. The row of Greek Revival houses, LaGrange Terrace, was often called "Colonnade Row" because of the recessed second floors with stately Corinthian columns and tall windows facing the street. Among the Delanos' neighbors were the Gardiners, who had been owners since the 1630s of Gardiners Island, situated between the two easternmost tips of Long Island; their ebullient and beautiful twenty-one-year-old daughter, Julia, had recently made news by marrying the forty-seven-year-old President of the United States, widower John Tyler. John Jacob Astor, who considered it sufficient that his door plate announce him only as "Mr. Astor," lived a few doors away, and his son William B. Astor resided across the street from the Delanos. Washington Irving, who had settled into his Hudson River estate, Sunnyside, near Tarrytown after years of living abroad, frequently visited his good friend Irving Van Wart a few doors away from the Delanos at number 33. Generally acknowledged as the leading American author of the time, he helped bring a touch of literary sophistication to the moneyed enclave.

Despite all these celebrities in Lafayette Place, it became clear that New York City was changing in the 1850s. Immigrants streamed into Manhattan in the largest numbers the city had ever experienced (proportional to the population already there), and the spiraling population put pressure on housing and schools. Streets filled with people and pushcarts. Conflicts pitting native-born American Protestants against newly arrived Catholics from Ireland and Germany often turned violent, and the riot at the Astor Place Opera House in May 1849 was within shouting distance of the Delano home. The trouble started when fans of the American actor Edwin Forrest broke up a performance by his English rival, William Macready, but very quickly all kinds of other prejudices and problems were injected into the fight. Militia and police finally managed to restore order but not before twenty-two people were killed and dozens more, including sixty policemen, were injured.

The Delanos' country estate, Algonac, about seventy-five miles up the Hudson River, near Newburgh, presented an idyllic alternative to chaotic Manhattan. The family began renting the property in

1851, and gradually over the next few years they made it their principal residence. Sara, born there in September 1854, was Catherine Delano's seventh child but only the fifth to live (and she would later have four more). For the next twenty-six years Sara called Algonac her home. Long trips abroad removed the entire Delano family for years at a time, but when they returned, it was to that elegant house, filled with English antiques and Chinese artwork, jutting out on a promontory above the Hudson River.

The Delanos might have continued that luxurious life had the depression of 1857 not made a dent in the family fortune. Disaster did not loom immediately—a staff of ten continued to tend the magnificent gardens and look after the riding stables—but Warren Delano decided he needed to make more money. In 1860 he returned to China, leaving his wife to manage the household in his absence. When Catherine rejoined him in 1862, she took along a sizable entourage, including their seven children (ranging in age from two to sixteen), a cousin to tutor them, and two nurses.

That four-month trip with her mother to China provided the basics of "Cosmopolitan 101" for Sara, age eight. After stopping at exotic ports along the way, the family finally arrived in Hong Kong, where Warren Delano had a luxurious villa waiting for them high above the harbor. Furnished in fine antiques and tended by a large staff, "Rose Wood" was the family home for the next two years. Tutored by their cousin, the children made friends with other foreigners their own age, but they remained isolated from much of the local culture. Warren Delano decreed that his children should not learn the local language so as to avoid exposure to what he considered the seedier aspects of the servants' lives.

Those two years in Hong Kong gave Sara a kind of special sophistication in her friends' eyes (and in her own). Alice Roosevelt Longworth later confessed to her biographer and friend Michael Teague that she always thought of the Delanos as a "fascinating family. Much more so than the Roosevelts. I was particularly interested in their trading connection with the Far East and was very impressed that Cousin Sally [Sara Delano] had actually sat on the knee of the famous Houqua in Canton."

None of the Roosevelt women came close to matching Sara Delano's global travels as a child. At age ten she, along with an older sister and a younger brother, was sent home from China to live with their grandparents. The Civil War was just ending, but Sara hardly had time to settle into American ways before her parents rejoined her, and off they all went on an extended European trip. Paris hosted the Universal Exposition that year, and the Delanos settled into a roomy apartment on l'avenue Imperatrice to see as much of it as possible. A parade that included such famous leaders as Czar Alexander II, Emperor Wilhelm I of Prussia, Count Otto von Bismarck—all in their splendid uniforms and colorful regalia—made such an impression on Sara that she never forgot it. When she took her grandchildren to visit Paris many years later, she pointed to the precise window where she had sat to watch the procession.

Sara's European education did not end in France, though she did attend school there with other young female expatriates. Her family went to Dresden for the winter, and when her parents returned to New York, she stayed on for two years, boarding with a German family and taking her lessons with the children of the house. Most girls her age would have rebelled at being left on their own (as Corinne Roosevelt did four years later), but Sara seems to have adapted to life on one continent as quickly as on another. Relatives living nearby took her to the North Sea islands during summer vacations, but she did not see her parents for more than two years. By the time she returned to New York in July 1870, the Franco-Prussian War had started—the same war that left Bamie feeling stranded at Mlle. Souvestre's school outside Paris.

Exactly when Bamie and Sara met is unclear, but by 1871, when they were both seventeen, they were visiting each other often. Sara would make the trip from Newburgh to Oyster Bay to spend a month with Bamie, her rambunctious siblings, and the friends who happened to be visiting—including Edith Carow.

Later, Sara recalled that she had gotten to know both of Bamie's parents and that Mittie had made a particularly strong impression; she was one of those rare adults who put such an indelible personal stamp on everything they do that young people find them fascinating and ally with them across big gaps in age. But it was Mittie's son Elliott, five years younger than Sara, who charmed her the most. (He became godfather to her only son. When that son, Franklin, grew up and married Elliott's daughter, Eleanor, the two families intertwined in a special way—and it was Sara who had started it.)

As an adult, Sara was one of the most beautiful women in New York. Standing five feet ten inches, she had the creamy skin and light brown hair so prized by her contemporaries. She attracted many admirers, including Stanford White, who would later become a partner of Charles McKim's. Still in his early twenties when he met Sara at the home of relatives who lived near her, White had not yet earned his enormous reputation as one of the finest architects of the century or as a notorious pursuer of young, beautiful women. Years later, in 1906, Harry K. Thaw, the husband of one of his conquests, shot the architect dead in the splendid roof restaurant of Madison Square Garden that White had designed. But even in the 1870s, Sara's father saw something he did not like in White, and he passed on to Sara his apprehensions about that "red-haired trial." To underline his desire to separate the two, Warren Delano sent Sara abroad. In the company of a married sister and her husband, she was entertained by family friends across western Europe and then sailed to China, where the couple was living. By the time she returned to Algonac, Stanford White had turned his attentions elsewhere. After one last visit to Sara, he began courting another young wealthy beauty.

A moneyed belle like Sara, flitting from continent to continent, might easily have developed into nothing more than an empty-headed social creature. Like most women of her class, she lacked models of women active in reform work or the arts, and she saw little of academe. But her intellectual curiosity and good health (she later recalled that her only serious illness had been a bout with rheumatic fever while she and her family were in Paris) dictated otherwise. During the time she spent in Europe, she worked hard at French and German, and learned to speak both languages fluently and without accent.

Sara Delano's intellectual bent showed itself in her stamp collection, a hobby requiring diligence and attention to detail and one that made use of her thorough knowledge of geography and history. It was a relatively uncommon interest for a girl at the time. Later she turned her stamps over to her younger brother Fred, who added to the collection. Fred passed it along to Franklin, who adopted it as his favorite pastime when polio sidelined him from all sports. It became a lifelong passion for him, and he spent hours meticulously cataloguing those tidbits from around the world. Even as President of the United States, when the problems of the Oval Office piled up until they seemed too much for one man to tackle, he still managed to find diversion in his stamp collection.

Why Sara waited so long to marry remains a subject for speculation. She may have been confused by a surfeit of offers. Her parents imposed some conditions—and Warren Delano held his daughters' suitors to high standards, especially when it came to the subject of net worth. Sara's older sister, Annie, could not marry until her fiancé amassed a sufficient fortune, and custom dictated that Sara wait. So much travel complicated courtship for the Delano daughters, and in the end it was Bamie who brought Sara together with the man she married.

ॐ

It was not an introduction in the usual sense of first meeting. Sara's father had known James Roosevelt as a Hudson Valley neighbor, and the two men, who were about the same age, crossed paths frequently when Sara was a child. Bamie knew him as a distant cousin, since James Roosevelt's roots went back, as hers did, to the same Dutch immigrant Claes Martenszen van Rosenvelt. It had been two of Claes's grandsons, Johannes and Jacobus, who headed up what later became known as the Oyster Bay and Hyde Park branches. As an adult, Bamie sometimes visited James and his first wife, Rebecca Howland, at Springwood, their home at Hyde Park, and three years after Rebecca died, when James was looking for a wife, Bamie set up a meeting between him and Sara. He was fifty-two and she was twenty-six, but the difference in their ages that had once seemed so large now appeared much less significant. What might have been written off as a May-December match of boring convenience turned into a romantic courtship for both partners.

Handsome, energetic James Roosevelt had apparently set his eyes first on Bamie. The father of an already married son, "Rosy" (the same man Bamie would later rescue in London), he was precisely the kind of older, considerate man that Bamie might have found appealing. A graduate of Union College and Harvard Law School, he sat on the boards of several companies. Dozens of letters to his first wife show how caring and kind he could be; he was a man who sent flowers and openly expressed his affection. But Bamie decided to wait for something better.

The matchmaking worked immediately, and the marriage occurred just a few months after Bamie brought James and Sara together. A small matter of political differences did emerge: James Roosevelt voted Democratic while Warren Delano was an avid Republican. To underline how inferior Delano judged Democrats to be, he was fond of saying that in his experience not all Democrats were horse thieves but all horse thieves were Democrats. But neither bride nor groom considered that a significant obstacle, and Sara happily adopted James's Democratic label and later accompanied him to Washington to visit his friend President Grover Cleveland and his young bride at the Executive Mansion.

After the marriage of Sara Delano and James Roosevelt in October 1880 at Algonac, they went on a long European honeymoon. Wedding trips of wealthy New Yorkers typically lasted a year in the nineteenth century, and Sara, who felt right at home on the Continent, had no objection to following tradition. Returning to the United States, she blithely moved with her new husband into the Hyde Park farmhouse, Springwood, that he had remodeled and shared with his first wife. A less secure woman might have bristled at constant reminders of her predecessor in her husband's affections, but Sara apparently saw no need to blot out the dead woman's memory. When Sara died sixty-one years later, Springwood had been renamed Hyde Park, but it still held pictures and platters from the time of the "first Mrs. James."

Soon after her marriage Sara got her own special place at Campobello Island, off the Maine coast in New Brunswick, Canada; she and her husband bought land and built there in the 1880s, but she was perfectly willing to take Springwood as she found it. She and James's first wife even ended up buried alongside him in a Hyde Park churchyard.

From the day she married James, Sara became a Roosevelt in more than name. Geoffrey Ward, one of Franklin's biographers, noted the symbolism of the twenty-mile ride she took from Algonac to Springwood after the wedding. The Delano carriage transported the newlyweds halfway, but then they were met by James's coachman, who drove them the rest of the way in a Roosevelt vehicle. Other signs confirmed the young woman's move into her husband's world. He was the third generation to live in Hyde Park, and she found herself surrounded with Roosevelts. Her husband's mother lived down the road, Rosy and Helen Roosevelt and their two little children next door, and James's brother's family a short distance away. Life for Sara's husband centered on the one-thousand-acre estate with its unassuming but sprawling white house alongside the river. Had she married a younger man, out to make his way, Sara might have been tempted to widen her social contacts and enlarge her horizons. But James had settled into the comfortable life of a country gentleman, enjoying what he had, and she seemed content with his choice.

By the time she returned from her honeymoon, Sara was four months pregnant, and in January 1882, at age twenty-seven, she gave birth to her first and only child. Although her husband's family had a long tradition of naming boys for ancestors and this baby was slated to be called Isaac, the parents named him for Sara's Uncle Franklin. She may have thought that her stepson, Rosy, whose given name was James Roosevelt Roosevelt, bore enough of that side of the family name for both boys. In any case, she got her side on the scoreboard twice with this boy: Franklin's middle name was Delano. Like most women of the time, whatever their economic level, Sara gave birth at home, in the big front bedroom at Springwood. It was a difficult delivery, and she was in labor for more than twenty-four hours, a fact that one biographer saw as significant in explaining her dedication to the child—but Sara would have doted on that boy if his delivery had been entirely painless.

Unlike Sara, who rarely admitted to any indisposition, Franklin was a sickly child. He got typhoid fever when his parents took him to London, then chicken pox on a subsequent trip abroad. But in his mother's mind he was the perfect child. Before he entered Groton at age fourteen, he studied with private tutors at home under her watchful eye. At Groton he was frequently in the infirmary with ailments ranging from bronchitis and measles to scarlet fever.

That fragile health and protected treatment as an only son may have combined to earn Franklin his reputation as slightly "sissy." It was a trait frequently commented on by the Theodore branch of the family. Alice Longworth, for example, noted that she and her siblings liked to read, but they detested sentimental books such as *Black Beauty* and *Little Lord Fauntleroy*. After they were all famous adults, Alice indirectly blamed Sara for starting Franklin down the wrong road: "Now, Franklin was encouraged to read *Little Lord Fauntleroy* as a child. We even suspected he dressed a little like him. It was THAT kind of difference [between him and us] which manifested itself at an early age."

But the difference did not stop there. Alice once recalled that Franklin was not at all like her brothers, and then, as though to clinch the distinction, she added that Franklin "sailed rather than rowed." During summer vacations at Campobello he became an avid sailor, spending entire days on his boat, *Half Moon*. But he showed little interest in the body-building competition or the rugged wilderness hikes that attracted Theodore's sons. With a touch of gleeful cruelty, his distant cousins wrote him off as "light-weight" and in a nod to his initials, F.D., they called him "Feather Duster" behind his back. A younger father might have encouraged Franklin to attempt more strenuous physical activity, but James Roosevelt was fifty-four when Franklin was born.

As the boy grew up, his father's health worsened. Sara tended her husband through every illness with the devotion and attention to detail that marks the younger wife, cognizant that her much older husband will probably die first but convinced that diligence on her part could alter the odds.

In one of James's bad spells, soon after Franklin entered Groton, Sara rushed home from a visit at her son's school to be with him and then wrote Franklin to reassure him: "My darling Boy, I found Papa better, I am thankful to say, it seems only a cold and chill which affected his stomach." So many of these episodes rendered each one a little less scary, and neither Sara nor her son was prepared for James's death when it came on December 8, 1900. They had been married for twenty years, and Sara's anguish and grief are evident in the diary entry she later made for that day: "All is over. At 2:20 he merely slept away. As I write these words I wonder how I lived when he left me."

But she still had Franklin, and having just turned forty-six herself, she could anticipate many years of full devotion to him. Since he had just begun his freshman year at Harvard, she took an apartment in Cambridge during his remaining winters there in order to see as much of him as possible. Such an arrangement was not unique. Nicholas Longworth, who married Theodore's daughter Alice, was thirteen years older than Franklin, but his widowed mother had also managed to live in Cambridge and keep a close watch on her only son. Both mothers could justify the moves as giving them the chance to explore Boston's art galleries and study music, but their primary focus remained their sons. Sara relished Franklin's every accomplishment, and when he graduated from Harvard in three years, she could not have been prouder if she had earned the sheepskin herself. (Edith Roosevelt's oldest son, Ted, and Eleanor's younger brother Hall both accomplished the same feat, making graduation from Harvard in three years something of a family tradition.)

Renting an extra apartment near Franklin presented no financial hardship for Sara. James Roosevelt left his young widow a large estate, including both land and investments. She turned some of the money over for management by her brothers and then watched as it grew. In 1928 she boasted to Franklin that a mere $2,000 investment was now worth $393,000, "a tremendous gain." Except for seeing that her income was spent wisely, she showed little interest in money. She did not have to—she had never known a world without it.

During Franklin's Harvard years and those that followed, Sara saw a lot of the Theodore branch. She continued her friendship with Bamie, by now married and with a son of her own, and she watched with satisfaction as Theodore's political star rose. At his inauguration as governor of New York in 1899, Sara and James sat proudly with other relatives in the audience. When the Rough Rider moved into the White House, the newly widowed Sara had an extra incentive to maintain contact with that branch of the family. She suggested that Franklin visit "Coz Bamie" as often as possible, and when an invitation arrived from Bamie's house in Washington, Sara insisted that he wire his acceptance immediately: "It is a delightful chance for you and I hope you have thought of my expressed wishes and not made other engagements." After one of Franklin's visits to Bamie in early January 1902, his mother wrote him: "I am so glad you had so 'rich and varied' an experience in Washington. . . . You certainly had great kindness and many pleasures. I wrote today to [thank] Cousin Bamie."

Not everything Theodore did as chief executive pleased Sara and her son. One of the President's first big showdowns came in the winter of 1902 when anthracite coal miners in Pennsylvania walked off their jobs and demanded a 20 percent pay raise and a cut in hours from the ten a day they had been working. With 140,000 men refusing to work, coal supplies dwindled during the winter, and some factories and schools had to close. In a move that won him many admirers in some quarters (and hostile attacks in others), Theodore Roosevelt summoned mine owners to the White House and threatened to take over the mines and operate them with federal troops. When the owners grudgingly consented to a 10 percent increase in wages and a one-hour reduction in workday, the miners went back on the job.

Young Franklin, still a student at Harvard, had not yet developed his trust in a strong executive, and he confessed to his mother that he thought the President had made a mistake. She agreed, although in tempered criticism. On October 28, 1902, she wrote Franklin: "I think you are perfectly right in your opinion that politically the President has made a mistake to interfere, but one cannot help loving and admiring him the more for it when one realizes that he tried to right the wrong, even though it may injure his own prospects." Sara also preferred limited government: "Personally I feel as I know your dear father felt two years ago, that if only the coal operators and companies could be left alone to work out the problem they would do it without help from either politicians, statesmen or 'financiers.'"

∽

The family fortune and her own beauty combined to get Sara almost everything she wanted, and when those did not suffice, she contributed her own iron will. Later, her daughter-in-law, Eleanor, and then Eleanor's biographers turned Sara's image into that of an interfering matriarch, but that interpretation needs context. From childhood, Sara had confidence, a trait that Eleanor acquired slowly and with great difficulty. Had they met in other circumstances, Sara might have become one of Eleanor's models—she was a lot like Bamie, whom Eleanor admired greatly.

It is true that even after her son became President of the United States, Sara rarely held her tongue, and she could be very blunt. The columnist Joe Alsop, Corinne's grandson and a cousin of both Eleanor and Franklin, recalled that Sara once hosted a large dinner at Hyde Park attended by Huey Long, the boisterous but popular Louisiana governor. He took no notice of her, but she zeroed in immediately on the contrast between Long's manners and those of a Hudson River squire. In a stage whisper audible to everyone present, she queried, "Who's that dreadful man sitting beside Franklin?"

Sara's reign at Hyde Park extended beyond the property line. She continued to entertain and be entertained by Delanos, especially the brothers and sisters who lived nearby, her entire life. But her role as a Roosevelt required a full schedule of charitable good works—of which Sara did more than she is usually credited with. As a young mother she organized a sewing club for Hyde Park schoolgirls and continued supporting it for thirty years. Another sewing club enrolled older women who made clothing for the town's indigent or taught villagers to sew for themselves. When a mass meeting in Manhattan featured Jacob Riis, the journalist known for exposing the horrible housing conditions of immigrants, Sara insisted on going to hear him. She became a contributing member, almost from its founding in 1902, of Greenwich House, the settlement house in Greenwich Village. Her donations were never as large as those of Corinne Robinson, who sometimes earmarked hundreds of dollars for Greenwich House, but Sara gave regular and sizable amounts.

Turn-of-the-century America saw many new organizations for women, some of them purely social and others political or philanthropic, but Sara showed little interest in them—she had a club of one in Franklin. In 1903 when wealthy New York women formed the Colony Club, modeled on the exclusive organizations of their husbands and brothers, Sara refused to join, saying she saw no need for it. The luxurious facilities located at Madison Avenue near Thirtieth Street—including a swimming pool, roof garden, library, and smoking room—might have appealed to others, but Sara never depended on the close cooperation of a community of women. She had female friends, including Bamie, but she did not require a Colony Club as a place to see them. Only later, when the club moved farther uptown and she needed a pied-à-terre in Manhattan, did she apply for membership.

Within the Roosevelt clan, praise for Sara Delano is almost universal among her own generation. Bamie, not known for suffering fools, welcomed visits with "Cousin Sallie" all her life. Sara even made a hit with Mittie, who made one of her rare trips up the Hudson to pay a call after Sara gave birth to Franklin. Corinne Robinson probably could not have listed all the roles that Sara played in her life: family friend, distant cousin by marriage, and stepgrandmother-in-law of Corinne's son Teddy after he married Helen Roosevelt in June 1904. Since the mother of the bride was dead, it fell to Sara, the stepmother of the bride's father, Rosy, to host the wedding party at Hyde Park. The entire clan turned out in force for the celebration, and the Robinsons stayed over for a few days. Later, they agreed that Sara had been a superb and thoughtful hostess—as usual.

Subsequent generations judged Sara more harshly; perhaps it is fairer to say that affection for her skipped a generation or two. Eleanor started out a devoted apostle of the sophisticated Sara but soon grew very tired of her insistence on "helping" her son's family so much, and both Shef Cowles and Corinne Alsop took Eleanor's side against Sara.

It was quite a different story among Sara's great-grandchildren, who found much to like in this energetic, smart dowager. Eleanor Seagraves recalled that Sara showed a warmth which Eleanor never matched. She was "terrific with the third generation, with her great-grandchildren. Very tolerant of all our childish idiosyncrasies. She used to read us the Sunday comics. We'd get in the big bed at Hyde Park and she read us all those silly things, Katzenjammer Kids and all of those."

Eleanor Seagraves was the oldest grandchild of Franklin and Eleanor, but Sara was already in her seventies by the time she was born in 1927. Sara could be "very strict" and "difficult," Seagraves recalled, but she did not deserve the "bad press" that she received. Pointing out that the "mother-in-law role when FDR and ER were younger" could not be easy, Seagraves continued: "I still think . . . she was a product of her social milieu" and that "people who write about her today simply have no understanding of her background. She could be haughty. . . . But she was not an unreasonable person. She never raised her voice." The best way to understand the dowager is to see her whole, someone who perceived Franklin and Eleanor as children even after they married, and much in need of her assistance.

More than just a doting matriarch, Sara also took a firm interest in government and politics. She relished a good campaign as much as anyone, and although her involvement might be dismissed as simply motherly concern, it showed itself long before Franklin entered politics. Their correspondence regarding Theodore while Franklin was still a student at Harvard and Theodore was in the White House is one example of this interest, but there were others reaching back to the days that she traveled and lived abroad. As a result of meeting leaders from many different countries, she felt comfortable exchanging opinions and was rarely daunted by power, whether in the form of the Chinese Houqua or a British prime minister. Many years spent outside the United States in her youth yielded a familiarity with governments and cultures of many nations, and this fed her confidence and curiosity.

After she was widowed, Sara continued to travel, making frequent trips to Europe until shortly before her death, and she liked to send her written impressions to Franklin. In August 1922 she added a postscript to her note from London to inform her son that James M. Cox, the Democratic presidential candidate with whom Franklin ran for vice president in 1920, was still receiving lots of press abroad. Then she moved on to a more controversial topic—the matter of debts that Great Britain had incurred during the Great War of 1914–18: "I wish the United States would lead the way in forgiving the debt. Other nations would follow. The first two years of the war, the U.S. made so much money and England borrowed not for herself but to [fight] the war. It would be a fine thing, I believe, and would do more than anything to bring some sort of help and settlement."

Sara's interest in government grew alongside Franklin's rise in politics. When it became clear that he would reenter the field despite his paralysis in 1921, she made it a point to attend political meetings. But sometimes her accounts of them took on a haughty tone. After a Democratic gathering in July 1925, she penned a report to "Dearest Son" that rendered his thirty-nine-year-old wife almost childlike: Everything "went off well," she assured him, "I think 200 people came. Eleanor presided and made several excellent little remarks in her charming way."

While many American women in the 1920s refused to take advantage of their newly earned right to vote, Sara not only voted herself but made sure others did. After the November 1925 election, she wrote Franklin that not only had she voted but she had provided a car to take others to the polls. She typically stayed up until the votes were counted even when the prospects were dim. After one disappointing showing she reported to Franklin that "the entire Democratic ticket of Hyde Park is defeated by a large majority." Then she added the good news: "All four amendments are voted for by a good majority, so that is something." When she could not remain at Hyde Park long enough to wire the results to her son in 1927, she made arrangements for someone else to see that he received word of the final count. In 1928, when Al Smith ran for president, Sara went to work to help him win. She had spent the summer in Europe, but after her return she went to Campobello, buttonholing as many people as she could to deliver a good word for Smith. To Franklin she wrote: "I have been working hard for Smith. . . . You would admire my eloquence."

Too shrewd to ignore the importance of good public relations, Sara reacted cautiously to attacks on Franklin. When a false rumor circulated in November 1930 that he was converting to Catholicism, she wrote it off as an obvious attempt by "some idiots" to "injure you in the opinion of our Protestant Church." The correct response would be a quick rebuttal, but she cautioned him not to sound prejudiced. Then she added, in a bit of overstatement considering her stand on Eleanor's hiring of African Americans, "I also am absolutely against bigotry."

Bringing her own perspective to the hurly-burly of politics, Sara objected to what she saw as "boss" support of her son. In July 1932, as the presidential campaign heated up, she contributed $5,000 to Franklin's campaign and then wrote him: "How proud I should be to have you elected without Tammany or [Al] Smith's help—You would be a wonderful President and follower of Cleveland and Wilson"—whom, of course, the Theodore branch detested.

When Sara's younger sister Kassie wrote from Washington a few weeks later that everyone in the capital expected Franklin to win, Sara gleefully passed that prediction on to him. Then she offered some motherly advice on how to perform. At a White House reception for the Bar Association not long before she wrote, President Hoover had quit shaking hands after greeting eighteen hundred people, leaving an even larger number disappointed. Sara sympathized with the reason given for stopping, a "bruised hand," but she thought the long receiving lines at the White House "a very barbaric custom." She suggested that Franklin "devise some thing better than hand shaking which now is out of all reason. Everyone feels it is a stupid idea."

Once Franklin won the presidency, his mother, who persisted in seeing herself as definitely not one of the rich, passed on to him her views on fiscal matters, though there is little evidence that he paid much attention to them. On June 5, 1933, she implored: "Darling, don't let the income taxes go up!" She had talked with a "good many people" who feared such an increase, and she felt she would suffer from any added tax: "To be personal, I must cut down if we have more income tax." To her mind an increased sales tax was preferable because "it would help some states very much where rich people go and pay no taxes."

Sara then passed on what she had been hearing from her friends and neighbors about the bonus bill for veterans from the Great War who were currently marching on Washington. The winter of 1932–33 had been the worst of the Great Depression, with more families dispossessed of their homes and more workers looking for jobs than ever before, and veterans argued that a bonus due them later should be paid immediately. By May 1933 thousands of them had set up their tents in the capital, but Franklin remained firm on not prepaying the bonus. He offered forestry jobs to the veterans, and Eleanor spoke words of encouragement, but the men adamantly refused to budge. Finally, after a representative group of veterans met with Franklin and learned that he continued to oppose any prepayment of the bonus, the veterans began to scatter. Some took forestry work, and others simply went home. Sara had not come up with a solution, but she made clear that she was aware of the problem.

As the time approached for Franklin to run for a second term in 1936, some parts of the nation seemed disappointed with his performance. In 1932 he had been elected by a wide margin and almost immediately began unfolding his New Deal, a program for recovery from the Depression that included more government in people's lives in the form of bank regulations and laws legitimizing unions, but basically it did not change the system. Four years later when many problems remained, including unemployment that stood at roughly 10 percent of the workforce, extremists of various persuasions castigated the President as too moderate. Father Coughlin, the bigoted "Radio Priest" who broadcast weekly from Detroit to a large audience, denounced Franklin as "the dumbest man ever to occupy the White House." Francis Townsend, a retired physician in California, urged the President to adopt his scheme to pump money into the pockets of the elderly with the requirement that they spend it at once. Louisiana governor Huey Long, the "Kingfish," a Populist demagogue who was assassinated in September 1935, insisted that Americans should "share the wealth." Long had in mind especially those like Sara Delano Roosevelt with family fortunes of more than $5 million or incomes of $1 million. For them he suggested a tax of 100 percent.

Sara took stock of the many threats to Franklin's reelection and then wrote him in sanguine terms about how she felt. In early April 1936 she met a friend of hers who had attended a "Republican affair" and came away disappointed. The friend admitted that the party had "*no* real plan and [showed] no sign that they realized how the world is changing." The conclusion was clear—Franklin would be reelected. Sara insisted that her interest in victory was not personal but issue-oriented: "I said 'I do not *care* except to see his [more moderate] theories *justified.*'"

⁂

All through her son's presidency Sara continued the charitable work she had begun as a young mother, but now she widened her horizons. She had first heard of Mary K. Simkhovitch in 1902, when she founded Greenwich House and Sara had become a contributor. Over the years the two women had met occasionally, but after 1918, when Simkhovitch bought a summer house in Maine, across the Bay of Fundy from the Roosevelts' Campobello, they saw more of each other, and Sara became even more supportive of Simkhovitch's efforts. In the 1930s when the need for settlement houses diminished because of a drop in immigration, Simkhovitch shifted her attention to national housing reform and insisted that the federal government take some responsibility for providing decent accommodations to all "deserving" Americans. This could be accomplished through renovation of dilapidated units or construction of new ones, but the national government had to pick up part of the tab, she insisted. Working with New York senator Robert Wagner and others, including First Lady Eleanor Roosevelt, Simkhovitch helped write the Federal Housing Act of 1938, providing for the debut of what would turn out to be an important role for the federal government in people's lives.

Older than Eleanor Roosevelt and younger than Sara, Simkhovitch, born in 1867, had the help of both in her housing struggle. Eleanor spoke at various housing conferences that Simkhovitch organized to change public opinion and bring Americans around to the idea that this was a legitimate role for government to play. Eleanor also gave money and used her "My Day" column to praise Simkhovitch's work. But few people realized that Sara Delano Roosevelt also allied with the reformer, performing less publicly but just as regularly. She sent checks and made sure the Roosevelt name appeared on the guest list at benefits that Eleanor was too busy to attend. Well into her eighties, Sara was a "regular" at Greenwich House events.

Sara's charity reached outside New York. Her years in Europe as a girl produced many friends there, and she continued to correspond with some of them to the end of her life. She knew Germany best of all, as a result of living there two years during her teens, and she spoke the language fluently. With shock and disbelief she witnessed Hitler's rise to power in the 1930s. In late 1938, when she was eighty-four and had many worries about her own family (including the marital difficulties of two of her grandchildren, who had recently obtained divorces), she still had the energy to consider what was happening in Germany. To Franklin she wrote in November 1938: "What can I do with very nice letters from Germany asking for help to get over here? It is all so awful for the Jews!" Sara's requests tended to be specific, offered in the name of her friends, but they were nevertheless genuine. Her assistance had been requested for a "Jewish family who have a shop!"

As the situation in Europe worsened, Sara joined many Americans hoping to avoid war. Like others, she stuck to that hope even after evidence came in to show it untenable. Following Hitler's move into

Austria in March 1938, which aroused virtually no protest abroad, he turned to Czechoslovakia, and Western European nations sent representatives to Munich in September to discuss what they should do. The notorious conclusion—to have "peace in our time" in exchange for silence—would later appear very wrong, but at the time it had its supporters, Sara among them. In early December she wrote Franklin that she knew some people who were "for" Anthony Eden, the British statesman who opposed the Munich Pact, but "I am for [Neville] Chamberlain!!!" the prime minister and architect of the "appeasement" policy.

At the same time, Sara referred to the economic crisis in France, another country she knew well. The economy had sagged there, and in May, Premier Edouard Daladier announced a devaluation plan as part of his program to get the country back on its feet. He added a spending program to make his suggestion more palatable but found insufficient public support. Finally, in October 1938, Daladier asked for decree power, which Parliament granted, to give him tighter control over production schedules. The franc gained slightly, but workers rebelled, and in late November the General Confederation of Labor ordered a nationwide strike. Violence erupted, and Daladier authorized the Public Works Minister to requisition mines and industries; then he took over the public utilities. The strike followed, and Daladier went on the radio to call for an end to it. Sara had followed events, and on December 1 she wrote Franklin: "Daladier seems to have been successful about the strike." Then she added modestly: "I try to read and think a little but am about as stupid as it is possible to be."

As Hitler continued to march across Europe, swallowing up one nation after another, Sara followed each move. Some Americans insisted that outsiders need not get involved because a revolt from within Germany would do the job more effectively than any foreign power ever could, but she doubted that. In 1940, after Italy entered the war and Franklin abandoned all pretense of neutrality on the part of the United States, Sara endorsed his stand, writing him: "I feel so sad for the poor Finns," who were struggling to maintain their own neutrality.

By that time word had spread around the world of the treatment of Jews in Germany and Austria. They were excluded from spas and places of entertainment, forbidden to perform in some theaters, and kept from many areas of trade. Books they wrote were burned, and their property was subjected to special requirements for registration and taxation. Sigmund Freud and other well-known Jews managed to flee, but others, less famous or not connected to power, had more difficulty. The United States' annual quota for German immigrants had been filled by mid-September 1938, so any new arrivals would need special authorization from Congress. Various groups and individuals came forward with proposals to help, and the New York State Jewish War Veterans Council suggested that each post accept responsibility for one refugee. But other Americans were less generous, and Father Coughlin helped fuel people's prejudices by ranting about the harm that Jews had done to the United States.

Not much attention was given to the concentration camps where Jews were imprisoned, but Sara was well aware of them. On December 7, 1940, she began a letter to Franklin by passing along a compliment from her friend Mr. Cartier, who "feels that your being President is everything for our country." Then Sara brought up the subject on her mind: "I hope [Mr. Cartier] will succeed in getting Claudel, his son in law, out of the internment camp and over here as he is [a] good and brave and useful man even in the camp." She was not relying entirely on Cartier for her judgment of the son-in-law. She had also spoken with a "man who does not even *know* the Cartiers," and he had agreed that Claudel deserved help. Complicating the situation was the fact that Claudel's wife refused to leave "her three babies somewhere in France," so the entire family had to be rescued. In the meantime, Sara feared for the health of her friend Mrs. Cartier, who seemed, Sara wrote in a mixture of pity and admiration, "pretty delicate and I think has almost *too* much to bear, but is brave."

Reaching beyond this one family whom she happened to know, Sara wanted to do something bigger. Her friend Cartier had a "plan," she wrote Franklin in late 1940, "which I think you will approve as he wants to do something for the *children* of France and *be one* of a committee of three [to work on this]." Sara suggested keeping the matter "between you and me" for the moment, but she assured him he would "hear [more] later." She had even taken it upon herself to guarantee an appointment at the White House for Cartier: "I have promised you will see him in Washington after

Christmas." Then, in an admission that her action in this matter went beyond what she usually did, she wrote: "You know I do not often 'put even my little finger into the pie.'"

∽

Before she had the chance to do much more, Sara Delano Roosevelt died, on September 7, 1941. Up until that time, observers frequently commented on her spunk and intelligence. Unabashedly biased in favor of her own class, she was hardly narrow or mean-spirited, and the newspaper and magazine coverage of her during her lifetime was generally kind. She left a long roster of admiring friends to mourn her death, and her great-grandchildren relished her energy and welcomed her generosity. Then her story got rewritten with a very different theme: first with Dore Schary's play "Sunrise at Campobello," and then through various biographies of Eleanor.

"Sunrise at Campobello" opened on Broadway on January 30, 1958, and a movie version opened two years later. Ironically, this piece of theater, which first appeared on the seventy-sixth anniversary of Sara's painful delivery of her son, portrayed her as an interfering and cruel mother-in-law, the butt of many jokes. Playwright Schary, who set out to dramatize Franklin's victory over polio, opened the action on the day Franklin was stricken at Campobello in 1921, and the curtain came down after his ebullient "Happy Warrior" speech for Al Smith at Madison Square Garden in 1924. But in between, the audience got a glimpse of Roosevelt family life, showing "Mama" as an unappealing individual. As Eleanor Seagraves noted, "If you're a playwright you have to have the protagonist and the antagonist, and Granny is always the antagonist. Everything's always exaggerated. It was just ghastly." This play was not simply a family's fight against a debilitating illness, it was, according to Seagraves, the portrayal of Sara Delano Roosevelt as a "harridan."

Schary, who asked Eleanor Roosevelt for permission to do the play, described Sara in the list of characters as "in her middle sixties, a strong, dominant vibrant figure of a woman . . . dressed in expensive and elegant clothes . . . at all times the Lady of the Manor." Anne Seymour, who played the role on Broadway, and Ann Shoemaker, who took it to Hollywood, both expanded the character beyond Schary's description and turned Sara into an unforgettable, domineering matriarch who shouts orders at the servants and countermands her son and daughter-in-law on how to raise their children. Entirely absorbed in her own importance, the Sara of "Sunrise" sees politics as an appalling endeavor for men and a shocking one for women. For many of the movie viewers, Sara's nastiness remained a more vivid image than Franklin's courage in fighting for his political life after contracting polio.

That play, even with a popular movie version to reinforce its message, could not have had such an impact had it not fit in with popular American views about mothers-in-law. But it had support from other quarters. Eleanor's many biographers, intent on pointing out her courage and achievements, overlooked Sara's redeeming characteristics, preferring to focus on her eccentricities and narrowness. In the process they helped reduce her to a cartoon figure—a sharp and convenient contrast to the benevolent, broad-minded Eleanor. A fuller picture of Sara would fill in the lines missing from the caricature, thus admitting her foibles along with her strengths. But for women marrying into the Roosevelt clan, a parody can sometimes substitute for proof.

∾

With the caricature torn away from Edith Carow and Sara Delano, they both seem to fit well a saying in the clan: "No one is more Roosevelt than a Roosevelt wife." Both women were complicated, and neither is entirely appealing, especially the snobbish, self-centered side of them. But their class consciousness, relegating most of the world to a lesser echelon, is much like that of Corinne and Bamie, who never had to answer for it, at least in any public way.

Stories abound of how Sara treated those she considered inferior as simply nonexistent. Hall Roosevelt's daughter Eleanor Roosevelt remembered that Sara wanted to "see Hall's daughter" one day at Hyde Park when the girl was about six. Pushed forward to comply with the command, Eleanor found herself "in front of Sara and my eyes were just about on the level of her bosom and the pearls. She turned me around and looked at my back and then gave me a slight push and I went back to my place. She said, 'So, that's Hall's daughter.'" The young woman met Sara afterward, but they never became friends: "That's the only thing she ever said to me."

Comments about Edith being "mean as a snake" or "in a snarkish mood" are underlined by her granddaughter's treatment of her in fiction. In 1950, Archie's daughter Theodora Keogh published *Meg*, a book her aunt Ethel found "horrifying [with its] accounts of perversion of every sort." The normally tolerant Alice Longworth drew the line at this book, insisting, "Thirty years ago it would not have been printed." The portrait of Edith was perfectly clear. She was described, according to Ethel, "in bed, playing solitaire in a lavender wrapper, her great nose standing out under her cap. Dreary Gloomy Sagamore."

The point is hardly whether Sara or Edith was the more difficult woman. The real question concerns the contradiction between the public and private records of the two. While criticism of Edith stayed within the family, Sara's bad press became the stuff of national comedy.

No photographer was engaged for Eleanor's wedding day in 1905, but her future mother-in-law, Sara Delano Roosevelt, arranged for this picture to be taken several weeks earlier.

CHAPTER FIVE

ELEANOR ROOSEVELT ROOSEVELT

(1884–1962)

HE BIG NEWS IN New York that day in 1905 was the Saint Patrick's Day Parade. For more than fifty years the Irish had been celebrating March 17 with a parade up Fifth Avenue, and as the Irish component of the city grew, the event became almost a citywide celebration. This particular parade gained more than the usual attention because the most popular president in decades, Theodore Roosevelt, was coming to New York to deliver two speeches, one to the paraders and one at a dinner afterward at Delmonico's, where members of the Hibernian Order were slated to celebrate.

Squeezed into that busy schedule, he would stop for a couple of hours at a brownstone on East Seventy-sixth Street, and there, in the presence of two hundred invited guests, he would, as *The New York Times* reported, give away in marriage his niece, who was "an orphan." The partition on the parlor floor had been taken down between the house of Susie Parish, Eleanor's cousin, and that of Susie's mother next door, forming one large space. Some guests failed to get in, however, because the crush of people at the parade and the large number of police officers assembled to control the crowds and protect the President combined to form a gigantic traffic jam. The buildup for the event had been enormous—more than three hundred wedding gifts had come in, and the names on the guest list looked like a *Who's Who* of New York—Burden, Mortimer, Vanderbilt, and lots of Roosevelts. Hardly anyone paid much attention to the bride and groom.

The President performed his official duty with a loud "I do," the bridal couple exchanged vows and rings, and then everyone, it seemed, followed the President into the library where he held forth in his usual ebullience with funny stories and political tidbits. When *The New York Times* reported the event the next day, the headline did not even mention Eleanor's name. It was "the President" who gave "the bride away" to his cousin, Franklin Delano Roosevelt.

The bevy of six bridesmaids—and an equivalent number of ushers—filled a large portion of the parlor, making the event look like a family reunion. Alice and Corinney represented Eleanor's paternal side, and from Franklin's side came two Delanos—Ellen and Muriel. Isabella Selmes, though not technically a relative, had been a part of the Roosevelt circle for so long that she seemed like a cousin, and Helen Cutting was a good friend.

Eleanor wore her mother's veil on this special day that was the anniversary of her birth, but so many aspects of that day seemed entirely removed from her control. The minister, the Reverend Endicott Peabody of Groton, was Franklin's choice. In his usual hearty style, the President kept most of the attention for himself. Alice once quipped that he always had to be at the center of the action—the "bride at every wedding, the corpse at every funeral"—and this was no exception. He did manage to congratulate Franklin on "keeping the name in the family," but he seemed completely oblivious to the fact that he had made Eleanor a bystander at her own wedding. In typical style she played the matter down, writing later that the "guests seemed more interested" in following the President than in anything else.

Thus began one of the most complicated marriages of all time. It lasted (in its fashion) almost forty years, through the births of six children and the death of one, two major wars and the Great Depression, and, most important, the strains produced by Franklin's wandering eyes and Eleanor's tight friendships with both men and women. Revealed in their marriage were most of the themes that mark the Roosevelt story: inordinate energy, strong commitment to public service, unusual achievement racked up during some very good luck and a substantial dose of misfortune.

I

THE ONE BLACK SHEEP among Theodore Sr. and Mittie's children was Eleanor's father, Elliott, who never measured up to the others, and she made it her business to burnish his image as soon as she got the chance. In 1933, when she had many obligations as First Lady, Eleanor took time out from other duties to collect her father's youthful letters in a book and publish them as *Hunting Big Game in the Eighties: The Letters of Elliott Roosevelt, Sportsman*. In the introduction she explained that she was the only one of her generation who remembered him well. She wanted people to see the adventuresome, charming side of Elliott Roosevelt, in contrast to his usual depiction as a failure. Struggling to be fair, she wrote: "He never accomplished anything which could make him of any importance to the world at large, unless a personality which left a vivid mark on friends and associates may be counted important." On her he left an "indelible impression" and became "the one great love of my life as a child. . . . Like many children I lived a dream life with him; so his memory is still a vivid, living thing to me."

Eleanor then recounted a family story to illustrate her father's generosity. When still quite young, Elliott went out for a walk on a cold winter day wearing a new overcoat, but when he returned an hour or so later, he was coatless. The family questioned him about what happened, and he replied that he had seen a "small and ragged urchin" who appeared to need the coat more than he did, and without a thought he took it off and gave it to him." Eleanor proudly cited that magnanimity as though it compensated for the many failures in other areas of his life. Anyone less biased than Eleanor might have reacted differently to hearing the story and wondered whether the "urchin" would have preferred some other assistance than a coat much too large for him. In any case, it was Elliott's parents who had to replace what he was quick to give away—and they had ample funds to do so without a murmur.

As a young man, Elliott charmed almost everyone he met, and his daughter benefited in some ways from his magnetism. While a student in England, she was befriended by her great-uncle Irvine Bulloch, Mittie's brother, and his wife, Ella, who had entertained Elliott on his travels through their country. Following Irvine's death, Ella continued loving contacts with Eleanor, who noted in *Hunting Big Game* that she had made every "slip worn by every girl baby" in the family, and in her will she left her most prized jewelry to Eleanor.

Eleanor's careful defense of her father did not extend to her mother or, indeed, to any of her mother's family. But in the beginning, the union of Elliott Roosevelt and Anna Hall was viewed within his family as the best thing that could have happened to him. In 1882, when he returned from his hunting trip to India, he had many exciting stories to tell but little else to show for his time. He did not, for example, as Theodore later did, try to publish an account of his exotic travel. In fact, Elliott seemed to find little to do. For a while he tagged along with Theodore, helping him campaign for the New York State Assembly and then accompanying him to explore ranching possibilities in the western states. But Elliott's life had such an aimlessness, all the more apparent alongside his older, very focused brother, that his family expressed considerable relief when he began courting the beautiful Anna Hall during the winter of 1882–83. Perhaps the responsibilities of a family would give his life some direction.

Three years younger than Elliott, Anna Rebecca Hall, born March 17, 1863, was the oldest of six children, but the strong sense of responsibility so evident in many firstborns completely eluded her. Whether she and her siblings were staying in their parents' brownstone at 429 Fifth Avenue (a few blocks north of the Astors) or in their sprawling country home, Oak Terrace, in Tivoli on the Hudson, they put the highest value on having a good time—perhaps a reaction to their stern and pious father. Like most people of their class, the Halls also made time for travel, and Anna took her first trip to Europe at age five. Her childhood was a carefree one, played out in pampered luxury, and as she grew up, the youthful pleasures became only slightly more mature. She and her three sisters all ranked as stunning beauties, and Anna was sometimes singled out as the most striking, so she had no dearth of invitations. An inspiring teacher might have brought out a more serious, intellectual side of her, but none appeared. Her parents were fiercely religious, but it was a religion centered more on piety than charity; the single bit of evidence supporting Anna's early interest in charity is a certificate of membership in the Children's American Missionary Society when she was about eight.

From the minute Elliott introduced Anna to his family, they vied among themselves to give her the highest approval rating. On June 24, 1883, as soon as she received news of the couple's engagement, Corinne sent exuberant congratulations to Anna saying how "delighted we are that you have made Elliott so grateful and happy a man." Corinne, who tended to side with sunny Elliott against the more serious Theodore in those days, concluded that he had found just the right woman: "He loves you with so tender and respectful a devotion that I who love my darling brother so dearly . . . cannot but feel that you as well as he have much to be thankful for." The already married Corinne proceeded to offer Anna some advice: "I think the best gift a woman can receive from her husband is his unfailing trust and confidence." Then she made her own prediction, remarkable for its error: "If Elliott is half so lovely in his new capacity as he has always been as brother, I do not believe you will ever regret your choice."

His mother and aunt also heartily approved Elliott's choice. Mittie sent a warm note and enclosed a pin that she had ordered specially made for the prospective bride. In a letter to Elliott, Aunt Anna Gracie explained she was thrilled to welcome into the family "dear, graceful, sweet, Anna, your chosen one, and my namesake! I feel that she is to become dearer and dearer to me, and that God has given her to you my beloved Ellie." The two Annas had attended a benefit for the newsboys, and the older woman had been immediately drawn to the twenty-year-old when she "laid her hand gently on me and looked into my face with her sweet innocent eyes." For Aunt Anna, who perceived divine intervention in so many corners of life, this match seemed made in heaven. But she, too, was very wrong.

The wedding on December 1, 1883, was singled out as "one of the most brilliant social events of the season," and for a while the young couple led an easy, carefree life. Elliott played polo while Anna socialized with other wealthy young matrons, and together they partied, often until dawn. The birth of their first child on October 11, 1884, ten months after their marriage, did little to alter that social whirl. Corinne rushed to see the newborn, christened Anna Eleanor but always called Eleanor, when she was three days old, and the rest of the family registered similar enthusiasm even though this was the third Roosevelt grandchild to be born in less than two years.

The playboy father quickly became Eleanor's greatest admirer, showering her with affectionate approval that she never forgot. On August 30, 1885, when she was not quite a year old, he wrote Bamie that he had just returned from Newport and was "spending my Sunday in town," but he could not resist boasting a bit. "Little Eleanor is looking so well," he wrote, "and her four little pearly front teeth have altered the entire expression of the face to quite a pretty one."

What Eleanor failed to see—either as a child or later—was that Elliott's drinking took over his life. He disappeared for hours or even days at a time, and when questioned about his actions, he became defensive, suggesting it was the questioner and not he whose behavior called for scrutiny. With the money inherited from both his parents, he had no need to work and could devote all his time to whatever he chose to do. What Elliott chose was having fun. Most nights he partied well into the morning hours, then tried to compensate for his lack of attention to his family by turning on his famous charm.

Anna Hall Roosevelt possessed few resources with which to confront her situation. Only twenty at the time of her marriage and a mother at twenty-one, she had been raised in a home where management skills had not been passed on from mother to daughter, partly because the mother did not possess them herself. Nor could Anna expect much help in dealing with an errant spouse. Her own mother, Mary Hall, widowed at thirty-six when Anna was seventeen, had never really been able to manage her children, leaving discipline matters to their father. When he died, she took to remaining alone in a darkened room for hours on end rather than facing up to her parental responsibilities. She had hired help, of course, but the management level was missing. After Anna married, within a year of her father's death, she was not likely to discuss husband problems with her mother, who was exhibiting her own form of depressive behavior.

Caught up in a full social schedule, Anna had more than she could handle. In 1890, when her daughter was six, Anna was singled out by Ward McAllister, New York's social arbiter, as "one of America's loveliest, most beautiful, and most graceful daughters." Such glowing accounts sounded a lot like those of Mittie a generation earlier, but Anna had a problem that Mittie never had to confront: a husband who drank too much. Using the only technique she knew, Anna advised willpower and abstinence, and she begged Elliott to stop drinking for her sake. They were not frequently apart for very long, but during one of her visits to her mother, Anna wrote "Poor old Nell" (as his family called Elliott), asking him to keep away from the bottle: "Please remember your promise not to touch any champagne tonight. It is poison truly & how I dread seeing you suffer."

Among their friends, Anna and Elliott appeared the contented couple. For their leisure time they preferred Meadow Brook Country Club on Long Island, a favorite watering place of the rich. Trips abroad exposed the pair to other aimless couples, and while they flitted about, enjoying themselves, relatives pitched in to care for Eleanor. The summer before she turned two, she stayed with Grandmother Hall, who, Aunt Anna Gracie reported in early August, was "*delighted* to have her, which I only know *too* well is true." Another year, Edith, busy with a new baby and her stepdaughter Alice, suggested that her own mother, Gertrude Carow, might be willing to look after Eleanor when she returned from Rome. If no other solution turned up and Anna did not make some provision for Eleanor, Edith volunteered: "I am perfectly willing to take the little thing this summer and care for her with Alice and Ted."

The summer of 1887 carried its own special trauma for Eleanor. Her parents had decided to return to Europe, taking along three-year-old Eleanor, her nurse, and one of Anna's sisters, Tissie. But an accident at sea caused a change in plans. A collision just outside the New York port required everyone on board to transfer to another ship, and little Eleanor, frightened at being tossed from one boat to another, made such a fuss that her parents delayed their departure long enough to leave her and the nurse at Oyster Bay with Anna Gracie. By now this woman, whom Eleanor later described as "my dearly beloved great aunt," was in her mid-fifties, and she turned the same attention to Eleanor that she had once shown to Elliott, her favorite nephew. In a pathetic attempt to cheer the forlorn child, Aunt Anna put together what she described as "the best tea I could to make up to her for her little lonely table with only one little person at it and had lovely stewed prunes and oatmeal wafers after her bread and butter." But Anna Gracie realized that this child needed other consolation, and she tried to oblige: "I had to stroke her little back after she said her prayers as some comfort to her," she wrote Corinne. Such observations make very clear that Eleanor was effectively orphaned long before her parents died.

✑

Eleanor's accounts of her earliest years raise interesting questions about memory—especially memories of her mother. One of her most repeated indictments of her inordinately beautiful mother concerns the embarrassment she expressed at having an unattractive daughter. To ridicule the girl, she called her "Granny." But in her book about her glamorous father, Eleanor notes that the first time her mother called her "Granny" was one day at Hyde Park when Elliott's family was visiting James and Sara Roosevelt. Eleanor was hardly two, too young to remember many specific details, and she herself, in recounting the rest of what happened that day, admits that she relied on others for the story about how four-year-old Franklin carried her around on his back that day "probably under protest."

As long as both of her parents lived, there was no question of removing Eleanor from their guardianship. It would have been unthinkable. More important, it would have confirmed that Elliott's drinking rendered him unsuitable as a parent—a fact his family hesitated to admit. At just what age Eleanor sensed that something ailed her father remains unclear. In *Hunting Big Game* she referred to his "gay sporting life" and a variety of ills that plagued him, including "a bad accident when riding in an amateur circus" and "Indian fever [which] never quite left him either."

But only in the most indirect terms did Eleanor concede that his condition impinged on her childhood. When he went to Europe seeking "cures to regain his health," she wrote, his wife and children accompanied him, and Eleanor was once put in a French convent for three months where she was, she admitted, "most unhappy." But she never found the voice to blame him.

That trip to Europe in 1890, the one that Bamie referred to as "the year that Elliott was ill," came as a last-ditch effort by his siblings to rescue him. In July 1889, Theodore had written Bamie that he was at his "wits end to know what else to do." Months later he was "distressed beyond measure" at the way Elliott was drinking, a "perfect nightmare." Anna was not likely to help much. According to Theodore she was "sweet" but "an impossible person to deal with. Her utterly frivolous life has, as was inevitable, eaten into her character, like an acid." Apparently oblivious to her situation, she "does not realize and feel as other women would in her place." About the only solution that Theodore could see was a cure trip to Europe, with Bamie in charge of Elliott and his entire family.

The trip itself was a sad marker in Elliott's decline. By the time he and Anna sailed, they had two children (young Elliott had been born in 1889), and she had already conceived again. As soon as Theodore learned that another baby was expected, he wrote a furious letter to Bamie, insisting that Anna and Elliott "must live apart. They have no right to have children now. It is a dreadful thing to bring into the world children under circumstances such as these. It must not be done. It is criminal."

But worse was yet to come. Sometime that year one of the family maids in New York, Catherine "Katie" Mann, informed Theodore that she had just given birth to Elliott's child. Methodically, Theodore first checked out Katie Mann's story by sending a representative to her home in Brooklyn to assess the evidence: look over the child and question the mother. The verdict came back that the boy was probably Elliott's, and Theodore would be wise to pay whatever it took to settle the case without a lawsuit. Since Elliott's wife gave birth to Hall Roosevelt three months after the Mann baby was born, it meant that Elliott had engaged in sexual relations with both women during the same period. It seems at that point most of Elliott's family gave up on the idea of ever being able to help him.

According to clippings marked "for Anna's children" and deposited in Eleanor's family papers at Hyde Park, Theodore and Bamie applied to the state courts to have Elliott committed for "lunacy." Anna Roosevelt had also reached the breaking point, and by the summer of 1891, when she returned to New York with her three little children, she had determined to separate from her husband. Elliott remained for a few months of treatment in France, then returned to the States and was immediately banished to the hills of western Virginia, where he worked for Douglas Robinson's land company while he tried to put his life back together. Cut off from her father, seven-year-old Eleanor could not have welcomed the move, but she later grasped at the idea that it had been a good experience for Elliott. In exaggeration completely uncharacteristic of her, she concluded her book on him by boasting that he "became one of the few most influential men" in that part of Virginia.

By June 1892 even the normally upbeat Corinne seemed close to giving up on Elliott, and she wrote Aunt Anna Gracie how "distressed" she was to hear about the family splitting up: "It is so hard for [Anna] and so unfortunate in every way." But just weeks later when Elliott went back to New York for a brief reunion with his wife, he turned on his candy-coated personality and Corinne's outlook changed. She observed that her brother and his wife were "so sweet together," and he seemed "so deeply content and so buoyantly happy that I cannot but feel satisfied about him." When Anna and Elliott and the children went to stay at Oak Terrace, Corinne took it as a sign that the worst was over.

But again she was wrong. Elliott's behavior did not meet the approval of Anna, and he returned to Virginia. In late November, when Anna required surgery, Elliott wrote her mother, asking permission to come to New York to see his wife, but the word came back that he was not wanted. Just days later Anna became ill with diphtheria, and she died on December 7, before Elliott reached her to say good-bye. It had been just nine years since their marriage at Calvary Church on Twentieth Street, and Mary Hall could not help but think that most of that time had been pure torture for her eldest daughter.

Subjects that had been only whispered about in the family now appeared in the newspapers, although there is no evidence that Eleanor, age ten, saw any of the articles. Even if she had, she was too devoted to her father to do anything but ignore them. Friends who had only surmised the extent of Elliott's impairment could now read about his family's commitment petition and how he had been described as "insane" and "alcoholic."

If the family hoped that such public accounts would shame Elliott into changing his ways, they were very wrong. His behavior became even more erratic and irresponsible after his wife died. Then, within another six months, he had to deal with the deaths of two other very close family members. His four-year-old son and namesake, Elliott Jr., died of diphtheria in May 1893, and just weeks later Aunt Anna Gracie, who had always been his staunchest defender, probably because she saw so much of the Bullochs in him, died at age sixty.

What had formerly been irresponsible, bizarre behavior in Elliott now became routine. Hallucinating about many parts of his past, he began moving around New York under an assumed name and took up residence in an apartment on West 102nd Street with a "Mrs. Evans." Nothing that any of his siblings could do had any effect, and Theodore's wife, Edith, wrote her mother that she was thankful that Aunt Anna Gracie had died before witnessing "the evil to come." The older woman would have suffered watching her favored nephew sink "to the lowest depths." Theodore, Bamie, and Douglas Robinson had all been receiving anonymous letters spelling out just how bad things had become for Elliott, and Edith feared that some of the scandal surrounding him would touch the others. "Poor fellow," she concluded the letter, "if only he could have died" instead of his wife.

After Elliott did die, on August 14, 1894, Corinne sounded almost relieved when she wrote Bamie in London. "It was a fearful shock," she admitted, "though I was not unprepared for some catastrophe." A few days earlier, word had reached her at Henderson House, where she was staying, that Elliott "had been using stimulants again" and "was having delusions." Now that he was dead, Corinne insisted, "I know it is *best.*... I know it makes his memory possible to his children . . . and yet my heart feels desperately sad for the brother I *knew*." The last few days of Elliott's life had been miserable, Corinne wrote Bamie, with "fearful nausea" and "convulsive attacks." But in the final hours of his life he had thought of Eleanor, according to Corinne. Apparently under the delusion that she was in the same building where he was living, he knocked at a door and "asked if Miss Eleanor Roosevelt was at home, and waited and then turned away and said, 'If she is out, will you tell her her father is so sorry not to see her.'"

For the rest of her life Eleanor retained only the fond memories of her father, and she blotted out the bad ones. He had made her feel important and pretty when he took her along on outings around the city, and somehow her mind conveniently failed to register the times his drinking led him to forget all about her. Once he left her on the steps of his club for hours, until an employee called a cab and sent her home. Her relatives became so concerned about his disregard for his children's safety that they instructed Eleanor to ignore him and reject all his invitations if she met him by chance on the street.

But such warnings had small effect on the daughter who loved this tragically erratic man above all others. In her childish dreams he was her gallant knight, and after her mother's death, she saw herself allied with him. "He and I were very close together and someday would have a life of our own together," she wrote in her autobiography of her young imaginings. In this dream life it was not clear, she admitted, how her brothers fit in—"perhaps they would have been our children."

Long after he died, Eleanor liked hearing the good accounts of her father's life, but she avoided the less savory ones. She dedicated the first volume of her autobiography, *This Is My Story,* published in 1937, to him but paid virtually no attention to her half-brother, the child of Katie Mann. Eleanor's good friend and superb biographer, Joseph Lash, doubted that she fully comprehended a letter she received in the White House that same year from a woman who identified herself as Eleanor Mann Biles, daughter of Elliott Roosevelt Mann, with the "Rooseveltian features." The First Lady replied in such vague terms— merely observing how nice it was to have someone named for her father—that she seems to have missed the significance of the message. Or she may have simply chosen to ignore the implications. A follow-up letter from Mrs. Biles received no response at all. This niece of Eleanor's later insisted that if the Roosevelts had ever paid anything toward the child's upbringing, none of it reached the Mann family.

Other communications that Eleanor received regarding her father were greeted much more favorably. She was particularly excited to receive photographs taken of him in his best days at the Meadow Brook Country Club in the 1880s. Anyone who sent such a picture or a recollection of Elliott at his most vibrant was likely to get an invitation to 1600 Pennsylvania Avenue. Her cousins, especially the children of Auntie Corinne, had many such stories. Although they were still very young when he died, they had often heard their mother insist that Elliott was "the most charming man she ever knew."

✂

Charming Elliott might have been, but Mary Hall could not forgive him for making her daughter's last years so miserable. Not a very forceful or interesting woman (Eleanor later singled out Grandmother Hall as one of the models to *avoid*), Mary Hall felt dutybound to remove Anna's children from the Roosevelt orbit. On her deathbed, in fact, Anna had assigned her three children to her mother, and Elliott's siblings could hardly challenge that arrangement without his cooperation. Mary Hall had tragically lost a daughter, but at least she had these grandchildren, and she was not about to hand them over—especially to Elliott's kin whom she could not help but hold partly responsible for failing to control his drinking and womanizing. Besides, with Elliott so alienated from his family, he would have fought any attempt they made to turn his children against him.

While living with Grandmother Hall, Eleanor was permitted limited visits to her Roosevelt relatives, but geography rendered them infrequent. Corinne Robinson's move to New Jersey after Elliott's death made her less accessible. Theodore was serving on the U.S. Civil Service Commission in Washington until 1895, so visits with his children were even more difficult to arrange. His move back to Sagamore Hill hardly improved matters. Moreover, by the time Elliott died, Theodore and Edith had their hands full with Alice and four children of their own. Concerned about Theodore's career and the medical problems of their own children, they would have hesitated to step forward and assume responsibility for Elliott's children. Bamie was even farther away, living in London.

Abundant evidence survives about what a very unpleasant place Grandmother Hall's household was for Eleanor and her little brother, whom she called "Brudie." In 1894, Mary Hall was only fifty, but Eleanor's cousin Corinney remembered that the grandmother seemed worn down, with more than she could manage—two "drunken sons and . . . very beautiful, fatiguing daughters." At the time, Anna's brothers, Valentine ("Vallie") and Edward, were in their mid-twenties, and her sisters, "Tissie," "Pussie," and Maud, ranged from twenty-six to seventeen—all eager to spend their nights partying and their days grumpily recovering from the effects of it. The house had a grim, shuttered look about it most of the time. Two years younger than Eleanor, Corinney found the Hall house so unappealing that she concocted excuses for not going there to stay with Eleanor. With its one lone gas jet in the hall and steeply inclined stairs, it had a sinister air about it. In the summers, the Hall household transferred to Tivoli, where the light and air were better, but Eleanor's aunts and uncles still engaged in all sorts of raucous behavior. One concerned nanny might have rescued her, but the one employed by her grandmother seemed to take pleasure in making Eleanor's life even more miserable—by criticizing and bullying her beyond all reason.

Bamie sent letters and presents from London, but the distance hampered close personal contact. Just about to marry for the first time, she had her own preoccupations and may have wanted to keep a distance from Eleanor so as to protect herself from the same kind of hurt she felt when she lost Alice. Whatever the reason, Bamie's communications with the orphaned Eleanor seem sadly distant. The year Elliott died, she sent Eleanor a set of books at Christmas, and the ten-year-old's dutiful note of thanks has a pathetic tinge. On black-bordered paper she wrote promptly on December 27: "Dear Aunty Bye, I thank you very much for the lovely set of Shakper you sent me. I have already begun it." Bamie sometimes resorted to sending checks, although she occasionally missed the exact date of a birthday. Toward the end of October one year, Eleanor wrote to thank her for the check she sent her and Hall. Then the precise little girl gently reminded her aunt: "My birthday comes on the 11 of October." She had a "very nice time" on the day itself, Eleanor wrote, and received many gifts, including a pony from Auntie Maud.

Grandmother Hall, who promised a saddle, had reneged, putting it off until the following year. Eleanor took the disappointment philosophically, explaining that her grandmother had delayed the purchase "because I would have so little use for it." In fact, Grandmother Hall gave almost exclusively gifts of a practical nature—penholders, rulers, pencils, schoolbags—the kinds of presents that could hardly delight a child, even a dutiful one like Eleanor.

Aunt Corinne's New Jersey household occasionally offered some escape, but the four Robinson cousins, ranging from a year older than Eleanor to five years younger, complained that she brought her sadness with her. They found her entirely too serious, devoid of any sense of humor. When she appeared at one of their parties wearing a dress Grandmother Hall had chosen for her but one much too juvenile for both her age and the occasion, her Robinson cousins urged Eleanor to change into something else; she refused, insisting that she had to settle for what she had.

Eleanor relished those visits, however, especially at holiday time, and just after New Year's 1897, when she was twelve, she wrote Bamie that she and Alice "all had great fun." Eleanor would have liked to see more of Alice: "I am so glad [she] is going to be in town this winter, I wish she went to school with me then I would see her every morning." Unlike her cousin, Eleanor liked school, but she enjoyed vacations even more.

In nearly every letter that survives from this period, Eleanor included a progress report on Brudie. Six years younger than Eleanor, the boy could remember very little about either his mother or father, and Eleanor seemed determined to make up for that big gap.

This would have been a good time—when Eleanor was between eleven and thirteen—for someone to take her to a good dentist and correct her protruding teeth. But orthodontics was still in its infancy in the late 1890s, and even after the father of the field, midwesterner Dr. Edward Hartley Angle, published the pioneering text on the subject in 1910, people on the East Coast were slow to line up for braces. The same people who, like Edith, put great faith in braces to straighten leg bones were reluctant to accept Dr. Angle's advice that straight teeth were important for proper chewing. Teeth braces appeared more a beauty measure—and moneyed easterners at that time shunned the very idea.

The bias was particularly evident among old, established families, such as the Roosevelts and the Halls, who saw hair dye and cosmetic surgery as beneath them—unworthy of their family line. Showgirls and photographers' models might need perfect teeth, but "young ladies" of "good" families need not concern themselves with such things. Popular magazines avoided the topic, so the Roosevelt circle would neither have read about orthodontics nor heard much about it from their wealthy friends. Even if they did, their class bias would have held them back from doing anything about Eleanor's protruding front teeth. Corinney later blamed Grandmother Hall for being too preoccupied with her children to take much notice of Eleanor's teeth. But the truth is probably more complicated.

Eleanor did what she could—what other young women of her class learned to do—to compensate. In her youthful posed photos, including those of her wedding in 1905, she kept her lips closed and held her head at an angle, thus concealing her noticeable overbite, or what in dentist jargon is a classic example of "Class 2, division 1 misalignment." Much later, after she became First Lady and was injured in an automobile accident, she had a complete rehabilitation of her mouth that improved her appearance. By then, attitudes on orthodontics had shifted. More important, the work was necessary for practical reasons—she needed teeth to chew properly and could proceed without any pangs of conscience about doing it merely for "vanity" or "beauty."

Her Roosevelt aunts were no help concerning the teeth, but they did help engineer Eleanor's temporary escape from the Hall household, although not until she was fifteen. Before Elliott's death, Edith and Bamie had become concerned about his children's schooling and exchanged worried notes about his legal right to take his children wherever he wished. Edith felt sure he would tire of the youngsters and let them go—and that would be the time to enroll Eleanor with the right teacher. Edith was clearly dubious. "I do not feel she has much chance," she wrote Bamie. But "if any thing *real* can be done for Eleanor it will be by a good school." Something in Edith's letter suggests she feared Eleanor stood more at risk in the Hall household than her brothers. Elliott could take his two sons to Virginia "with a really good nurse and not much harm can come to them," she continued in her letter to Bamie, leaving unsaid why Eleanor needed different attention. Bamie agreed concerning the need for a good boarding school for Eleanor and even had a specific place in mind—Mlle. Souvestre's school, Allenswood. Eventually, Grandmother Hall agreed to let her enroll there, and she sent one of her daughters to accompany Eleanor on the Atlantic crossing in the fall of 1899. Eight-year-old Hall, for whom Eleanor felt so much responsibility, remained in New York, a sign that Bamie also considered Eleanor's situation the more precarious of the two.

Now it was Eleanor's turn to write from England to her aunt, who had moved back to the States with her husband and had a one-year-old son, Sheffield. In one letter from Allenswood, she reported she was glad "baby is well" and thanked Bamie for sending letters from Alice, Corinne, and Teddy: "I enjoyed them *so* much but they made me quite envious for I wanted to be with them so much." Eleanor had just returned from a holiday trip through the Continent with Mlle. Souvestre, who had taken Bamie's niece under her wing, and she welcomed the opportunity to get her room in shape before classes started: "I like being back soon for it gives you lots of time to get settled and this term I am sleeping with two other girls so the room will be a mess."

For the next three years Eleanor's life centered on Allenswood. Except for one trip home in the summer of 1901, she remained with Souvestre and became her protégée. That trip to the States proved an extremely painful one due to the insensitivity of one of her mother's sisters, Pussie. Mercurial and unpredictable but very beautiful, Eleanor's aunt evidently became annoyed with her one day and blurted out that she was an "ugly duckling" and would "never have the beaux that the rest of the women in the [Hall] family had." Then to cinch Eleanor's unhappiness, Pussie told her in some detail about Elliott's decline into drunkenness at the end of his life. Shocked and hurt, Eleanor could not wait to get back to the refuge of Allenswood, and on her own she engaged a chaperone to accompany her on the sailing—a move she later admitted was completely out of character for her. The chaperone acted in name only, as far as Eleanor could recall, and succumbing to seasickness on her first day out, she did not show her face for the duration of the trip.

In the spring of 1902, just before Eleanor finished at Allenswood, her cousin Corinney joined her, and the two girls renewed the friendship that had waned during their separation. Almost eighteen years old, Eleanor was becoming an elegant young woman, and except for her teeth, she was pretty. She had abundant honey-colored hair, long legs, and a slim waist, but everyone agreed that her sky blue eyes were her best feature. Much later her daughter Anna pointed out that it was only Eleanor who insisted she was homely. Alice's granddaughter underlined that interpretation: Alice did not think she was beautiful; "she was dark and had legs that were different sizes," and she envied Eleanor her good skin and blue eyes.

The time at Allenswood marked a turning point in Eleanor's life, and she repeatedly referred to the important influence of Mlle. Souvestre. Others agreed. Corinney judged that Eleanor's "salvation" was going to Allenswood, where the headmistress "loved and understood the girl, made a fuss over her and gave her responsibilities." The intense relationship that Souvestre had with the Italian teacher, whom Corinney identified only as "Signorina," evidently did not bother Eleanor as it did Corinney, and in the few weeks that the two cousins overlapped at Allenswood, they formed a special bond.

Eleanor's workbooks from Allenswood, labeled with her school nickname "Totty," give some idea of how she filled her days and what she was thinking. In elegant penmanship she constructed sample letters that a wealthy matron might have to write in Italian to a tailor, to rent a house, or to inquire about a prospective servant. But more revealing of the woman she would become were her short pieces entitled "My First Joy" and "My First Sorrow." In the former she wrote: "I was five years old when I went for the first time on horseback and I still remember as though it were yesterday my joy. . . . I have had other joys but it seems to me that the first one was the most perfect." Her "greatest sorrow" also comes from the realm of objects rather than human beings: the orphaned teenager wrote about "leaves changing on trees" rather than of the losses that must have cut more deeply in her memory.

Her instructors' comments indicate Eleanor performed competently but not exceptionally. One German instructor mentioned a need to improve spelling; her Latin teacher reported only "good results"; and her music teacher, with whom Eleanor studied ten hours a week (including a brief trial with the violin), acknowledged that Eleanor made "a satisfactory beginning." Her English literature instructor, Dorothy Strachey, judged her intelligent but "not quite up to the level of the class she is in." In the subject of "Danse," Eleanor showed more determination than talent, reflected in the teacher's comment: "Much improved; takes great pains." Only in general conduct did Eleanor excel, and here Mlle. Souvestre wrote that Eleanor was "excellent" and "the most amiable girl" she had come across in her many years of teaching.

As Eleanor prepared to return to live in New York in the summer of 1902, Souvestre summed up her remarkable effect on the other students (although she misspelled her name as "Elinor"). The headmistress waxed enthusiastic about how she "had the most admirable influence on the school and gained the affection of many, the respect of all. To me personally I feel I lose a dear friend in her."

By early July when Eleanor actually left England to return to New York, Souvestre was traveling on the Continent. She sent a farewell telegram from Geneva, that went astray, and a few days later she complained: "See how little luck I have with you. The day you left I wired you a single word which expressed all my hope and all my desire, 'au revoir'." But the telegram had bounced back, undelivered, and Souvestre wrote, "Once more this very warm remembrance of my friendship for you, of my regrets, did not reach you." The teacher remained convinced that Eleanor's time at Allenswood had been fruitful, and she correctly predicted: "I am happy in the thought that these three years of such sustained and productive work on your part have also been a period of joy and rest for you and that they will ... be a period you will look back to for a long time with satisfaction and serenity."

Souvestre knew enough about the kind of home life Eleanor would face back in New York that she tried to boost her confidence and prepare her for a difficult time: School days will "disappear quickly," she wrote, and "your life which is entirely new and entirely different and in several respects entirely contradictory, is going to take you and drag you into its turmoil." Souvestre's advice was specific: "Protect yourself ... my dear child, protect yourself ... in these next years to sustain the strain of this worldly rush." She warned Eleanor about giving too much of her energy to the "worldly pleasures which are going to beckon to you." Then, with more accuracy than she ever lived to know, she predicted: "When success comes, as I am sure it will, bear in mind that there are more quiet and enviable joys than to be among the most sought-after-women at a ball or the woman best liked by your neighbor at the table, at luncheons and the various fashionable affairs."

Souvestre knew that Eleanor would be living again at her grandmother's but that Aunt Pussie, still unmarried at age twenty-nine, was making many of the decisions. Sometimes cruel, as she had been to Eleanor in the summer of 1901, Pussie was most commonly described as "erratic." To make matters worse, she had become such a presence in Brudie's life that Eleanor felt she had been displaced. Gingerly, Souvestre requested news about the situation: "Tell me how you have found your grandmother and your little brother. The latter does not yet know the value of your warm sisterly tenderness; but he will learn that gradually and you will become for him what you desire to be."

Just weeks later she again wrote from Switzerland to reply to Eleanor's admission that she had wanted a photograph of her teacher but had been too shy to ask. Souvestre seemed flattered by the request but sorry that Eleanor had held back: "Why didn't you ask for it? I would have given it to you immediately, and with such pleasure! But I never offer to give one." She continued that some people prefer to remember others in their mind, rather than via a representation that can never adequately recreate the real person.

Souvestre closed the letter with words that could only have warmed the heart of the lonely Eleanor: "I would like to have you with me. I miss you every day of my life, but it is a selfish regret for which I reprove myself. You fulfill your destiny more where you are than you would near me. . . . Till soon, dear child. I love you and kiss you." A few weeks later, when Corinne Robinson came to Allenswood to visit her daughter, Souvestre gave her the picture Eleanor had requested. Then she wrote the girl, "If by chance she should forget to give it to you, ask her for it, for she will surely have it among her belongings."

Other teachers also kept in touch with Eleanor after she returned to New York. In September 1902 her French teacher sent a list of recommended reading (in French) to "Ma chère petite Totty" and promised a celebration if Eleanor returned for a visit to Allenswood. When another former student wrote a glowing recollection of Eleanor, Souvestre forwarded it to her, adding, "It portrays you, in your surroundings as you wouldn't present yourself."

Corinney, who remained that year at Allenswood, had her doubts about how her older cousin was fitting into the New York scene. Corinney always seemed to find something humorous or out of place in her cousin, and in a letter to her father she asked "how Eleanor was getting on." Corinney's expectations were limited: "I would so like to see her out in society for I am sure it must be very funny."

∽

At first the news from New York was good. Auntie Corinne reported that she had spoken with Susie Parish, a cousin of Eleanor's mother, who confirmed that the young woman looked "very sweet in her low necked gowns" and seemed to get along well with people. It was Eleanor's "coming out" year, and her social calendar was filled with engagements. She attended a dinner dance on December 9 and another "big dinner" a few days later. Her proud Aunt Corinne noted that eighteen-year-old Eleanor "looks very smartly in all her pretty French clothes," and then she reported that the rest of the family concurred. One cousin commented that she had "never seen anyone so improved in looks" as Eleanor.

Eleanor very quickly showed clear signs of discontent with how her life was going, but in her usual reticent style she kept the reasons quiet. On her visit to the White House in early January 1903, she seemed moody and unsure of herself. Auntie Corinne, whose stay overlapped with hers for ten days, reported to her daughter: "I am sorry to say that Eleanor did not make as good an impression on your aunt and uncle [Edith and Theodore] as I should have wished. She apparently gave them the feeling that she took very little interest in anything American, and went out walking in the midst of the New Year's reception, did not want to receive at the Admiral of the Navy's and altogether made one or more rather unfortunate mistakes." Aunt Corinne placed the blame more on the Halls than on Eleanor: "Poor child! She has lived almost entirely alone with Pussie. . . in a most erratic way, and . . . she has become less careful about things on account of her environment." Aunt Corinne had no complaints about how Eleanor treated her: "She is always sweet and thoughtful with me, and I think has enjoyed her winter though not wildly." But the aunt was "really distressed about the Washington impression."

Corinney understood that Eleanor had committed a gaffe, and she knew it would cost her. From Allenswood she wrote her mother in early February 1903: "I was awfully sorry to hear from you about Eleanor Roosevelt making so many foolish mistakes in Washington because those sort of things always do leave a bad impression."

Eleanor was cutting herself off from more than White House receptions that winter. She also seemed to ignore Mlle. Souvestre for a time. Corinney, who was left to face her teachers' inquiries about Eleanor and why she had not written, had no answers, and she admitted to her mother that she sometimes prevaricated a bit. When one of the teachers inquired what Eleanor had said about her, Corinney fibbed that she had not yet read her mail completely and did not know. Souvestre expressed her disappointment directly to Eleanor:

"Yesterday quantities of letters from you arrived at Allenswood. There were none for me among the ones I distributed but I hope I shall be luckier next week."

Corinne's letters to her daughter confirm how hard Eleanor found that first winter back in New York. The high point may have come in late January when the Robinsons gave a dinner, and Eleanor and Franklin were both among the guests for what the hostess summed up as "really . . . a very nice time." But a few weeks later when Eleanor got her aunt alone, she told her how difficult she had found the previous months. In a letter to her daughter, Auntie Corinne warned: "Do not say anything about it, but the child [Eleanor] has had a hard winter in many ways." While Grandmother Hall stayed most of the time at Oak Terrace, Pussie ran the Manhattan house, and she "is so inconsiderate," Corinne continued, "that Eleanor's path is not all roses." It was during that talk that Eleanor "burst into tears and cried, 'Auntie, I have no real home' in such a pathetic way," Corinne continued, "that my heart simply ached for her." What Corinne apparently did not know was that Eleanor feared her uncles, especially when they were drunk, and that she had installed multiple locks on her bedroom door to keep them out.

Invitations still came to Eleanor from the Roosevelts. In March 1903, Bamie entertained her niece in the capital, though she worried that the young woman would find her stay dull with no one there her own age. To Corinne, Bamie expressed her reservations about their niece's upcoming visit: "Eleanor is as dear and sweet as possible and I hope may enjoy her stay, but I feel always that being just with Will and me is a little lonely for a young girl. She has no personal friends here." Edith tried inviting her, writing to Bamie during the visit: "I want Eleanor to lunch any day before she goes that it is convenient just because I think Theodore ought to see her—*not* for her amusement." In comparison with the rebellious Alice, who was then making headlines as the President's fun-loving daughter, Eleanor offered quiet relief. "I love having her," Bamie wrote of the upcoming visit. "She is such a fine young creature."

By the time Eleanor left Washington, Bamie felt confident she could handle her difficult living situation. On April 7 she wrote Corinne: "I am worried for Eleanor but the child has such a strong character and is so calm in her decisions that I feel she is doing what is wisest and best." Bamie understood that Eleanor felt so strongly her responsibility for Brudie that she would not leave him. But with the Halls unlikely to relinquish guardianship of either of Anna's children, all that Bamie could do was stress that both of them were welcome either in Washington or in Farmington, where the Cowleses spent the summer months.

Conditions did not immediately improve, and Bamie continued to worry. In an undated letter to Corinne, she wrote that she was "dreadfully worried about Eleanor. She looks badly and is in a *very* difficult position." Both Eleanor and her brother seemed particularly vulnerable at Oak Terrace, where their thirty-five-year-old uncle Vallie acted like a delinquent teenager, shooting wildly at passersby whenever he felt like it. Bamie recognized that Tivoli and "the life that is being led" there was no place for the boy. "I have heard that things occur at the Tivoli house and they are exactly what happened with Elliott." And yet she recognized that Eleanor could not remove her brother until she had a "home of her own."

Eleanor later showed some resentment at being saddled with so much responsibility at a very young age. When a mother of teenagers wrote to the mature Eleanor asking for advice on how to deal with young people who are "crazy, irresponsible, insolent," Eleanor replied: "I have always regretted that in my own teen-age I had so much responsibility that I never knew what it was to be carefree. It is in those years that one acquires a real joie de vivre, and it is a pity to miss out on it."

Corinne and Bamie, who would have opened their homes to their niece, found their hands tied. Bamie even considered legal action, asking Douglas Robinson to find out whom Elliott had designated "*legally* guardian" of the children. According to Bamie, Anna had really wanted her children to be brought up by Bamie, "but as Elliott was living [she] could not make it legal." Since he had outlived his wife and never renounced guardianship of his children, his right as a parent presumably outweighed everyone else's. But how could anyone make sense out of the tangled mess? In considering her options, Bamie wondered if Mrs. Hall would fight any move to take the grandchildren from her. In the meantime, "Eleanor can do nothing herself until she knows how matters really are."

Mlle. Souvestre had counseled Eleanor to spend more time with her Roosevelt aunts, noting that Corinne Robinson had assured her that both she and Bamie would be happy to take Eleanor "as often as possible." Gingerly, Souvestre inquired why Eleanor did not accept these invitations, and she hinted that Eleanor might be staying with Grandmother Hall simply because she hesitated to hurt her feelings. Or perhaps it was the money situation. Souvestre wanted to know whether Eleanor received "a definite sum" or relied on someone else to "pay your expenses." Struggling to brighten Eleanor's world with words, she wrote from gray London, "I wish you what we lack: light and sun."

Eleanor continued to find refuge at Auntie Bye's, whom she later described as "one of the most interesting women I have ever known." For her part, Bamie enjoyed her niece's visits to Washington, partly because they reminded her of the days that she and Corinne had "dropped in" on each other "at a moment's notice" and then gotten caught up in "profound analytical discussions." On the social front, Bamie reported that Eleanor had made progress in the capital: "Every one likes her and though it must seem frightfully quiet to her, she seems happy and we both accept our separate invitations or stay home calmly as the case may be."

∽

Part of Eleanor's improved attitude came from the turn her relationship with Franklin had taken during the prior few months. There were many ties between the two, and they intersected and overlapped in more ways than either of them could easily describe. They had known each other since infancy, their fathers had been distant cousins, and their parents had been friends. But after Eleanor returned from Allenswood, Franklin took a new look at her and quickly zeroed in on her best features. The romance could not have been very far along in the winter of 1902–03 or Eleanor would not have confided to her aunt Corinne how miserable she was.

But the situation changed over the next few months, and by July 1904 they had come to an agreement to marry—a secret they kept to themselves. Corinney, who had returned from England and was visiting family friends in Islesboro, Maine, at the same time as Eleanor, had no idea how serious the two had become, and she later pulled out a diary she had kept in 1904 that showed Franklin's

Her trips to China—here she is shown at age nine in Hong Kong—gave Sara Delano a special sophistication in the eyes of some of the other Roosevelts.

Sara Delano Roosevelt (right) was fond of saying that she mothered Franklin and Eleanor's children more than Eleanor did. At Campobello in the summer of 1913, she posed with Franklin (lower left) and two of his sons, James and Elliott.

At the time this grim family photo was taken at Hyde Park in 1924, Franklin (seated center) had already regained enough strength to deliver his famous "Happy Warrior" speech for Al Smith at the 1924 Democratic National Convention, but his own political future and that of Eleanor (seated left) remained uncertain. Sara Delano is seated on right; daughter Anna Dall is at Franklin's right shoulder; sons John and FDR Jr., seated front; son-in-law Curtis Dall is on Eleanor's right; James and Elliott are standing in the rear.

In 1939, two years before her death, a proud Sara Delano Roosevelt attended a birthday party for her son, Franklin, at the Waldorf-Astoria.

Eleanor's mother, Anna, was the eldest of four exceptionally beautiful daughters of Valentine and Mary Hall. At age twenty she married Elliott Roosevelt, Mittie's third-born child, and nine years later, after giving birth to three children, she died.

Just months before their mother died in 1892, Eleanor posed with her brothers, Elliott Jr. (left) and Hall (right).

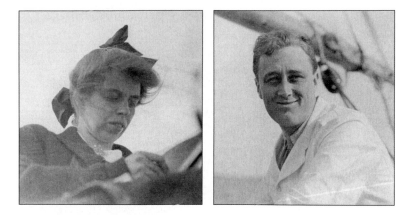

This picture of young Eleanor Roosevelt—surely one of the least flattering ever made of her—is rarely reproduced, but she used it in her 1937 autobiography, where it appears just below one of Franklin at his most debonair.

At 22, Eleanor Roosevelt, shown with Franklin, daughter Anna, and dog "Duffy," already had one child and was pregnant with a second.

Known as the "Flying First Lady," Eleanor Roosevelt showed a zest for travel that was characteristic of the Roosevelt women.

Before Eleanor Roosevelt traveled to the South Pacific in 1943, several of her cousins, including the young Alice Roosevelt, had already made celebrated trips to the Far East.

Few of the people who applauded Eleanor Roosevelt's strong stands on civil rights knew that her grandmother came from a slave-holding family in Georgia.

Sixty years old when Franklin died in 1945, Eleanor Roosevelt went on to accept the important role of representing the United States at the United Nations.

courtship of Eleanor went almost undetected. As Corinney saw it, the attraction was heavily one-sided, with Franklin acting the part of the pathetic pursuer. Noting that Eleanor seemed to reciprocate so little of Franklin's devotion, Corinney speculated that Eleanor had her eyes on someone else.

When Franklin and his mother showed up in Washington early that November, they dined at Bamie's while Eleanor was also a guest. But the Hyde Park contingent stayed "at a hotel," Bamie explained, "as I have no room for them." By Thanksgiving the Roosevelt family learned of Eleanor's engagement to Franklin, although it was "not to be spoken of outside as yet." Aunt Edith approved the match, though her stated reasons had little to do with the bride and groom: "I think it is such a splendid thing and now poor little Hall will have a home with a good man at the head of it."

Sara Delano Roosevelt had finally come around to accepting the marriage, but with great misgivings. In her eyes Eleanor and Franklin were both much too young. While she found it perfectly reasonable that her step-granddaughter Helen would announce her engagement to Teddy Robinson before he graduated from Harvard, she still saw Franklin, at age twenty-three, as her little boy. She had not married until age twenty-six, and she liked to point out that her father had waited until he was thirty-three to take a wife. In an effort to divert Franklin and gain some time, she had taken him and a school friend of his on a Caribbean cruise the previous winter and even negotiated (unsuccessfully) for a job for Franklin in a foreign embassy.

Sara gradually overcame her misgivings, though, and began to show an interest in the daughter of her old friend Elliott who, after all, had been Franklin's godfather. Sara's attentions to the young Eleanor have been portrayed by her biographers as excessively intrusive, but Eleanor seemed to revel in them. The prospective mother-in-law, a sophisticated world traveler, easily spotted blemishes in the twenty-year-old so lacking in self-confidence, and she took her under her wing. During the courtship, Eleanor lunched with Sara several times a week, shopped with her, and followed her advice on the social niceties. She could not see enough of her or do quite enough to please. In early December 1903 Eleanor wrote to "Dearest Cousin Sally" to "thank you for being so good to me yesterday. I know just how you feel and how hard it must be, but I do so want you to learn to love me a little. You must know that I will always try to do what you wish for I have grown to love you very dearly during this past summer. It is impossible for me to tell you how I feel toward Franklin. I can only say that the great wish is always to prove worthy of him. I am counting the days to the 12th when I hope Franklin and you will both be here again and if there is anything which I can do for you, you will write me, won't you? With much love dear Cousin Sally, Always devotedly, Eleanor."

Like a doting aunt, Sara attended to Eleanor's needs. When the prospective bride badly cut two of her fingers, Sara made a trip to Manhattan from Hyde Park to oversee treatment. Then she informed her son: "I am thankful to say she is better—one finger was taken in time to prevent it's getting bad, her thumb seems to be improving a little and the doctor thinks she can go to Tivoli tomorrow." The two women had lunched at Corinne Robinson's and then "after lunch, Eleanor went about with me in a hansom and I drove her home at six, having had tea at Sherry's. . . . I think country air and rest will do her good." When the young couple remained adamant about marrying, Sara pitched in to help and seemed to delight in taking over many of the arrangements that would have ordinarily fallen to the Halls. She arranged for engagement pictures to be taken of the bride, then noted proudly in her diary that Eleanor looked "charming." On the big day, Sara apparently stayed in the background—at least *The New York Times* noted only that "Mrs. James Roosevelt was in white silk, covered with black lace."

II

NOT SURPRISINGLY, Eleanor operated almost entirely within the Roosevelt orbit during the first ten or fifteen years of her marriage. She saw a lot of Bamie, Corinne, and especially Sara Delano who, with her considerable inheritance and a single son to dote on, proved a generous in-law. A few months after the marriage she sent the young couple a sketch, showing a city house of four floors, alongside her own handwritten cryptic note announcing: "A Christmas present to Franklin and Eleanor from Mama. Number and Street not yet quite decided—19 or 20 feet wide." Any mention of the adjoining house that she had built for herself at the same time is missing from that note, and she apparently did not see it as relevant. She later told her biographer, Rita Kleeman, that it would never have occurred to her to live with her son's family—next door did not count.

In fact, Eleanor and Franklin lived in an apartment for the first few months of their marriage, while he completed Columbia Law School, and then they moved into a rented house on East Thirty-sixth Street, where they lived—without Sara—for more than two years. The house Sara built for them—on Sixty-fifth Street near Madison Avenue—was technically their residence after it was completed in 1908, but they used other places for at least part of many years while Franklin served in the Albany legislature or in Washington, D.C.

Sara could always be depended on to pay the bills. Her note about a "present" from "Mama" set the tone for her relationship with her son and daughter-in-law for the rest of her life. Until she died in 1941, she took care of Eleanor's household expenses as well as other family finances. The repair of a broken pipe in New York or a leaking roof at Campobello got paid for by "Mama." The children's nurses or their trips to Europe were almost as likely to come from Sara as from their parents. Why Eleanor permitted—even depended on—this largesse is not known. At the time of her marriage she had an annual income from her father's estate that was clearly higher than Franklin's. Between them they received about $12,500 annually, enough to manage easily without Sara's help.

Just how deeply Sara's purse strings reached also remains unclear, though the evidence points at least to Franklin's depending on his mother's support. In 1918, when Eleanor's marriage came close to breaking up, her mother-in-law's money may have played a part in keeping it together. That fall, when the entire nation was reeling from the great flu epidemic and the final months of the war in Europe, Eleanor faced a trauma that loomed larger for her personally than any national disaster. Her husband, then serving as assistant secretary of the Navy, had returned sick from an official trip to Paris, and as she unpacked his bags, she discovered a cache of love letters written to him by a woman she knew very well. The "other woman" was Lucy Mercer, whom Eleanor had hired as her social secretary when she and

Franklin first moved to Washington. The contents of the letters made clear that this was not a case of a younger woman having a one-sided crush on Franklin. The relationship was intimate, and he reciprocated her feelings. Family members later confirmed that Eleanor offered Franklin a divorce at that time.

When the couple convened with Sara, she made it quite clear that she wanted her son to remain with Eleanor. Aside from Sara's objection, divorce had two other drawbacks: Lucy was Roman Catholic and would have difficulty marrying a divorced man; and Franklin's close adviser Louis Howe, whom he trusted for his political savvy, argued that a ruptured marriage could affect Franklin's political career. But alongside these was Sara with the money she threatened to withhold if her son displeased her. Franklin would never inherit a cent from her, she warned, and he would never inherit the family estate, Springwood. Sara's stand may not have been the deciding factor, but it must have figured in the decision. Just how much Eleanor appreciated Sara's support remains unclear, but when Eleanor's four sons and one daughter later went through multiple divorces, she did not intervene in the same way.

Sara's stand against a divorce for Franklin, especially when taken with the other evidence on her relationship with Eleanor, suggests that she did not dislike her daughter-in-law. But having known Eleanor since the days when she had come as a toddler with her parents to Hyde Park, she had trouble seeing her as a mature woman. That weakness is hardly unique: Sara Delano was not the first mother-in-law to experience a certain blindness in assessing the competence of the next generation, especially in a daughter-in-law. Eleanor's lack of self-confidence, even after exposure to the assertive Mlle. Souvestre, called out for help, and Sara responded with a surfeit of advice on clothes and behavior. Like a strong, well-meaning teacher whose zeal ignores the possibility of offending, she criticized her in front of others. Corinney thought Sara's reprimands had little to do with Eleanor. She would have behaved that way with any woman Franklin married: "I've never seen such possession in my life," Corinney told historian Hermann Hagedorn when discussing Sara's relationship with Franklin.

Yet Sara could be caring and attentive. When Eleanor prepared to travel to Campobello with Franklin and their new baby in July 1906, Sara, who had gone on ahead of them, reminded him to take precautions so that his wife would not get sick. Writing from the train on her way to Eastport, Maine, where she would get a boat to the island, Sara instructed Franklin to "please get some educator biscuits or something of that sort for Eleanor to eat when she first wakes on the train. They 'saved my life' this morning. If I had not had them I do not like to think of what might have happened."

In the beginning of her adult association with Sara, Eleanor clung to her as she had to Mlle. Souvestre. Why wouldn't she? Here was a sophisticated, experienced woman, a favorite of Eleanor's aunts and an admirer of Eleanor's beloved father. Sara also showed real concern for Eleanor's brother, who had shed the nickname Brudie in favor of Hall. In 1907, after inquiring about the health of the sixteen-year-old, Sara urged Eleanor to bring him for a visit so he "can be quiet and have good air." The possibility of Eleanor and Hall forming a family with Sara, of being nurtured and encouraged, must have seemed liked a miraculous deliverance from the chaotic household of Grandmother Hall. Eleanor latched on to her mother-in-law in a way that her cousin Corinney deemed silly and unnecessary. But to Eleanor the relationship made a lot of sense. Marriage gave her the chance to have a home of her own—it is no wonder that she accepted Franklin's offer at once.

After the marriage, Eleanor kept Sara informed of every detail of her activities whenever the two were separated—an attention that prompted Sara to call her an "angel." During the first summer that Eleanor and Franklin spent at Campobello with two small children, she offered such a complete account that Franklin could only add: "Eleanor has told you about everything and must have a strong wrist to escape the horrors of writer's cramp." Then he volunteered his own tempered evaluation of his young wife's state of mind: "The only thing that she hasn't told you is that she is well and doesn't seem unhappy." About himself he was surer: "I am ditto as to health and can vouch for the state of my feelings." He signed himself "FDR," while his usually reticent wife sent "Ever so much love." In spite of that closing, Eleanor rarely revealed in letters to Sara how she felt about things that mattered, confining herself to a list of sailing and swimming activities or a progress report on the children's growth.

As her grandchildren matured, Sara doted on them and spoiled them in a way their mother resented but felt helpless to stop. The

JOHNSTON PUBLIC LIBRARY
JOHNSTON, IOWA 50131

five that survived (one boy died at nine months) divided naturally into two batches as a result of the spacing of their births. Anna (born in 1906), James (1907), and Elliott (1910) were grouped together as the "older" children, while Franklin Jr. (1914) and John (1916) were often called the "little boys," at least into their late teens.

Eleanor thought her mother-in-law especially indulgent with the latter group, but Sara showed considerable largesse and patience with the older ones as well and took the oldest two on their first trip to Europe in the summer of 1922. The daughter, Anna, later insisted that Eleanor had let her mother-in-law have the pleasure of showing the children around Europe because she herself could not afford it. But that summer Eleanor had a seriously disabled husband— Franklin had contracted polio the previous summer—and five children under the age of sixteen, so she was hardly in a position to relax on a trip abroad. In fact, she had more than she could manage, which might help explain why she lost control of an automobile she was driving near Hyde Park. Her mother-in-law (who never learned to drive) tried to reassure her, writing from Paris that Eleanor should not worry about "running into our gate post . . . so long as you were not hurt." With time, Eleanor would become "an expert chauffeur," and Sara insisted that learning to drive "is the only thing to do . . . and if I were not 100 years old I would learn!"

Even while in Europe, Sara kept up with expenses at home. From Paris she sent a check to Eleanor with a note saying that she knew Franklin would be short on the first of the month. (Later, she helped bankroll his spa at Warm Springs, Georgia, where he hoped that other "polios" like himself could get back their full mobility.)

On the trip to Europe, Sara tried hard to please her grandchildren and cater to their whims, even having new clothes tailored for them. At the age of sixty-seven she mustered the stamina to conduct long, energetic guided tours, and when Anna and James appeared "fed up with the sights," she decided to skip Holland.

With the two older children away, Eleanor found herself burdened with more tasks than she could easily manage. The three youngest boys required her attention, and she helped Franklin arrange medical visits and therapy sessions, but she still dutifully wrote her mother-in-law. In August, Sara wrote Eleanor from London that "your long delightful letter . . . made me happy . . . and is like the sort you accustomed me to many years ago, but I still don't see how you had time to write it." Franklin had put high hopes on aquatic exercises to help him regain his strength, but Eleanor had passed on the information that a lack of coal prevented heating of the pool. Sara, accustomed to getting what she wanted, offered to buy "a carload" if the current strike would not prevent delivery.

All through those years of close association with Sara, Eleanor continued to see a lot of her father's sisters. After 1908, when Auntie Bye began spending more time in Connecticut, she visited her niece and Franklin often. Eleanor's marriage actually strengthened her tie to Bamie because the aunt always showed a special fondness for Franklin. As the son of her good friend Sara, he seemed more a nephew than a distant cousin, and as he matured, she sought his company with or without his wife. In mid-July 1909, while Eleanor struggled with three young children (including a sickly infant) at Campobello, Bamie invited Franklin to Oldgate "for a Saturday and Sunday as Eleanor and your mother are out of reach." She gave him the option of staying longer but recognized that he might prefer a more exciting setting: "It is perfectly dull and quiet for a young gentleman from town." She lined up the enticements: "Ted Roosevelt is generally here and I have a small automobile so you could wander about—it would be too good to have you but only if a convenience to you because I have no reason to wish you to sacrifice yourself for any inducement."

During those years when her children were young, Eleanor spent her summers on Sara's turf at Campobello. Before air-conditioning, when even the Hudson River Valley sweltered during July and August, Campobello and the Bay of Fundy offered a cool refuge. Temperatures after sundown regularly dropped down into the fifties (and sometimes lower), making blankets a necessity. The water remained invigorating right through Labor Day. Spartan accommodations, with narrow cotlike single beds and cold water showers, seemed more adventure than hardship, and Eleanor saw her family's transfer there each summer as a relief from the heavy social schedule of the city. This was clearly Sara's territory even after Franklin and Eleanor acquired their own cottage, but the easy outdoor living, with lots of sailing and picnicking, encouraged the matriarch to relax her standards. Indoor meals were taken on a rough wooden table, which was not a conducive setting for lectures on etiquette.

One of Eleanor's children, Franklin Jr., was born on the small island, although she had not planned it that way. Someone erred in calculating the due date, and after Franklin had to set out in the *Half Moon* to fetch the doctor, he vowed never again to "trust" Eleanor's "mathematics!" But that was only one night of that very busy summer. Isabella Selmes Ferguson had come to stay for a few weeks, and after she left, Sara wrote her to boast how "splendidly" Eleanor had delivered the baby. Then she filled in Isabella about some other recent guests. Sara's stepson, Rosy, and his new wife had stayed a week, Sara wrote, and the bride "is *very* nice and of course absolutely unselfish and devoted to him and he seems devoted to her." Widowed since 1893, Rosy had finally married Elizabeth Riley, an Englishwoman of very modest origins with whom he had been involved for many years. Riley had been as much responsible for the delay as Rosy because she feared she did not measure up to the famous Roosevelts. The liaison took on more color because of Rosy's son, who had married a New York prostitute known as "Dutch Sadie" several years earlier and permanently distanced himself from his entire family at that time. Now that Rosy had decided to make his long-standing relationship with Elizabeth Riley legal, Sara quickly fell into line and invited him and his bride to Maine. Eleanor's assessment of the whole situation, however, was less enthusiastic. She wrote Isabella that she found it "so funny at times for such a respectable conventional family to be mixed up [with such women] that I occasionally pinch myself to make sure it is true." Eleanor then added her own endorsement of the bride, whom she found "a very unselfish, sweet woman."

After giving birth in August 1914, Eleanor remained at Campobello for the month of September to recuperate, and Bamie suggested that Franklin visit her in New York. She wrote in mid-September to "Dearest Franklin" inviting him to stop and see her at the Hotel Belmont, where she was staying. Lunch or dinner together would give her the chance to catch up on news, both family and political, which Bamie typically mixed in the same sentence: "I would simply love seeing you and hearing of Eleanor and the new son but also of the Senate and the navy."

Bamie's ties with Franklin and Eleanor had grown stronger since 1913 when he became assistant secretary of the Navy. Just days after his appointment he lunched with Auntie Bye, and Eleanor immediately turned to her for advice. Not only had the older woman lived in the capital for several years, but she also knew her way around foreign capitals where Eleanor and Franklin might be called upon to go now. Eleanor knew she had a lot to learn, and she wrote her aunt that Franklin was "of course . . . delighted" with his new job "as it's the thing of all things he's most interested in." But she saw problems for herself: "Now I have to write and bother you for all kinds of advice and information." She and Franklin had decided to rent temporary quarters in the capital but then asked if the house Bamie owned at 1733 N Street might be available. Eleanor had not seen it since Bamie had renovated it, and she inquired about the number of rooms and servants' quarters. She also sought advice on the social scene: "I don't know a soul in Washington and I am afraid I'll make all kinds of stupid mistakes."

Bamie's house was available, and as soon as the couple decided to rent it, she wrote from Connecticut to "Eleanor darlingest of nieces" that she wanted to be "a little business like." Then she spelled out the terms: rental amounting to $2,250 per year would be paid quarterly; if the renters wished to give up the house, they were to notify the owner three months in advance "as we have no real estate agent." This price was only possible, Bamie pointed out, if repairs were minimal. In case Eleanor and Franklin found something missing that "would add much to your comfort" or if the family remained in the house for several years, Bamie would be willing to "discuss what could be done." Somewhat apologetically, she reminded Eleanor: "This is only business, darling," and then she offered to ease the move to Washington by sending a "list of trades people and addresses." She signed herself "Devotedly Auntie Bye."

The arrangement continued for four years, but Franklin and Eleanor were not always careful to keep Bamie informed of their intentions. One summer, while Eleanor was preparing to move her family to Campobello, Franklin received a letter from Bamie asking what was happening. She had received a list of requested improvements from Eleanor and took this as a sign they wanted to stay, but she wanted to be sure. "I suppose this means you wish to remain at 1733," she wrote, and then persisted, "Is this the case?" The birth of their last son, John, in March 1916 stretched the house's capacity, and Franklin reluctantly informed Bamie that they would have to move. He regretted leaving the house, he wrote, because it had been home to them all for several years, and Bamie also disliked seeing them go: "I hate to feel you will no longer be at 1733 as it always gave me a homey sensation. Thanks for the check." After they moved out, she made a trip to Washington to move the furniture back where she had left it, complaining to Corinne "how queer tenants are. Every single room has some of its furniture in another and perfectly inappropriate place!"

While Eleanor and Franklin and the children lived in Washington, Sara could not walk through the doors that divided her quarters from theirs, as she had been able to do in the connecting houses that she built for herself and Franklin in Manhattan. But she had not had much opportunity to do that anyway. In 1911, when Franklin took his seat in the New York State Senate, he and Eleanor rented a house in Albany, and they retained that house until moving to Washington. They still spent time at Hyde Park and Campobello, but Eleanor had ample opportunity during the first fifteen years of her marriage to exert her own authority over the management of her household. The question is why she did not do so but left so many decisions to her mother-in-law.

Because of her strong personality, Sara stood out as the most important member of Eleanor's family, especially to relatives who had known her and liked her for years. On hearing of Franklin's nomination as vice president in 1920, Bamie wired congratulations not to his wife but to his mother. Realizing her gaffe, Bamie later dictated a note to "My very dear Eleanor" about how she had neglected to write and then could not remember the address for a telegram. But she hoped her niece would understand. "You surely know," Bamie continued, "that I always think of you in the great moments of your life and Franklin's nomination comes under that head." Franklin had been getting excellent coverage in the newspapers, and Bamie knew that Eleanor "must feel very proud for we all do." She insisted her letter "needs no answer and merely takes you oceans of love."

Auntie Corinne also offered Eleanor emotional support during the first decades of her marriage, and if the niece was chafing from too many intrusions of her mother-in-law, Corinne failed to notice.

In May 1911, after inviting several women, including Eleanor, to lunch, she wrote her daughter that she and Eleanor "had a little chat. She seems so well, bright and happy." Corinne occasionally entertained Franklin's clan without Sara, and in May 1916, while they were living in the capital, she invited them to her place in Washington County, Virginia, for a few days' stay.

Sara enlarged the main house at Hyde Park that summer, and by the fall, Auntie Corinne traveled up from her home in Orange, New Jersey, "to see Eleanor and Sallie . . . for a cup of tea." After assessing the new third floor, Corinne mused over the fact that she would have liked a similar space for her own grandchildren. But by now Corinne was less confident that her niece was doing well. Eleanor had given birth just six months earlier, and Auntie Corinne thought she "*looked* very fragile but seems well just the same."

Those were the years that Auntie Corinne was making a national reputation for herself as a public speaker and poet, and her niece could not help but notice her accomplishments and compare them with Grandmother Hall, who was, of course, several years older. Rather than confronting the world, the latter had lived by withdrawing, keeping mostly to herself at home. Eleanor mused after her grandmother's death in 1919 that she had some talent as a painter and would have been far happier and contented with her life had she developed that talent rather than just given in to grief.

The Roosevelt aunts offered a stark contrast—examples of strong women who acted even in the face of personal suffering and hardship. In early 1918, Eleanor wrote Isabella Ferguson that Auntie Corinne was becoming an accomplished "public speaker and it seems to agree with her." Bamie offered inspiration of a different sort. Although severely crippled with arthritis and dependent on others to move her from room to room, she retained her razor-sharp wit and intellect. People old and young still relished the chance to sit at her side and hear her dissect the latest political intrigue or newly published book. Eleanor once observed that Bye's mind "worked as a very able man's mind works," and she was always "full of animation, always the center of any group she was with." Her magic held even as her health declined, and Eleanor marveled: "Courage like hers is wonderfully inspiring, one couldn't be a coward over minor trials after seeing her."

✑

Even with these powerful examples close at hand, Eleanor began to distance herself from her Roosevelt kin after 1920. Gradually developing new confidence, she started shaping an important place for herself in the national spotlight—but among Franklin's Democrats rather than Theodore's Republicans. When Franklin was nominated to run for vice president on the national ticket in 1920, his wife had such a low profile that Louis Howe had to beg her for a photograph. Now, very quickly, her name was in the news.

The discovery of Franklin's affair with Lucy Mercer evidently speeded up the metamorphosis, partly because most of the adults in the family were privy to the matter, a subject Eleanor wanted to avoid. The affair, which Franklin agreed to end in 1918, certainly had a profound effect on her, and she later told her friend Joe Lash that when she discovered the relationship, "the bottom dropped out of my own particular world and I faced myself, my surroundings, my world honestly for the first time."

Much about the affair struck close to home. Eleanor had hired Lucy as her own social secretary, but she had hired her on the recommendation of Auntie Bye, who had previously employed her. Cousin Alice Longworth had known about the affair and seemed to encourage it by inviting Franklin and Lucy to dinner parties while Eleanor was out of town. When riding in the country one day, Alice inadvertently came upon the lovers, and rather than registering disapproval, she joked with Franklin about the "lovely lady" he was with. For an insecure woman like Eleanor, whose troubled childhood left her craving affection and approval, Franklin's infidelity cut very deeply, and she later destroyed his courtship letters that had promised eternal devotion. But she might also have wondered about how she had contributed to the affair. In 1916, after the birth of their son John, she ended sexual relations with Franklin, according to her son Elliott who insisted that Franklin and Eleanor never again "lived together as man and wife."

By that time Eleanor had given birth to six children (including the son who had died in infancy), far outdoing most of her relatives. Aunt Corinne Robinson had four, cousins Ethel and Corinney each had four, while Bamie and Alice Longworth both stopped at one.

Although only thirty-two years old in 1916 (Franklin was thirty-four), Eleanor might well have concluded that she had more than done her "duty." But then, discovering his liaison with Lucy, she might also have wondered if her own veto on sex could have served as an invitation for him to seek intimacy outside marriage.

Franklin's infidelity might have had other consequences. Instead of looking outward and becoming involved in public life, Eleanor might have taken to a darkened room as Grandmother Hall had done when widowed. But Eleanor was pushed into action from many sources. In addition to her aunts' example, she had observed the changes caused by World War I, coinciding almost exactly with Grandmother Hall's death and her discovery of Franklin's affair. With their men fighting or otherwise involved in the war, women of all economic levels pitched in to do their part. Some ran trolley cars and delivered mail; others sewed bandages and nursed soldiers. First Lady Edith Wilson arranged for a herd of sheep to graze on the White House lawn, and then when the sheep were shorn, she had the wool auctioned off to the highest bidder, bringing in a total of $50,000 for the benefit of injured and weary soldiers. These and other examples spurred Eleanor on. As she explained to Joe Lash, "I loved it. I simply ate it up."

Within the Roosevelt clan, the sense of competition was strong among the men to enlist first and perform most bravely. Theodore, in his late fifties and ill, ran a spirited campaign to convince President Wilson to permit him to lead a company of soldiers into battle. Between the two men, who had fought each other for the White House in 1912, lay a special enmity that exceeded the normal limits of political foes. Wilson understood that the still popular Roosevelt could easily enlarge his national standing through exploits in battle, and he firmly refused to permit him to participate in the biggest war of his adult years. According to one widely told story, Theodore complained to a friend about Wilson's cowardice and lack of cooperation. When Theodore noted that he himself was more than willing to die for his country, the friend, who knew how much Wilson detested him, inquired, "Did you make that perfectly clear to the President?"

Among the next generation of Roosevelt men, most took an active part. In the summer of 1915, before the United States entered the fighting, several of them joined the voluntary training camp in upstate New York. After April 1917, when Wilson finally asked for a declaration of war, Ted, Theodore's eldest son, could hardly wait to get into action, and his brother Archie was just as enthusiastic. Archie later wrote in a memoir for his son: "Since our earliest days, it had been the ambition of my brother [Ted] and I to 'beat out father' as we called it."

They did not have long to wait—both sailed to Europe in June 1917—and before the war ended in November 1918, Ted was a lieutenant colonel and Archie a captain. Brother Kermit was close behind. With his father pulling strings to arrange a commission in the British army for him, he sailed to England in July 1917, headed for Mesopotamia. Their youngest brother, Quentin, left his studies at Harvard to join up, and his cousin Sheffield Cowles dropped out of Yale to enlist. Corinne Robinson's two surviving sons, Teddy and Monroe, also fought. Franklin did not serve in battle, although one family member recalled that he regretted it. On the trip back from France after the Versailles peace conference in 1919, Franklin confided to Sheffield that he wished he had resigned as assistant secretary of the Navy to become an officer on a destroyer. "It would have been much better for my future," he pointed out.

Surrounded by all this war activity, the Roosevelt women could hardly sit back and wait—or continue their lives as though nothing unusual was happening. Almost as soon as the slaughter began in Europe in August 1914, Eleanor's cousin Ethel Derby left with her physician husband to assist wounded soldiers in France. Ethel's sister-in-law, Eleanor Butler Alexander Roosevelt (sometimes called the "other Eleanor"), may have been inspired by Ethel's example. In the summer of 1917, just before American authorities banned wives joining their soldier husbands abroad, she signed up with the YMCA and sailed to France, where Ted had just landed with American forces. Living in an apartment in Paris often used by family members for rest and reunions, the young woman helped organize recreation spots for men on furlough. Even Emily Carow, who had shown little interest in any cause, donned a nurse's uniform and helped care for wounded soldiers in Italy.

Back in the United States, other Roosevelt women performed more traditional tasks, such as rolling bandages and serving in canteens. Corinney, busy with four young children on a farm in Connecticut, organized a food program to help conserve supplies. Even the normally self-centered Alice volunteered to help. In early April 1918, Eleanor wrote Isabella Ferguson that Alice "has been here twice in two days to ask if I want her to work anywhere and I'm going to try to get her interested. It is a pity so much energy should go to waste!"

Eleanor admired the courage of the women who found some way to get near the fighting front, but she kept her own activities closer to home. At canteens in the capital she dispensed cheer and refreshments six days a week, even during the summer when Washington could be stiflingly hot and humid. To Isabella she wrote immediately after the United States entered the war that she would not be going west for a visit as planned because she had promised to help in Washington while the "chicks" spent those weeks at Hyde Park. The children would be supervised by "5 farmerettes from Vassar College ... in their blue bloomers"; these farmerettes had volunteered to help a local farmer by substituting for the young men who were off fighting. With her children in the country, Eleanor concentrated on her volunteer work in Washington, and after the war ended, she accompanied Franklin, who had been ill with pneumonia and influenza, to Paris for the peace conference. But she did all this in a wifely, background role.

With both the war and the vote for women won by 1920, all sorts of changes shaped and altered people's lives during the next decade. The increase in the number of automobiles and household appliances changed how people used their time; dress lengths and hair styles both became shorter and easier to manage; the divorce rate rose. A kind of frivolity dominated the national psyche as Americans vied with each other for the silliest phrase ("Yes, we have no bananas") or the most senseless joke ("How many people can cram into a telephone booth?") or aimless expenditure of energy (dance marathons that lasted for days). A kind of lawlessness, obvious in the flagrant disobedience of prohibition laws, linked up with a sense of relief among Americans that they had helped win the "war to end all wars."

Against this strong tide of buoyancy, some voices spoke out for serious reform in how Americans lived. Calling for protective laws to make factories safer and hours shorter, these same voices advocated special benefits for mothers and babies. Eleanor Roosevelt, now in her mid-thirties, saw 1920 as a turning point for women, and she quickly moved into the reform stream.

Always sympathetic to the underdog, she had other reasons to take this side. Franklin's role in the Democratic Party introduced her to some of the party's leading women, who helped move her toward reform, and she also feared the dire consequences if some changes were not made. In 1920 she wrote to Isabella Ferguson that Washington was changing: the "gay side, in the shape of French and English officers, has disappeared," and more and more people are predicting "strikes and labor questions." Eleanor preferred dealing with the problems before they worsened: "I realize more and more that we are entering on a new era where ideas and habits and customs are to be revolutionized if we are not to have another kind of revolution."

Franklin's nomination as vice president in 1920 marked an important turning point for the entire clan—as the Hyde Park branch of Roosevelts pulled ahead of those from Oyster Bay. Theodore's unexpected death in January 1919, when he was only sixty, deprived that side of the family of its most charismatic leader before his eldest son, Ted, had developed the capacity to fill his shoes. Franklin's elevation from the relatively obscure job of assistant secretary of the Navy to a national ticket did not come as a complete surprise to everyone. Earlier that year, when Isabella wrote from her ranch in New Mexico to thank Eleanor for the family photo she had sent at Christmas, she added: "It looks alarmingly like the [photos] of families that end up in the White House, and I am not sure I would wish that for anyone I love." But within the Theodores, Franklin's ascendancy cut deep—they had been caught unprepared.

Franklin's polio derailed his political career, but not for long. From the time he became ill in the late summer of 1921 until he ran for governor of New York State in 1928, he rarely absented himself from the political world for very long. Complete recovery remained his objective for a while, and he retained a buoyant confidence that he would find a treatment to give full life back to his atrophied leg muscles. When a more pessimistic verdict finally settled on him and he realized that he would never again walk without assistance, he turned his energies to a contest he could dominate without legs—the winning of political office. By 1924 he was speaking out for other candidates, and after long hours of frustrating practice with his crutches, he was able to stand long enough to arouse the enthusiasm of delegates at the Democratic National Convention when he gave his "Happy Warrior" speech nominating Al Smith.

Her husband's illness and long recuperation propelled Eleanor into a much more active role in Democratic politics. In moving to that side of the political aisle, she acted as Franklin's substitute, but she also underscored her "outsider" perspective as far as her family was concerned. Her grandfather Roosevelt had voted Republican, and her uncle Theodore always ran as a Republican (except for his brief revolt in 1912). Auntie Corinne and Auntie Bye were tightly identified with the Republican Party, and cousins Alice, Corinney, and Ethel all took the GOP label. Now that Eleanor was making a name for herself in the political opposition, the family would have to reconcile that fact with their own strong sense of family.

During the 1920s, Eleanor forged many more friendships with forceful, independent women in the Democratic Party. Her irreverent cousin Alice summed up the change as "the years that Eleanor went public," and, indeed, she did devote increasing attention to public rather than private or family needs. Two of her sons were under ten years of age, and Franklin still struggled to overcome his paralysis, but Eleanor's calendar began to fill with appointments that had little to do with any of them. The seeds for this intellectual migration had lain dormant—except to perceptive eyes like those of Marie Souvestre and Isabella Ferguson, who both predicted that Eleanor would become a leader—but now they grew quickly.

Eleanor gravitated to women far bolder than herself about speaking, writing, and advocating change. After venturing into politics through the nonpartisan League of Women Voters (where Corinney was already a leader), Eleanor consented in 1920 to head up that organization's national legislation committee. Through that work she met Elizabeth Read, an activist and attorney, and together the two women perused the *Congressional Record*, looking for issues on which the league could focus its efforts. Through Read, Eleanor encountered Esther Lape, a professor who lived with Read in Greenwich Village, a mecca for women experimenting with new lifestyles in the 1920s. Alongside poets such as Edna St. Vincent Millay lived entrepreneurs, such as Lila Wallace who worked with her husband to start *Readers' Digest*, lawyers, and doctors, all challenging old stereotypes about appropriate roles for women.

It was not surprising that Eleanor Roosevelt, whose family had been involved in politics for nearly half a century, would turn her talents to the same arena. In 1922, when Nancy Cook asked her to speak at a fund-raising luncheon for Democratic women, she first demurred and then agreed, thus beginning a long, close friendship with this dynamic administrator. Cook and her partner, Marion Dickerman, had served as Red Cross volunteers in London during the war, and after they returned to New York, Dickerman ran for the New York State Assembly. Aristocratic and well educated, Dickerman lost that election in a torrent of name calling and violence aimed at her liberal views, but she retained her faith in her ability to help achieve change. She took a job as a college dean but continued to work in Greenwich Village with other reformers such as Mary Simkhovitch.

In a time of such rapid change, it is easy to get caught up in the excitement, and sometimes Eleanor seemed almost giddy with her newfound world and the women who inhabited it. With them she found the acceptance and sense of worth that had eluded her in her own family. She spent more and more time in Greenwich Village with Dickerman, Cook, Lape, Read, and their circle. Teaming up with Dickerman and Cook, she opened a private girls' school on the Upper East Side, and after she began teaching history there, she admitted she liked that job more than anything she had ever done. Through her new friends, Eleanor met women such as Rose Schneiderman, the labor leader whose family's poverty sent her out to work at age thirteen. Eleanor had not been unaware of the fact that most Americans lived in a considerably less comfortable world than her own, but these new acquaintances impressed her with the need to make changes.

Sara Delano Roosevelt viewed Eleanor's migration, both in intellect and affections, with mixed feelings. In writing to Corinne Robinson in 1924, she noted that Eleanor had been spending less time at Hyde Park and that she often brought Nancy Cook and Marion Dickerman with her. Sara had too much energy and curiosity to simply write off her daughter-in-law and her new friends, so she struggled to keep up with them, even inviting Cook and Dickerman to lunch or dinner when Eleanor was absent. Both Cook and Dickerman came from well-to-do Protestant families, so Sara could accept them, but she showed less interest in Eleanor's Jewish or working-class associates, such as Schneiderman, and Eleanor rarely brought them with her to Hyde Park.

Eleanor's friendships with several lesbian couples—and later with the journalist Lorena Hickok—have raised questions about her own sexual orientation and whether her friendship with women who preferred women partners meant that she did, too. Certainly she had close emotional ties to important women, some of whom lived in lesbian partnerships. Without a doubt Eleanor welcomed their approval and support, and she enjoyed their lively conversations and fun, but she left unanswered the question of how physical her relationships with them became. A niece who knew Eleanor well has pointed out that she typically attached herself to a couple (such as Dickerman and Cook or Lape and Read)—another case of her being the outsider. With Lorena Hickok, with whom Eleanor did have a close relationship in the 1930s without a third woman being involved, the niece saw a special friendship in which each woman gave the other confidence and worth, but then it changed. Since the years that she studied with Marie Souvestre, Eleanor had been attracted to people on a different social stratum from her own and curious about their lives, and she found the outspoken midwesterner interesting—a welcome contrast to so many women she knew. By the last decades of her life, however, Hickok became a pitiful figure, sick and dependent on her famous friend for money and attention.

Whatever the relationships, Eleanor's increasingly hectic life with her new friends left much less time for "Mama." In the early years of her marriage, Eleanor's diary noted almost daily that she dined "with Mama" or "F and I dined with Mama." But in the 1920s new names, often women's names with strong political affiliations, filled Eleanor's diary. In 1924, when Sara was closing down the big house for a year, Franklin encouraged Eleanor to build her own place in partnership with Nancy Cook and Marion Dickerman. By the following summer a small fieldstone house, named "Val-Kill" for a neighboring stream on the Hyde Park property, was ready for occupancy by Cook and Dickerman. Eleanor joined them on weekends.

Throughout the 1920s, while Franklin struggled to walk again and spent much of his time in the milder climate of Georgia or Florida, his mother kept reminding him what his busy wife was doing. In March 1927, Sara informed Franklin that Eleanor had dropped in on her at her Sixty-fifth Street house "for ten minutes and then went to her office." On another occasion, she noted pointedly that Eleanor "dined out." When Sara invited some of her own Delano kin to dinner, she observed that Eleanor might join them but only if she happened to be free.

This heightened activity was all the more baffling since Eleanor remained—to Sara's eyes—the young, inexperienced girl who needed help. In 1930, when Eleanor was forty-six years old and the wife of the governor of New York, her mother-in-law was still offering advice on what to wear—and to remember that with a gray dress "wear 'jewels' to give it life!"

Auntie Bye added her own word on Eleanor's appearance. In fact, she seemed more upset by the style of Eleanor's new companions than by their political views. Bamie, unconventional about so many aspects of life, put great stock in dressing conservatively and well. She bought expensive clothes, always in the most acceptable color and cut, and then felt free to "break all the rules" in more significant ways. By the early 1920s she could not help but notice that Eleanor and her friends were wearing the new styles.

After one visit from her niece and Nancy Cook, Bye wrote to Corinne, "I just hate to have Eleanor let herself look as she does. Though never handsome, she always had to me a very charming effect, but Alas and alackaday! since politics have become her choice interest, all her charm has disappeared, and the fact is emphasized by the companions she chooses to bring with her." Bamie then went into some detail about how she had always insisted that a woman could accomplish more if she looked good than if she "assumed an uncompromisingly plain aspect." Little did she know how much Eleanor would accomplish even with her "plain aspect."

III

BY MARCH 1933, when Eleanor and Franklin moved into the White House after four years in Albany, few members of her father's generation survived to witness the event. Corinne and Bamie and Theodore were all dead, and of their spouses, only Theodore's widow, Edith, survived. Since the former First Lady campaigned openly for Herbert Hoover in 1932, the relationship between her and Eleanor was somewhat strained. Over the ensuing years the two women exchanged condolence messages when there was a death in the family or humorous notes when one of them received mail intended for the other, but they saw little of each other. Each of Edith's children and grandchildren received a wedding gift from Cousin Eleanor, often a beautifully engraved silver bowl from "Eleanor and Franklin"—but rarely a visit. "Poor Eleanor" had now become both powerful and popular, and few of the Theodore branch found that transition easy.

Sara Delano Roosevelt, proud of her son as she was, tried to adjust to a situation over which she had little control. She had always huddled over the Hyde Park branch as though she knew what was best for them all, monitoring everyone's health as if any frailty reflected on her. Just after Franklin's election to the presidency, she reminded him that she wanted Eleanor and granddaughter Anna to get more rest and fresh air: "I hate being told how badly my family looks. I feel quite responsible." Too shrewd to ignore the fact that her role in the family was becoming more and more peripheral, she fought hard against the implications by continuing to give her own opinions. In 1935, when the First Lady made headlines by going down into a coal mine, Sara wrote Franklin that she had read Eleanor "has emerged from the mine—and that is something to be thankful for."

Although Sara must have realized that she no longer held the reins, she stubbornly refused to relinquish the driver's seat, and she used her money to make her point. Eleanor objected that her lavish gifts to the grandchildren undermined the parents' relationship with them, but Sara had trouble seeing the reason for her anger. When Anna married in 1926, her grandmother gave her an apartment in Manhattan, but without fully informing Eleanor, a lapse that hurt. Later, after Anna's first baby was born, Sara wanted to pay for a nurse, but this time she wisely arranged matters so that the gift appeared to come from Franklin. At Hyde Park dinners she sat opposite Franklin (while Eleanor took a place at the side), and in the big hall her chair was paired with his in front of the fireplace.

But in more important matters the tables had turned, and Eleanor stood in a position to counsel Sara. As the mother of the President,

Sara was often approached for a statement or the use of her name, and Eleanor advised her about situations that might embarrass Franklin. Occasionally, Eleanor invited Sara to go along on a trip that she thought might interest her. Now secure enough to risk disappointing her mother-in-law, Eleanor felt free to refuse invitations and appearances that Sara urged her to accept. In early 1937, for example, when Sara asked her daughter-in-law to attend a recital in Washington, thus potentially boosting the young artist's audience, Eleanor replied that she would be out of town and could not oblige.

Within the family, Sara retained her strong energy well into her eighties. She gave large dinner parties, mixing young guests with older ones so that people did not get too "tired of the same old lady." Still intent on lavishing expensive gifts on her grandchildren, she now had to rely on Eleanor for a list of their wishes. Complaining to Franklin that she was "too tired" to shop, Sara added, "Eleanor, like an angel, offered to do it for me (with all *she* has to do!)." Most of the time the family settled for checks, but at Christmas 1939, Eleanor instructed her mother-in-law in a typewritten note that two of her sons wanted new suits.

Visits between the two women became shorter, less frequent, and often in the company of other people. In 1936, Sara wrote: "I had a glimpse of Eleanor on Sunday. She came over with Nancy Cook." In another, undated note, Sara wrote to Franklin: "It is such a comfort to have Eleanor and a few peaceful days with her beloved children will do her no harm! She accomplishes so much in her quiet way, and is always so sweet and cheerful, never nervous or cross and I just count on these few days."

On occasion, Sara substituted for Eleanor at a ceremonial event. On June 9, 1938, she collected an honorary degree for the First Lady from New York University and seemed thrilled with her role. When Eleanor had to give up the idea of going, "I went and got her little parchment and they were all very kind to me, in spite of their disappointment," she wrote Franklin. The President's mother still commanded considerable attention. In preparation for the 1939 visit of the British king and queen to the United States, *Life* ran a large article, complete with sixteen photos of Hyde Park, and put Eleanor's photo on the cover. But the title of the piece must have grated on

Eleanor: "The President's Wife Is Hostess at Hyde Park but the President's Mother Is Mistress There."

When Sara died in September 1941, such a huge crowd was expected for the funeral that Corinney decided not to attend—she feared she would not get in. In a note to Eleanor, Corinney observed that "the strain falls on you continually and you have such courage and such strength and yet I feel you must feel it all far more than any of us can see." Corinney would have gladly "spent the day motoring over" to Hyde Park "and having a delicious time thinking of those of the past generation and how thrilling they were," had she had the identification to get in.

When Eleanor wrote to thank Corinney for her kindness, she filled in the details of Sara's death in very matter-of-fact tones, as though she were writing about a person she hardly knew rather than one whose life intertwined with hers over more than forty years: "Mama had been rather frail all summer and the end came peacefully and suddenly. Franklin was at Hyde Park and had had a good day with her before this sudden turn came."

By that time Eleanor's prominence—not just in the Democratic Party but in the entire nation—was assured, and she had less reason to review with her cousin her long, complicated relationship with Sara. When Eleanor made her first tentative attempts in politics, such as trying to present women's suggestions to the Platform Committee of the Democratic Party in 1924, she had been ignored. But by the mid-1930s she confidently expressed her ideas on many issues and knew that she carried weight. Years earlier, Isabella Ferguson called Eleanor a "magic politician," and now she seemed fully deserving of the title. In fact, as far back as 1913, Isabella had foreseen the day when Eleanor's daughter would be telling her own children about the "extraordinary life led by their grandmother!" In preparation for the time when Eleanor became famous, Isabella vowed to save "every scrap of your writing."

Isabella Ferguson had one giant advantage—she knew Eleanor's relatives and the groundwork they laid for her remarkable metamorphosis. From childhood, Eleanor watched her aunts converse easily with senators; she knew they traveled on their own and cultivated their separate circle of friends, both male and female. Physical feats intrigued Auntie Corinne as much as they did her brothers, and the idea of publishing in her own name or giving a speech to thousands of people appeared no more daunting than a strenuous morning hike. Auntie Bye boasted that she had acted "against all the rules" in London society (and had gotten away with it). Both sisters exemplified the notion that thinking women could lead lives every bit as full and exciting as their men. In July 1936, when the First Lady outlined her suggestions for how the presidential campaign should proceed that year, she emphasized how wrong it was to take victory for granted—she had heard that the Republicans were well organized. The suggestions sound a lot like those outlined by Auntie Corinne years earlier.

As for Corinney, Eleanor continued to see a lot of her even though they stood on opposite sides of a prominent political fence, with Eleanor the most famous woman in the Democratic Party and Corinney a leader among the Republicans. When Eleanor made national news in her own right, quite apart from Franklin, her cousin stood first in line to congratulate her. In the spring of 1939, after the Daughters of the American Revolution turned down a request for the famous African-American contralto Marian Anderson to perform in their Constitution Hall, Eleanor decided to take a stand: she resigned her membership in the organization in protest. With help from others, she then arranged for Anderson to perform on the steps of the Lincoln Memorial in a poignant recital that drew an audience of thousands. Corinney applauded her cousin's decision: "I want you to know how proud I was of you the other day— *very* proud of being a first cousin! Tolerance without a certain soft flabbiness is hard to achieve and you were tolerant and fair and frank and yet maintained your own point of view. You are the first lady of the land in your own right!"

During the 1940 presidential election, the relationship between the two cousins became strained when Corinney (along with prominent Democrats, including Isabella Ferguson) openly opposed a third term for Franklin. When he won, Corinney waited several weeks— until she wrote her Christmas letter— before getting in touch. After apologizing for not sending "congratulations" on Franklin's "great personal triumph," Corinney explained the reason: "I felt it would seem hypocritical as I was strongly opposed to a consecutive third term and many of the internal policies of the New Deal."

Corinney continued that she had thought of Eleanor and Franklin "*so* much" and that their relationship endured through all disagreements. "Political differences seem so unimportant," she wrote, promising to visit Eleanor if she got to Washington. With Europe already at war, Corinne noted: "A *Merry* Christmas seems almost an impossibility in a world black with hate and destruction but Christmas does typify the conquest of the 'world' by love and we must make much of it." She signed herself, "Devotedly, Corinne."

Eleanor responded with her usual generosity: "I loved your letter and, as you know, I never let political differences enter into my personal relationships." She had not been keen about spending four more years in the White House, she admitted to her cousin in characteristic self-effacement, "but if Franklin is willing to shoulder the responsibility and do so much work, my wishes are unimportant."

∽

Eleanor and Corinney shared more than they could easily cite. They had played together as children and made some of the same friends at Allenswood. They had sat at the same holiday dinner tables and commiserated over the illnesses in the family. In what seemed like a remarkable coincidence, Corinney's nephew Teddy Robinson was stricken with polio in 1927 while Franklin still struggled to live with the crippling effect of the disease. They also shared a love for Corinne Robinson. Before Corinne died in 1933, Eleanor had formed such a strong attachment to her aunt that she was still sending flowers to mark the anniversary of that loss more than a decade later.

What tied the two cousins most pathetically may have been their almost identical struggles with their errant, alcoholic brothers. Alcoholism had troubled many different Roosevelts, but one son out of each family seemed doomed by the disease and their sisters had to deal with it: Corinne Alsop's brother Monroe Robinson; Eleanor's brother, Hall Roosevelt; and Ethel Derby's brother, Kermit Roosevelt. All three brothers were, Corinney wrote Eleanor, "victims of something that cannot be understood."

Eleanor certainly tried to help Hall, especially in his early years, but he had followed pretty much in his father's footsteps, drinking excessively and behaving in ways no one could understand. Brilliant and unpredictable, Hall led a tortured life, leaving Eleanor to pick up the pieces. He had escaped Grandmother Hall's household when he went to Groton, but the influence of his maternal uncles, especially the volatile Uncle Vallie, cannot be discounted. Only eight years old when Eleanor left him to go to school in England, he may have felt abandoned by her as well.

After graduating with honors from Harvard in three years and marrying at twenty, Hall drifted from job to job, showing very little sense of responsibility. With his first wife, Margaret Richardson, he had three children (a fourth died in infancy), but after he divorced her in 1920, he had so little to do with their children that Eleanor took it upon herself to arrange meetings between him and them. The one daughter from that marriage recalled that her aunt would book a car and send father and daughter off on an evening in New York, but the daughter would become so embarrassed by her father's behavior that she could not wait for the evening to end.

Eleanor played an equally important role with Hall's second family, so that by the time she died, it seemed that she had raised not only an orphaned brother but also both his families. With his second wife, Dorothy Kemp, Hall had three daughters, but he left them soon after the third was born in January 1930 and never went back. The estrangement was so complete that when he encountered the eldest at a White House celebration in 1941, he did not know who she was.

It is difficult to imagine how this second family would have managed if Eleanor had not volunteered to help. She arranged for her sister-in-law, a pianist, to perform in Washington, an obvious boost for a struggling artist. Then she found her a job in her home state, Michigan. Later, when Dorothy Kemp Roosevelt ran for Congress (becoming the first woman to win nomination for a major office in that state), Eleanor helped campaign. When the nieces were old enough, she invited them to Hyde Park, and she later paid part of their college bills. The girls admired her enormously, and one of them admitted, years after Eleanor's death, "She was always there for us." While most people could find no redeeming traits in the lanky, tall brother who looked remarkably like her, Eleanor refused to give up on him no matter what he did. He had inherited the same incredible charm that guaranteed his father an audience of admirers, but with his sister he could be petty and cheap. He asked her to reimburse him for small amounts he had spent on her behalf (sometimes less than one dollar) and more than once for the same item. After she became First Lady, he boasted that his sister lived in the White House and imposed on her to furnish his friends with invitations to important events. But when he wrote a book about sailors in the family, she gamely contributed an endorsement.

By September 1941, not long after he turned fifty, Hall's physical condition had deteriorated. When Corinney wrote Eleanor to thank her for inviting Monroe to the White House at what was for him "a very crucial time," Eleanor played down her part. She had been "delighted to see Monroe and I think it is grand that he has been strong enough to fight the urge." Her own brother had not done as well, she wrote. He was "very seriously ill at Walter Reed Hospital, and I have very little hope that he will recover. His liver is in very bad shape."

That letter arrived the same day that Corinney read in the newspaper of Hall's death on September 25. She wrote Eleanor that she had had no idea of "Hall's condition and I am so sad." The death had caused her to rethink the odd contradictions among the Roosevelts. "Our family is such a strange one in many ways. Dynamic genius—brilliance—power—action and with all this—a reckless self destruction. Hall was all this to the last degree. I can see him now at Henderson [House]—so fascinating—such a thrilling companion— so reckless of life and limb in a large powerful motor dashing around corners in those narrow roads—so unpredictable, so brilliant." Corinney had last seen Hall at the wedding of one of his daughters a few months earlier, and she admitted: "I was naturally horribly shocked when I saw him . . . a stark tragedy; this self-destruction."

Corinney knew that Hall's last few days had been painful for Eleanor, "waiting and watching at the hospital," but she wanted to convey her own admiration for the steadfast devotion Eleanor had shown over half a century since brother and sister were orphaned. "You have been so wonderful with Hall—you have given of your devotion and understanding without stint," and she knew that both his wives and all his children "love and admire all that you have done." Eleanor had treated Hall as her own son, one with "great promise. Magnificent in many ways and tragic in this same self destruction." Corinney regretted that she had not been at Eleanor's side during "those long last moments. They are often so long—even when there is no hope." In closing she noted that the letter required no answer—it was just a declaration of support and love.

But of course Eleanor did answer. Corinney was one of the few people in the world who knew how very much she had suffered with Hall—worried over his failures and agonized at his losses. On October 1 she replied: "Dearest Corinne . . . I know that you realize better than most people how there is something we can not understand in men like Hall and Monroe and Kermit. They start with so many wonderful qualities and so much ability, and yet this weakness causes them and many others so much unhappiness." Hall had suffered from "wretched health for a long time," but the last three weeks were especially painful "for me as well as for him." Then she observed that Monroe "seemed so well this summer," and she hoped "he has learned from the experience of others." As for Kermit, she held little hope: He is "pretty badly off and my heart aches for Belle." This letter she signed with uncharacteristic emotion, "Much love."

When the time came for Corinney to bury her brother in December 1944, Eleanor made it a point to be at the funeral even though she had to rearrange her hectic schedule. In spite of failing health, Franklin had just been reelected for an unprecedented fourth term, and in addition to preparing for his inauguration in January, Eleanor also had many extra demands on her because of the war. Afterward, Corinney wrote her that it was "more than lovely [for you] to wait over for Monroe's funeral and I was glad to have you with us. You and I have had the same unique brother and sister relationship throughout our lives and I know you could understand better than anyone."

On a happier note, the two cousins laughed over memories of Allenswood. When the First Lady visited England in 1942, she called on some of the old school friends they had shared, and Corinney admitted that she laughed "with glee" over the report, "and it brought me back with delight to Allenswood." Once again Corinney observed how Eleanor had been a favorite of Mlle. Souvestre's while she had been "the cousin that followed you [and] was loved—but I am afraid not admired to the same degree!"

Eleanor and Corinney had other reasons for keeping in touch during the war. Lunching at an apartment that Eleanor kept on Washington Square in Greenwich Village, they discussed what roles they (and other women) could play in victory. After talking over the value of a national land army, an association of civilians to coordinate food production while many men were away fighting, Corinney returned to Connecticut and started a state branch. Whenever she wished to discuss the progress of the organization, she went straight to Washington and talked things over with either Franklin or Eleanor.

Sometimes Corinney's requests came on behalf of others who lacked her direct access to the White House. In October 1944 she wrote Eleanor's secretary asking for information about a Connecticut woman's brother whose plane had been shot down a month earlier. It took a second letter from the Alsop household before Eleanor replied in her own hand at the end of November, telling what she had learned about the ill-fated plane. Corinney's in-laws also considered themselves entitled to special access to the Roosevelt White House—which they approached through the First Lady.

In the many communications between Eleanor and her various Roosevelt cousins, it is difficult to separate the favors from the genuine affection. At Christmas 1944, Teddy and Helen Robinson sent Eleanor the book *Gypsy in the Sun*, and she reciprocated with a box of pecans, along with regrets that they could not all gather in Washington as they had in previous years: "It was always such fun." But some of the relatives inundated the busy First Lady with copies of their own books or books by friends, along with a specific request that she mention them in her nationally syndicated newspaper column or in a speech that would attract wide attention. Somehow Eleanor had to sort out the ones to boost and the ones to ignore, fully aware that a plug in "My Day" was more valuable than a costly advertisement.

∞

Franklin's death in April 1945 did not significantly change Eleanor's relationship with the Roosevelt clan. Over the years she had moved out of the "Theodores" and into the "Franklins." She even took with her Hall's children, who were born "Theodores" through their father but aligned with the Hyde Park branch through Eleanor. One of Hall's daughters, Diana Jaicks, later admitted that she hardly knew her cousins from her father's side of the family, while she had warm memories of summer vacations at Hyde Park. Her sister, Janet Katten, echoed that recollection. She romped as a youngster in the presence of Uncle Franklin but had little knowledge of her great-uncle Theodore or of his children and grandchildren, many of them about her age.

At life's biggest markers—marriages and deaths (especially deaths)—the two branches still communicated, at least as long as Eleanor lived. In response to a letter from Ted's widow—the "other" Eleanor—at the time of Franklin's death, Eleanor wrote that she thought of her often and "getting your sweet note gives me a chance to tell you." Then she went ahead to compare notes on widowhood and wrote, in what might have been an unconscious slip, "It has not been hard to adjust my own life." She continued that she felt compelled to assist with the "work in the world that Franklin wanted to help."

Aunt Edith, now in her mid-eighties, acknowledged Franklin's death in a telegram of only seven words: "Love and deep sympathy from Aunt Edith." When Eleanor replied a few days later, it was in businesslike tones on paper imprinted "1600 Pennsylvania Avenue, Washington, D.C."—an interesting usage since it had been her uncle Theodore who had officially changed the mansion's name to "The White House." Penning the words herself, Eleanor wrote: "Dear Aunt Edith, Many thanks for your kind wire. It was a shock, but I am glad he died working, without pain or long illness. Affly yours, Eleanor Roosevelt." Even Edith's address on the envelope is in Eleanor's hand, a mark of rare attention from the busy widow.

✑

Eleanor's prediction about her years alone proved notoriously incorrect. When a journalist approached her after her husband's death and asked what she planned to do with the rest of her life, she replied, "The story is over." But of course it was not, and anyone familiar with the examples of the preceding generation of Roosevelt women would have known why not. It was not a family tradition for wives to fold up their tents and disappear after their husbands died. Some became inveterate travelers, such as her aunt Edith. Others, such as Auntie Corinne, gained national reputations as speakers and writers. Those who were too crippled to move, such as Auntie Bye, or not inclined to move, such as Cousin Alice, nurtured their own salons where they attracted the wittiest and most gifted people. Eleanor took a little from all their books, continuing with her speaking, writing, and traveling, but she did far more.

Appointed by President Truman in 1947 as the U.S. delegate to the United Nations, Eleanor was never a figurehead there. When the Universal Declaration of Human Rights, largely shaped by her, passed the General Assembly on December 10, 1948, she became an international symbol of the fight for human rights. The election of a Republican president, Dwight Eisenhower, in 1953 led her to resign the U.N. post, but she continued to travel and speak all over the world on the need for international cooperation and respect for human dignity. She continued playing an active role in the national Democratic Party, favoring Adlai Stevenson as a candidate in both 1952 and 1956, and reluctantly endorsing John F. Kennedy in 1960. In 1961, President Kennedy appointed her to chair the Commission on the Status of Women, work that she continued to pursue until just months before her death.

It was during her years as a widow, the last seventeen years of her life, that she was dubbed "First Lady of the World." They were busy years indeed, requiring a separate volume when Joe Lash wrote her biography. Her enormous reputation resulted partly from the fact that she lived in the White House longer than any other president's wife and during a time of tremendous uncertainty and trauma for the nation. But it is also true that no other president's widow went on to achieve in the same way.

Eleanor's five children continued to have their share of difficulties, both personal and professional. Elliott obtained his third divorce in 1950; Anna had been divorced for the second time in 1949. None of the sons seemed to find an appropriate career niche, and Anna's attempt to run a newspaper, the *Seattle Post-Intelligencer*, was not successful. Like many children of famous, successful parents, all five fell short in equaling their relatives' achievements. While they might have led happy lives without the glitter of the White House or the glow of public adoration, they did not seem contented with what they had. Elliott, in particular, often singled out as his mother's favorite, seemed distressed with his lot.

Eleanor could take criticism of herself and Franklin in stride, but she bristled when one of her children was attacked—even if the criticism came from inside the family circle. In the fall of 1946, for example, she took to task Corinney's son, Joe Alsop, already a famous columnist, for his unflattering comments about Elliott. In his new book *As He Saw It*, Elliott had not only listed his father's views but he had gone on to show how he disagreed with them, and Joe Alsop, along with many other Americans, thought he had gone too far.

Eleanor informed Joe that she was "horrified," and when he tried to explain himself, she charged that Joe did not understand Elliott and had not "known him for a very long time." Joe hoped that this disagreement would not rupture their friendship, and she assured him it would not: she had "every desire to continue what I look upon not simply as a cousinly relationship but a really friendly one. I am quite capable," she continued, "of liking people even when we differ." But the uncharacteristically sharp tone in those letters indicates that Joe had hit a very tender spot.

Eleanor had many calls on her time, of course, and she stretched to do as much as possible. She hired secretarial help but preferred to pen some letters herself. Her family had always been letter writers, so she thought nothing of answering several correspondents in one sitting, often at two or three in the morning. By using small note sheets and a large script, she could fill a page with just a few words and conclude a message in less than a minute. Yet every one of them had her own personal touch, the flurry of her pen across the page, and the individualized signature, "Affly, Eleanor."

Her niece Eleanor, Hall's eldest daughter, later spoke about how she treasured even a few minutes in the company of her busy aunt. When the former First Lady phoned her niece, who lived near Hyde Park, and invited her to come to Val-Kill for a quick lunch, the niece jumped at the chance to accept, and she was glad she did because Eleanor could accomplish a lot in very little time. "In just 15 minutes, she had asked all the questions, found out about everybody in the family . . . and off she went. It was great," the niece recalled.

Eleanor's busy schedule continued up to a few months before she died, on November 7, 1962. The first of the four cousins to marry and have a family, she was also the first to die. Alice Longworth and Corinne Alsop both made the trip to Hyde Park for the funeral, but

Ethel Derby, the youngest of the four cousins and the one Eleanor was least close to, decided not to attend. Ethel explained to her daughter, "One goes to funerals because one loves someone dearly, or because it will make a difference to the survivors, or because one thinks that there won't be many there. None of these applied."

Ethel correctly predicted a huge turnout. No woman in American history ever drew a more prestigious assembly. For most former first ladies, a sprinkling of presidents' wives turn up, but for Eleanor Roosevelt, the presidents themselves came in force: incumbent John F. Kennedy and his wife, Jacqueline; former presidents Harry S Truman and Dwight D. Eisenhower; and Vice President Lyndon B. Johnson, who would become chief executive thirteen months later. Their combined presence at Eleanor's funeral made the occasion seem more a day of national mourning than of rites for a private citizen. In the slight drizzle of that dreary November day, few of those present could have explained how a shy, unremarkable girl matured into the most famous woman of the twentieth century—unless they knew her family and the extraordinary women who paved her way.

During Theodore Roosevelt's presidency, Eleanor was routinely singled out as his favorite niece, but Corinne Robinson, his only other niece, never seemed to mind.

CHAPTER SIX

CORINNE ROBINSON ALSOP

(1886–1971)

N JUNE 10, 1936, when Corinne Robinson Alsop stood up in Cleveland to second the nomination of Alf Landon, many of her fellow Republicans could remember her mother's speech in Chicago sixteen years earlier. At fifty, Corinney was younger than her mother had been then but every bit as good a speaker. Unfortunately, the audience, numbering about twelve thousand or, as one newspaper put it, as many as could crowd into the Municipal Auditorium, responded with less enthusiasm—not because of what she said about the governor of Kansas but because of the dismal prospects for winning the presidency back on November 3. The Democrats had not yet met to make it official, but few people doubted that Franklin Roosevelt would be renominated and then win the general election by a landslide.

In a move that historians would later dub "the second New Deal," the President had begun to respond to his critics by embracing reforms that addressed their needs. Instead of the stopgap or "relief" measures of his first two years in office, he had, in the next two years, endorsed reforms and social programs that would reshape the role of government in people's lives: public works programs, rural electrification, the National Youth Administration (providing work and school for young people), and the Wagner Act (legalizing collective bargaining and thus legitimizing unions). In combination these reforms and others drew support away from dissidents all over the nation who had attacked FDR: the flamboyant Louisiana senator Huey Long and his program to "Share Our Wealth"; the bigoted "radio preacher" Charles Coughlin in Detroit; United Mine Workers president John L. Lewis, looking for more tangible benefits for his miners; and others.

With the most vocal of FDR's critics muted, many Americans saw him in a more favorable light than did some of his Roosevelt kin. Bamie's son, Sheffield Cowles, thought Franklin had gone much too far to the left, and he placed the blame on something that happened when Franklin was a student at Harvard. He failed to make the prestigious club Porcellian (which admitted other Roosevelts), and Sheffield saw the New Deal as his payback to "all those bankers who had shut him out back then." Theodore's daughter Ethel and her husband, Richard Derby, had no use for Franklin's intervening government (though they were less sure than Sheffield Cowles about his motivation). Corinne Alsop preferred keeping power on the state level rather than in Washington, D.C.; Alice Longworth managed to find some objection to just about anything Franklin tried to do, as well as the style in which he did it.

In announcing that Corinne Alsop would speak at the 1936 Republican convention, newspapers noted that she was a "distant relative of President Roosevelt." In fact, the relationship was not so distant. First cousin to Eleanor Roosevelt, Corinney was a fifth cousin to Franklin, and she had known him since childhood. When one reporter pointedly reminded Corinney that she had served as a bridesmaid at their wedding, she bristled but then explained that she liked the Republican nominee, Alf Landon, and his record as Kansas governor. She added, "As to my relationship with the Franklin Roosevelts, we are and I hope we always will be friends, but I do not like their political program."

In spite of her stout defense of Landon, Corinney evidently felt a bit used by the Republicans that year. By putting her in such visible opposition to her cousins, they implied a breach in the family that she liked to disregard. She may also have disliked reminders about how badly her candidate lost. Except for Maine and Vermont, Franklin won every state, including Landon's home state. Whatever her reasons, Corinney's youngest son recalled that whenever he wanted to tease her or get her angry, he got out the gramophone recording of her 1936 nominating speech and played it for her.

By the time of that election, Corinne Alsop stood out in her family as the biggest political achiever—just as Eleanor stood out in hers. The parents of both women were dead, as were all their brothers—except for Hall and Monroe, who had already shown they were not likely to win much notice from either political party. Monroe Robinson had managed to stay "dry" after his mother's death in 1933, but it was too late to shape a career for himself either in business or writing, both of which he tried. With two siblings so obviously failures, Corinney and Eleanor seemed all the more remarkable—vibrant and confident, one a leader in the Democratic Party and the other in the Republican.

Neither of the women ranked as a beauty, but they treated the subject differently. While Eleanor tended to appeal for sympathy by describing how her beautiful mother made her feel unattractive as a child, Corinney made a joke of her looks. She remembered herself as "a terribly dull child, plain as a hedge fence." Her mother corroborated that view by recalling that when she first glimpsed her newborn daughter "on the very hottest day in July," she turned to her husband and said, "I *think* I can love her." In fact, the girl (and later the woman) resembled her father in appearance, and almost everyone agreed that Douglas Robinson was "the plainest man in the world." His daughter, who had his very large, curved nose and straight, "dark hair that had the strength and rigidity of a poker," sometimes joked about how much better she would have looked if her hair had curled instead of her nose. Behind the humor lay the self-assurance that none of this mattered one bit.

I

After Cousin Eleanor became famous, historians routinely referred to her as Theodore Roosevelt's "favorite" niece. In fact, he had only one other niece—the second child (and only daughter) born to his sister Corinne Robinson. All four Robinson children carried their father's first name as their middle name, and the daughter was no exception. To distinguish her from her mother, she was variously referred to as Corinney, Corinne Jr., or by some adjective showing relationship, such as Cousin Corinne or Auntie Corinne's Corinne or, after her marriage, Corinne Alsop.

Being the only sister of three brothers had its rewards. Corinney remembered that when the family read Shakespeare plays aloud, she held a monopoly on the heroine roles. But in this rather loud and overpowering family she found it difficult to make her mark and insisted that she never learned to speak until she turned sixteen and left home because both her parents talked so much and they were "all so bright and . . . clever."

The lively Robinson household offered a companionship that cousins Eleanor and Alice enjoyed only as guests. The skating parties organized at the Robinsons' estate in Orange, New Jersey, and the tennis and boating outings at Henderson House, their "Scottish castle" in the Adirondacks, drew friends of all ages. Even when her parents traveled, Corinney had an attentive nanny at home, and she never had to be packed off to relatives as Alice and Eleanor did.

What most distinguished Corinney from her female cousins, however, was the very close relationship she had with her mother. Between the two Corinnes was a long, loving bond that neither Eleanor nor Alice had the chance to develop with their own mothers. Alice's stepmother formed close ties with both Alice and her birth daughter, Ethel, nurturing them and loving them (in her way), but she remained a bit awesome, her self-control too daunting to invite intimacy. Corinney's connection with her mother was anything but distant, and the hundreds of loving letters exchanged between the two women over several decades attest to a strong, mutual devotion.

Corinney did not share all her mother's interests, but she stood in awe of her energy and enthusiasm. When her mother's good friend Frances Parsons came to visit, Corinney was furnished with binoculars and expected to join the two women on long exploratory walks through what they called the "lush meadow." Much as she tried, she could never seem to spot a single bird.

The mother offered a heroic example on other fronts. On the ocean voyage home, after Corinne attended Bamie's wedding in 1895, the ship encountered a terrible storm that made almost all the passengers, including Corinne Robinson, miserably seasick. But she refused to give in. As the ship reeled, she stoically kept reading aloud to her children as a way of keeping them from getting sick, too. Both the name of the book and the plot were soon forgotten, but their mother's "heroism made a deep impression," and Corinney included it in the autobiography that she wrote but never published years later.

The first long separation between mother and daughter occurred in the spring of 1902 when Corinney, just short of her sixteenth birthday, enrolled at Allenswood. Besides the 1895 European expedition, when Corinne Robinson had her four children join her for part of the trip, Corinney had not traveled outside the United States. Her education, like that of most of her friends, had been limited to dancing classes and home instruction. But because Cousin Eleanor was completing her third year at Allenswood and could ease the transition, the decision was made that she should join her there. Corinne Robinson never studied with Mlle. Souvestre, but the two had met through Bamie, and the Frenchwoman occasionally turned to Corinne to host her friends who came to the United States. Just exactly what the American thought of Mlle. Souvestre remains unclear. After seeing Souvestre when she accompanied her daughter to Allenswood, Corinne wrote Edith, reporting that the institution was "as nice as a school could possibly be," but the headmistress was a little "too much like Grandmother," meaning Douglas's formidable mother, for her tastes.

Once enrolled, Corinney made a good impression on the headmistress, who evaluated her as "unusually" intelligent and "*va tres bien.*" But Corinney had mixed feelings. She complained about the "abominable" weather and the sports program, which she judged "very slow" with few students who measured up to her level in tennis or cricket. On the musical front, things went a bit better with an instructor that Corinney judged not a very good performer but "interesting as a teacher."

Unlike Cousin Eleanor, who singled out Marie Souvestre as an important influence on her life, Corinney found her a bit bizarre. Although obviously intelligent and interesting, Souvestre played favorites, a habit that Corinney found objectionable even when she benefited from it. When Souvestre held her up as an example for her classmates to emulate, Corinney cringed: "I nearly sank through the floor when she said it." Moody and unpredictable, the headmistress would fly into a rage, especially on days when her partner, the Signorina, was absent. Even to sixteen-year-old Corinney, the relationship between the two teachers seemed out of the ordinary, and she wrote her mother that Souvestre "always seems restless and ragey when the [Signorina] is not here." Small infractions, such as letting a door bang, could send the headmistress off on a shouting spree, Corinney reported. She had no use for sports of any kind but patiently spent hours with her students on matters of the mind, reading to them in French and introducing them to her intellectual friends.

Allenswood offered the kind of international environment that Corinney enjoyed as much as her mother. Although the majority of the two dozen or so students were English, others came from Germany, France, Holland, and the United States. Since Souvestre was French, the school had a continental flair, and Corinney had two French lessons every day except Friday when she had one.

Among the French friends that Corinney made that year was one whose life would later intersect with hers in a special way. Nearly forty years later, a Jewish classmate from Allenswood sought Corinney's help in arranging her family's escape from France. Corinney phoned the White House, and through the intervention of the President and First Lady, the entire family was able to immigrate to America, where the sons later showed their gratitude in a variety of ways. One of them supported Corinney's son John in his race for governor of Connecticut. Another, a banker, looked after her eldest son's business affairs with all the kind concern of a brother.

While at Allenswood during the winter of 1902–03, Corinney missed her family back in New York. She spent Christmas with some Robinson relatives west of London, and Monroe came from Harrow to join her. Although their hosts made every effort to entertain them, this was the first Christmas away from their family, and both young people were homesick. Corinney wrote to her mother about the stockings they had hung, but then she added wistfully: "Our jokes are not quite so witty as yours."

By the end of December, Corinney, accompanied by a friend and a chaperone, headed south to see the art treasures of Italy. She wrote to her mother, using the family code for menstruation, that she was starting the trip "unwell. . . . Isn't it too mean? Happily I feel pretty much myself so it doesn't matter so much." After a rough channel crossing in heavy rain, she and her party sat up all night on a train before they reached Italy. Corinney had her mother's appreciation for fine architecture, and she judged the Duomo in Milan magnificent, with its "perfect statues" and "simply wonderful glass." Her only complaint regarded the chaperone, a distant cousin on her father's side. The woman knew nothing about art or literature and left off all her g's, which "drives me crazy." Besides, she was stingy with money and refused to tip, causing both her charges considerable embarrassment.

The teenagers persevered, however, seeing as many sites as they could in their short visit. In Florence they admired the art at the Uffizi but found the Duomo "horribly bare . . . so very little like a great religious centre" and a great disappointment after Milan, which was "so wonderfully quiet and holy." On most matters the girls agreed, but Raphael was an exception: "I simply love nearly all his things and she dislikes nearly all his things so we have great fights over him," Corinney noted.

Enthusiastic as she was about her art trip, Corinney sought all the news she could get from New York. She was so ingrained with feelings of civic responsibility that she could not forget about what she might have been doing had she not gone abroad. Since its founding by Theodore Sr. (and others), the Orthopaedic Hospital had been a pet project of the Roosevelts, and the women helped raise funds for it and entertained the patients. Now that Eleanor was back in New York, she joined in the effort, leaving Corinney feeling a little left out, as she related in a letter home: "I feel awfully jealous of Eleanor going up there one day a week."

After completing her Italian trip by throwing a coin in the fountain of Trevi in Rome, Corinne returned to Allenswood to finish out the academic year. By early March she had decided to return to New York at the end of the term rather than spend three years as Eleanor had. But the question of where Corinne would continue her studies had not been answered. She could either take classes at home or go to Brearley, a private school for girls in New York City that her friends favored. Studying with young women her own age would be fun, she decided, but she could learn more with a private tutor. She finally decided to leave the decision up to her mother, although she stipulated that she wanted to avoid Latin, algebra, and geometry in favor of history and literature. She still lacked confidence on several fronts and confessed to her mother that she fell apart after a disastrous performance on the piano: "I had sort of half hysterics and could not keep myself from simply howling. . . . I never felt such an idiot in all my life and yet could not stop." But she was ready to go home.

The fact that she would be leaving Monroe behind bothered her. Eighteen months her junior, he had left his American school because of academic and discipline difficulties, and now he seemed to have trouble fitting into Harrow. Corinney, though not much older, acted the part of little mother, reporting home how he was doing. He was getting along all right, she concluded by the spring of 1903, except for cricket—"and at Harrow there does not seem to be anything of any account which the boys do apart from cricket." She noted other difficulties. Monroe stuttered occasionally, and although she thought he would grow out of that, she was not so sure about his social skills. "He is in rather a discontented frame of mind," she wrote her mother, and, as Corinne had feared, "doesn't seem to have made any real friends." It was a shrewd and accurate account of a young man who was already showing signs of eccentric, out-of-control behavior. No one ever diagnosed what ailed him, just as no one had diagnosed his uncle Elliott, but since he acted strangely even at this young age, before he began to drink, his problem no doubt went beyond alcoholism.

From New York, Corinne Robinson wrote that she and Douglas would be coming to England to travel with Corinney and then escort her home. Before sailing on July 11, Corinne opened up Henderson House, visited her youngest son, Stewart, at his boarding school, spent a fortnight with Bamie at Farmington, and then returned briefly to Henderson House. The crossing gave her time to rest before beginning the ambitious itinerary she had set for her daughter and husband through the Scandinavian countries and Russia. Suffering from a combination of asthma and skin rashes, Corinne felt miserable most of the time, but in family tradition, she refused to shorten the trip by even one day.

Back in New York by September, Corinney had a busy schedule. She started classes at home, as Corinne had decided was best, visited her ailing grandmother Robinson (whom she described as seeming "very well though extremely irritable with the servants"), and caught up with her friends. After a year's absence from New York, she found herself showered with invitations and sometimes received two or more for the same day. After committing for lunch on one day, she had to turn down both opera and skating invitations, thus missing "the two things that I would simply adore doing." Without the time to accept a December invitation to the White House, she left it up to her mother to convey her love to "the whole presidential family."

II

F OR CORINNEY, the winter of 1903–04 was an interim period, full of preparations for being "presented" to society. Although she completed what she called "the last lap of my very superficial education" by studying with a private tutor, a "Miss Davidge," she did not prepare for college. In fact, the prospect was never seriously considered even though her eldest brother was finishing up at Harvard, and Monroe and Stewart were preparing to follow him there. She might have shown some interest in the Women's Annex (later called Radcliffe) or in any of the women's colleges that had recently opened, but contemporaries of her social standing rarely did. With her family resources, she would never have to earn her own way, and the intellectual stimulation that she might have found at college could be duplicated every day of the year in her own home. College courses were for others of lesser means— those who wanted to prepare for the day when they might have to support themselves or their children.

Social activities filled Corinney's "coming out" calendar that first year back in New York. Now old enough to have a place at her mother's dinners, she also traveled to Auntie Bye's in Washington, where she accompanied the older woman to dinners at the homes of cabinet members. At Aunt Edith's White House musicales she met "lots of funny little Dips," that is, diplomats. Theater parties in New York, yacht trips to Boston, and weekends in the country all combined to fill those months.

In July 1904, Corinney turned eighteen, and her debut took place that December, on a Thursday evening just three days before Christmas. By the standards of their time, it was not an extravagant event. The party that Corinne and Douglas Robinson gave for their only daughter at the St. Regis Hotel in New York was, according to *The New York Times*, "not a large affair." About sixty of the honored guest's young women friends and a dozen young men sat down to dinner at 8:30 at tables decorated with garlands of holly and bouquets of red roses. In the center of the banquet room, three tables, slightly larger than the others, were presided over by the debutante, her mother, and her cousin Eleanor. At Corinne's table were guests of her own generation, including her very good friend Charles Allen Munn, Auntie Bye, and, of course, Douglas. At the honoree's table sat several of her contemporaries, including Alice, who had recently been dubbed "Princess Alice" by the press, and good friend Isabella Selmes. When the dancing began at 11:00, additional young men came to even out the numbers, and among them was Franklin Roosevelt. He was, Alice later quipped, the "kind of young man that you invite to the dance but not the dinner."

The debut itself was only one part of an elaborate social ritual that went on for months. Lunches and dinners preceded it and followed it, all to be sandwiched in among the invitations to her friends' parties celebrating their debuts. These all had to be juggled with appointments for dress fittings and hair settings (when a male beautician came to her home to "ondule" Corinney's straight hair). A steady beau was not part of the picture because she and her friends scorned the idea of "going steady" or "keeping company," a practice they considered for the "uneducated only." In her set the preference was for "adventuring" so that they could "flirt . . . dance, ride, drive in the buggy and play tennis" with a steadily changing roster of admirers.

About the time she turned nineteen, in July 1905, Corinney wrote her mother that she felt "very old" and could "hardly believe that my first year of 'coming out' is over." The next few years rolled along in the same lazy, pleasurable way. During the summers she visited cousins and young friends on Long Island, in Maine, or in the Adirondacks, where several family friends had homes. Or she invited them to Henderson House. Money rarely concerned her.

Both parents were generous, and for her twentieth birthday her mother sent her a check for $100 that even a daughter accustomed to generosity had to acknowledge as a big surprise—one that went beyond her "wildest dreams."

As her friends married, Corinney moved closer to that step herself. She was particularly dumbfounded in July 1905 when Isabella Selmes, whom she regarded as one of her closest friends, suddenly married Bob Ferguson, Bamie's longtime admirer. Most of the couple's friends were caught offguard, but Corinney had just spent three weeks at the Selmes estate in Kentucky with Isabella, who had given no hint of her plans. It "was an absolute surprise to me," Corinney wrote her mother, "I never even suspected it was possible." The decision may have been a sudden one, and many of the couple's friends got word of the marriage after it took place, but it also made Corinney think more seriously about choosing a husband herself. Cousin Eleanor had married the previous year, and Alice's name was frequently linked with one or another eligible bachelor, so it is not surprising that Corinney began seeing a lot of one particular man, George Draper, in the fall of 1906.

George's family sounded a lot like the Robinsons. His father, William Henry Draper, was a well-known New York physician, and his mother, Ruth Dana Draper, was the daughter of Charles Dana, the editor of the *New York Sun*. One of the four Draper daughters, Ruth, about eighteen months older than Corinne, had already started giving character sketches in her friends' homes, and eventually she made the dramatic monologue an important art form. Whether Corinne met George through Ruth or Ruth through George is not clear, but the talented and energetic Ruth remained a lifelong friend.

Corinney's romance with George, solidified by an engagement sometime in late 1906, did not prevent her from accompanying her parents to Europe the following spring for what she later described as a "fantastic, triumphant tour with red carpets strewn in front of us, and entertainments everywhere we went." With Uncle Theodore in the White House, Corinney found all doors open to her: she met queens, princesses, and the Pope, and she attended countless dinner parties and fancy balls. That fall she and a friend went to England, where she caught up with some of her Allenswood classmates. At twenty-one, Corinney was writing in more mature tones, and letters between mother and daughter have the quality of communications between equals. Almost no one called her Corinney anymore—she was Corinne—and relishing her maturity, she began her birthday letter to her mother, "Dearest little birthday girl."

Corinney's tastes had also matured. When she went on to Paris, her friend shopped for clothes while she looked for old books and bought a five-volume set of Molière. She scoured the print shops (although she did not buy) and then noted, as other Roosevelt women were apt to do, that she had an unerring eye for the most expensive items: "I am afraid that as my appreciation grows for lovely things I become a more luxurious-desiring nature."

These two European trips, each lasting several weeks, gave Corinney time to reconsider her relationship with George Draper, and in the spring of 1908 she broke off her engagement. "She was crazy about him," her son later recalled hearing, "but finally decided he was a little too loose around the edges." In other words, he lacked a certain solidness that the Roosevelt women liked in their men.

Writing to Isabella (now the mother of a baby boy), Corinney used phrases very similar to those her mother adopted at the time Douglas Robinson was pursuing her. The engagement had been broken, Corinney wrote, although she found it "far too sacred a thing to discuss and all that I can say to even my dearest friends—is that it is best." In a letter to her mother about the same time, she sounded despondent about ending her relationship with "my most intimate friend and very closest companion," but she remained convinced that she had done the right thing. The blame was entirely hers, she admitted: "I can never feel anything but sorrow that something is lacking in me that does not respond in the right way." Besides, she had already met a new candidate, though she did not see him as such at the time.

Cousin Alice suggested that Corinney join her party on a trip through the western states that summer. The Democrats would convene in Denver in early July to choose a presidential nominee, and although Alice and her group took no part in it, they liked the excitement surrounding the convention. Indeed, Corinney enjoyed herself immensely. In Denver she met people with a wide range of political views, from the Socialist Joe Patterson to Ruth Bryan Leavitt, the daughter of the Democratic nominee William Jennings

Bryan. Corinney's letters to her mother make it sound as though the Democratic conventioneers made no distinctions on the basis of political affiliation—Corinney found herself invited to more lunches and dinners than she could accept. At the end she summed it up: "I was bored part of the time, and hot and tired but I wouldn't have missed it for worlds."

By August, when Corinney returned east, George Draper had receded into the past, and she began seeing more of a man she had met through Auntie Bye two years earlier. At that time Joe Alsop, a bachelor farmer nearing thirty, had shown no romantic interest in Corinney, who was a full ten years younger. But by the spring of 1908 they began seeing more of each other at Oldgate, and Corinney pronounced Joe "delightful." During one of her visits to Auntie Bye, she wrote her mother, "I really feel that he is a friend of mine and yet the fact of his being here as Auntie Bye's friend and my not seeing him in a personal way has made it possible for it to be a perfectly natural easy thing. If he had come as *my* friend it would have been a different situation."

Originally from Middletown, Connecticut, Joe Alsop had wandered around a bit before deciding to buy land a few miles from his birthplace. After graduating from Yale with a degree in engineering, he studied for a year in Berlin, then tried Denver, Colorado, before going into partnership with an elderly female relative and buying a seven-hundred-acre farm near Avon, just six miles north of Oldgate. Before long he was riding over on horseback to visit Bamie, and he became part of her coterie of young admirers—one of what the family affectionately termed her "Joe-Bobs."

Hardly a typical farmer, Joseph Wright Alsop IV was one of those men, his wife later wrote, who "looked distinguished even covered with fertilizer and smelling to high heaven." Descended from some of the nation's earliest settlers, he came from a family that, like the Roosevelts, was both wealthy and political. His father, a physician, had served as a Connecticut state senator, and he ran on the Republican ticket for lieutenant governor in 1891. So it is not remarkable that Joe got bitten by the political bug, too. Just about the time he met Bamie, he won a seat in the Connecticut House of Representatives. Though one of the smallest states, Connecticut had a huge legislature—45 members of the state senate and 255 of the house—so Joe might have gone unnoticed. But this self-confident young man rarely melted into the background. As a member of the majority party (the Republicans held huge margins in both branches of the legislature), he had an opportunity to move in powerful circles, and he went on to serve in the state senate and play a central role in Republican affairs the rest of his life.

Not everyone thought so highly of Joe as Corinney. Cousin Ethel met him at Auntie Bye's in the fall of 1908, and she wrote Isabella that Corinney "cares for him" for reasons Edith could not fathom. "I don't think he is so wonderful at all. He's slouchy and messy and thinks a lot of himself." To Ethel's mind, her cousin could use some help from the naturally sophisticated Isabella: "I don't think Corinney looks at all well. . . . I wish you could give her some lessons."

Corinney showed no great haste to marry. She spent five days in Washington in January 1909 when her uncle was finishing his second presidential term and Ethel was making her debut, and afterward Corinney wrote Isabella that it had been such a hectic time, "how I lived through it I do not know." Bob and Isabella had moved to Saranac Lake, New York, partly because of his poor health, and Corinney made a trip to visit them before returning to Washington with her mother to attend several White House dinners. "I talked to a little Belgian and a wee Austrian at dinner and a weeer Italian after dinner," she wrote Isabella. "They all had good manners and delicious little birdlike pleasure loving dispositions and such funny little characters."

Within days Corinney's life dramatically changed, and it would be a long time before she regained the lightness revealed in that note to Isabella. The following Saturday night, Stewart fell out of his Harvard dorm window to his death. The entire Robinson household reeled in shock, and among themselves they admitted they were never quite the same again. Stewart had been Corinney's favorite among her three brothers, and she grieved deeply for him, but at twenty-three she also recognized a need to move on with her life. Escaping the grief in her parents' home, she visited more often at Auntie Bye's where her path again crossed with that of Joe Alsop.

By May 1909, Joe was bringing his sister to Oldgate, and Corinney was struck by the contrast in the sister's very plain appearance and her amiable personality. After dinner, conversation divided into twos, and she wrote her mother that "Joe and I had a perfectly easy time but Auntie Bye [who chatted with the sister] looked distinctly bored." The next day Corinney went with Bamie to see the improvements that Joe had made at the farm, and she returned—again with Bamie—to see "some engravings he had inherited." Her accounts of those visits give so little hint of romance that it is difficult to conclude she had marriage in mind. She even considered leaving Bye's and going back to her mother's because she had so many other things she wanted to do.

Over the summer her feelings obviously changed because by mid-September she and Joe were planning a November wedding. In the joint letter that they composed for the Fergusons on September 20, Corinney joked that her fiancé was "a fine person (Auntie Bye has often told me so anyway) and I am going to marry him on November 4 . . . unless I think of something better to do." About the same time Bamie wrote Corinne that she hoped the engagement would be announced "as near as possible to the wedding." But she voiced only praise for the choice: "I believe your little girl has chosen a man who is as dear and high minded as they come."

In her choice of bridegroom, Corinney acted very much in the family tradition. All three of her cousins took their husbands from circles close to the clan. Franklin, of course, was a distant blood relative of Eleanor's as well as her father's godson. Nicholas Longworth, Alice's husband, had worked as a political associate of Theodore's for more than a decade before he and Alice married, and his sister had been an early backer of Theodore's. Four years after the Alsop marriage, Ethel wed Richard Derby, a young physician whom she had met through her brother. Although these were not actually arranged marriages in the technical sense, in each instance the parents, if given the chance, could well have made the very same choice as the daughters did.

Because of Stewart's death, Corinney's wedding had to be small. Indeed, the mood surrounding the event was not particularly celebratory, however compatible the partners. The ceremony did take place on November 4, as planned; it was hosted by the bride's eldest brother, Teddy, and his wife, Helen, at their Park Avenue apartment. Auntie Bye insisted it was the "loveliest in every way" of any wedding she had "ever been to," but she probably erred on the generous side in making that judgment.

The bride's family was under great strain at the time. In addition to Stewart Robinson's death, they mourned the loss of Eleanor and

Franklin's six-month-old son, Franklin Jr., just three days before the Robinson-Alsop ceremony. The baby had been sickly since birth, but that hardly eased the pain. In a letter to the Fergusons just after her marriage, Corinney wrote that she was "heart broken for . . . Dear Eleanor . . . she is suffering so intensely." To add to all their other worries, a false report came in just after the wedding that Theodore had been killed in Africa (where he was hunting wild game with Kermit), and until the family learned that the report had no foundation, they could concentrate on little else.

Post-ceremony activities were also somewhat muted. The bride and groom left in an "electric" to go to the railroad station, where they caught a train south. Douglas Robinson owned thousands of acres in the very westernmost tip of Virginia, where even in November the hill country could be beautiful, and it was there that Joe and Corinney decided to take a ten-day honeymoon. Corinney took one maid, and she later recalled that it had been "an odd, Victorian first night of marriage" since the bride and groom had separate accommodations on the train.

The bride's letters from Virginia sounded as if it were perfect bliss. The house itself was a simple farmhouse, but it fit the Alsops' needs perfectly. Corinney could hardly believe her luck. Joe had taken to the Virginia hills "as I knew that he would and we have had such glorious rides and walks and we have sat on the little piazza reading and talking and it is altogether the only place to come for a honeymoon." Perhaps her father could make money by renting the place out to other honeymooners, she joked. As for herself, she seemed ecstatic and announced that Joe was "the most beautiful thing that has ever come into my life."

The return trip was something of an odyssey. After stopping in Orange, New Jersey, to see Corinney's parents, the newlyweds proceeded to New Haven by train and saw the Yale-Harvard football game. Then they went by automobile—this time a gasoline-powered FIAT, more suitable for the unpaved roads than an "electric"—to Joe's farm about forty miles north. Joe had instructed one of his Italian workers how to drive the FIAT, and he was at the wheel as the newlyweds began their slow trip over the dirt roads. A tire had to be changed, the acetylene lights went out, but finally—four hours later—the car pulled slowly into Woodford Farm, and Joe carried his bride over the door sill of the unimposing farmhouse where she would live the rest of her life.

A modest white house, it had been built about one hundred years earlier for the Woodford family. Downstairs it had a kitchen, dining room, and parlor—used rarely except for funerals—and there were three bedrooms upstairs—hardly the kind of home that Corinne was accustomed to living in or even visiting. Joe had already installed running water, a furnace (requiring considerable attention), electricity, and a telephone, but with four other families on the party line, they could hardly count on using the phone very often. Eventually, more rooms were added—a large children's wing in 1914 and then, ten years later, a separate servants' cottage with five bedrooms—but it never looked like anything more than a relatively prosperous farmhouse. When Aunt Edith came to visit, she described it as "a dear quaint little house." Corinney concurred in that assessment. With its "old portraits, disreputable, ancient rugs, battered chairs and hundreds of old and somewhat disheveled books," it looked like "a second class hotel."

In preparation for his bride's arrival, Joe informed the house staff, including "the waitress, the chambermaid and the cook," that he was marrying "Miss Corinne Robinson from New York." All three employees were devoted to Joe and his dog, but the cook, whom Corinney later described as "a deaf sinister little gnome and one of the best cooks I have ever known," was particularly upset at what she saw as an intrusion, and she muttered in response to Joe, "She won't last."

The maid stubbornly refused to call her anything but "Miss Robinson," despite Joe's frequently referring to her in a loud voice as "Mrs. Alsop." Emma Schenk, the cook, barely acknowledged Corinney's presence and muttered, "Perfect foolishness," when Joe asked to have his breakfast with his wife in her bedroom. On days when Joe went out early in the morning to oversee workers, Corinne slept late—too late, in the cook's opinion—and she got burnt toast on her breakfast tray as a sign of disapproval.

After about three weeks in the farmhouse, Corinne despaired of ever taking charge. Writing her mother, she admitted that Emma "has the most utter contempt for me. I cannot manage her at all now, she having lost any respect she once had. She never had much." Corinne and Joe had even had one of the first disagreements of their married life on the subject of Emma, who angered Corinne by telling Joe one day that his wife slept too much. That night, when it was time to go to bed, Corinne announced that if the cook became too disagreeable she would have to be dismissed, to which he replied, "If Emma goes, I go too!!" Then the two of them "giggled and went to sleep."

Only the fact that Emma adored Joe made her continued employment possible. Some years later, when Joe lost a lot of money and confessed to the entire household that he was "ruined," Emma appeared silently one evening in the parlor and put two bankbooks in front of him. They represented her entire life savings, and she was offering them to her boss in his time of need. Such loyalty deserved recognition in Corinne's book, and she patiently endured all the contempt for Joe's sake, even finding a retirement home for Emma and visiting her regularly in her final years. Not sure that her forbearance had ever been recognized, Corinne once suggested for herself a simple epitaph: "She kept her husband's cook."

Relatives of the bride trooped out to Avon to size up life on the farm. Auntie Bye came over often, although some weeks passed after the honeymoon before Corinne could write that the two of them had "mealed." Aunt Edith came for tea with her daughters, Ethel and Alice, and then observed dryly that the couple seemed "perfectly contented tho it does not strike me as a romantic love match." She may well have been referring to what few in the family seemed to see—that most of the Roosevelt women married convenient men who seemed more like their cousins or brothers than their lovers. Edith's own marriage was quite different, and everyone who knew her and Theodore commented on their close, loving relationship. But for most of the female Roosevelts, marriage involved little obvious, consuming passion. After Joe's death, Corinne Alsop described her own married life as "delicious" and her husband as someone "with whom I was never bored, whom I always loved, and who gave me the opportunity to live a fascinating life." But that was not how Edith saw things, and Corinney's comments carry connotations of reasoned maturity rather than great ardor.

⚭

The early months of the Alsop marriage were still marked by the shadow of Stewart's untimely death. In late November, shortly after

Corinne, Douglas, and Monroe left on their round-the-world trip, she wrote her mother that it was "torture saying good bye to you yesterday," but she knew the journey would be therapeutic and her parents would come home "stronger." To cheer herself up, Corinne made an excursion to New York to lunch with friends at Sherry's, and she indulged in long talks with Alsop relatives about the possibility that Joe and his brothers might inherit millions—if only they could find a way to deliver a car to a woman in Europe, a wealthy cousin of Joe's. When her husband left on a three-day trip to Maine to buy Guernsey cows, Corinney decided not to accompany him. She preferred staying home, and if a friend whom she had invited did not come to stay with her, she could always go visit Auntie Bye, she wrote her mother.

Christmas that year was a family affair—even with three of the Robinsons thousands of miles away. The Alsops spent the holiday at Oldgate with Auntie Bye and Uncle Will, whose son, Shef, had just turned twelve. Other relatives gathered there, including Teddy and Helen and their two little boys. Joe gave his bride a camera, and her father sent her a "cheque" for $50. From Auntie Bye came an "enchanting spring silk cover for my bed or sofa," Corinney wrote her mother. Some of the rooms were still unfurnished, and to help the new bride put her own decorating touch on the farmhouse, she was going to redo her own bedroom with "plain white paper," adding "white and pink chintz and . . . a lovely new rug from Aunt Edith which will make it look very dainty."

Just after New Year's 1910, while Will Cowles was in Washington, Bamie became so ill with an unspecified disease that a doctor was called from New York. Her face broke out in a disfiguring rash, appearing to affect her eye, but the patient, in characteristic fashion, insisted she had only a touch of "grippe and rheumatism." Corinne confided to the Fergusons that the situation was much more serious, requiring her and Joe to stay at Oldgate for several days. Bamie's energy apparently never flagged, because Corinne wrote Isabella, "She is most awfully bored by her enforced incarceration and no wild horses could keep her from going to Washington on Feb 1st for two gay weeks if her eye is in possible condition."

The Alsops were preparing to sail to Naples at the end of January on an extended wedding trip, since the time in Virginia had not really counted as a proper honeymoon. Joe purported to dread long trips, although he had taken several as a young man, and like most farmers, he disliked leaving his land, even in winter when work lulled. But with a new wife eager to travel and her parents paying the bill, he had trouble refusing, and so they left—on the only trip to Europe that the two of them ever took. Corinne thought she might be pregnant just before leaving, but when it turned out to be a false alarm, she was pleased. She had looked forward to the trip and admitted that she "should have felt a little worried about taking any risks and going if in that other condition." Getting pregnant immediately would also have meant that she would deliver during the summer, thus precluding any long stay with her mother at Henderson House, "and that is another good reason."

Just before their ship, the *Berlin*, sailed out of New York Harbor on January 29, the Alsops spent a few days seeing friends in Manhattan and shopping for an automobile (or, as Corinney called it, a "machine") to deliver to Joe's wealthy relative living in Switzerland. Corinney and Joe had researched the purchase, cutting out advertisements about various models and prices. They considered an eighteen-horsepower town car that had been used only one winter, but the owner refused their first offer of $2,600 and held firm at $3,000, an enormous amount of money at the time. Later, in a hurry to leave the city, he reconsidered and in the end accepted $1,800, still a very hefty sum and more than three day laborers could earn in a year. Corinne took advantage of their stay in New York to confer with the family physician, who assured her that she was in excellent shape to go abroad. But he recommended that she be careful if "I go over my time."

The winter crossing was rough. Corinne got sick—the first time she had ever suffered while sailing—and in the clinical style that her eldest son later described with amusement, she sized up the other passengers and found most of them lacking: "There are very few possible people on board." Arriving in Naples in early February, she and Joe drove north. They stopped briefly in Rome, saw two of Joe's aunts and some of the tourist sights, and then proceeded to Florence and on to the Italian Riviera, where they had the car overhauled and delivered it to its new owner on February 26.

All their trouble got them little reward. Shortly after delivering the car, Corinney wrote her mother that the woman who received it informed Joe that she had cut him out of her will. "He was to have $40,000 outright and be her residuary legatee," but now all that had changed. "She has been with some other cousins, and she is making *them* her heirs and says the reason is that Joe did not marry an 'absolutely penniless girl.'" The woman's penchant for volatility had already aroused their suspicions that she might make such a switch, and they tried to take it in stride. "Joe has been very cheerful and calls me his hundred thousand dollar girl! and I ask him all the time whether I am worth it and he answers pretty satisfactorily."

Continuing on their way, the Alsops went from the Riviera to Paris and on to Guernsey, the Channel Island that had given its name to Joe's preferred dairy cows. When they reached London, Corinney took time to visit with some old friends from her Allenswood days. But both of them were ready to return home, and Corinney had a particular reason—she was pregnant.

After the Alsops returned to Woodford Farm, Bamie insisted that Corinney had never looked better. The facts, however, were not so rosy. She suffered with severe back pain and general fatigue throughout her pregnancy and spent a lot of time in bed. Careful attention from Joe's family cheered her. Although Joe was one of seven children, none of them had yet produced an heir, Corinney wrote her mother, so they were excited about the idea of having a niece or nephew. She thrived on the attention and admitted that she felt as though she were delivering an heir to a throne.

Joe Alsop's letters to his new mother-in-law overflowed with praise for his wife. Marveling at how well she adjusted to the farm and handled her pregnancy, he wrote that she was "looking more lovely every day. . . . I am just amazed at her dexterity. All the school children have adopted her for their goddess and bring her flowers and come to see her all the time." Following the Roosevelt tradition that mixed the personal and the professional in the same paragraph, he referred to his own upcoming campaign for the state senate: "Politics look pretty good, too, I am glad to say." Then he signed himself, "Yours affectionately, JWA."

Corinne Robinson was overjoyed at the prospect of this grandchild, and while still on her long journey, she wrote her daughter about how she wanted "this world to have another Corinne in it— loyal and brave and strong and true, ready to laugh, and be merry, strong, to cheer and tender to uphold." As a precaution, Corinne advised her daughter not to drive "the machine" because of the strain of putting on the brake. That warning about the car proved unnecessary—Corinne considered the big FIAT that Joe owned so difficult to crank that only a "female Samson could have budged it." She preferred walking anyway and continued to amble around Avon during her pregnancy. Years later she recalled that women in her condition were expected to keep out of sight, and shortly before her first son was born, she had met a neighbor on the street who looked her up and down, and then said, "You had better go home."

Since the projected delivery date coincided with the November election season, Corinne feared that her husband would be out campaigning when her time came: "Joe will have to be doing politics hard and we will probably have to telephone him at a large political meeting to return to his little house and wife." Since this was her first baby—but not her husband's first campaign—she and Cousin Eleanor might have profitably compared notes, and that is apparently what they did. Eleanor had just given birth for the fourth time when Franklin, deep in his first campaign for the New York State Senate, took time off and brought the entire family up to Oldgate for a visit with the Cowleses and the Alsops. Cousin Alice and her husband could not join the group—Nick Longworth was running for his fifth term representing his Ohio district in the U.S. House of Representatives.

When Corinney's delivery time arrived, her fears went unfounded, and Joe was at her side. She later recalled how they had shared the "many hours of labor and his two strong hands held my right hand during the last two hours." Her mother had engaged a famous obstetrician, who had to come from a distance, but when the projected delivery date came and passed, he returned to his own city, leaving another doctor in charge. Corinney declined the chloroform in order to be conscious during the delivery, and she was always grateful "for the wonderful experience" of seeing her child come into the world." The pain itself she considered "unique. It is not static, merely to be endured," she later wrote. "It has the quality of rhythm like great waves of the sea when the tide comes in. It progresses with purpose and rises from a strange gnawing sensation to an agony of pain and then sinks as, helpless, the woman reacts not with apprehension but with anticipation for the next wave of pain to carry her nearer her destination." In the end she felt "a part of the violent forces of nature, a sensation of being torn apart in the midst of a giant upheaval, a blasting and pounding, a tornado, an earthquake inside my body and a final tremendous explosion coupled with ecstasy when the baby was born."

Joseph Wright Alsop, Jr., weighed in at ten pounds. Arriving on October 11, 1910, he beat his father's election by about three weeks. Two weeks after the delivery, the new mother was up and about, with her "corsets on," assessing her wardrobe to see what she needed to purchase for the winter season. Her strength came back slowly, however, and she informed her mother that the doctor had prescribed a variety of medicines and meals to build her up.

The new baby helped brighten Christmas that year (the first the family had celebrated together since Stewart's death). Joe Jr. quickly developed a colorful personality of his own, according to his great-aunt Bye. His grandmother Corinne offered advice about weaning him, travel, and other family arrangements. His first summer, she kept him at Henderson House, establishing a pattern that all the Alsop children would follow during much of their lives. Until after they reached adulthood and their grandmother died, they spent part of every summer in the hills of Herkimer County. Because her husband would not leave the farm, Corinney traveled back and forth between Woodford Farm and Henderson House, spending a few weeks with her mother and a few weeks at home.

After trying a succession of baby nurses and finding them all lacking, Corinney went to New York City when Joe Jr. was about a year old and engaged a young immigrant from Scotland. Agnes Guthrie had come to America as a single woman looking for a new life, and the life she found was in the Alsop home. For forty-seven years, until her death, Aggie was a fixture at Woodford Farm, looking after the children and then remaining as companion to Corinne. It was Aggie, according to one of the Alsop sons, who provided a permanent anchor for the children. She was always there, ready to arbitrate the children's disputes and administer just punishment to the culprits. As much as she relied on Aggie, Corinney may have learned from her cousin Eleanor that it was best to develop some confidence in her ability to care for her babies rather than entrust them entirely to paid help. Taking advantage of the nurse's occasional absence, Corinne became "quite nonchalant" with her baby and boasted that she had tended him "calmly myself."

Like Eleanor, Corinney wasted no time producing a family. Before Joe Jr. celebrated his first birthday, she was pregnant with a second child, and the others arrived in quick succession: Corinne Roosevelt Alsop on March 14, 1912; Stewart Johonnot Oliver Alsop on May 17, 1914; and John deKoven Alsop on August 4, 1915. Delivering and supervising the care of four children born in a little less than five years took its toll. In a family where sentimentality was fairly common, she did not exult over the pleasures of motherhood, and she amused Corinne by commenting that the romance of it was much exaggerated.

∽

Those first years of her marriage were, however, the most important of Corinne Alsop's life. With her husband spending time in Hartford on legislative business, she was on her own much of the time. The change required considerable adjustment, and she later explained why she thought she had been able to manage it. The "precious time" between meeting Joe and marrying him had given her a chance to mature into the kind of woman who could make a success of life on his farm. Had she married earlier, she would never have been content in the small world of Avon, Connecticut; the "pastures would have seemed far greener in the great world, . . . but I had *had* the chance to see them, to know them, to evaluate, and to choose an isolated farm."

For transportation, she had only the FIAT (which she could not crank) and two "impossible" ponies, one "the epitome of inertia and the other prone to running away." Left with "endless hours" to herself, she developed "inner resources" that she never knew she had, leading her to write a children's history of the world (never published and later lost), dabble with paints, read widely, and play the piano. It all added up to "nothing," she admitted, "except the two things of importance: I knew how to be alone and never be bored—and had time to know the people in Avon." She walked all over the town, stopping at the houses of Italian gardeners and Irish laborers, chatting with native New England doctors as comfortably as with immigrant workers. It was at this time that she developed her remarkable skill at sizing up election prospects, which enabled her to predict with remarkable accuracy the outcome of every election held in Avon during her lifetime.

Even while delivering babies at short intervals, Corinne maintained a keen interest in politics. In the spring of 1912, during her second pregnancy, she followed Uncle Theodore's activities, culminating in his decision to run again for the presidency. In January she wrote "Mother dearest" about how amused she was at the description of him at one of the Robinsons' dinners: "Nothing could have been more delicious." But most of her energy went to preparing herself and her household for the new baby. Besides getting her journal and ledger in order, she updated her diary, inventoried her medicine chest, hired a new "waitress" for the house, and made a list of flower seeds that she would plant as soon as she was up and around. This time she hoped for another boy. To Isabella Ferguson she confided that her firstborn needed a playmate and companion and "a possible bully" because she feared he would be spoiled if he continued to get his way all the time. He needed someone "to snatch his toys away from him." Adding that she had recently seen Eleanor and found her "looking very well," Corinney told Isabella that she and Joe were planning to go to Albany "for a couple of days" to see Franklin and her brother Teddy, both of them now serving in the state legislature.

That year saw many changes in the Alsop household besides the birth of the latest Corinne, whom everyone called Sis. Corinney acquired her first automobile—a Model T Ford—for her birthday on July 2, and the next day she had a driving lesson. Joe lacked all patience for instructing, and as he shrieked directions, she became more and more confused. At the end of the ordeal she could not crank the car into action, had not yet learned where the brakes were, and could stop it only by turning off the ignition. Despite that limited progress, she had to get back in the driver's seat the next day and accompany him to a breakfast meeting in Farmington, and then, while he went out to play golf, drive home by herself to nurse her infant daughter. It was the roughest ride of her life, she later admitted, as she careened on one wheel around the curves and then bumped along the dirt road. But she had formed a permanent attachment to the Model T and drove fearlessly for the rest of her life. Joe, whose first automobile had the license number 79, had tried to get her a contiguous number, but when none was available, he settled for the first two he could get: 162 and 163. Corinne and he used these numbers the rest of their lives, and since license numbers can be passed down in the family in Connecticut, their youngest son, John, and his wife were still using those numbers in the 1990s.

In many ways the Alsops spent their time like other farm families: they mingled with other residents of Avon and took active part in the Grange. Joe played King Arthur in one of the dramatic productions, "and he sang!!" Corinney wrote her mother, even though he "cannot keep one note to save his soul." The show was hardly professional quality, with costumes made "out of the cheapest things," but she found them "perfectly wonderful" and pronounced the show "the greatest possible success." Corinney settled contentedly into rural life. When Joe was absent, she delighted in the joys of the farm, the abundance of fresh smells, and the rhythms of planting and harvesting the crops. On the other hand, she confessed that she never realized "how much I must miss the companionship of women until I realize how much I enjoy it when it is there," and when she felt really lonesome, she drove over to "Auntie Bye's for an intimate chat."

Not all women interested Corinne Alsop as much as Auntie Bye did. After a visit with her husband's relatives in Middletown, Corinney complained to her mother: "I have done my duty by calling on all Joe's family's old friends—most of them spinster ladies leading refined spinster lives." She found the Alsop family home there "charming—a fascinating old house," but she could not imagine why anyone would want to live in the town, which she described as "half alive." It had two sides, neither of them attractive to her—the "dead but rather charming old element" and then the "dashing . . . young married set . . . doing nothing but dress in ugly very expensive clothes and talk about the others belonging to the little circle. Their seem to be about 6 couples with much money and nothing to do. . . . Well, you can't judge other peoples lives," she mused in conclusion.

Just after their daughter was born, Corinne and Joe decided they needed some time on their own. They had not been away together since their European trip in early 1910, and now they decided to leave the newborn and the toddler under Corinne Robinson's care and go to the Caribbean. After stopping in Trinidad for a short day tour, they drove through Barbados, where Corinney showed little sympathy for the extremely poor. She described to Isabella how they had "motored through endless acres of sugar cane and endless negroes all begging with an English accent—a penny for a pension—the contrast was most amusing." She concentrated on the natural beauty, including "a glorious bath in the bluest, clearest water I have ever seen." The island of Martinique "where color runs riot" intrigued her, especially the flowers and the "little narrow streets . . . with a strange babble of French."

After Stewart's birth in May 1914, Corinney apparently suffered a bout of postpartum depression. Or perhaps her mood was affected because she became pregnant again within six months. About the time that Stewart was due to be weaned, she commiserated with her mother: "I just hate myself for getting into this foolish condition but I do not seem to be able to help it." She begged Corinne not to overreact: "Do not be worried about me for it is only the past weeks that I have begun to feel this 'tissue papery' way."

During her fourth pregnancy, Corinney decided to cheer herself up with another trip. This time it was an extended journey through the western states, including California and New Mexico, where the Fergusons had recently settled on a small ranch in Tyrone. Corinne went into rapturous praise of the beauties of the Southwest and the simple style in which the Fergusons lived, but she had to admit to herself that she still preferred the excitement of the East Coast. After returning to New York and dining with her parents, her uncle Theodore, and Senator Henry Cabot Lodge, she wrote Isabella: "You can imagine how interesting the discussions were—war [and] politics . . . were all brought up and with a brilliancy that was indescribable." She decided that both Theodore and the Senator could be cutting and sarcastic about the incumbent Democratic President Wilson, but they clothed their barbs in equally "aristocratic and diplomatic style."

Isolated on a farm with a family now grown to include John, Corinne persisted with several interests. After practicing at the piano, she proudly announced that she was good enough to substitute at Grange meetings when the regular pianist was absent. She made it a point to resume studying languages and even got a gramophone to help her with her German pronunciation. Italian came more easily because she could practice with native speakers who worked on the farm. On one of his European trips before she met him, Joe had returned with a young couple from the Lake Garda area to work for him. Other Italians followed, and eventually Avon had a substantial Italian population, mostly from the Veneto region but a few from Arezzo, south of Florence.

Whenever Joe was gone, Corinney had to deal with the men who worked the tobacco fields and tended the dairy cattle, and with the women who gardened and laundered. One day when two of the men set about harnessing a horse for her to ride, she realized that they had very little idea of what they were supposed to do. One martingale was left hanging down and only one girth was fastened. After adjusting them herself, she instructed the men to hold the horse's head, but, she wrote her mother, she had hardly put one foot in a stirrup when the horse "plunged and reared and careened over the yard with the two much frightened Italians still manfully hanging on." Matching her mother's prowess at physical feats, Corinne refused to be "daunted," and although frightened, she immediately tried again while the Italians muttered words that sounded a lot like "curses but perhaps . . . were blessings." This time the horse behaved better, giving her a good ride. Proud of having succeeded at what she set out to do, she was amused to overhear the Italians telling her husband that evening: "She Mrs. Alsop she not afraid of anything." For her part, she concluded "it was worthwhile to gain their respect."

The young Mrs. Alsop took great pride in every accomplishment and victory of her husband. Although a Yale graduate, he managed to fit right in with people of much less education. Once she overheard him giving instructions about the shipment of a cow: "Send her Wednesday. She ain't the kind that travels good." After accompanying him to a farmers' meeting seventy miles from home, she boasted to her mother that he had been made president of the Connecticut Guernsey Club, and "I heard one of [the farmers] say—He's a mighty nice young feller." Like most of the Roosevelt women, she enjoyed talking with men more than with their wives: "I had a very chatty time with all the farmers. To me they are the most delicious people in the world—only very few wives were present—they, poor things, are not so delicious."

Corinne employed the politician's tactic of listening to everyone without revealing her own feelings. At one farmers' meeting, where she had met a man she "couldn't stand," she listened intently as he went on and on about the previous election and then "stuck" to her "like a leach." He had won her attention by announcing that he thought Joe ought to be governor, and two others mentioned him for Congress. In response to such predictions, she refused to commit herself. Later she described her reaction to Corinne: "I smile sweetly but am sure that Woodford Farm is the place that he will probably be for quite a long while to come." Her prediction was correct. In 1912, when he followed Uncle Theodore out of the Republican Party and ran for the U.S. Senate under the Progressive Party banner, he suffered a disastrous defeat and never won another election.

Joe did continue to speak out on public issues, and when he was invited to Wellesley College in 1913, Corinney accompanied him to Massachusetts. To her mother she carefully described the occasion and then detailed her own reactions to the women's college. The sight of Joe surrounded by "1500 unmarried females" was "a bit appalling," but he performed well, she wrote. Corinney appeared surprisingly biased against the students at Wellesley, especially since her only formal education had been in a girls' school. She described the students as "strange" and "rather unattractive" although the campus was "too lovely" and all the traditions connected with it were "fascinating."

The faculty, who were Joe's audience that day, came in for special censure from his wife, who pronounced them "perfectly charming, though of course not good to look upon and without a certain charm that is meant to be woman's." She was convinced that what was lacking in them was "exactly the same thing which I am sure comes from the lack of contact with men." She envied them the intellectual exchanges but was so repulsed by their appearance that she insisted she would never send her daughter there. The Alsops had been met at the station by Emily Balch, already an eminent economist and sociologist—the same woman who later would win the Nobel Peace Prize—but Corinne dismissed her as a "very thin faced [woman] who knows all about something I don't remember what." Considering Corinney's considerable interest in politics and her respect for matters of the mind, it is a surprising dismissal, and it suggests that one's appearance, though not evaluated in traditional terms of beauty, was very important.

It had already become clear—to Corinney, at least—that she lacked some of the inordinate energy exuded by most of the Roosevelt clan. Eleanor, for example, thrived on three or four hours of sleep per night, but Corinney liked to get up late in the morning or crawl back into bed for an additional hour or two. She understood that her mother was different and commiserated with an old family friend, Frances Parsons, who returned from a trip with Corinne and reported how she felt traveling "with one of the tribe of Superman—alias Roosevelt: the early starts, the lectures, that fearful desire! not to miss one thing that one could see, hear or understand—the hurried meals!" In spite of the schedule, Parsons had thoroughly enjoyed herself, "'the delicious long talks with the most fascinating person in the world . . . the late retiring hours and ever more the early start.'" Corinney assured her mother: "I know just how much she loved it and also just how tired she was." On another occasion she chided her mother, who occasionally penned her letters at five in the morning, for starting "the day in truly Rooseveltian-Hendersonian fashion." Corinney admitted that she rarely felt up to such a schedule.

On the other hand, in one of the rare cases of a Roosevelt woman complaining about feeling hampered by her sex, Corinney regretted that she could not fight in a war. In mid-May 1915, after the sinking of the passenger ship *Lusitania* precipitated calls for the United States to enter the war in Europe, Joe and some of his male friends went to Virginia to drill for military service. Corinney, six months pregnant, remained at home, but she wrote her mother: "What an extraordinary and terrible epoch of history we are living in." The atrocities at sea made her want to fight, too, and "if my figure were not of the shape that it is . . . I should probably be with Joe also." Instead, she had to content herself with looking after the farm and the three children while Joe was away.

As debates about possible American participation in the war grew, Corinney, like most of the Roosevelts, was calling for action. Her uncle Theodore was attempting to form a brigade of volunteers, a move that she approved. "If he does get up a brigade of volunteers or whatever it is," she wrote her mother in 1916, "I am sure Joe will volunteer and I would not keep him for anything." A large force could make it a much shorter war, she reasoned. But when the United States did enter the war, Joe ended up staying home.

From Woodford Farm, Corinney had little opportunity to undertake the same kind of war-related work that Eleanor did in Washington, but she did help recruit women laborers for the few factories in her state. By 1918, when many states—but not Connecticut—appeared willing to add women to the voters' rolls, Corinney helped start the Connecticut League for Republican Women, a forerunner of the nonpartisan League of Women Voters. During those first years in Avon, when she liked walking around town talking to anyone she met, she developed a firm interest in politics. There were only about three hundred registered voters, and she must have known every one of them. The Republican town chairman, whom she later described as "a strong slippery character," controlled everything, giving no notice of upcoming caucuses except to "six of his henchmen." According to gossip she heard at the time, he derived enough power from the generous favors he passed out—in the form of whiskey and even cash—to elect anyone he chose. In those days, of course, women had no vote, being classed in an old seventeenth-century Connecticut law as ineligible, "along with criminals and the insane," and Corinney went to work to change that.

III

As the nation settled into "normalcy" after the end of the war in 1918, Corinne Alsop's world still centered on Woodford Farm. Her father had died in September, just weeks before the armistice. But, because her relationship with him had never been close, his death made even less of a ripple in her life than in her mother's. In the memoir she wrote for her children, Corinney later described her father as a blustery man, so loud that he sometimes appeared drunk to people who did not know him. Easily irritated by small things, he was known for outbursts that sent his children into tears. Corinne was the "mainspring" of her children's lives, while Douglas, who "did not like little children" and was jealous of his wife's attentions to them, stayed in the background. Even after his four children became adults, when Corinney believed she gained a better understanding of him, he remained curiously disconnected from them, and Corinney insisted that Monroe "hated" him.

Douglas apparently rarely visited the Connecticut Valley farm where the Alsops raised tobacco and dairy cattle. Tobacco had flourished in that part of New England since long before English settlers arrived, but most of it was consumed close to where it was grown. That changed in the early nineteenth century when American exports to the rest of the world increased and Connecticut farmers got their chance to profit. Cigars gained in popularity, and the particular tobacco produced in Connecticut made excellent cigar wrappers. The heyday was brief, however: Sumatra soon entered the world market with an equally good wrapper leaf at a fraction of the Americans' price, and in spite of efforts to specialize and mechanize, Connecticut growers lost their advantage. After a particularly bad year in 1921, when farmers produced more than they could sell, they decided to unite in a cooperative organization they called the Tobacco Growers' Association.

Joe headed the organization, at a very generous salary for the time— $30,000—and his wife proudly passed on reports she heard from various people about the good job he was doing. But Joe's plush salary was doomed from the start, and after two years at the helm, he was gradually obliged to take a 30 percent cut. With tobacco prices spiraling downward, his job was in jeopardy by 1925. Members of the association, frustrated by matters beyond their control, turned their anger on Joe Alsop. They made such bitter comments about his leadership to the press, and the publicity became so bad at one point in 1926, that Corinney felt obliged to reassure her mother: "Joe and I are well," she wrote, "and particularly . . . Joe has been superb. I have never admired him so much in my life." When a drought threatened their financial well-being even more, she reasoned, "Mother darling, material things are not happiness. That is one thing I have learnt in my life." If hard times came, she would see that the children shared them since "it would do them more good to share them than to be saved from sharing them. . . . Public school would not hurt any of them for a couple of years."

Joe Jr. might actually benefit from a change in circumstances, his mother speculated. A big, overweight boy, he had a "wonderfully developed" mind, and his mother thought that exposure to the underside of life would do him good. He needed to develop "initiative, responsibility . . . [and] see that work is a part of life—not simply a momentary insistence on the part of a dragon-like mother." She may have worried a bit that though just a teenager he had already taken on some of the excessive self-assurance that later marked him as a fixture in Washington, D.C.

Even as a thirteen-year-old, Joe Jr. had a knack for poking fun at pretentious people who exaggerated their blood lines. In May 1923, after a visit with Grandmother Robinson, he wrote to thank her for "my fun in New York," and then he sought some information about the "Alsop Coat of Arms." Having just read in the *Ladies' Home Journal* an "extremely 'highbrow' and terribly snobbish article" written by a woman with "no other charms," the boy wanted to distance himself from her as much as possible, though she "is some very distant relative of ours." Noting that the Alsops had distinguished themselves in America long before the Astors, he speculated that one of the Astors had probably mended furs for one of his forebears.

Corinne Robinson helped the Alsop children in more ways than filling in the family ancestry. She took great pride in Joe's brilliance, especially on learning that he finished at Groton with "Highest Honors" in English, actually a perfect score and an achievement not matched in twenty years. When he wanted to go to Idaho in the summer of 1924, she sent $300, providing money for the ticket, his accommodations, and some left over for miscellaneous expenses. "Sis" got music lessons and tennis coaching, courtesy of Grandmother Robinson, who also paid for camp, deposited hundreds of dollars in the children's school accounts, and bankrolled more than one trip to Europe in the 1920s. During one vacation, when Corinney took the two oldest children abroad, she wrote to thank her mother "a thousand times for helping me in this adventure. I am homesick but I know it is a good thing for the children." Another year she took Stewart, who wrote his grandmother from aboard a ship on the French Line to thank her. One of the Alsop sons later speculated that Corinne Robinson had been living far beyond her means—not only was she subsidizing her daughter's family, but she was still maintaining two homes of her own, where she often entertained many guests. But she died before exhausting her considerable fortune.

When Joe Alsop faced the prospect of losing his job at the Tobacco Growers' Association, his wife tried to think beyond her own household. "Mad as possible" about his situation, Corinney deemed the "question of our finances . . . for some unknown reason a minor thing." Confident that Joe would find "some business interest," she worried about others: "The vital, ghastly thing is the smashing of these great possibilities for the whole tobacco industry and the cooperative plan." Her husband had been under such stress that it had become "unbearable" for him, and she saw a "bright side" to the failure of the association—a different job would cause less of the "terrible strain." When Corinne did eventually have to cut down on the number of servants, she insisted she did not care "in the least" for herself, but she feared that her "beloved family would feel that they should not trouble me by coming to the farm and that would really depress me."

Joe did eventually lose his job when the association gradually fell apart in the late 1920s, but he continued to collect his small salary as a member of the Connecticut Public Utilities Commission, a position he had been first appointed to in 1917. His first six-year term overlapped with his leadership of the Tobacco Growers' Association, but he was reappointed several times and served a total of twenty-six years, including twelve as chairman, before retiring in 1943. The commissioner's salary was only a fraction of what he earned as head of the association—he started at $4,000 per year, then earned an extra $1,000 as chair—but the commission wielded enormous power in the state. Trained as an engineer at Yale many years earlier, he could now use his expertise in important decisions on roadways, power lines, and other matters affecting the lives of people throughout Connecticut.

∽

During the same years that Joe struggled at the tobacco association, Corinne began shaping a larger public life for herself. Her children were growing up, and she admitted that the prospect of an "empty nest" made her feel "sick at heart and lonely." To occupy herself, she turned to the same activities that concerned her mother: politics and public speaking on a list of topics as diverse as that of her mother—education, libraries, and, of course, government. People who heard the two Corinnes often compared them. After giving a speech in nearby Litchfield, Corinney reported proudly to her mother that one woman in the audience looked her "squarely in the eye and said, 'You don't mind my telling you. I do like to hear you speak but I just *love* to hear your dear Mother! She's a wonder!'"

In November 1924, Corinney did something that neither her mother nor any of the female Roosevelt cousins ever attempted: she ran for public office and won. In January 1925, at age thirty-eight, she took her seat in the State House of Representatives representing Avon—the very same job that Joe had held when she first met him. She joined fifteen other women in the huge legislature where her Republican Party held a whopping majority, outnumbering the Democrats by about six to one. Like Corinney, most of the other female legislators were married and listed their occupations as "housewife" or "housekeeper," but their contingent also included one teacher, one editor, an "investigator," and an unmarried farmer. When time came for committee assignments, most of the women ended up on Education or other panels deemed suitable. Corinney was so displeased with her assignment that she dropped in on those where she was not expected—thus annoying the party chairman, but friction between her and the boss went back many years.

Immediately after women got the vote in Connecticut in 1920, Corinney had gone to work. Privy to the fact that the local party boss was holding a caucus, she went through Avon "like Paul Revere," encouraging women to attend it. When the big night came, 139 of them showed up instead of the half-dozen men the chairman expected; a new chairman was elected, and Corinney became vice-chairman. Over the next four years she stepped up her political work, speaking out on issues that affected women and Avon, and her election to the legislature marked the culmination.

After one two-year term, Corinne Alsop left the legislature for reasons she never made clear. Her son later speculated that she might have gotten tired of bucking the boss; and the meager pay, so paltry it hardly paid for the gasoline to attend the sessions, must have grated. But she decided to run again in 1929, and this time she served four more years, finally getting assigned to the powerful Finance Committee. Her voice sounded loudest on matters of local interest, such as better roads, and she took as one of her slogans

"Let's get the farmers out of the mud." Vigilant about keeping taxes low—especially real estate taxes—she was wary of much government intrusion in people's lives. The ideal society, she sometimes said, was one that "provided a foundation for everyone and a ceiling for no one." It would soon become apparent that, though she and Eleanor shared a vision of what could be done, they disagreed drastically on how to do it.

In a family with a long history of winning elections, Corinne's stint in Connecticut's House of Representatives attracted little comment, even though she was the first female Roosevelt to hold office. Aging Auntie Bye seemed to take it in stride, though she admitted to her sister early in 1925 that she did not quite understand the attraction her niece saw in the work.

Bamie might have been a bit miffed that Corinney had taken such a different stand on woman suffrage. After all, the two women lived only a few miles from each other, but while Bamie was being named as the "token" antisuffragist on a committee, her niece was making headlines for the other side. Since much of Bamie's objection to giving women the vote came out of her disapproval of the style of the suffragists (frumpy, in her view) and their arguments (unsound), she may have found it easy to distance her niece from the others. Bamie had never objected to women's voicing strong opinions or participating in political discussions—as long as the opinions were well formed—so she could easily incorporate Corinney's work into what she and Corinne had been doing since Theodore made his first run for office.

Loyalty to the GOP ran deep in Corinney's book. Registering as an independent was foolish, she argued: "Without party affiliation, you lose 50 percent of your voting rights." On another occasion she pointed out: "The most important part of the franchise is choosing the proper candidate, something an independent does not have." Cousin Eleanor disagreed, stressing the independent voter's freedom to move back and forth between parties.

Corinne Alsop's years in the state legislature coincided with the beginning of the Great Depression, a time when her own family as well as her constituents had additional needs. Corinne, ever generous, repeatedly reassured her daughter, saying in one letter that "every suffering or joy or anxiety of yours is deeply shared by your own Mother." With Joe at Harvard and the two younger boys at

Groton, school costs were high, and in 1930, when the prospect reappeared of having to put some of them in public schools, Corinne wrote that she was ready to help and "do anything you want after the primaries on the 16th." She even offered to close down Henderson House and come stay with her daughter, "sharing your expenses by cutting down here in every way."

But Corinney refused to feel desperate. Things could be worse, she joked, if her husband took to drink or if he ran off with some other woman. And at least Monroe, who always had trouble holding a job, was working at arranging exhibits for Arnold Constable, the New York department store.

The Alsop children all reached maturity during the Great Depression. Joe Jr. finished at Harvard, with help from a scholarship, and the other two boys went to Yale, but Sis never enrolled in college. She briefly considered Barnard, but her mother objected to her living in a dorm. Above all, Corinney feared that her daughter might take her studies too seriously: "If she were a different type," Corinney informed her mother, "I should much prefer to have her stay at Bryn Mawr but she needs less rigidity instead of more—less conscience, if one can put it that way, rather than more, and people—not books—should be the main diet." In the end, the girl opted to work as a secretary, but only briefly. On May 28, 1932, just after celebrating her twentieth birthday, she married Percy Chubb of New Jersey, a member of the wealthy insurance family. The bride's great-aunt Ethel Derby wrote her own mother, Edith: "It's so nice to hear about Corinne and her Chubb." But the Depression had made itself felt on the Derbys, and Ethel mused: "I am so far behind in wedding presents. Oh my!"

That year marked changes in the lives of all four cousins. Alice's husband, Nick, had died the previous April, and she struggled with the financial pressures of paying estate taxes and managing on her own. Ethel Derby, who had returned from another extended stay in Europe, resettled on Long Island. Corinney was serving her third term in the Connecticut legislature. But, of course, it was Eleanor who made the biggest transformation—when Franklin won the White House in November.

The Alsops still had some reservations about Franklin as president, though Corinne Robinson had broken with the Oyster Bay

Roosevelts and voted for him. None of the Sagamore Hill crowd had much regard for either his intellect or his character, and the demands of the nation in the middle of the worst depression in its history seemed too much for any one human being to solve, especially one they had long ago written off as "Feather Duster." During his first term, Corinney and Joe kept their political distance, but after 1936 the two couples began seeing more of each other. Franklin won reelection, a sign of public approval, but, more important, Joe Jr. moved from New York to Washington, giving his parents added impetus to visit the capital and see more of Cousin Eleanor.

At the time he graduated from college in 1932, Joe Jr. had no idea what kind of work he wanted to do, and so, as he recalled hearing— because he was not invited—a family meeting was held at his grand-mother's Manhattan house. After some discussion, when other options were discarded as unsuitable, Corinne volunteered that his let-ters to her had been unusually good and perhaps he should go into journalism. The suggestion was quite extraordinary, Joe later admit-ted, because no one in the family had ever gone into journalism. Their writing had always been a sideline job, while business or gov-ernment, for example, were their careers. Corinne went even further: she would speak with her good friend Helen Reid, whose family owned the *New York Herald Tribune*, to see about a job for him there.

While many young people continued to look for work in 1932, Joe Jr. started at the *Herald Tribune*, and he liked journalism so much that he stayed in it for the rest of his life. In late 1935, when the newspa-per assigned him to Washington, he profited from family intervention once again: his mother lost no time informing "Dearest Eleanor" that he would be in the capital, and although he had not yet located a place to live, he could be reached at the newspaper. Corinney emphasized that she had not wanted to bother the busy First Lady, but she did not feel quite right about her son being so close to the White House without letting Franklin and Eleanor know.

Corinney had been too prominent in the political opposition to have eluded Eleanor's notice, but now she tried to mend fences when she wrote to the First Lady: "The fact that I disagree with you [and Franklin] politically very frequently does not change my affection one iota. I wish I could sit down with you both this minute and dis-cuss any thing under the sun—from politics to the last grandchild!"

Corinney had decided not to try for another term in 1932, partly because she wisely recognized the tide was running against her party label and partly because she wanted to devote more time to the next generation. Her daughter followed family tradition, quickly producing two children, and by 1936, Corinney was writing Eleanor, "I know much more about grandchildren than I do about politics now . . . the babies are a passion!"

With Joe Jr. working in Washington, his mother visited frequently, thus finding herself caught in a rift between Eleanor and Alice—one that had developed earlier but gained steam since Franklin took office. It was common knowledge in the capital that Alice delighted in imitating Eleanor's high-pitched voice and her noble sentiments, and newspapers, always eager to report fractures within a famous family, began relaying these stories to a wider public. Finally, in 1936, her name was dropped from White House guest lists. Since she still visited both cousins, Corinney had a problem, and when Eleanor invited her to stay at the White House, she had to admit that she had already accepted Alice's offer. Fashioning a compromise that she hoped would not offend either cousin, Corinney wrote Eleanor that she would try to find "a moment," while Alice was busy with her own engagements, to get together. Aware that Alice had plans for one particular evening, Corinney suggested that might be a good time, "or I shall gladly join any group you may be having at tea and catch a glimpse of you that way."

Corinney tried to mediate family differences, as her mother had done, and play them down: "How strange all our family is. Real personalities with strong, vital and frequently divergent views," she wrote Eleanor. Even among the Alsops, points of view differed, and Corinney tried to emphasize how little they mattered: "Joe and Stewart and I discussed government problems Christmas night until we began to laugh—we had felt so differently on so many questions and became so intense that it became ludicrous." Not wanting to cause too much trouble for anyone as busy as the First Lady, Corinne tempered her request for an invitation: "I know that in casually saying I want to see you I am treating you as 'Eleanor' and not quite as the mistress of the White House and I am always finding myself shy in so doing." She suggested that Eleanor's secretary reply regarding the best date for a meeting, and she signed herself, "Devotedly, Corinne."

Eleanor's reply, although typed, was firmly personal: "For Heaven's sake, why shouldn't you treat me as Eleanor! I never think of myself as mistress of the White House with casual people, much less with my family." She offered several possibilities for getting together, including a "Congressional reception. You might be interested to be at it." In case Alice could not host Corinney for the entire time she wished to stay in Washington, she was welcome to move into the White House. Or, the First Lady suggested, Corinney might wish to go along on a short trip Eleanor would be making to West Virginia. In either case, she concluded, it would be "lovely to see you."

Favors between the cousins ran both ways. When Eleanor needed something done, she often looked to her relatives to act for her. In June 1937, when an editorial ran in a Connecticut newspaper, *The Republican*, Eleanor objected that the last line made a strong attack on FDR. Furious and ready to reply herself, Eleanor consulted Stephen Early, the President's press secretary, who sympathized with her anger but counseled that anything she wrote would not make much difference. Early suggested another approach. Why not find somebody else to write for her, a respected "local resident, a man of reputation for honesty and fair play, a Republican rather than a Democrat. Such a man, I believe, is Joseph Alsop." If Eleanor sent Joe the editorial, he could act far more effectively than she—especially, Early pointed out, if he had any business dealings with the newspaper.

Eleanor took Early's advice. Writing to ask if Joe knew the editor, she enclosed a memo of what a letter to him might include. Its general tone was one of warning: if editors continued such attacks on people in office, no one would want to enter the field. Joe thought that the attack called for a public apology from its author, and he relayed that view to both Eleanor and the editor of the paper. But she demurred. "I would not dream of a public apology," she wrote. "I just felt that probably it was some perfectly hard boiled person who had a feeling that personal remarks of that kind were entirely justified." She followed up with a letter to the newspaper, emphasizing that a public apology was not what she wanted, but the point had been made—Joe Alsop, a respected Connecticut Republican, had warned one of the local papers that it had gone too far in criticizing FDR.

Even though Corinney worked for Franklin's opponent in 1936, she felt no qualms about attending his inauguration in January

1937. Realizing that she would be in the capital at the time, she wrote her cousin "on the spur of the moment" about being included in some of the events. Not everyone was so magnanimous about people who walked on both sides of the political aisle, and a report got back to Corinney that described how she had "charged down on Washington—demanded tickets for everything . . . and bothered [Eleanor] to death." Fully "distressed" by the charge—which she traced to Katherine Delano, a cousin of Franklin's mother, a woman "I do not think I know . . . though I may"—Corinney wrote Eleanor that she hoped she had not caused any inconvenience. During her two days in Washington she had not even tried to see Eleanor "so as not to bother you" but had attended a lunch where the First Lady presided "and enjoyed it and was as always so impressed the way you received everybody." To see Eleanor so confidently managing such events brought back many memories for Corinney: "You often remind me of Mother."

Eleanor assured her that the entire matter had been blown out of all proportion. On February 26, 1937, she wrote, "Dearest Corinne: How extraordinary it is the way people like to stir up trouble! Certainly I never for a single minute felt that you had asked for anything, and I was only too happy that you could be here for inauguration. I certainly never made any comment to anyone, for I had none to make. It is always a joy to see you."

When Corinney returned to Washington in April 1938, with a group of "lady legislators," her cousin could not schedule a meeting with them, but the President did, and Corinney later informed Eleanor how several of the women remarked on "how enthusiastic they were about Franklin's courtesy to them and about the tea and about the White House and how sad they were not to see you." Another friend, not part of that delegation, visited the White House at about the same time, and she returned, Corinney wrote Eleanor, "thrilled and enchanted and thinks you are the eighth wonder of the world."

When the First Lady mentioned Joe Jr. in "My Day," it gave a tremendous boost to the young journalist. In September 1938 he wrote to thank her for her "great kindness. . . . And it was most generous of you to put your compliment in print." He saw her often, and when he wrote her, he mixed family news with professional courtesy, inquiring about her children, catching her up on his own ailments, and apologizing for occasionally turning down one of her invitations to the White House.

All through the 1930s, when both Eleanor and Corinney had many calls on their time and energy, they continued to exchange information about their troubled brothers, both of whom remained erratic and as needy as ever. Monroe had somehow managed to stop drinking after his mother's death, but Hall continued as before, his health and professional reputation suffering from it. Neither sister ever gave up the idea that change might come, and Eleanor was particularly generous with invitations for Monroe to come to the White House.

The deep affection between Eleanor and Corinney was tested more than once by gossip and innuendo. In June 1939, after Eleanor had received a letter from a man she did not know, claiming that Corinne Robinson had once made some very critical comments about Eleanor and Franklin, the First Lady sent the letter to Corinney to get her version, in order for Eleanor to answer "intelligently." Corinney replied that if she were Eleanor, she would not even deign to answer "such a silly letter." She had met the man only twice in her life, would not know him if she saw him, and she had no recollection of a conversation between her mother and him. The statement, she wrote, "seems idiotic to me. I, who talked to Mother intimately, would not think of quoting her. I could not be sure of what she said. I remember only one thing and that was her frequent assertion that she was devoted to both you and Franklin." Corinne concluded with the advice: "Dearest love, Take care of yourself and pay no attention to a person who makes a statement that anybody would know he had no right to make." Eleanor answered in relieved tones: "I was sure your mother never made any such statement."

Sometimes the communications between the First Lady and Corinne concerned requests from other people. In October 1939, Eleanor asked about a Florida woman who claimed she had once worked for Corinne Robinson and now desired a job as housekeeper. Corinney vaguely recalled hearing her mother talk about the woman (and the orange marmalade that she made), but she felt unable to vouch for her in any way. Occasionally, Corinney would request an autograph for someone who was too shy to ask herself.

After the United States entered the war in 1941, Corinne and Eleanor shared their worries about their own sons. All seven of them—Corinne's three and Eleanor's four—were in uniform fighting on various continents. Neither mother had obstructed her sons' participation. Corinney even pulled some strings at the White House to get Stewart into the British army when his high blood pressure prevented his joining the American forces, and then transferred back to the American army when he married and needed the higher pay that the Americans received. But Eleanor did show a twinge of regret when she wrote Corinney that she would have liked for some of their sons to stay out of the fight, thus preparing themselves for the rebuilding that would be necessary once the war ended.

The war engaged both Corinney and Eleanor in other than maternal roles. Corinney's efforts to increase agricultural output, through the organization of the Connecticut Land Army, gave her the chance to communicate with Eleanor on that subject. As the director the group in her state, Corinney had her own secretary, but she wrote in her own hand to assure Eleanor of her influence: "In the midst of the agonizing nightmare of destruction—with your boys in continual danger—you are a joy and a great inspiration to me—your calm—your tolerance—your capacity for work—challenged me to go home and 'do likewise'!" Despite Eleanor's status, when she and Corinney got together, they might as well have been schoolgirls back at Allenswood. "I loved our windy walk and I felt we picked up threads that I was so delighted to pick up," Corinney wrote her after one visit.

When the First Lady arranged important contacts in the capital for her cousin, the latter traveled to Washington, and then, in expressing her thanks, she insisted that she felt much better prepared to attack the work ahead. On one of those visits Corinney also saw Franklin, who had a cold, and she admitted she had been reassured by his healthy appearance: "I should have been more troubled by the sound of his voice on Monday night [on the radio] if I had not had a glimpse of him." The speech itself was "very fine," and the letter he sent about the same time to the Senate objecting to an agricultural bill that would have affected price controls on farm products "was splendid." Not surprisingly, Corinne held firm views on the farm bill: "I hope he vetoes the damned thing if the House follows the Senate."

After the war's end, life at Woodford Farm continued in the comfortable routine established over decades—the rhythms of work set by the seasons and weather. Throughout the country, modernization continued to change how people did their jobs, bent over loud machines that could be set to run without regard for human fatigue and limitations. But on the farm, ageless considerations—the amount of sunshine and rain, the timing of temperature drops below freezing or soars into the 90s, insects and animal diseases—continued to dominate life. Tobacco production fell far short of what it had been in the early 1920s, but dairy cows still grazed on the pastures. Corinney's enthusiasm for rural life seemed undiminished, and when her cousin Ethel saw her at a summer wedding in 1946, she found her "in good form, very relaxed." Later that day the Derbys toured the Alsop farm and saw their prized dairy cattle, including a "thousand dollar bull." Another time, when Corinney agreed to visit the Derbys, she had to "tear . . . herself away from her 'cow ladies'" to make it.

In addition to being active members of the American Ayrshire Breeders Association, where Joe served as president, the Alsops had many other interests. He was on the boards of two insurance companies: the Hartford County Mutual Fire Insurance Company and the Connecticut Valley Mutual Hail Insurance Co. She helped on the boards of the Avon chapter of the Red Cross, the state's Children's Services, and Newington Children's Hospital. These were, of course, in addition to their activities for the Republican Party.

By this stage in their lives Ethel and Corinney had become closer than ever before. With their children all grown and more time for themselves, they seemed to relish their visits. After spending a night at the Alsop farm in April 1949, Ethel wrote her daughter that it was "glorious." Corinney was keeping Stewart's children, "who are darlings," while their parents went around the world. Following a later visit, Ethel wrote her eldest daughter that she found "the greatest joy and satisfaction" in seeing Corinney. She continued: "You will find when you are older that it is v[ery] nice to see family and be able to talk about family things."

When the Alsops went to the Derbys', Ethel could hardly find enough compliments. After one visit she wrote, "Cousin C is to me the most utterly sympathetic person." A little over a year after that, she noted that Corinney was a model house guest who amuses herself "away from her hosts for happy hours," and when in their presence, she is "utterly fascinating." Few other people in the world could convey that comfortable combination, and "next to you children," Ethel wrote her daughter, "I get this heavenly feeling with her. There is the mixture of gaiety, and complete sympathy and under- standing that I do not find elsewhere." Ethel put great stock in find- ing the lighter side of life, and she advised her daughter to share that view: "Hold on to gaiety. . . . I realize that it is rare, . . . cherish it."

In their view of world affairs, Corinney and Ethel teamed up against the pessimism of Alice Longworth. After a visit to Washing- ton, Corinney stopped at Ethel's on Long Island and there reported how she had stood up to Alice on the matter of the need for the United Nations. Then Ethel passed the word on: When Alice "undertook to deride good high minded silly people such as Father and myself for our attitude toward one eventual world, Cousin C suddenly got mad and said [to] put her right in that class, we might be silly," but people like Alice who failed to see things the same way were "damn fools."

⌒

The quiet rhythm of the Alsops' life ended with Joe's death in March 1953 at age seventy-six. Corinne's health had actually seemed the more precarious of the two, and earlier that year she traveled to Johns Hopkins in Baltimore for surgery on a throat tumor. When doc- tors discovered a growth in her ear as well, they prescribed radiation treatments. Partly to recuperate from her ordeal, she and Joe sched- uled a short vacation to Charleston, South Carolina, and it was there that he died in "the way people ought to die," his son pointed out, "after playing golf and enjoying a good dinner." Joe and Corinney had spent nearly forty-four years together.

The funeral was in Avon, and Corinne made a point to invite Eleanor. "I know how busy you are," she wired, but "should you be planning to come to Joe's funeral," she was invited to the lunch before it. Burial took place in Middletown, at the cemetery where other Alsops were buried.

Relatives speculated that the sixty-six-year-old widow might want to make a change and find a place of her own—as many of the Roo- sevelt women had done when their husbands died. But Corinney quickly set everyone straight. Although described by her relatives as very thin and frail at the time of Joe's death, she was determined to continue with "the same kind of life" she had been living. She had always liked the stillness of rural roads and rolling pastures, and even at the darkest times she had described "this peaceful Connecti-cut valley [as] far away from . . . reality."

Her youngest, John, agreed to run the farm, but no one expected him to continue that indefinitely. He had already tested the waters for political office, and Ethel Derby predicted that "he will go far." Joe's death gave Ethel the opportunity to speculate on some of the differences in Corinne Robinson's grandchildren, and she concluded that the Alsops were the stars. In contrast to Teddy Robinson's chil-dren, who had not fulfilled their promise, the Alsops had all carved out full, successful lives for themselves: Joe and Stewart were two of the nation's most respected and widely read syndicated columnists; Sis was the wife of a successful insurance executive and mother of six children; and John was a rising star in the Republican Party.

In addition to his other accomplishments, John Alsop can be remembered for adding a word to the political lexicon. In 1952 he had served as vice-chairman of the Connecticut committee to elect Dwight Eisenhower, whose Democratic opponent for the presidency was Illinois governor Adlai Stevenson. When Stewart Alsop asked John what the Republicans could do about all the intellectuals who were deserting Eisenhower for Stevenson, John Alsop shot back: "Oh yes, we'll lose the eggheads, but how many eggheads are there?" The phrase may have come spontaneously, as John once explained, but only someone from a family adept at catchy phrases would have had the confidence to use it.

In the last part of her life, Corinney Alsop retained the stubborn-ness and absentmindedness that had both amused and infuriated her family for years. All four of the female cousins shared a tendency to appear slightly distracted and unobservant, as though most rules and regulations applied only to others. Even Ethel Derby, the most centered of the four, had a hint of that, and in early 1954 her hus-band discovered that her driver's license had expired some time before. He immediately insisted that she renew it, citing dire conse-quences if she failed to act. Ethel was almost persuaded, but then she talked the subject over with Corinney, who announced that she had no idea where her license was or, indeed, if she had ever had one—although she had been driving all over Connecticut for forty years.

In the 1950s it was Corinney's sons who debated public questions with Eleanor. In early 1953, when Joe Jr. wrote an article in the *Saturday Evening Post* on the dangers of Communism, it elicited a long, analytic reply from Eleanor. She was "very much interested in your article," she wrote him, and thought it a "brilliant analysis," but she retained the belief that suspicion and disunity posed a national danger. She admitted that "much of the communist fear" was fueled by the need to get Americans to accept new taxes for rearmament, but then "it was seized upon by Senators [Pat] McCarran and [Joseph] McCarthy to be used politically for different reasons, nevertheless for their own political reasons." She was convinced that the fear was excessive, and "unless we stop being afraid of American communists in our midst, we are going to be a weakened country that will not be able to give any kind of leadership in the world." She understood that Joe "probably will not agree with me," but she wanted him to know her thinking, "because I admire what you are doing very much and I think you are gaining enormously in influence."

Joe replied almost immediately: "Nothing heartens me more than encouragement from you." Then he explained that he had made very much the same point as she had when he first drafted the article, but he had taken it out "because I wanted to avoid the appearance of exploring internal policy questions." After dismissing outgoing President Truman "as too small for the job" and expressing doubts "that I am going to be able to admire Eisenhower," he closed with the hope that he could see her when she next came to Washington. Both had busy schedules, but they persevered and found a mutually acceptable lunch date, which they sealed with a "hoorah."

∽

In 1956, three years after the death of Joe Alsop, Sr., Corinne became the only one of the four female cousins to remarry. Her wedding to Francis Cole, a Hartford businessman, hardly came as a surprise. He and his wife had been friends of the Alsops for years, and Corinney once confessed to Ethel that the Coles house was one of the very few in Hartford where she always felt at home. Now that both Francis Cole and Corinne Alsop were widowed, they decided to marry, dividing their time between Hartford, where he had a home and a law practice, and her farm at Avon. The marriage seemed to bring happiness to both partners, and when they visited Ethel, she reported that Corinney was "her usual completely dear self, gay and interesting and amusing and so lovely."

In many ways Francis Cole came from almost within the family circle—as had Joe Alsop. A "real New Englander," he was three years older than Corinney. A Harvard graduate and attorney, he sat on the boards of several important corporations. The year before he married Corinney—when a merger formed Chase Manhattan Bank, the second largest in the nation and the biggest in New York City— he became one of its directors.

By the spring of 1966, Corinne Alsop Cole was in frail health. At age eighty she had already outlived her mother, Auntie Bye, and Cousin Eleanor. After being hospitalized in May with a heart problem, she was released and then almost immediately had to return to the hospital. Later that year Francis Cole died, and Ethel Derby, in writing to her daughter, expressed mixed feelings about his passing. Although he was "old and unhappy," Ethel wrote, "cousin Corinne will miss him." Ethel's mother had often said that losing a spouse was difficult because it meant "not being first in anyone's life," and Corinney had liked to quote her. Now that it applied to her, Ethel mused, "I'm sorry she said it," but she had had two husbands and "was clearly first with both of them."

Corinney's health continued to deteriorate over the next five years. She still took part in many public activities, at one point teaming up with Eric Sevareid to narrate a film about Eleanor, and she continued the work she had begun earlier with the Committee of One Hundred to raise money for a new library at the University of Hartford. She was proud of her children but always refused to value the achievements of one of them above the others: "I'm delighted that all four have the kinds of lives that lead to contributions to others and at the same time are interesting."

Although she was still accepting invitations to give public speeches at the age of eighty-five, Corinne did not feel up to the task one day in June 1971 and asked her son John to substitute for her. He delivered a speech, and then when he stopped afterward to see her, he realized how very ill she was. He summoned his siblings, and they gathered around her bed as she quietly stopped living on June 23. In her obituary the *Hartford Courant* called her the "grand old lady" of Connecticut's Republican Party, but inside the family the reaction was much more poignant. Ethel confided to her daughter that she missed her cousin greatly. She "was like a sister, not an Auntie Sister [Alice Longworth] who is in a class by herself, but a contemporary sister, so to say." Memories of Corinney surfaced at the oddest times—when Ethel made applesauce (one of her cousin's favorites) and when she burned trash. Corinney always threw her cigarette packs in with other things, insisting they would burn, but Ethel noted that of course they would not.

Part of Ethel's greatest grief no doubt came from the realization that the ranks were rapidly being depleted. Of the four Roosevelt cousins, only two survived—herself and the indomitable Alice.

Ethel, the only daughter of Theodore and Edith, was as poised and unflappable as a young girl as she remained throughout her life.

CHAPTER SEVEN

ETHEL CAROW ROOSEVELT DERBY

(1891–1977)

N A COLD DECEMBER NIGHT IN 1908, more than four hundred guests milled outside the east entrance to the White House waiting for a chance to greet the President's daughter. Still too young to come out in 1902 as Alice and Eleanor did, Ethel Carow Roosevelt was now ready, several months short of her eighteenth birthday, to have her own party. Her father's second presidential term would be ending in just a few months, and if Ethel was going to make her formal entry into society from 1600 Pennsylvania Avenue, now was the time to do it.

The only daughter of Edith and Theodore Roosevelt, Ethel had kept a low profile throughout her father's tenure due as much to her own personality as to her mother's counsel and efforts. At the time of her graduation from Washington's Cathedral School for Girls in 1906, Ethel read about herself in the newspapers and decided she did not like the attention—particularly some of the fan letters. Security concerns had already altered life at the White House, and all mail for the President's family routinely went through inspection before they ever saw it—surely an annoying invasion of privacy for a teenager. Among the letters that did get through to Ethel was a request from a woman "newspaper correspondent" in Boston, for a "recent picture" of the President's daughter. If none was available, she would send a "young man" to take one. What displeased Ethel most was the newspaper woman's promise to publish the picture on the society page under a caption, "Belle of the White House." To her aunt Emily Carow, Ethel complained that she considered such publicity "perfectly horrid."

Coming out carried its own connotations of maturity and independence, so Ethel went along with her mother's plans to make it a very special party. When guests began filing in at the then fashionable hour of 10:00 P. M., they proceeded first to the Oval Room on the main floor, where they greeted the guest of honor and her mother. Ethel's sturdy figure was unremarkable, but she had vivacious spontaneity that singled her out even had she not been the guest of honor. Like Eleanor, she had a peachy complexion and silky blond hair that complemented her blue eyes, usually singled out as her best feature. But she lacked Eleanor's long legs and slim waist, and as she stood there in debutante white, accented by the black velvet neck ribbon that she wore instead of jewelry, she made a girlish contrast with her mother. Edith, in blue satin set off by a diamond pendant, appeared every inch the chaperone strategically placed to guard the younger generation against excess. After she had greeted each one, the guests danced to the music of the Marine Band and milled around until midnight when supper was served on the ground floor.

Not since Alice's debut six years earlier had the White House been the setting for such merriment, and newspapers could not resist comparing the President's younger daughter to her irrepressible half-sister, who had spent her White House years seeking the attention that Ethel detested. Some papers tended toward obvious exaggeration, with one New York headline holding Ethel up as the "Most Interesting Figure in Washington Society This Season." The three-column-wide article in *The New York Times* actually described a tame version of the unpredictable Alice. In the two years or so that she had been attending White House receptions—she had even attended her first "grown-up dinner"—Ethel had impressed observers, according to this article, as "modest and retiring to the verge of bashfulness," a person who had "the simplest tastes" and "the most innocent pastimes," making her "a really old-fashioned girl." In her "girlish and inexpensive" outfits, she was "vivacious, healthy minded," devoted to outdoor sports and exercise, and, "of course, an excellent horsewoman." This was a young woman who looked after her pets, feeding and watering them herself, and she could be seen almost any morning frolicking on the White House lawn with "her latest favorite, a beautiful bull terrier pup."

Looking for something distinctive about the debutante, the *Times* singled out her artistic bent and concluded vaguely: "Rarely poetic, and strongly imaginative, she is deeply moved by the beautiful in all arts of which she is a sincere follower." A Washington newspaper zeroed in on the same trait, reporting that the debutante "showed talent as a pianist" and planned to study abroad, but on both counts the article was wrong. Ethel never showed exceptional musical ability, and when she left the United States the following spring, it was for a European tour with her mother—not for study at one of the universities or conservatories that admitted women.

What none of the newspapers managed to convey was the special niche that Ethel had carved out for herself as responsible and reliable. At the Cathedral School, which she entered in 1902, she had thrived as a day student, unlike Alice who had balked at the thought of any organized classes. Her schoolmates liked her so much that they elected her one of their class officers in her junior year. Only seventeen at the time of graduation, she agreeably signed up for lessons at home with a private tutor, Marie Young, whom she described as "a walking Encyclopedia Britannica. After a day with her I really feel like a 'lunatic at large' as if I had absolutely no brain at all." Even at that young age Ethel had defined herself as very different from Alice, and historians would later focus on that difference, calling one the "asset" daughter and the other the "liability."

In comparison with Alice, Eleanor, and Corinney, Ethel moved several steps behind in the ways that women's lives were usually measured. Eleanor, married for nearly four years, already had two children and was six months pregnant with a third. Alice had not yet produced an heir after nearly three years of marriage to Nicholas Longworth, but she kept a busy social schedule in Washington as the wife of an ambitious and popular congressman. Corinney remained single at age twenty-one, but marriage was clearly on the horizon, and she came to Washington for Ethel's party—but in a spectator role. Yet of the four, it was Ethel whom the family considered the most congenial. Each of the others could be a little "too"—too serious, too frivolous, too something—but Ethel was evidently considered just right. Anyone researching her story would have trouble finding a negative word about Ethel.

I

WHILE STILL A TODDLER, Ethel laid claim to the robust build of her Dutch ancestors rather than the fragile beauty of Mittie's line. Edith sometimes complained that she could not find appropriate dresses for the child, who looked best in those without a waistline. As Ethel grew, the sturdiness became a metaphor not only for her appearance but also for her personality. Her mother, no weak willow herself, found the stocky offspring a little intimidating, and in one of Edith's many letters to her sister, she commented that she was "almost afraid" when the three-year-old "comes near me." Never obese or even chubby, Ethel was simply solid.

A cheerful, self-confident personality underlined that physique and emphasized it, and Ethel felt no need to engage in the kind of behavior that got Alice so much attention. Her aunt Corinne Robinson paid tribute to Ethel with a poem about the time of her debut: "She is fair / She is sweet / She is young / She is rare / But her sweetness is strength / and her strength is not bleakness / and her youth is not weakness. / She is girl, she is woman / She is brave, she is human / She is sweet / She is fair / She is young / She is rare!"

In her teens, Ethel found her mother beginning to depend on her almost as though she were another adult. When the family moved from Washington to Sagamore Hill for the summer, Ethel would sometimes go on ahead of her mother to supervise the younger boys and oversee purchases and staff. One summer when faced with a butcher's bill that she considered questionable, Ethel sought advice. "I think it is too much," she wrote her mother. "We have been here 10 days with 8 or 9 people each day. Will you please tell me if [a bill for $28.32] is too much." Her father frequently praised Ethel's cheerful management of the "little boys," as though she played an assistant role to Edith. If it is true that in every large family one child acts as the sane center, in this family it was Ethel—reliable and good-natured, and, people said, a lot like Bye.

In many ways Ethel was the typical "middle" child. With Alice and her two older brothers—Ted was four years her senior and Kermit, two—she was the "kid" sister, but with the two younger brothers, Archie and Quentin, she acted like the bossy older sibling. She bonded especially with Kermit, and long after his death, following a pilgrimage to his grave in Alaska, she wrote her daughter, "I don't think anyone but you now knows how dearly Uncle Kermit and I loved each other."

In a family where distinction did not come easily, Kermit stood out, for his deep sensitivity and for his love of adventure. A favorite of both parents, he accompanied his father wild game hunting in Africa and collaborated with his mother on a book about her family. Soon after he graduated from Harvard, his sister reminded him: "Really, Kerm, its wonderful to see what you are to Mother and Father. They are both so proud of you, and we talk over all you have accomplished and gloat." Without his older brother's intense egotism (that sometimes bordered on the obnoxious), Kermit showed a genuine, deep interest in other people and their ideas. Immediately after graduation from college, he went to live and work in Brazil, where he delved into railroad construction and investment. His sister emphatically agreed that he had made the right choice, though she disliked having him so many miles away. She held the highest hopes for his future, and to Bob and Isabella Ferguson she bragged, "Very few people could do what he's doing and I'm sure he'll make a lot of it."

To the end of her life Ethel insisted that Kermit's attitudes had helped shape hers. "I think often of [our] connected interests and of how much I learned from him." She saw her childhood relationship with him as ideal and hoped to duplicate it for her own family. To the Fergusons, with whom she had a specially close relationship since Bob was her godfather, she wrote that she wanted a place like Sagamore Hill where her children could "live a real little life and have such times as Kermit and I had."

The relationship between Ethel and Kermit may have been sealed during the White House years when they delighted in leading their teenage friends in all kinds of fun. Archie and Quentin both gained attention for their many pranks—playing tricks on the security guards, hobbling on stilts through the parlor rooms, and startling important guests with their menagerie of animals and insects. Quentin gained particular attention when he led his pony into the White House elevator for the trip upstairs to cheer up Archie, who was sick in bed. In contrast, Ethel's doings seem practically grown up, but nevertheless they sometimes brought down the wrath of Edith.

In one of her many letters to the Fergusons, Ethel explained one such incident, revealing how very differently her parents disciplined their children. She and Kermit had returned to the White House from a party and decided at about 2:00 A.M. to take their young friends up on the roof, forgetting "how comparatively near we were to family, and [we] barn danced up and down singing Harrigan." Just as the party was warming up, they heard "the sound of bare feet" and looked up to see the President of the United States "paddling crossly up in his pajamas to greet us!"

One of the teenage guests blurted out, "Look, here comes Cupid," and then realized his gaffe and "was covered with shame." Theodore took it all in stride, as though he was used to being called "Cupid" by his children's friends. He even suggested that the party adjourn to the pantry for a snack. But then Edith appeared, and it was a different story. Ethel could not even bring herself to repeat the words of her mother's reprimand, "but we all flew to our rooms . . . [and] Kerm and I 'got it.'"

The bond between brother and sister was so strong that Ethel refused to fault Kermit when he later declined into alcoholism and left his wife, Belle, for another woman of considerably lower social status. Ethel placed part of the blame on Belle, who was, Ethel maintained, "too strong a character for him, and dominated him, and he did not like it, and took obscure revenge, by misbehaving in various ways. She wanted SOCIETY and it was not his dish."

In the beginning, Ethel and Belle had been good friends. They had met in Washington, where Belle's family owned the famed Willard Hotel just a few steps from 1600 Pennsylvania Avenue. In 1912, when the Willards invited Ethel to join them on a motor trip through Canada, she wrote the Fergusons about the trip and described Belle as "a little southern lady whom Kerm is very fond of too."

The fact that Belle's father, Joseph Edward Willard, was an active Democrat, a southerner, and "a strong Wilson man" mattered little, though Ethel admitted she had tried to convert Belle to the Progressive cause. The 1912 presidential campaign, when Theodore angered many Republicans by running on the Progressive Party ticket, was a difficult time for the whole family but particularly for Ethel. It was the first campaign in which she had really gotten involved, and she did so with gusto. To Kermit in Brazil she explained how several people, including "Uncle Douglas," had given "huge sums" for the campaign, but others had not "given a thing." To pay back the donors, Ethel had helped organize a canvass, surely one of the first of its kind. Many New Yorkers still received and made their telephone calls at their local drugstore, and Ethel and her friends organized their drive around telephone exchanges. "We divided all New York up by telephone centrals," she explained to Kermit, "and then for instance I took Madison Square and went to all the drugstores." Some parts of the fund-raising were clearly more pleasant than others. "It's really very interesting for you get a good idea of the people," she noted, but then continued, "I must say it makes me feel dreadfully embarrassed but never mind." It had been partly to remove Ethel from the stresses of campaigning that Edith had encouraged her to take the trip with the Willards.

After the election was over, Ethel quickly turned to other matters. Earlier that year she had met Richard Derby, a tall, slim surgeon who had graduated from Harvard in 1903 and from Columbia College of Physicians and Surgeons in 1907. Kermit had befriended him first when the two encountered each other while Quentin was undergoing minor surgery in a New York City hospital, and Kermit had taken an immediate liking to the soft spoken doctor. Within weeks Kermit presented him to Ethel, who at twenty-one was quickly passing the age at which most upper-class women, especially Roosevelt women, married. Before many months elapsed, she agreed to marry him. Corinney reported to the Fergusons that a trip to New York had revealed very little gossip except that "Dick Derby is going to marry Ethel R."

Ethel later told her own daughters that her mother had rushed her into the marriage at least a year before she was ready, but at the time she seemed ecstatic. To the Fergusons she wrote, "You're the first people I want to tell that I'm going to marry Dick Derby . . . and oh he's awfully nice." Then she paid him the highest compliment by comparing him to her brother: "Father and Mother and I think that he's like Kermit in a queer way. You know the funny little companiony way Kerm has. Dick's just the same." About the same time she wrote to "My dearest Auntie Bye" about her "very wonderful" engagement. "Tell Uncle Will that I've found *the* brother." The prospective bridegroom was just the person to "sit on the sofa with . . . and talk and talk and talk and then roast marshmallows." Edith endorsed her daughter's choice, especially since it had been made with the family's assistance. To her son Kermit, still working in Brazil, she wrote: "I do hope that you got Ethel's cable about her engagement. . . . It is a comfort when you are so far away to feel that you like Dick and had picked him for Ethel."

The date selected—Friday, April 4—turned out to be "lovely," according to the mother of the bride who wrote a description of the wedding to Kermit. "I don't think there was a single hitch anywhere. Ethel's cheeks were pink and she looked as pretty as possible—not in the least tired." Immediately afterward, the Derbys sailed to Europe for an extended honeymoon. Theodore's letters to them predicted great happiness—almost, but not quite, the same happiness he had known with Edith. "I believe you'll be," he wrote, "with the exception of mother and myself, the happiest married couple." He insisted that he could picture them as he wrote, sitting on a "balcony looking at Vesuvius." Only the matter of "Dick's headaches" marred what looked like a perfect trip.

During the honeymoon Ethel toyed with the idea of doing social work when she returned—a new profession attracting many young women at the time. But by the time the Derbys returned to New York, Ethel was pregnant, and morning nausea caused her to abandon plans to accompany Dick on his hospital rounds and do some volunteer work with sick children. Instead, she concentrated on settling into their Manhattan apartment. She had not really wanted to live in an apartment, even a large one such as theirs on the Upper East side of New York, but Dick persuaded her by pointing out that he could also have his office there. Money was no problem. In addition to his income from a thriving medical practice, he had a private income of between $12,000 and $14,000 a year.

Ethel busied herself at home. She bought a piano because she missed having one "so much and especially now it would be such a pleasure to strum a little myself." For the summer she wanted to rent a house "somewhere on L[ong] I[sland] of course!!" Her father would be leaving on his South American expedition in the fall, and Edith would accompany him part of the way, so Ethel tried to sneak in as much time as possible with both of them before they left. There was, of course, no question of her going along, though she would have welcomed a chance to spend more time with Kermit, whose relationship with Belle Willard had now progressed to the point that they were planning to marry. In December 1913, when Ethel first heard the news, she expressed surprise, and Belle's cable from Madrid a short time later gave few specific details. Ethel prayed for a ceremony in Richmond, Virginia, where the Willards had a family home, but guessed correctly that it would take place in June in Madrid since Belle's father was serving as American ambassador there. The date was particularly bad timing for Ethel. Her baby was born on March 7, almost exactly eleven months after her marriage. When time came to name the boy, no hint of the Roosevelt line crept in: he was Richard Derby, Jr.

ॐ

Regardless of her decision to forgo the Madrid wedding, Ethel packed her bags soon afterward for an extended stay in Paris. Almost immediately after war broke out in Europe, in August 1914, Dick signed up to treat people needing medical attention, many of them wounded soldiers. When he sailed in September, Ethel went with him, leaving their infant son behind with her parents and a nurse. She was no doubt motivated by the desire to help, and like most of her family, held strong views on the war, but the chance to travel and live abroad should not be discounted as motivation. Aboard ship she sounded like an exuberant tourist, writing to her mother that she and Dick wanted to learn "French perfectly—[and] get all we can out of this in every way—it certainly comes high." Ethel, who had never witnessed the effects of war, felt that she had no stomach for them, and she vowed to "see as little of the horrors as possible."

On their arrival in Paris, however, the Derbys were shocked by the reality of war. All around them were gravely injured soldiers, some of them missing a limb, others frightened by the prospect of returning to homes that had been destroyed or to families scattered. Dick went to work at the American Ambulance Hospital, where he soon became very popular. As Ethel wrote her mother: "It is perfectly wonderful to see the way the men in D[ick]'s ward adore him. They always say, 'Well, anything the tall Dr. does is alright' and [they] try to escape from the others." She did not discount the possibility that Dick would gain professionally from the experience, noting that it would be "a wonderful thing for him."

Ethel pitched in to help where she could, taking charge of the dispensary in the mornings because "they are terribly short of nurses." The rest of the day she filled in wherever needed, removing bandages, making splints, and accompanying wounded men to the X-ray room. Much as she had vowed to avoid seeing suffering, she could not do so, though she observed that the patients, mostly English, were "wonderfully brave." She could not witness their pain without severe discomfort herself: "I don't go much in the wards because I cannot bear it. Such appalling wounds. . . . Nearly everything is infected."

For living quarters the Derbys were "comfortably installed in a dear little hotel—Hotel Belmont" on rue Bassano. The tiny bedroom and sitting room on the first floor (with its own "nice bathroom") cost more than they wanted to pay, but since it was close to the hospital, they could both come home for lunch. Ethel moved the furniture around, and to ward off the winter chill and make the place cozy, she kept a fire burning. They had looked for an apartment but failed to find one, and in the end Ethel thought this the better solution. Dick wouldn't worry about her if he had to work late, and, besides, their schedules left them little free time.

Ethel's world centered on the patients. Shortly after she arrived, she wrote home how "devoted" she had become "to my men at the hospital." When one of her distant cousins sent her some money to use wherever she saw a need, she knew immediately that she wanted to "buy a new leg for a boy from Tipperary." When his leg was amputated, the young soldier had become distraught, moaning to Ethel about how he had "an understanding with a girl" back home and now she would never marry him. Trying to cheer him up, Ethel suggested the possibility of an artificial leg, but he rejected the idea as "too expensive" for him. Later, after talking the matter over with Dick, Ethel promised that she would find some way to get the $200 for the leg and that when the young man got home, no one would see the difference. The change in his attitude was immediate: "He is so happy now that it's pathetic." Her problem would not end there—five other men needed the same expensive prosthesis, but in her characteristically optimistic manner, she remained convinced: "We'll get the money *somehow*."

News from home arrived irregularly, but Ethel had already assured her mother while aboard ship that she would not worry even if long intervals occurred between letters. Struggling to keep up with the many changes in her little boy, she could only guess at what she was missing, and she wrote her parents that he probably "has cut a tooth. I suppose he already is doing new things. Probably he tries to sit up now and laughs out loud more often." When she felt a twinge of nostalgia for her "good bunny," she suggested that her mother play patty-cake, "for he loves having his paddies slapped together and laughs out loud. Also peek-a-boo." Both Edith and the nurse she hired to care for the baby kept the parents informed about changes—how he cut that first tooth and when he first managed to eat off a spoon—but it was not the same as witnessing these milestones firsthand.

Ethel never seemed to question or regret her decision to go to Paris with her husband rather than stay behind with her baby. Ironically, she was the first in the family to become directly involved in the war, and her dedication to helping the wounded ran just as deep as any of the men's determination to get involved in the fighting. Her four brothers would later go to Europe to fight, and her father tried to go, but she was every bit as revolted by the slaughter as they were eager to take part in it. To her mother Ethel wrote: "I cannot believe that men should do such things to each other."

When word reached the general American public about the work that the daughter of the former President was doing, many contributions and special requests came in. A church group in Oyster Bay collected clothing for Ethel to distribute as she thought appropriate, but other people were not so generous. One woman in Idaho wrote "My dear Ethel" to compliment her on her efforts but also to request a child for adoption. Specifically, the woman wanted a child "under five years old ... good helthy attractive." Needless to say, Ethel did not oblige.

By Christmas, Ethel was back in New York, reclaiming her son and resuming family life in an apartment on East Seventy-ninth Street. But she could not help noticing that pressure was building for the United States to enter the war, especially after the sinking of the *Lusitania* in May 1915. When a group of volunteers set up their own military training camp in Plattsburg, New York, Dick Derby joined several thousand men from across the nation who paid their own way to go there and prepare to fight. Besides getting the men into good physical condition, such a camp impressed on the nation the need for the United States to resist isolation and help determine the outcome of the war. Dick was not away many weeks, but in the first separation of their married life, Ethel felt a little lost. He reciprocated the feeling, writing her on March 9, 1916: "It isn't until you go away that I realize how dependent I am on you, darling." Now that Sagamore Hill, where Ethel and young Richard stayed with her parents, had its own telephone (number OB60), the two of them could occasionally talk with each other.

By the time the United States entered the war, in April 1917, Ethel, seven months pregnant with her second child, was unable to join her husband when he went to do military training in Tennessee. Unlike the other camp, this one was official, sponsored by the U.S. government, and as much as Ethel endorsed Dick's decision to enlist, she could hardly go with him—at least until after June 17 when daughter Edith was born. Weeks later Ethel left the infant and the three-year-old with her parents because, as she explained to Kermit, housing was tight and Chattanooga "is no place for a bottle baby and a convalescing child." Trying to make herself useful around the base where help was scarce, she did domestic chores and instructed young people how to milk a cow, a skill she had picked up along the way as part of her general introduction to farm animals and pets. Patriotic commitment aside, her biggest reason for being there was to be with her husband in the center of action, which was far more appealing to her than staying home with young children.

Ethel's stay in Chattanooga lasted less than two months. On October 31 a telegram arrived ordering Medical Corps Major Richard Derby to proceed to Hoboken, New Jersey, "for transportation abroad." The government had already banned wives from joining their soldier husbands in Europe, but Ethel made it very clear that nothing would deter her if she decided to reach Dick: "Dearest, if you are wounded I shall get to you if I have to divorce you first and then marry you on the other side."

With her husband and brothers involved in the fighting, Ethel had plenty to worry about, and to divert her attention a bit, her father took her with him on a speaking trip through Canada. Ethel's relationship with her father had always been close. With her he showed none of the guilt that marked his dealings with Alice, and after she became an adult with children of her own, she found extraordinary comfort in his presence. With Dick in France, she spent more and more time at Sagamore Hill.

Separated by an ocean, Dick and Ethel wrote each other about what they would do when the fighting ended. While keeping him informed about each child's latest accomplishment, she often apologized for putting too much of the "concrete" in her letters. Sometimes husband and wife speculated on Dr. Derby's career, and when he revealed his decision in March 1918 to accept appointment as regimental surgeon, she expressed misgivings: "I cannot say I am glad of your decision but dear Heart, I can say that I know well how you feel and am infinitely proud of your spirit." Ethel had entertained higher hopes: "I do feel a little that with all your knowledge and all your French and what you have learnt since being over, that a [regimental surgeon] is not important enough place for you or, to express it better, that you could be of even more use doing different work." In the short run, she could accept his decision, but "I hope you won't feel you must be one too awfully long. Just get the experience." Her letter's closing left no doubt, however, that she would stick by him, no matter what he decided.

At Sagamore Hill, little Edith quickly became Theodore's favorite among her generation. Ethel observed that her father doted on the infant, and when some friends came to Sagamore Hill and admired four-year-old Richard, pointing out how much he looked like his father, Theodore immediately "picked up Edith from her carriage outside, and brought her in to be admired. He adores her." Ethel's mother confided that Theodore had the same special feeling for his son Archie but that "she has never seen him care for any other child . . . the same way." To hear Theodore talk, "there is *the* Baby and the rest of them are just babies." Little Edith returned his affection in full measure: She "loves him," Ethel wrote her husband, "and waves her arms and legs and all her little self with delight when he comes into the room."

The children provided a little diversion from the effects of the war—all too apparent by the spring of 1918. Ethel reported that she saw a "great change in the country's realization of the war. We have had various shortages, and most of all the casualty lists are beginning to be read with poignant anxiety all over the country." But in many ways life went on in mundane regularity—caring for children and waiting for mail and learning to type. Partly to keep her in touch with other young women friends but also to help in the war effort, Ethel accepted the vice presidency of the local Junior League.

Within the family, the bad news started in March when they learned that Archie had been seriously wounded. Dick, who was not far away from him, rushed to his side to monitor his condition and treatment. A respected surgeon had already operated on Archie, and now the prognosis was good. Dick reassured Ethel: "The very worst that can happen is a stiff knee joint." On the plus side, Archie would be "out of it for months and perhaps for good. I sincerely hope so." Ted had been gassed, though he was expected to recover with no permanent disability. Dick had a close call himself in early June when "a large shell exploded so near to me that I felt the hot waft of air and was toppled over against the hedge." One man and a mule standing within fifteen feet of him were killed and another man badly wounded, but Dick reported proudly: "I never got a scratch." It had been his reaction to danger that pleased him most: "I was glad it happened for it proved to me to my satisfaction that I am not afraid to die—something of which I had never been sure before."

Worse news was yet to come. On July 17, word reached Sagamore Hill that Quentin, who had managed to get into action as an airman in spite of his bad eyes, was missing in action. Dick wrote his own version from France, reporting to Ethel that Quentin's plane "had descended in flames back of the German lines," but since the news had not been "authenticated at headquarters," everyone could nurture the slim hope that Quentin might have made a safe landing and was being held prisoner somewhere. Dick, Kermit, Archie, and Ted all managed to gather at the Paris apartment of Ted's wife, Eleanor, to wait for some verification. On July 20 the word came—Quentin had died of two shots to the head at Chamery, near Rheims. It was a time, Richard wrote home, "when we all needed one another's company and moral support so much."

Trying to console his wife, Dick wrote her on July 21, "I am so sorry for you and Mother and Father, dearest. My heart aches for the grief that you must feel and I feel most particularly for Mother." But in family tradition, Dick emphasized the satisfaction the family should feel because of how Quentin died: "My grief and yours too must be lessened by that wonderful feeling of pride that comes for such valor and utter fearlessness."

Ethel could not reconcile herself to this, death's first break in their tight family circle. The fact that it hit the youngest of the children, and a great favorite with all of them, only underscored its impact. "Until I heard he was actually buried I could not believe he was dead," Ethel wrote her husband. "I still feel he is alive." She had accompanied her parents to church, observing how "terribly hard" it was for her mother, but added defiantly, "She is not going to wear black." Theodore's grief went beyond anything Ethel had ever observed in him. To Archie he bemoaned the fact that "the young must die and not the old."

As though the family did not have enough to bear, Ted suffered another injury, this time from machine-gun fire to his left knee. After examining him, Dick took him to a specialist, who found the nerve "to be all right" but saw evidence of a "slight paralysis." Ted, who was an impressionable eleven-year-old when his father made headlines in Cuba, never seemed to think he measured up to him and stubbornly resisted taking any gain from his battle exploits. Now Dick Derby counseled him to change: "He should most certainly get a Lt. Col. or a Col. after all that he has done." Dick had "been lecturing him good and hard" and had finally gotten him to agree to accept an increase in rank "if offered him." The war had altered Ted, in Dick's eyes, and for the better: "[He is] very much changed in some ways, very much the same small boy Ted in others. . . . He is much more a friend of all the world."

When the armistice was signed in November 1918, Ethel still had a number of hurdles to overcome. Almost all the men in the family were fighting or sick, leaving many decisions to the women. Her father's health was failing, and Ethel tried to assist her mother in making decisions about his care. Quentin's death was still a fresh wound when Auntie Corinne's husband, Douglas Robinson, died suddenly in September. Cousin Eleanor's Franklin had hardly gotten over pneumonia when he got the flu, and Corinney Alsop's Joe was also ill.

With two little children to supervise, Ethel could only hope that her husband would return as soon as possible. He had not yet arrived on January 6 when Theodore died at Sagamore Hill, and Ethel had to write him the details, including how Alice had come up from Washington to lend her moral support. While she tried to help her mother through the first few days, Ethel unloaded her own grief on Dick. "I cannot believe we never more will [all] meet at Sagamore," she wrote. "How terribly sad it will be." Her grief was more than personal—she saw her father's death as a great loss to the country. "The whole country mourns him and I mourn for the country. There's no one now to say what we want said."

II

WITH DICK DERBY'S RETURN from the war in 1919, the family appeared started on a new phase. Just before he shipped out, he and Ethel had bought the Old Adams House, a large Georgian structure in Oyster Bay, and now, with his return, they settled in there and he began work at the Glen Cove hospital nearby. A third child, Sarah Alden, named for one of the Derby ancestors and always called by both names, was born in December 1920, joining little Richard and Edith. During the summers Ethel would take the children to visit Auntie Corinne's Henderson House, and throughout the year the Derby children were frequent callers at their grandmother Roosevelt's.

That tranquil, comfortable life broke apart suddenly in October 1922 when eight-year-old Richard Derby died of septicemia, commonly called blood poisoning. He had suffered the usual childhood illnesses but seemed healthy until an infection in a chest gland—something easily curable after antibiotics came into use—ran out of control. Hospitalized on Sunday, he died the next day. For any parent to lose a child is traumatic, but for a physician-father, the loss was apparently multiplied since he was involved in the medical treatment.

The impact on Ethel was enormous and deep, much like Auntie Corinne's reaction to Stewart's death in 1909. She continued caring for her family and gave birth to a third daughter, Judith Quentin, in December 1923, but her son's death left a large gap. For the rest of her life she commemorated his birthday and often referred to him as though no one else mattered as much as he. Five years after his death, in a letter to her mother, Ethel commiserated about the pain they shared, having both lost a son. That Ethel also lost a brother seemed especially unfair, and she mused: "If only I had Richard it would comfort me for losing [Quentin]. [I]t always did, somehow." Then she implied that losing a son cut more deeply than losing a daughter: "I suppose that idea of 'carrying on' [the family name] which is never the same with girls."

The effect of young Richard's death on his father was even more disastrous: he was devastated. Perhaps Dick could not quite accept the fact that his medical expertise had given him no particular advantage. Or this may have been an old fragility exposed to new tests. Since the beginning of his marriage, he had suffered debilitating headaches, but now, with his grief, he could not function. He complained of blinding pain, digestive problems, and, most disturbing of all, deep depression. Work became nearly impossible, and he struggled to meet appointments.

Travel offered one hope, and in September 1925 he set out on a trip west, through Montana to Seattle and then Alaska. Ethel, who took her three little girls up to Henderson House, wrote him long, encouraging letters and shared her own pain over their loss. She recognized her good fortune to have three perfectly healthy little girls, but they never compensated for one little boy: "It is sometimes impossible to think of him as away for always from this life."

Ethel's immediate concern, however, was finding a cure for her husband, and she hoped the trip west would boost his spirits. It would be a "wonderful rest" for him, she wrote Kermit, putting him in a new setting, far removed from the scene of their son's death, and exposing him to a part of the world he had never seen. As for herself, continually worried about him and their future, it represented a bonus: "I feel as if it were a form of health insurance too."

For a while the change in scenery seemed to help. Dick became "absorbed in moving picture cameras" and sought advice on what kind of equipment Kermit had used on his recent excursion to central Asia. When Dick returned at the end of November, laden "with guns and movie cameras," he looked "better than I have ever seen him," Ethel wrote Kermit. Though hampered by rain and overcast skies in shooting pictures, he had a "most splendid time" and photographed "three bears, and two sheep, not particularly big ones." Taking a leaf from the Roosevelt book, he wrote two articles on his trip, which his wife pronounced "very good," and Kermit invited him to publish them in a book he and his mother were putting together on travel.

For some months Ethel retained her optimism about Dick's improvement. She had noticed a change herself, and her husband's physician agreed. Dr. Thomas Salmon, one of New York's leading psychiatrists (or, as they were still called at the time, alienists), predicted that Dick "will be entirely well, and better than he has been for years," she wrote Kermit. Dick seemed to like and respect his doctor, whom he playfully referred to as "The Chief Nut Cracker." But Ethel feared that the Christmas holidays in 1926 would bring a relapse, and she begged Kermit to help protect Dick from anything that might upset him—that is, don't let anyone talk about bothering things to him."

Dr. Salmon's prediction proved premature. Dick was able to work some but his depression had not lifted, and Ethel scurried to find more trips to divert him. When his doctors suggested that he escape the winter cold, she traveled with him to Florida and then left him there with Dr. Salmon while she returned north. Dick continued to complain of fatigue, and she felt unsure about what summer plans to make. Europe was a possibility if Dick felt better, but Dr. Salmon "thought it would be unwise to spend the summer at O[yster] B[ay]," she wrote Kermit in April 1927. She suggested Pine Knot, the rustic cabin that her mother, while First Lady, had bought near Charlottesville, Virginia, but Dr. Salmon opposed the idea.

For a few months the family tried a rural setting in Cornish, New Hampshire, but Dick's spirits did not improve. Finally Ethel, who was committed to putting more distance between them and the house where little Richard died, moved the family to Europe. It was the first of three long trips, each lasting at least several months, and although the first was largely convalescent for Dick, the journeys gave Ethel the chance to satisfy her own desire for travel and also expose their daughters to Europe. She had toured the Continent in 1909 when she was eighteen, but she wanted to give their three daughters an earlier start.

By November 1927 the Derbys had settled into a small hotel apartment in Lausanne, and Ethel wrote her sister-in-law Belle that she was really worried about her husband. Marking one section of her letter "Private," Ethel revealed: "Dick has been miserable. . . . Ever since Cornish, things had not been going so well, and for the last 3 weeks, steadily worse, headaches, sleeplessness, tired, and consequent depression."

Ethel refused to abandon the idea that some previously undiagnosed physical ailment was at the base of all her husband's suffering. He went from doctor to doctor, and she finally reported brightly that a new physician "found a liver and digestive condition to account for the headaches and he promises swift improvement." But if this approach should fail, Ethel would not know where to turn: "It has been a period of cold terror and not over yet," she wrote Belle. Separated from her mother and brothers, she felt "entirely alone" but definitely not incapacitated. Although she continued to worry about her husband, she considered taking some courses herself at the university.

By January 1928, Dick entered a Swiss clinic where he seemed to improve. After visiting him there, Ethel described the setting as "an excellent place for him . . . deliciously sunny, one skates with only a light sweater, no coat, and yet it is high and bracing." After six weeks there he would be back to normal, she hoped, and then she mused that he seemed to do best in cold weather, but his American physician had always prescribed warm climes. Dick was well enough to add his own note to Belle, though it quickly faded as he predicted, "There is no ink worse than the French." Ethel's letters still carried an occasionally optimistic note—about buying herself a new fur jacket or how well the girls were doing—but this was definitely one of the low points in her life.

By June, Dick's condition had not significantly improved, and she explained to Kermit why she had kept her counsel on her husband's

health although she was usually forthright and open about her feelings: "I despise people who won't face things and are Pollyannas but
it's almost worse to be forever dreary. So silence seemed best." Now
that the situation appeared dire, she had to speak out, and instead
of cryptic notes marked "Private," she wrote openly of what was
happening to Dick. Always slender, he was losing weight at an
alarming rate, and when his physician suggested that he spend the
summer in a Swiss hotel "for a change," she decided to take their
three daughters back to the States. Leaving Europe would mean
withdrawing an invitation she had extended to her least favorite
aunt, Emily Carow, but Ethel decided to endure the "canniption
fits" that her mother's sister would throw since "anything is better
than being joined by her!"

༄

By the time Dick returned to Long Island that fall, he was able to
resume a full schedule at Glen Cove Community Hospital, and family life settled into a kind of routine. Edith, age eleven, and Sarah
Alden, seven, went to local schools, and Ethel became active in the
local Red Cross. She had been very critical of that organization's
efforts during the time she spent in Paris in 1914. Bandages arrived
too wet to use, and shipments were erratic and undependable. But
now she made the Red Cross her primary volunteer effort.

Some of their relatives thought they should have sold the Old
Adams House, with all its reminders of little Richard, but her time
away from it had convinced Ethel otherwise. In a letter to her mother
she mused that, instead of associating the house with bad memories,
she had come to value it as the place where her son remained alive for
her. "Richard's death was not a *side* effect," she had written her
mother from Paris, "it's part of the happy and the sad and I don't feel
that he's dead when I'm there." In characteristic fashion, she welcomed differing opinions but insisted on putting her husband's health
ahead of all else: "An outside p[oint] of v[iew] is often illuminating
and I do want to do the wisest and best of things for Dick."

The house had many advantages. It was close to Dick's work and
to Sagamore Hill, and its spacious yard and access to the water
accommodated almost any sport that her daughters and their friends
wanted to try. The girls got a pony, which the two youngest could

ride bareback at the same time, using as a blanket an old opera cloak that once belonged to Corinne Robinson. When a new French governess, more gentle and understanding than a previous one, came to teach them, Ethel was so grateful that she volunteered to teach her how to drive an automobile. The governess spoke a clear and distinct French and seemed to "love the USA," causing Ethel to conclude that she was too good to be true: "Neat, good discipline. It really does not sound possible."

But the idea of travel still drew Ethel away, and in late 1931 the Derbys returned to Europe. As soon as she settled the rest of the family into a "silly little chalet" in Switzerland, Ethel made her way south to Italy and the hill towns of Umbria. She felt completely at ease in France, where she had many friends and spoke the language, but the Italian landscape brought out the poet in her. How lucky she felt, she wrote Kermit, to be "exploring hill towns and seeing pictures and having picnic lunches under olive [trees]." Here, where no one could reach her easily, she felt freed: "It is blessed to be away from the telephone and not to feel the uncertainty hanging over you every minute of the night and day."

Now that the Great Depression had taken its toll on her income, Ethel found she liked European prices better: "Everything is very cheap in Italy, room and meals at excellent hotels cost $4.50 a day—except gas which is 50 cents a gallon!" Dick's investment income had fallen along with the income from his medical practice, so she kept a close eye on the family's bankbook. In early December 1931 she wrote Belle that she could manage as long as they stayed on that side of the Atlantic: "The hard pull may be when we get back." Then she joked, "And perhaps we shall all be penniless by then anyway." The economic situation looked worse from afar: "You must all be having a very anxious time in NY. From here it all looks horrid." Unable to understand what had brought about this calamity, she queried: "Where has the money gone to? and all our natural resources behind us?" Then she added facetiously, "Why don't we have leather money like the Carthaginians?"

The girls, now fourteen, eleven, and eight, were all of school age, and Ethel had to make arrangements for each of them. She found a teacher from Tuscany for Edith and then supplemented the formal study with a trip that she and Edith took to northern Italy in

November. By Christmas the Derbys were reunited and the holidays went well, except that Ethel thought Dick looked tired and puffy-eyed. When Nick Longworth arrived for a visit after Christmas, she encouraged him to go skiing with Dick.

Ethel continued to observe news from America closely, especially when it involved a member of the family. Her relationship with Ted had become increasingly strained since the war years, especially after he and Eleanor began moving in more fashionable circles than the Derbys cared for. After Ted's unsuccessful run for governor of New York in 1924, he had struggled to find a new niche and finally got himself an appointment abroad by the Republican president Herbert Hoover. He had hoped to follow up his governorship of Puerto Rico (1929–32) with an equally prestigious assignment to the Philippines, but this time Hoover lagged in making a decision. Finally, when the nomination seemed assured in January 1932, Ethel wrote her mother that she was glad but she doubted Ted would be satisfied there for long: "His eyes are elsewhere." He would find the job difficult "but most interesting," she predicted, "and the kind of thing he will do splendidly." Ethel evidently had additional reasons for wanting Ted moved from his current location; she added that the new job would "keep him away from certain petticoats."

Archie and Ethel had never been close, though for some reason he was named godfather to her Edith, and even Kermit was losing his favored status with her. He and Belle were spending too much time with Ted and Eleanor, she felt, and they all were too much enthralled with the rich and famous. Ethel could not believe the kind of friends they made, and to her mother she wrote, "How can they love the Du Ponts!" With her three surviving brothers giving her so little to feel satisfied about, Ethel's thoughts turned repeatedly to memories of Quentin, dead now about thirteen years. On his birthday she always wired her mother from wherever she was, using only the simplest phrase to convey her grief. When she traveled where people had known Quentin, she made a point of contacting them, and she talked about him with her daughters so that they would have some sense of how special he had been. She continued to link Quentin in her thoughts with her dead son and noted in one letter to her mother, "I ever remember Quentin putting his arms around [Richard] . . . hugging him with that curious Peter Grimm quality when they said 'good-bye.'"

Throughout the Great Depression, the Derbys watched expenses, but in comparison with most families, they lived luxuriously. On Long Island, where they rented out their house during their absence, they kept a staff of five, including four house workers and one gardener–handy man. In Switzerland their employees earned much less than the Americans, but Ethel still had to meet a sizable payroll for one governess, one cook, one maid, and one handyman. In addition to the rent for the chalet, food, clothing, and medical bills, she also paid school costs. Tuition for Edith, now enrolled in a private school, was high, and though the two younger girls went to a less expensive school, Ethel knew those costs would go up as they got older. To her mother, who frequently sent her checks, Ethel was forever grateful, and she wrote her: "I feel still all protected and safe— with mother between me and the world."

In an attempt to cut expenses, Ethel experimented with washing her own hair, but after obtaining dismal results, she resolved to go back to a professional. She had skin problems, and after reading in *The New Yorker* about a new remedy, she decided that the treatments must be worth "every bit of the $50" that each one cost. Then, in jest to her mother, she suggested that she might have to stop the children's school payments to meet the cost of the skin care: "That is what we shall come to, I see: Stop lessons and take to beauty doctors every time!"

By January 1932, however, Ethel realized that she would have to cut back. The Long Island staff was asking for more, and she despaired of being able to pay. The handyman had already agreed to one cut, and now, as Ethel faced the prospect of making another decrease, she worried: "I don't want anyone to think we would abandon him at such a time." She had gone over her own accounts and found it "depressing work." Her husband's income had continued to fall, and all predictions were for a further decline the following year. Ethel's income from investments had been cut in half, and with "taxes going up," she calculated that she would have "instead of $1,300 a month" something more like "$850—we'll just see how it turns out." She considered dismissing the handyman and the upstairs maid but then wavered: "That may be too drastic or not enough." It really came down to choosing between tuition for her daughters and one employee: "I don't see how we can keep Joseph and send the children to schools." As long as her family remained in Europe, she could manage "for it's all so much less expensive." Kermit, head of his own steamship company, could help her get cheap tickets home, and they always had her mother's home, "the House on the Hill [to] shelter us," until they were able to settle back into the Old Adams House.

Money was only one concern. Her son's death still haunted Ethel, and a decade afterward she admitted, "I am never reconciled." All other adversities would diminish if only he had survived, she wrote her mother. "If Richard were here it would have been alright." Dick had not fully recovered his health, and in March 1932, when a physician in Paris diagnosed a pancreas malfunction and prescribed insulin, Ethel hoped for the best.

Ethel also worried about her mother, but in some ways Edith, now in her seventies, continued as a dauntless model for her daughter. In 1932, while traveling in France, Ethel had an attack of indigestion "as violent as it is the rare times it attacks me." But then she had gathered her strength, and "with a heroism worthy of my mother, conceal[ed] it from my hosts."

Ethel made little use of unsolicited advice from relatives about how to manage her family. She and her three female cousins had worked out such different kinds of marriages that they hardly gained from comparison. Alice's had been an "open" marriage, and well before Nick Longworth's death, she nurtured her own circle of friends and admirers. Eleanor's friendships in both political and feminist circles escalated in the 1920s, moving her farther away from Franklin and his mother and certainly farther from Ethel, who had limited use for such causes. During the war she had written Dick a scathing account of what she called the "Superwoman who now inhabits New York. They are very good [and] do an enormous amount of work," but she thought most of them looked down on "a mere worm like myself." Ethel had no complaints about Corinney, who had taken her seat in the Connecticut legislature where she worked with colleagues of both sexes on both sides of the political aisle. But Ethel fancied no such role for herself.

It may have been partly their differing circumstances that caused Ethel to muse on the general topic of women's relationships with their men. In early December 1928 she wrote her mother about changes she had observed and then questioned whether it was "a general change, that of women to their husbands, perhaps arising from the great change in the position and opportunities of women," or something that affected only a few people. "It does seem very strange," she continued, and then asked, "Would you want to go to Bermuda with female friends? Or even would you feel you had the right to come abroad with your parents, leaving your husband at home to grapple with children?"

After less than two years back in Oyster Bay, Ethel was ready to travel again in the fall of 1934. This time Dick remained behind, looking after his work at the Glen Cove hospital while she took the girls to Italy, enrolling them in classes in Florence. En route they stopped in Venice to see the art museums and the Ducal Palace, arranging to do the sightseeing on Sunday when admission dropped from twelve lire to one. In Florence, where they stayed at a *pensione,* Ethel found a school she judged just right; it was run by a "New England school marm" with strict "Dalton" rather than looser "Montessori ideas." The emphasis was on language study, with Italian lessons daily, French three times a week, and German twice—at least for Edith, now seventeen, while the younger girls had slightly less rigorous schedules.

Ethel described their *pensione* as providing "excellent service" though it was admittedly "shabby." Then, poking fun at herself, she added, "But so is my house." She had bargained a bit on the price, and when the proprietor accepted her offer of $11 per day for all four of them *"tutto compresso,"* Ethel reported proudly: "[It] shows you that Florence is adjustable to any purse."

Dick Derby joined them in December, taking time off from his work for an extended Christmas vacation and bringing another generous check from Ethel's mother. Young Edith wrote her grandmother in her very precise, almost mechanical, penmanship that since her father's arrival "Mother has been just like a little girl. . . . I don't think we realized how awful it was for her without him. She is so cunning about him and won't let him out of her sight for a minute." He had experienced a smooth sailing to Naples, but he appeared tired to his daughter, who wrote: "I think this holiday will do him a world of good." As for herself, she still felt "awful periods of homesickness" but remained convinced that she was going to "get through this winter quite well."

Ethel gave a slightly different picture. She confided to her mother that she had awakened in the night with a "breathless attack which

I have not had for so long." But she concentrated on each day's activities. She and Dick heard a violin concert, visited art galleries, and planned a ski trip over the Christmas holiday. Now in an apartment rather than the *pensione,* they found the living arrangements more comfortable, although Edith still described it as "on the cold side." She and her mother were studying Italian history together and taking lots of side trips, including one to the Etruscan capital city of Volterra. Even eleven-year-old Judith was writing to her grandmother in Italian, describing the Ponte Vecchio and other sights.

By the spring of 1935 the last of the three long European trips ended, and the Derbys took up residence again in Oyster Bay. Edith, now college age, mulled over the idea of whether or not she should go. Ethel even started putting money aside for it, then jokingly suggested that a couple of lucrative cases for her surgeon husband could improve the family's finances. "I almost hope for some polo accidents!!!!" she wrote her mother. Dick Derby, confronted with the usual teenage silliness, tended to "brood ... rather irritably," according to Ethel, who countered that it is "much better to worry because [Edith] is too gay than because she is not gay enough." He had already announced that he did not think that Edith was the "college type," and Ethel immediately replied, "That's one of the real reasons I want her to go. She has that curious quality of Sister's [Alice Longworth] of acceptance and laziness, and I don't want her to sleep and smoke and fritter about with girls all day and movies and boys at night." Ethel thought this was just a phase Edith would soon pass through; she had an "unusually good mind and really enjoys herself when she has a course mapped out for her to do." A friend of Edith's had suggested that the two of them take a course at Columbia University the following winter, and Ethel approved it as a "good solution" because it would entail "no campus life, and separation from the family, but [offer] something to keep her going." In fact, Edith went for one year to Barnard and then insisted she *"couldn't stand it."* So she went "out and got a job." She had also considered Bryn Mawr but rejected it, she later recalled, because she had no desire to be in that "terrible women's atmosphere."

Ethel was beginning a very satisfactory part of her life—even for a person who tended to find the bright spots during the bad patches. With Dick earning the respect of his colleagues at the Glen Cove hospital and rapidly becoming one of its outstanding physician-administrators, she could direct more of her energies to the kind of volunteer work she had wanted to do just after marrying two decades earlier. Her daughters still claimed a large chunk of her time and attention, but she found she had more space for herself. In the Red Cross work she got involved, as was inevitable, in the personal rivalries common to any organization and threaded her way through them with ease, making many friends along the way. Dick reported admiringly that she was "tackling all sorts of difficult questions and getting them solved in such a capable manner. . . . On the subject of the Nurses Aides at the hospital, she got right to the bottom of the trouble that we have been having, which nobody else had been able to discover. I was filled with admiration over the way she handled the matter." Hers was a world centered on a small town on Long Island and on her family—husband, daughters, mother, and many friends.

III

THE FACT THAT HER COUSIN Franklin was now President of the United States caused Ethel some misgivings. Something about his jaunty personality always jarred her, and she once confided to her daughter Edith that whenever the two of them met, Franklin insisted they were "kissing cousins" and proceeded to act accordingly, while she would have preferred keeping more distance. Much more important, she judged him ineffectual and superficial as a leader, and she saw no reason to alter that judgment just because he lived in the White House. In July 1933 she wrote Dick, who was traveling in Canada: "I think that Franklin is stupid and sees very little. He does see one or two obvious things, and thinks that those must be done. The rest flits over his head." The fact that he presided over a nation in the midst of an economic crisis made the matter more worrisome, and she had cautioned her mother in 1934, "We must be patient and not allow ourselves to get so indignant that we poison our minds entirely. After all, the country likes FDR and it's too big a country to ruin in a few years. Pazienza [Patience]."

Those few years turned into more than a dozen, during which Franklin and Eleanor both received enormous national attention, but the Derbys saw very little of them. Perhaps the most poignant exchanges between the Hyde Park and Oyster Bay branches came at times of death when neither personality nor political differences could build a barrier large enough to block communication.

Death cut heavily into the Roosevelt ranks between 1940 and 1945, a time in which Eleanor and Corinney both lost their last surviving siblings, and Ethel lost two of her brothers within a year. On June 4, 1943, while on active military duty in Alaska, Kermit, lonely and depressed, put a gun to his head and ended his life. Though shaken by the death, Ethel could hardly be surprised. Kermit had been drinking heavily for a long time, and the attempted interventions of Ted and Archie had been as ineffective as those of their father and Auntie Bye in the case of Elliott a generation earlier. Within the family there was some hope that military life might sober him up, but that failed, too, especially after he was assigned to the remote outpost in Alaska.

The following summer, Ted, a brigadier general, led American troops ashore in the famous D-day invasion of France, and under heavy fire he commanded his own men and helped others land safely. Singled out for unusual courage, he won the Congressional Medal of Honor, making him one of very few men to win every combat medal given by the U.S. Army. Fatigued by battle but insistent on remaining in the field until the enemy was driven back, he suffered a fatal heart attack and died on July 12 at Sainte-Mère-Eglise in Normandy, at the age of fifty-six.

Of Ethel's four brothers, only Archie survived—her least favorite sibling. His political views were too far right for Ethel, who considered herself a liberal Republican, and he had always been far too close with his money. As an example of the latter, Ethel noted that Archie and his wife, Grace, solved the acute shortage of servants after the war in a most unusual way—they hired parolees from a New Jersey reformatory for $50 per month. Not only was the price right but obedience was almost guaranteed. Ethel explained to her daughter Edith how Grace became their "appointed keeper and has complete power over them! They tremble at her nod and their one desire is to please."

Differences between Ethel and Archie grew as they had to deal with an increasingly unpredictable mother. In her eighties, Edith Roosevelt started showing more of the disagreeable traits that she had once succeeded in concealing. Before Ted died, the normally tolerant Ethel wrote him: "Mother seems to distribute rather impartially her displeasure. It will be lovely to have you up here to share it." But worse was yet to come. During the next few years Edith became even more petty and unpredictable. She would give a favorite ring to one granddaughter and then ask that it be returned so she could give it to another. During the gas rationing of World War II, she insisted that members of her family take a long circuitous route through the grounds of Sagamore Hill because she did not want to hear or see their cars. Ethel tended her patiently and tolerated her caprices, but it must have been at least partly a relief when she died in 1948.

The task of going through her possessions fell to Ethel and Archie, who spent days sorting pictures and housewares. They devised a special system for the linen: they divided sheets and tablecloths into even piles and then drew lots for the piles. It was the same procedure, Ethel explained to her daughter, that the Egyptian government used in dividing the findings of foreign expeditions. Then Ethel set about turning Sagamore Hill into a historic site. When it opened to the public in 1953, opinion was unanimous that her hard work made it possible.

Although Archie seemed oblivious to his obligations as godfather to Edith Derby, Ethel took seriously her own godmother role to Archie's firstborn son, Archie Jr. She sent generous checks to him and his wife, Selwa, known as Lucky, who recalled that both she and her husband "loved Aunty Ethel. She was extremely motherly and had a benign sweetness about her." Lucky Roosevelt mused after Ethel's death that there had been times when her generosity "made a huge difference in our lives." Unexpectedly, without any hint from them, she "would just send a check." In Lucky's opinion, Ethel could never have an enemy because "she was the most generous and kind woman." After one especially large gift, Ethel explained that she preferred giving while she was alive rather than making a provision for them in her will.

With Archie Sr., Ethel differed on other matters besides godparenting. Convinced that he showed little respect for her opinions, she cringed at the views he expressed during the McCarthy era. The Theodore Roosevelt Association, founded just months after Theodore's death in 1919, had always been a favorite project of the Oyster Bay clan, and its annual dinner was a time for them to gather as a family. But in 1959, when

Archie addressed the group, word passed to the relatives not in attendance that his performance had been "very embarrassing." He also displayed his frugal side, looking for loopholes to avoid paying out of his own pocket. After he and Ethel had agreed to supplement the retirement of their mother's former servants, he came up with a scheme to meet this obligation through the Theodore Roosevelt Association, but Ethel balked, objecting that it was not right.

Alice Longworth, whose reputation for sarcasm might have put her at odds with Ethel, proved a supportive friend. Everyone who knew them insisted that they got along well despite their very different personalities. Unlike Archie, Alice, who held very definite opinions on most subjects, permitted others to disagree, showing a latitude that Ethel appreciated.

In their early years, the seven-year difference in their ages cast Alice in a quasi-parental role, but after their respective marriages, the tables turned and the resolute Ethel assumed a mentor position. She had the more stable marriage, and had produced four children before Alice had one. By the time Alice's only child, Paulina, was born in 1925, the Derbys were living on Long Island, and Alice sought ways for the cousins to get together. In August 1926 she wrote Ethel from Cincinnati that she planned to return to Washington via Oyster Bay so that her eighteen-month-old daughter could see Ethel's girls. "I long, I really long to have her meet Edith, Sarah, and Judith."

The camaraderie between Ethel and Alice grew over the next half-century. Near the end of her life, Ethel still could not quite explain how two such different personalities were able to enjoy each other's company so much. She wrote her daughter Edith: "Auntie Sister [Alice] called and we had a long talk the other night. And laughed at our obvious incompatibility, and our deep and close affection and understanding. She goes out to dine and dazzles everyone, and pays for it by being really laid up for a couple of days afterward." When preparations began for a large celebration of Alice's ninetieth birthday in February 1974, Ethel agreed to write a tribute, although she found such things difficult: "I don't think I can and I must." And she did.

∽

Far closer to Ethel than any of her siblings were her three daughters, very different from one another but close to each other and to her. Edith, who turned out to be the most politically involved, married Andrew Murray "Mike" Williams, Jr., in June 1941. Their first child was born eighteen months later, but the uncertainties connected with the war evidently caused them, like many young people, to rethink the wisdom of having more. In January 1944, Edith received a letter from her mother pointing out how important it was to persevere even in the midst of a barbarous war: "If people such as you and Mike were afraid to have children, it would be the end for our country. That's the dangerous thing which hit France. People were afraid of life. I think of it often." Then the inveterate optimist added, "Life is an adventure anyway you look."

After the war ended, the Williams family moved to the Seattle area, thus putting a continent between mother and daughter. It made little difference in their closeness. By 1947, when Edith had three children, she was keeping her mother so fully informed of their problems and accomplishments that the two women might just as well have been living in the same town. Every Sunday morning Ethel sat down at her desk in Oyster Bay to write, and after Edith received the letter on Wednesday, she penned her reply in time for the post office to deliver it on Saturday. For three decades the letters continued—except when the women were together—and they detail that time better than most diaries ever could.

Each of the children's exploits and failings was reported to Ethel, who replied with careful, sagacious advice, much of it gleaned from her own parents and siblings. In August 1946, when her daughter confided that five-year-old Andrew was afraid of the dark, Ethel consoled her that "fear of the dark does not arise from being frightened." It was "an inexplicable thing. Perhaps something with which we are dowered." Then she reminded her daughter that "fear is a part of life, and it has its useful place, as a quickener of our enjoyments, a stimulus to life itself. The shadow which brings warmth to the sunlight." She concluded that perhaps "you would not call it fear."

In November 1951, when one of the Williams boys got into some mischief, Ethel reminded her daughter: "It was a saying in our family that you could not bring your boys up to be eagles, and then expect them to behave like chickens." Ethel also had some advice for the harried young mother who sometimes lost her patience with the children. Such an outburst "certainly does not hurt children, probably is good for them once in a while." They would encounter such situations later in life "and might well begin adjusting to it now. . . . I wish we were placid creatures with neither nerves nor tempers," the down-to-earth Ethel wrote, "but we're not."

As the children matured, Grandmother Derby observed all the milestones. In June 1965, when Sarah Gilmore Williams graduated from the Cathedral School for Girls in Washington, President Lyndon Johnson spoke, and Ethel noted proudly, "My old school you know." For Sarah's wedding in 1974, Ethel made the long trip to the West Coast to be present. She offered advice on the boys' choice of college, their scrapes with the law, and their misgivings over being related to anyone with the name of Roosevelt.

Much of the advice was purely practical, and it came with checks to make things work. In April 1949, when Ethel was offering one of her generous gifts to the Williamses—for new cars and riding lessons or camp for the boys—she insisted her daughter accept the money. "In a few years," she joked, Mike Williams, a lawyer, would be earning much more and "sending us on little trips to Sardinia, or the Tian Shan Mountains . . . and I shall hate to feel that I cannot accept them."

Household help was not as cheap or available in postwar America as Ethel had found it when her own children were young, and she had to accept the fact that the Williamses had to do much of the work themselves. Accustomed to having a cook and the leisure to "dress" for dinner, Ethel struggled to counsel Edith how to manage. In meal planning, she suggested repetition: "Find something one can do, and then repeat." When it came to choosing between reading a book or cleaning the house, the book should win: "I am more than ever convinced that we must concentrate our energies on the things men live by. Just so a house looks neat, and the dirt does not rise up to greet you, I ask no more. Once a week is plenty to clean. With the veriest whisk in between, where dust bothers one."

The same kind of advice was no doubt dispensed to Sarah Alden, but because she always lived much closer to her parents and saw her mother frequently, there are fewer letters available to illustrate. Her older sister's distaste for college may have influenced Sarah Alden because, instead of getting a bachelor's degree, she chose to work as a secretary for New York City councilman Joseph Clark Baldwin. When he moved to Washington as a congressman in 1941, she went, too. Her great-aunt Alice provided her with room and board, a generous gesture to the nineteen-year-old who later described the period as "a great time." The Washington job was brief, however, because when her fiancé, Robert Gannett, a young soldier from Vermont, was scheduled to ship out to fight, they decided to marry before he left.

After the war, when Bob Gannett finished law school and he and Sarah Alden settled in Brattleboro, they saw a great deal of her parents. The Derbys' purchase in 1949 of a simple farmhouse near Cavendish, about forty miles north of Brattleboro, made the visits even easier and more frequent. With his father-in-law, Bob shared an avid interest in fishing, and as long as the older man was able, they indulged in that sport together. Ethel could watch the three Gannett children go through their school graduations and mark important birthdays.

Politics also drew the Gannetts and the Derbys together. After 1952, when Bob Gannett attended his first Republican National Convention as an Eisenhower delegate, he became enthusiastic about the idea of running for office himself. Sarah Alden did not make that meeting because she was seven months pregnant, but she fully supported her husband's decision to combine elective office with his law practice. He served in the Vermont House of Representatives from 1953 to 1961, and then returned to serve in the Vermont State Senate in 1973. An enthusiastic political wife, Sarah Alden sat in on debates "that interested me," she later said, especially on topics such as capital punishment, which both she and Bob vigorously opposed. But she insisted that she never entertained the idea of running for office herself. With her three children and her many community projects, she found herself fully occupied, and in her seventies, she summed it all up as a "wonderful life." She could hardly find adequate words to praise her parents. They had been, she insisted, the most loving parents that anyone could wish for.

The youngest Derby daughter, Judith Quentin, remained the most enigmatic of the three, although relatives insisted that she resembled her mother in both appearance and charm. Born when her parents were still reeling from the death of their son, Judith had trouble finding her niche, and her life followed a tragic pattern similar to that of some of her Roosevelt relatives. Both older girls had known their parents before the trauma of their brother's death, but Judith never did.

Named after her uncle Quentin, Judith had health problems from an early age. When she was only six months old, her mother wrote Kermit that Judith had suddenly turned blue and the baby nurse feared she would die, but then the doctor gave her "adrenalin, and hypodermics and hot mustard baths and just worked over her" until she recovered. The diagnosis—"acute asthmatic bronchitis"—discouraged Ethel because so many of the Roosevelts battled asthma. Theodore had suffered terribly as a child, and everyone in the family knew that Auntie Corinne Robinson sometimes had to excuse herself from her dinner guests to hook up to lung-clearing vapors. Now Ethel despaired that her youngest daughter would be equally disabled, but the first few years were relatively uneventful.

After high school graduation and a year at Bryn Mawr, Judith went to work in Washington at the State Department in a job so secret that she could not discuss it with her parents. The stress related to that work worried her mother, who finally resolved to go down to Washington and look the situation over herself. To her eldest daughter Ethel wrote, "I've had her on my mind and you know how it is when I get one of you on my mind." Judith left that job and took another one with the United Nations in New York.

Her entire family seemed intent on finding Judith a husband. In December 1943, just after her twentieth birthday, her mother lamented the missed opportunities: "I only deplore if she strews broken hearts along the way." Ethel filled in her other daughters on the "unfortunate" young men that Judith had dropped, and she spent hours exploring marriage prospects with Judith. The three of them—Ethel, Edith, and Sarah Alden—exchanged worried letters about each new candidate that Judith brought home, including those who had to be "discarded" in favor of a "new line up."

Judith seemed reluctant to make choices—or perhaps she liked the idea of remaining single a little longer than was common in the family. She took a cross-country train trip in the spring of 1947 to visit Edith's family near Seattle, then returned east contemplating more college courses or some kind of charity work. Judith thrived on outdoor activities, including tennis, and her enthusiasm was contagious. After she got her mother back on the court, long after she had put tennis aside as a "thing of the past," Ethel was delighted to realize that she still enjoyed the game, and she boasted to Edith that she could "still run like a lamp lighter."

In spite of her joy in her daughter's frequent companionship, Ethel did not consider her "settled" until she was married with a family of her own. At the top of her New Year's resolutions in 1948, Ethel listed finding a husband for Judith. At twenty-four, she was practically a confirmed spinster, at least in comparison to the other young women in her family. All the daughters of her mother's female cousins had married before they could vote. Eleanor's Anna, the oldest of them all, married Curtis Dall in 1926 when she was barely twenty. Cousin Corinney's daughter, Sis, also older than any of Ethel's girls, married in 1932, two weeks after she turned twenty. Even Paulina Longworth, who was more than a year younger than Judith, had found a husband by the time she was nineteen, and by 1946 she had a daughter. With both her older sisters and all her female cousins married, Judith looked like the laggard, especially in postwar America where large families and "wives in the kitchen" were held up as the ideal arrangement.

The fact that Ethel persevered as matchmaker seems curious, especially since she had described how her own mother rushed her into marriage before she was ready. The next generation would rewrite the rules, many of the women delaying matrimony or living their lives as single women, but for this generation of cousins, the custom still held. They may have been asserting their own independence and their desire to get homes of their own, as two of them stated, or they may have reasoned that by having their families early, they would have more years later, after the children were grown, to pursue their own interests and travel the world.

Whatever the reason, Judith went along with her mother's plans. By mid-1948, six months after Ethel made her resolution, the engagement was set. Judith had stayed that spring as a house guest with the Ameses, old friends of her parents, giving her the chance to become reacquainted with their son Adelbert III, known as "Del," who was just finishing medical school. The two young people had known each other since childhood, and it did not take them long to decide to marry. By the time Judith's parents returned from a summer vacation through the western states, wedding plans were under way. Dick Derby insisted that Judith's attitude toward Del had always been different from her attitude toward the "also rans" and that in many ways this was a union of the two sets of parents. In a long letter that Dick wrote Edith about the upcoming wedding, he noted that when he and Ethel sat down with the Ameses to talk about how long they had known each other and then about the pleasure of seeing their children "indispensable to one another," they were "almost on the point of tears."

The wedding, first scheduled for September 9, 1948, ran into several obstacles. Andrew Williams, the six-year-old nephew of the bride, had to be hospitalized in Washington State, and not until he improved could his mother make plans to come east for the wedding. Then the bride got mononucleosis, and a new date was set for five weeks later. As if this were not enough to mark the marriage as jinxed, the condition of the bride's grandmother worsened. At eighty-seven, Edith Roosevelt could no longer continue living on her own at Sagamore Hill, and she was moved to the Derbys' for the winter.

By late September, Edith's condxition worsened, and on the thirtieth she died, but Ethel had already decided, once the invitations went out, to proceed with the wedding on October 16—no matter what. If absolutely necessary, some phone calls could be made at the last minute to alter the details. Ethel was very clear that Judith's interests came first. "I feel so strongly that Judith is starting out, and that she is the one to think of," Ethel wrote Edith. Such a view was completely in tune with the time-honored family dictum, "Live for the living and not the dead," and that is what they did.

On the financial side, it was clear that both families would have to help out the young couple. Del Ames had just started his medical residency the previous summer, and the $40 a month that he earned could hardly support a family. Edith Williams, who had been receiving a regular monthly check from her mother, offered to forgo it temporarily in favor of Judith, but her mother insisted that was not necessary. Judith would get $75 per month from her mother.

As it turned out, money was the least of the newlyweds' problems. Within six months Del was hospitalized with tuberculosis, and in the summer of 1949, accompanied by his pregnant wife, he went to the sanitarium at Saranac Lake, New York, to recuperate. By September 1950 his X rays showed that he had made a complete recovery, and he returned to a medical career that led to research and teaching at Harvard Medical School. With a son born in November 1949 and a daughter born two years later, the young Ames family might have matched the stability of Judith's sisters, but Ethel still worried. She referred to her youngest daughter as "little Judith," conveying a kind of protectiveness that she never showed toward the other two. She counseled all her daughters to keep some time strictly for themselves, untouched by family duties, but between her and Judith there was a special pledge—that neither of them would let others boss them around.

Judith's problems were far bigger than those of an ordinary harried mother of young children. Her mother thought she detected signs of recurring mononucleosis in 1954, and immediately after giving birth to a healthy son in March 1955, Judith became ill with pneumonia. Ethel thought money might help. She had been generous with all three daughters, passing out a total of nearly $30,000 by 1955, but the amounts had not been equal. Edith had received more than twice what her sisters got, and Ethel now decided to even up the accounts.

But money could no more help Judith's real problems than it had helped her cousins Hall Roosevelt and Monroe Robinson or her uncle Kermit. For the rest of her life she battled a combination of physical and mental complaints. Alcoholism played a part, but who could say whether it developed out of other weaknesses or was itself the cause of them? In December 1956, Ethel thought that Judith looked "fairly well but [is] not really well or strong." Struggling to understand herself, Judith had decided, according to Ethel, "that for some reason she must give in to this and not fight as is our instinct." In the summer of 1957 she managed to give up smoking for several weeks, but by October, her mother noted, Judith was "smoking again. . . . I am sad and discouraged and worried."

Like her father decades earlier, Judith could not throw off the feeling that life held little for her. But unlike him, she had not lost a child and could not point to any one event as a cause for her feelings. Her mother, who had witnessed years of her husband's depression, kept hoping that time would make a difference as it had for him. But time only seemed to make things worse for Judith. The old asthma attacks returned, and somehow it seemed easier to avoid seeing her parents than to make the four-hour drive to Long Island or Vermont, depending on the season.

The family began to divide on the best approach to Judith's recovery. Her husband, the Harvard professor of medicine, favored hands-off and insisted that she had to decide to change—no one else could do it for her. Ethel concentrated on boosting her confidence by telling her how well she was managing "everyone, husband, doctors and all." When Judith tried to reassure her parents that she was actually improving, her mother took heart, writing Edith in Seattle, "It shows how she has been fighting this thing."

The "thing" that no one wanted to name was alcoholism. In early July 1959, Judith checked in to Silver Hill, an exclusive clinic in New Canaan, Connecticut, famous for treating wealthy alcoholics. One doctor suggested it might be a "strange metabolic thing which will eventually disappear," and another mentioned allergies. Ethel continued to hope that the problem was "physical," just as she had hoped with her husband, and she retained her sense of humor. In the very same letter that detailed Judith's problems, Ethel joked that Archie's daughter, Nancy Jackson, had just given birth to a fifth daughter, "as yet unnamed." The first four girls were Miranda, Melissa, Melanie, and Melinda, and someone had suggested for this one "Mercy."

As for Judith, Ethel searched her own memories for some clue about how she might have contributed to her daughter's difficulties. Judith had insisted that her two older sisters had "freed" themselves from their mother far sooner than she had, and Ethel mused, "It's hard for a mother to realize that she either asks, or just plain *Is* too much for a growing child." Judith complained that Ethel had over-protected her children, but Ethel failed to see it and noted that she felt as though she "always leaned heavily on any child whose shoulder was available and also asked advice."

⁂

While Ethel worried about Judith, she also had a sick husband to care for. Dick Derby had gradually reduced his medical practice and finally retired completely in the late 1950s. But like most people deeply involved in their work, he found it difficult to give it up. Ethel noted a restlessness about him, and she encouraged him to find other interests, but, nearing eighty, that was not easy. His health began to worsen, and by January 1959 he was clearly ill. Always a good letter writer, he stopped corresponding with his daughter in Seattle, and he became more and more withdrawn. By Christmas 1961, when Edith came east for the holidays, he was beginning to faint frequently.

One of the brighter spots in Ethel's life was travel—something she continued to do even as her husband became more frail. She often invited one of her daughters to join her or sometimes she went with a friend, leaving Dick in a hospital or under the care of the trusted housekeeper, Clara. In October 1961 she reported to Edith that she had her itinerary for the London trip—including a train ride through the countryside. She continued to attend "exhibitions and the museums and the very best plays and movies." As she wrote to Edith: "These are the things I love to do."

Several years into his retirement, in April 1962, his hospital, renamed Community Hospital, honored Dr. Derby by naming a new laboratory for him. Since he was too ill to attend the dedication, Ethel went in his stead. Always able to find the bright spot in the most depressing picture, she observed that people could not have "said all those nice things about him had he been present."

That summer Ethel moved her household to Vermont for the summer months as she always did. By October, when she prepared to transfer back to Long Island, she craved a few days alone. Relieved that Clara could accompany Dick while she remained behind to pack up, "oblivious to time," Ethel wrote Edith that the prospect reminded her of something Edna St. Vincent Millay once wrote about how nice it was to meander peacefully and slowly in one's own rhythm after the men had left, taking all their troubles with them.

In March 1963, when Edith called her mother on the anniversary of little Richard Derby's birthday, always a difficult time for Ethel, she found her father not at all well. He was trying a new medication, but Ethel had failed to see any improvement. The strain of caring for him at home was enormous, but Ethel would not hear of doing it any other way. She wrote her daughter that she was "learning to live with this and to accept it. This is my precious duty and responsibility. I turn to you in all crises. But the road is mine." Then she added that she looked forward to an upcoming visit from her daughter "more than I can say."

With spring, the Derbys returned to Vermont, and Ethel's thoughts turned to the prospect that she would have to live alone: "I cannot even imagine what life would be like without every waking moment turning to Father. But it will be like a child learning to walk, and it's a new turn of the road." As she looked toward the upcoming summer and what plans she might make, she wrote, "There is always the hope that F[ather] may be much better. Or," she added with chilling realism, "not as well."

By June it was clear that the latter prediction would prove the accurate one. Edith Williams came east to be with her parents, and on June 5, Dick Derby had a severe stroke and was taken to a hospital in Brattleboro, where he remained until his death on July 21. Ethel's sister Alice had been widowed more than forty years earlier, and cousins Eleanor and Corinney had both lost their husbands as well. Now it was Ethel's turn. Wrestling with questions about her husband's estate, she observed that after fifty years of marriage, she never thought of possessions as being anything but joint: "[W]e were so removed from 'mine' and 'thine.'" Consoling herself that "those years of suffering and the terrible terrible last months are over," she was reminded of a widowed friend who had once advised Ethel "'never to beguile sorrow,'" but to "'try and master it'" and "'peradventure in time, we shall be good friends with sorrow and death and dwell together.'"

Dick's regard for his wife had always been clear, and several years after his death when Ethel was going through some papers of his, she found a note written long before about how he was always so "proud" of her and how, whenever they met somewhere, he had a "little jumpy feeling of how nice" it was to be married to her. But from her side, she always felt she had failed him by not giving him another son. He was, she mused, "so especially a man's man. . . . How many things he would have shared with Richard which we [as wife and daughters] could not give him. . . . And he never showed it."

All through Dick Derby's final illness, Judith continued to battle her own demons. A full fifty years younger than her father, she should have been at the peak of health and vitality, but she looked frail and ill. Ethel worried that Del Ames failed to realize "how weak she is.... Judith is such a gentle person ... our darling Judith." Ethel went to the Ames home in Cambridge just weeks after her husband's death and found Judith "miserable." After treatment for a lung ailment, she seemed to improve, and by mid-September 1963 her mother was writing that Judith looked better than at any time in recent years. A month later there was a relapse, and it was "last summer all over again."

The remainder of Judith's life piled one calamity on top of another. She quit smoking again, but then gained enough weight to make her feel uncomfortable with her body. Her teenage children rebelled in the style of many of their contemporaries in the 1960s, and Del Ames's permissive approach confused Ethel, who much preferred her own mother's "firm" stand on discipline. After Judith was stopped by the police for weaving in traffic, she lost her driver's license, causing Ethel to suggest Alcoholics Anonymous as a solution for her daughter, who seemed "afraid or too proud to acknowledge the sin or the problem and conquer it."

Throughout the 1960s, Judith found some satisfaction in her volunteer work at a mental health center in Concord, Massachusetts. Her curious mind and quirky sense of humor helped her through some of the bad times, and after one visit with her, her mother remarked: "There is no one who reads funny things aloud as she does." Mother and daughter ranged over a wide variety of subjects, from poetry to religion to cybernetics, which Ethel admitted she found confusing.

These were the rare bright spots in an otherwise dismal life, soon to be rendered more dismal by fatal illness. By September 1970, Judith was back at Silver Hill, where she was treated intermittently over the next eighteen months. After being diagnosed with cancer, she was hospitalized at Massachusetts General Hospital in Boston, where she began a series of treatments. Her mental problems became impossible to separate from the physical, as doctors speculated on some previous illness or damage that might be implicated in her condition. By April 1972, Ethel reported that Sarah Alden saw Judith as largely cut off from the world, in "a deep [depression, and] she does not want or is unable to communicate."

Ethel refused to accept what seemed clear to almost everyone else, and when friends inquired about Judith, she brushed off their queries with a simple "improving." For a while it did seem as though there was a change for the better. Judith talked about wanting to take a college course or sign up to work for Common Cause. But that winter saw her growing steadily worse, and by the spring she was more confused and talked of dying. When Sarah Alden visited her in March 1973, she reported to her mother that Judith talked "incessantly of suicide, its different aspects . . . and would wake from sleep crying." Ethel insisted that the medicines prescribed for her had taken a toll—"This is not our Judith."

As Judith's death became more imminent, Ethel watched in despair. In July she wrote Edith that the patient "lives in a timeless world now." She could no longer read, and the thought of losing that special pleasure made Ethel cry. Always so precise about so many things, the eighty-two-year-old Ethel herself began to lose track of days and could not even be sure of the date when she sat down to write a letter. Even the prospect of corresponding daunted her: "How can one put into words or even into thought the place where Judith is going now." Ethel preferred thinking of the time after death "as Love and Peace and fulfillment," but she could not console herself that Judith's life had been easy or joyful: "Sometimes that hurts the most of all, that she has had such hard times . . . darling Judith." Ethel tried to marshal her strength and go visit Judith in August 1973, but she was advised to wait.

A month later, on September 26, 1973, Judith Quentin Derby Ames died in Concord, Massachusetts, after what the newspaper obituary, in classic understatement, called a "long illness." Just months short of her fiftieth birthday, she left three children, ages eighteen to twenty-four. Ethel began to have nightmares in which her sick daughter played a central part, and she admitted to Edith "how strange that was." She complained that the Williams children had too much reserve to even mention their aunt's death—a reserve that Ethel proudly noted she did not share. To Edith she wrote, "[T]alking about reserve . . . many people have it, and my family did not and I am thankful that neither you nor I have it. But your boys have, for neither has mentioned Judith to me."

Christmas that year held little joy. In late December, Ethel explained that she had found it hard to be the only one "of all the family who had [once] been there, at the Christmas Carol service."

She took some solace in hearing from Sarah Alden that she had felt it necessary to resort to her bedroom to "sob and weep. That comforted me."

⟋⟋⟋

After Theodore's death, Edith Roosevelt had written about setting out to see "the wide world," and throughout her life her daughter showed the same zest for trading the comforts of a familiar home for the adventure of being on the road. Edith and Sarah Alden later recalled that Ethel was indomitable, even in her mid-seventies, reading about some exotic place and then making up her mind to go there. An article in *The Saturday Review of Literature* might carry a headline such as "How would you like to go to Timbuktoo on Friday?" and Ethel rushed to reply in the affirmative. At the Mayan ruins of Machu Picchu in Peru, she encountered a friend of her grandson's, trekking the same altitudes as she was. In the mid-1960s, when Ethel stayed on a houseboat with Sarah Alden and Edith in Kashmir, the daughters decided to give her a rest and go on a fishing expedition of their own. They returned that evening to hear that her day was far more adventurous than theirs. A boatman described how Ethel asked to be taken to the other side of the lake. From there she climbed to the top of the mountain "all by herself" although it was "very steep." She negotiated the most difficult parts by asking some English boys that she met along the way to give her a boost. Then, at the end of her hike, she had to find her way back to the houseboat on her own. Such escapades were common for her brothers in their youth—and even for her father in his fifties—but Ethel did some of her most exciting travel in the last decades of her life.

Ethel would not have been a Roosevelt if she had not found time to reach out and help her community. She abhorred the idea of publicity surrounding such efforts, just as she had once abhorred being called the "belle of the White House," and she could not entirely separate in her own mind Cousin Eleanor's many good works from the gain she received for doing them. After observing Eleanor conduct a meeting of the Human Rights Commission at the United Nations in April 1950, Ethel wrote her daughter, "Cousin Eleanor presided with dignity, decision, and charm." But when Ethel mentioned to her companion how much she admired Eleanor's "endless patience and devoted labours," the friend had "sniffed and said that she got $12,000 a year, her luxurious quarters, and living conditions, and all traveling expenses paid so not to be too admiring." In relaying her friend's assessment without disagreeing with it, Ethel seemed to conclude that the friend had a point.

Preferring a lower profile than Eleanor's, Ethel worked on a more local level, involving herself in a variety of community service projects near Oyster Bay. She had earned her ribbon for twenty-five years of work with the Red Cross in 1950, but she was in Boston at the time of the ceremony and seemed glad to have missed it. "Don't hold with those things," she explained to Edith, but she held with the hard work and continued it for the rest of her life.

Whether their southern grandmother entered into their feelings or not, both Eleanor and Ethel worked determinedly for civil rights, but on very different levels. Eleanor spoke at national events and her photograph was on the front pages, while Ethel endorsed integration more quietly but no less firmly. At the time of the *Brown* v. *Board of Education* decision by the Supreme Court in 1954, ordering the integration of public schools, Ethel was ecstatic. "Wasn't it exciting about the Non Segregation bill going through the Supreme Court," she wrote Edith. "I realize well how difficult it is going to be for many places in the South, but am sure it was right."

Given the chance, she spoke out, even if it meant clashing with Archie. When the board of the Theodore Roosevelt Association considered sending $1,000 to the Southern Christian Leadership Conference as a memorial to the recently assassinated Reverend Martin Luther King, Jr., two board members objected. Ethel favored the action and refused to budge, writing her daughter, "I thought of all the trouble I would have with Uncle A[rchie]. But only for a moment because I shall speak firmly back to him."

Too sophisticated to believe that all problems of inequality could be easily solved, Ethel turned her attention to matters closer to home, inequities that she might correct. When she suspected that African Americans were being discriminated against "by charging them excessive rents," she questioned how to act: "Should I struggle?" Then, in tempered, analytic family fashion, she decided that "much ground work" needed to be done before she could expect

Corinne (known to her family as Corinney) Robinson married Connecticut farmer and politician Joseph Alsop in 1909. She had met him through her aunt Bamie. Here, the four young Alsops—from left, John, Stewart, Corinne (called Sis), and Joe—line up for a photo in a pose that had become a family tradition.

*Not long before her three sons left for World War II, Corinne Alsop (seated)
posed at Woodford Farm with her husband, Joe, and their children: (left to
right, standing) John, Corinne, Stewart, and Joe.*

*Corinne Robinson Alsop achieved a considerable reputation as a public
speaker and Republican legislator and leader in Connecticut before her sons
Joe and Stewart Alsop achieved national fame as political commentators.*

Ethel Roosevelt (center) lived in the White House for nearly eight years, leaving in 1909 just before she turned 18. From left, Ted Jr., Archie, Theodore, Ethel, Edith, Quentin, and Kermit.

Twenty-six-year-old Ethel Derby, mother of two small children, saw her husband, Dr. Richard Derby, off to France in 1917. Three years earlier she had accompanied him to Paris, where she assisted him in his work treating the war wounded.

During the last of the Derby family's three long stays in Europe, Ethel (center) posed with her husband and their daughters, Sarah Alden (left), Edith (right), and Judith Quentin (front), in Florence, Italy.

When Ethel Derby (center in hat) toured Theodore Roosevelt National Park in the North Dakota Badlands in 1954, she was accompanied by her husband (standing behind her), two of their daughters, Edith Williams (left) and Sarah Alden Gannett (center), and four grandchildren.

MISS ALICE ROOSEVELT

Postcards such as these, mailed around the time of Alice Roosevelt's marriage to Nicholas Longworth in 1906, illustrate her "Princess Alice" status. The one reads: "Friend, Are you the next in line?"

In 1961, when Alice Longworth attended the International Horse Show with President Kennedy and the First Lady, she had been a Washington fixture for more than sixty years and was sometimes referred to as "the OTHER Washington Monument."

Donald Graham (right) welcomes Alice Longworth and her cousin, colum-nist Joe Alsop, to a garden party given by his mother, Katharine Graham.

any big changes. Quietly, effectively, she did her part. In 1968 when many of her neighbors opposed the building of low-income housing in their town, she called her friends together and changed some minds. According to the local housing authority chairman, she "made it possible for low-income housing to be built in Oyster Bay."

Ethel liked to quote her father, who once said that the United States would never demonstrate itself to be a "democracy . . . until we will have had both a Negro and Jewish president," but she shuddered to think of how far Archie had moved from such a view. She wrote to her daughter about the book she had heard he was putting together: "You will not find that in it."

Ethel approached her final years with incredible zest. When someone asked her to host the Tanzanian ambassador for a weekend at her home in Oyster Bay, she responded, "Yes, of course." In 1968 she established a scholarship at Harvard in honor of her husband, and when the first student winner was selected, she insisted on meeting him personally. Afterward she delivered the supreme compliment: both Dick Derby and her father would have liked him. More popular as a speaker than Archie, Ethel was called on often to address one group or another on her father's legacy. "Auntie Ethel used to give a good speech," her grandniece Susan Roosevelt Weld insisted, and she seemed to take her many public appearances in stride.

The new drug culture mystified Ethel, but instead of turning her back on it, she tried to comprehend its attractions. In early 1969 she considered the new popularity of marijuana and decided it presented no problem because it was not addictive, though she admitted that the "phantasies or dream visions were not beneficial." The big drawback "was the people it brought you in touch with."

Of the four cousins, Ethel was the most quietly involved in politics. Every American knew about Eleanor's work, and most of them knew that Alice gathered together the nation's most powerful men and women in her salon in Washington. Some of them knew about Corinney Alsop, whose reputation reached beyond Connecticut. Ethel, a close friend of Leonard Hall, leader of the national Republican Party, kept abreast of what was happening in the party, but she showed no desire to see her name in headlines. While daughter Edith served as Republican committeewoman in the State of Washington and spoke at the 1960 national convention, following in the footsteps of

Corinne Robinson and Corinne Alsop, Ethel was only a proud onlooker. In 1964, after Leonard Hall wrote her an interesting evaluation of the party's candidates and asked her to destroy the letter, Ethel seemed relieved that she remained on the sidelines. As for the upcoming convention, she would be glad to watch it on television.

Ethel had been around campaigns too long to ignore the presidential candidates of both parties, and she had firm opinions about them all. In 1972 she judged Richard Nixon's acceptance speech "lousy" and the Democratic nominee, George McGovern, a disappointment: "I thought he would be better than he is." Nixon was "no hero of mine," she told Edith, but he was "dignified," and that counted for something. After Nixon's reelection by a landslide, she became more and more interested in how his mind worked. Her own eight years in the White House as a young girl had convinced her of the weight of the presidency on any one human being, and she recognized that the job had become much more onerous by the 1970s. Her father had never had to consider dropping bombs on other nations, but now that method of ending the Vietnam War was gaining favor. Ethel looked to the public to object: "If [the President] renews the bombing I think the country will protest." She knew that Nixon struggled with feelings of personal isolation in the Oval Office. Her cousin Stewart Alsop told her that he had once discussed this very problem with Nixon, who insisted that he felt there was no one in whom he could confide. When Stewart suggested that he surely could talk with his wife, Richard Nixon persisted, "No, not to her either." It all added up to quite a different presidency than the one Ethel had known as a young girl.

Besides her interests in politics, travel, and community service, Ethel showed one other important family trait—an almost foolhardy disregard for pain. One of her relatives recalled how a car door slammed on her hand as she was on the way to a political meeting. Instead of admitting what had happened, she concealed it so that none of those with her had any idea she had been injured. She was, after all, the daughter of Theodore Roosevelt, who insisted on giving an hour-long speech after he was shot in the 1912 presidential campaign. It was almost a family credo that only sissies cried.

By the fall of 1977 it was clear that Ethel was losing some of her famous vitality. The Roosevelt legacy did not include exceptional longevity, and although this was particularly true for the men, few of the women before Ethel's generation survived into their seventies. Mittie died at forty-eight, her sister Anna at sixty. Neither Bamie nor Corinne made it to eighty. But like the population in general, members of this family were living longer. Eleanor died in 1962 at seventy-eight; Corinney, in 1971 at eighty-four. Ethel outdid both of them, but by her eighty-sixth birthday in the summer of 1977, she seemed to be fading out of life.

That November she received a very special visit. Susan Roosevelt Weld, wife of William Weld and granddaughter of Ethel's brother Ted, came to Oyster Bay with her newborn daughter. Susan had grown up there, along with her two sisters, after their widowed mother moved in with Ted's wife in the late forties. Susan had developed a great admiration for Ethel, and she wanted her first daughter to be named Ethel, though it was, she admitted, "very unfashionable" at the time. So there would be no misunderstanding, the child was "Ethel Derby Weld." Even if she had wanted to, the little girl could hardly ignore the origin of her name: the Weld house was "studded" with references to Ethel Derby, according to Susan Weld, and the girl was "mainlined with Auntie Ethel." It all seemed very appropriate because she was "the dominant force in all our lives."

Toward the end of 1977, Ethel's normally chatty letters to Edith got shorter and the writing shaky. In November she began using postcards to write just a few words, and the last one, written on November 30 and ending "So Bed time," is nearly illegible. On December 10 she died. Of the four cousins, only Alice survived—still going strong at ninety-three.

This 1904 postcard of Alice shows a glamorous twenty-year-old who had already made headlines for her rebellious ways.

CHAPTER EIGHT

ALICE ROOSEVELT LONGWORTH

(1884–1980)

JUST BEFORE CHRISTMAS IN 1902, a New York newspaper, *The American*, ran a long article on "The Roosevelt Sextette" of debutantes. "It is a Roosevelt year in society," the gushy piece began, when six "pretty lucky maidens" take "American society by storm . . . every one of them, wealthy and witty and happy to be presented to society's smartest set." Each one of the young women had individual charms, but in a group they were impressive: "all jolly good chums and they have a little clannish way all their own of keeping together at dances and teas as much as possible."

Only two of the sextette came from Mittie's line: Alice and Eleanor. The other two female cousins on that side of the family would have to wait for their entrance into society: Corinney was only sixteen and still attending school in England, and Ethel had not yet celebrated her twelfth birthday.

In 1902 it was Helen Roosevelt, the only daughter of Franklin's half-brother, Rosy, and the same young woman that Bamie had looked after, who stood out as "probably the most interesting of the Roosevelt debutantes." Described as an "heiress . . . worth more than one million dollars," she came by most of her money through her mother's family, the Astors. This "healthy happy outdoor girl" was out of the running for suitors, however. She had already paired off with her distant cousin Theodore Douglas Robinson, Corinne's eldest son, and it was assumed that they would soon marry.

Close behind Helen, according to *The American*, came "Princess Alice." Her family had lived in the White House for little more than a year, but she had already attracted notice as someone "born to lead," a characteristic the newspaper traced to her father. Other talents included an "artistic" flair, and the ability to "ride, drive, shoot, play golf and tennis and manage her own automobile . . . swim like a duck and walk to keep up with her father."

Behind these two headline grabbers the other four Roosevelt debutantes merited little attention. Three of them—Dorothy Quincy Roosevelt, Elfrieda Lowell Roosevelt, and Christine Kean Roosevelt—received brief but kind coverage, and then at the end came Eleanor. Dismissed as the "niece of the President" who still made her home with her maternal grandmother, she was summed up in the single innocuous adjective, "charming."

With time this evaluation of the young Roosevelts would be proven very wrong. Helen, dubbed "the most interesting," would virtually disappear from history, while Eleanor and Alice made headlines. With her tireless efforts for human rights and her attempts to make government more responsive to people's needs, Eleanor eventually helped change ideas about what the nation could be. But Alice's fame came earlier. As women all over America chose "Alice blue" as their favorite color, her name became a household word, and one of her biographers called her the "first female American celebrity of the twentieth century." She became a fixture at White House events, regardless of the President's party affiliation, and by her own calculation averaged three White House dinners a year for more than sixty years.

What often got lost in the coverage of Eleanor and Alice was their connection to their aunts, Bamie and Corinne. In their phenomenal energy (requiring only a few hours of sleep each night) and their keen intelligence (which permitted them to read over a wide range and remember what they read), both Eleanor and Alice—as well as their younger cousins, Corinney and Ethel—resembled their aunts.

All the women mixed politics with parenting in a seamless day—as though a child's cough deserved no more, nor any less, attention than a Senate debate. Alice outlived all the cousins, and in her own unique style she made a reputation that was solely hers. Motherless as an infant, she struggled to assert herself as a rebellious teenager, and did not become a mother herself until the age of forty-one. In her many meetings with presidents and other powerful people, she saw no reason to camouflage her own strong views. Yet when she died in 1980, it was difficult to list exactly what she had done to merit the attention she received.

Alice was most famous for her caustic wit, and her comments became legend. She wrote off Republican presidential candidate Thomas Dewey as resembling the little man on the wedding cake. His predecessor Wendell Willkie, who strove for the "common man" image, fell far short, according to Alice, who mocked him as someone who "sprang from the grass roots of American country clubs." She quipped that Calvin Coolidge looked as if he had been weaned on a pickle. Although she later insisted that she had not invented all these phrases but merely gave them "currency," they are exactly the kind of observations for which she gained fame.

Big names never intimidated Alice. At the peak of his power, Senator Joseph McCarthy sidled up to her at a dinner party, put his arm around her, and announced, "I'm going to call you Alice." "No," she corrected him. "You are NOT going to call me Alice. The truckman, the trashman, and the policeman on the block may call me Alice but you may not." With some people she preferred to keep her distance, and in this case her method worked. She never saw the Wisconsin senator again.

When riled up or siding with the underdog, this aristocratic matron could match epithets with anyone on the street, having learned from Auntie Bye how to skewer the most pompous. Once, toward the end of her life, while Alice's African-American chauffeur was driving her to an appointment in New York City, he angered a taxicab driver by pulling in front of him. The latter caught up, rolled down his window, and shouted, "What do you think you're doing, you black bastard?" The chauffeur, who had been driving Mrs. Longworth for years and had enough experience with such comments to know the wisdom of ignoring them, kept his eyes straight ahead and his mouth shut. But not Alice. She rolled down her window and from the backseat shot back: "He's driving me to my destination, you white son-of-a-bitch."

I

No one could have predicted such a strong character when Alice entered the world as her mother and grandmother exited it in February 1884. Her first three and a half years were spent with Bamie, while her father played a very small role in her upbringing. He sent "many kisses" from his ranch in the Dakotas, but they were paper kisses that delivered little comfort. Alice's maternal grandparents, the Lees, took her for weeks at a time at their home just outside Boston, where they let her do just as she pleased. She later recalled that she jumped on the sofa in her shoes and then gleefully observed their tight-lipped glances as they could not bring themselves to reprimand the only offspring of their dead daughter. The child may have felt a little uncomfortable, realizing that the Lees inevitably connected her to her mother. She later ridiculed them as lacking in culture, a judgment that Auntie Corinne considered unfair. In comparing the Lees and the Roosevelts, Corinne found both families enjoyed their share of fun and social activities, but she conceded the Roosevelts held a slight advantage in the number of books owned.

Bamie's Manhattan house, where Alice spent most of her first years, had more than books—it offered both solace and sophistication, and Alice later recalled that people came calling in "droves." Bamie's tall butler, Chamberlain, and the caliber of dining both impressed Alice, who later described the food as "by far the best in [the] family." After Alice married, she patterned her own elegant tea hours on Bamie's. The brew had to be Earl Grey from a particular shop in London, and she poured it into delicate porcelain cups or tall glasses with silver holders, Russian style. More than one guest commented on Alice's skill at buttering bread across the top and then slicing it paper thin, but few knew she had learned that trick from Bamie. As Alice grew up, she matched her aunt's intellectual curiosity and her delight in witty conversation, but hard as she tried, she admitted she could never duplicate Bamie's distinctive handwriting.

Between aunt and niece there developed a deep bond that went beyond books and tea rituals. Alice could be scathing about nearly anyone when the mood struck her, but no one remembered her saying anything even mildly critical of Auntie Bye. Near the end of her life Alice told her biographer-friend Michael Teague that Bye had been the "single most important influence" on her childhood. Bamie had gone on record years earlier with similarly warm sentiments about Alice.

The change from Bamie's house to Edith's in 1887 was a big one for a young child, and it made a permanent impression. Bamie had managed Theodore's Oyster Bay house for him before his remarriage, and Alice remembered it as a fun-filled place with many exciting visitors. Under Edith's supervision the mood changed; the house became tightly run, on a careful budget, and with many rules.

Within a few months of taking Alice to live with them, Theodore and Edith had a son of their own, Ted. The proud father insisted that Alice delighted in having a new brother and joined in caring for him, but sharing center stage was a new experience. Edith soon became pregnant again, miscarried, then gave birth to Kermit. In short order, Alice saw a drop in her status from reigning princess at Bamie's to one of a flock of three at Sagamore Hill. Ted quickly picked up the fact that her place in the family did not quite equal his, and in his childish attempt to set her apart, he settled on a graphic image. As Edith breast-fed Kermit, a precocious two-year-old Ted taunted Alice: "Sissy had a sweat nurse."

Not surprisingly, Alice welcomed visits from other relatives. Aunt Anna Gracie and her husband, who lived nearby, came often to Sagamore Hill. With Cousin Eleanor, whose parents had just built a new house not far away from Oyster Bay, Alice could exchange frequent visits. After Aunt Corinne had her daughter, Corinney, in 1886, the girl cousins numbered three, and for a short while they formed a jolly coterie. With their parents or their nurses, they partied and played together, unaware of how the years ahead would draw them into opposing camps.

Most of Alice's time was spent in a household that was quickly growing. Ethel was born in 1891, and Archie in 1894. Had she been a completely healthy child, Alice might have forged her own niche in this sizable clan much earlier, but the problem with her foot and leg held her back. As an adult she would insist that she had had polio, but Edith's letters give a different account of why Alice started wearing a heavy metal brace during the winter she turned nine. It was "nothing serious," Edith wrote her sister, and she thought Alice rather enjoyed the attention she received from the other children because of the brace. Alice remembered it differently. She hated the brace and once told a friend that only enormous willpower prevented her from walking with a limp.

By the time she was wearing the brace, Alice could no longer hope to find quick refuge at Bamie's because she lived an ocean away, engrossed in her own new life in London. After her move there in late 1893, Bamie communicated mostly by letter and could provide little comfort when Alice struggled to establish her place in the family. Bamie may have found herself a bit out of touch with how preteens thought and what they wanted. For Christmas she sent identical sets of Shakespeare to Eleanor and Alice, and the restraint in Alice's thank-you note suggests she was not thrilled with the selection.

Alice's relationship with her stepmother was complicated. Edith struggled to do right by all her children, including Alice, but something seemed to be missing. Alice later suggested that in spite of the "enormous effort" her stepmother made with her, "I think she was bored by doing so." Eventually, the two became "very good friends" anyway, in Alice's opinion, because they shared New England roots. They laughed at the same things and made the same wry comments about others. Ethel Derby once remarked on how much Alice resembled her stepmother, "whom she accepts," Ethel wrote, "as her own."

Alice had an even more complicated relationship with her father. Stung by what she perceived as a lack of interest in her and bewildered by the fact that he never mentioned her mother's name in her presence, Alice insisted that she had "great affection for him but tended to worship from afar." But, she said, he felt "guilty" about her because she reminded him of his first wife and the fact that he had remarried after her death rather than remaining dedicated to her memory. Alice also speculated that he considered her a burden on Edith, who, Alice felt, saw the stepdaughter as living evidence that she was second choice. For an insecure little girl who understood that Edith's "birth children" held some kind of advantage over her, Theodore's reticence was more than puzzling—it was infuriating. Later, Alice mused: "The curious thing is that he never seemed to realize that I was perfectly aware of it and developing a resentment."

Theodore fed her anger with his exhortations about physical feats. Ever the taskmaster about challenging exercises, he seemed oblivious to the fact that she detested them. Swimming did not come easy for her, but her father would egg her on, no matter how cold the water or how high the jump. "Dive, Alice, now dive" still rang in her ears long after he was dead. To her, his insistence that she attempt what frightened her felt like persecution.

Between the ages of ten and fourteen Alice learned that the same headstrong determination that she admired in Auntie Bye would help her get what she wanted. When time came for her to enroll at Miss Spence's boarding school in New York City, Alice rebelled, and, after her loud sobs and verbal outbursts, the idea was dropped, leaving her to continue lessons with a governess at home. Much of her education came from perusing the family library, where she had full freedom to choose whatever book caught her fancy. Her sex education came from literature, she maintained, and from watching her pets. But when she tried to share some of that knowledge with Eleanor, the latter recoiled in horror and insisted that Alice was "blasphemous" in her interpretation of the biblical verb "begat." The contrast between the curious, rebellious Alice and the more straitlaced Eleanor had already become clear, but it would play itself out in curious ways.

Soon after Bamie moved back to the United States in 1897, Theodore and Edith began to recognize that they could no longer manage thirteen-year-old Alice. In the spring of 1898, as a weak Edith recovered from surgery and a patriotic Theodore prepared to lead his Rough Riders in Cuba, they decided to split up their five children temporarily. The three youngest could be managed by their nurses, but Alice was, according to Theodore, "running riot" with her young friends. Even though Bamie was several months pregnant, she agreed to take Alice and Ted into her home in New York.

The new environment resulted in immediate change for the better. Alice's attitude improved so much that her surprised father offered to ship her piano and bicycle to her. She proved a "good letter writer," according to Theodore, and phrased reports that were both "interesting and amusing." Bamie tried to assure her brother that Alice's unruliness was merely a phase and that her feelings for the family remained strong—a judgment that Theodore wanted to accept. He wrote his sister that he agreed with her that Alice "really does love Edith and the children and me" but that she had been led astray by her mischievous young friends who had "driven everything else out of her head."

The plaudits were not permanent. Alice soon had a much larger arena in which to perform. Almost as soon as Theodore returned in triumph from Cuba, he was elected governor of New York State, and in September 1901 he became President of the United States— only six months after being sworn in as vice president. Suddenly his entire family stood exposed in the nation's limelight, and for teenager Alice, still trying to figure out who she was, the timing could not have been worse. She thrived on attention and resented her father's advice to keep a more reserved distance from photographers and fans. When she waved exuberantly to friends at his inauguration, he chided her, "But this is MY inauguration," and she was left to conclude that he wanted to relegate her to the background.

By the time of her debut in 1902, Alice made very clear that she did not intend being corseted—not by her parents or by attitudes about how young women should behave. She found her own way to shock, mixing rebellious behavior with disdain and boredom, so that nothing seemed worthy of her serious attention. Showing only contempt for most of the young men whose names filled her dance card, she later pointed out that in those pre-deodorant days, their body odors could be very strong. She preferred older men, a propensity she explained as "a father complex coming out, presumably. I didn't particularly like boys." Theodore chastised her for "gallivanting with society" and not making the kind of serious friends that Eleanor had, but Alice reminded him that she had other models: "Auntie Bye wasn't like that at all. She had a tremendously good time with everyone. So did Auntie Corinne."

Theodore's commands carried little weight. When he decreed that no daughter of his would smoke under his roof, Alice climbed up to the White House roof and puffed away. The automobile was then a daring new mode of transportation, and most women who drove stuck to the "electric," which was cleaner, quieter, and slower than the gasoline "machine." But Alice liked to speed, and with a woman friend she made headlines by driving from Newport to Boston, covering the distance in six hours with only one stop. The term "jet set" had not yet been invented, but Alice certainly headed the equivalent of her time. Even Ethel, the normally patient little sister, found some of this behavior baffling, and when Alice installed "the latest fad," a telephone, in her bedroom, Ethel complained to Kermit, "She locks all her doors and there telephones for years."

Alice seemed unsure as to how to direct the intelligence and energy that came with the family name. She detested "do-gooders" but enjoyed the limelight, and she eventually shaped a special niche for herself. But it took time to carve out that role, and Edith wrote to family friend Cecil Spring-Rice that, at eighteen, Alice had "a remarkably steady head though in some ways [is] very child like." Many years later, historian Stacy Cordery made a similar point, concluding that in her youth, Alice chased after an elusive goal, "somewhere between Auntie Bye's politically popular salon" and Grace Vanderbilt's "carefree, footloose, cosmopolitan and unimaginably wealthy life."

More than one of her relatives objected to Alice's youthful shenanigans. In June 1903, when she was planning to visit Auntie Bye in Farmington, the older woman laid down some rules. She would be delighted to see her niece, she wrote, and to welcome the girl's young friends, but Alice had to look after her own guests and "conform to the life and rules of my home." Bamie disliked taking such a stern tone, but guided by past experience, she decided it was wise to be clear. On a previous visit, nineteen-year-old Alice had brought some of her male friends with her, and Bamie reminded her: "You did anything but make the time pleasant for them and consequently unpleasant for me and this must never occur again." Then she closed on an amiable note, writing how much she wanted to see Alice and hear what she had been doing.

In spite of such admonitions, Bamie found much to compliment in Alice. She wrote Corinne that their niece was "very well and handsome." Bamie considered footing the bill so that Alice could summer in Newport, then the most fashionable resort on the East Coast, because it was "the place she really enjoys." But on second thought,

Bamie concluded it might be advisable to keep the girl away from that social hot spot and instead put her "with the proper friends."

Money was not an issue—Alice had enough of her own to go where she wanted. Her mother's family always provided handsomely for her, paying for her medical care, extravagant wardrobes, and ponies and carts. Theodore once even jokingly remarked to Edith that they should be good to Alice because they might have to borrow money from her. The Lee inheritance became significantly greater when Grandfather Lee died, leaving a large estate, half of it designated for his widow and the rest to their six children, with Alice receiving her mother's share.

Alice had carefully laid the groundwork so as to maximize her inheritance. As she explained it, she learned at an early age "from heaven knows where about the difference between leaving money per stirpes as opposed to per capita," and she primed her grandparents to write their wills accordingly. In a "per capita" distribution, the money is divided among the many heirs, with each of the grandchildren, for example, receiving an equal share no matter how many siblings each has. A "per stirpes" arrangement divides an estate according to connections to the source, and in Alice's case, it meant she received her mother's sixth since she was her only child. Alice recalled: "I constantly reminded my grandfather of it. 'Remember, Grandpa,' I would say, 'per stirpes, not per capita.' I must really have been an odious child. . . . Anyway it worked."

The grandfather's death was only the first step. After his widow died, her estate was divided into six parts, with Alice again receiving her mother's share.. Bamie, writing to Corinne, reported the inheritance with satisfaction and noted that "Alice is thoroughly provided for." This legacy was particularly welcomed since Theodore and Edith were not in a position to settle money on their children. In Bamie's opinion it would have been hard for Alice had she not received the Lee inheritance.

Unfortunately, the money from her mother's family did little to diminish Alice's disdain for them. She wrote them off as parochial and limited, and while she thrived in her new celebrity status, she found less and less time for them. Grandmother Lee recognized that her famous granddaughter operated in a sphere far removed from her own. In August 1905, while twenty-one-year-old Alice was on a much publicized trip halfway around the world, her grandmother wrote her from Magnolia, Massachusetts, where she was visiting friends: "Of course this note from such a quaint place will seem very tame, but we can't all go or do as you are doing."

Edith tried unsuccessfully to cope with Alice, and in the process she appeared brusque if not harsh. When Alice visited Cuba in March 1902, she sent back a picture of herself, which Edith examined and then responded that it was not very flattering—but "I am glad to have it anyway." The two women tangled on money. When Alice spent freely, sometimes exceeding the generous allowance that she received from the Lees, Edith cautioned restraint, and Alice shot back that the money was hers, to spend as she wished. In August 1904, while the girl was off visiting friends in Maine, Edith admitted that the decision was up to her: "My 'scolding' now would be both silly and useless. If you have debts, they must be paid. I can only remind you that it is neither honest nor wise to incur them." Then she signed herself, "Your affectionate Mother." On another occasion Edith's warnings about profligate spending were even more dire. She warned Alice that if she did not cut down on expensive clothes, she might endanger her brothers' futures: "How would you like to have Archie give up college to pay your debts?"

Other differences loomed between the two women. Alice thrived on attention while Edith loathed it. For the round of coming-out parties in December 1902, Edith advised Alice to invite different young men to escort her so that her name would not be linked with any one of them—thus putting "a stop to all possible gossip." She might have saved her breath. Alice exalted in gossip.

Even Corinne Robinson, who was not entirely averse to the limelight, decided Alice went too far. In October 1902, Corinne wrote to her daughter, away at Allenswood, that Alice was "dear and sweet but . . . she has gotten sadly beyond control." A few months later, when Corinne visited the White House, she reiterated her displeasure. "Alice is dear," she wrote Corinney, "but I deplore the change in her. She cannot be interested in anything unless it happens to excite her and she is terribly bored unless she is the centre of everything. Poor child. It is the natural result of her unfortunate position. She is always madly gay, or bored to death, and wishes to be outre in every way."

One of Alice's plays for attention featured her pet snake, Spinach Emily. Nothing delighted Alice more than frightening White House guests by approaching them with the snake twirled around her arm. Finally Theodore forbade such exhibitions, but Corinne still worried: "She is always sweet to me and I do not mean to be disloyal to her but I am so sorry to see the kind of attitudes she has toward everything." When Owen Wister, the famous author, asked his good friend Theodore why he did not keep a tighter reign on Alice, he replied that he could "either run the country or control" Alice but he "could not possibly do both."

Since Alice's favorite adjective was *boring* and since wit and the ability to have a good time ranked high on her list of attractive features, she found plenty to fault in Eleanor. Corinney once observed that duty was central to Eleanor's life, while Alice did not understand the meaning of the word. During Eleanor's years at Allenswood, they saw little of each other, but when Eleanor married in March 1905, she chose Alice as one of her bridesmaids. Alice was not thrilled. She complained to a family friend that she "had to be bridesmaid for my cousin Eleanor" and then the next week had to "do the same trick all over again" for another wedding "which is a fearful bore."

As the debutante daughter of the President of the United States, Alice found many doors open, but some were closed. In sections of the country where Theodore had critics, his daughter suffered the consequences. In January 1903, for example, she traveled to New Orleans but was not invited to the Mardi Gras ball because of strong feeling against Theodore in that part of the country. The President had angered some southerners with his invitation to Booker T. Washington to dine at the White House, and they vented their anger on Alice. The year before, when protocol questions arose about her attending the coronation of Edward VII in London, she had to settle for a trip to Cuba instead. There her father's hero status guaranteed Alice royal treatment.

⌒

Even the journey Alice made to the Far East in 1905—which she later described as "by far the most exciting one I ever made"—was characterized by her at the time as "a fearful bore." But the trip was far from boring because she got her first chance to spend extended time with Nicholas Longworth, a bachelor congressman from Cincinnati, Ohio. Fifteen years her senior, he was just enough older to seem worldly without the stigma of belonging to her parents' generation, and Alice had had her eye on him for some time. Slim and always elegantly dressed, he was a superb violinist and, by virtue of the fact that his family owned a large vineyard, a connoisseur of fine wine and food.

The Longworths had been prominent in southern Ohio for several generations, and as the only son, Nicholas had entree to the most select society. He graduated from Harvard in 1891, then briefly attended Harvard Law School before returning to Ohio to earn his LLB at the Law School of Cincinnati College in 1894. Family wealth permitted an early entry into politics, and while still in his twenties, he won election to the city board of education and then to the state legislature in 1899. Ascension was swift, and by 1903, when he was thirty-four years old, he had a seat in the U.S. House of Representatives. As a Republican he soon met the Roosevelts, including Alice. Along with her friend Marguerite Cassini, the Russian ambassador's daughter, Alice pretty much dictated who got accepted into the capital "fast crowd." In Washington, Alice shared Nick's attentions with several other young women, but on the trip she had him almost entirely to herself.

In July 1905, Theodore and Edith welcomed the chance to remove Alice from her partying companions by sending her with an American delegation on a four-month-long trip to the Far East. The group of eighty or so was led by Nick's fellow Republican from Cincinnati, Secretary of War William Howard Taft, who had just returned from a stint as governor-general of the Philippines. Alice did not relish the idea of being herded about by the avuncular Taft, but she liked the prospect of taking her first extended trip abroad, and with several large trunks and many suitcases, she boarded ship with her fellow travelers.

At no time was the "Princess Alice" title more appropriate than on this trip. Royal leaders in Japan and China vied with each other to give her the most valuable present. One acquaintance later described the trip as "Alice in Plunderland." With her knack for talking about her adventures in a witty, descriptive way, she had a bonanza with this trip and later described her stay in Tokyo as including "a rather grand garden party . . . [where] all the Japanese ladies wore big floppy hats and carried parasols. . . . We look[ed] like a slightly stoned version of the Ascot scene from 'My Fair Lady.'" The long trip catapulted her to international attention, and when Mrs. Taft tried to rejoin the American delegation in London, she had trouble convincing hotel staff of her identity until she blurted out that she was the woman whose husband "is traveling now with Miss Alice Roosevelt."

As the delegation toured the sites and attended parties over several months, Nick and Alice were frequently seen together, and American newspapers began speculating that the two were engaged. Finally, Mr. Taft, who disliked confrontation, mustered the courage to ask Alice directly if she and Nick had come to some decision, but she refused to be specific, leaving him no more enlightened than before he asked.

Back in Washington at the end of October, Nick and Alice knew they would have to approach her parents with their intention to marry, although a formal announcement would come later. Theodore was delighted with the prospect of a son-in-law who had all the right credentials: a Harvard man and even a member of the same Harvard club, Porcellian, that had admitted Theodore but turned down Franklin. The difference in the ages of Nick and Alice gave Theodore no pause—he welcomed a mature influence on his rebellious daughter.

Best of all, Nick was 100 percent American—not some foreign mogul. Theodore had feared Alice might marry one of those minor royal figures or titled nobility that so many wealthy Americans sought in order to add a bit of dash to their family dollars. Consuelo Vanderbilt offered a case in point. She had married the Duke of Marlborough—for the explicit reason that her parents wanted a title in the family—and Theodore shuddered at such a prospect for Alice. His own resources might be limited, but he placed his Knickerbocker heritage on an echelon superior to any foreign title or any amount of "new" money.

Alice had flirted with more than one titled European suitor. When Prince Henry, the brother of the German kaiser, gave her an expensive diamond bracelet, she saw no reason to refuse it. Cousin Eleanor, who had strict rules on accepting presents, lectured Alice on what gifts were acceptable: "yes" to flowers and books but definitely "no" to jewelry. Alice later mused, "I listened to her earnest discourse, fingering all the while a modest string of seed pearls that an admirer had given me the week before." An engagement to Nick would presumably put an end to such shenanigans.

Back in Cincinnati, the Longworths showed little enthusiasm for Nick's impending marriage to Alice. Others might see them as merely equal to an alliance with the Roosevelts, but they zeroed in on what they believed made them superior. Belmont, their Cincinnati estate, with its well-tended gardens and wide marble steps leading up to a portico, ranked as the city's grandest private dwelling, and it had few rivals in the nation. The Longworths had settled in the Ohio Valley when land was cheap, and by 1900 they were very wealthy. Their vineyard produced 150,000 bottles of fine wines every year.

In addition to wealth, the Longworths held a privileged social status in Cincinnati. Nick's mother claimed direct descent from *Mayflower* passenger William Brewster. Widowed in 1890 when she was only forty-five, she devoted her time and energy to her only son who was at Harvard. Taking an apartment near him in Cambridge, she dined with him frequently and thus anticipated by a decade the same arrangement that Sara Delano Roosevelt worked out with Franklin. Mrs. Longworth had helped found the law school from which her son graduated, and she played an active role in the city's arts programs.

Nick's two sisters were also forces with whom Alice had to reckon. The elder, Maria Longworth Storer, following the example of her cultural arbiter mother, helped start a summer opera season in the Queen City and raised funds for its new Music Hall. But she also found time to dabble in politics, even before Ohio granted the vote to women. In 1896 she contributed the generous sum of $10,000 to the presidential campaign of fellow Ohioan William McKinley, and when he won, she suggested various candidates for appointments, including the young New Yorker Theodore Roosevelt. He became assistant secretary of the Navy, and four years later gained a place on McKinley's ticket as his running mate. Although Theodore's ambition would probably have propelled him to the top without Mrs. Storer's help, he could hardly ignore the fact that she singled him out at such an early point in his career, and he liked the idea of Alice's becoming her sister-in-law.

Clara de Chambrun, Nick's other sister, had her own curiously mixed credentials. Married to a French count, she kept up with public affairs in the United States and wrote books on Shakespeare. Although she may have chafed at the disadvantages of trying to publish as a woman (and signed her books "Clarence Brownfield" to disguise her sex), she had little use for feminist reforms. Like her mother, she opposed the vote for women. Alice, used to going her own way, was not likely to become a close friend of either sister.

None of the Longworth women cared much for Alice—or perhaps it is more accurate to say that they did not make the fuss over her that she felt she deserved. They may well have been one of the few families in the nation that could view marriage into President Roosevelt's family as a step down. Nick's mother treated Alice with a smugness that infuriated her and made clear that "Princess Alice" came into *her* domain if she married Nick.

On the Roosevelt side, not everyone shared Theodore's enthusiasm for the match. Edith had mixed feelings about Nick, though she thought it high time that Alice married. Although Edith herself had not married until age twenty-six and her only sister never married, she favored young marriages and worked hard to get her female progeny mated early. Alice later pointed out that she wed Nick when she did—only a few days after her twenty-second birthday—partly because her family expected it. Eleanor had already beaten her to the altar, and Alice later recalled that she felt the pressure: "In those days [if] one had been 'out' for two or three years, one was expected to marry. If you didn't, you ended up with a thermos of tea in your room, alone, like my poor Aunt Emily." Alice remembered Emily as "one of those wizened virgins from birth. I can still hear my stepmother say when poor Aunt Emily requested tea, 'If Miss Emily wants tea, she can have tea. In a thermos. In her room.'" Alice was determined not to end up like Emily; she wanted to get "out of the house and into [her] own spot."

Edith's reservations about the match centered on whether Nick was the right man. Always a shrewd judge of character and particularly wary of men who drank too much, probably because of her father's alcoholism, she warned Alice that Nick liked his booze. That observation, like so many others delivered to Alice, had no perceptible effect.

The engagement, announced in December 1905, was brief for the time. On February 17, 1906, in a fifteen-minute ceremony, the marriage was solemnized in the East Room of the White House. One thousand invited guests watched as Alice walked to the improvised altar on the arm of her father, without any attendants at all. Eleanor's six bridesmaids had impressed on Alice the wisdom of having none, thus concentrating all the attention on herself. As she approached her bridegroom, she could only think, she later admitted, how very "midwestern" he looked as he stood there waiting for her. Among the guests were many Roosevelts, including Franklin, and when the bride needed someone tall enough to adjust her veil for the photographs, it was Franklin who "popped up to do the job." Years later, after he broke many precedents as president, Alice mused: "I wish I had a picture of that." Eleanor, already six months pregnant with her first child, had remained at home.

The wedding proved an ordeal for Edith. In addition to her regular White House duties, always heavier in January, she had to orchestrate the staging of this major event. Alice, still her rebellious self, was of little help, and more than half a century later she was still chuckling about how she had kept the assembled guests waiting that day. When Alice turned to her stepmother following the ceremony to thank her for the job done, Edith, weary but relieved, shocked everyone within hearing by replying: "I want you to know that I'm glad to see you leave. You have never been anything but trouble." The comment became much quoted, evidence of Edith's cruelty to her stepdaughter. But Alice had a different interpretation—that the outburst was explainable by stress. Alice took it in stride, saying, "That's all right, Mother," she replied. "I'll be back in a few weeks and you won't feel the same way." Later, Alice recalled she had been correct.

Expensive wedding gifts came in from leaders around the world, and although Alice tossed them off as "the sort of presents that any girl gets from her relatives and friends and friends of the family . . . with the exception of a few from foreign potentates," they were hardly commonplace. They included mosaic tables, antique jewelry, and bolts of brocaded cloth. Cuba sent a "superb string of pearls" after carefully considering and then rejecting the idea of giving her a set of bedroom furniture inlaid with semiprecious stones. Wealthy Americans came up with silver services, sewing machines, and seasoned wood, and Local 8 of the Pennsylvania United Mineworkers sent a carload of coal. Alice laughingly conceded that she was not particular: "I'll accept anything except a red hot stove."

For their wedding trip, Alice and Nick went first to Friendship, an eighty-acre estate in northwest Washington that lots of wealthy Republicans later made their playground, and then to Cuba, site of Alice's celebrated 1902 visit. When they arrived back at the capital, everything seemed rosy. Fifteen-year-old Ethel, who now claimed Alice's large bedroom in the White House, wrote her godfather, Bob Ferguson, that he would be "surprised at the difference" in Alice. "She is cunning and perfectly devoted to Nick."

The next few years would show how very wrong Ethel's judgment had been. At twenty-two, Alice's life might have taken a turn with marriage. The motherless girl, always looking for someone in whose life she came first, now had a husband. She could move on from being "Princess Alice" to the serious business of adulthood—engaged in important issues and working for change. But maturity was not Alice's objective. Much later she mused to one of her biographers, "I'm amused and, I hope, amusing. I've always believed in the adage that the secret of eternal youth is arrested development."

II

For a time, the Longworth marriage appeared happy. In 1907, Ethel described Nick and Alice as having a "beautiful" time, a "sort of second honeymoon." But Alice recognized almost immediately that she had erred in marrying Nick. By the time she returned from the honeymoon, her granddaughter later reported, she knew that life with Nick was not what she wanted, and for the rest of their time together they were "not married in any real sense." But divorce in 1906 was so uncommon—and its repercussions on political families so enormous—that she stuck with Nick, even going out to campaign for him that November when he ran for reelection.

As the daughter of a popular president, Alice drew crowds in Ohio, where she and Nick were obliged to live at least part of the year. Her father also took an interest in the campaign, and early on, he inquired of his daughter about prospects for victory. When told that his son-in-law was expected to win "hands down," he expressed delight. After the votes were counted, he congratulated Alice and Nick "upon the successful way in which both of you have run your campaign. I tell you I felt mighty pleased with my daughter and her husband, especially comparing them with certain other American girls and their spouses, as for example, the Duke and Duchess of Marlborough, of fragrant presence!"

The real picture of Alice and Nick Longworth was grimmer. They shared very few interests, and his excessive drinking bothered her, partly because she understood that it put a limit on how high he might go in political office. She later quipped that he would "rather be tight than be President." Rumors circulated in the capital that he continued to see other women, and these stories evidently reached Alice. She once showed an overnight guest of hers the window that Nick had jumped out of in his attempt to conceal his visit to the Belgian ambassador's daughter. Nick had some admirable traits—for instance, he was popular with colleagues in the House of Representatives—but to Alice, his philandering and drinking made him an unsuitable husband. They had produced no children, and after three years of waiting for a niece or nephew, Ethel wrote to Bob Ferguson to arrange a loan: "I wish you'd lend Sister one of [your] children. She has only one small . . . Pekinese poodle."

Few people knew how unhappy Alice was with the marriage. She refused to discuss it, but after Nick's death, she told a friend: "Some things are too bad to talk about. If you must lick your wounds, do it in private."

Alice turned elsewhere for the satisfaction she did not find in her marriage, directing some of her energy to shrewd observation and candid, even cruel, descriptions of others. Terrified of public speaking, she was an excellent mimic, and with the superb timing of an accomplished actress, she delivered her lines like a pro. Helen Taft, who replaced Edith as First Lady in 1909, became one of Alice's favorite targets. The woman who four years earlier had found herself traveling in Alice's considerable wake had unintentionally annoyed Alice by offering her a ticket to William Howard Taft's inauguration—a move that only someone who felt she had full run of the capital without an invitation would find offensive. The payback came swiftly: Alice delighted Washingtonians with a naughty imitation of Mrs. Taft, complete with elevated chin and snooty tone. Edith, who knew as much about sarcasm as anyone, counseled caution in doing imitations of the President's wife. "Your account of it was most amusing," Edith wrote Alice, but "remember for Nick's sake to be really careful what you say for people are only too ready to take up and repeat the most trivial remarks."

In addition to offering counsel that was not always welcome, Edith continued to be sharply terse with Alice. In September 1909, while traveling through Europe with Theodore after his African game hunt, Edith responded to Alice's news that she had lost fifteen pounds. But if Alice expected a word of praise, she did not get it. "I feel sure could you lose 30 you would do no more than attain your ideal," Edith wrote her, "so I shall only hope that you may feel perfectly well and strong without regaining the lost 15." As for Alice's complaints about having to spend time with Grandmother Lee, Edith showed little sympathy: These "are just plain duties to which you certainly should attend."

Marriage to Nick did have the advantage of keeping Alice in the thick of politics. When he ran for reelection in 1910, she wrote Auntie Bye in September that she was optimistic about the outcome: "This district is supposed to be safe but nevertheless I shall have a distinctly nervous feeling until it is all over." She had been around politicians too long to ignore her own role, and she kept quiet on sensitive issues, such as the woman suffrage question. But as the 1914 campaign approached, she resolved to speak her mind if Nick lost, thus evening the score with his mother, whom Alice called "ma-in-law . . . an amazing old female." Set to become "an active suffragist just to spite her," Alice admitted that the elder Mrs. Longworth was "violently on the other side. This is nasty of me . . . but she has been so outrageous." Nick did win reelection, so Alice apparently had to hold her tongue.

After 1913, when the Democrat Woodrow Wilson took up residence in the White House, Alice began focusing more of her attention on the Republican Congress. She became a regular in the Senate gallery and took an avid interest in the debates about entering the war in Europe. Along with most of her family, she declared President Wilson cowardly in holding out against the United States' entry into the war. After the armistice she opposed joining up with the League of Nations, at least in the form proposed by Wilson. In her opinion the archenemy Wilson was moving in on Theodore's turf, claiming too much credit for initiating the idea of an international organization. When Theodore gave a belated acceptance speech in 1910 for the Nobel Peace Prize he had won in 1906, he urged the establishment of a "League of Peace," and now Wilson's League of Nations sounded a lot like it.

But Alice's objection to Wilson ran much deeper than that. She saw him as rigid and preachy—and much preferred his Republican opponent, Auntie Corinne's great friend, Senator Henry Cabot Lodge of Massachusetts. But in general Alice found few heroes in the legislature: "On the whole they are such a stagnant lot, our 'statesmen,' . . . pretty depressing," she opined in a letter to Auntie Bye, who had recently accompanied her on one of her visits to the Senate.

None of the politicians she encountered measured up to her father, and months after his death in 1919, Alice admitted that she missed him more and more "as time goes on . . . if that were possible." The nation faced serious decisions, and President Wilson, who had recently suffered a stroke, did little to resolve them. Besides the problem with the peace treaty, "labor [was] in a desperate snarl," she wrote Auntie Bye, and nobody did anything. Alice heard her father's name invoked on all sides: "his name on their lips and his memory in their hearts. I had to write to you darling Auntie Bye. . . . I long to see you and tell you about everything as I see it."

Although Bamie was increasingly crippled by arthritis and found travel difficult, she continued to go to Washington, where Alice introduced her to witty, energetic folk, including the remarkable Ruth Hanna McCormick, who played an important part in Alice's life later. As the daughter of Ohio Republican Mark Hanna, Ruth apprenticed in politics as a teenager when she traveled with her father during his management of William McKinley's 1896 presidential campaign. Her marriage to Chicago newspaper publisher Medill McCormick in 1903 only whetted her appetite for more of the political game. With her husband she worked for social reforms in Illinois—even going to live for a while at a Chicago settlement house—and took a prominent role in Republican contests. When Medill McCormick ran for office himself, first on the state level in Illinois and later to represent his state in the U.S. House and the Senate, Ruth campaigned for him. She avidly supported the vote for women, a view that Bamie did not share but apparently did not object to in others, because after lunching with Ruth in 1918, Bamie admitted that she found her "so interesting." Bamie's only regret was that she had learned late in their conversation about the success of "her farming experiments with women workers."

Other friends of Alice's, far less political than Ruth Hanna McCormick, also met with Bamie's approval. Evalyn Walsh McLean, the mining heiress, had lived in Washington since the age of twelve (with intervals of study and travel abroad), so her path had frequently crossed that of Alice, two years her senior. Not long after Alice married Nick, Evalyn eloped with Ned McLean, the spoiled son of the wealthy family that owned *The Washington Post*. The union was even less successful than that of Alice and Nick, and far more stormy, but the McLeans kept a gay and exciting social schedule at their large estate just outside Washington—the same place that Nick McLean's family had lent the Longworths to begin their honeymoon in 1906.

Hobnobbing with the nation's leading Republicans and amusing themselves with extravagant parties and purchases, including the Hope diamond, Evalyn and Ned continued to make headlines, at least in the social columns, and they counted Alice among their friends. When Auntie Bye came visiting, Alice arranged for her to see Evalyn, and though it is difficult to understand what Bamie would like about such a frivolous person, something about her vitality was appealing. After lunch and an afternoon of bridge at the McLean estate, an enormous spread that boasted its own golf course and required a house staff of thirty, Bamie wrote glowingly of the setting and the company. The McLeans' third son was just a month old, and Bamie pronounced him "adorable." Evalyn won even higher accolades. She was, according to Bamie, "one of the smartest young women I have met for ages and really good and true."

Beneath her cheerful exterior, Alice still struggled in a marriage that she wanted to escape. In 1912 she seriously considered divorce, but her family talked her out of it. As she later told a biographer: "I remember telling my family in 1912 that I wanted [a divorce] and although they didn't quite lock me up, they exercised considerable pressure to get me to reconsider."

Her timing was partly dictated by the split that year in the Republican Party. When Theodore left the regular Republicans and ran for president on the Progressive ticket, he put his son-in-law between a rock and a hard place. If Nick stuck by his father-in-law, he risked alienating colleagues whom he might need in the future. Besides, the Republican nominee, William Howard Taft, was a fellow Ohioan from Nick's hometown, Cincinnati. For Alice the choice was easy, but Nick must have wished he could just go into hibernation and wake up after the votes were counted. Theodore urged him to stick with the party and protect his future, and that is what he tried to do.

Alice had a more difficult time. She kept an uncharacteristically low profile during the campaign—until an event over which she had no control pulled her into full view. On October 14, during a campaign stop in Milwaukee, a man in the crowd shot Theodore at close range. Had it not been for a metal eyeglass case and a thick manuscript folded into his breast pocket—where the bullet lodged—the wound might well have been fatal. Although bleeding profusely, Theodore insisted on going ahead and giving the speech he had prepared, asking the crowd only to keep a little quieter than usual so as to hear him. Finally, his concerned aides managed to get him to stop, and then they took him to Chicago where he was hospitalized. It was then that Alice came out of obscurity, rushing to his bedside and drawing attention to her close relationship with the man whom many blamed for making possible what would assuredly be a Democratic victory.

When the votes were counted, Nick lost by ninety-seven—the only defeat of his career—and Theodore failed to win back the White House. Family morale plummeted, especially in the Longworth household. Even before the outcome was clear, Alice was obviously unhappy, causing Edith to write to Corinne that Alice would welcome a "private visit" with her aunt. "She is having a hard time poor dear." Bamie also saw the signs of stress and wrote her old friend Bob Ferguson that Alice had had "a hard winter and spring—feeling against Theodore in Washington official circles having run very high and Alice being absolutely interested in her Father."

By the time Ethel married Dick Derby the following April, Alice's dissatisfaction was evident to everyone. Even the bride picked up her sister's disenchantment and, while on her honeymoon, wrote to her

mother to thank her for making every detail of the wedding so perfect. Then Ethel added, "Bad boy Sister—I don't think she was very
happy over the wedding. She seemed so unnatural." Alice had generously lent the bride some traveling clothes, and Ethel wrote her
mother that she had nearly *"lived* in Sister's dark blue suit which we
almost didn't bring." Between the two sisters, any mention of Nick's
family became taboo, as Ethel indicated when she wrote her husband, "Sister and I never mentioned Cincinnati except that she said
she had hated it."

Having decided to stick out the marriage, Alice leavened her life
with a good dose of politics. She was shrewd at discerning the big
picture, and in the 1916 election she observed that a change in only
two thousand votes in key states would have given the victory to the
Republican candidate, Charles Evans Hughes, rather than return the
detested incumbent Wilson for another four years. The intricacies of
the electoral college would have made this possible, prompting her
to begin questioning the feasibility of the system.

Some of her most caustic comments were reserved for political figures—whom she socialized with one day and ridiculed the next.
About Warren Harding, with whom she played poker, she said, "He
wasn't a bad man, just a slob." In fact, the higher the office, the
more Alice delighted in puncturing the pompous. Humble folk were
never the brunt of her jokes—unless they were relatives. Late in both
their lives, her brother Archie, whose personality had not sweetened
with time, came to visit her in her Washington home, and on the
way out he fell down a flight of stairs. Alice never budged from her
chair, merely observing: "I never liked him anyway."

✺

One senator who escaped Alice's wrath was William E. Borah
from Idaho, and by the early 1920s their names were linked in more
ways than concerned the Senate. A burly midwesterner seventeen
years her senior, he seemed an unlikely ally for Alice. He represented
the complete opposite of Nicholas Longworth, and except for his
highly polished shoes, for which he was well known, he showed little of Nick's sartorial flair. Born in poverty in Illinois, Borah worked
his way through college in Kansas and then taught school and prac-
ticed law. By his mid-twenties he had made his way farther west, for

reasons not entirely clear. One story had it that he fled to escape a young woman whose child he was accused of fathering.

The decision to settle in Idaho evidently came by chance—Borah had exhausted his money by the time he reached Boise and could go no farther. He managed to make friends in the right circles very quickly. His marriage to the Governor's daughter provided a good entree into the state's top political circles, and in 1907, at age forty-two, he was elected to the U.S. Senate, a job he held until his death in 1940. For nine of those years (1924–33) he chaired the powerful Senate Foreign Relations Committee, during a time when important questions were being debated about war reparations, armaments reductions, and international debts.

A booming and magnetic speaker, Borah attracted spectators to the Senate gallery just to hear him—Alice Longworth and his wife, Mamie, among them. Physically, the two women resembled each other, both wiry and rather glamorous, but Alice held the edge in personality. While Mamie Borah was diplomatic to the point of insipidness, Alice still liked to add spice to her comments. The Senator apparently needed both of them, and while he remained married to Mamie until his death, he also saw a lot of Alice. The relationship was no secret to Alice's family, who complained to one another that the Senator held too much influence on her. One relative even quipped that Alice was "completely Borahized."

For her part, Alice described her relationship with Borah as that of "close friends," and she noted that he and the labor leader John L. Lewis, with whom her name was also linked later, were "remarkably similar in looks and also, to some extent, in temperament. They had the same large, shaggy heads and they both alternated between being very stimulating or very taciturn. They were NEVER boring. Humor was the great bond between us." She might also have noted that they were both extremely powerful at the time she found them interesting.

Neither Senator Borah nor his wife referred to his relationship with Alice as inappropriate or showed that they considered it threatening to their marriage. In 1932, when he became ill and feared he was dying, he dictated a will leaving everything to Mamie, and when she wrote her own story of their marriage, she made only the kindest references to Alice and her graciousness. For Mamie, whom

Washington wags dubbed "Little Borah," a background role in her husband's career seemed sufficient, and she appeared far more pre-occupied with her enormous collection of miniature glass elephants than with anything else.

The Senator's relevance to Alice's story became the subject of much speculation in 1924 when, after eighteen years of marriage, she became pregnant for the first time at age forty. Tongues wagged in the capital about who had fathered the child. For her relatives, paternity was less an issue than Alice's health and welfare. The details of her own birth and her mother's death still haunted them, and to make matters worse, the baby was due in February, around the time of Alice's birthday.

The mother-to-be seemed adamant about keeping control of events. Rather than confide in any of the relatives, she turned to her good friend Ruth Hanna McCormick, who made arrangements for the baby to be born in Chicago under the direction of a noted obste-trician. With Alice so far away, her relatives' anxiety increased as the due date approached. Finally, Bamie could not restrain herself, and she wrote Corinne: "I am waiting every day with such anxiety and love to hear of my blessed Alice." Nick, who showed every anxiety common to the expectant father, could not leave Washington, she noted, "as the House is in the final throes of the session, and he comes up in the Speakership contest on the 27th," so it looked as though Alice would have to manage on her own. "Should the baby come, as the doctors thought possible, sooner, he may not get there," Bamie worried. Then, aware that she did not have to spell out the dreadful chain of events that had saddened the Roosevelt household in February 1884, Bamie added only the cryptic: "Yes-terday was [Alice's] birthday."

Edith traveled to Chicago for the baby's birth, and had only praise for the doctor who delivered the baby on February 14, the anniversary of the older Alice's death. Edith reported to the family back East that Alice's labor pains had started before dawn, and Ruth McCormick drove her to the hospital at six; by the time Edith arrived at 10:30, the baby was born. "Such a satisfactory baby," Edith wrote, then added tersely, "apart from its sex." She judged the newborn looked "exactly like Alice," except for its brow, and thought Alice looked "younger than she had done in years."

The name for the new baby had not yet been chosen. Edith hoped for another Alice but then observed that was about the only name not under consideration. The matter was finally settled to everyone's relief, and Edith conveyed the news to Bamie, who wrote to Corinne on February 24: "Apparently the small child is to be called Paulina. The reason given in the newspapers is that St. Paul was Alice's favorite character in the Bible. "For anyone as nonreligious as Alice, the explanation verged on the ridiculous, but at least Paulina was preferable to Lalage, one of the possibilities considered. According to Bamie, "Her only object apparently was to avoid recalling any relationship with any of our family." Even more appalling was the prospect that the child might have been called Deborah, a name sure to have titillated those who were speculating about Alice and Senator Borah.

The entire family, and much of Washington, watched to see how Alice performed as Mama. She was such a society figure, entertaining and being entertained by world and national leaders, that few people believed she could be happy in the nursery, but the first reports were good. Her brother Kermit visited her in Washington in March 1925 and then wrote Auntie Bye that "Sister" seemed to adore the baby. "Of course it has changed Sister's whole method of living," he continued, "but she doesn't seem to mind that a bit." Corinne Robinson gave a similarly enthusiastic account when she visited her two-month-old grandniece. She found the new mother looking "so attractive, and the baby was brought down so cunning and compact and *so* like Alice as a baby and it seemed like a fairy story to see Alice hovering over her."

But this contentedly maternal stage would not last long, and gradually people noted a change in Alice. Ethel thought she detected a diminished energy and a "strange mood" when she visited Alice in May 1926. "She does absolutely nothing," Ethel wrote Dick, adding, "It's fairly amazing that so energetic minded a person at times . . . can be so lazy." No laggard herself, Ethel puzzled: "I suppose she is storing up energy to release on us poor ones who are constantly using up our own." To Ethel's mind, Alice showed interest in only two things: "Paulina and the World Court," and more of the latter than the former.

When Alice continued to mull over her mistake at not getting out of her marriage earlier, Ethel counseled her to forget the past and make the best of what she had. She would only worsen her situation by dwelling on what she could not change, and with an infant daughter to consider, divorce as an option was even less practical. Besides, any such move would be seen as a "betrayal of the trust of the American people, so to speak," according to Ethel, whose advice did little to cheer Alice. More and more Alice kept to herself, going out rarely in the evening and occupying herself, Ethel wrote, "doing little things."

Nick received superb marks as a father. He doted on Paulina, and she adoringly tagged behind him wherever he went. Even before she could walk, he toted her to the Capitol, and Ethel reported: "Paulina is a sweet thing—very sunny and gay and it's too amusing to see her conducting her Father to the Capitol—he is very proud of her." Colleagues found him such an attentive parent that they could hardly object when he adjourned the House of Representatives in order to preside over a birthday party.

Like many children of indulgent parents, Paulina was subject to infinite assessment and unreasonable praise. In May 1926, Bamie wrote Corinne that she had just received from a mutual friend of theirs in Washington "the most irresistible description of Alice Longworth with Paulina dropping in at 6 P.M." while other guests were having tea. "She said Paulina was perfectly adorable with no end of character, and Alice, as usual, absolutely absorbed in her." In 1930, when the proud mother informed Ethel about Paulina's enrolling in school, she added, "She loves it, and I am all a twitter watching her learn to read."

Motherhood did not seriously dent Alice's stake in politics, but she continued to accentuate the negative. When Corinne visited Washington in July 1927, she confessed to Ethel that she had not been entirely pleased with Alice, who had "attacked Stimson and Nicaragua and Coolidge." To Corinne's mind, Alice was entirely under the influence of the Idaho senator and "not as interesting as if she were herself." But she could still pinpoint a person's flaws with lightning speed.

Not long after Paulina's birth, the Longworths moved from the M Street house where they had lived for many years into what newspapers at the time described as a "palatial house" on Massachusetts Avenue. The four-story, yellow sandstone building, with servants' quarters on the ground floor and Alice's salon upstairs on the third, would be her home for the rest of her life. Over the fifty-plus years that she lived there, the luxurious fabrics of her wedding presents faded and frayed, and the animal skins inherited from her father shredded and tattered, so that the house had a worn look about it but also one of elegance and great style. No object in the place seemed to lack its own amusing story. Some of the animal skins, for example, had come into her possession after her father's death when she and Ethel played poker to see who got them. Ethel won, but when Alice pouted, the ever-thoughtful younger sister offered to split the bounty, and Alice quickly accepted.

Not many congressmen could afford such a grand house in Washington, and this one underlined the Longworths' prominence. Nick had won election as speaker of the House of Representatives the same year that Paulina was born, thus raising his already significant standing in the city's social and political hierarchy. Alice had rarely been out of the news since she moved into the White House with her family in September 1901. Paulina, a naturally shy child, became accustomed to reporters following her around and photographers recording every move. *The New York Times* published her photograph on the front page and relayed her clever remarks, including her response when her mother chastised her for reading comics rather than more serious books. The little girl, completely unaware of the link between her mother and Borah, replied: "I notice you spend a lot of time in the Senate."

But Nick's career, except for the term he lost in the 1912 election, was in the House of Representatives. After starting out as a young man, he rose to become Republican floor leader in 1923 and then, two years later, to the top job in the Republican-controlled legislature. In spite of his strong showing at most elections, Alice never took victory for granted. When Nick faced an unsavory opponent in 1930, she admitted to "one moment [in which] it looked as if Nick might have been beat." In her inimitable fashion, Alice summed up the other candidate as "an almost completely half witted individual whose sole speech, repeated over and over" consisted of a taunt regarding Nick's soft stand on prohibition repeal. The opponent kept calling Nick "a pussy-footer!" and would croon during speeches: "Pussy, Pussy, Pussy, come out of your tent." Nick personally favored repeal of the Eighteenth Amendment (banning the sale of alcohol), but he tried to avoid mentioning the subject so as not to embarrass his Republican colleagues running in "dry" districts in Ohio. He felt confident that his own district would remain loyal, no matter what his view on alcohol, but he almost miscalculated. So much for "security," Alice complained. "The district fell for the pussyfooting charge, and Nick won by a slim 3,500 votes, compared to 30,000 two years ago."

The tougher the fight, the better Alice liked it. After holding on to his seat in the House that year, Nick still faced competition for the speaker post, leading his wife to write a relative that no one is "sure of how the House or Senate will organize until the next Congress meets! Isn't it fantastic but it will be all kinds of fun—for anyone with a taste for chaos." When Nick retained the speakership, it marked one more sign of the high regard in which his fellow Republicans held him, in spite of the many stories that circulated about his own personal life or his wife's outspokenness.

Nick's womanizing was no secret, although it hardly marked him as unusual in a legislature where powerful men sometimes took for granted their right to private trysting on public property, including their offices in the Capitol building. According to William "Fishbait" Miller, longtime doorkeeper of the House, Nick stood out as "one of the early swingers" and "one of the greatest womanizers in history on Capitol Hill."

His own lighthearted openness on the topic probably helped Nick overcome criticism. According to one story, a young congressman, trying to make a point about Nick's behavior, taunted him by saying that Nick's "pretty bald head" reminded him of "my wife's behind." Swiping his hand across Nick's head, in order to "be sure," he announced with some satisfaction that "yes, it does feel just like my wife's behind." Instead of squirming or looking embarrassed, Nick ran his own hand across his bald head and quipped: "I'll be damned if it doesn't."

According to Miller, Nick made no attempt to conceal his very active sex life. One man visiting his office started to help himself to a cigarette from a box on the desk, and then he realized that what looked like cigarettes were actually condoms. This was the 1920s when attitudes about sexual behavior were changing, but Nick still raised some eyebrows among his more conservative colleagues. Around

Washington the Longworth marriage was considered "open," and Nick and Alice would arrive together at parties, then leave separately.

The two were not together on April 9, 1931, when Nick had a heart attack in Aiken, South Carolina. Alice, who was in Cincinnati, where Paulina attended school in Nick's district, immediately went to him, but she arrived too late; he had died at the age of sixty-one, leaving Alice a widow at forty-six and Paulina fatherless at six. Rumor had it that Alice burned his Stradivarius.

III

THE FIRST OF THE four cousins to be widowed, Alice must have felt some relief since she had been toying with the possibilities of getting out of the marriage almost as soon as she had gotten into it. She no longer had to placate Nick's constituents by making Cincinnati her official residence, thus putting herself in the hostile orbit of Nick's relatives. Now she could settle into the house on Massachusetts Avenue where she could carve out her own niche in Washington, which she described as a "small, cozy town . . . global in scope." From the time she first went there as a child of eight, during the time her father served as a civil service commissioner, she made it her turf, and short sojourns in New York or in Cincinnati were only interruptions. The nation's capital, with its mixture of big-time politics and small-town social life, fit her, and she fit it—as illustrated when she was dubbed "Washington's other monument."

Much about the city had changed, of course, now that the Republicans controlled neither the legislative nor the executive branch; both of them were now held by what Alice termed "the opposition." That the big shift should come under the aegis of Franklin and Eleanor—family faces that she knew so well—made it all the more unpalatable. With the 1932 election, the "Theodores" suddenly found themselves the "out of season Roosevelts." Up until that time, and especially in the late 1920s when Nick served as speaker of the House, Alice could claim a front seat for herself at the capital's most important social functions, even vying for top billing with the Vice President's sister during the Hoover years. Now, with Nick gone, that all changed, and she had to garner recognition in her own right.

That her own status should be cut, just as her newly emboldened cousin Eleanor was becoming the most conspicuous woman in town, added to Alice's sense of displacement.

As the slightly older of the two cousins, Alice had started out with a small advantage, helped by her wit and sharp tongue. But the two women were so clearly opposite and their priorities so different that they could hardly have been compatible. While Eleanor concentrated on helping others and performing public duties, Alice devoted herself to her private salon and her circle of witty friends. Having mastered the skill that many of the Roosevelt women possessed to size up a personality and mimic a key trait, she could sometimes be cruel. Eleanor had no use for either the mimicry or the cruelty.

Fully cognizant of the difference between herself and Eleanor, Alice sometimes told a story to illustrate it. As a young wife in Washington, Eleanor left a party early while Franklin remained "to enjoy himself alone." Arriving home, according to Alice, Eleanor realized that she had forgotten her key, but rather than wake up the servants or call her husband away from his fun, she simply "lay down on the mat in the vestibule so that when Franklin came back in the small hours of the morning all flushed with wine and good cheer, he was greeted by this apparition, looking like a string bean that had been raised in a cellar. . . . She could be quite maddening that way and she always seemed to manage to hold Franklin back from having a good time."

Anyone who knew Alice could have listed the many ways that story would have ended if she had been the central figure. For a start, she was not in the habit of leaving parties early, and if she had and then discovered she had forgotten her key, she would have returned to the party with great fanfare—to demand that the key be turned over on a silver platter. Or "Alice style" might have played out a little differently—she would have phoned the police and asked them to go to the party in sirened vehicles and handcuff her husband, remove the key, and deliver it to her in a posse of police cars. Whatever route she took, it would call attention to herself and make a joke of her plight rather than asking for sympathy. When the family learned about Franklin's affair with Lucy Mercer, Alice is said to have quipped that Franklin "deserved a good time. He was married to Eleanor."

In the beginning of Franklin's presidency, Alice tried to have it both ways. In front of an admiring audience she would imitate Eleanor's high-pitched voice and her "do-good requests," then accept invitations to White House dinners and receptions where she met the same people for whom she had performed. Just because Franklin held the highest office in the land did not protect him from Alice's wit, and she liked to poke fun at those who made too much fuss about him. To Vice President John Nance Garner she gleefully confided that at the Hyde Park Church favored by Franklin, a young pastor had amended the sign out front to read "The President's Church," and someone quickly penciled in underneath, "Formerly God's."

When enough of these stories got back to Franklin, he grew exasperated and decreed that he did not want to see Alice's face. Eleanor, left with the task of enforcing the dictum, found a gracious way out. In a note to Alice she said she realized how very "busy" Alice was, and she would not impose on her time by issuing invitations that Alice might feel "obliged" to accept. Outfoxed, Alice had to live with temporary banishment from the most important residence in Washington.

Competition between the two cousins continued. Just before Eleanor began writing her regular column, "My Day," in 1936, Alice agreed to write a column of her own, "Capital Comment." The columns resembled each other in content and size, and for a while the cousins vied with each other for the larger number of newspapers carrying their bylines. In the beginning, Alice appeared to win, but when readers discovered that the sharp observations that came so spontaneously off her tongue did not transfer well to the printed page, her readership dwindled. Alice's interest flagged, and she stopped writing the column, while Eleanor's "My Day" continued to appear in newspapers throughout the country until August 1962, only months before her death.

Writing of any kind did not come easily to Alice. When well-known editor Maxwell Perkins first suggested that she pen her memoirs, she rejected the idea, saying she had "never written anything longer than a postcard." But Perkins persisted, the money sounded good, and Alice sat down to tell the story of her life. She rejected the idea of a collaborator or ghostwriter, telling Ethel, "If I err, it will not be on the side of the angels." When *Crowded Hours* came out in 1933, almost everyone agreed that, except for its apt name, it was disappointing; it had many errors and few insights into how Alice made her choices. Four years later she teamed up with her brother Ted to edit *Desk Drawer Anthology*, a compilation of short poems they solicited from people around the country. She also updated an old book on the White House, recycling from her autobiography in a style fitting for young readers. But none of the books did particularly well or brought her the fame or the money she desired.

Playwrights and humorists still found Alice good material. In one rendition that must have delighted Alice, a character very much like her was featured as the title personage in a play, *First Lady,* that opened in New York in November 1935 and ran for 234 performances. Although the central figure, Lucy Chase Wayne, was clearly based on Alice Longworth, it had just enough differences to support the pretense of being fiction. Alice basked in the attention the play brought her, including that implied in one line of the play about Mrs. Wayne being "the woman who owned Washington." Being Alice, she commented to one of the playwrights, George Kaufman, "Too bad the property values are down these days." Alice's pleasure in the publicity was only heightened by the realization that, while her cousin was the real First Lady, Alice got the attention of the playwrights. That the play helped popularize the title First Lady by focusing on the personality of a woman who never held it could not have escaped either of the cousins.

At the same time the play was running in New York, Alice published an article in the popular *Ladies' Home Journal* entitled "Ideal Qualifications for a President's Wife." Although it did not explicitly condemn Eleanor's handling of the job she had held for three years, the article implied as much. A photo of Lou Hoover, Eleanor's Republican predecessor, appeared above the caption, "First to take a public part on her own," while under Eleanor's picture was only, "Here, there and everywhere." Such comments could only titillate people interested in the rift between the cousins, and it helped harden the division between the two branches of Roosevelts.

∽

By the time Eleanor was beginning a second term as First Lady, Alice had been on her own for six years. She had to manage with limited moral support from her family since the Roosevelt circle had diminished and scattered. Auntie Bye's death just months after Nick's, and then Auntie Corinne's two years later, both hit hard. Ethel, preoccupied with her own family, did not see Alice often, partly because she objected to Alice's preference for the social, moneyed set and so much attention for herself. Upon learning that Alice and Kermit were taking time to dine with the socialite Elsa Maxwell in the midst of the Great Depression, Ethel pronounced it "strange" and entirely too frivolous for her. Weeks later, on hearing that Alice had decided to write a newspaper column, Ethel was "filled with admiration," she wrote Kermit, that Alice was finally doing something "of her own self, not exploiting any one else's name, or her society position." But the two sisters led such different lives in the 1930s that their paths rarely crossed for very long. Nick's sisters saw even less of her. When one of them wrote his biography, *The Making of Nicholas Longworth: Annals of an American Family*, she dedicated it to Paulina but ignored Alice in both the text and photos.

Alice continued to seek the company of powerful men. Even before William Borah died, she began spending considerable time with John L. Lewis, the charismatic leader of the United Mine Workers. Dining together, at her home on Massachusetts Avenue or at his in Alexandria, they had "great fun," she later recalled. She found him "courtly and friendly," and pronounced herself "lucky in my middle age to find a new delightful companion." As for marriage, "I think it was in the wind," she admitted. "But I didn't take it seriously. I wouldn't have married anybody. Once is enough, but for me, he was the best company there ever was."

One of Alice's biographers, Carol Felsenthal, implied the relationship with Lewis was more intimate, though she noted that Lewis was devoted to his wife until her death. Lewis and Alice shared a birthday (along with Abraham Lincoln), but little else about their lives seemed similar. He was born in Iowa of parents whose families had been miners in Wales, and when John reached working age, he went into the mines as his father had done before him. Unlike his ancestors, John spoke out against the system that exacted a quota each day and left him grimy, fatigued, poor, and sick at the end. Although he had little schooling, he excelled at debate and quickly emerged as a leader, whether managing the local baseball team or exhorting his fellow workers to unite to improve their lives.

At twenty-one, when Alice was flitting around the eastern seaboard with her fun-loving friends, John Lewis quit his mining job in Iowa and began traveling through the western states. In 1906, the year she married, he returned to Lucas, Iowa, and won the right to represent the miners' union at the next national convention. The next year he married a local teacher, Myrta Edith Bell, who is often credited with helping him shape his thoughts, and he quickly climbed to the top of the United Mine Workers of America, becoming vice president in 1917. Two years later he was president, a job he kept for the next two decades.

Generally considered one of the most magnetic union leaders in American history, the big, bushy-eyebrowed Lewis could move the most obdurate audience with his vivid descriptions of what it meant to be poor. To Alice, who could not even bring herself to give the briefest speech in public, his ability must have looked like magic. One of his legendary orations, sometimes dubbed the "crust of bread" speech, began with a description of mealtime in a poor miner's home. Lewis would contrast the mine workers with the mine owners, and note that the former were not asking for very much— not the yachts and fancy autos that the employers took for granted, not expensive meats or rich desserts—but only a "crust of bread."

Lewis's power and influence went far beyond miners, and in the 1930s he helped form the powerful Congress of Industrial Organizations (CIO), an amalgam of previously separate unions of workers laboring in heavy industry jobs and generally less skilled than those in the American Federation of Labor (AFL). It is fair to say that by the late 1930s, John L. Lewis had the kind of national visibility that Nicholas Longworth enjoyed a decade earlier: his name frequently made headlines in the largest newspapers, and he wielded enormous power in unions that affected the lives of millions of Americans.

From Alice's point of view, it was not only his power that made Lewis attractive but also his stand on Franklin. In 1936 the union leader supported the Democrat's reelection, but in 1940 he adamantly opposed a third term. Even the giant George Washington stopped at eight years, and Lewis (along with many others) thought Franklin should hope for no more. John L. Lewis and Franklin Roosevelt had already tangled during the 1937 steel strike when an exasperated President, lashing out at both workers and steel executives, pronounced his famous "plague on both your houses." The articulate Lewis, remembering labor's support of FDR in 1932 and 1936, responded that it "ill behooved one who had supped at labor's table" to castigate labor and employers in the same tones.

In 1940, Lewis changed his party affiliation to Republican in order to support that party's nominee, Wendell Willkie. So strong was his objection to FDR's reelection that Lewis threatened to resign the presidency of the CIO if the members went for FDR. When they did, he made good on his promise but kept his job with the miners. Lewis insisted that the Democrat would lead the nation into war, a view that Alice shared.

With so many issues drawing John L. Lewis and Alice Longworth together, it is not surprising that rumors circulated about them. Luvie Pearson, the wife of columnist Drew Pearson, told an interviewer that she recognized them driving together in the Virginia countryside, and since it was during a time of gas rationing, she thought it suspicious that they failed to give her a lift—they must have had something to hide. Others gave evidence on both sides, with some noting that the Lewises' long marriage appeared happy and free of scandal, and some recalling how Alice liked to talk about John's "tremendous animal appeal."

Any speculation should take into account the family models that Alice had. Auntie Bye nurtured a circle of male admirers for much of her life, though no hint of scandal attached itself to her or her youthful "Joe-Bobs." Auntie Corinne included Senator Henry Cabot Lodge, editor Charles Munn, and attorney-poet Charles Erskine Scott Wood among her closest friends while she was married to Douglas Robinson, and she traveled extensively with Munn. Cousin Eleanor would play her own version of this family game by forming long, involved relationships with younger men such as Joe Lash and Earl Miller. Alice differed from the other women in preferring older men, but they may well have formed the same kind of "serial" relationship that, even if platonic, fulfilled a need for companionship and fun.

∽

The evidence on Alice's mothering is even less clear. When Nick died in 1931, Paulina was only six, and she lost her biggest booster just when she needed him most. Like Eleanor a generation earlier, she withdrew into a world bounded by her own shyness. The effect of her father's death on Paulina was, if anything, even more pronounced than Elliott's death was on Eleanor in 1894. Eleanor was motherless, but Paulina had a very visible, much applauded, witty mother whom she could never match in words or looks. Another person might have played down the comparison and set out to excel in the things she did best, but Paulina lacked the confidence to try. She was not unattractive, but her stuttering speech and uncoordinated physical movements would have rendered her awkward in almost any family. To suffer these disabilities as the daughter of one of the nation's quickest wits was excruciating.

Like most of her female relatives, Paulina chose to marry as quickly as possible. After graduating from high school and spending two years at Vassar, she married twenty-one-year-old Alexander Sturm in August 1944, when she was nineteen. The bulky, eccentric bridegroom had already published two books, but little else about him could have appealed to Alice, and he, apparently, was one of the few people who ever met her and was not even a little bit intimidated. It may have been her displeasure with the match or perhaps a need to set the record straight that moved Alice to make a remarkable confession to the bride on the evening before the wedding. It had been thirteen years since Nick died, but Paulina adored him, and she must have been taken aback by Alice's revelation that Nick was not her father. Earlier statements had seemed calculated to shock—especially one that Alice made about not having slept in the same bed with a man since many years before Paulina's birth but this one clearly hurt.

Alexander Sturm was probably the worst possible choice for a shy, insecure young wife. He drank heavily, showed little direction in his life, and did nothing to boost Paulina's opinion of herself. The birth of a daughter in July 1946 hardly helped matters, and Paulina followed her mother's cue by choosing a name that, although very long, had nothing at all to do with the Roosevelts: Joanna Mercedes Alessandra Sturm.

If maternity was meant to validate Paulina's life, it did not work. She showed less than full devotion to the child and continued to accompany her husband to late-night parties and on heavy drinking sprees. In November 1951, when Alexander died at age twenty-eight of cirrhosis of the liver, family letters referred to his illness vaguely as "jaundice." Left to manage on her own, Paulina seemed worse off without him than with him. Although few in her family could understand what drew the two together, they had made a life for themselves, albeit one termed an "absorbing queer life" by Aunt Ethel. They were "devoted to each other," Ethel wrote her daughter Edith, and now the young widow would have to construct on her own a life for herself and Joanna, who was almost exactly the same age that Paulina had been when Nick Longworth died.

Although never close to her son-in-law, Alice recognized that his death would have enormous consequences for Paulina, who seemed confused about her future. Alice knew that her daughter and granddaughter could hardly move in with her, and other relatives agreed that the three should not live under the same roof. But Paulina had difficulties on her own and continued to drink. In May 1952 she entered a sanitarium for an indefinite period, leaving Joanna with her paternal grandparents in Connecticut. The Sturms had not been generous, according to family letters, and there was talk that they had made Paulina pay the wages for her daughter's nurse as well as room and board for the child. In other areas of their lives, the Sturms spent freely. They were, according to the ever-tolerant Ethel, "the champagne cocktail type," but they were tight-fisted with their granddaughter. At least the nurse was excellent, exactly the kind of competent woman who can "bring up" Joanna, Ethel wrote.

By the end of that summer, though Paulina was able to leave the sanitarium on weekends and looked forward to full release within a matter of weeks, she had not fully recovered. In addition to the alcoholism, she battled other demons, the exact description of which eluded the family. Alice worried that the cure was temporary, and she confided to her sister that she feared her daughter's antagonism toward her might be behind all the problems. Even Paulina's persistent stutter might have been caused, in Alice's judgment, by the animosity she felt for her mother.

By the winter of 1952–53, Paulina was out of the sanitarium and seeking help in religion. For some time she had been drawn to Roman Catholicism, with its formal ritual and confession, and in the spring of 1953 she and Joanna converted to that faith. Clare Booth Luce, much in the news as the newly named ambassador to Italy, was one of their sponsors.

Ethel, who visited Washington about that time, failed to perceive that mother and daughter had benefited from their change in religion. Paulina was "still remote and with the same vague appealing smile" while Joanna was "an attractive little girl whom Auntie S[ister] loves and cherishes and longs to see that she is in happy surroundings." The situation in the Sturms' Georgetown household worsened when Paulina's priest, who might have offered counsel and comfort, died suddenly one evening after having dinner with her. Ethel thought remarriage might help, but no prospects appeared, partly because Paulina did little socializing with adults. She went to bed at the same time as her daughter and then got up in the early morning hours—a schedule that would have kept her from seeing much of Alice, who rarely rose before noon and liked to stay up until dawn.

During her waking hours, Alice had always kept a busy schedule. She read obscure, dense books and performed acrobatic feats that included curling her big toe up to meet her ear. In her large-brimmed hats and outdated but elegant clothing, she seemed "above style." Ethel, who tended to more mundane pleasures, found a visit to Alice, where "the unusual is usual," a heady experience. On one occasion, when sixteen sat down to dinner at Alice's house and the talk turned to a whole range of international issues, Ethel marveled. Later she informed her daughter Edith: "I heard things discussed and lightly thrown aside which seemed to me of grave moment and things which I never even knew about and other things from entirely new angles. Such fun." After everybody else had left, the two sisters talked on until 3:30 A.M.

With the new Eisenhower administration in place by early 1953, Ethel judged it "certainly much more 'our Washington.'" Now Alice could mix important guests from both parties. At one dinner Vice President Nixon and the columnist Arthur Krock sat down to eat with Massachusetts senator John Kennedy "to represent the Dem[ocratic] part." Ethel enjoyed herself immensely: "Everyone was at their best and I heard so much of interest." She had been seated next to the young Vice President and reported that she liked his wife "very much indeed."

In 1956, Alice missed the Republican National Convention, causing her brother Archie to inquire what had happened. She had undergone surgery, she replied, but only later would she reveal exactly what kind—a mastectomy for breast cancer. Months later she faced a far greater tragedy.

On January 27, 1957, she received word that Paulina had died at home. That Sunday afternoon Paulina had sent ten-year-old Joanna to play with a friend, and when the child returned, she found her mother slumped unconscious in a chair in the living room. Medical help was summoned, but it was too late—Paulina was pronounced dead at the age of thirty-one.

Now the family's concern focused on Alice and how she might react to the loss of the daughter with whom she had had such a complicated relationship. Ethel spelled out some of the questions in a letter to her own daughter: "You can imagine Auntie Sister's despair. . . . There are so many things we don't know." How did the conversion to Catholicism fit in? Why had Paulina recently discussed with her mother appointing guardians for Joanna "in case" something happened to her? So much bewildered Ethel that she hesitated to go near Washington: "I was not even sure that Auntie S[ister] would want me and said to her that the lines were so clear between us . . . [but] she said to come."

After spending a few days with Alice, Ethel reported to her daughter that it had been "the strangest, saddest, darkest week. Most people will believe that Paulina committed suicide but I do not think that Auntie Sister believes this." Then Ethel produced the evidence for that conclusion: there was no empty pill bottle by her chair, she had been in apparently good spirits that morning, and the funeral was at a Catholic church—something that would not have been permitted had the evidence been clear that she had taken her own life.

Among themselves the family cited the evidence for concluding that, even if Paulina had not intentionally taken her life, she had mixed her medicines in a way that flirted with death. Ethel explained: "Paulina had been drinking periodically, fighting it hard, and she had been drinking the day she died and perhaps took tranquilizers or sleeping pills, which is a deadly combination." Ethel could only speculate on the true cause of the tragedy: "There must have been some deep psychosis there."

Now the problem was Joanna, who was "extrovert, highly intelligent and used to riding her bike around everywhere." Ethel did not think Alice's home would be right for the child, and yet arrangements had to be made. This time Alice responded more wisely than she had done with her own daughter. Though she enjoyed an indolent schedule, sleeping late and planning her hours to suit only herself, she was ready to alter her ways to accommodate a young child. But perhaps mindful of the trauma involved in her own uprooting from Bamie many years earlier, she took her time to win Joanna's affection and trust. The girl stayed with Bazy Tankserslee, a family friend who had a daughter about Joanna's age, and Alice had her chauffeur drive her out there for brief visits with the girl. Only after Joannna developed an attachment to Alice did she move into the house on Massachusetts Avenue.

Leaving to her housekeeper the mundane matters of preschool breakfasts and laundry for Joanna, Alice made space in her life for this child until the two became devoted companions. Now in her mid-seventies, Alice entertained her granddaughter's young friends and in the summers made the long train trip across the continent so that Joanna could ride horses in Wyoming. Ethel had to admit that the two seemed loyal companions and that Alice had "worked out a satisfactory relationship with Joanna, who is as oddly independent and removed as ever her Mother was." When it came time for college, Alice respected her daughter's conversion to Catholicism by enrolling Joanna in the Jesuit-run Boston College, from which she graduated in 1967.

Ethel Derby attended the graduation ceremony, giving her a chance to catch up with Alice. Her sister looked "really remarkable," Ethel decided, adding that she appeared "younger than I and is in fine form." The graduation exercise itself focused so little attention on each of the graduates that Ethel was reminded of the times she used to watch her own daughter ride in a horse show. Far more interesting were Alice's observations on an array of topics, from family matters to the United Nations and what was happening in the Middle East. But the day belonged to Joanna—the person who would figure most prominently in Alice's last years.

∽

Throughout her final decades, Alice maintained her celebrity status. Her salon drew the cream of the capital city, no matter what their politics. The Democratic Kennedys were particularly attentive. When Ethel visited her in March 1962, she wrote her daughter: "Auntie Sister . . . is having a marvelous time, in the inner Circle, with the Kennedys. Not part of them and not blinded by them, but frankly thoroughly enjoying them."

A decade later when Gerald Ford became president, he trooped over from the White House for her ninetieth birthday party and managed to get hit on the head by one of the young Roosevelts swinging a balloon. Alice was not particularly drawn to Ford, but like other presidents, he came to pay homage to the rather emaciated woman who kept a cushion by her side, its message clearly visible: "If you don't have anything good to say about somebody, come sit by me." When Alice favored her guests with one of her imitations of Cousin Eleanor or Helen Taft, she was, her sister wrote, "apparently uninhibited, gay, clever and wicked." Even young Joanna "enjoyed herself thoroughly."

Alice did not limit her imitations of Eleanor to private parties in her own home. After her cousin's death in 1962, she felt fewer inhibitions about mimicking her in public, and in the spring of 1969 she agreed to "take off" both Eleanor and Helen Taft in a taped segment for the television program *60 Minutes*. When Ethel saw a preview of the tape about a month before it was broadcast, she knew other family members might not approve: "She says things which will certainly wound here and there." But the total performance was so "uninhibited, so absolutely natural" that Ethel could not bring herself to condemn it. Alice touched a sensitive nerve when she talked in less than reverent terms about her father, and Ethel confessed, "I never feel quite sure of what picture she will present." But all in all she had to admit that Alice "handles herself so well, picking up and going on."

By Christmas 1975 both Ethel and Alice recognized that they were failing. Alice, at ninety-one, had trouble keeping things straight, and when she could not remember exactly where her younger sister was living, she would inquire "with great interest" again and again. The two women joked about their frailties and about the disadvantages of living so long. They would have preferred taking after their father's side in longevity rather than Edith's branch, which typically survived well past eighty. "Auntie Sister and I laugh about taking after G[rand]M[other]'s who she accepts as hers also," Ethel explained to her daughter.

The decline was all the more noticeable because Alice had long enjoyed a reputation as one of the healthiest, most limber of the Roosevelts. Into her late seventies she amazed even Ethel, who reported after one visit that Alice was "marvelous. Reads the small print in a telephone book without glasses, hears a whisper two blocks away, limber as a kitten, deeply interested in all that goes on." Even after a second mastectomy, Alice seemed undaunted, and she quipped that she was Washington's only topless nonagenarian.

The spotlight still drew Alice like a moth to a flame. Even when she knew she would raise eyebrows, she could not restrain herself. When an interviewer from *Newsweek* inquired about her impressions of the current sexual mores in 1970, she replied that she had "nothing much to say on that subject except if one wishes to talk about bodily functions, my philosophy is 'Fill what's empty, empty what's full, and scratch where it itches.'" Alice acknowledged the exhibitionist side of her personality in a 1974 interview for *Time* magazine when she admitted, "I'm just one of the show-off Roosevelts. I'm like an old fire horse. I just perform. I give a good show."

Some of her friends and relatives occasionally lamented that she could have done more with her life, that she had squandered her talent and energy. Toward the end of her life, her cousin, Stewart Alsop, observed to a friend that "Alice wasted her life being a spectator. She is bright; she is able, she could have done a great many things and done them well, and instead, she chose the role of spectator." But she was hardly a spectator when her name was almost synonymous with witty repartee.

Many people had trouble defining exactly what made her special. After observing her magnetism at a large party, Stalin's daughter, Svetlana Alliluyeva, queried the hostess: "Who was that woman?" After a long answer explaining Alice's relationship to Theodore, Nicholas Longworth, and Eleanor, Alliluyeva remained as puzzled as before. "But what has *she* ever done?"

The problem of finding just the right adjective for Alice persisted for decades. Writing in the *Chicago Tribune* in 1924, Anne Hard admitted that whenever she thought of Alice, she quickly exhausted her vocabulary without finding a word that seemed to suit. It was more than "power" or "energy," but nothing else came close.

That search continued after February 20, 1980, when Alice Roosevelt Longworth died, just days after her ninety-sixth birthday and nearly a century after the death of Mittie, another Roosevelt woman who eluded description.

E P I L O G U E

ALICE LONGWORTH'S DEATH IN FEBRUARY 1980 offered a good opportunity for Mittie's progeny to gather and take stock. Nearly a century had passed since she died, and now that all her children and grandchildren were also gone, it was time to assess the next generations—to see the course their lives were taking. The assembly would have been huge. Mittie's great-grandchildren totaled forty, and in the next generation the numbers just about doubled. Some had already preceded Alice in death, but the survivors would have brought spouses, partners, and children. Such a gathering never took place, however. Alice had decreed that she wanted no funeral, and Joanna followed her wishes.

It was probably a wise decision. Speaking at that funeral would have been a tough assignment. The pious life summary, so common on such occasions, would have been inappropriate for Alice, and her witty observations would have been hard to match. Instead of a tribute, the speech would have ended up quoting the deceased—unless the speaker wanted to take another option and look at the changes that had occurred in that family during Alice's long life. Reaching even further back in the clan's history, the funeral oration could have mentioned Mittie and how little Alice's life resembled hers. The contrast between Mittie and her great-granddaughters was even more pronounced, and it would continue to grow in the 1980s and 1990s.

Far removed from the Victorian disabilities of the nineteenth century, Mittie's great-granddaughters redefined what it meant to be a Roosevelt woman. She had played with life's boundaries by leaving her native Georgia to live in New York City, but they went much further afield. A family that once confined itself to within a one-hundred-mile radius of Manhattan followed the national trend after

World War II and took up residence in many states. Sisters could no longer drop in on each other, as Bamie and Corinne liked to do when they lived within a few blocks of each other in Manhattan. Nor could the extended family gather for weekly suppers as they had done at the house of C.V.S. Roosevelt during the Civil War.

Gender still mattered, but it mattered less than in Mittie's time. None of her daughters or granddaughters had gone to college, but the next generation began experimenting with a year or two, and by the time their daughters reached eighteen, college was taken for granted for girls as well as boys. In at least two cases, a sister finished college while her brother did not—something that would have been almost inconceivable to Bamie. College attendance helped push marriage age off and hold down the number of children so that few of the post-1945 Roosevelts equaled the family norm for earlier generations. Some women delayed marriage until their late twenties, reflecting the national trend, while others remained single into middle age. One chose to have a child without marrying, and divorce was common. All of these changes would have caused Mittie to blink, and Alice—who had been told that getting a divorce amounted to "betrayal of the trust of the American people"—would have chuckled at how much things had altered.

Class still mattered, but less so. Dilution of the family fortune meant that few women in the fourth and fifth generations had inheritances to match those of Eleanor or Alice. In the face of new attitudes about work and a reduced supply of domestic workers, few of them could count on having a full-time cook. Marriages across ethnic and class lines had changed the picture so that the *New York Social Register* no longer served as the family's telephone directory and address book.

Government service and politics still attracted, but as in the previous generations, the Roosevelt women figured more in the role of supportive spouses and volunteers than as candidates themselves. None had equaled Eleanor's visibility, but in 1994, Susan Roosevelt Weld found herself in an interesting position. Her husband, Republican William Weld, running for governor of Massachusetts, defeated Democratic Mark Roosevelt, her cousin. At the same time, on the West Coast, Bruce Chapman, husband of another of Edith's great-granddaughters, Sarah Williams Chapman, was making a name for himself in Washington State as—according to his Web site—"editorial writer, publisher and public policy fellow."

Volunteer work still drew Roosevelt women of the fourth and fifth generations—as the newsboys' dinners had two generations before them. Eleanor's niece, Diana Jaicks, ran a food distribution program in San Francisco and helped her daughter organize fundraisers for striking or locked-out workers. In New Jersey, Corinne Alsop Chubb took an important role in the Chubb family's foundation, serving as board member and, later, trustee in an organization that gave away more than $1 million—a sum that would have boggled the mind of her grandmother, Corinne Robinson.

Much of what used to be charitable or volunteer work had, however, become professionalized by the late twentieth century: it required a degree and yielded a paycheck. The easy acceptance of women working outside their homes would have puzzled Sara Delano. But startling as it may have been to see a great-granddaughter become a librarian and other young Roosevelts go into teaching or social work, the focus of the jobs was not unfamiliar. Anna Curtenius Roosevelt, an anthropologist who earned a "genius" MacArthur grant for her studies of South American peoples, followed in the adventuresome footsteps of her great-uncle Kermit. Her sister, Susan Weld, echoed another old family interest—including one of Sara Delano's—when she chose to write her doctoral dissertation on blood rituals in China.

No one ever added up the phenomenal number of words published by Eleanor and her aunt Corinne, or the reams written by Corinney and Ethel in family letters, but later generations appeared dedicated to equaling it. Most wrote nonfiction, and though none had a syndicated column like Eleanor and Alice, Margot Hornblower's articles for *Time* magazine in the late 1980s earned her a reputation as an outstanding reporter. Like many of her cousins, Margot, a granddaughter of Archie, obscured her connection to the Roosevelts by using her married name. But the wide range of topics she covered had more than a hint of the Roosevelt. She wrote with equal confidence about sports and international finance, Paris fashions and South American fiction.

Although no one showed much interest in equaling Corinne Robinson's six volumes of poetry, several of the women wrote fiction. Margot's aunt, Theodora Keogh, published four novels between

1950 and 1954, all drawing heavily on her own experience and that of her ancestors. Elizabeth Winthrop, the only daughter of Corinne Robinson Alsop's son Stewart, published a long list of children's books before she wrote for adults: *In My Mother's House* (1988) and *Island Justice* (1998). Another cousin did not write herself, but, as the wife and literary agent of one of America's most elusive authors, she was never far from the writing world.

The family's high energy level showed up in other ways. The travel bug still bit, but with more Americans now traveling, the effects made less of a splash. In the trade-off that every traveler knows, giving up the comfort of the familiar for the excitement of the unknown, most Roosevelts were quick to choose. In 1997, her eightieth year, Edith Williams went off happily to China, echoing the kind of spirit that Edith Kermit Roosevelt described in "Odyssey of a Grandmother," an account of the many trips she took in the 1920s.

By the time of Alice's death, the old rift between the Franklins and the Theodores was beginning to heal. In 1989 members of the clan—including many from outside the circle of those considered here—began gathering every three years for a long weekend of talking and remembering. At first it was mostly Franklins who came, but then a sprinkling of Theodores joined in, and by 1997 it was an amalgam, including dozens of Mittie's descendants, questioning and celebrating what it means to be a Roosevelt.

A NOTE ON SOURCES

PUBLISHED SOURCES

In the endnotes I have listed published sources in abbreviated form, but the full citation of books and dissertations can be found in the selected bibliography. The scholarship on the Roosevelts is enormous. Rather than list the hundreds of books and dissertations available on the subject, I have cited those that were most valuable to me in writing this book or so obscure that they may be difficult to find. Magazine and newspaper articles are listed only in the endnotes, but with complete citations.

UNPUBLISHED SOURCES

Because I have relied heavily on family letters, it is appropriate to explain how I have dated them. Some of the originals were completely dated, with day, month, and year, but many had only a cryptic "Thursday" or lacked the year. Sometimes a letter was begun one day and then added on to over a period of several days. This was particularly true of letters written "on the road" or aboard ship. When the internal evidence made the date fairly clear, I have speculated and added "probably." In some cases I had to settle for a month or year or note simply "no date." Only when the archived letter was clearly filed incorrectly—making it difficult for other researchers to find it—did I note that, as in the important letter from Corinne Roosevelt Robinson to Anna Roosevelt Cowles on March 5, 1905.

Several of the Roosevelt women wrote memoirs for their children but never published them. They proved invaluable, though problematic, to use and cite. These memoirs were usually typed by a secretary so that spellings of names are inconsistent or sometimes wrong. The memoir of Anna Roosevelt Cowles has several segments, some paged or dated, others lacking both page and date. The same story is sometimes told more than once in slightly differing versions. I have been as specific as possible about the location of the quotations I used. Fortunately, all segments that I know of are at the Theodore Roosevelt Collection, Houghton Library, Harvard University. Corinne Roosevelt Robinson's Papers form an important part of the Theodore Roosevelt Collection. Her memoir on Henderson House is in the possession of her grandson, John Alsop.

Corinne Alsop left several autobiographical segments that I found rich in detail. She titled three of them: Autobiography, "Letter for Stewart," and Diary. I refer to the fourth segment, which she left untitled, as "Recollections" to distinguish it from the other three. All four segments are in the possession of her son, John Alsop.

INTERVIEWS

John Alsop

Martha Ferguson Breasted

Maureen Corr (telephone)

Alexandra Roosevelt Dworkin

Diana Roosevelt Jaicks

Janet Roosevelt Katten

Dorothy Robinson Kidder

Eleanor Roosevelt (Wotkyns)

Mary "Polly" Gaddis Roosevelt

Selwa Roosevelt

Eleanor Seagraves

Joanna Sturm

Susan Roosevelt Weld

Elizabeth Winthrop (telephone)

NOTES

ABBREVIATIONS USED IN NOTES

ARC	Anna "Bamie" Roosevelt Cowles
ARL	Alice Roosevelt Longworth
CRA	Corinne Robinson Alsop
CRR	Corinne Roosevelt Robinson
EDW	Edith Derby Williams
EKR	Edith Kermit Carow Roosevelt
ERD	Ethel Roosevelt Derby
ERR	Eleanor Roosevelt Roosevelt
FDR	Franklin Delano Roosevelt
MBR	Martha "Mittie" Bulloch Roosevelt
SDR	Sara Delano Roosevelt
TR	Theodore Roosevelt (1858–1919)
TR, Sr.	Theodore Roosevelt (1831–1878)

NYT	*The New York Times*
MBTR	*My Brother Theodore Roosevelt*

AHS	Arizona Historical Society, Tucson
FDRL	Franklin D. Roosevelt Library, Hyde Park
LC	Manuscript Division, Library of Congress, Washington, D.C.
MHS	Massachusetts Historical Society, Boston
TRC	Theodore Roosevelt Collection, Houghton Library, Harvard University

INTRODUCTION

"The old lion": Sylvia Jukes Morris, *Edith Kermit Roosevelt: Portrait of a First Lady* (1980), p. 434.

"I wish Rebecca West": ERD to EDW, Jan. 11, 1948, TRC.

Sylvia Morris's book: *Edith Kermit Roosevelt,* published in 1980.

Blanche Wiesen Cook's biography: *Eleanor Roosevelt: 1884–1933*, published in 1992.

Doris Kearns Goodwin's account: *No Ordinary Time: Franklin and Eleanor Roosevelt: The Home Front in W.W. II*, published in 1994.

"upstart Dutch": Howard Teichmann, *Alice: The Life and Times of Alice Roosevelt Longworth* (1979), p. 243.

"peasants": Michael Teague, *Mrs. L: Conversations with Alice Roosevelt Longworth* (1981), p. 18.

"Very common": Timothy Field Beard and Henry B. Hoff, "Introduction," *The Roosevelt Family in America: A Genealogy*, Part I, p. 5 (Sagamore Hill, NY: Theodore Roosevelt Association, 1990). Also published as *Theodore Roosevelt Association Journal*, winter 1990.

handful of millionaires : Peter Collier (with David Horowitz), *The Roosevelts: An American Saga* (1994), p. 28.

$1 million: David McCullough, *Mornings on Horseback* (1981), p. 126. I am indebted to Richard Sylla, professor of economics and financial history at New York University, for converting the inheritance to its 1998 equivalent.

"to live in tarnished magnificence": Dixon Wecter, *The Saga of American Society: A Record of Social Aspiration, 1607–1937* (1937), reprinted 1970), p. 331.

"because all the better people": Joseph W. Alsop (with Adam Platt), *I've Seen the Best of It* (1992), p. 19. Theodore Roosevelt stubbornly continued to be Dutch Reformed, attending Reformed churches in Albany and Washington, D.C. But in Oyster Bay, where there was no Dutch Reformed church, he went to the Episcopalian church with Edith.

"all sorts of do's and don'ts": Joseph W. Alsop (with Adam Platt), *I've Seen the Best of It* (1992), p. 20. The entire first chapter of Alsop's book deals with this topic.

always had a cook: EDW and Sarah Alden Derby Gannett, interview with author, June 16, 1994.

"the romance of young motherhood": CRA is quoted in a letter of CRR to CRA, Nov. 7, 1910, TRC.

"I would not have my daughters": TR wrote admiringly of large families in 1916 in "The Ranchland of Argentina and Southern Brazil." At one point he noted: "The woman who shirks from motherhood is as low a creature as a man of the professional pacifist or poltroon type who shirks his duty as a soldier." See *The Works of Theodore Roosevelt* (Memorial Edition, 1923–1926) vol. IV, p. 78.

"no one like Auntie Bye": ARL, interview with Joseph Lash, Apr. 6, 1966, FDRL.

against the "shoe-horn" approach: Susan Roosevelt Weld to author, Nov. 10, 1994.

"posterity" letters: ARL, quoted in Michael Teague, *Mrs. L*, p. 44.

"part of a clan": P. James Roosevelt, quoted in David McCullough, *Mornings on Horseback*, p. 12.
"sisterhood of pain": CRA to EKR, May 10, 1943, TRC.

CHAPTER 1: MARTHA "MITTIE" BULLOCH ROOSEVELT

"and not a day sooner": MBR to TR Sr., Dec. 3, 1853, TRC.
"more moonlight white": CRR, *MBTR*, p. 18.
"Like most northern people": Margaret Mitchell, "Bridesmaid of 87 Recalls Mittie Roosevelt's Wedding," *Atlanta Journal* magazine, June 10, 1923, p. 5.
Ice cream, known in England: International Association of Ice Cream Manufacturers, *The History of Ice Cream* (1958), pp. 5–6.
"Everybody packed up": Mitchell, "Bridesmaid of 87," p. 5.
"only person who could so suit": MBR to TR Sr., Dec. 3, 1853, TRC.
first glimpse of land—a tropical island: Jack C. Ramsay, Jr., "Archibald Stobo, Presbyterian Minister," *Journal of the Presbyterian Historical Society*, vol. 36, no. 3, Sept. 1959, pp. 129–42. I am indebted to Margaret Riddle for supplying me with this article.
one of its delegates: See Joseph G. Bulloch, M.D., *A History and Genealogy of the Families of Bulloch, Stobo, DeVeaux, Irvine*, etc. (Savannah, GA: Braid and Hutton, 1892.) Also see *Genealogy of the Pendarvis-Bedon Families of South Carolina, 1670–1900*, compiled by James Barnewell Heyward (Atlanta, GA: Foote and Davies Company, 1905).
name for himself in the War of 1812: Howard K. Beale, "Theodore Roosevelt's Ancestry, a Study in Heredity," *New York Genealogical and Biographical Record*, Oct. 1954, p. 202.
Savannah ranked among the top: David Goldfield, "Pursuing the American Dream," in *The City in Southern History*, edited by Blaine A. Brownell and David Goldfield (Port Washington, NY: Kennikat Press, 1977), pp. 84–85.
great-grandson of the original James Bulloch: Clarece Martin, *A Glimpse of the Past: The History of Bulloch Hall and Roswell Georgia* (1973), p. 4.
hesitated to take his only daughter: ARC, Memoir, p. 4, TRC.
"hung down to her belt": ARC, Memoir, p. 4, TRC.
Savannah on May 8: Genealogical Committee of Georgia Historical Society, *Marriages of Chatham County* (Savannah, GA: 1993, 2 vols.), vol. 1, p. 103.
"never knew the difference": CRR, *MBTR*, p. 10.
"My grandmother Roosevelt's family": CRR, typescript describing Roosevelt family trip abroad, 1869–70, TRC.
she made the journey from Savannah: Clarece Martin, *A Glimpse of the Past*, p. 8

"the one in whose grandmother's pew": ARC to CRR, May 10, 1926, TRC.

her descendants liked to emphasize: ARC, Memoir, p. 5, TRC.

"my heart felt tender": CRR to CRA, Mar. 14, 1912, TRC.

"incredible": ARC, Memoir, Part 3, TRC.

Federal census takers in 1850: Seventh Census of U.S., 1850, Georgia Slave Schedule for Cobb County, lists nineteen slaves, including seven males and six females of working age (fourteen or over) and six children, including a male one month old.

how the moon "crawled": CRR, *MBTR*, p. 11.

not unusual rendering of "justice,": ARC, Memoir, part 3, TRC.

he left his wife: Howard K. Beale, "Theodore Roosevelt's Ancestry, a Study in Heredity," p. 201.

"fifth wheel to the coach": CRR, *MBTR*, p. 3.

"those five horrid boys": CRR, *MBTR*, p. 3.

down the middle of Canal Street": ARC, Memoir, no page, TRC.

"fascinating looking": CRA, interview with Hermann and Mary Hagedorn, Nov. 23, 1954, p. 4, TRC.

sent her a gold thimble: CRA, interview with Hermann and Mary Hagedorn, Nov. 23, 1954, p. 4, TRC.

by the name of "Stuart": TR Sr. to "Lizzie," Nov. 1851, TR Papers, LC.

"I have never interfered": Martha Bulloch to TR Sr., May 1853, TRC.

marriage as a "trap": TR Sr. to George Morris, Roosevelt Family Papers, LC.

loved him "tenderly": MBR to TR Sr., Dec. 3, 1853, TRC.

"rush away and be alone": MBR to TR Sr., July 26, 1853, quoted in CRR, *MBTR*, pp. 13–14.

her father-in-law was known: Howard K. Beale, "Theodore Roosevelt's Ancestry, a Study in Heredity," p. 200.

"a foreign manner": ARC, Memoir, Aug. 19, 1929, p. 2, TRC.

"dignified": ARC, Memoir, Oct. 28, 1924, p. 5, TRC.

tried to reassure her: TR Sr. to MBR, July 23, 1853, TRC.

"I should hate to have married": Archibald Butt, *Letters of Archie Butt: Personal Aide to President Roosevelt.* Edited and with a biographical sketch of the author by Lawrence F. Abbott (Garden City, NY: Doubleday, 1924), p. 279.

"I cannot express": MBR to TR Sr., May 12, 1855, TRC.

"enormous quart bottle": TR Sr. to MBR, May 8, 1855, TRC.

"I feel as tho": MBR to TR Sr., May 17, 1855, TRC.

"more than any other person": MBR to TR Sr., May 23, 1855, TRC.

"dedicated to the memory": TR Sr. to MBR, May 6, 1855, TRC.

"devoted servants": CRA, interview with Hermann and Mary Hagedorn, Nov. 23, 1954, p. 5, TRC.

"the most charming aunt": CRR, *MBTR*, p. 1.

"more spiritually minded": CRA, interview Hermann and Mary Hagedorn, Nov. 23, 1954, p. 3, TRC.

"everything about Georgia": Archibald Butt, *Letters,* p. 279.
special fondness for the book *Porgy:* ARC to CRR, Feb. 9, 1926, TRC.
the "big stick" phrase: Sylvia Jukes Morris, *Edith Kermit Roosevelt,* p. 18.
"old Mrs. Badeau": ARC to CRR, May 10, 1926, TRC.
they hid a mouse: ARC to CRR, May 10, 1926, TRC.
"I am so glad": ARC to CRR, May 10, 1926, TRC.
"discovered it when the snow": ARC to CRR, May 10, 1926, TRC.
Aunt Lizzie kept soothing: ARC, Memoir, Oct. 28, 1924, p. 1, TRC.
"it had to have its legs": ARC, Memoir, Oct. 28, 1924, p. 2, TRC.
Fortescue children: "The Roosevelt Family in America: A Genealogy," *Theodore Roosevelt Association Journal* (1990), Part I, pp. 37–38, lists the Fortescue children as children of Robert B. Roosevelt and Maria Theresa O'Shea. Also see Nathan Miller, *Theodore Roosevelt: A Life* (1992), p. 51 note.
"the 'nursery'" included: CRR, *MBTR,* p. 1.
"beautiful use of the English language": ARC, Memoir, p 4.
"Our letters are sometimes meddled with": Martha Bulloch to Susan West, no date, TRC.
"for a long time never came to the dinner table": Archibald Butt, *Letters,* p. 279.
"almost unbearable to her": ARC, Memoir, p. 5, TRC.
None of his brothers served: Howard K. Beale, "Theodore Roosevelt's Ancestry, a Study in Heredity," p. 201.
for the newly formed Union League Club: The Union League Club, located on Union Square, was formed in 1863.
allotment commissioner, charged with seeing: CRR, *MBTR,* p. 20; ARC, Memoir, p. 5, TRC.
contracted typhoid fever: ARC, Memoir, no date, p. 5, TRC.
"I do not want you": CRR, *MBTR,* p. 23.
captured sixty-three Union vessels: Clarece Martin, *A Glimpse of the Past,* p. 26.
fought on land until his discharge: Clarece Martin, *A Glimpse of the Past,* p. 26.
"If I may judge": Martha Bulloch to Susan West, Nov. 1861, TRC.
"Oh it is hopeless": Martha Bulloch to Susan West, Nov. 1861, TRC.
shipping via Nassau: Martha Bulloch to Susan West, Oct. 1863, TRC.
she collected: Martha Bulloch to Susan West, Oct. 1863, TRC.
"grind the Southern troops": CRR, *MBTR,* p. 17.
sew a "drawerful": Martha Bulloch to Susan West, Jan. 1864, TRC.
invent war games: ARC, Memoir, Oct. 28, 1924, p. 7, TRC.
suffered the destruction of six city blocks: David Goldfield, "Pursuing the American Dream," *The City in Southern History,* p. 92.
in deference to a fellow Mason: Clarece Martin, *A Glimpse of the Past,* p. 32.
It contained paper silhouettes: ARC, Memoir, Oct. 28, 1924, p. 8, TRC.
When Theodore Roosevelt was president, a Union veteran sent him a

book that had been taken from Bulloch Hall when Roswell served as Union headquarters.

died of a pulmonary illness: Clarece Martin, *A Glimpse of the Past*, p. 26.

"This must be from Irvine": CRR, *MBTR*, p. 36.

recount the saga: ERD to EDW, Apr. 15, 1955, TRC.

"a wonderfully constructed creature": CRR, *MBTR*, p. 43.

"panting over you": CRR, *MBTR*, p. 43.

"The carpet," she informed her sister: CRR, *MBTR*, p. 43.

too quick to plant big kisses: H. W. Brandes, *T.R.: The Last Romantic* (1997), p. 22. Even when TR returned to England with his bride, Alice, in 1881, he wrote that the visit was marred only by "the everlasting slobbering . . . the kissing . . . simply disgusting." TR to MBR, June 5, 1881, TRC.

returned with a "Hip! Hurrah": H. W. Brandes, *T.R.*, p. 25.

Over "an enormous crinoline": ARC, Memoir, Aug. 19, 1929, pp. 4–5, TRC.

"seemed somehow to convey a waft of violets": Constance (Mrs. Burton) Harrison, *Recollections Grave and Gay* (1911), pp. 278–79.

the next three months on the Nile: CRR, *MBTR*, p. 55.

The high point of the trip for Bamie: CRR, *MBTR*, p. 62.

"an 'all-round' man": CRR, *MBTR*, p. 3.

"To be with [him was]": Monroe Robinson, "Mother Bore Her Part," no page, TRC.

"How much this time?" CRR, *MBTR*, p. 5.

"'Theodore, you are right'": CRR, *MBTR*, p. 5.

"as the son of your father": CRR, *MBTR*, p. 6.

"vague" and "nebulous": Helen R. Robinson, interview with Mary Hagedorn, Nov. 17, 1954, p. 25, TRC. Alice Longworth described Mittie as "distant." See Michael Teague, *Mrs. L*, p. 20.

Her solution was to summon the butler: Monroe Robinson, "Mother Bore Her Part," TRC.

she would be "perfectly beautiful": Helen R. Robinson, interview with Mary Hagedorn, Nov. 17, 1954, p. 25, TRC.

amounted to only "respectable poverty": Ward McAllister, *Society As I Have Found It* (1890), p. 349. The New-York Historical Society has copy #352, annotated in red by the author.

"witty but very ugly": ARC, Memoir, p. 2, TRC.

she credited him with bringing gaiety: ARC, Memoir, p. 2, TRC.

"Mrs. Theodore Roosevelt . . . seemed . . . easily the most beautiful": Constance (Mrs. Burton) Harrison, *Recollections Grave and Gay*, p. 278.

"One asks oneself": Constance (Mrs. Burton) Harrison, *Recollections Grave and Gay*, pp. 278–79.

"Little Motherling": TR to MBR, Sept. 14, 1879, TRC.

she "had fascinating little ways": Rita Halle Kleeman, *Gracious Lady: The Life of Sara Delano Roosevelt* (1935), p. 99.

remarkable mimic and storyteller: Edmund Morris, *The Rise of Theodore Roosevelt* (1979), p. 36.

open and close a house: David McCullough, *Mornings on Horseback*, p. 226. McCullough estimated that in one nine-month period MBR hosted twenty dinner parties and at least that many teas.

"didn't have it": CRA, interview with Hermann and Mary Hagedorn, Nov. 23, 1954, p. 2, TRC.

"stormy love affairs": ARC, Memoir, p. 4, TRC.

"one of the greatest works of art": CRR, *MBTR*, pp. 47–48.

handcarved staircase had to be remade: ARC, Memoir, p. 1, TRC.

"terribly, terribly extravagant": CRA, interview with Hermann and Mary Hagedorn, Nov. 23, 1954, p.1, TRC.

found no evidence: David McCullough, *Mornings on Horseback*, p. 135.

"Life was completely changed": ARC, Memoir, p. 2, TRC.

could not have managed: MBR to ARC, Aug. 24, 1870, TRC.

Elliott who pronounced the house "cursed": Henry F. Pringle, *Theodore Roosevelt; A Biography* (1931), p. 51.

"There was no dissipation": ARC, Memoir, Oct. 28, 1924, p. 3, TRC.

"I never felt that I was childless": Anna Bulloch Gracie to ARL, Mar. 25, 1884, TRC.

"I *love* a little *girl*": Anna Bulloch Gracie to ARL, Mar. 25, 1884, TRC.

chosen as the baby's godmother: Anna Bulloch Gracie to ERD, 1891, TRC.

"like an extra set of parents": Helen R. Robinson, interview with Mary Hagedorn, Nov. 17,1954, TRC.

get "along well with Teddy": Anna Bulloch Gracie to CRR, Oct. 27, 1886, TRC.

"her little sides shook": Anna Bulloch Gracie to CRR, June 13, 1886, TRC.

"married the dolt": Anna Bulloch Gracie to CRR, Oct. 6, 1890, TRC.

"the sob which will not be restrained": Anna Bulloch Gracie to CRR, Sept. 16, 1892, TRC.

"Our southern blood runs strong": ERD to EDW, Oct. 8, 1972, TRC.

"'Sweeted himself away'": ERD to EDW, Apr. 12, 1964, TRC.

"practical in her own strange way": CRA, interview with Hermann and Mary Hagedorn, Nov. 23, 1954, TRC.

"small, vague and feminine": Edmund Morris, *The Rise of Theodore Roosevelt*, p. 35.

"the most fascinating of them all": David McCullough, *Mornings on Horseback*, p. 38.

"Dearest" or "Darling": See letters of TR Sr. to MBR, 1853 and 1855, TRC.

"I have always been accustomed to think": TR Sr. to MBR, June 3, 1873, TRC.

"My own little Girl": TR Sr. to MBR, July 17, 1873, TRC.

"I wish I could kiss you": TR Sr. to MBR, Sept. 21, 1874, TRC.

She wrote remarkably intelligent: MBR, Diary, Aug. 26–Sept. 29, 1869, TRC.

if *"the money matters are going on well"*: MBR to TR Sr., July 13, 1873, TRC.

"look them over very carefully": MBR to TR Sr., July 20, 1873, TRC.

"Mr F was in doubt about furniture": MBR to TR Sr., June 15, 1873, TRC.

"temporary carpet for my own room": MBR to TR Sr., Aug. 10, 1873, TRC.

CHAPTER 2: ANNA "BAMIE" ROOSEVELT COWLES

"Oh Energy": TR to ARC, Apr. 1, 1877, TRC.

"the energy" of Bye: Susan Weld to author, Nov. 10, 1994.

"been a man": Nicholas Roosevelt, *A Front Row Seat*, (1953), p. 53.

"I always believed": Michael Teague, *Mrs. L: Conversations with Alice Roosevelt Longworth* (1981), p. 22.

"too smart by half": Anna Gracie, quoting a friend, in letter to ARC, no date, TRC.

"Doh pack": Michael Teague, *Mrs. L*, p. 22.

"Anna E.": ARC to Anna Bulloch Gracie, 1869, TRC.

"four great and hideous swine": Anna Gracie to EKR, Aug. 30, 1890, TRC.

"had no particular girlhood": Mrs. Richard Aldrich [née Margaret Chanler], interview with Mary Hagedorn, Mar. 30, 1955, p. 2, cites interview of Mrs. Richard Bissell with Mary Hagedorn, Mar. 30, 1955, TRC.

"Instead of the terrible": ARC, Memoir, p. 5, TRC.

"became very strong": ARC, Memoir, p. 5, TRC.

"possessing an immense capacity": Lloyd C. Griscom, *Diplomatically Speaking* (1940), p. 66.

"charming afternoon" . . . "amusing memories cling": ARC to Robert Ferguson, Apr. 1891, Ferguson Papers, Box 2, Folder 25, AHS.

"When we reach": ARC to TR, July 24, 1873, TRC.

"There is always": Michael Teague, *Mrs. L* (1981), p. 22.

"It all seems": ARC, Memoir, TRC.

"It was the fashion" . . . parents sent her: ARC, Memoir, TRC.

"with mingled feelings": ARC, Memoir, TRC.

On Bamie not wearing glasses, see interview of Mrs. Richard Bissell with Mary Hagedorn, May 23, 1955, p. 10, TRC.

"She is a woman": Mrs. Richard Bissell, interview with Mary Hagedorn, May 23, 1955, p. 10, TRC.

"From then on": ARC, Memoir, TRC.

Bamie would have taken no note: Joyce Antler, "'After College, What': New Graduates and the Family Claim," *American Quarterly*, fall 1980, pp. 409–34.

"The curtains": TR, *Letters from Theodore Roosevelt to Anna Roosevelt Cowles, 1870–1918* (1924), p. 12.

"It has really": TR, *Letters* (1924), p. 18.

"For joy or for sorrow": quoted in H. W. Brandes, *TR: The Last Romantic* (1997), p. 163.

he relied on his sister: TR, *Letters*, p. 54.

"listened to": TR, *Letters*, p. 55.

"political career finished": TR, *Letters*, p. 68.

"a perfect nightmare": ARC, Memoir, p. 2, TRC.

"I always insisted": ARC, Memoir, p. 3, TRC.

"additions to our limited list": TR to ARC, Apr. 1886, TRC.

"politics . . . dull husbands": TR to ARC, Apr. 1886, TRC.

"our friends": TR to ARC, Apr. 1886, TRC.

"I am delighted": TR to ARC, June 28, 1886, TRC.

"which I suppose": TR, *Letters*, p. 85.

"to become a teacher": TR to ARC, June 28, 1886, TRC.

"railroad scheme": TR to ARC, June 28, 1886, TRC.

"really to my mind": TR to ARC, Aug. 11, 1886, TRC.

"She is very well read": TR to ARC, Aug. 11, 1886, TRC.

"best love": TR to ARC, Apr. 29, 1886, TRC.

"cunning little": TR to ARC, June 28, 1886, TRC.

"It was very much": ARC, Memoir, p. 3, TRC.

"pretty nearly ideal": TR to ARC, Apr. 1886, TRC.

"most ideal way of traveling": ARC, Memoir, p. 4, TRC.

"a mass of bloom": For an account of the trip, see ARC, Memoir, p. 4, TRC.

"nothing is more common": David McCullough, *Mornings on Horseback* (1981), p. 357.

"savagely irritated" . . . "face to face": TR to ARC, Sept. 20, 1886, TRC.

"utterly disbelieve[d]" . . . "on my shoulders": TR to ARC, Sept. 20, 1886, TRC.

"Eight years": TR to ARC, Sept. 20, 1886, TRC.

"As regards" . . . "paying the expense": TR to ARC, Sept. 20, 1886, TRC.

"hold" and role of Douglas Robinson in campaign, see ARC to EKR, Oct. 23, 1886, TRC.

"I will never forget": ARC, Memoir, p. 4, TRC.

"undauntedly": ARC, Memoir, p. 2, TRC.

"You dearest sister": TR to ARC, Dec. 1886, TRC.

"I hardly know" . . . "many kisses": TR to ARC, Jan. 10, 1887, TRC.

"there was a wonderful feeling": Michael Teague, *Mrs. L*, p. 28.

"It almost broke my heart": ARC, Memoir, p. 3, TRC.

"Sine my little Alice" . . . "despair": ARC to Robert Ferguson, no date, Ferguson Papers, Box 3, Folder 54, AHS.

"at his very best" . . . "exerting all his powers": ARC to EKR, Oct. 23, 1886, TRC.

"perfectly enchanting": ARC, Memoir, no date, p. 2, TRC.

"one of the most exclusively aristocratic": ARC, p. 3, TRC.

Wharton's characters: ARC to CRR, May 16, 1925, TRC.

"there is really" . . . "platform is not": TR to ARC, July 8, 1888, TRC.

"a big man": Michael Teague, *Mrs. L*, p. 10.

"I wish Caution": TR to ARC, May 27, 1887, TRC.

"Alice's wish" . . . "frankly about it": TR to ARC, July 15, 1888, TRC.

"an odd-job man": ARC, Memoir, p. 4, TRC.

"Edith has just had" . . . "over a week": TR to ARC, Aug. 8, 1888, TRC.

"Hell-roaring" . . . "in those days": ARC, Memoir, Oct. 27, 1925, p. 1, TRC.

"perfectly disreputable": ARC, Memoir, Oct. 27, 1925, p. 2, TRC.

dangled the prospect: ARC to Robert Ferguson, Oct. 28, 1890, Ferguson Papers, Box 2, Folder 24, AHS.

"hate to think": ARC to Robert Ferguson, Sept. 17, 1893, Ferguson Papers, Box 2, Folder 27, AHS.

"overfatigue" . . . "absolutely necessary": ARC to Robert Ferguson, Aug. 31, 1893, Ferguson Papers, Box 2, Folder 27, AHS.

"Your room": ARC to Robert Ferguson, Aug. 31, 1893, Ferguson Papers, Box 2, Folder 27, AHS.

"Bob if ever": ARC to Robert Ferguson, Sept. 1893, Box 2, Folder 27, AHS.

"business is really": ARC to Robert Ferguson, Aug. 31, 1893, Ferguson Papers, Box 2, Folder 27, AHS.

difficult drunk: ARL put the date much earlier. In an interview with Joseph Lash, Feb. 6, 1967, FDRL, ARL said: "I think Elliott was already a drunkard when he went on his round-the-world trip."

"it was against": ARC, Memoir, Oct. 23, 1925, p. 1, TRC.

"became my home": ARC, Memoir, Oct. 23, 1925, p. 1, TRC.

"in a strange": ARC, Memoir, Oct. 23, 1925, p. 1, TRC

"loved" . . . "feeding the birds": ARC to CRR, Aug. 7, 1925. For biographical information on Thomas Reed, see Samuel W. McCall, *The Life of Thomas Bracket Reed* (1914) and U.S. Congress, *Biographical Directory of the American Congress, 1774–1989*, p. 1702.

"heartily": TR, *Letters* (1924), pp. 119–20.

"decidedly older" . . . "with trembling": ARC to Robert Ferguson, undated, Ferguson Papers, Box 2, Folder 25, AHS.

"glittering autumn day": ARC to Robert Ferguson, Sept. 1893, Ferguson Papers, Box 2, Folder 27, AHS.

"There is very very much": ARC to Robert Ferguson, Sept. 24, 1893, Ferguson Papers, Box 2, Folder 27, AHS.

Columbian Exposition: Neil Harris, William de Wit, James Gilbert, and Robert W. Rydell, *Grand Illusions* (1993) and John W. Findling, *Chicago's Great World's Fair* (1994).

"perfectly wonderful": ARC, Memoir, Oct. 23, 1925, p. 2, TRC.

Women's Building: Harris et al., *Grand Illusions*, p. 289.

official sculptor: Harris et al., *Grand Illusions*, p. 152.

"I never will forget": ARC, Memoir, Oct. 23, 1925, p. 2, TRC.

"life would not be worth": ARC, Memoir, Oct. 23, 1925, p. 2, TRC.

"wonderful college settlement": ARC to Robert Ferguson, Dec. 8, 1893, Ferguson Papers, Box 2, Folder 27, AHS.

"knew every foot" . . . "I should be": TR to ARC, Nov. 1893, TRC.

"did not recognize": ARC, Memoir, Oct. 23, 1925, p. 2, TRC.

"unequal to facing": ARC to Robert Ferguson, Nov. 24, 1893, Ferguson Papers, Box 2, Folder 27, AHS.

"it is selfish" . . . "pleasant side": ARC to Robert Ferguson, Nov. 24, 1893, Ferguson Papers, Box 2, Folder 27, AHS.

"Bob dear" . . . "at that time": ARC to Robert Ferguson, Nov. 24, 1893, Ferguson Papers, Box 2, Folder 27, AHS.

"marvelous and overwhelming" . . . "I return": ARC to Robert Ferguson, Dec. 1, 1893, Ferguson Papers, Box 2, Folder 27, AHS.

"as late as possible": ARC to Robert Ferguson, Dec. 1, 1893, Ferguson Papers, Box 2, Folder 27, AHS.

"it is dreadful" . . . "was bad": ARC to Robert Ferguson, Dec. 8, 1893, Ferguson Papers, Box 2, Folder 27, AHS.

"time of crying": ARC to Robert Ferguson, Dec. 8, 1893, Ferguson Papers, Box 2, Folder 27, AHS.

"very pretty French": Helen R. Robinson, interview with Mary Hagedorn, Nov. 17, 1954, p. 2, TRC.

"so that everything": Helen R. Robinson, interview with Mary Hagedorn, Nov. 17, 1954, p. 3, TRC.

"immediately caught on" . . . "what to do": Helen R. Robinson, interview with Mary Hagedorn, Nov. 17, 1954, pp. 3–4, TRC.

"knew instinctively" . . . "adored her": Helen R. Robinson, interview with Mary Hagedorn, Nov. 17, 1954, pp. 4–5, TRC.

Bamie's loss of hearing: Helen R. Robinson, interview with Mary Hagedorn, Nov. 17, 1954, pp. 14–15, TRC.

"No good looks" . . . "It was contagious": Helen R. Robinson to Mary Hagedorn, Nov. 17, 1954, p. 10, TRC.

"curiously stiff": Helen R. Robinson, interview with Mary Hagedorn, Nov. 17, 1954, p. 10, TRC.

"You are doing": TR to ARC, Dec. 1893, TRC.

"dear": ARC to TR, Jan. 18, 1894, TRC.

"back with me": ARC to Robert Ferguson, Apr. 27, 1894, Ferguson Papers, Box 2, Folder 28, AHS.

to relay his view: TR, *Letters* (1924), p. 143.

"our economic thinkers" . . . "stable basis": TR, *Letters*, pp. 141–42.

"a hopeless snarl" . . . "Presidential nomination": TR, *Letters*, p. 142.

"Theodore is so good": ARC to Robert Ferguson, Apr. 27, 1894, Ferguson Papers, Box 2, Folder 28, AHS.

"Corinne in a vague way": ARC to Robert Ferguson, Apr. 27, 1894, Ferguson Papers, Box 2, Folder 28, AHS.

"very good spirits": ERK to Gertrude Carow, Jan. 1895, TRC.

"a darling" . . . "such adoration": Helen R. Robinson, interview with Mary Hagedorn, Nov. 17, 1954, p. 6, TRC.

"I don't think": Helen R. Robinson, interview with Mary Hagedorn, Nov. 17, 1954, p. 6, TRC.

The Cowleses . . . "remarkably intellectual": Calvin Duvall Cowles, *Genealogy of the Cowles Families in America* (1929), p. 268.

"It took the solitude": ARC, Memoir, p. 4, TRC.

"To say": TR to ARC, July 4, 1895, TRC.

"I have always felt": TR to ARC, July 4, 1895, TRC. On Cabot Lodge, see ARC, Memoir, Part 4, TRC.

Allen Thurman was dead: Herman Dieck, *Life and Public Services of Our Great Reform President Grover Cleveland* (1888), passim. On Thurman's career, see U.S. Congress, *Biographical Directory of the American Congress*, pp. 1938–39.

"full written report" . . . "in California": TR to ARC, July 19, 1895, TRC.

"bigamous" . . . "at an end": TR to ARC, July 19, 1895, TRC.

"*probably* get relief" . . . "if I do not write as plainly": TR to ARC, July 19, 1895, TRC.

"little more hopeful" . . . "would go" TR to ARC, July 23, 1895, TRC.

"insisted on my writing" . . . "wreck your life": TR to ARC, Aug. 5, 1895, TRC.

"I have devoted" . . . "always be remembered": TR to ARC, Sept. 8, 1895, TRC.

"without regard": TR to ARC, Sept. 15, 1895, TRC.

"in the district": TR to ARC, Nov. 10, 1895, TRC.

"dumbfounded": TR to ARC, Nov. 10, 1895, TRC.

"It seems so funny": ERR to ARC, Nov. 15, [1895], TRC.

"dishonorable": TR to ARC, July 5, 1895, TRC.

"I see the wisdom": EKR to ARC, Nov. 1895, TRC.

"this autumn somewhere" . . . "minor difficulties": ARC to Robert Ferguson, Aug. 1895, Ferguson Papers, Box 2, Folder 29, AHS.

"did me a world of good" . . . "at least": ARC to Robert Ferguson, Oct. 1895, Ferguson Papers, Box 2, Folder 29, AHS.

"ridiculous": ARC, Memoir, Part 4, TRC.

"so excited": CRR to ARC, Oct. 1895, TRC.

"She is wonderfully natural": CRR to TR, Nov. 25, 1895, TRC.

"as executive as usual" . . . "really happy": CRR to TR, Nov. 25, 1895, TRC.

"beautifully" . . . "she was delayed": CRR to TR, Nov. 25, 1895, TRC.

the American side: Lilian Rixey, *Bamie* (1963), p. 92.
"A spark would": Lilian Rixey, *Bamie*, p. 89.
"suffered in Abyssinia": ARC to Robert Ferguson, Mar. 14, 1896, Ferguson Papers, Box 2, Folder 30, AHS.
"with all his naval matters": ARC to Robert Ferguson, Mar. 14, 1896, Ferguson Papers, Box 2, Folder 30, AHS.
"told me to fondly": ARC to Robert Ferguson, May 16, 1896, Ferguson Papers, Box 2, Folder 30, AHS.
"bursting with pride": Douglas Robinson to Robert Ferguson, Sept. 1896, TRC.
"turned out to be": . . . always "Anna": Helen R. Robinson, interview with Mary Hagedorn, p. 11, TRC.
"a merry couple of weeks": ARC to CRR, Feb. 14, 1925, TRC.
"cloth doll": ARC to CRR, July 15, 1922, TRC. It should be noted that Bamie used the cloth doll image also for herself.
"determination": John Alsop to author, Oct. [15, 1997.
considered the possibility: EKR to ARC, 1893, TRC.
"You furnish the pictures": Thomas F. Bailey, *The American Pageant* (4th ed., 1971), p. 657.
"cowboys, ex-polo players": Thomas F. Bailey, *The American Pageant*, p. 662.
"petrified" . . . "safely to us": ARC to Robert Ferguson, Sept. 10, 1898, Ferguson Papers, Box 2, Folder 32, AHS.
"Bob dear": ARC to Robert Ferguson, Sept. 10, 1898, Ferguson Papers, Box 2, Folder 32, AHS.
"good people" . . . "ARC": Lilian Rixey, *Bamie*, p. 130.
named him: He, in turn, would also have one son and recycle the name once more. Only in the next generation when the fourth William Sheffield Cowles (born in 1923) added substantially to the family tree by fathering five sons and one daughter did the Roosevelt name reappear in Bamie's line.
"to fairly smirk": ARC to EKR, Jan. 29, 1903, TRC.
"is much more boyish looking": EKR to Kermit Roosevelt, Nov. 9, 1902, Papers of Belle and Kermit Roosevelt, LC.
"a little difference": EKR to Emily Carow, July 1904, TRC.
services of a specialist: This insistence on specialists was something of a family tradition. Joanna Sturm later reported that she hesitated to complain about some physical ailments because her grandmother, Alice Longworth, would immediately seek the best expert on the subject.
choose to live: TR, *Letters*, p. 207.
whether or not he should run: TR to ARC, Jan. 23, 1900, TRC.
"Bamie met us": EKR to Emily Carow, Mar. 8, 1901, TRC.
"damned cowboy": Thomas F. Bailey, *The American Pageant*, p. 676.
"I shall have to trust": TR *Letters*, p. 251.

walk a narrow line . . . "involves so much": ARC to CRR, Apr. 16, 1902, TRC.

"the worst disaster": Clipping of Apr. 13, 1904, in Folder 371, ARC Papers, TRC.

"an outrage" . . . "for us all": ARC to CRR, Apr. 1904, TRC.

"Theodore I see" . . . "entirely alone": ARC to CRR, Nov. 21, 1901, TRC.

"hard on us all": ARC to CRR, Jan. 2, 1903, TRC.

Democratic candidates: TR to ARC, Aug. 30, 1904, TRC.

her attempt to influence: TR to ARC, Oct. 16, 1902, TRC.

"in the last stages": ARC to CRR, July 20, 1909, TRC.

"machine-made sensation": ARC to CRR, 1891, during German trip.

"*cannot* be cured": ARC, quoted in letter of CRR to CRA, Oct. 19, 1910, TRC.

"what solitary confinement": ARC to CRR, July 15, 1911, TRC.

"far too much": ARC to CRR, Sept. 3, 1913, TRC.

"the busiest person in the house": ARC to Robert Ferguson, Dec. 18, 1916, Ferguson Papers, Box 2, Folder 51, AHS.

reported to Congress: *NYT,* Dec. 23, 1909, p. 3.

"absconded with the suffrage bill": CRA, interview with Hermann and Mary Hagedorn, Dec. 28, 1954, p. 31, TRC.

Bamie noted that Catt: ARC to CRR, Nov. 1, 1926, recalls event of 1914 in which Bamie came up against the suffragists. On the complexities of the suffrage movement and how class differences mattered, see Ellen Carol DuBois, "Working Women, Class Relations and Suffrage Militance: Harriot Stanton Blatch and the New York Woman Suffrage Movement, 1894–1909," *Journal of American History,* June 1987, pp. 34–58.

"strongly against it": CRR to Robert Ferguson, June 18, 1895, Ferguson Papers, Box 15, Folder 344, AHS.

"the faint aroma": ARC to ERR, July 14, 1917, FDRL.

"not regard it": TR to ARC, June 29, 1911, TRC.

"only the tiniest fraction": TR to ARC, June 29, 1922, TRC.

"huge woman suffrage meeting" . . . like a weapon: TR to ERD, May 1, 1913, TRC.

"stupid vote": Sylvia Jukes Morris, *Edith Kermit Roosevelt: Portrait of a First Lady* (1980), p. 98.

"just wasn't attuned": Helen R. Robinson, interview with Mary Hagedorn, Nov. 17, 1954, p. 30, TRC.

Connecticut . . . did not ratify: See *New York World-Telegram,* June 11, 1932, p. 2; it reviewed events of 1920 when the necessary number of states (thirty-six) had not yet ratified the Nineteenth Amendment and suffragists asked the governors of Vermont and Connecticut to call special sessions of their state legislatures to ratify.

"just exactly" . . . "in Connecticut": CRA, interview with Hermann and Mary Hagedorn, Dec. 28, 1954, p. 31, TRC.

"a wistful look": ARC to CRR, Aug. 28, 1917, TRC.

"gay as a bird": CRA to EKR, letter enclosed in EKR to ERD, Jan. 1919, TRC.

"A visit to New York" . . . "tukee": ARC to CRR, Feb. 15, 1917, TRC.

"I truly think": ARC to Robert and Isabella Ferguson, Sept. 21, 1906, Ferguson Papers, Box 2, Folder 41, AHS.

"I feel quite like": ARC to Joe Alsop, Feb. 1, 1908, TRC.

"naturally bursting with pride": CRA to CRR, Apr. 1911, TRC.

"Poor Sheffield": ERR to Isabella Selmes Ferguson, June 27, 1914, Ferguson Papers, Box 15, Folder 360, AHS.

"If he comes back": ERR to Isabella Selmes Ferguson, Feb. 24, 1918, Ferguson Papers, Box 2, Folder 53, AHS.

"working hard at New Haven": ARC to Robert Ferguson, Jan. 23, 1919, Ferguson Papers, Box 3, Folder 53, AHS.

"one of the most notable": *NYT*, July 10, 1921, p. 22.

"I feel as though" . . . used kitchen stove: ARC to CRR, Sept. 19, 1922, TRC.

"beloved grandson": ARC to CRR, Aug. 9, 1925, TRC.

"too adorable" . . . "perfectly adorable": ARC to CRR, Dec. 11, 1923, TRC.

"I have felt sure": ARC to CRR, Sept. 9, 1926, TRC.

colorful cast of guests: ARC to CRR, Feb. 9, 1926, TRC.

"the limit I could stand": ARC to CRR, Feb. 9, 1926, TRC.

"withered away": ARC to CRR, Oct. 15, 1924, TRC.

"felt absolutely creepy": ARC to CRR, May 17, 1926, TRC.

"a pleasant bridge table": ARC to CRR, Feb. 14, 1925, TRC.

"a very worn out, decrepit": ARC to CRR, Aug. 26, 1926, TRC.

"I think that she combines" . . . "was the word": ARC to CRR, Aug. 7, 1925, TRC.

"[There was never] one bit": Helen R. Robinson, interview with Mary Hagedorn, Nov. 17, 1954, pp. 16–17, TRC.

"The first time": ARC to CRR, Apr. 24, 1902, TRC.

"She certainly accomplished": ARC to CRR, Aug. 26, 1926, TRC.

"live on bitter tonics": ARC to CRR, Sept. 10, 1929, TRC.

One story: CRA to Hermann and Mary Hagedorn, Dec. 28, 1954, p. 27, TRC.

"rather a man's mind" . . . "financial interests": Sheffield Cowles, interview with Hermann and Mary Hagedorn, Dec. 28, 1954, pp. 21–22, TRC.

"That is nothing": Sheffield Cowles, interview with Hermann and Mary Hagedorn, Dec. 28, 1954, p. 24, TRC.

sharpness in her manner: Helen R. Robinson, interview with Mary Hagedorn, Nov. 17, 1954, p. 16, TRC

"a certain quality of significance": ERD to EDW, Apr. 26, 1958, TRC.

"leave a life": ARC to CRR, June 25, 1910, TRC.

"I have rather an odd sensation" . . . "painful possibilities": ARC to CRR, Sept. 1922, TRC.
"Blessed Corinne": ARC to CRR, Mar. 10, 1926, TRC
"She . . . seems": EKR to CRR, June 8, 1929, TRC.
"perspiration run down": ARC to CRR, July 31, 1931, TRC.
"Of course every thing": CRR to CRA, Mar. 6, 1930, TRC.
"I cannot face": CRA to CRR, Sept. 1930, TRC.
"I always had the feeling": Mrs. Richard Bissell, interview with Mary Hagedorn, May 23, 1955, TRC.

CHAPTER 3: CORINNE ROOSEVELT ROBINSON

"Vote against the Republican Party": *NYT,* June 10, 1920, p. 8.
"There's not enough money": Samuel Adams, *Incredible Era: The Life and Times of Warren Gamaliel Harding* (1939), p. 132.
"deferentially escorted" . . . "sister of Theodore Roosevelt": *NYT,* June 12, 1920, p. 2.
"Her gestures": *NYT,* June 12, 1920, p. 2.
Roosevelt "type": Frederick M. Davenport, "Conservative America," *Outlook*, vol. 125, p. 377.
"You can imagine": ARC quoted Lodge in letter to CRR, June 29, 1920, TRC.
She "longed" to learn: CRR, *MBTR*, p. 131.
She later singled out: *Mentor*, June 15, 1920, p. 7.
"two young ladies": Elliott Roosevelt to James Gracie, May 2, 1873, TRC.
"I have written": CRR to TR Sr., July 1873, TRC.
"We are No Asses": CRR, *MBTR,* pp. 71–72.
"over or under": Monroe Robinson, "Mother Bore Her Part," TRC.
"how very old" . . . "I am glad": CRR to EKR, Aug. 6, 1878, TRC.
"a sword of Damocles": CRA, interview with Hermann and Mary Hagedorn, Nov. 23, 1954, p. 13, TRC.
"I think you will be able": CRA, interview with Hermann and Mary Hagedorn, Nov. 23, 1954, p. 13, TRC.
Bamie . . . better match: CRR to Douglas Robinson, May 1, 1881, TRC.
"Sometimes I think": CRR to Douglas Robinson, Mar. 23, 1881, TRC.
"strong and tender": CRR to Douglas Robinson, Feb. 13, 1881, TRC.
"both say we would like": CRR to Douglas Robinson, 1881, TRC.
"or I would not have the horror": CRR to Douglas Robinson, Mar. 30, 1881, TRC.
"bluer than indigo": TR to Alice Lee Roosevelt, Mar. 28, 1881, TRC.
"Nihilism (deep)": CRR to Douglas Robinson, Mar. 26, 1881, TRC.
"tremendous collision": CRR to Douglas Robinson, Mar. 14, 1881, TRC.
"like pieces of dirt": CRA, interview with Hermann and Mary Hagedorn, Nov. 23, 1954, p. 16, TRC.

One . . . dropped dead: CRA, interview with Hermann and Mary Hagedorn, Nov. 23, 1954, p. 16, TRC.

"a literary society of great renown": CRR to Douglas Robinson, Mar. 21, 1881, TRC.

"true and strong": CRR to Douglas Robinson, Mar. 21, 1881, TRC.

"a real saint of a woman" . . . "sad and dull": CRR to Douglas Robinson, Mar. 26, 1881, TRC.

"You *must* be naturalized": CRR to Douglas Robinson, ca. 1881, TRC.

"much excited": CRR to Douglas Robinson, July 3, 1881, TRC.

"I married your father": Monroe Robinson, "Mother Bore Her Part," TRC.

"two or three men": CRA, interview with Hermann and Mary Hagedorn, Nov. 23, 1954, p. 13, TRC.

"convenient": Dorothy Robinson Kidder to author, Oct. 17, 1994.

same physical problem: CRA reported that her mother had to have a "tiny" operation before child number two.

"He loves you": CRA, interview with Hermann and Mary Hagedorn, Nov. 23, 1954, p. 19, TRC.

"the catechism so far": Douglas Robinson to CRR, Sept. 17, 1901, TRC.

Robinson estate: For a description of life at Orange, see CRA, interview with Hermann and Mary Hagedorn, Nov. 23, 1954, pp. 11–12 and 21–22, TRC.

"Moses, poor Moses": CRA, interview with Hermann and Mary Hagedorn, Nov. 23, 1954, p. 11, TRC.

"madly in love" . . . "ready to kill": CRA, interview with Hermann and Mary Hagedorn, Nov. 23, 1954, p. 23, TRC.

"I know that I am": CRR to Douglas Robinson, May 1892, TRC.

"If you do": CRR to Douglas Robinson, May 1895, TRC.

"Mr. Briggs" . . . "friends anyway": CRR to Douglas Robinson, May 1895; letter appeared unopened in 1992 when author came across it in the TRC.

"Roosevelts . . . wide awake": CRR to Douglas Robinson, May 1895, TRC.

"not find me attractive": CRR to Douglas Robinson, summer 1902, TRC.

"nothing second cut": Douglas Robinson to Robert Ferguson, May 22, 1894, Ferguson Papers, Box 15, Folder 357, AHS.

"whether in Orange or New York" . . . "door was shut": CRA, Autobiography, p. 13. I am indebted to John Alsop for permitting me to read his mother's unpublished autobiography.

"really best times": CRR to Douglas Robinson, Feb. 3, 1903, TRC.

"very sunny character": CRA, interview with Hermann and Mary Hagedorn, Dec. 28, 1954, pp. 40–41, TRC.

"very able in his studies": CRR to Douglas Robinson, Sept. 14, 1902, TRC.

"I am filled with yearning tenderness": CRR to Douglas Robinson, Sept. 14, 1902, TRC.

JOHNSTON PUBLIC LIBRARY
JOHNSTON, IOWA 50131

"Of course I said nothing": CRR to Douglas Robinson, Oct. 2, 1902, TRC.

"because that's how he tested" ... "document before": CRR to Douglas Robinson, Oct. 2, 1902, TRC.

"The President of the U.S.": CRR to Douglas Robinson, Oct. 1902, TRC.

"looking very much like Humpty Dumpty": CRR to EKR, June 8, 1902, TRC.

"The President's Sister": Headline quoted in CRR to CRA, Oct. 1902, TRC.

"This is one of the penalties" ... "very mad": CRR to Robert Ferguson, Jan. 18, 1909, Ferguson Papers, Box 15, Folder 351, AHS.

"just as they were": CRR to CRA, Nov. 28, 1902, TRC.

"really magnificent room" ... "Ethel [his goddaughter] cavorted": CRR to CRA, Nov. 28, 1902, TRC.

"gave out the candy": CRR to CRA, Jan. 1903, TRC.

"the most enormous creature" ... "inclusion in *Punch*": CRR to CRA, Jan. 1903, TRC.

"I'll never forget": Monroe Robinson, "Mother Bore Her Part," TRC. CRR describes her wrestling technique in *MBTR*, pp. 145–46.

"brilliant evening" ... "as usual": CRR to CRA, Jan. 1903, TRC.

"very bright and well": CRR to CRA, Jan. 1903, TRC.

"I have just seen Bamie": EKR to CRR, Dec. 19, 1904, TRC.

"defiling" the White House: Quoted in Nathan Miller, *Theodore Roosevelt: A Life* (1992), p. 362.

Corinne ... entertained Washington: Note from Booker T. Washington to CRR, accepting her invitation for lunch, Apr. 27, 1903, TRC.

"Haven't we had fun": CRR, *MBTR*, p. 194.

"or at least I asked": CRR, *MBTR,* p. 216.

"with one strong stroke": CRR, *MBTR*, p. 234.

"no problem, no difficulties": CRA, interview with Hermann and Mary Hagedorn, Dec. 28, 1954, p. 40, TRC.

the fall resulted: Joseph W. Alsop (with Adam Platt), *I've Seen the Best of It* (1992), p. 69. Robert Merry gives the same account in *Taking On the World: Joseph and Stewart Alsop, Guardians of the American Century*, (1996), p. 12.

"was very much in love": CRA, interview with Hermann and Mary Hagedorn, Dec. 28, 1954, p. 40, TRC.

"Everything seems to have gone": CRR to CRA, Nov. 1909, TRC.

"To part with you": CRR to CRA, Dec. 1, 1909, TRC.

"pleasant people" ... "particularly strong": CRR to CRA, Dec. 1909, TRC.

"a motor trip might": CRR to CRA, early 1910, TRC.

"about art": CRR to CRA, early 1910, TRC.

"Wasn't that exactly": CRR to CRA, Dec. 7, 1909, TRC.

"horrid spot" ... "and he loved it": CRR to CRA, Dec. 20, 1909, TRC.

"Many of his interesting letters": CRR to ERR, Feb. 28, 1910, FDRL.

"I saw it early": CRR to CRA, Feb. 1910, TRC.

"I know I am nervous": CRR to CRA, Sept. 30, 1910, TRC.

"All the high muck a mucks": CRR to CRA, Mar. 28, 1910, TRC.

"pink cloud of happiness": CRR to CRA, May 2, 1910, TRC.

"able, agreeable Englishmen": CRR to CRA, Mar. 1910, TRC.

"incarnation of youth": CRR to CRA, May 2, 1910, TRC.

"perpetual Cheshire cat smile" . . . "made me ill": CRR to CRA, Apr. 18, 1910, TRC.

bored by such events: CRR to CRA, May 2, 1910, TRC.

"poisoned" system: CRR to CRA, May 2, 1910, TRC.

"'very large man'": CRR to CRA, May 2, 1910, TRC.

"have a new household": CRR to CRA, May 2, 1910, TRC.

"I both long and dread": CRR to Henry Cabot Lodge, May 27, 1910, MHS.

"I longed for you": CRR to CRA, Nov. 25, 1910, TRC.

"to consult the 'Big Stick'": CRR to CRA, July 18, 1910, TRC.

"as full of that wonderful vigor": CRR to CRA, Nov. 19, 1911, TRC.

"sat by the Library fire": CRR to CRA, Jan. 12, 1912, TRC.

"I am not a candidate" . . . "he had had it": CRR to CRA, Jan. 12, 1912, TRC.

"constantly" . . . "last ditch": CRR to CRA, spring 1912, TRC.

"I had to sweep out" . . . "quiet evening together": CRR to CRA, spring 1912, TRC.

when Corinne first met him: CRR Diary, Sept. 26, 1890, TRC.

"perfectly inadequate" . . . "what they understand": Charles Erskine Scott Wood to CRR, July 27, 1913, TRC.

"really and truly" . . . "but not mine": Charles Erskine Scott Wood to CRR, July 27, 1913, TRC.

"infinitely shocking" . . . to disappointment: Charles Erskine Scott Wood to CRR, July 27, 1913, TRC.

"literary and poetical love affair": Erskine Wood, *Life of Charles Erskine Scott Wood* (1978), p. 116. I am indebted to Dona Munker for calling this book to my attention.

"but I do not remember": Charles Erskine Scott Wood to CRR, July 27, 1913, TRC.

Bought a starched one: Erskine Wood, *Life of Charles Erskine Scott Wood*, p. 54.

"elements of popular success": Edith Wharton to CRR, Sept. 1907, TRC.

"verses have a fine militant" . . . "described in detail": Edith Wharton to CRR, ca. 1912, TRC.

"This was the day" . . . "seared my soul": CRR, *The Call of Brotherhood* (New York: Charles Scribner's Sons, 1912), pp. 87–93. Corinne dedicated the book to Frances Theodora Parsons, "the friend to whose inspiration and companionship I owe my happiest hours with books and nature."

"last of our lives": CRR to Henry Cabot Lodge, May 23, 1916, MHS.

"a portion of my life": Henry Cabot Lodge to CRR, Sept 3, 1909, TRC.

material for two volumes: TR, *Selections from the Correspondence of Theodore Roosevelt and Henry Cabot Lodge, 1884–1918* (1925).

"his public friends": CRR to Henry Cabot Lodge, Apr. 24, 1898, MHS.

"It is a heavy blow": Henry Cabot Lodge to CRR, Mar. 7, 1900, TRC.

"seemed to wake up my dormant brain": CRR to Henry Cabot Lodge, May 11, 1910, MHS.

"behind the scenes" . . . "political reasons": CRR to Henry Cabot Lodge, May 11, 1910, MHS.

"a gift of saying": Henry Cabot Lodge to CRR, Jan. 22, 1911, TRC.

"Your love, your sympathy": Henry Cabot Lodge to CRR, Jan. 22, 1911, TRC.

"would be glad of any criticism": CRR to Henry Cabot Lodge, June 25, 1913, MHS.

"too long for their favor": CRR to Henry Cabot Lodge, May 23, 1916, MHS.

"emboldened": CRR to Henry Cabot Lodge, June 24, 1916, MHS.

"O Poetess": Edith Wharton to CRR, Sept. 3, 1911, TRC.

"I hope you are still": Edith Wharton to CRR, June 9, 1912, TRC.

it was common gossip: Patricia O'Toole, *The Five of Hearts* (1990), pp. 217–20.

"I never saw": Henry Cabot Lodge to CRR, July 2, 1916, TRC.

"'ultimatums' do not 'ultimate'": CRR to Henry Cabot Lodge, May 23, 1916, MHS.

"happiness and a comfort": Henry Cabot Lodge to CRR, July 2, 1916, TRC.

"Apparently the only certain": CRR to Henry Cabot Lodge, Nov. 8, 1916, MHS.

"Chicago on Thursday": CRR to CRA, Nov. 1920, TRC.

"He even went": Joseph Alsop to CRR, Sept. 1918, TRC.

"the adjective, especially . . . of admiration": *NYT,* Sept. 25, 1921, p. 13.

"Mrs. Robinson loved her brother": *Literary Review,* Oct. 15, 1921, p. 84.

praised *Service* in its monthly column: *Literary Digest,* May 17, 1919, p. 39.

The other two poems . . . "and still": *Literary Digest,* May 17, 1919, p. 39.

focused on Corinne: *Literary Digest,* Dec. 19, 1914, p. 1235.

nation's most prominent women writers: *Mentor,* June 15, 1920, p. 7.

"You must know" . . . "so little time remains": Henry Cabot Lodge to CRR, Jan. 5, 1919, TRC.

"I long to see you": Henry Cabot Lodge to CRR, Jan. 11, 1919, TRC.

"to Cabot for several days": CRR to CRA, Jan. 21, 1921, TRC.

"distinguished nephew": Henry Cabot Lodge to CRR, no date, TRC.

glowing tribute: *Outlook,* Dec. 10, 1924, pp. 609–10.

"Mrs. Douglas Robinson" headed the list: *NYT,* Apr. 4, 1924, p. 27.

"pain in the loss": CRR to CRA, July 2, 1924, TRC.

After he met Sara: Erskine Wood, *Life of Charles Erskine Scott Wood*, p. 121.

"Where's your platform": CRR to CRA, Nov. 3, 1921, TRC.

"as it was a paying one": CRR to CRA, Oct. 30, 1922, TRC.

"the mass of women": CRR to CRA, May 24, 1924, TRC.

"as usual after about two hours": CRR to CRA, Apr. 5, 1923, TRC.

"hundreds were turned away" ... "some of my questioners": CRR to CRA, Oct. 30, 1923, TRC.

"Let there be light": CRR's poem, "On an Operating Table," is in her last volume of poetry: *Out of Nymph* (New York: Charles Scribner's Sons, 1930), p. 28. She dedicated the volume to the memory of Charles Scribner.

"perfectly splendid": ARC to CRR, Aug. 28, 1917, TRC.

"the tragedy of drink": CRA, interview with Hermann and Mary Hagedorn, Nov. 23, 1954, pp. 6–7, TRC.

"It was just like a bowl": CRA, interview with Hermann and Mary Hagedorn, Nov. 23, 1954, p. 18, TRC.

"Darling, if I get to the age": CRR to CRA, June 28, 1930, TRC.

"I cannot realize": CRR to CRA, Nov. 15, 1931, TRC.

"There is no one on earth": SDR to CRR, Nov. 17, 1928, TRC.

"all wishes for happiness": Charles Erskine Scott Wood to CRR, June 3, 1932, TRC.

CHAPTER 4: EDITH KERMIT CAROW ROOSEVELT AND SARA DELANO ROOSEVELT

"perpetual jog-trot" ... "not born a Roosevelt": CRR, *MBTR*, p. 220.

"whole thing has been most mysterious": CRR to ARC, Aug. 13, 1888, TRC.

"The atmosphere was one": CRR, *MBTR*, pp. 223–25.

"I know I was very wrong": CRR to ARC, Mar. 5, 1905 (misdated as 1909), TRC.

"pledged friends from birth": CRR, *MBTR*, p. 44.

"There we were": Michael Teague, *Mrs. L: Conversations with Alice Roosevelt Longworth* (1981), p. 159.

"I can't possibly imagine": Geoffrey Ward, *Before the Trumpet: Young Franklin Roosevelt, 1882–1905* (1985), p. 61.

"Fifth cousin": Michael Teague, *Mrs. L*, p. 159.

"Because his mother": Mrs. Theodore Roosevelt, Jr., *Day Before Yesterday: Reminiscences of Mrs. Theodore Roosevelt, Jr.* (1959), p. 301.

"never made a mistake": Amy La Follette Jensen, *The White House and Its Thirty-Three Families* (rev. ed., 1962), p. 191.

Rumor had it: Sylvia Jukes Morris, *Edith Kermit Roosevelt: Portrait of a First Lady* (1980), p. 15; Alice Longworth made the same point, quoted in Michael Teague, *Mrs. L*, p. 30.

called him "an angel": Sylvia Jukes Morris, *Edith Kermit Roosevelt*, p. 72.

"been all around the world in one of Papa's ships": EKR to TR, Nov. 9, 1869, TRC.

"almost a gift": Michael Teague, *Mrs. L*, p. 37.

"almost Oriental": Hermann Hagedorn, *The Roosevelt Family of Sagamore Hill* (1954), p. 10.

"While Theodore's personality": Margaret (Mrs. Winthrop) Chanler, *Roman Spring: Memoirs* (1934), p. 203.

years "had been unhappy": Michael Teague, *Mrs. L*, p. 30.

"the Mediterranean menace": Sylvia Jukes Morris, *Edith Kermit Roosevelt*, p. 115.

"whiskered brigand": Sylvia Jukes Morris, *Edith Kermit Roosevelt*, p. 471.

"Only one, one tiny room": P.O.R.E notebook quoted in Sylvia Jukes Morris, *Edith Kermit Roosevelt*, p. 54.

"most cultivated, best-read": TR Diary, Nov. 16, 1879, LC.

She attended . . . gave a party: Sylvia Jukes Morris, *Edith Kermit Roosevelt*, pp. 64 and 69.

excursion to Montreal: In Papers of ARL in TRC is the only photograph ever taken evidently of Edith Carow, Alice Lee Roosevelt, Bamie, and Corinne. For comment on photo, see Michael Teague, *Mrs. L*, p. 30.

"have bored [him] to death": Michael Teague, *Mrs. L*, p. 37.

"were rather concerned": Michael Teague, *Mrs. L*, p. 36.

"Mother never took any prisoners": William Sheffield Cowles, Jr., to Sylvia Jukes Morris, quoted in *Edith Kermit Roosevelt*, p. 195.

"the long head in politics": Sylvia Jukes Morris, *Edith Kermit Roosevelt*, p. 4, quotes Nicholas Roosevelt, *Theodore Roosevelt: The Man as I Knew Him* (1967), p. 28.

"nothing in the world": Sylvia Jukes Morris, *Edith Kermit Roosevelt*, p. 200.

"wonderful silky private part": Theodora Rauchfuss to Sylvia Jukes Morris, Feb. 1979, quoted in Sylvia Jukes Morris, *Edith Kermit Roosevelt*, p. 4.

Two more miscarriages: Sylvia Jukes Morris, *Edith Kermit Roosevelt*, p. 265.

"perfectly strong and healthy": EKR to Emily Carow, Aug. 30, 1894, TRC.

"bustling person" . . . "comes near me": EKR to Emily Carow, June 17, 1894, TRC.

"fat": EKR to Emily Carow, spring 1895, TRC.

"like a little guttersnipe": EKR to Emily Carow, Sept. 1894, TRC.

"none of them": EKR to Gertrude Carow, no date, TRC.

"most appalling looking": EKR to Emily Carow, Nov. 14, 1894, TRC.

"mean as a snake": Joanna Sturm to author, Oct. 20, 1994.

"I like to see their little faces": Sylvia Jukes Morris, *Edith Kermit Roosevelt*, p. 463.

better than she had treated: Michael Teague, *Mrs. L*, p. 30.

earned from writing articles: In the 1890s, Theodore Roosevelt published about fifty articles on subjects ranging from ranching to civil service reform. The exact number depends on whether book reviews are included.

"I think she 'done'" . . . "worth anything": EKR to Emily Carow, Jan. 3, 1895, TRC.

"liked the butter": ERD to EDW, Aug. 11, 1957, TRC.

"deadly dull": EKR to Emily Carow, Feb. 6, no year, TRC.

"I do not think": EKR to Emily Carow, Mar. 8, 1901, TRC.

"very blowsy": EKR to Emily Carow, no date, TRC.

"of losing my temper": EKR to ARL, Sept. 1909, TRC.

"snarkish mood": ARC to CRR, Sept. 1927, TRC.

but the record shows: William Seale, *The President's House* (Washington, D.C., 1986, 2 vols.), vol. 2, pp. 653–84.

A delegate of Steinway: Elise K. Kirk, *Music at the White House: A History of the American Spirit* (1986), p. 217.

"they mean just what they did": EKR to Cecil Spring-Rice, Jan. 27, 1902, quoted in Sylvia Jukes Morris, *Edith Kermit Roosevelt*, p. 233.

"very cleverly": Quoted in Sylvia Jukes Morris, *Edith Kermit Roosevelt*, introductory note, no page.

"We used to think": Margaret (Mrs. Winthrop) Chanler, *Roman Spring*, p. 203.

"stands in abject terror": Quoted in Sylvia Jukes Morris, *Edith Kermit Roosevelt*, p. 126.

published an admiring article: Mabel Potter Daggett, "Mrs. Roosevelt: The Woman in the Background," *The Delineator*, Mar. 1909, p. 394.

"Why Mrs. Roosevelt": Helen McCarthy, "Why Mrs. Roosevelt Has Not Broken Down," *Ladies' Home Journal*, Oct. 25, 1908, p. 25.

Historians would later rank: Betty Boyd Caroli, *First Ladies* (1987; expanded ed., 1995), p. 421.

"[Cabot] is one of the few men": TR to ARC, Feb. 12, 1893, TRC.

"had great literary taste": Michael Teague, *Mrs. L*, p. 18.

Her topic was "Social Service" . . . "Spend and be Spent": Newspaper clippings, Jan. 26, 1924, from Osaka, Japan, TRC.

"born public speaker" . . . "make them cry": Sylvia Jukes Morris, *Edith Kermit Roosevelt*, p. 489.

"in giving life and fostering it": Mrs. Theodore Roosevelt, Sr., Mrs. Kermit Roosevelt, Richard Derby, and Kermit Roosevelt, *Cleared for Strange Ports* (1927), p. 5.

"last chance to be a boy": Joseph R. Ornig, *My Last Chance to Be a Boy: Theodore Roosevelt's South American Expedition of 1913–1914* (1994).

"Last night I began to feel": EKR to ERD, Feb. 7, 1919, TRC.

"jade green ocean": Sylvia Jukes Morris, *Edith Kermit Roosevelt*, p. 453.

"an ever-present fear" . . . "must be content": Sylvia Jukes Morris, *Edith Kermit Roosevelt,* p. 460.

"I still cannot understand" . . . "unfailing respect": CRR to William Thayer, Mar. 18, 1919, TRC.

"During my present sister-in-law's": CRR to William Thayer, Mar. 18, 1919, TRC.

"half out of his mind": CRR to Henry Pringle, Sept. 22, 1930, TRC. Pringle took CRR's advice about how to describe the incident. On sensitive matters he listed her in his book as "Confidential Source No. 1." See Henry F. Pringle, *Theodore Roosevelt: A Biography* (1931), pp. 43–46. EKR did not like the book. On November 8, 1931, she wrote to ERD: "Pringle's book has come and on each page is a sneer or a slap at Father. I cannot read it. . . . I should like to burn it and mail the ashes to its author. Nothing has made me as angry for a long time." Letter is in TRC.

once described the poignant scene: Jacob Riis, "Mrs. Roosevelt and Her Children," *Ladies' Home Journal,* Aug. 1902, p. 5.

"terribly" . . . "my own for": EKR to ARC, Sept. 28, 1894, TRC.

"She has so lived": ERD to Richard Derby, Jan. 6, 1919, TRC.

"Every enrolled Republican": EKR to ERD, Nov. 3, 1928, TRC.

"worth publishing": EKR to ERD, Jan. 1927, TRC.

"been much in my mind" . . . "I find it so": EKR to ERD, Dec. 1927, TRC.

"In these days": EKR to ERR, July 3, 1943, FDRL.

trace her American roots: For details of Warren Delano's early years, see Geoffrey Ward, *Before the Trumpet,* pp. 67–74.

"I do not pretend": Geoffrey Ward, *Before the Trumpet,* p. 71. On the role of American merchants in China, see Jacques M. Downes, "American Merchants and the China Opium Trade, 1800–1840," *Business History,* winter 1968, pp. 418–42.

Catherine Lyman, the youngest daughter: Geoffrey Ward, *Before the Trumpet,* pp. 78–80.

Gardiners Island: Robert Seager, *And Tyler Too: A Biography of John and Julia Gardiner Tyler* (1963), p. 8.

Riot at Astor Place: Kenneth T. Jackson, ed., *Encyclopedia of New York City* (1995), p. 1007.

"fascinating family": ARL in Michael Teague, *Mrs. L,* p. 156.

"red-haired trial": Geoffrey Ward, *Before the Trumpet,* p. 102.

Dozens of letters: See letters of James Roosevelt to Rebecca Howland Roosevelt, FDRL.

not all Democrats: Geoffrey Ward, *Before the Trumpet,* p. 63.

it still held pictures and platters: I am indebted to Diane Boyce of the Franklin D. Roosevelt Historic Site who took the time to show me the traces of Rebecca Howland that remain at Hyde Park, Aug. 13, 1992.

"Now, Franklin was encouraged": ARL in Michael Teague, *Mrs. L,* p. 46.

"My darling Boy": SDR to FDR, no date, FDRL.

"All is over": SDR to FDR, Dec. 8, 1900, FDRL.

"a tremendous gain": SDR to FDR, Jan. 28, 1928, FDRL.

"It is a delightful chance": SDR to FDR, no date, FDRL.

"I am so glad": SDR to FDR, Jan. 8, 1902, FDRL.

the miners went back on the job: Thomas F. Bailey, *The American Pageant* (4th ed., 1971), p. 693.

"I think you are" . . . "statesmen or 'financieres'": SDR to FDR, Oct. 28, 1902, FDRL.

"Who's that dreadful man": Many versions of this story exist. For one variation, see Laura Delano, interview with Joseph Lash, June 25, p. 2, FDRL.

organized a sewing club: Rita Halle Kleeman, *Gracious Lady: The Life of Sara Delano Roosevelt* (1935), p. 134. SDR apparently went over Kleeman's manuscript. Geoffrey Ward pointed out that the printed version is somewhat different from the manuscript.

hundreds of dollars for Greenwich House: Greenwich House Annual Report, 1902–1929, located at Robert F. Wagner Archives, New York University.

"terrific with the third generation": Eleanor Seagraves to author, May 13, 1994.

"very strict" . . . "never raised her voice": Eleanor Seagraves to author, May 13, 1994.

"I wish the United States": SDR to ERR and FDR, Aug. 28, 1922, FDRL.

Everything "went off well": SDR to FDR, July 27, 1925, FDRL.

used her car . . . "that is something": SDR to FDR, Nov. 1925, FDRL.

"I have been working hard": SDR to FDR, Sept. 1928, FDRL.

"some idiots" . . . "against bigotry": SDR to FDR, Nov. 1930, FDRL.

"How proud I should be": SDR to FDR, July 26, 1932, FDRL.

"bruised hand" . . . "stupid idea": SDR to FDR, July 26, 1932, FDRL.

"Darling, don't let" . . . "no taxes": SDR to FDR, June 5, 1933, FDRL.

"the dumbest man": John A. Garraty, *The American Nation* (2nd ed., 1971, 2 vols.), vol. 2, p. 350.

suggested a tax of 100 percent: John A. Garraty, *The American Nation*, vol. 2, p. 347.

"I said 'I do not care'": SDR to FDR Apr. 4, 1936, FDRL.

used her "My Day" column: ERR, "My Day," July 2, 1943.

a "regular" at Greenwich House: Annual Reports of Greenwich House, Robert Wagner Archives, New York University.

"Jewish family who have a shop": SDR to FDR, Nov. 15, 1938, FDRL.

"I am for [Neville] Chamberlain": SDR to FDR, Dec. 1, 1938, FDRL.

"Daladier seems": SDR to FDR, Dec. 1, 1938, FDRL.

"I feel so sad": SDR to FDR, Mar. 13, 1940, FDRL.

Annual quota for German immigrants: *NYT*, Sept. 13, 1938, p. 3.

for one refugee: *NYT*, Aug. 30, 1938, p. 2.

"feels that your being President" ... "but is brave": SDR to FDR, Dec. 7, 1940, FDRL.

"which I think you will approve" ... "'finger into the pie'": SDR to FDR, Dec. 7, 1940, FDRL.

"If you're a playwright": Eleanor Seagraves to author, May 14, 1994.

"in her middle sixties": Dore Schary, "Sunrise at Campobello" (1957), p. 60. In the foreword, Schary describes Sara Delano Roosevelt as "matriarchal," a woman "who had contempt for politics."

to "see Hall's daughter" ... "ever said to me": Eleanor Roosevelt (Wotkyns) to author, Dec. 6, 1994.

Published *Meg*: Theodora Keogh, *Meg: A Novel* (1950). Reviewers tended to side with Ethel and Alice. The reviewer for *Time* (Mar. 13, 1950, p. 102) wrote: "Meg is the story of a little girl, but it is not for little girls."

"horrifying [with its] accounts": ERD to EDW, Mar. 12, 1950, TRC. ARL's comment is quoted in ERD's letter.

"in bed, playing solitaire": ERD to EDW, Mar. 12, 1950. TRC. Several words in this letter are crossed out with a heavy black pen.

CHAPTER 5: ELEANOR ROOSEVELT ROOSEVELT

The New York Times reported: *NYT,* Mar. 18, 1905, p.1.

"guests seemed more interested": ERR, *This Is My Story* (1958), p. 126.

Hunting Big Game: Elliott Roosevelt, *Hunting Big Game in the Eighties: The Letters of Elliot Roosevelt, Sportsman* (1933).

"He never accomplished": Elliott Roosevelt, *Hunting Big Game*, p. viii. For a discussion of the effect of her father's alcoholism on Eleanor, see Hugh Davis Graham, "The Paradox of Eleanor Roosevelt: Alcoholism's Child," *Virginia Quarterly Review,* spring 1987, pp. 210–30. Graham concluded that Eleanor looked to the public for self-esteem she never had as a child.

"small and ragged urchin": Elliott Roosevelt, *Hunting Big Game*, p. ix.

"slip worn by every girl baby": Elliott Roosevelt, *Hunting Big Game*, p. 141.

Children's American Missionary Society: Papers of Anna Hall Roosevelt, Box 6, Folder 7, FDRL.

"He loves you with so tender": CRR to Anna Hall Roosevelt, ERR Family Papers, FDRL.

"dear, graceful, sweet": Anna Bulloch Gracie to Elliott Roosevelt, ERR Family Papers, FDRL.

"laid her hand": Anna Bulloch Gracie to Elliott Roosevelt, June 26, 1883, ERR Family Papers, FDRL.

"one of the most brilliant": Clipping in Papers of Anna Hall Roosevelt, FDRL.

"Little Eleanor": Elliott Roosevelt to ARC, Aug. 30, 1885, TRC.

"one of America's loveliest": Ward McAllister, *Society As I Have Found It* (1890), p. 380. In the printed text, McAllister does not name her, but in the annotated copy (#352) at New-York Historical Society, he wrote in the margin "Mrs. Elliott Roosevelt."

"Poor old Nell": Quoted in Blanche Wiesen Cook, *Eleanor Roosevelt, 1884–1933* (vol. 1, 1992), p. 47.

"*delighted* to have her": Anna Bulloch Gracie to CRR, Aug. 9, 1886, TRC.

"I am perfectly willing": EKR to ARC, spring 1888, TRC.

taking along three-year-old: Elliott Roosevelt, *Hunting Big Game*, p. 158.

"the best tea": Anna Bulloch Gracie to CRR, Sept. 9, no year, TRC.

"Granny" . . . "under protest": Elliott Roosevelt, *Hunting Big Game*, p. 34.

"gay sporting life": Elliott Roosevelt, *Hunting Big Game*, p. 167.

"a bad accident": Elliott Roosevelt, *Hunting Big Game*, p. 166.

"Indian fever": Elliott Roosevelt, *Hunting Big Game*, p. 167.

"cures to regain": Elliott Roosevelt, *Hunting Big Game*, p. 167.

"wits end": TR to ARC, July 1889, TRC.

"distressed beyond measure": TR to ARC, Jan. 24, 1890, TRC.

"sweet" . . . "women would in her place": TR to ARC, Apr. 30, 1890, TRC.

"must live apart": TR to ARC, Jan. 25, 1891, TRC.

committed for "lunacy": Folder 12, ERR Family Papers, FDRL.

"became one of the few": Elliott Roosevelt, *Hunting Big Game*, p. 167.

"It is so hard for [Anna]": CRR to Anna Bulloch Gracie, June 21, 1892, TRC.

"so sweet together": CRR to Anna Bulloch Gracie, July 3, 1892, TRC.

"insane" and "alcoholic": Clippings marked "for Anna's children," 1893, in Box 6, Folder 7 of ERR Family Papers, FDRL. Geraldine Hawkins, currently working on a biography of Elliott Roosevelt, kindly shared with me her insights on his role in the family.

before witnessing "the evil" . . . instead of his wife: Sylvia Jukes Morris, *Edith Kermit Roosevelt: Portrait of a First Lady* (1980), p. 142.

"It was a fearful shock" . . . "not to see her": CRR to ARC, Aug. 15, 1894, TRC.

"He and I were very close: ERR, *This Is My Story*, p. 20.

"Rooseveltian features": Joseph P. Lash, *Love, Eleanor: Eleanor Roosevelt and Her Friends* (1982), p. 10.

"most charming man": Monroe Robinson to ERR, Feb. 1937, FDRL.

Two "drunken sons": CRA, interview with Hermann and Mary Hagedorn, Dec. 28, 1954, p. 6, TRC.

making Eleanor's life even more miserable: ERR, *This Is My Story*, p. 18; she describes a French maid who taunted Eleanor and threatened to expose her small transgressions—such as buying sweets when she had been instructed not to.

"Dear Aunty Bye": ERR to ARC, Dec. 27, 1894, TRC.

"My birthday": ERR to ARC, Oct. 26, no year, TRC.

"because I would have": ERR to ARC, Oct. 26, no year, TRC.

devoid of any sense of humor: CRA, interview with Hermann and Mary Hagedorn, Dec. 28, 1954, p. 5, TRC.

"all had great fun": ERR to ARC, Jan. 3, 1897, TRC.

"I am so glad": ERR to ARC, Nov. 15, 1895, TRC.

Dr. Edward Hartley Angle: I am indebted to Dr. Irwin Mandel, professor emeritus of dentistry at Columbia University, and Dr. Sidney Horowitz, also of Columbia University, for their insights into the class bias against orthodontics at the turn of the century.

Corinney later blamed: CRA, interview with Hermann and Mary Hagedorn, Dec. 28, 1954, p. 7, TRC.

"I do not feel": EKR to ARC, no date, probably 1893, TRC.

"I enjoyed them *so* much": ERR to ARC, Jan. 21, no year, probably 1900, TRC.

"I like being back": ERR to ARC, Jan. 21, no year, probably 1900, TRC.

"ugly duckling": ERR, *This Is My Story*, pp. 17–18.

"she was dark": Joanna Sturm to author, Oct. 20, 1994.

"salvation" was going: CRA, interview with Hermann and Mary Hagedorn, Dec. 28, 1954, p. 2, TRC.

"My First Joy": ERR, Journal and Composition Books, FDRL.

"good results": ... "most amiable girl": Marie Souvestre, ER's report cards, FDRL.

"had the most admirable influence": Marie Souvestre, Report card for ERR, May-July 1902, FDRL.

"Once more this very warm": Marie Souvestre to ERR, July 7, 1902, FDRL.

"disappear quickly" ... "various fashionable affairs": Marie Souvestre to ERR, July 7, 1902, FDRL.

"Tell me how you have found": Marie Souvestre to ERR, July 7, 1902, FDRL.

"Why didn't you ask?": Marie Souvestre to ERR, Aug. 17, 1902, FDRL.

"I would like": Marie Souvestre to ERR, Aug. 17, 1902, FDRL.

"If by chance": Marie Souvestre to ERR, Oct. 5, 1902, FDRL.

"Ma chère petite": Mlle. Maître to ERR, Sept. 10, 1902, FDRL.

"It portrays you": Marie Souvestre to ERR, Oct. 5, 1902, FDRL.

"how Eleanor was getting on": CRA to Douglas Robinson, no date, probably late 1902. TRC.

"very sweet": CRR to CRA, Oct. 31, 1902, TRC.

"looks very smartly": CRR to CRA, no date, probably late 1902, TRC.

"never seen anyone": CRR to CRA, no date, probably late 1902, TRC.

"I am so sorry to say" ... "the Washington impression": CRR to CRA, Jan. 1903, TRC.

"I was awfully sorry": CRA to CRR, Feb. 8, 1903, TRC.

"Yesterday quantities of letters": Marie Souvestre to ERR, Oct. 5, 1902, FDRL.

"really . . . a very nice time": CRR to CRA, Jan. 30, 1903, TRC.

"Do not say anything" . . . "ached for her": CRR to CRA, Apr. 6, 1903, TRC.

feared her uncles: CRA, interview with Joseph Lash, Apr. 21, 1967, p. 7, FDRL.

installed multiple locks: Geoffrey Ward to Blanche Wiesen Cook, as reported in *Eleanor Roosevelt*, vol. 1, p. 517.

"Eleanor is as dear": ARC to CRR, Mar. 20, 1903, TRC.

"I want Eleanor": EKR to ARC, no date, probably Mar. 1903, from White House, TRC.

"I love having her": ARC to CRR, Mar. 20, 1903, TRC.

"I am worried": ARC to CRR, Apr. 7, 1903, TRC.

"dreadfully worried" . . . "home of her own": ARC to CRR, no date, TRC.

"I have always regretted": ERR, *It Seems to Me* (2nd ed., 1954), p. 61.

"but as Elliott was living": ARC to CRR, about 1903, TRC.

"Eleanor can do nothing": ARC to CRR, about 1903, TRC.

"a definite sum" . . . "light and sun": Marie Souvestre to ERR, Oct. 5, 1902, FDRL.

"one of the most interesting": ERR, *This Is My Story* (1937), p. 57.

"at a moment's notice" . . . "as the case may be": ARC to CRR, Nov. 6, 1904, TRC.

Corinney speculated: CRA, interview with Joseph Lash, Apr. 27, 1967, p. 3, FDRL.

"at a hotel": ARC to CRR, Nov. 6, 1904, TRC.

"not to be spoken of": EKR to Kermit Roosevelt, Nov. 24, 1904, Papers of Kermit and Belle Roosevelt, LC.

"Dearest Cousin Sally": ERR to SDR, Dec. 2, 1903, FDRL.

"I am thankful" . . . "do her good": SDR to FDR, no date, FDRL.

Eleanor looked "charming": SDR, Diary, Jan. 20, 1905, FDRL.

"Mrs. James Roosevelt was in white silk": *NYT*, Mar. 18, 1905, p. 2.

"A Christmas present": SDR to FDR and ERR, Christmas 1905, FDRL.

it would never have occurred: Rita Halle Kleeman, *Gracious Lady*, p. 246.

Eleanor offered Franklin a divorce: CRA, interview with Joseph Lash, Apr. 27, 1967, p. 2, FDRL. A similar version is in ARL to Michael Teague, quoted in *Mrs L: Conversations with Alice Roosevelt Longworth* (1981), p. 158.

"I've never seen such possession": CRA, interview with Hermann and Mary Hagedorn, Dec. 28, 1954, p. 14, TRC.

"please get some educator biscuits": SDR to FDR, July 18, 1906, FDRL.

"can be quiet": SDR to ERR, 1907, FDRL.

silly and unnecessary: CRA, interview with Joseph Lash, Apr. 17, 1967, p. 3, FDRL. CRA's exact words: "In those early days you always felt she was a slave to her mother-in-law. I've always been interested in the 'why' of that."

"angel": SDR to FDR, Aug. 9, 1909, FDRL.

"Eleanor has told you" ... "Ever so much love": FDR to SDR, summer 1907, FDRL.

"running into our gate post": SDR to ERR, early July, 1922, FDRL.

sent a check: SDR to ERR, July 31, 1922, FDRL.

"fed up with the sights": SDR to ERR, July 31, 1922, FDRL.

"your long delightful" ... "a carload": SDR to ERR, Aug. 9, 1922, FDRL.

"for a Saturday and Sunday": ARC to FDR, July 15, 1909, FDRL.

"trust" ... "mathematics": FDR to Isabella Ferguson, Aug. 19, 1914, Ferguson Papers, Box 15, Folder 360, AHS.

"splendidly" ... "devoted to her": SDR to Isabella Ferguson, Aug. 19, 1914, Ferguson Papers, Box 15, Folder 360, AHS.

"so funny at times" ... "unselfish, sweet woman": ERR to Robert Ferguson, Sept. 28, 1914, Ferguson Papers, Box 15, Folder 360, AHS.

"Dearest Franklin": ARC to FDR, Sept. 17, 1914, FDRL.

Franklin was "of course ... delighted" ... "stupid mistakes": ERR to ARC, Mar. 10, 1913, TRC.

"Eleanor darlingest" ... "Auntie Bye": ARC to ERR, Apr. 13, 1913, FDRL.

"I suppose this means": ARC to FDR, June 26, 1914, FDRL.

"I hate to feel": ARC to FDR, July 5, 1917, FDRL.

"how queer tenants are": ARC to CRR, June 22, 1918, TRC.

"My very dear Eleanor": ARC to ERR, July 19, 1920, FDRL.

"had a little chat": CRR to CRA, May 5, 1911, TRC.

"to see Eleanor and Sallie": CRR to CRA, Oct. 21, 1916, TRC.

"public speaker and it seems": ERR to Isabella Ferguson, Feb. 10, 1918, Ferguson Papers, Box 15, Folder 360, AHS.

"worked as a very able man's mind": Quoted in David McCullough, *Mornings on Horseback* (1981), p. 353.

"Courage like hers": ERR to Isabella Ferguson, Feb. 10, 1918, Ferguson Papers, Box 15, Folder 360, AHS.

had to beg her for a photograph: Telegram from Howe to ERR, July 20, 1920, FDRL.

"the bottom dropped out": Joseph P. Lash. *Love, Eleanor*, p. 66.

"lived together as man and wife": Elliott Roosevelt, *An Untold Story: The Roosevelts of Hyde Park* (1973), p. 81. Also see Joseph P. Lash, *Love, Eleanor*, p. 71.

"I loved it": Joseph P. Lash, *Love, Eleanor*, p. 67.

"Since our earliest days": Peter Collier (with David Horowitz), *The Roosevelts: An American Saga* (1994), p. 197.

"It would have been much better" Sheffield Cowles, interview with Hermann and Mary Hagedorn, Dec. 28, 1954, p. 48, TRC.

"has been here twice": ERR to Isabella Ferguson, Apr. 2, 1918, Ferguson Papers, Box 15, Folder 360, AHS.

"5 farmerettes": ERR to Isabella Ferguson, spring 1917, Ferguson Papers, Box 15, Folder 360, AHS.

"gay side": ERR to Isabella Ferguson, Sept. 16, 1920, Ferguson Papers, Box 15, Folder 360, AHS.

"It looks alarmingly": Isabella Ferguson to ERR, Jan. 1920, FDRL.

Eleanor consented in 1920 to head up: Blanche Wiesen Cook, *Eleanor Roosevelt, 1884–1933*, p. 292.

even inviting Cook and Dickerman: SDR to FDR, Oct. 1925, FDRL.

found the outspoken midwesterner interesting: Eleanor Roosevelt (Wotkyns) to author, Dec. 6, 1994.

"for ten minutes": SDR to FDR, Mar. 1927, FDRL.

"wear 'jewels'": SDR to ERR, May 28, 1930, FDRL.

"I just hate": ARC to CRR, Dec. 11, 1923, TRC.

"I hate being told": SDR to FDR, Nov. 1932, FDRL.

"has emerged from the mine": SDR to FDR, May 22, 1935, FDRL.

"tired of the same old lady": SDR to ERR, Jan. 30, 1937, FDRL.

"Eleanor, like an angel": SDR to FDR, before Christmas 1938, FDRL.

a typewritten note: ERR to SDR, before Christmas 1939, FDRL.

"I had a glimpse": SDR to FDR, no date, 1936, FDRL.

"It is such a comfort": SDR to FDR, no date, FDRL.

"I went and got her little parchment": SDR to FDR, June 9, 1938, FDRL.

"The President's Wife Is Hostess": *Life*, May 29, 1939, pp. 61–67.

"the strain falls on you": CRA to ERR, Sept. 1941, FDRL.

"Mama had been rather frail": ERR to CRA, Sept. 1941, FDRL.

"magic politician": Isabella Ferguson to ERR, June 11, 1924, FDRL.

"extraordinary life led": Isabella Ferguson to ERR, July 1913, FDRL.

Republicans were well organized: Memo written by ERR, July 16, 1936, FDRL.

"I want you to know": CRA to ERR, Mar. 13, 1939, FDRL.

"great personal triumph": CRA to ERR, Dec. 17, 1940, FDRL.

"A *Merry* Christmas": CRA to ERR, Dec. 17, 1940, FDRL.

"I loved your letter": ERR to CRA, about Christmas 1940, FDRL.

"victims of something": CRA to ERR, soon after the death of Hall Roosevelt, 1941, FDRL.

embarrassed by her father's behavior: Eleanor Roosevelt (Wotkyns) to author, Dec. 6, 1994.

did not know who she was: Janet Katten to author, Dec. 5, 1994.

"She was always there": Diana Jaicks to author, Dec. 5, 1994.

a book about sailors: Hall Roosevelt, *Odyssey of an American Family: An Account of the Roosevelts and Their Kin as Travelers, from 1613 to 1938* (1938).

"very seriously ill": ERR to CRA, Sept. 1941, FDRL.

"Hall's condition" . . . "this self-destruction": CRA to ERR, about Sept. 26, 1941, FDRL.

"You have been so wonderful" . . . "no hope": CRA to ERR, about Sept. 26, 1941, FDRL.

"Dearest Corinne" . . . "aches for Belle": ERR to CRA, Oct. 1, 1941, FDRL.

"more than lovely": CRA to ERR, Dec. 1944, FDRL.

"with glee" . . . "to the same degree": CRA to ERR, Dec. 1942, FDRL.

Corinney's in-laws: For example, see letter of Mrs. Francis Alsop to ERR, spring 1935, FDRL, identifying the writer as "a sister-in-law of Corinne Alsop."

"It was always such fun": ERR to Helen Robinson, Dec. 1944, FDRL.

hardly knew her cousins: Diana Jaicks to author, Dec. 5, 1994

Little knowledge of her great-uncle Theodore: Janet Katten to author, Dec. 5, 1994

"getting your sweet note" . . . "wanted to help": ERR to Eleanor Butler Alexander Roosevelt, July 23, 1945, Papers of Theodore Roosevelt, Jr., LC.

"Dear Aunt Edith": ERR to EKR, Apr. 17, 1945, TRC.

requiring a separate volume: Joseph P. Lash, *Eleanor: The Years Alone* (1972).

not "known him for a very long time": ERR to Joe Alsop, Dec. 29, 1946, FDRL.

"In just 15 minutes": Eleanor Roosevelt (Wotkyns) to author, Dec. 6, 1994.

"One goes to funerals": ERD to EDW, Nov. 11, 1962, TRC.

CHAPTER 6: CORINNE ROBINSON ALSOP

"all those bankers": Sheffield Cowles, interview with Hermann and Mary Hagedorn, Dec. 28, 1954, p. 41, TRC.

"distant relative of President Roosevelt" . . . "their political program": *NYT,* June 3, 1936, p. 2.

get her angry: John Alsop to author, Oct. 15, 1997.

"a terribly dull child": CRA, interview with Hermann and Mary Hagedorn, Nov. 23, 1954, p. 11, TRC.

"I *think* I can love her": CRA, interview with Hermann and Mary Hagedorn, Nov. 23, 1954, p. 12, TRC. A similar account appears in CRA's unpublished Autobiography, pp. 1–2.

"the plainest man in the world": CRA, interview with Hermann and Mary Hagedorn, Nov. 23, 1954, p. 12, TRC.

"dark hair that had the strength": CRA, unpublished Autobiography, p. 2. I am indebted to John Alsop for permitting me to read his mother's autobiography.

monopoly on heroine roles: CRA, interview with Hermann and Mary Hagedorn, Nov. 23, 1954, p. 11, TRC.

"all so bright": CRA, interview with Hermann and Mary Hagedorn, Nov. 23, 1954, p. 11, TRC.

"heroism made a deep impression": CRA, Autobiography, p. 15.

"as nice as a school could possibly be": CRR to EKR, June 8, 1902, TRC.

"va tres bien": Marie Souvestre to CRR, July 10, 1902, TRC.

"interesting as a teacher": CRA to CRR, undated letter from Allenswood, TRC.

"I nearly sank through the floor": CRA to CRR, no date, TRC.

"always seems restless": CRA to CRR, no date, TRC.

Another, a banker: John Alsop to author, Oct. 15, 1997.

"Our jokes are not quite": CRA to CRR, after Christmas 1902, TRC.

"unwell. . . . Isn't it too mean?": CRA to CRR, Dec. 30, 1902, TRC.

"drives me crazy": CRA to CRR, Jan. 1903, TRC.

"horribly bare" . . . "fights over him": CRA to CRR, Jan. 1903, TRC.

"I feel awfully jealous": CRA to CRR, Jan. 1903, TRC.

"I had sort of half hysterics": CRA to CRR, May 1903, TRC.

"and at Harrow": CRA to CRR, spring 1903, TRC.

"doesn't seem to have": CRA to CRR, May 20, 1903, TRC.

"the two things": CRA to CRR, Dec. 1903, TRC.

"the last lap": CRA, Memoir, p. 2. I am indebted to John Alsop for sharing this unpublished memoir with me.

"lots of funny little Dips": CRA, Memoir, p. 4.

"not a large affair": *NYT,* Dec. 23, 1904, p. 9.

"kind of young man": ARL, interview with Joseph Lash, Apr. 5, 1966, p. 2, FDRL.

"ondule" . . . "going steady": CRA, Unpublished Memoir, p. 3.

"hardly believe": CRA to CRR, July 1905, TRC.

"wildest dreams": CRA to CRR, July 1906, TRC.

"was an absolute surprise": CRA to CRR, July 20, 1905, TRC.

she made the dramatic monologue: Muriel B. McKenna, entry for Ruth Draper, *Notable American Women: The Modern Period,* ed. by Barbara Sicherman and Carol Hurd Green (1980), p. 201.

"fantastic, triumphant tour": CRA, Diary, p. 1. John Alsop generously shared his mother's unpublished diary with me.

"Dearest little birthday girl": CRA to CRR, Sept. 1907, TRC.

"I am afraid": CRA to CRR, Oct. 1907, TRC.

"She was crazy about him": John Alsop to author, Oct. 15, 1997.

"far too sacred": CRA to Isabella Ferguson, Mar. 8, 1908, Ferguson Papers, Box 1, Folder 5, AHS.

"I can never feel": CRA to CRR, about Mar. 1908, TRC.

Ruth Bryan Leavitt: Ruth Bryan's marriage to William Leavitt ended in 1909, and she subsequently married Reginald Owen and then Borge Rohde. This last marriage took place at the home of Eleanor and Franklin Roosevelt

"I was bored": CRA to CRR, July 1908, TRC.

"I really feel": CRA to CRR, spring 1908, TRC.

"looked distinguished": CRA, Recollections, p. 5. This typescript, in possession of John Alsop (and quoted with his kind permission), has no title, but I have called it "Recollections" in order to distinguish it from the segments that CRA called Diary, Memoir, and "For Stewart."

"I don't think" . . . "lessons": ERD to Isabella Ferguson, Nov. 22, 1908, Ferguson Papers, Box 5, Folder 126, AHS.

"how I lived through it": CRA to Isabella Ferguson, Jan. 16, 1909, Ferguson Papers, Box 1, Folder 6, AHS.

"I talked to a little Belgian": CRA to Isabella Ferguson, Feb. 17, 1909, Ferguson Papers, Box 1, Folder 6, AHS.

"Joe and I had": CRA to CRR, May 1909, TRC.

"some engravings": CRA to CRR, May 1909, TRC.

"a fine person": CRA and Joe Alsop to Isabella and Bob Ferguson, Sept. 20, 1909, Ferguson Papers, Box 1, Folder 6, AHS.

"I believe your little girl": ARC to CRR, Sept. 1909, TRC.

"heart broken . . . for Dear Eleanor": CRA to Robert and Isabella Ferguson, Nov. 1909, Ferguson Papers, Box 1, Folder 6, AHS.

"an odd, Victorian": CRA, Recollections, p. 7.

"as I knew that he would": CRA to CRR, Nov. 1909, TRC.

"a dear quaint little house": EKR to Kermit Roosevelt, Nov. 28, 1909, Papers of Kermit and Belle Roosevelt, LC.

"old portraits": CRA, Recollections, p. 11.

"She won't last": CRA, Recollections, p. 12.

"Perfect foolishness": CRA to CRR, Nov. 1909, TRC.

"has the most utter contempt": CRA to CRR, Dec. 7, 1909, TRC.

"If Emma goes": CRA to CRR, Dec. 7, 1909, TRC.

"She kept her husband's cook": CRA, Recollections, p. 13.

two of them had "mealed": CRA to CRR, Nov. 1909, TRC.

"perfectly contented": EKR to Kermit Roosevelt, Nov. 28, 1909, Papers of Kermit and Belle Roosevelt, LC.

"delicious" . . . "fascinating life": CRA, Autobiography, p. 1.

come home "stronger": CRA to CRR, about Nov. 30, 1909, TRC.

"enchanting spring silk cover": CRA to CRR, Christmas 1909, TRC.

"grippe and rheumatism": CRA to Isabella Ferguson, Jan. 7, 1910, Ferguson Papers, Box 1, Folder 7, AHS.

"should have felt" . . . "good reason": CRA to CRR, Jan. 1910, TRC.

"I go over my time": CRA to CRR, Jan. 1910, TRC.

"There are very few": CRA to CRR, Feb. 1910, TRC.

"He was to have" . . . "satisfactorily": CRA to CRR, no date, TRC.

"looking more lovely" . . . "glad to say": Joe Alsop to CRR, July 1910, TRC.

"this world to have": CRR to CRA, May 10, 1910, TRC.

"female Samson": CRA, Recollections, p. 17.

"You had better go home": CRA, Memoir, p. 22.

"Joe will have to be doing politics": CRA to CRR, June 1910, TRC.

"many hours of labor": CRA, Recollections, p. 23.

"for the wonderful experience": CRA, Recollections, pp. 22–23

Joseph Wright Alsop, Jr.: Joe Jr. was technically Joseph Wright Alsop V.

It was Aggie: John Alsop to author, Oct. 15, 1997.

"quite nonchalant": CRA to CRR, no date, about 1911, TRC.

"pastures would have . . . isolated farm": CRA, Recollections, p. 5.

"endless hours" . . . "people in Avon": CRA, Recollections, pp. 17–18.

"Nothing could have been": CRA to CRR, about Jan. 23, 1912, TRC.

"a possible bully": CRA to Isabella Ferguson, Jan. 1912, Ferguson Papers, Box 1, Folder 9, AHS.

"out of the cheapest things": CRA to CRR, 1910, TRC.

"how much I must miss": CRA to CRR, 1911, TRC.

"I have done my duty": CRA to CRR, 1911, TRC.

"motored through endless acres": CRA to Isabella Ferguson, 1912, Ferguson Papers, Box 1, Folder 9, AHS.

"I just hate myself": CRA to CRR, penciled note, no date, TRC. Stewart, born in May, 1914, weighed nearly fourteen pounds at the time CRA wrote this note, and John was born in August 1915.

"aristocratic and diplomatic style": CRA to Isabella Ferguson, Mar. 20, 1915, Box 1, Folder 10, AHS.

"She Mrs. Alsop": CRA to CRR, about 1911, TRC.

"Send her Wednesday": CRA, written "For Stewart," p. 9. This autobiographical note, written for her son Stewart, was shown to me by her son John. I am grateful for the opportunity to read it.

"I had a very chatty time": CRA to CRR, about 1911, TRC.

"I smile sweetly": CRA to CRR, about 1911, TRC.

accompanied him to Massachusetts . . . "I don't remember what": For a description of Wellesley and her impressions, see CRA to CRR, May 22, 1913, TRC.

"delicious long talks": CRA to CRR, no date, cites letter from Parsons to ARC, TRC.

"the day in truly Rooseveltian-Hendersonian fashion": CRA to CRR, May 10, 1915, TRC.

"if my figure were not": CRA to CRR, May 10, 1915, TRC.

"If he does get up a brigade": CRA to CRR, 1916, TRC.

only about three hundred: CRA, "For Stewart," p. 6.

"along with criminals and the insane": CRA, "For Stewart," p. 6.

sent his children into tears: CRA, Autobiography, p. 19.

"mainspring": CRA, Autobiography, p. 13.

Monroe "hated" him: CRA, interview with Hermann and Mary Hagedorn, Nov. 23, 1954, p. 15, TRC.

"Joe and I are well": CRA to CRR, penciled note, Sept. 1926, TRC.

"Mother darling": CRA to CRR, no date, TRC.

"wonderfully developed" mind: CRA to CRR, no date, TRC.

"my fun in New York": Joe Alsop, Jr., to CRR, Apr. 1923, TRC.

"a thousand times for helping": CRA to CRR, no date, probably 1923 aboard ship, TRC.

before exhausting her considerable fortune: John Alsop to author, Oct. 15, 1997.

"Mad as possible" . . . "terrible strain": CRA to CRR, penciled note, Sept. 1926, TRC.

"beloved family would feel": CRA to CRR, no date, envelope says Oct. 17, 1932, but may be wrong, TRC.

"squarely in the eye": CRA to CRR, no date, about 1926, TRC.

thus annoying the party chairman: John Alsop to author, Oct. 15, 1997.

"like Paul Revere": CRA, "For Stewart," p. 7.

reasons she never made clear: John Alsop speculated what her reasons might have been, interview with author, Oct. 15, 1997.

"Let's get the farmers out of the mud": Elizabeth Winthrop to author, Apr. 24, 1998.

"provided a foundation for everyone": John Alsop to author, Apr. 24, 1998

"Without party affiliation": Clipping of *Hartford Courant,* June 25, 1971, TRC.

"every suffering or joy": CRR to CRA, Aug. 18, 1930, TRC.

"sharing your expenses": CRR to CRA, Aug. 18, 1930, TRC.

"If she were a different type": CRA to CRR, Apr. 26, 1930, TRC.

"It's so nice to hear": ERD to EKR, Mar. 15, 1932, TRC.

Corinne went even further: Joseph W. Alsop (with Adam Platt), *I've Seen the Best of It* (1992), p. 71.

"I know much more about grandchildren": CRA to ERR, Dec. 27, 1935, FDRL.

"or I shall gladly join any group": CRA to ERR, Jan. 10, 1936, FDRL.

"Joe and Stewart and I": CRA to ERR, Jan. 10, 1936, FDRL.

"For Heaven's sake" . . . "lovely to see you": ERR to CRA, Jan. 15, 1936, FDRL.

"local resident": Stephen Early, memo to ERR, June 24, 1937, FDRL.

"I would not dream": ERR to Joe Alsop, July 8, 1937, FDRL.

"charged down on Washington" . . . "remind me of Mother": CRA to ERR, Feb. 1937, FDRL.

"Dearest Corinne": ERR to CRA, Feb. 26, 1937, FDRL.

"how enthusiastic": CRA to ERR, about Apr. 1938, FDRL.

"great kindness": Joe Alsop to ERR, Sept. 20, 1938, FDRL.

"intelligently" . . . "any such statement": ERR to CRA and CRA to ERR, June 1939, FDRL.

needed the higher pay: John Alsop to author, Oct. 15, 1997.

"In the midst of the agonizing nightmare": CRA to ERR, Feb. 26, 1942, FDRL.

"I loved our windy walk": CRA to ERR, Feb. 26, 1942, FDRL.

"I should have been more troubled" . . . "House follows the Senate": CRA to ERR, Feb. 26, 1942, FDRL.

"in good form": ERD to EDW, July 8, 1946, TRC.

"tear . . . herself away": ERD to EDW, Nov. 11, 1948, TRC.

"glorious" . . . "are darlings": ERD to EDW, Apr. 3, 1949, TRC.

"the greatest joy and satisfaction": ERD to EDW, June 4, 1950, TRC.

"Cousin C is to me": ERD to EDW, Jan. 13, 1952, TRC.

"away from her hosts" . . . "cherish it": ERD to EDW, Sept. 6, 1953, TRC.

"undertook to deride": ERD to EDW, Oct. 11, 1953, TRC.

"the way people ought to die": John Alsop to author, Oct. 15, 1997.

"I know how busy": Wire from CRA to ERR, May 18, 1953, FDRL.

"this peaceful Connecticut valley": CRA to EKR, May 1941, TRC.

"Oh yes, we'll lose the eggheads": John Alsop verified this version in an interview with the author, Oct. 15, 1997.

"very much interested": ERR to Joe Alsop, Jan. 21, 1953, FDRL.

"Nothing heartens me": Joe Alsop to ERR, Jan. 28, 1953, FDRL.

"her usual completely dear self": ERD to EDW, May 14, 1955, TRC.

"old and unhappy" . . . "with both of them": ERD to EDW, Dec. 11, 1966, TRC.

"I'm delighted": Quoted in her obituary, *Hartford Courant,* June 25, 1971, TRC.

"was like a sister": ERD to EDW, Sept. 12, 1971, TRC.

CHAPTER 7: ETHEL CAROW ROOSEVELT DERBY

"newspaper correspondent" . . . "perfectly horrid": ERD to Emily Carow, 1906, TRC.

"Most Interesting Figure": *NYT,* Nov. 15, 1908, VI, p. 6.

"Rarely poetic": *NYT,* Nov. 15, 1908, VI, p. 6.

"showed talent": Undated clipping, *Washington Post,* TRC.

"a walking Encyclopedia": ERD to Robert and Isabella Ferguson, Oct. 7, 1907, Ferguson Papers, Box 5, Folder 26, AHS.

"asset": Carol Felsenthal, *Princess Alice: The Life and Times of Alice Roosevelt Longworth* (1988), p. 70.

"almost afraid": EKR to Emily Carow, June 17, 1894, TRC.

"She is fair": Typescript of poem in CRR's writings, TRC.

"I think it is too much": ERD to EKR, no date, TRC. Among the letters that refer to the subject of household management, one dates from June 1904, when Ethel was twelve, and others to 1906, when she was fourteen.

"I don't think anyone": ERD to EDW, June 6, 1971, TRC.

"Really, Kerm": ERD to Kermit Roosevelt, Nov. 1911, Papers of Kermit and Belle Roosevelt, LC.

"Very few people": ERD to Robert and Isabella Ferguson, Aug. 18, 1912, Ferguson Papers, Box 5, Folder 130, AHS.

"I think often": ERD to EDW, June 4, 1972, TRC.

"live a real little life": ERD to Robert and Isabella Ferguson, about Nov. 1, 1915, Ferguson Papers, Box 5, Folder 132.

"how comparatively" . . . "'got it'": ERD to Robert and Isabella Ferguson, Jan. 14, 1909, Ferguson Papers, Box 5, Folder 127, AHS.

"too strong": ERD to EDW, June 4, 1972, TRC.

"little southern lady": ERD to Robert and Isabella Ferguson, Aug. 18, 1912, Ferguson Papers, Box 5, Folder 130, AHS.

"Uncle Douglas" . . . "never mind": ERD to Kermit Roosevelt, Oct. 4, 1912, Papers of Kermit and Belle Roosevelt Papers, LC.

she had met Richard Derby: Family lore had it that Ethel first met Richard Derby at the White House when she was just a little girl on stilts, and the ten-year difference in their ages made her seem a child to him. EDW confirmed this story in a letter to the author, June 1, 1998.

"Dick Derby is going to marry": CRA to Robert and Isabella Ferguson, Jan. 2, 1913, Ferguson Papers, Box 1, Folder 8, AHS.

at least a year before she was ready: EDW and Sarah Alden Gannett to author, June 16, 1994.

"You're the first people": ERD to Robert and Isabella Ferguson, Feb. 10, 1913, Box 5, Folder 131, AHS.

"Tell Uncle Will": ERD to ARC, Feb. 11, 1913, TRC.

"I do hope": EKR to Kermit Roosevelt, Feb. 14, 1913, Papers of Kermit and Belle Roosevelt, LC.

"I don't think": EKR to Kermit Roosevelt, Apr. 6, 1913, Papers of Kermit and Belle Roosevelt, LC.

"I believe you'll be": TR to ERD, May 1, 1913, TRC.

$12,000 to $14,000: Sylvia Jukes Morris, *Edith Kermit Roosevelt: Portrait of a First Lady* (1980), p. 394.

"so much" . . . "of course": ERD to EKR, fall 1913, TRC.

"French perfectly". . . "as possible": ERD to EKR, aboard ship, Oct. 1914, TRC.

"It is perfectly". . . "for him": ERD to EKR, Oct. 10, 1914, TRC.

"they are terribly short" . . . "everything is infected": ERD to EKR, Oct. 10, 1914, TRC.

"comfortably installed": ERD to EKR, Oct. 10, 1914, TRC.

"devoted" . . . "*somehow*": ERD to EKR, after Oct. 10, 1914, TRC.

"has cut a tooth": ERD to EKR, Oct. 10, 1914, TRC.

"good bunny": ERD to EKR, aboard ship, 1914, TRC.

"I cannot believe": ERD to EKR, Oct. 10, 1914, TRC.

"under five years old": EKR to ERD, clipping from sometime in Nov. 1914, TRC.

"It isn't until": Richard Derby to ERD, Mar. 9, 1916, TRC.

"is no place": ERD to Kermit Roosevelt, Aug. 31, 1917, Papers of Kermit and Belle Roosevelt, LC.

"for transportation abroad": Cable with ERD letter, no date, TRC.

"Dearest, if you are wounded": ERD to Richard Derby, Mar. 16, 1918, TRC.

"I cannot say" . . . "get the experience": ERD to Richard Derby, Mar. 16, 1918, TRC.

"picked up Edith" . . . "into the room": ERD to Richard Derby, Mar. 22, 1918, TRC.

"great change": ERD to Richard Derby, Mar. 22, 1918, TRC.

"The very worst" . . . "hope so": Richard Derby to ERD, Mar. 12, 1918, TRC.

"a large shell" . . . "sure before": Richard Derby to ERD, June 7, 1918, TRC.

"had descended in flames": Richard Derby to ERD, July 17, 1918, TRC.

"when we all needed": Richard Derby to ERD, about July 20, 1918, TRC.

"I am so sorry" . . . "utter fearlessness": Richard Derby to ERD, July 21, 1918, TRC.

"Until I heard" . . . "wear black": ERD to Richard Derby, July 21, 1918, TRC.

"the young must die": Note from TR to Archie Roosevelt, in possession of Selwa Roosevelt and quoted with her permission.

"He should" . . . "all the world": Richard Derby to ERD, July 21, 1918, TRC.

"I cannot believe" . . . "want said": FRD to Richard Derby, letter started Jan. 6, 1919, TRC.

"If only I had" . . . "with girls": ERD to EKR, Dec. 3, 1927, TRC.

"It is sometimes impossible": ERD to Richard Derby, Sept. 21, 1925, TRC.

"wonderful rest" . . . "insurance too": ERD to Kermit Roosevelt, Aug. 10, 1925, Papers of Kermit and Belle Roosevelt, LC.

"absorbed in moving picture" . . . "big ones": ERD to Kermit Roosevelt, Dec. 1, 1925, Papers of Kermit and Belle Roosevelt, LC.

he wrote two articles: Richard Derby's two articles appear as two chapters in *Cleared for Strange Ports,* edited by Mrs. Theodore Roosevelt, Sr., et al.: "With Rifle and Camera on the Kenai," pp. 117–30; "The Beach-Combing Bears of Sukluk," pp. 131–44. Both are dated 1925.

"will be entirely well": ERD to Kermit Roosevelt, Christmas 1926, Papers of Kermit and Belle Roosevelt, LC.

"The Chief Nut Cracker": ERD to Kermit Roosevelt, Christmas 1926, Papers of Kermit and Belle Roosevelt, LC.

"that is, don't let": ERD to Kermit Roosevelt, Christmas 1926, Papers of Kermit and Belle Roosevelt, LC.

"thought it would be unwise": ERD to Kermit Roosevelt, Apr. 9, 1927, Papers of Kermit and Belle Roosevelt, LC.

"Dick has been miserable": ERD to Belle Roosevelt, Nov. 18, 1927, Papers of Kermit and Belle Roosevelt, LC.

"found a liver" . . . "entirely alone": ERD to Belle Roosevelt, Nov. 18, 1927, Papers of Kermit and Belle Roosevelt, LC.

"an excellent place" . . . "than the French": ERD to Belle Roosevelt, Jan. 28, 1928, Papers of Kermit and Belle Roosevelt, LC.

"I despise people": ERD to Kermit Roosevelt, June 11, 1928, Papers of Kermit and Belle Roosevelt, LC.

"for a change" . . . "joined by her": ERD to Kermit Roosevelt, June 11, 1928, Papers of Kermit and Belle Roosevelt, LC.

"Richard's death" . . . "for Dick": ERD to EKR, Nov. 14, 1928, TRC.

"Neat, good discipline": ERD to EKR, Sept. 19, 1930, TRC.

"exploring hill towns" . . . "night and day": ERD to Kermit Roosevelt, Nov. 22, 1931, Papers of Kermit and Belle Roosevelt, LC.

"Everything is very cheap": ERD to Kermit Roosevelt, Nov. 22, 1931, Papers of Kermit and Belle Roosevelt, LC.

"The hard pull" . . . "like the Carthaginians": ERD to Belle Roosevelt, Dec. 6, 1931, Papers of Kermit and Belle Roosevelt, LC.

"His eyes" . . . "certain petticoats": ERD to EKR, Jan. 11, 1932, TRC.

"How can they" . . . "said 'good-bye'": ERD to EKR, Nov. 14, 1931, TRC.

"I still feel": ERD to EKR, Nov. 14, 1931, TRC.

"every bit of the $50" . . . "every time": ERD to EKR, Nov. 29, 1931, TRC.

"I don't want" . . . "children to schools": ERD to EKR, Feb. 1932, TRC.

"for it's all" . . . "shelter us": ERD to EKR, Feb. 1932, TRC.

"I am never reconciled" . . . "been alright": ERD to EKR, Feb. 1932, TRC.

"as violent" . . . "from my hosts": ERD to EKR, Feb. 1932, TRC.

"Super woman" . . . "like myself": ERD to Richard Derby, Mar. 1918, TRC.

"a general change" . . . "grapple with children": ERD to EKR, Dec. 2, 1928, TRC.

"New England school marm": ERD to EKR, Oct. 1934, TRC.

"excellent service" . . . "any purse": ERD to EKR, Oct. 1934, TRC.

"Mother has been" . . . "quite well": EDW to EKR, Dec. 6, 1934, TRC.

"breathless attack": ERD to EKR, Dec. 6, 1934, TRC.

"on the cold side": EDW to EKR, Dec. 11, 1934, TRC.

"I almost hope": ERD to EKR, Mar. 11, 1935, TRC.

"brood . . . rather irritably" . . . "boys at night": ERD to EKR, Mar. 11, 1935, TRC.

"unusually good mind" . . . "keep her going": ERD to EKR, Mar. 11, 1935, TRC.

"*couldn't stand it*" . . . "terrible women's atmosphere": EDW author, June 16, 1994.

"tackling all sorts": Richard Derby to EDW, Dec. 18, 1943, TRC.

"kissing cousins": ERD to EDW, Nov. 21, 1976, TRC.

"I think that Franklin": ERD to Richard Derby, July 1933, TRC.

"We must be patient": ERD to EKR, Oct. 22, 1934, TRC.

"appointed keeper": ERD to EDW, Jan. 6, 1946, TRC.

"Mother seems": ERD to Ted Roosevelt, Aug. 27, 1943, Papers of Theodore Roosevelt, Jr., LC.

"loved Aunty Ethel" . . . "generous kind of woman": Selwa Roosevelt to author, Oct. 20, 1994.

"very embarrassing": ERD to EDW, Oct. 23, 1960, TRC.

"I long": ARL to ERD, Aug. 14, 1926, TRC.

"Auntie Sister" ERD to EDW, July 8, 1973, TRC.

"I don't think I can": ERD to EDW, Sept. 16, 1973, TRC.

"If people such as you": ERD to EDW, Jan. 12, 1944, TRC.

"fear of the dark" . . . "not call it fear": ERD to EDW, Aug. 1946, TRC.

"It was a saying": ERD to EDW, Nov. 12, 1951, TRC.

"certainly does not hurt" . . . "but we're not": ERD to EDW, Apr. 1946, TRC.

"My old school": ERD to EDW, June 13, 1965, TRC.

"In a few years": ERD to EDW, Apr. 21, 1949, TRC.

"Find something": ERD to EDW, Mar. 24, 1946, TRC.

"I am more than ever": ERD to EDW, Mar. 28, 1948, TRC.

"a great time": Sarah Alden Gannett to author, June 16, 1994.

"that interested me": Sarah Alden Gannett to author, June 16, 1994.

"wonderful life": Sarah Alden Gannett to author, June 16, 1994.

"adrenalin, and hypodermics": ERD to Kermit Roosevelt, May 24, 1925, Papers of Kermit and Belle Roosevelt, LC.

"I've had her on my mind": ERD to EDW, June 22, 1946, TRC.

"I only deplore": ERD to EDW, Dec. 18, 1943, TRC.

"discarded": ERD to EDW, Aug. 25, 1946, TRC.

"thing of the past": ERD to EDW, July 18, 1946, TRC.

"indispensable to one another": Richard Derby to EDW, June 27, 1948, TRC.

"I feel so strongly": ERD to EDW, Sept. 19, 1948, TRC.

"little Judith": ERD to EDW, Feb. 26, 1950, TRC.

Others boss them around: ERD to EDW, Aug. 24, 1952, TRC.

"fairly well": ERD to EDW, Dec. 9, 1956, TRC.

"that for some reason": ERD to EDW, Dec. 9, 1956, TRC.

Judith was "smoking again": ERD to EDW, Oct. 6, 1957, TRC.

managing "everyone" . . . "fighting this thing": ERD to EDW, June 28, 1959, TRC.

"strange metabolic thing": ERD to EDW, July 21, 1959, TRC.

"It's hard for a mother": ERD to EDW, Jan. 29, 1962, TRC.

"always leaned": ERD to EDW, Dec. 23, 1962, TRC.

"These are the things": ERD to EDW, Dec. 10, 1962, TRC.

"said all those nice things": ERD to EDW, Apr. 29, 1962, TRC.

"oblivious to time" . . . troubles with them: ERD to EDW, Oct. 7, 1962, TRC.

"learning to live" . . . "more than I can say": ERD to EDW, Apr. 20, 1963, TRC.

"I cannot even imagine" . . . "not as well": ERD to EDW, May 18, 1963, TRC.

"[W]e were so removed": ERD to EDW, Sept. 29, 1963, TRC.

"those years of suffering": ERD to EDW, Oct. 6, 1963, TRC.

"little jumpy feeling": ERD to EDW, Nov. 9, 1969, TRC.

"so especially a man's man": ERD to EDW, Mar. 10, 1971, TRC.

"how weak she is": ERD to EDW, Aug. 11, 1963, TRC.

found Judith "miserable": ERD to EDW, Aug. 18, 1963, TRC.

"last summer all over again": ERD to EDW, Oct. 13, 1963, TRC.

"afraid or too proud": ERD to EDW, Apr. 19, 1970, TRC.

"There is no one": ERD to EDW, July 23, 1967, TRC.

" deep [depression]": ERD to EDW, Apr. 3, 1972, TRC.

"incessantly of suicide" . . . "not our Judith": ERD to EDW, Mar. 25, 1973, TRC.

"lives in a timeless world": ERD to EDW, July 8, 1973, TRC.

"How can one" . . . "darling Judith": ERD to EDW, July 30 or 31, 1973, TRC.

"how strange that was": ERD to EDW, Nov. 18, 1973, TRC.

"[T]alking about reserve": ERD to EDW, Nov. 25, 1973, TRC.

"of all the family": ERD to EDW, Dec. 30, 1973, TRC.

"all by herself" . . . "very steep": EDW and Sarah Alden Gannett to author, June 16, 1994.

"Cousin Eleanor" . . . "not to be too admiring": ERD to EDW, Apr. 9, 1950, TRC.

"Don't hold with those things": ERD to EDW, Jan. 22, 1950, TRC.

"Wasn't it exciting": ERD to EDW, June 13, 1954, TRC.

"I thought of all the trouble": ERD to EDW, Apr. 14, 1968, TRC.

"by charging them excessive rents": ERD to EDW, Jan. 16, 1962, TRC.

"made it possible": Jesse Harmon, quoted in *Theodore Roosevelt Association Journal,* winter 1978, p. 5.

"democracy" . . . "not find that in it": ERD to EDW, Jan. 4, 1970, TRC.

"Yes, of course": ERD to EDW, Jan. 20, 1968, TRC.

"Auntie Ethel used to give": Susan Weld to author, Nov. 10, 1994.

"phantasies or dream visions" . . . "in touch with": ERD to EDW, Jan. 5, 1969, TRC.

watch it on television: ERD to EDW, July 5, 1964, TRC.

"lousy": ERD to EDW, Sept. 2, 1972, TRC.

"dignified": ERD to EDW, Sept. 24, 1972, TRC.

"If [the President] renews" . . . "not to her either": ERD to EDW, Jan. 7, 1973, TRC.

"very unfashionable" . . . "in all our lives": Susan Weld to author, Nov. 10, 1994.

"So Bed time": ERD to EDW, Nov. 30, 1977, TRC.

Chapter 8: Alice Roosevelt Longworth

"It is a Roosevelt year": Clipping, *The American*, Dec. 21, 1902, TRC.

"probably the most interesting": Clipping, *The American*, Dec. 21, 1902, TRC.

"born to lead": Clipping, *The American*, Dec. 21, 1902, TRC.

"niece of the President": Clipping, *The American*, Dec. 21, 1902, TRC.

"first female American celebrity": Stacy Rozek Cordery, "Alice Roosevelt Longworth: Life in a Public Crucible," unpublished Ph.D. dissertation, University of Texas at Austin, 1992, p. iv.

"sprang from the grass roots": Barbara Howar, *Laughing All the Way* (1973), p. 225.

gave them "currency": Michael Teague, *Mrs. L: Conversations with Alice Roosevelt Longworth* (1981), p. 170.

"I'm going to call you Alice": Various versions of this story circulated. This one is from Michael Teague, *Mrs. L*, pp. 197–99.

"What do you think you're doing": Alice Longworth evidently told different ent versions of this story. For one version, see Barbara Howar, *Laughing All the Way*, p. 225.

"many kisses": TR to ARC, Nov. 23, 1884, TRC.

number of books owned: CRR to Henry F. Pringle, Sept. 22, 1930, TRC.

"droves": ARL to ARC, Jan. 7, 1917, TRC.

"by far the best": ARL, quoted in Michael Teague, *Mrs. L*, p. 22.

Russian style: Michael Teague, *Mrs. L*, p. ix.

distinctive handwriting: Michael Teague, *Mrs. L*, p. 25.

"single most important": Michael Teague, *Mrs. L*, p. 12.

"Sissy had a sweat nurse": Michael Teague, *Mrs. L*, p. 18.

had polio: Michael Teague, *Mrs. L*, p. vii.

"nothing serious": EKR to Emily Carow, Feb. 25, 1893, TRC.

enormous will-power: Michael Teague, *Mrs. L*, p. vii.

"enormous effort": Michael Teague, *Mrs. L*, p. 30.

Ethel Derby often remarked: ERD to EDW, Dec. 21, 1975, TRC.

never mentioned her mother's name: Alexandra Dworkin to author, Nov. 22, 1994.

"great affection" ... "guilty": Michael Teague, *Mrs. L*, p. 109.

"The curious thing": Michael Teague, *Mrs. L*, p. 109.

"Dive, Alice": Howard Teichmann, *Alice: The Life and Times of Alice Roosevelt Longworth* (1979), p. 103.

governess at home: Michael Teague, *Mrs. L*, p. 54.

biblical verb "begat": Michael Teague, *Mrs. L*, p. 54.

"running riot": TR to ARC, Feb. 23, 1898, TRC.

"good letter writer": TR to ARC, Feb. 23, 1898, TRC.

"really does love": TR to ARC, Feb. 23, 1898, TRC.

"But this is MY inauguration": Michael Teague, *Mrs. L*, p. 72.

"a father complex": Michael Teague, *Mrs. L*, p. 76.

"Auntie Bye": Michael Teague, *Mrs. L*, p. 77.

quieter, and slower: Elizabeth Norris kindly shared with me her considerable knowledge on early automobiles and why the "electric" was considered "more womanly."

"She locks all her doors": ERD to Kermit Roosevelt, early 1905, Papers of Kermit and Belle Roosevelt, LC.

"remarkably steady head": EKR, quoted in Sylvia Jukes Morris, *Edith Kermit Roosevelt: Portrait of a First Lady* (1980), p. 233.

"somewhere between Auntie Bye's": Stacy Rozek Cordery, "Alice Roosevelt Longworth," (1992), p. 133.

"conform to the life" . . . "never occur again": ARC to ARL, June 23, 1903, ARL Papers, LC.

"very well and handsome" . . . "proper friends": ARC to CRR, Apr. 7, 1903, TRC.

"from heaven knows" . . . "Anyway it worked": Michael Teague, *Mrs. L*, p. 14.

"Alice is thoroughly provided for": ARC to CRR, May 19, 1910, TRC.

"Of course this note": Caroline Haskell Lee to ARL, Aug. 13, 1905, TRC.

"I am glad to have it": EKR to ARL, Mar. 1902, TRC.

"My 'scolding'": EKR to ARL, Aug. 2, 1904, TRC.

"How would you like": EKR to ARL, no date, TRC.

"a stop to all possible gossip": EKR to ARL, Dec. 2, 1902, TRC.

"dear and sweet": CRR to CRA, Oct. 31, 1902, TRC.

"Alice is dear": CRR to CRA, Jan. 20, 1903, TRC.

"She is always sweet": CRR to CRA, Jan. 20, 1903, TRC.

"either run the country": The original version of this often repeated phrase is in Owen Wister, *Roosevelt: The Story of a Friendship, 1880–1919* (1930), p. 87.

Corinney once observed that duty was central: CRA interview with Joseph Lash, Apr. 27, 1967, p. 2, FDRL.

"had to be bridesmaid" . . . "fearful bore": ARL to John Greenway, Mar. 15, 1905, Papers of John and Isabella Greenway, Box 89, AHS. Isabella Selmes Ferguson married John Greenway after the death of Robert Ferguson in 1922.

they vented their anger: CRR to CRA, Jan. 30, 1903, TRC.

trip to Cuba instead: Michael Teague, *Mrs. L*, p. 84.

"by far the most exciting": Michael Teague, *Mrs. L*, p. 84.

"a fearful bore": ARL to John Greenway, Mar. 15, 1905, Papers of John and Isabella Greenway, Box 89, AHS.

extended trip abroad: Carol Felsenthal, *Princess Alice*, p. 80.

"Alice in Plunderland": Michael Teague, "Alice Roosevelt's 1905 State Visit to China," *Vogue*, Feb. 1, 1972, pp. 156–58. "Alice in Plunderland" was the title of a poem that a family friend, Willard Straight, wrote at the time of Alice's trip.

"a rather grand garden party": Michael Teague, "Alice Roosevelt's 1905 State Visit to China," p. 156.

"is traveling now": Helen Taft, *Recollections of Full Years* (1914), p. 294.

"I listened to her earnest discourse": Michael Teague, *Mrs. L*, p. 151.

Their vineyard produced: Stacy Rozek Cordery, "Alice Roosevelt Longworth," p. 184.

"In those days": Michael Teague, *Mrs. L*, p. 129.

"one of those wizened virgins": Michael Teague, *Mrs. L*, p. 73.

"out of the house":In an interview with the author, Nov. 22, 1994, Alexandra Dworkin recalled that ARL used these words.

How very "midwestern" . . . "picture of that": Michael Teague, *Mrs. L*, p. 128.

kept the assembled guests waiting: Lady Bird Johnson, *A White House Diary* (1970) p. 65.

"I want you to know" . . . "the same way": Michael Teague, *Mrs. L*, p. 128.

"the sort of presents" . . . "red hot stove": Howard Teichmann, *Alice*, pp. 56–57.

For their wedding trip: Stacy Rozek Cordery, "Alice Roosevelt Longworth," p. 204.

"surprised at the difference": ERD to Robert Ferguson, Mar. 1906, Ferguson Papers, Box 5, Folder 124, AHS.

"I'm amused": Michael Teague, *Mrs. L*, p. 199.

"beautiful" . . . "second honeymoon": ERD to Robert Ferguson, Oct. 7, 1907, Ferguson Papers, Box 5, Folder 125, AHS.

"not married in any real sense": Joanna Sturm to author, Oct. 20, 1994.

win "hands down": TR to ARL, Oct. 16, 1906, TRC.

"upon the successful way": TR to ARL, Nov. 7, 1906, TRC.

"rather be tight": Joan Braden, *Just Enough Rope: An Intimate Memoir* (1989), p. 89.

Belgian ambassador's daughter: Joan Braden, *Just Enough Rope*, p. 84.

"I wish you'd lend": ERD to Robert Ferguson, Apr. 20, 1909, Ferguson Papers, Box 5, Folder 127, AHS.

"Some things are too bad": June Bingham, "Before the Colors Fade," *American Heritage*, Feb. 1969, p. 74.

"Your account of it": EKR to ARL, Mar. 10, 1909, TRC.

"I feel sure": EKR to ARL, Sept. 1909, TRC.

"are just plain duties": EKR to ARL, Sept. 1909, TRC.

"This district": ARL to ARC, Sept. 27, 1910, TRC.

"ma-in-law" . . . "so outrageous": ARL to ARC, Jan. 31, 1914, TRC.

"On the whole": ARL to ARC, Jan. 17, 1917, TRC.

"as time goes on" . . . "as I see it": ARL to ARC, Oct. 27, 1919, TRC.

"so interesting" . . . "women workers": ARC to CRR, Jan. 28, 1918, TRC.

"adorable" . . . "good and true": ARC to ARL, Jan. 28, 1918, TRC.

"I remember telling": Michael Teague, *Mrs. L*, p. 158.

"private visit": EKR to CRR, Aug. 22, 1912, TRC.

"a hard winter": ARC to Robert Ferguson, July 13, 1912, Ferguson Papers, Box 2, Folder 47, AHS.

"Bad boy Sister": ERD to EKR, Apr. 1913, TRC.

"*lived* in Sister's dark blue suit": ERD to EKR, Apr. 1913, TRC.

"Sister and I": ERD to Richard Derby, Dec. 2, no year, probably 1915, TRC.

"He wasn't a bad man": ARL, *Crowded Hours: Reminiscences of Alice Roosevelt Longworth* (1933), p. 325.

"I never liked him anyway": Joanna Sturm to author, Oct. 20, 1994.

child he was accused of fathering: Carol Felsenthal, *Princess Alice*, p. 147 cites two Borah biographers who told Felsenthal about their sources for this version of Borah's early life.

"completely Borahized": ERD to EKR, July 20, 1927, quotes CRR, TRC.

"close friends" . . . "bond between us": Michael Teague, *Mrs. L*, p. 187.

"Little Borah": Carol Felsenthal, *Princess Alice*, p. 188.

enormous collection of miniature elephants: Mary Borah titled her autobiography *Elephants and Donkeys* (1976).

Tongues wagged: Ralph Martin, *Cissy* (1979), p. 211.

"I am waiting" . . . "[Alice's] birthday": ARC to CRR, Feb. 13, 1925, TRC.

"Such a satisfactory baby" . . . "done in years": EKR to ARC, Feb. 1925, TRC.

"Apparently the small child" . . . "with any of our family": ARC to CRR, Feb. 24, 1925, TRC.

name sure to have titillated: Carol Felsenthal, *Princess Alice*, p. 157.

"Of course it has changed": Kermit Roosevelt to ARC, Mar. 1925, TRC.

"so attractive": CRR to CRA, Apr. 1925, TRC.

"strange mood" . . . "World Court": ERD to Richard Derby, May 1926, TRC.

"betrayal of the trust" . . . "doing little things": ERD to Richard Derby, May 1926, TRC.

"Paulina is a sweet thing": ERD to Isabella Ferguson Greenway, June 1925, Papers of John and Isabella Greenway, AHS.

such an attentive parent: NYT, Nov. 28, 1926, p. 25; Mar. 5, 1929, p. 5; July 13, 1930, VI; Jan. 9, 1931, p. 24.

"the most irresistible description": ARC to CRR, May 1926, TRC.

"She loves it": ARL to ERD, Nov. 1930, TRC.

"attacked Stimson" . . . "as if she were herself": ERD to EKR quotes CRR, July 20, 1927, TRC.

split the bounty: Several different versions exist, but see Howard Teichmann, *Alice*, p. 132, for one version based on an interview with Ethel Derby.

"I notice": Howard Teichman, *Alice*, p. 157.

"one moment" . . . "30,000 two years ago": ARL to ERD, Nov. 1930, TRC.

"sure of how the House": ARL to ERD, Nov. 1930, TRC.

"one of the early swingers": William Miller and Frances Spatz Leighton, *Fishbait* (1977), p. 104.

"one of the greatest womanizers": William Miller and Frances Spatz Leighton, *Fishbait* (1977), p. 103.

"pretty bald head". . . "damned if it doesn't": William Miller and Frances Spatz Leighton, *Fishbait*, pp. 103–04.

actually condoms: William Miller and Frances Spatz Leighton, *Fishbait*, p. 104.

burned his Stradivarius: Carol Felsenthal, *Princess Alice*, p. 168.

"small, cozy town": Michael Teague, *Mrs. L*, p. 199.

"Washington's other monument": It is not exactly clear who first used this term, but Ethel Derby endorsed it in a letter to her daughter on April 24, 1966, and Carol Felsenthal made it a chapter title in *Princess Alice*, pp. 242–70.

"out of season Roosevelts": Howard Teichmann, *Alice*, p. 155; cites Alexander Woollcott.

"to enjoy himself" . . . "a good time": Michael Teague, *Mrs. L*, p. 160.

"deserved a good time": Ted Morgan, *F.D.R.: A Biography* (1985), p. 206.

"The President's church": Howard Teichmann, *Alice*, p. 175.

"My Day": ERR signed the contract in December 1935, but the column first appeared in January 1936.

"Capital Comment": Titles varied on ARL's columns. See Carol Felsenthal, *Princess Alice*, p. 177.

"never written anything longer": Howard Teichmann, *Alice*, p. 158.

"If I err": Howard Teichmann, *Alice*, p. 158.

in a play, First Lady: Howard Teichmann, *Alice*, p. 166.

One of the playwrights: The play is by Katherine Dayton and George S. Kaufman (1935).

"Too bad the property values": Howard Teichmann, *Alice*, p. 166.

"Ideal Qualifications": *Ladies' Home Journal*, Feb. 1936, p. 8.

pronounced it "strange": ERD to EKR, Feb. 11, 1935, TRC.

"filled with admiration": ERD to Kermit Roosevelt, Mar. 25, 1935, TRC.

"great fun": ARL to ERD, Aug. 11, 1926, TRC.

"courtly and friendly": Howard Teichmann, *Alice*, p. 192.

relationship with Lewis was more intimate: Carol Felsenthal, *Princess Alice*, p. 193, cites friends of the Lewises.

"crust of bread" speech is described in the entry for Lewis in *Current Biography*, 1942.

"ill behooved one": *Current Biography*, 1942.

something to hide: Carol Felsenthal, *Princess Alice*, p. 193.

"tremendous animal appeal": Carol Felsethal, *Princess Alice*, p. 193.

confession to the bride: Carol Felsenthal, *Princess Alice*, pp. 216–17.

choosing a name: ERD to EDW, July 18, 1946, TRC.

"jaundice": ERD to EDW, Nov. 14, 1951, TRC.

"absorbing queer life": ERD to EDW, Nov. 14, 1951, TRC.

under the same roof: ERD to EDW, Nov. 18, 1951, TRC.

"the champagne cocktail type" . . . "bring up" Joanna: ERD to EDW, May 23, 1952, TRC.

animosity she felt: ERD to EDW, May 23, 1952, TRC.

converted to that faith: ERD to EDW, Aug. 17, 1952, TRC.

Clare Booth Luce, a sponsor: ERD to EDW, Mar. 1, 1953, TRC.

"still remote" . . . "happy surroundings": ERD to EDW, Mar. 14, 1953, TRC.

"the unusual is usual" . . . "Such fun": ERD to EDW, Jan. 11, 1948, TRC.

"certainly much more 'our Washington'": ERD to EDW, Mar. 1, 1953, TRC.

"to represent the Dem[ocratic] part": ERD to EDW, Mar. 14, 1953, TRC.

Paulina had died at home: For details of Paulina's death, see Carol Felsenthal, Princess Alice, pp. 234–35.

"You can imagine" . . . "she said to come": ERD to EDW, Jan. 28 [?], 1957, TRC.

"the strangest, saddest, darkest week": ERD to EDW, Feb. 3, 1957, TRC.

"Paulina had been drinking" . . . "some deep psychosis there ": ERD to EDW, Feb. 3, 1957, TRC.

"extrovert, highly intelligent": ERD to EDW, Feb. 3, 1957, TRC.

"worked out a satisfactory relationship": ERD to EDW, Jan. 6, 1958, TRC.

"really remarkable": ERD to EDW, June 3, 1967, TRC.

"Auntie Sister": ERD to EDW, Mar. 18, 1962, TRC.

"apparently uninhibited": ERD to EDW, Feb. 15, 1969, TRC.

"She says things": ERD to EDW, Apr. 13, 1969, TRC.

"I never feel quite sure" . . . "going on": ERD to EDW, Apr. 13, 1969, TRC.

"with great interest": ERD to EDW, Dec. 21, 1975, TRC.

"Auntie Sister and I laugh": ERD to EDW, Dec. 21, 1975, TRC.

"marvelous. Reads the small print": ERD to EDW, May 7, 1961, TRC.

"nothing much to say": Howard Teichmann, *Alice*, p. 237, quotes *Newsweek*, May 18, 1970.

"I'm just one": Howard Teichmann, *Alice*, p. 235; quotes *Time*, Feb. 18, 1974.

"Alice wasted her life": Joan Braden, *Just Enough Rope*, p. 90.

"Who was that woman": Carol Felsenthal, *Princess Alice*, p. 270.

more than "power": Howard Teichmann, *Alice*, p. 242.

Adams, Samuel. *The Incredible Era: The Life and Times of Warren Gamaliel Harding.* Boston: Houghton Mifflin, 1939.

Alsop, Joseph W. (with Adam Platt). *I've Seen the Best of It.* New York: Norton, 1992.

Auchincloss, Louis. *The Vanderbilt Era: Profiles of a Gilded Age.* New York: Scribner's, 1989.

Bailey, Thomas F. *The American Pageant.* Lexington, MA: D.C. Heath, 1956; 4th ed., 1971.

Balsan, Consuelo Vanderbilt. *The Glitter and the Gold.* New York: Harper, 1952.

Beasley, Maurine, ed. *The White House Press Conferences of Eleanor Roosevelt.* New York: Garland, 1983.

Birmingham, Stephen. *America's Secret Aristocracy.* Boston: Little, Brown, 1987.

Boatwright, Eleanor Miot. *Status of Women in Georgia, 1783–1860.* Brooklyn, NY: Carlson, 1994.

Boettiger, John R. *A Love in the Shadow: The Story of Anna Roosevelt and John Boettiger, Told by Their Son.* New York: Norton, 1978.

Borah, Mary. *Elephants and Donkeys.* Boise, ID: University of Idaho Press, 1976.

Boyd, Elizabeth French. *Bloomsbury Heritage: Their Mothers and Their Aunts.* London: Hamish Hamilton, 1976.

Braden, Joan. *Just Enough Rope: An Intimate Memoir.* New York: Villard, 1989.

Brandes, H. W. *T. R.: The Last Romantic.* New York: Basic Books, 1997.

Brownell, Blaine A., and Goldfield, David R., eds. *The City in Southern History: The Growth of Urban Civilization in the South.* Port Washington, NY: Kennikat Press, 1977.

Bulloch, James Dunwody. *The Secret Service of the Confederate States in Europe, or, How the Confederate Cruisers Were Equipped.* London: R. Bentley and Son, 2 vols., 1883.

Butt, Archibald. *Letters of Archie Butt: Personal Aide to President Roosevelt.* Edited and with a biographical sketch of the author by Lawrence F. Abbott. Garden City, NY: Doubleday, 1924.

Camhi, Jane Jerome. *Women against Women: American Anti-Suffragism, 1880–1920*. Brooklyn, NY: Carlson, 1994.

Caroli, Betty Boyd. *First Ladies*. New York: Oxford University Press, 1987; expanded ed., 1995.

Cassini, Marguerite. *Never a Dull Moment*. New York: Harper, 1956.

Chambrun, Clara Longworth de. *The Making of Nicholas Longworth: Annals of an American Family*. New York: Ray Long & Richard Smith, Inc., 1933.

Chanler, Margaret (Mrs. Winthrop). *Roman Spring: Memoirs*. Boston: Little, Brown, 1934.

Collier, Peter (with David Horowitz). *The Roosevelts: An American Saga*. New York: Simon and Schuster, 1994.

Cook, Blanche Wiesen. *Eleanor Roosevelt, 1884–1933*. New York: Viking, 1992.

Cordery, Stacy Rozek. "Alice Roosevelt Longworth: Life in a Public Crucible." Unpublished Ph.D. dissertation, University of Texas at Austin, 1992.

Dalton, Kathleen. "The Early Life of Theodore Roosevelt." Unpublished Ph.D. dissertation, Johns Hopkins University, 1979.

Dieck, Herman. *Life and Public Services of Our Great Reform President Grover Cleveland*. San Francisco: J. Dewing, 1888.

Duncan, Bingham. *Whitelaw Reid: Journalist, Politician, Diplomat*. Athens, GA: University of Georgia Press, 1975.

Faber, Doris. *The Life of Lorena Hickok, ER's Friend*. New York: Morrow, 1980.

Faust, Drew Gilpin. *Mothers of Invention: Women of the Slaveholding South in the American Civil War*. Chapel Hill: University of North Carolina Press, 1996.

Felsenthal, Carol. *Princess Alice: The Life and Times of Alice Roosevelt Longworth*. New York: St. Martin's Press, 1988.

Ferguson, James. *History of the Ferguson Family in Scotland and America*. New York: Times Presses, 1905.

Fleming, Karl, and Fleming, Anne Taylor. *The First Time*. New York: Simon and Schuster, 1972.

Garraty, John. *The American Nation*. New York: Harper & Row, 1966; 2nd ed., 1971.

Genealogical Committee of Georgia Historical Society. *Marriages of Chatham County, Georgia*. Savannah, GA: The Society, 1993.

Goodwin, Doris Kearns. *No Ordinary Time: Franklin and Eleanor Roosevelt: The Home Front in World War II*. New York: Simon and Schuster, 1994.

Gordon, Linda, ed. *Women, the State and Welfare*. Madison: University of Wisconsin Press, 1990.

Gould, Lewis. *The Presidency of Theodore Roosevelt.* Lawrence, KA: University Press of Kansas, 1991.

Griscom, Lloyd C. *Diplomatically Speaking.* Boston: Little, Brown, 1940.

Hagedorn, Hermann. *The Roosevelt Family of Sagamore Hill.* New York: Macmillan, 1954.

Harrison, Constance (Mrs. Burton). *Recollections Grave and Gay.* New York: Scribner's, 1911.

Hickok, Lorena. *Eleanor Roosevelt: Reluctant First Lady.* New York: Dodd, Mead, 1962.

Hoff-Wilson, Joan, and Lightman, Marjorie, eds. *Without Precedent.* Blooomington: Indiana University Press, 1984.

Howar, Barbara. *Laughing All the Way.* New York: Stein and Day, 1973.

International Association of Ice Cream Manufacturers. *The History of Ice Cream.* Washington, DC: Privately printed, 1958.

Jablonsky, Thomas J. *The Home, Heaven, and Mother Party: Female Anti-Suffragists in the United States, 1868–1920.* Brooklyn, NY: Carlson, 1994.

Jackson, Kenneth T., ed. *Encyclopedia of New York City.* New Haven, CT: Yale University Press, 1995.

Jensen, Amy La Follette. *The White House and Its Thirty-Three Families.* New York: McGraw-Hill, 1958; 2nd ed., 1962.

Johnson, Lady Bird. *A White House Diary.* New York: Holt, Rinehart, Winston, 1970.

Keogh, Theodora. *The Double Door.* New York: Creative Age Press, 1950.

———. *The Fascinator.* New York: Farrar, Straus & Young, 1954.

———. *Meg: A Novel.* New York: Creative Age Press, 1950.

———. *Street Music.* New York: Farrar, Straus & Young, 1951.

Kirk, Elise K. *Music at the White House: A History of the American Spirit.* Urbana: University of Illinois Press, 1986.

Kleeman, Rita Halle. *Gracious Lady: The Life of Sara Delano Roosevelt.* New York: D. Appleton Century, 1935.

Lash, Joseph P. *Eleanor and Franklin: The Story of Their Relationship, Based on Eleanor Roosevelt's Private Papers.* New York: Norton, 1971.

———. *Eleanor: The Years Alone.* New York: Norton, 1972.

———. *Love, Eleanor: Eleanor Roosevelt and Her Friends.* Garden City, NY: Doubleday, 1982.

Longworth, Alice Roosevelt. *Crowded Hours: Reminiscences of Alice Roosevelt Longworth.* New York: Scribner's, 1933.

Longworth, Alice Roosevelt, and Roosevelt, Theodore, compilers. *The Desk Drawer Anthology.* Freeport, NY: Books for Libraries Press, 1937. Also Garden City, NY: Doubleday, 1938.

Martin, Clarece. *A Glimpse of the Past: The History of Bulloch Hall and Roswell, Georgia.* Roswell, GA: Lake Publications, 1973 and 1987.

Martin, Ralph. *Cissy.* New York: Simon and Schuster, 1979.

McAllister, Ward. *Society As I Have Found It.* New York: Cassell, 1890.

McCall, Samuel W. *The Life of Thomas Brackett Reed.* Boston: Houghton Mifflin, 1914.

McCullough, David. *Mornings on Horseback.* New York: Simon and Schuster, 1981.

McKenna, Marian C. *Borah.* Ann Arbor: University of Michigan Press, 1961.

Merry, Robert W. *Taking On the World: Joseph and Stewart Alsop, Guardians of the American Century.* New York: Viking Penguin, 1996.

Miller, Nathan. *Theodore Roosevelt: A Life.* New York: Morrow, 1992.

Miller, William, and Leighton, Frances Spatz. *Fishbait.* Englewood Cliffs, NJ: Prentice-Hall, Inc., 1977.

Morgan, Ted. *F.D.R.: A Biography.* New York: Simon and Schuster, 1985.

Morris, Edmund. *The Rise of Theodore Roosevelt.* New York: Coward, McCann & Geoghegan, 1979.

Morris, Sylvia Jukes. *Edith Kermit Roosevelt: Portrait of a First Lady.* New York: Coward, McCann & Geoghegan, 1980.

Myers, Robert. *Children of Pride.* New Haven, CT: Yale University Press, 1972.

Nagel, Paul C. *The Adams Women: Abigail, Louisa Adams, Their Sisters and Daughters.* New York: Oxford University Press, 1987.

Nasaw, David. *Children of the City.* New York: Oxford University Press, 1986.

Ornig, Joseph R. *My Last Chance to Be a Boy: Theodore Roosevelt's South American Expedition of 1913–1914.* Mechanicsburg, PA: Stackpole Books, 1994.

O'Toole, Patricia. *The Five of Hearts.* New York: Clarkson N. Potter, 1990.

Parsons, Frances. *Perchance Some Day.* Privately printed, 1951.

Pringle, Henry F. *Theodore Roosevelt: A Biography.* New York: Harcourt, Brace, 1931.

Putnam, Carleton. *Theodore Roosevelt: The Formative Years.* New York: Scribner's, 1958.

Rixey, Lilian. *Bamie.* New York: David McKay, 1963.

Robinson, Corinne Roosevelt. *My Brother Theodore Roosevelt.* New York: Scribner's, 1921.

Roosevelt, Edith Kermit, and Roosevelt, Kermit. *American Backlogs: The Story of Gertrude Tyler and Her Family, 1660–1860.* New York: Scribner's, 1928.

Roosevelt, Eleanor. *Eleanor Roosevelt's My Day.* New York: Pharos Books, 1989–1991, 3 vols.

——. *If You Ask Me.* New York: D. Appleton-Century, 1946.

——. *It Seems to Me.* New York: Norton, 1949; 2nd ed., 1954.

——. *It's Up to the Women.* New York: Frederick A. Stokes, 1933.

——. *Mother and Daughter: The Letters of Eleanor and Anna Roosevelt,* edited by Bernard Asbell. New York: Coward, McCann & Geoghegan, 1982.

———. *On My Own.* New York: Harper, 1958.

———. *This I Remember.* New York: Harper, 1949.

———. *This Is My Story.* New York: Harper, 1958.

Roosevelt, Elliott. *Hunting Big Game in the Eighties: The Letters of Elliott Roosevelt, Sportsman,* edited by his daughter Anna Eleanor Roosevelt. New York: Scribner's, 1933.

———. *An Untold Story: The Roosevelts of Hyde Park.* New York: Putnam, 1973.

Roosevelt, Hall. *Odyssey of an American Family: An Account of the Roosevelts and Their Kin as Travelers, From 1613 to 1938.* New York: Harper, 1938.

Roosevelt, James. *My Parents: A Differing View.* Chicago: Playboy Press, 1976.

Roosevelt, Nicholas. *A Front Row Seat.* Norman: University of Oklahoma Press, 1953.

———. *Theodore Roosevelt: The Man As I Knew Him.* New York: Dodd, Mead, 1967.

Roosevelt, Theodore. *Letters from Theodore Roosevelt to Anna Roosevelt Cowles, 1870–1918.* New York: Scribner's, 1924.

———. *Selections from the Correspondence of Theodore Roosevelt and Henry Cabot Lodge, 1884–1918.* New York: Scribner's, 1925, 2 vols.

———. *The Works of Theodore Roosevelt.* New York: Scribner's, 1926. Similar to this collection (known as the National Edition) is the Memorial Edition, also published by Scribner's, 1923–1926.

Roosevelt, Mrs. Theodore Sr.; Roosevelt, Mrs. Kermit; Derby, Richard; and Roosevelt, Kermit. *Cleared for Strange Ports.* New York: Scribner's, 1927.

Roosevelt, Mrs. Theodore Jr. *Day Before Yesterday: Reminiscences of Mrs. Theodore Roosevelt, Jr.* Garden City, NY: Doubleday, 1959.

Schary, Dore. *Sunrise at Campobello.* New York: Random House, 1957.

Seager, Robert. *And Tyler Too: A Biography of John and Julia Gardiner Tyler.* New York: McGraw-Hill, 1963.

Silverman, Elaine Leslau. *Theodore Roosevelt and Women: The Inner Conflict of a President and Its Impact on His Ideology.* Unpublished Ph.D. dissertation, University of California, Los Angeles, 1973.

Steinberg, Alfred. *Mrs. R: The Life of Eleanor Roosevelt.* New York: Putnam, 1958.

Sturm, Alexander. *From Ambush to Zig-Zag.* New York: Scribner's, 1942.

Taft, Helen. *Recollections of Full Years.* New York: Dodd Mead, 1914.

Teague, Michael. *Mrs. L: Conversations with Alice Roosevelt Longworth.* Garden City, NY: Doubleday, 1981.

Teichmann, Howard. *Alice: The Life and Times of Alice Roosevelt Long-worth*. Englewood Cliffs, NJ: Prentice-Hall, 1979.

Thayer, William. *Theodore Roosevelt: An Intimate Biography*. Boston: Houghton Mifflin, 1919.

U.S. Congress. *Biographical Directory of the American Congress, 1774–1989*. Washington: U.S. Government Printing Office, 1988.

Vinovskis, Maris, ed. *Studies in American Historical Demography*. New York: Academic Press, 1979.

Ward, Geoffrey. *Before the Trumpet: Young Franklin Roosevelt, 1882–1905*. New York: Harper & Row, 1985.

———. *First Class Temperament: The Emergence of Franklin Roosevelt*. New York: Harper & Row, 1989.

Wecter, Dixon. *The Saga of American Society: A Record of Social Aspiration, 1607–1937*. New York: Scribner's, 1937 and 1970.

Winthrop, Elizabeth. *In My Mother's House*. Garden City, NY: 1988.

———. *Island Justice*. New York: Morrow, 1998.

Wister, Owen. *Roosevelt: The Story of a Friendship, 1880–1919*. New York: Macmillan, 1930.

Wood, Erskine. *Life of Charles Erskine Scott Wood*. Vancouver, WA: Rose Wind, 1978.

Youngs, William T. *Eleanor Roosevelt*. Boston: Little, Brown, 1985.

PHOTOGRAPH CREDITS

CHAPTER OPENERS

Chapter 1: Mittie Roosevelt, in hat. Personal Collection of Joseph W. Alsop VI

Chapter 2: Anna "Bamie" Roosevelt in lace and velvet. Franklin D. Roosevelt Library

Chapter 3: Corinne Roosevelt Robinson, in ball gown. Personal Collection of John Alsop

Chapter 4: Edith Kermit Carow Roosevelt, "the goddess" photo (*top*). Theodore Roosevelt Collection, Harvard College Library; (*bottom*) Sara Delano in dark dress. Franklin D. Roosevelt Library

Chapter 5: Eleanor Roosevelt in bridal gown. Franklin D. Roosevelt Library

Chapter 6: Corinne Alsop, in white dress and black hat. Personal Collection of John Alsop

Chapter 7: Ethel Roosevelt as young girl. Theodore Roosevelt Collection, Harvard College Library

Chapter 8: Postcard of "Princess Alice." Franklin D. Roosevelt Library

FIRST INSERT

Mittie in white plumed hat. Theodore Roosevelt Collection, Harvard College Library

Portrait of Anna Bulloch Gracie. Theodore Roosevelt Collection, Harvard College Library

Bulloch Hall. Theodore Roosevelt Collection, Harvard College Library

Tranquillity. Theodore Roosevelt Collection, Harvard College Library

Bamie, with her father. Theodore Roosevelt Collection, Harvard College Library

Bamie and Alice. Theodore Roosevelt Collection. Harvard College Library

Bamie and her family in Farmington. Cowles Family Archives, Courtesy of Brie Quinby and Evan Cowles

Corinne Roosevelt with doll. Theodore Roosevelt Collection, Harvard College Library

Group photo of P.O.R.E. (Paradise of Ravenous Eaters). Theodore Roosevelt Collection, Harvard College Library

Portrait of Corinne Roosevelt. Theodore Roosevelt Collection, Harvard College Library

Portrait of Corinne Roosevelt Robinson. Personal Collection of John Alsop

Henderson House. Personal Collection of John Alsop

Group photo of Corinne Robinson's New Year's Party. Theodore Roosevelt Collection, Harvard College Library

Edith Roosevelt at desk. Library of Congress

Family photo with Edith, Theodore, and Ethel Derby. Theodore Roosevelt Collection, Harvard College Library

Edith Roosevelt speaking at 1932 rally. Sagamore Hill National Historic Site.

Edith Roosevelt in Lisbon. Theodore Roosevelt Collection, Harvard College Library

SECOND INSERT

Sara Delano at age 9 in Hong Kong. Franklin D. Roosevelt Library

Sara Delano Roosevelt with FDR and two of his sons. Franklin D. Roosevelt Library

FDR family at Hyde Park. Franklin D. Roosevelt Library

Sara Delano Roosevelt in 1939 at the Waldorf-Astoria. Franklin D. Roosevelt Library

Eleanor's mother, Anna Hall Roosevelt. Theodore Roosevelt Collection, Harvard College Library, and the kind permission of John Alsop

Eleanor with her two brothers, Elliott Jr. and Hall. Franklin D. Roosevelt Library

Eleanor from her 1937 autobiography. Franklin D. Roosevelt Library

Franklin "at his most debonair." Franklin D. Roosevelt Library

Eleanor with Franklin, daughter Anna and dog "Duffy." Franklin D. Roosevelt Library

Eleanor standing beside airplane. Franklin D. Roosevelt Library

Eleanor with Maori woman. Library of Congress

Eleanor accompanying two African-Americans supporters. Library of Congress

Eleanor (with suitcase) as a representative to the United Nations. Franklin D. Roosevelt Library

THIRD INSERT

Both photos of the four Alsop children in a row. Personal Collection of John Alsop.

Alsop family at Woodford Farm. Personal Collection of Joseph W. Alsop VI

Corinne Robinson Alsop speaking at the Statler Hilton. Personal Collection of John Alsop

Theodore Roosevelt and family. Theodore Roosevelt Collection, Harvard College Library

Ethel Derby with her husband, Dr. Richard Derby. Theodore Roosevelt Collection, Harvard College Library

Derby family in Florence, Italy. Theodore Roosevelt Collection, Harvard College Library, and the kind permission of Edith Derby Williams

Derby family in the North Dakota Badlands. Theodore Roosevelt collection, Harvard College Library, and the kind permission of Edith Derby Williams

Both postcards of Alice Roosevelt Longworth. Elizabeth Norris Personal Collection

Alice Longworth with President Kennedy and the First Lady. John F. Kennedy Library

Donald Graham greeting Alice Longworth at garden party. Personal Collection of Joseph W. Alsop VI

INDEX